NTC's
ENGLISH
IDIOMS
Dictionary

Richard A. Spears

Betty Kirkpatrick

National Textbook Company
NTC a division of *NTC Publishing Group* • Lincolnwood, Illinois USA

Published by National Textbook Company, a division of NTC Publishing Group.
© 1993 by NTC Publishing Group, 4255 West Touhy Avenue,
Lincolnwood (Chicago), Illinois 60646-1975 USA.
2 3 4 5 6 7 8 9 0 VP 9 8 7 6 5 4 3 2 1

Contents

TO THE USER

Every language has phrases or sentences that cannot be understood literally. Even if you know the meanings of all the words in a phrase and understand the grammar of the phrase completely, the meaning of the phrase may still be confusing. Many proverbs, informal phrases, and common sayings offer this kind of problem. A phrase or sentence of this type is said to be idiomatic. This dictionary is a collection of the idiomatic phrases and sentences that occur frequently in the varieties of English that follow the British standard.

HOW TO USE THIS DICTIONARY

1. First, try looking up the complete phrase in the dictionary. Each expression is alphabetized under the first word of the phrase. For example, **in so many words** will be found in the section dealing with the letter "i." Entry phrases are never inverted or reordered, e.g., **so many words, in; words, in so many;** or **many words, in so.** Initial articles, *a, an, the* are not part of the entry except in the case of proverbs or other complete sentences, where the choice of article is invariant.

2. If you do not find the phrase you want or if you cannot decide exactly what the phrase is, look up any major word in the phrase in the Phrase-Finder Index, which begins on page 365. There you will find all the phrases that contain the key word you have looked up. Pick out the phrase you want and look it up.

3. An entry head may have one or more alternate forms. The entry head and its alternates are printed in **boldface type**, and the alternate forms are preceded by "AND." Two or more alternate forms are separated by a semicolon. For example:

> **bear a grudge (against someone)** AND **have a grudge against someone; hold a grudge (against someone)** to have an old resentment for someone; to have continual anger for someone. □ *She bears a grudge against the judge who sentenced her.* □ *I have a grudge*

against my landlord for overcharging me. □ *How long can a person hold a grudge? Let's be friends.*

4. Many of the entry phrases have more than one major sense or meaning. These senses or meanings are numbered with boldface numerals. For example:

stand for something 1. to endure something. □ *The teacher won't stand for any whispering in class.* □ *We just can't stand for that kind of behaviour.* **2.** to signify something. □ *In a traffic signal, the red light stands for "stop."* □ *The abbreviation "Dr." stands for "doctor."* **3.** to endorse or support an ideal; to represent a quality. □ *The mayor claims to stand for honesty in government and jobs for everyone.* □ *Every candidate for public office stands for all the good things in life.*

5. Individual numbered senses may have additional forms that appear in boldface type, in which case the "AND" and the additional form(s) follow the numeral. For example:

set something aside 1. to discard or reject something. □ *The judge set the ruling aside and released the prisoner.* □ *I have to set aside your opinion. I think you're wrong.* **2.** AND **lay something aside; put something aside** to put something apart or to the side. □ *Take part of the cooking juices and set it aside for later use.* □ *Lay that glass aside because it's cracked.*

6. Some entries have additional related forms within the entry. These are introduced by "ALSO:" and are in boldface type. For example:

scare someone stiff to scare someone severely; to *frighten someone to death.* (*Stiff* means dead.) □ *That loud noise scared me stiff.* □ *The robber jumped out and scared us stiff.* ALSO: **scared stiff** badly frightened. (See also *scared to death* at *frighten someone to death.*) □ *We were scared stiff by the robber.*

7. The boldface entry head (together with any alternates) is usually followed by a definition. Alternate definitions are separated by a semicolon (;). These additional definitions are usually given to show slight differences in meaning or interpretation. Sometimes an alternate definition is given when the vocabulary of the first definition is difficult. For example:

dead on one's or its feet exhausted; worn out; no longer effective or successful. □ *Ann is so tired. She's really dead on her feet.* □ *He can't teach well anymore. He's dead on his feet.* □ *This inefficient company is dead on its feet.*

8. Some entries are followed by instructions or suggestions to look up some other phrase. For example:

scarcer than hen's teeth See *(as) scarce as hen's teeth.*

9. A definition may be followed by comments in parentheses. These comments tell about some of the variations of a phrase, explain what it alludes to, give other useful information, or indicate cross-referencing. For example:

> **desert a sinking ship** AND **leave a sinking ship** to leave a place, a person, or a situation when things become difficult or unpleasant. (Rats are said to be the first to leave a ship which is sinking.) □ *I hate to be the one to desert a sinking ship, but I can't stand it around here any more.* □ *There goes Tom. Wouldn't you know he'd leave a sinking ship rather than stay around and try to help?*

10. When the comments apply to all the numbered senses of an entry, the comments are found before the first numbered sense. For example:

> **sew something up** AND **sew up something** (See also *get something sewed up.*) **1.** to sew something; to stitch closed a tear or hole. □ *I had better sew this rip up before it tears more.* □ *Please sew up this hole in my sock. My toe keeps coming out.* **2.** to finalize something; to secure something. (Informal.) □ *The manager told me to sew this contract up, or else.* □ *Let's sew this contract up today.*

11. Some definitions are preceded by additional information in square brackets. This information clarifies the definition by supplying details about the typical grammatical context in which the phrase is found. For example:

> **serve someone right** [for an act or event] to punish someone fairly (for doing something). □ *John copied off my test paper. It would serve him right if he fails the test.* □ *It'd serve John right if he got arrested.*

12. Some entries are cross-referenced to similar idiomatic phrases that are related in form or meaning. For example:

> **in the black** not in debt; in a financially profitable condition. (Compare to *in the red. In* can be replaced with *into.* See comment at *in a jam* and the examples below.) □ *I wish my accounts were in the black.* □ *Sally moved the company into the black.*

13. Sometimes the numbered senses refer only to people or things, but not both, even though the entry head indicates both someone or something. In such cases, the numeral is followed by "[with *someone*]" or "[with *something*]." For example:

> **set about someone or something** **1.** [with *someone*] to attack someone. □ *The thieves set about the night watchman with knives.* □ *The older boys set about Tom on his way home.* **2.** [with *something*] to begin something; to tackle something. □ *He doesn't know how to set about repairing the bike.* □ *She set about the task right away.*

14. Entry heads and their variants appear in **boldface type**. Examples are introduced by a □ and are in *italic type*. An entry head appears in *slanted type* whenever the phrase is referred to in a definition or cross-reference.

15. Some entry heads stand for two or more idiomatic expressions. Parentheses are used to show which parts of the phrase may or may not be there. For example: **all set (to do something)** stands for **all set** and **all set to do something.**

TERMS AND SYMBOLS

☐ (a box) marks the beginning of an example.

ALSO: introduces additional forms within an entry that are related to the main entry head.

AND indicates that an entry head has variant forms that are the same or similar in meaning as the entry head. One or more variant forms are preceded by AND.

compare to means to consult the entry indicated and examine its form or meaning in relation to the entry head containing the "compare to" instruction.

entry head is the first word or phrase, in boldface type, of an entry; the word or phrase that the definition explains.

formal indicates an expression that is literary in origin or usually reserved for writing.

informal refers to a very casual expression that is most likely to be spoken and not written.

see means to turn to the entry head indicated.

see also means to consult the entry head indicated for additional information or to find expressions similar in form or meaning to the entry head containing the "see also" instruction.

see under means to turn to the entry head indicated and look for the phrase you are seeking *within* the entry indicated, usually after AND or ALSO:.

ABOUT THIS DICTIONARY

NTC's English Idioms Dictionary is designed for easy use by life-long speakers of English, as well as the new-to-English speaker or learner. A controlled vocabulary is used in both the definitions and the examples, while special features make this dictionary uniquely effective for language learners. The dictionary covers over 6500 different forms in approximately 5500 entry blocks in 6000 definitions.

This is a dictionary of form and meaning. It focuses on the user's need to know the meaning, usage, and appropriate contexts for each idiomatic phrase. The definitions and examples provide sufficient information to allow a person trained in English grammar to parse the idiomatic expressions. Persons who do not understand English grammar or English grammar terminology and who cannot themselves parse the idiomatic expressions or example sentences do not derive much benefit from grammatical explanations. The dictionary relies on clarity, simplicity, and carefully written examples to lead the user to the meaning and appropriate usage of each idiomatic expression.

The special features that make this book useful for learners do not detract from or interfere with its usefulness for the life-long English speaker, and should, in fact, add to its usefulness. Specialized knowledge of English lexical and sentential semantics and English grammar is not used in indexing, defining, or explaining the idiomatic phrases.

Idioms or idiomatic expressions are often defined as "set phrases" or "fixed phrases." The number of idiomatic expressions that are totally invariant is really quite small, however, even when the English proverbs are included in this category. Most such phrases can vary the choice of noun or pronoun and most select from a wide variety of verb tense and aspect patterns. Adjectives and some adverbs can be added at will to idiomatic phrases. Furthermore, the new-to-English user is faced with the difficulty of isolating an idiomatic expression from the rest of the sentence and determining where to find it in a dictionary of idioms. If the user cannot extract the essential idiomatic expression, the likelihood of finding it in *any* dictionary is reduced considerably.

In dictionaries that list each idiomatic expression under a "key word," there may be some difficulty in deciding what the "key word" is. In phrases such as **button, on the** or **cards, on the,** the key word, the only noun in the phrase, is easy to determine if one has correctly isolated the phrase from the sentence in which it was found. In phrases that have more than one noun, such as **all hours of the day and night, drive a coach and horses through something,** or **All roads lead to Rome,** deciding on a "key word" may be more difficult. It is even more difficult when the only noun in the phrase is one of the variable words, such as with **go around with** *her old friends*, **go around with** *Jim*, **go around with** *no one at all*.

This dictionary uses the Phrase-Finder Index to avoid the problems users face with trying to isolate the complete idiom and predicting its location in the dictionary. Simply look up any major word—noun, verb, adjective, or adverb—in the Phrase-Finder Index, and you will find the form of the entry head that contains the definition you seek.

For instance, in trying to unravel the sentence "This one is head and shoulders above the others," the idiomatic expression **head and shoulders above someone or something** will be listed in the index under *head, shoulders,* and *above*. The Phrase-Finder Index allows the user to determine which portion of the sentence is the idiom as well as the form of the idiom chosen to be an entry head.

Another important feature for the learner is the use of object placeholders indicating human and nonhuman. This means that there is an indication of whether an object can be a person, a thing, or both.

Typical dictionary entries for idiomatic phrases—especially for phrasal verbs, prepositional verbs, and phrasal prepositional verbs—omit the objects, as in **put on hold; bail out,** or **see through.** This dictionary uses the stand-in pronouns *someone* and *something* to indicate whether the verb in the phrase calls for an object, where the object should go in the sentence, whether the object can be human or nonhuman, and if there are different meanings dependent on whether the object is human or nonhuman. All of that information is vital to learners of English, although it seems to come perfectly naturally to life-long English speakers. For example, there is a big difference between **put someone on hold** and **put something on hold,** or between **bail someone out** and **bail something out.** There is also a great difference between **see something through** and **see through something.** These differences may never be revealed if the entry heads are just **put on hold, bail out,** and **see through,** with no object indicated.

Many idioms have optional parts. In fact, a phrase may seem opaque simply because it is really just an ellipsis of a longer, less opaque phrase. This dictionary shows as full a form of an idiom as possible with the frequently omitted parts in parentheses. For example: **all set (to do something); back down (from something); be all eyes (and ears);** etc.

A

A bird in the hand is worth two in the bush. a proverb meaning that something you already have is better than something you might get. □ *Bill has offered to buy my car for £3,000. Someone else might pay more, but a bird in the hand is worth two in the bush.* □ *I might be able to find a better offer, but a bird in the hand is worth two in the bush.*

(a case of) the blind leading the blind a situation where people who don't know how to do something try to explain or demonstrate it to other people. □ *Tom doesn't know anything about cars, but he's trying to teach Sally how to change the oil. It's a case of the blind leading the blind.* □ *When I tried to show Mary how to use a computer, it was the blind leading the blind.*

A fool and his money are soon parted. a proverb meaning that a person who acts unwisely with money soon loses it. (Often said about a person who has just lost a sum of money because of poor judgement.) □ *When Bill lost a £400 bet on a horse-race, Mary said, "A fool and his money are soon parted."* □ *When John bought a cheap used car that fell apart the next day, he said, "Oh well, a fool and his money are soon parted."*

A friend in need is a friend indeed. a proverb meaning that a true friend is a person who will help you when you really need someone. (Compare to *fair-weather friend*.) □ *When Bill helped me with geometry, I really learned the meaning of "A friend in need is a friend indeed."* □ *"A friend in need is a friend indeed" sounds silly until you need someone very badly.*

A little bird told me. learned from a mysterious or secret source. (Often given as an evasive answer to someone who asks how you learned something.) □ *"All right," said Mary, "where did you get that information?" John replied, "A little bird told me."* □ *A little bird told me where I might find you.*

A little knowledge is a dangerous thing See the following entry.

A little learning is a dangerous thing. AND **A little knowledge is a dangerous thing.** a proverb meaning that incomplete knowledge can embarrass or harm someone or something. (From a line in Alexander Pope's "An Essay on Criticism.") □ *After one week's apprenticeship John thought he could mend my electric drill. A little learning is a dangerous thing.* □ *The doctor said, "Just because you've had a course in first aid, you shouldn't have treated your own illness. A little knowledge is a dangerous thing."* □ *John thought he knew how to care for the garden, but he killed all the flowers. A little knowledge is a dangerous thing.*

A penny for your thoughts. I notice you are thinking about something.; I would be happy to know what you are thinking about. (As if to say, "I will give you a penny for your thoughts." Note variation.) □ *You look sad. A penny for your thoughts.* □ *You were lost in thought. A penny for them.*

A penny saved is a penny earned. a proverb meaning that money saved through thrift comes to the same thing as money earned from employment. (Sometimes used to explain meanness.) □ *"I didn't want to pay that much for the book," said Mary. "After all, a penny saved is a penny earned."* □ *Bob put his money in a new bank which pays more interest than his old bank, saying, "A penny saved is a penny earned."*

A rolling stone gathers no moss. a proverb which describes a person who keeps changing jobs or residences and, therefore, accumulates no possessions or responsibilities. □ *"John just can't seem to stay in one place," said Sally. "Oh well, a rolling stone gathers no moss."* □ *Bill has no furniture to bother with because he's always on the move. He keeps saying that a rolling stone gathers no moss.*

A stitch in time (saves nine). a proverb meaning that early action to repair something damaged can save a lot of time because if the damage is left to get worse the repair will take longer. □ *Get the roof repaired when there's only one slate missing. A stitch in time saves nine.* □ *You should replace the rotten floorboards before the rot spreads. You know—a stitch in time.*

A watched pot never boils. a proverb meaning that when one is waiting for something to happen, the time taken seems longer if one is constantly thinking and worrying about it. (Refers to the seemingly long time it takes water to boil when you are waiting for it.) □ *John was looking out the window, waiting eagerly for the mail to be delivered. Ann said, "Be patient. A watched pot never boils."* □ *Billy weighed himself four times a day while he was trying to lose weight. His mother said, "Relax. A watched pot never boils."*

abandon oneself to someone or something to give up and accept a situation; to yield to a person; to allow oneself to be completely controlled by someone or something. □ *Ann gave up and abandoned herself to grief.* □ *Bill saw the gun and abandoned himself to the robber.* □ *Bill abandoned himself to the music.*

ABC of something the basic facts or principles of something. □ *I have never mastered the ABC of car maintenance.* □ *The book claims to be a guide to the ABC of cooking.*

abide by something to follow the rules of something; to obey orders. □ *John felt that he had to abide by his father's wishes.* □ *All drivers are expected to abide by the rules of the road.*

able to breathe again able to relax and recover from a busy or stressful time. (*Able to* can be replaced with *can.*) □ *Now that the annual sale is over, the sales staff will be able to breathe again.* □ *Final exams are over, so I can breathe again.*

able to do something blindfold AND **able to do something standing on one's head** able to do something easily and quickly. (Informal. *Able to* can be replaced with *can.*) □ *Bill boasted that he could pass his driver's test blindfold.* □ *Mary is very good with computers. She can program blindfold.* □ *Dr. Jones is a great surgeon. He can take out an appendix standing on his head.*

able to do something standing on one's head See the previous entry.

able to take a joke able to accept ridicule good-naturedly; willingly to be the object or butt of a joke without taking offence. (*Able to* can be replaced with *can.*) □ *Let's play a trick on Bill and see if he's able to take a joke.* □ *Better not tease Ann. She can't take a joke.*

able to take something able to endure something; able to endure abuse. (Often in the negative. *Able to* can be replaced with *can.* See also the previous entry.) □ *Stop shouting like that. I'm not able to take it any more.* □ *Go ahead, hit me again. I can take it.* ALSO: **able to take just so much** able to endure only a limited amount of discomfort or distress. (*Able to* can be replaced with *can.*) □ *Please stop hurting my feelings. I'm* able to take just so much. □ *I can take just so much.*

about to do something ready to do something; to be on the verge of doing something. □ *I think our old cat is about to die.* □ *The apple tree is about to bloom.*

(above and) beyond the call of duty in addition to what is required; more than is required by the terms of one's employment. □ *We didn't expect the police officer to drive us home. That was above and beyond the call of duty.* □ *The English teacher helped pupils after school every day, even though it was beyond the call of duty.*

above-board in the open; visible to the public; honest. □ *Don't keep it a secret. Let's make certain that everything is above-board.* □ *The police inspector had to make certain that everything was above-board.*

above one's station higher than one's social class or position in society. □ *He has been educated above his station and is now ashamed of his parents' poverty.* □ *She is getting above her station since she started working in the office. She ignores her old friends in the warehouse.*

above someone's head too difficult or clever for someone to understand. (Treated grammatically as a distance above one's head or understanding.) □ *The children have no idea what the new teacher is talking about. Her ideas are away above their heads.* □ *She started a physics course, but it turned out to be miles above her head.*

above suspicion in such a position of respect that one would not be suspected of wrongdoing. □ *The general is a fine old man, completely above suspicion. He would not be involved in espionage.* □ *Members of the police force should be above suspicion, but sometimes a few of them are found guilty of corruption.*

absent without leave AND **AWOL** absent from a military unit without permission; absent from anything without permission. (**AWOL** is an abbreviation. This is a serious offence in the armed services.) □ *The soldier was taken away by the military police because he was absent without leave.* □ *John was AWOL from school and got into a lot of trouble with his parents.* ALSO: **go AWOL** to become absent without leave. □ *Private Smith went AWOL last Wednesday. Now he's in a military prison.* □ *Peter decided to go AWOL from school camp.*

according to all accounts AND **by all accounts** from all the reports; judging from what everyone is saying. □ *According to all accounts, the police were on the scene immediately.* □ *According to all accounts, the meeting broke up over a very minor matter.* □ *By all accounts, it was a very poor performance.*

according to one's (own) lights according to the way one believes; according to the way one's conscience or inclinations lead one. □ *People must act on this matter according to their own lights.* □ *John may have been wrong, but he did what he did according to his lights.*

Achilles' heel a weak point or fault in someone or something otherwise perfect or excellent. (From the Greek hero Achilles, who had only one vulnerable part of his body, his heel, by which his mother held him to dip him in the River Styx to make him invulnerable. See also *chink in one's armour*.) □ *He was very brave, but fear of spiders was his Achilles' heel.* □ *She was a wonderful wife, but extravagance was her Achilles' heel.*

acid test a test whose findings are beyond doubt or dispute. □ *Her new husband seems generous, but the acid test will be if he lets her mother stay with them.* □ *The MP isn't very popular just now, but the acid test will be if he gets re-elected next election.*

acquainted with someone or something knowing someone or something by name, not necessarily well; knowing of the existence of someone or something. □ *I'm acquainted with John, but I've only met him once.* □ *I'm acquainted with the street you describe, but I don't know how to get there.*

acquire a taste for something to develop a liking for food, drink, or something else; to learn to like something. □ *One acquires a taste for fine wines.* □ *Many people are not able to acquire a taste for foreign food.* □ *Mary acquired a taste for art when she was very young.*

across the board equally for everyone or everything. □ *The government raised the pay of all the teachers across the board.* □ *The council cut the budget by reducing the money for each department 10 percent across the board.*

act of faith an act or deed demonstrating religious faith; an act or deed showing trust in someone or something. □ *He lit candles in church as an act of faith.* □ *For him to trust you with his car was a real act of faith.*

act of God an occurrence (usually an accident) for which no human is responsible; an act of nature such as a storm, earthquake, or windstorm. □ *My insurance company wouldn't pay for the damage because it was an act of God.* □ *The thief tried to convince the judge that the broken shop-window was an act of God.*

act of war an international act of violence to which war is considered a suitable response; [figuratively] any hostile act between two people. □ *To bomb a ship is an act of war.* □ *Can spying be considered an act of war?* □ *"You just broke my stereo," shouted John. "That's an act of war!"*

act one's age to behave more maturely; to act as grown-up as one really is. □ *Come on, John, act your age. Stop throwing stones.* □ *Mary! Stop teasing your little brother. Act your age!*

act something out AND **act out something** to perform an imaginary event as if one were in a play. □ *Bill always acted his anger out by shouting and pounding his fists.* □ *The psychiatrist asked Bill to act out the way he felt about getting sacked.*

act the goat deliberately to behave in a silly or eccentric way; to play the fool.

(Informal.) □ *He was asked to leave the class because he was always acting the goat.* □ *No one takes him seriously. He acts the goat too much.*

act up to misbehave; to behave in a troublesome or unco-operative way. (Informal.) □ *John, why do you always have to act up when your father and I take you out to eat?* □ *My arthritis is acting up. It really hurts.* □ *My car is acting up. I could hardly get it started this morning.*

Actions speak louder than words. a proverb meaning that it is better to do something about a problem than just talk about it. □ *Mary kept promising to find work. John finally looked her in the eye and said, "Actions speak louder than words!"* □ *After listening to the MP promising to cut government spending, Ann wrote a simple note saying, "Actions speak louder than words."*

add fuel to the fire AND **add fuel to the flame** to make a problem worse; to say or do something which makes a bad situation worse; to make an angry person get even more angry. □ *To spank a crying child just adds fuel to the fire.* □ *Bill was shouting angrily, and Bob tried to get him to stop by laughing at him. Of course, that was just adding fuel to the flame.*

add insult to injury to make a bad situation worse; to hurt the feelings of a person who has already been hurt. □ *First, the basement flooded, and then, to add insult to injury, a pipe burst in the kitchen.* □ *My car barely started this morning, and to add insult to injury, I got a flat tyre in the driveway.* □ *First of all he asked John's girlfriend out and then, to add insult to injury, he applied for his job.*

add something up AND **add up something; total something up; total up something** to make a mathematical total; to combine facts in order to come to a conclusion. (See also the following entry.) □ *I've got to finish adding the figures up.* □ *Hurry and add up the* numbers. □ *When you total up all the facts, you see things entirely differently.*

add up (to something) to mean something; to signify or represent something; to result in something. (Informal.) □ *All this adds up to trouble! □ I don't understand the situation. It just doesn't add up.*

advanced in years See *up in years.*

afraid of one's own shadow easily frightened; always frightened, timid, or suspicious. □ *After Tom was robbed, he was afraid of his own shadow. □ Jane has always been a shy child. She has been afraid of her own shadow since she was three.*

after a fashion in a manner which is just barely adequate; not very well. □ *He thanked me—after a fashion—for my help. □ Oh yes, I can swim, after a fashion.*

after all anyway; in spite of what had been decided. (Often refers to a change in plans or a reversal of plans.) □ *Mary had planned to go to the bank first, but she came here after all. □ It looks like Tom will study law after all.*

after all is said and done when everything is settled or concluded; finally. □ *After all was said and done, the wedding was a lovely affair. □ After all is said and done, things will turn out just as I said.*

after hours after the regular closing time; after any normal or regular time, such as one's bedtime. □ *John was arrested in a bar after hours. □ The soldier was caught sneaking into the barracks after hours. □ Ted found employment sweeping floors in the bank after hours.*

after the fact after a crime or offence has taken place. (Primarily a legal phrase.) □ *He was not involved in the actual robbery. He was an accomplice after the fact. □ Because she gave the thief shelter she may well be charged with being an accessory after the fact.*

after the style of someone or something in the manner or style of someone or something; in imitation of someone or something. □ *She thinks her painting is after* the style of the Impressionists. □ *The parish church was built after the style of a French cathedral.*

against someone's will without a person's consent or agreement. □ *You cannot force me to come with you against my will! □ Against their will, the men were made to stand up against the wall and be searched.*

ahead of one's time having ideas or attitudes that are too advanced to be acceptable to or appreciated by the society in which one is living. □ *People buy that artist's work now, but his paintings were laughed at when he was alive. He was ahead of his time. □ Mary's grandmother was ahead of her time in wanting to study medicine. Women were supposed to stay at home and do nothing until they were married.*

ahead of time beforehand; before the announced time. □ *If you turn up ahead of time, you will have to wait. □ Be there ahead of time if you want to get a good seat.*

aid and abet someone to help someone, especially in a crime or misdeed; to incite someone to do something which is wrong. □ *He was scolded for aiding and abetting those boys who were fighting. □ It's illegal to aid and abet a thief.*

aim to do something to mean to do something; to intend to do something in the future. □ *I aim to paint the house as soon as I can find the time. □ He aims to take a few days off and go fishing.*

air one's dirty linen in public AND **wash one's dirty linen in public** to discuss private or embarrassing matters in public, especially when quarrelling or complaining. (Figurative.) □ *John's mother had asked him repeatedly not to air the family's dirty linen in public. □ Mr. and Mrs. Johnson are arguing again. Why must they always wash their dirty linen in public?*

air one's grievances to complain; to make a public complaint. □ *I know how you feel, John, but it isn't necessary*

5

to air your grievances over and over. □ *I know you're busy, sir, but I must air my grievances. This matter is very serious.*

airs and graces proud behaviour adopted by one who is acting as though one were more important than one is in order to impress others. □ *She is only a junior secretary, but from her airs and graces you would think she was managing director.* □ *Jane comes from a very humble background despite her airs and graces.*

alive and kicking well and healthy. (Informal.) □ JANE: *How is Bill?* MARY: *Oh, he's alive and kicking.* □ *I thought the firm was in trouble, but apparently it's alive and kicking.*

alive with someone or something covered with, filled with, or active with people or things. (Informal.) □ *Look! Ants everywhere. The floor is alive with ants!* □ *When we got to the scene of the crime, the place was alive with police activity.* □ *The campground was alive with campers from all over the country.*

all and sundry everyone; one and all, indiscriminately. □ *Cold drinks were served to all and sundry.* □ *All and sundry came to the village fair.*

all better now improved; cured. (Childish.) □ *My leg was sore, but it's all better now.* □ *I fell off my tricycle and bumped my knee. Mummy kissed it, and it's all better now.*

all day long throughout the day; during the entire day. □ *The sun shone brightly all day long.* □ *I can't keep smiling all day long.*

all dressed up dressed in one's best clothes; dressed formally. (See also *dress up; get (all) dolled up.*) □ *We're all dressed up to go out to dinner.* □ *I really hate to get all dressed up just to go somewhere to eat.*

all for something very much in favour of something. (*For* is usually emphasized.) □ *Bill is all for stopping to get ice-cream.* □ *Mary suggested that they sell their house. They were far from all for it, but they did it anyway.*

all hours (of the day and night) very late in the night or very early in the morning. □ *Why do you always stay out until all hours of the day and night?* □ *I like to stay out till all hours partying.*

all in 1. tired; exhausted. (Informal.) □ *I just walked all the way from town. I'm all in.* □ *"What a day!" said Sally. "I'm all in."* **2.** with everything included in the price. □ *If that's the price all in, I can afford the holiday.* □ *The cost of staying there is £50 per night all in.*

all in a day's work part of what is expected; typical or normal. □ *I don't particularly like to cook, but it's all in a day's work.* □ *Putting up with rude customers isn't pleasant, but it's all in a day's work.* □ *Cleaning up after other people is all in a day's work for a chamber-maid.*

all in all considering everything which has happened. □ *All in all, it was a jolly good party.* □ *All in all, I'm glad that I visited Oxford.*

all in good time at some future time; *in good time;* soon. (This phrase is used to encourage people to be patient and wait quietly.) □ *When will the baby be born? All in good time.* □ MARY: *I'm starved! When will Bill get here with the fish and chips?* TOM: *All in good time, Mary, all in good time.*

all in one breath spoken very rapidly, usually while one is very excited. □ *Ann said all in one breath, "Hurry, quick! The procession is coming!"* □ *Jane was in a play, and she was so excited that she said her whole speech all in one breath.*

all in one piece safely; without damage. (Informal.) □ *Her son came home from school all in one piece, even though he had been in a fight.* □ *The package was handled carelessly, but the vase inside arrived all in one piece.*

all manner of someone or something all types of people or things. □ *We saw all manner of people there. They came from every country in the world.* □ *They* *were selling all manner of things in the little shop.*

all my eye (and Betty Martin) nonsense; not true. □ *Jane is always talking about her wonderful childhood, but it's all my eye.* □ *He pretends to have great plans, but they're all my eye and Betty Martin.*

all night long throughout the whole night. □ *I couldn't sleep all night long.* □ *John was sick all night long.*

all of a sudden suddenly. □ *All of a sudden lightning struck the tree we were sitting under.* □ *I felt a sharp pain in my side all of a sudden.*

all out effort a very good and thorough effort. □ *We need an all out effort to get this matter finished on time.* □ *The government began an all out effort to reduce the budget.*

all out war total war, as opposed to minor warlike acts or threats of war. □ *We are now concerned about all out war in the Middle East.* □ *Threats of all out war caused many tourists to leave the country immediately.*

all over 1. finished; dead. (Compare to *all over with.*) □ *The affair is all over. He's going out with someone else.* □ *It's all over. He's dead now.* 2. everywhere. □ *Oh, I just itch all over.* □ *She's spreading the rumour all over.*

all over bar the shouting decided and concluded; finished except for the formalities. (Informal. An elaboration of *all over,* which means "finished.") □ *The last goal was made just as the final whistle sounded. Tom said, "Well, it's all over bar the shouting."* □ *Tom has finished his exams and is waiting to graduate. It's all over bar the shouting.*

all over the place everywhere; in all parts of a particular location. (Informal. An elaboration of *all over.*) □ *Tom, stop leaving your dirty clothes all over the place.* □ *We keep finding this kind of problem all over the place.*

all over with finished. (See also *all over.*) □ *His problems are all over with now.*

□ *It's all over with him now. He's been sacked.*

all right well, good, or okay, but not excellent. (Informal. This phrase has all the uses that *okay* has.) □ *I was a little sick, but now I'm all right.* □ *His work is all right, but nothing to brag about.*

all right with someone acceptable to someone. (Sometimes used ironically.) □ *If you want to ruin your life and marry Tom, it's all right with me.* □ *I'll see if it's all right with my father.*

All roads lead to Rome. a proverb meaning that there are many different routes to the same goal. □ *Mary was criticizing the way that Jane was planting the flowers. John said, "Never mind, Mary, all roads lead to Rome."* □ *Some people learn by doing. Others have to be taught. In the long run, all roads lead to Rome.*

all set (to do something) prepared or ready to do something. □ *Are you all set to cook the steaks?* □ *Yes, the fire is ready, and I'm all set to start.* □ TOM: *Is everything ready?* JANE: *Yes, we are all set.*

all skin and bones See *nothing but skin and bones.*

all systems go everything is ready. (Informal. Originally said when preparing to launch a rocket.) □ *The factory opens tomorrow. Then it's all systems go.* □ TOM: *Are you lot ready to start playing?* BILL: *Sure, Tom, all systems go.*

all talk talking about doing something, but never actually doing it. (See also *Actions speak louder than words.*) □ *Bill keeps saying he'll get a job soon, but he's all talk.* □ *Jack won't take part in a fight. He's just all talk.*

All that glitters is not gold. a proverb meaning that many attractive and alluring things have no value. □ *The used car looked fine but didn't run well at all. "Ah yes," thought Bill, "all that glitters is not gold."* □ *When Mary was disappointed about losing Tom, Jane re-*

minded her, "All that glitters is not gold."

all the livelong day throughout the whole day. (Literary.) □ *They kept at their work all the livelong day.* □ *Bob just sat by the river fishing, all the livelong day.*

all the rage in current fashion. (Informal.) □ *A new dance called the "floppy disc" is all the rage.* □ *Wearing a rope instead of a belt is all the rage these days.*

all the same AND **just the same** 1. nevertheless; anyhow. □ *They were told not to bring presents, but they brought them all the same.* □ *His parents said no, but John went out just the same.* 2. See the following entry.

all the same (to someone) of no consequence to someone; immaterial to someone. □ *It's all the same to me whether we win or lose.* □ *If it's all the same, I'd rather you didn't smoke.*

all the time 1. continuously throughout a specific period of time, often referring to an act of secrecy or deception. □ *Bill was stealing money for the last two years, and Tom knew it all the time.* □ *Throughout December and January, Jane had two employers all the time, although she said she had no work.* 2. at all times; continuously. □ *Your blood keeps flowing all the time.* □ *That electric motor runs all the time.*

all thumbs very awkward and clumsy, especially with one's hands. (Informal.) □ *Poor Bob can't play the piano at all. He's all thumbs.* □ *Mary is all thumbs when it comes to gardening.*

all to the good for the best; for one's benefit. □ *He missed his train, but it was all to the good because the train had a crash.* □ *It was all to the good that he died before his wife. He couldn't have coped without her.*

all told totalled up; including all parts. □ *All told, he earned about £700 last week.* □ *All told, he is a musician of talent.*

all walks of life all social, economic, and ethnic groups. □ *We saw people there from all walks of life.* □ *The people who came to the art exhibit represented all walks of life.*

All work and no play makes Jack a dull boy. a proverb meaning that one should have recreation as well as work. (*Jack* does not refer to anyone in particular, and the phrase can be used for persons of either sex.) □ *Stop reading that book and go out and play! All work and no play makes Jack a dull boy.* □ *The doctor told Mr. Jones to stop working on week-ends and start playing golf, because all work and no play makes Jack a dull boy.*

all worked up (over something) AND **all worked up (about something)** excited and agitated about something. (Informal.) □ *Tom is all worked up over the threat of a new war.* □ *Don't get all worked up about something which you can't do anything about.* □ *Bill is all worked up again. It's bad for his health.*

all year round throughout all the seasons of the year; during the entire year. □ *The public swimming-pool is enclosed so that it can be used all year round.* □ *In the South they can grow flowers all year round.*

allow for someone or something 1. to plan on having enough of something (such as food, space, etc.) for someone. □ *Mary is bringing Bill on the picnic, so be certain to allow for him when buying the food.* □ *Allow for an extra person when setting the table tonight.* 2. to plan on the possibility of something. □ *Allow for a few rainy days on your holiday.* □ *Be certain to allow for future growth when you plant the rose-bushes.*

All's well that ends well. a proverb meaning that an event which has a good ending is good even if some things went wrong along the way. (This is the name of a play by Shakespeare.) □ *I'm glad you finally got here even though your car had a flat tyre on the way. Oh well. All's well that ends well.* □ *The groom was late for the wedding, but everything* *worked out all right. All's well that ends well.*

alongside (of) someone or something as compared to a person or a thing. (Informal.) □ *Our car looks quite small alongside of theirs.* □ *My power of concentration is quite limited alongside of yours.*

amount to something [for someone or something] to be or to become valuable or successful. □ *Most parents hope that their children will amount to something one day.* □ *I put £200 in the bank, and I hope it will amount to something in twenty years.* □ *I'm glad to see that Bill Jones finally amounts to something in the firm.*

An eye for an eye (and a tooth for a tooth). a punishment or act of revenge that is of the same degree as the crime or offence committed. (A biblical quote.) □ *His mother told him to hit the boy who had hit him. An eye for an eye.* □ *I don't feel bad about reporting him for being late when he did the same to me last week. After all—an eye for an eye and a tooth for a tooth.*

and the like and other similar things. (Informal.) □ *Whenever we go on a picnic, we take roast chicken, bread, cheese, wine, and the like.* □ *I'm very tired of being shouted at, pushed around, and the like.*

and then some and even more; more than has been mentioned. (Informal.) □ *John is going to have to run like a deer and then some to win this race.* □ *He needs all the money he can earn and then some.*

and what have you and so on; and other similar things. (Informal.) □ *Their garage is full of bikes, sledges, football boots, and what have you.* □ *The newsagent sells writing-paper, pens, string, and what have you.*

answer someone's purpose AND **serve someone's purpose** to fit or suit someone's purpose. □ *This piece of wood will answer my purpose quite nicely.* □ *The new car serves our purpose perfectly.*

answer to someone to justify one's actions to someone. (Usually with *have to*.) □ *If John cannot behave properly, he'll have to answer to me.* □ *You'll have to answer to her father if you take Mary home late.*

any number of someone or something a large number; a sufficiently large number. □ *Any number of people can vouch for my honesty.* □ *I can give you any number of reasons why I should join the army.* □ *I ate there any number of times and never became ill.*

any port in a storm a phrase indicating that when one is in difficulties one must accept any way out, whether one likes the solution or not. □ *I don't want to live with my parents, but it's a case of any port in a storm. I can't find a flat.* □ *He hates his job, but he can't get another. Any port in a storm, you know.*

apple of someone's eye someone's favourite person or thing. □ *Tom is the apple of Mary's eye. She thinks he's great.* □ *Jean is the apple of her father's eye.*

arm in arm linked or hooked together by the arms. □ *The two lovers walked arm in arm down the street.* □ *Arm in arm, the row of dancers kicked high, and the audience roared its approval.*

armed to the teeth heavily armed with weapons. □ *The bank robber was armed to the teeth when he was caught.* □ *There are too many guns around. The entire country is armed to the teeth.*

(a)round the clock continuously for twenty-four hours at a time. □ *The priceless jewels were guarded around the clock.* □ *Grandfather was so sick that he had to have nursing care round the clock.* ALSO: **(a)round-the-clock** constant; day and night. □ *Grandfather required around-the-clock care.*

as a duck takes to water easily and naturally. (Informal.) □ *She took to singing just as a duck takes to water.* □ *The baby adapted to the feeding-bottle as a duck takes to water.*

as a (general) rule usually; almost always. □ *He can be found in his office as a general rule.* □ *As a general rule, Jane plays golf on Wednesdays.* □ *As a rule, things tend to get less busy after suppertime.*

as a last resort as the last choice; if everything else fails. □ *Call the doctor at home only as a last resort.* □ *As a last resort, she will perform surgery.*

as a matter of course normally; as a normal procedure. □ *In hospital, the nurse always takes your temperature as a matter of course.* □ *You are expected to make your own bed as a matter of course.*

as a matter of fact in addition to what has been said; in reference to what has been said. (See also *matter-of-fact*.) □ *As a matter of fact, John came into the room while you were talking about him.* □ *I'm not a poor worker. As a matter of fact, I'm very efficient.*

as a rule See *as a (general) rule*.

as a token of something symbolic of something, especially of gratitude; as a memento of something. □ *He gave me a rose as a token of the romantic time we spent together.* □ *Here, take this £100 as a token of my appreciation.*

as bad as all that as bad as reported; as bad as it seems. (Usually expressed in the negative.) □ *Come on! Nothing could be as bad as all that.* □ *Stop crying. It can't be as bad as all that.*

(as) black as one is painted as evil or unpleasant as one is thought to be. (Usually negative.) □ *The landlord is not as black as he is painted. He seems quite generous.* □ *Young people are rarely black as they are painted in the media.*

(as) black as pitch very black; very dark. □ *The night was as black as pitch.* □ *The rocks seemed black as pitch against the silver sand.*

(as) blind as a bat with imperfect sight; blind. □ *My grandmother is as blind as a bat.* □ *I'm getting blind as a bat. I can hardly read this page.*

(as) bold as brass brazen; very bold and impertinent. □ *She went up to her lover's wife bold as brass.* □ *The girl arrives late every morning as bold as brass.*

(as) bright as a button very intelligent; extremely alert. □ *The little girl is as bright as a button.* □ *Her new dog is bright as a button.*

(as) busy as a bee very busy. □ *I don't have time to talk to you. I'm as busy as a bee.* □ *Whenever there is a holiday, we are all busy as bees at the hotel.*

(as) calm as a millpond [for water to be] exceptionally calm. (Referring to the still water in a pond around a mill in contrast to the fast-flowing stream which supplies it.) □ *The English Channel was calm as a millpond that day.* □ *Jane gets seasick even when the sea is calm as a millpond.*

(as) clean as a whistle very clean. □ *The wound isn't infected. It's clean as a whistle.* □ *I thought the car would be filthy, but it was as clean as a whistle.*

(as) clear as crystal **1.** very clear; transparent. □ *The stream was as clear as crystal.* □ *She cleaned the window pane until it was clear as crystal.* **2.** very clear; easy to understand. □ *The explanation was as clear as crystal.* □ *Her lecture was not clear as crystal, but at least it was not dull.*

(as) clear as mud not understandable. (Informal.) □ *Your explanation is as clear as mud.* □ *This doesn't make sense. It's clear as mud.*

(as) cold as charity **1.** very cold; icy. □ *The room was as cold as charity.* □ *It was snowing and the moors were cold as charity.* **2.** very unresponsive; lacking in passion. □ *Their mother keeps them clean and fed but she is cold as charity.* □ *His sister is generous and welcoming, but he is as cold as charity.*

(as) cool as a cucumber calm and not agitated; with one's wits about one. (Informal.) □ *The captain remained as cool as a cucumber as the passengers boarded the lifeboats.* □ *During the fire the owner of the house was cool as a cucumber.*

(as) cunning as a fox clever in a devious way. □ *The police won't get a confession from him. He's cunning as a fox.* □ *You have to be as cunning as a fox to outwit me.*

(as) dead as a dodo dead; no longer in existence. (Informal.) □ *Yes, Adolf Hitler is really dead—as dead as a dodo.* □ *That silly old idea is dead as a dodo.*

(as) dead as a doornail dead. □ *This fish is as dead as a doornail.* □ *John kept twisting the chicken's neck even though it was dead as a doornail.*

(as) different as chalk from cheese See the following entry.

(as) different as night and day AND **(as) different as chalk from cheese** completely different. □ *Although Bobby and Billy are twins, they are as different as night and day.* □ *Their styles of painting are as different as chalk from cheese.*

(as) dull as dish-water very uninteresting. □ *I'm not surprised that he can't find a partner. He's as dull as dish-water.* □ *Mr. Black's speech was dull as dish-water.*

(as) easy as falling off a log AND **(as) easy as pie** very easy. □ *Passing that exam was as easy as falling off a log.* □ *Getting out of jail was easy as falling off a log.* □ *Mountain climbing is as easy as pie.* □ *Making a simple dress out of cotton cloth is easy as pie.*

(as) easy as pie See the previous entry.

(as) far as anyone knows AND **so far as anyone knows** to the limits of anyone's knowledge or understanding. (The *anyone* can be replaced with a more specific noun or pronoun.) □ *As far as anyone knows, this is the last of the great herds of buffalo.* □ *These are the only keys to the house so far as anyone knows.*

as far as it goes as much as something does, covers, or accomplishes. (Usually said of something which is inadequate.) □ *Your plan is fine as far as it goes. It doesn't seem to cover everything, though.* □ *As far as it goes, this law is*

a good one. It should require more severe penalties, however.

as far as possible AND **so far as possible** as much as possible; to whatever degree is possible. □ *We must try, as far as possible, to get people to stop smoking in buses.* □ *As far as possible, the police will issue tickets to all speeding drivers.* □ *I'll follow your instructions so far as possible.*

as far as someone is concerned AND **so far as someone is concerned** for all someone cares; if one is to make the decision. □ *As far as he's concerned, you can just go away.* □ *You can take your old dog and leave as far as I'm concerned.* □ *So far as I'm concerned, you're okay.*

(as) fit as a fiddle healthy and physically fit. (Informal.) □ *Mary is as fit as a fiddle.* □ *Tom used to be fit as a fiddle. Look at him now!*

(as) flat as a pancake very flat. (Informal.) □ *The punctured tyre was as flat as a pancake.* □ *Bobby squashed the ant flat as a pancake.*

as for someone or something regarding someone or something. □ *As for the mayor, he can pay for his own dinner.* □ *As for you, Bobby, there will be no dessert for you tonight.* □ *As for this chair, there is nothing to do but throw it away.*

(as) free as a bird carefree; completely free. □ *Jane is always happy and free as a bird.* □ *The convict escaped from jail and was as free as a bird for two days.* □ *In the summer holidays, I feel free as a bird.*

as good as done much the same as being done; almost done. (Many different past participles can replace *done* in this phrase: *cooked, dead, finished, painted, typed,* etc.) □ *This thing is as good as done. It'll just take another second.* □ *Yes sir, if you employ me to paint your house, it's as good as painted.* □ *When I hand my secretary a letter to be typed, I know that it's as good as typed right then and there.*

(as) good as gold very well-behaved. □ *The baby was as good as gold all evening.* □ *The children were as good as gold on the bus trip.*

as good as one's word obedient to one's promise; dependable in keeping one's promises. □ *He was as good as his word. He lent me the books as promised.* □ *She said she would baby-sit, and she was as good as her word.*

(as) happy as a lark visibly happy and cheerful. (Note the variations in the examples.) □ *Sally walked along whistling, as happy as a lark.* □ *The children danced and sang, happy as larks.*

(as) happy as a sandboy AND **(as) happy as Larry; (as) happy as the day is long** very happy; carefree. □ *Mary's as happy as a sandboy now that she is at home all day with her children.* □ *Peter earns very little money, but he's happy as Larry in his job.* □ *The old lady is happy as the day is long so long as she can sit by the window.*

(as) happy as Larry See the previous entry.

(as) happy as the day is long See *(as) happy as a sandboy.*

(as) hard as nails cold and cruel; mean. (Refers to the nails which are used with a hammer.) □ *His new girlfriend hates children. She's as hard as nails.* □ *Sarah was unpleasant and hard as nails.*

(as) high as a kite drunk or drugged. (Informal.) □ *Bill drank beer until he got as high as a kite.* □ *The thieves were high as a kite on drugs.*

(as) hot as hell very hot. (Informal.) □ *It's as hot as hell outside. It must be near 38 degrees.* □ *I hate to get into a car that has been parked in the sun. It's hot as hell.*

(as) hungry as a hunter very hungry. □ *I'm as hungry as a hunter. I could eat anything!* □ *Whenever I jog, I get hungry as a hunter.*

(as) innocent as a lamb guiltless; naive. □ *"Look! You can't throw me in jail," cried the robber. "I'm innocent as a lamb."* □ *Look at the baby, as innocent as a lamb.*

(as) large as life in person; actually, and sometimes surprisingly, present at a place. □ *I thought Jack was away, but there he was as large as life.* □ *Jean was not expected to appear, but she turned up large as life.*

(as) large as life (and twice as ugly) an exaggerated way of saying that a person or a thing appeared in a particular place. (Informal.) □ *The little child just stood there as large as life and laughed very hard.* □ *I opened the door, and there was Tom large as life.* □ *I came home and found this cat in my chair, as large as life and twice as ugly.*

(as) light as a feather of little weight. (Informal.) □ *Sally dieted until she was as light as a feather.* □ *Of course I can lift the box. It's light as a feather.*

(as) likely as not probably; with an even chance either way. □ *He will as likely as not arrive without warning.* □ *Likely as not, the match will be cancelled.*

(as) luck would have it by good or bad luck; as it turned out; by chance. □ *As luck would have it, we had a flat tyre.* □ *As luck would have it, the cheque came in the mail today.*

(as) mad as a hatter crazy. (From the character called the Mad Hatter in Lewis Carroll's *Alice's Adventures in Wonderland.*) □ *Poor old John is as mad as a hatter.* □ *All these screaming children are driving me mad as a hatter.*

(as) mad as a March hare crazy; silly. (From the name of a character in Lewis Carroll's *Alice's Adventures in Wonderland.*) □ *Sally is getting as mad as a March hare.* □ *My Uncle Bill is mad as a March hare.*

(as) mad as hell very angry. (Informal.) □ *He made his wife as mad as hell.* □ *Those terrorists make me mad as hell.*

(as) near as dammit very nearly. (Informal.) □ *He earns sixty thousand pounds a year as near as dammit.* □ *She was naked near as dammit.*

(as) nutty as a fruit-cake silly; crazy. (Slang. A fruit-cake usually has lots of nuts in it.) □ *Whenever John goes on holiday, he gets as nutty as a fruit-cake.* □ *Sally has been acting as nutty as a fruit-cake lately.*

(as) old as the hills very old. □ *The children think their mother's as old as the hills, but she's only forty.* □ *That song's not new. It's old as the hills.*

as one as if a group were one person. (Especially with *act, move,* or *speak.*) □ *All the dancers moved as one.* □ *The chorus spoke as one.*

(as) plain as a pikestaff very obvious; clearly visible. (*Pikestaff* was originally *packstaff*, a stick on which a peddlar's or traveller's pack was supported. The original reference was to the plainness of this staff, although the allusion is to another sense of plain: clear or obvious.) □ *The 'no parking' sign was as plain as a pikestaff. How did he miss it?* □ *It's as plain as a pikestaff. The children are unhappy.*

(as) plain as the nose on one's face obvious; clearly evident. (Informal.) □ *What do you mean you don't understand? It's as plain as the nose on your face.* □ *Your guilt is plain as the nose on your face.*

(as) pleased as Punch very pleased or happy. (From the puppet-show character who is depicted as smiling gleefully.) □ *The little girl was pleased as Punch with her new dress.* □ *Jack's as pleased as Punch with his new car.*

(as) poor as a church mouse very poor. □ *My aunt is as poor as a church mouse.* □ *The Browns are poor as church mice.*

(as) pretty as a picture very pretty. □ *Sweet little Mary is as pretty as a picture.* □ *Their new house is pretty as a picture.*

(as) proud as a peacock very proud; haughty. □ *John is so arrogant. He's as proud as a peacock.* □ *The new father was proud as a peacock.*

(as) pure as the driven snow very pure; as pure and virtuous as snow is white. (Compare to *(as) white as the driven snow.*) □ *She wouldn't do anything wicked. She's pure as the driven snow.* □ *He's not without principles, but he's not exactly as pure as the driven snow.*

(as) quick as a flash very quickly; very rapidly. □ *The dog grabbed the meat as quick as a flash.* □ *The summer days went by quick as a flash.*

(as) quick as (greased) lightning very quickly; very fast. □ *Jane can really run. She's as quick as greased lightning.* □ *Quick as greased lightning, the thief stole my wallet.*

(as) quiet as a mouse very quiet; shy and silent. □ *Don't shout; whisper. Be as quiet as a mouse.* □ *Mary hardly ever says anything. She's quiet as a mouse.*

(as) quiet as the grave very quiet; silent. □ *The house is as quiet as the grave when the children are at school.* □ *This town is quiet as the grave now that the offices have closed.*

(as) rare as hen's teeth very scarce or nonexistent. (Informal. Chickens don't have teeth.) □ *I've never seen one of those. They're as rare as hen's teeth.* □ *I was told that the part needed for my car is rare as hen's teeth, and it would take a long time to find one.*

(as) regular as clockwork dependably regular. (See also *go like clockwork.*) □ *She comes into this shop every day, as regular as clockwork.* □ *The same guests come every year, regular as clockwork.*

(as) right as rain fine; all right. □ *Your mother is as right as rain after the operation.* □ *John has recovered now. He's right as rain.*

(as) safe as houses completely safe. □ *The children will be as safe as houses on holiday with your parents.* □ *The dog will be as safe as houses in the boarding-kennels.*

(as) sharp as a razor **1.** very sharp. □ *The penknife is sharp as a razor.* □ *The carving knife will have to be as* sharp as a razor to cut through this meat. **2.** very sharp-witted or intelligent. □ *The old man's senile, but his wife is as sharp as a razor.* □ *Don't say too much in front of the child. She's as sharp as a razor.*

(as) sick as a dog very sick; sick and vomiting. □ *We've never been so ill. The whole family was sick as dogs.* □ *Sally was as sick as a dog and couldn't go to the party.*

(as) sick as a parrot very disappointed or envious. □ *Tom was sick as a parrot when Dick won the match.* □ *When Sally married Jim, Bill was as sick as a parrot.*

(as) slippery as an eel devious; difficult to catch. □ *Tom can't be trusted. He's as slippery as an eel.* □ *It's hard to catch Joe in the act of playing truant. He's slippery as an eel.*

(as) snug as a bug (in a rug) cosy and snug. (Informal.) □ *Let's pull up the covers. There you are, Bobby, as snug as a bug in a rug.* □ *What a lovely little house! I know I'll be snug as a bug.*

(as) sober as a judge not drunk; alert and completely sober. □ *John's drunk? No, he's as sober as a judge.* □ *You should be sober as a judge when you drive a car.*

(as) soft as a baby's bottom very soft and smooth to the touch. □ *This cloth is as soft as a baby's bottom.* □ *No, Bob doesn't shave yet. His cheeks are soft as a baby's bottom.*

(as) sound as a bell in perfect condition or health; undamaged. □ *The doctor says that old man's heart's as sound as a bell.* □ *I thought the vase was broken when it fell, but it was sound as a bell.*

(as) steady as a rock very steady and unmoving; very stable. □ *His hand was steady as a rock as he pulled the trigger of the revolver.* □ *You must remain as steady as a rock when you are arguing with your enemies.*

(as) strong as an ox very strong. □ *Tom lifts weights and is as strong as an*

ox. □ *Now that Ann has recovered from her illness, she's strong as an ox.*

(as) stubborn as a mule very stubborn. □ *My husband is as stubborn as a mule.* □ *Our cat is stubborn as a mule.*

as the crow flies straight across the land, as opposed to distances measured on a road, river, etc. □ *It's twenty miles to town on the M4, but only ten as the crow flies.* □ *Our house is only a few miles from the lake as the crow flies.*

(as) thick as thieves very close-knit; friendly; allied. (Informal.) □ *Mary, Tom, and Sally are as thick as thieves. They go everywhere together.* □ *Those two families are thick as thieves.*

(as) thick as two short planks very stupid. (Informal.) □ *Jim must be as thick as two short planks, not able to understand the plans.* □ *Some of the children are clever, but the rest are as thick as two short planks.*

(as) thin as a rake very thin; too thin. □ *Mary's thin as a rake since she's been ill.* □ *Jean's been on a diet and is now as thin as a rake.*

(as) tight as a tick very drunk. (Informal. Refers to a tick which has filled itself full of blood.) □ *Her husband was as tight as a tick after the office party.* □ *The woman behind the bar was tight as a tick.*

(as) tough as old boots (Informal.) **1.** very tough. □ *This meat is tough as old boots.* □ *Bob couldn't eat the steak. It was as tough as old boots.* **2.** very strong; not easily moved by feelings such as pity. □ *Margaret is never off work. She's as tough as old boots.* □ *Don't expect sympathy from the headmistress. She's as tough as old boots.*

(as) ugly as sin very ugly. □ *The new building is as ugly as sin.* □ *The old woman is ugly as sin, but she dresses beautifully.*

(as) warm as toast very warm and cosy. (Informal.) □ *The baby will be warm as toast in that sleeping-suit.* □ *We* were as warm as toast by the side of the coal fire.

(as) weak as a kitten weak; weak and sickly. □ *John is as weak as a kitten because he doesn't eat well.* □ *Oh! Suddenly I feel weak as a kitten.*

(as) white as a sheet very pale. □ *Jane is white as a sheet after her illness.* □ *Mary went as white as a sheet when she heard the news.*

(as) white as the driven snow very white; of a very pure white. (Compare to *(as) pure as the driven snow.*) □ *I like my bed linen to be as white as the driven snow.* □ *We have a new kitten whose fur is white as the driven snow.*

(as) wise as an owl very wise. □ *Grandfather is as wise as an owl.* □ *The old woman in the village is wise as an owl.*

aside from someone or something not including someone or something. □ *Aside from a small bank account, I have no money at all.* □ *Aside from Mary, I have no friends.*

ask for something to do something which will cause trouble. (See also *ask for trouble.*) □ *Don't talk to me that way! You're really asking for it.* □ *Anyone who acts like that is just asking for a good talking-to.*

ask for the moon to ask for too much; to make great demands. □ *When you're trying to get a job, it's unwise to ask for the moon.* □ *Please lend me the money. I'm not asking for the moon!*

ask for trouble to do or say something which will cause trouble. □ *Stop talking to me that way, John. You're just asking for trouble.* □ *Anybody who threatens a police officer is just asking for trouble.*

ask someone out AND **ask out someone** to ask a person for a date. □ *Mary hopes that John will ask her out.* □ *John doesn't want to ask out his best friend's girl.*

asleep at the wheel not attending to one's assigned task; failing to do one's duty at the proper time. □ *I should* have spotted the error. I must have been asleep at the wheel. □ *The management must have been asleep at the wheel to let the firm get into such a state.*

at a loose end restless and unsettled; unemployed. (Informal.) □ *Just before school starts, all the children are at a loose end.* □ *When Tom is home on the week-ends, he's always at a loose end.* □ *Jane has been at a loose end ever since she lost her job.*

at a loss for words unable to speak; speechless. □ *I was so surprised that I was at a loss for words.* □ *Tom was terribly embarrassed—really at a loss for words.*

at a pinch if absolutely necessary. □ *At a pinch, I could come tomorrow, but it's not really convenient.* □ *He could commute to work from home at a pinch, but it is a long way.*

at a premium priced high because of some special feature; in demand and therefore difficult to obtain. □ *Since the new factories were built, houses around here are at a premium.* □ *With the increase in the numbers of elderly people, places in the old people's homes are at a premium.*

at a rate of knots very fast. (Informal.) □ *They'll have to drive at a rate of knots to get there on time.* □ *They were travelling at a rate of knots when they passed us.*

at a snail's pace very slowly. □ *When you watch a clock, time seems to move at a snail's pace.* □ *You always eat at a snail's pace. I'm tired of waiting for you.*

at a stretch continuously; without stopping. □ *We all had to do eight hours of duty at a stretch.* □ *The baby doesn't sleep for more than three hours at a stretch.*

at all costs AND **at any cost** regardless of the difficulty or cost; no matter what. □ *I intend to have that car at all costs.* □ *I'll get there by six o'clock at all costs.* □ *Mary was going to get that job at any cost.*

at an early date soon; some day soon. □ *The note said, "Please call me at an early date."* □ *You're expected to return the form to the office at an early date.*

at any cost See *at all costs.*

at any rate anyway. (Informal. Frequently used as an introduction to a conclusion or a final statement.) □ *At any rate, we had a nice time at your party. We are grateful that you asked us.* □ *It's not much at any rate, but it's the best we can do.*

at best See *at (the) best.*

at close range very near; in close proximity. (Usually used in regard to shooting.) □ *The hunter fired at the deer at close range.* □ *The powder burns tell us that the gun was fired at close range.*

at cross purposes with opposing purposes or aims; [of two people or groups] misunderstanding each other's purposes or aims. □ *We are arguing at cross purposes. We aren't even discussing the same thing.* □ *Bill and Tom are working at cross purposes. Bill has bought modern furniture and Tom antique for the same room.*

at death's door near death. (Euphemistic.) □ *I was so ill that I was at death's door.* □ *The family dog was at death's door for three days, and then it finally died.*

at ease relaxed and comfortable. □ *I don't feel at ease driving when there is lots of traffic.* □ *Mary is most at ease when she's near the sea.*

at every turn everywhere; everywhere one looks. □ *There is a new problem at every turn.* □ *Life holds new adventures at every turn.*

at first glance when first examined; at an early stage. □ *At first glance, the problem appeared quite simple. Later we learned just how complex it really was.* □ *He appeared quite healthy at first glance.*

(at) full blast using full power; as loudly as possible. □ *The neighbours had*

their televisions on at full blast. □ *The car radio was on full blast. We couldn't hear what the driver was saying.*

at full speed AND **at full tilt** as fast as possible; very quickly. □ *The motor was running at full speed.* □ *Things are now operating at full speed.* □ *The car ran into the wall at full tilt.*

at full stretch with as much energy and strength as possible. □ *The police are working at full stretch to find the murderer.* □ *We cannot accept any more work. We are already working at full stretch.*

at full tilt See *at full speed.*

at half-mast half-way up or down. (Primarily referring to flags. Can be used for things other than flags as a joke.) □ *The flag was flying at half-mast because the general had died.* □ *We fly flags at half-mast when someone important dies.* □ *The little boy ran out of the house with his trousers at half-mast.*

at hand close by. (Used with both time and distance.) □ *I don't happen to have your application at hand at the moment.* □ *With the holiday season at hand, everyone is very excited.*

at home with someone or something comfortable with someone or something; comfortable doing something. (Informal. Especially with *be* or *feel.*) □ *Tom is very much at home with my parents.* □ *Sally seems to be very much at home with her new car.* □ *Mary feels at home with selling shares for a large brokerage house.*

at it again doing something again. (Informal. Usually with *be.*) □ *I asked Tom to stop playing his trumpet, but he's at it again.* □ *They are at it again. Why are they always fighting?*

at large free; uncaptured. (Usually said of criminals running loose.) □ *At midday the day after the robbery, the thieves were still at large.* □ *There is a murderer at large in the city.*

at length **1.** after some time; finally. □ *At length, the roses bloomed, and the* *tomatoes ripened.* □ *And at length, the wizard spoke.* **2.** AND **at some length** for quite a long time. □ *He spoke on and on at some length.* □ *He described the history of his village at length.*

at liberty free; unrestrained. □ *You're at liberty to go anywhere you wish.* □ *I'm not at liberty to discuss the matter.*

at loggerheads (with someone) in opposition; at an impasse; in a quarrel. □ *Mr. and Mrs. Jones have been at loggerheads with each other for years.* □ *The two political parties were at loggerheads during the entire legislative session.*

at (long) last after a long wait; finally. □ *At last the hostages were released.* □ *Sally earned her diploma at long last.*

at most See *at (the) best.*

at odds (with someone) in opposition to someone; *at loggerheads (with someone).)* □ *Mary is always at odds with her father about how late she can stay out.* □ *John and his father are always at odds, too.*

at one fell swoop AND **in one fell swoop** in a single incident; as a single event. (This phrase preserves the old word *fell*, meaning "terrible." Now a cliché, sometimes with humorous overtones.) □ *The party guests ate up all the snacks at one fell swoop.* □ *When the stock-market crashed, many large fortunes were wiped out in one fell swoop.*

at one's best in the best of health, temper, or condition. (Often in the negative.) □ *I'm not at my best in the morning.* □ *He's at his best after a good nap.*

at (one's) leisure at one's convenience, without regard to time. □ *Choose one or the other at leisure.* □ *Please look at the photographs at your leisure.*

at one's wits' end at the limits of one's mental resources. □ *I'm at my wits' end trying to solve this problem.* □ *Tom could do no more to earn money. He was at his wits' end.*

at present now; *at this point in time.* □ *We are not able to do any more at present.* □ *We may be able to lend you money next week, but not at present.*

at random without sequence or order. □ *Sally picked four names at random from the telephone directory.* □ *The gunman walked into the crowded restaurant and fired at random.* □ *Jane will read almost anything. She selects four novels at random at the library each week and reads them all.*

at sea (about something) confused; lost and bewildered. □ *Mary is all at sea about the process of getting married.* □ *When it comes to maths, John is totally at sea.*

at second hand from another person or source, not directly from personal experience or observation. □ *I wasn't present at the riot. I heard about it at second hand.* □ *Frank tell stories about the Gulf War, but he got them at second hand. He wasn't actually in the desert with the troops.*

at sixes and sevens disorderly; completely disorganized. (Informal.) □ *Mrs. Smith is at sixes and sevens since the death of her husband.* □ *The house is always at sixes and sevens when Bill's home by himself.*

at some length See under *at length.*

at someone's beck and call always ready to obey someone. □ *What makes you think I wait around here at your beck and call? I live here, too, you know!* □ *It was a fine hotel. There were dozens of maids and waiters at our beck and call.*

at someone's doorstep AND **on someone's doorstep** in someone's care; as someone's responsibility. □ *Why do you always have to lay your problems at my doorstep?* □ *I shall put this issue on someone else's doorstep.* □ *I don't want it on my doorstep.*

at someone's earliest convenience as soon as it is easy or convenient for someone. (This is also a polite way of saying immediately.) □ *Please stop by my office at your earliest convenience.* □

Bill, please have the oil changed at your earliest convenience.

at someone's mercy See *at the mercy of someone*.

at someone's request in response to someone's request; on being asked by someone. □ *At his mother's request, Tom stopped playing the saxophone.* □ *At the request of the police officer, Bill pulled his car over to the side of the road.*

at sometime sharp exactly at a named time. □ *You must be here at twelve o'clock sharp.* □ *The plane is expected to arrive at 7:45 sharp.*

at stake to be won or lost; at risk; hanging in the balance. □ *That's a very risky investment. How much money is at stake?* □ *I have everything at stake on this wager.*

at that rate if that is the case. □ *At that rate we'll never get the money which is owed us.* □ *They say that he resigned. At that rate he won't get another job in the firm.*

at (the) best AND **at (the) most** taking the most favourable point of view; with the most positive judgement. □ *I believe her to be totally negligent. At best, her actions were careless.* □ *At best, we found their visit pleasantly short.* □ *The dinner was not at all pleasant. At the best, the food was edible.* □ *At the most, she was careless, if not criminal.* □ *We shall do fifty miles per hour, at most.*

at the bottom of the ladder at the lowest level of pay and status. □ *Most people start work at the bottom of the ladder.* □ *When Ann was declared redundant, she had to start all over again at the bottom of the ladder.*

at the break of dawn See the following entry.

at the crack of dawn AND **at the break of dawn** at the earliest light of the day. □ *Jane was always up at the crack of dawn.* □ *The birds start singing at the break of dawn.*

at the drop of a hat immediately and without urging. □ *John was always ready to go fishing at the drop of a hat.* □ *If you need help, just call on me. I can come at the drop of a hat.*

at the eleventh hour at the last possible moment. (See also *eleventh-hour decision*.) □ *She always handed her term essays in at the eleventh hour.* □ *We don't worry about death until the eleventh hour.*

at the end of one's tether at the limits of one's endurance. □ *I'm at the end of my tether! I just can't go on this way!* □ *These children are driving me out of my mind. I'm at the end of my tether.*

at the end of the day 1. when the day has finished; at the end of the business day. □ *I leave here at the end of the day.* □ *How much was left at the end of the day?* 2. when everything else has been taken into consideration. □ *At the end of the day you will have to decide where you want to live.* □ *The committee interviewed many applicants for the post, but at the end of the day made no appointment.*

at the expense of someone or something to the detriment of someone or something; to the harm or disadvantage of someone or something. □ *He had a good laugh at the expense of his brother.* □ *He took employment in a better place at the expense of a larger income.*

at the last minute at the last possible chance. (Compare to *at the eleventh hour*.) □ *Please don't make reservations at the last minute.* □ *Why do you ask all your questions at the last minute?*

at the latest no later than. □ *Please pay this bill in ten days at the latest.* □ *I'll be home by midnight at the latest.*

at the mercy of someone AND **at someone's mercy** under the control of someone; without defence against someone. □ *We were left at the mercy of the arresting officer.* □ *Mrs. Franklin wanted Mr. Franklin at her mercy.*

at (the) most See *at (the) best*.

at the outset at the beginning. □ *It seemed like a very simple problem at the outset.* □ *At the outset, they were very happy. Then they had money problems.*

at the outside at the very most. (Informal.) □ *The car repairs will cost £300 at the outside.* □ *I'll be there in three weeks at the outside.*

at the point of doing something See *on the point of doing something.*

at the present time AND **at this point (in time)** now; *at present.* (Used often as a wordy replacement for *now.*) □ *We don't know the location of the stolen car at the present time.* □ *At this point in time, we feel very sad about his death.* □ *Yes, it's sad, but there is nothing we can do at this point.*

at the same time nevertheless; however. □ *Bill was able to pay for the car repairs. At the same time, he was very angry about the size of the bill.* □ *We agree to your demands. At the same time, we object strongly to your methods.*

at the top of one's voice with a very loud voice. □ *Bill called to Mary at the top of his voice.* □ *How can I work when you're all talking at the top of your voice?*

at (the) worst taking the worst point of view; with the most negative judgement; the worst one can say about something.

□ *At worst, Tom can be seen as greedy.* □ *Ann will receive a ticket for careless driving, at the worst.*

at this point (in time) See *at the present time.*

at this rate if things continue like this. (Compare to *at any rate* and *at that rate.*) □ *Hurry up! We'll never get there at this rate.* □ *At this rate, all the food will be gone before we get there.*

at this stage AND **at this stage of the game** at the current point in some event; currently. (The second phrase is an informal elaboration of the first phrase.) □ *We'll have to wait and see. There isn't much we can do at this stage of the game.* □ *At this stage, we are better off not calling the doctor.*

at times sometimes; occasionally. □ *I feel quite sad at times.* □ *At times, I wish I had never come here.*

at will whenever one wants; freely. (Compare to *at liberty.*) □ *You're free to come and go at will.* □ *You can eat anything you want at will.*

avoid someone or something like the plague to avoid someone or something totally. (Informal.) □ *What's wrong with Bob? Everyone avoids him like the plague.* □ *I don't like opera. I avoid it like the plague.*

AWOL See *absent without leave.*

B

babe in arms an innocent or naive person. (Informal.) □ *He's a babe in arms when it comes to taking girls out.* □ *Mary has no idea how to fight the election. Politically she's a babe in arms.*

babe in the woods a naive or innocent person; an inexperienced person. (From a children's story about two children who go into the woods unaware of the dangers.) □ *Bill is a mere babe in the woods when it comes to dealing with plumbers.* □ *The young couple are both very clever, but they are babes in the woods when it comes to buying a house.*

back and forth backwards and forwards repeatedly; first one way and then another way. (See also *to and fro*.) □ *The young man was pacing back and forth in the hospital waiting room.* □ *The pendulum on the clock swung back and forth.*

back down (from something) to withdraw or abandon an opinion, claim, accusation, or course of action. □ *Jane was forced to back down from her position on the budget.* □ *John agreed that it was probably better to back down than to risk getting shot.* □ *Bill doesn't like to back down from a fight.* □ *Sometimes it's better to back down than to get hurt.*

back in circulation socially active again. (Informal.) □ *Now that Bill is divorced, he's back in circulation again.* □ *Tom was in the hospital for a month, but now he's back in circulation.*

back of the beyond the most remote place; somewhere very remote. (Informal.) □ *John hardly ever comes to the city. He lives at the back of the beyond.* □ *Mary likes lively entertainment, but her husband likes to holiday in the back of the beyond.*

back out (of something) to withdraw from something you have agreed to do; to break an agreement. □ *The buyer tried to back out of the sale, but the seller wouldn't permit it.* □ *Please don't back out of our arrangement.* □ *Mary backed out at the last minute.*

back someone or something up AND **back up someone or something** to support someone or something; to agree with someone. □ *Please back me up in this argument.* □ *I would like you to back up John in this discussion.*

back to the drawing-board time to start over again; it is time to plan something over again, especially if it has gone wrong. (Also with *old* as in the examples.) □ *The scheme didn't work. Back to the drawing-board.* □ *I failed English this term. Well, back to the old drawing-board.*

back to the salt mines time to return to work, school, or something else which might be unpleasant. (Informal.) □ *It's eight o'clock. Time to go to work! Back to the salt mines.* □ *School starts again in the autumn, and then it's back to the salt mines again.*

bad-mouth someone or something to say bad things about someone or something; to libel someone. (Slang.) □ *Mr.*

Smith was always bad-mouthing Mrs. Smith. They didn't get along. □ John bad-mouths his car constantly because it doesn't run.

bag and baggage with one's luggage; with all one's possessions. (Informal.) □ Sally showed up at our door bag and baggage one Sunday morning. □ All right, if you won't pay the rent, out with you, bag and baggage!

bag of tricks a collection of special techniques or methods. (Informal.) □ What have you got in your bag of tricks that could help me with this problem? □ Here comes Mother with her bag of tricks. I'm sure she can help us.

bail out (of something) See bale out (of something).

bail someone or something out AND **bail out someone or something** 1. [with someone] to deposit a sum of money which allows someone to get out of jail while waiting for a trial; to get a person out of trouble. □ John was in jail. I had to go down to the police station to bail him out. □ You lot are always getting in trouble. Do you really expect me to bail out the whole gang of you every time you have a problem? 2. AND **bale something out** [with something] to remove water from the bottom of a boat by or scooping. □ Tom has to bail the boat out before we get in. □ You should always bale out a boat before using it.

balance the books to determine through accounting that accounts are in balance or that all money is accounted for. □ Jane was up all night balancing the books. □ The cashier was not allowed to leave the bank until the manager balanced the books.

bale out (of something) AND **bail out (of something)** 1. to jump out of an aeroplane (with a parachute). □ John still remembers the first time he baled out of a plane. □ When we get to 8,000 feet, we'll all bail out and drift down together. We'll open our parachutes at 2,000 feet. 2. to abandon a situation; to get out of something. (Informal.) □ John got

tired of classes, so he just baled out of school. □ Please stay, Bill. You've been with us too long to bail out now.

bale something out See under bail someone or something out.

ball and chain a person's special burden; a person's employment. (Informal. Prisoners are sometimes fettered with a chain attached to a leg on one end and a heavy metal ball on the other.) □ Mr. Franklin always referred to his wife as his ball and chain. □ Tom wanted to leave his job. He said he was tired of that old ball and chain.

ball of fire a very active and energetic person who always succeeds. (Informal.) □ Sally is a real ball of fire—she works late every night. □ Ann is no ball of fire, but she does get everything done.

bandy something about to utter or speak gossip freely; to spread rumours or tell secrets. □ They bandied the story about until everyone in the town had heard it. □ It's being bandied about that he's having an affair.

bang one's head against a brick wall See beat one's head against the wall.

bank on something to count on something; to rely on something. □ The weather forecast said it wouldn't rain, but I wouldn't bank on it. □ My word is to be trusted. You can bank on it.

baptism of fire a first experience of something, usually something difficult or unpleasant. □ My son's just had his first visit to the dentist. He stood up to the baptism of fire very well. □ Mary's had her baptism of fire as a teacher. She had to take the worst class in the school.

bargain for something to plan for something; to expect something. □ We knew it would be difficult, but we didn't bargain for this kind of trouble. □ I expected a few cancellations, but there were far more than I bargained for.

barge in (on someone or something) to break in on someone or something; to interrupt someone or something.

(Informal.) □ *Oh! I'm sorry. I didn't mean to barge in on you.* □ *They barged in on the church service and caused a commotion.* □ *You can't just barge in like that!*

bark up the wrong tree to make the wrong choice; to follow the wrong course. □ *If you think I'm the guilty person, you're barking up the wrong tree.* □ *The players blamed their bad record on the bowler, but they were barking up the wrong tree.*

bawl someone out AND **bawl out someone** to scold someone in a loud voice; to criticize someone severely. (Slang.) □ *The teacher bawled the pupil out for arriving late.* □ *Teachers don't usually bawl out pupils in public.*

be a cold fish to be a person who is distant and unfeeling. □ *Bob never cuddles his children. He's a real cold fish.* □ *Jane didn't cry when her parents died. She's a cold fish.*

be a copy-cat to be a person who copies or mimics what someone else does. (Informal.) □ *Sally wore a pink dress just like Mary's. Mary called Sally a copy-cat.* □ *Bill is such a copy-cat. He bought a coat just like mine.*

be a dead duck to be finished; to have failed or lost a contest; to be dead. (Slang.) □ *He missed the exam. He's a dead duck.* □ *Yes, John's a dead duck. He got drunk at work.*

be a drag to be a burden to someone; to be a bore. (Slang.) □ *It's a drag having to go to school today.* □ *Don't invite Peter. He's a real drag.*

be a fan of someone to be a follower or admirer of someone. □ *My mother is still a fan of the Beatles.* □ *I'm a great fan of the mayor of the town.*

be a goner to be dead or finished; to be as good as dead or nearly dead. (Slang.) □ *The boy brought the sick fish back to the pet shop to get his money back. "This one is a goner," he said.* □ *John thought he was a goner when his parachute didn't open.*

be a must to be something that you must do; to be something that you should see, attend, etc. (Informal.) □ *When you're in London, see the changing of the guard. It's a must.* □ *Wearing a school uniform is a must at my daughter's school.*

be a past master at something to have been proven extremely good or skillful at an activity. □ *Mary is a past master at cooking omelettes.* □ *Pam is a past master at the art of complaining.*

be a thorn in someone's side to be a constant source of annoyance to someone. □ *This problem is a thorn in my side. I wish I had a solution to it.* □ *John was a thorn in my side for years before I finally got rid of him.*

be about one's business to get busy doing something. □ *Why are you still in the pub? It's time to be about your business.* □ *Goodbye, Jane. I must be about my business.*

be abreast (of something) See *keep abreast (of something).*

be ahead (of someone or something) See under *get ahead (of someone or something).*

be all ears to be listening eagerly and carefully. (Informal. See also the following entry.) □ *Well, hurry up and tell me. I'm all ears.* □ *Be careful what you say. The children are all ears.*

be all eyes (and ears) to be alert; to await eagerly for something to happen or for someone or something to appear or be heard. (See also the previous entry.) □ *There they were, sitting at the table, all eyes. The birthday cake was soon to be served.* □ *Nothing can escape my notice. I'm all eyes and ears.*

be an end in itself to exist for its own sake; to serve no purpose but its own existence. □ *For Bob, art is an end in itself. He doesn't hope to make any money from it.* □ *Learning is an end in itself. Knowledge does not have to have a practical application.*

be an unknown quantity to be a person or thing about which little is known. □ *John is an unknown quantity. We don't know how he's going to act.* □ *The new shop assistant is an unknown quantity. Things may not turn out all right.*

be at someone's service to be ready to help someone in any way. (This is rarely meant literally.) □ *The count greeted me warmly and said, "Welcome to my home. Just let me know what you need. I'm at your service."* □ *The young woman at reception said, "Good morning, madam. I'm at your service."*

be becoming to someone [for something] to be complimentary to someone; [for something] to enhance someone's good looks. (Usually refers to clothing, hair, and other personal ornaments.) □ *That hair-style is very becoming to you.* □ *Your new fur coat is becoming to you.*

be bent on doing something to be determined to do something. □ *Jane was bent on having her own flat.* □ *Her mother was bent on keeping her at home.*

be beside oneself to be excited; to be disturbed; to be emotionally uncontrolled. □ *He was beside himself with grief.* □ *She laughed and laughed until she was beside herself.*

be better off doing something to be in a better or more advantageous position if something were done. □ *She'd be better off selling her house.* □ *They are better off flying to Detroit.*

be better off somewhere to be in a better or more advantageous position somewhere else. □ *They would be better off in Florida.* □ *We'd all be better off over there.*

be bursting at the seams See under *burst at the seams.*

be bursting with joy See under *burst with joy.*

be bursting with pride See under *burst with pride.*

be bushed to be tired or exhausted. (Slang.) □ *I can't go on, Mary. I'm just bushed.* □ *Oh, John, you look bushed! Whatever have you been doing?*

be careful not to do something to use care in avoiding difficulties. □ *Please be careful not to discuss politics with Mr. Brown.* □ *Please be careful not to break the vase.*

be careful (with something) to treat or handle something with caution. □ *Please be careful with the vase. It's old and valuable.* □ *That's too big a load. Be careful!*

be curtains for someone or something to be the death, end, or ruin of someone or something. (Informal. From the lowering or closing of the curtains at the end of a stage performance.) □ *If the car hadn't swerved, it would have been curtains for the pedestrians.* □ *If they can't get into the export market, it's curtains for the firm.*

be death to something to be very harmful to something. (Informal or slang.) □ *The salt they put on the roads in the winter is death to cars.* □ *Business lunches are death to his work schedule.*

be done with someone or something to be finished with someone or something. (Informal.) □ *Mary is done with Bill. She has found another boyfriend.* □ *I can't wait until I'm done with school forever.* □ *I agree. I'll be glad when we are done with all this work.*

be even-steven to be even (with someone). (Informal.) □ *Bill hit Tom; then Tom hit Bill. Now they are even-steven.* □ *Mary paid Ann the £100 she owed her. Ann said, "Good, we are even-steven."*

be flying high See *fly high.*

be for something to support or be in favour of someone or something. □ *I'm for abandoning the scheme.* □ *Mary is running for office, and the whole family is for her.*

be getting on for something to be close to something; to be nearly at something, such as a time, date, age, etc. (Informal.) □ *It's getting on for midnight.* □ *He must be getting on for fifty.*

be given a big send-off See *get a big send-off.*

be given a free hand (with something) to be granted complete control over something. □ *I wasn't given a free hand with the last project.* □ *John was in charge then, but he wasn't given a free hand either.* ALSO: **give someone a free hand (with something)** to give someone complete control over something. □ *They gave me a free hand with the project.* □ *I feel proud that they gave me a free hand. That means that they trust my judgement.*

be given a hard time to be presented with or experience unnecessary difficulties. (Informal. Also with *have*.) □ *James is being given a hard time by the new boss.* □ *I had a really hard time when the new manager came.* ALSO: **give someone a hard time** to give someone unnecessary difficulty. □ *Please don't give me a hard time.*

be given to understand See under *give someone to understand something.*

be half-hearted about someone or something to be unenthusiastic about someone or something. □ *Ann was half-hearted about the choice of Sally for manager.* □ *Don't take the English course if you're going to be half-hearted about it.*

be into something to be interested in something; to be involved in something. (Slang. See also *get into something.*) □ *Did you hear? Tom is into sky-diving!* □ *Too many people are into drugs.*

be involved with someone or something See under *get involved (with someone or something).*

be of age to be old enough to marry or to sign legal agreements. (See also *come of age.*) □ *Now that Mary is of age, she can buy her own car.* □ *When I'm of age, I'm going to get married and move to the city.*

be of service (to someone) to help someone; to be of assistance to someone. □ *Good morning, madam. May I be of service to you?* □ *Welcome to the Bedford Hotel. May I be of service?*

be off 1. to be spoiled; to be rotten; to be sour. (Informal.) □ *Oh! I'm afraid that this meat is off. Don't eat it.* □ *The milk is off.* 2. to leave; to depart. □ *Well, I must be off. Goodbye.* □ *The train leaves in an hour, so I must be off.*

be off on the wrong foot See under *get off on the wrong foot.*

be off to a bad start See under *get off on the wrong foot.*

be old hat to be old-fashioned; to be outmoded. (Informal.) □ *That's a silly idea. It's old hat.* □ *Nobody does that any more. That's just old hat.*

be oneself again to be healthy again; to be calm again; to be restored. □ *After such a long illness, it's good to be myself again.* □ *I'm sorry that I lost my temper. I think I'm myself again now.*

be poles apart to be very different, especially in opinions or attitudes; to be far from coming to an agreement. □ *Mr. and Mrs. Jones don't get along well. They are poles apart.* □ *They'll never sign the contract because they are poles apart.*

be so See *be to.*

be the last person to be the most unlikely person of whom one could think in a particular situation; the most unlikely person to do something. □ *Bob was the last person for Tom to insult. He's so hot-tempered.* □ *Mary was the last person to ask to chair the meeting—she's so shy.*

be the spit and image of someone AND **be the spitting image of someone** to look very much like someone; to resemble someone very closely. □ *John is the spit and image of his father.* □ *You are the spitting image of a girl I used to know.*

be the spitting image of someone See the previous entry.

be the teacher's pet to be the teacher's favourite pupil. (Informal.) □ *Sally is the teacher's pet. She always gets special treatment.* □ *The other pupils don't like the teacher's pet.*

be through with something to have finished with something. (Informal. Compare to *get through something*.) □ *You can use this pencil when I'm through with it.* □ *Can I have the salt when you're through with it?*

be too AND **be so** to be something (despite anything to the contrary). (An emphatic form of *is, am, are, was, were.* See also *do too, have too.*) □ MOTHER: *Billy, you aren't old enough to be up this late.* Billy: *I am too!* □ *I was so! I was there exactly when I said I would be!*

be up to something (Informal.) **1.** to be occupied in some activity, often something secret or wrong. □ *Those kids are up to something. They're too quiet.* □ *Goodness knows what that child will be up to next.* **2.** to be capable of something; to be fit enough for something. □ *John's not up to doing a job of that kind.* □ *Mary's mother's been ill and is not up to travelling yet.* **3.** to be as good as something; to be good enough for something. □ *This work's not up to the standard of the class.* □ *Your last essay was not up to your best.*

be with someone to be on someone's side; to be allied with someone. (Also used literally.) □ *Keep on trying, John. We are all with you.* □ *Remember that I'm with you in your efforts to win re-election.*

bear a grudge (against someone) AND **have a grudge against someone; hold a grudge (against someone)** to have an old resentment for someone; to have continual anger for someone. □ *She bears a grudge against the judge who sentenced her.* □ *I have a grudge against my landlord for overcharging me.* □ *How long can a person hold a grudge? Let's be friends.*

bear fruit to yield results; to give (literal or figurative) fruit. □ *Our apple tree didn't bear fruit this year.* □ *I hope your new plan bears fruit.* □ *We've had many good ideas, but none of them has borne fruit.*

bear one's cross AND **carry one's cross** to carry or bear one's burden; to endure one's difficulties. □ *It's a very bad disease, but I'll just have to bear my cross.* □ *I can't help you with it. You'll have to carry your own cross.*

bear someone or something in mind See *keep someone or something in mind.*

bear something out AND **bear out something** to demonstrate or prove that something is right; to support or confirm something. □ *I hope that the facts will bear your story out.* □ *I'm certain that the facts will bear out my story.* □ *The evidence of the witness bore out what the accused said in his statement.*

bear the brunt (of something) to suffer or withstand the worst part or the strongest part of something, such as an attack. □ *I had to bear the brunt of her screaming and shouting.* □ *Why don't you talk with her the next time? I'm tired of bearing the brunt.*

bear up to endure; to hold up in a bad situation; to retain strength and continue supporting yourself or something else. □ *This is such a trying time. I don't see how she can bear up.* □ *Bear up! The exams will soon be over.* □ *How long will that bridge bear up under all that heavy traffic?*

bear with someone or something to be patient with someone or something; to endure someone or something. □ *Please bear with me while I fill out this form.* □ *Please bear with my old car. It'll get us there sooner or later.*

beard the lion in his den to face an adversary on the adversary's home ground. □ *I went to the solicitor's office to beard the lion in his den.* □ *He said he hadn't wanted to come to my home, but it was better to beard the lion in his den.*

beat a (hasty) retreat to retreat or withdraw very quickly. □ *We went out into the cold weather, but beat a retreat to the warmth of our fire.* □ *The cat beat a hasty retreat to its own garden when it saw the dog.*

beat a path to someone's door [for people] to come to someone in great numbers. (So many people will wish to come and see one that they will wear down a pathway to one's door.) □ *I have a product so good that everyone is beating a path to my door.* □ *If you really become famous, people will beat a path to your door to get your autograph.*

beat about the bush to avoid answering a question or discussing a subject directly; to stall; to waste time. □ *Let's stop beating about the bush and discuss this matter.* □ *Stop beating about the bush and answer my question.*

beat one's brains out (to do something) to work very hard (to do something); to struggle with a difficult task. (See also *beat someone's brains out.*) □ *I beat my brains out to solve the problem.* □ *That's the last time I'll beat my brains out trying to think of an excuse for you.*

beat one's head against the wall AND **bang one's head against a brick wall** to waste one's time trying to accomplish something which is completely hopeless. □ *You're wasting your time trying to repair this house. You're just beating your head against the wall.* □ *You're banging your head against a brick wall trying to get that dog to behave properly.*

beat someone to it See the following entry.

beat someone to the draw AND **beat someone to it** to do something before someone else does it. (Informal.) □ *I wanted to have the first new car, but Sally beat me to the draw.* □ *I planned to write a book about computers, but someone else beat me to it.*

beat someone up AND **beat up someone** to harm or subdue a person by beating and striking. (Informal.) □ *The robber beat me up and took my money.* □ *He's beaten up several people already.*

beat someone's brains out to beat someone severely. (See also *beat one's brains out (to do something).*) □ *If I catch him, I'll beat his brains out.* □ *Take it easy. Don't beat his brains out.*

beat the band very much; very fast. (Informal. This has no literal meaning.) □ *The carpenter sawed and hammered to beat the band.* □ *They baked biscuits and pies to beat the band.*

beat the living daylights out of someone AND **beat the stuffing out of someone** to beat or spank someone, probably a child. (Informal.) □ *If you do that again, I'll beat the living daylights out of you.* □ *The last time Bobby put the cat in the refrigerator, his mother beat the living daylights out of him.* □ *He wouldn't stop, so I beat the stuffing out of him.*

beat the stuffing out of someone See the previous entry.

Beauty is only skin deep. a proverb meaning that looks are only superficial and so are of no real value. □ BOB: *Isn't Jane lovely?* TOM: *Yes, but beauty is only skin deep.* □ *I know that she looks wonderful, but beauty is only skin deep.*

bed of roses a situation or way of life that is always happy and comfortable. □ *Living with Pat can't be a bed of roses, but her husband is always smiling.* □ *Being the boss isn't exactly a bed of roses. There are so many problems to sort out.*

beef something up AND **beef up something** to make something stronger; to supplement something. (Slang.) □ *The government decided to beef the army up by buying hundreds of new tanks.* □ *I wish they'd beef up the newspaper with more international coverage.*

before you can say Jack Robinson almost immediately. □ *And before you could say Jack Robinson, the bird flew away.* □ *I'll catch a plane and be there before you can say Jack Robinson.*

before you know it almost immediately. □ *I'll be there before you know it.* □ *If you keep spending money like that, you'll be penniless before you know it.*

beg off to ask to be released from something; to refuse an invitation. □ *I have an important meeting, so I'll have to beg off.* □ *I wanted to go to the affair, but I had to beg off.*

beg the question to evade the issue; to carry on a false argument where one assumes as proved the very point which is being argued. □ *Stop arguing in circles. You're begging the question.* □ *It's hopeless to argue with Sally. She always begs the question.*

beggar description to be impossible to describe well enough to give an accurate picture; to be impossible to do justice to in words. □ *Her cruelty to her child beggars description.* □ *The soprano's voice beggars description.*

Beggars can't be choosers. a proverb meaning that one should not criticize something one gets for free. □ *I don't like the old hat that you gave me, but beggars can't be choosers.* □ *It doesn't matter whether people like the free food or not. Beggars can't be choosers.*

begin to see daylight to begin to see the end of a long task. (See also *see the light at the end of the tunnel*.) □ *I've been working on my thesis for two years, and at last I'm beginning to see daylight.* □ *I've been so busy. Only in the last week have I begun to see daylight.*

begin to see the light to begin to understand (something). (See also *see the light*.) □ *My algebra class is hard for me, but I'm beginning to see the light.* □ *I was totally confused, but I began to see the light after your explanation.*

behind someone's back in secret; without someone's knowledge. □ *Please don't talk about me behind my back.* □ *She sold the car behind his back.*

behind the scenes privately; out of public view. □ *The people who worked behind the scenes are the real heroes of this project.* □ *We don't usually thank the people who are behind the scenes.*

believe it or not to choose to believe something or not. □ *Believe it or not, I just got home from work.* □ *I'm over fifty years old, believe it or not.*

belt something out AND **belt out something** to sing or play a song loudly and with spirit. (Slang.) □ *She really knows how to belt out a song.* □ *When she's playing the piano, she really belts the music out.*

bend over backwards to do something See *fall over backwards to do something*.

bend someone's ear to talk to someone at length, perhaps annoyingly. (Informal.) □ *Tom is over there bending Jane's ear about something.* □ *I'm sorry. I didn't mean to bend your ear for an hour, but I'm upset.*

beside the point irrelevant. □ *That's very interesting, but beside the point.* □ *That's beside the point. You're evading the issue.*

best bib and tucker one's best clothing. (Informal.) □ *I always put on my best bib and tucker on Sundays.* □ *Put on your best bib and tucker, and let's go to the city.*

bet one's bottom dollar AND **bet one's life** to be quite certain (about something). (Informal. A *bottom dollar* is one's last dollar.) □ *I'll be there. You bet your bottom dollar.* □ *I bet my bottom dollar you can't swim across the pool.* □ *You bet your life I can't swim that far.*

bet one's life See the previous entry.

better late than never better to do something late than not at all. □ *I wish you had come here sooner, but better late than never.* □ *She bought a house when she was quite old. Better late than never.*

between the devil and the deep blue sea faced with having to choose between two courses of action, both equally risky or undesirable. □ *He* didn't want to go out with Jane or Margaret. *He was between the devil and the deep blue sea.* □ *Mary's been offered two jobs, but one is miles away and one is badly paid. She's really between the devil and the deep blue sea.*

betwixt and between undecided; not settled. □ *I wish she would choose. She has been betwixt and between for three weeks.* □ *Tom is so betwixt and between about getting married. I don't think he's ready.*

beyond measure more than can be measured; in a very large amount. □ *Her contribution to the work was beyond measure.* □ *A mother's love for her children is beyond measure.*

beyond one's ken outside the extent of one's knowledge or understanding. □ *Why she married him is beyond our ken.* □ *His attitude to others is quite beyond my ken.*

beyond one's means more than one can afford. □ *I'm sorry, but this house is beyond our means. Please show us a cheaper one.* □ *Mr. and Mrs. Brown are living beyond their means.*

beyond reasonable doubt almost without any doubt. (A legal phrase.) □ *The jury decided beyond reasonable doubt that she had committed the crime.* □ *She was also found guilty beyond reasonable doubt.*

beyond the call of duty See *(above and)* beyond the call of duty.

beyond the pale unacceptable; outlawed. (The Pale historically was the area of English government around Dublin. The people who lived outside this area were regarded as uncivilized.) □ *Your behaviour is simply beyond the pale.* □ *Because of Tom's rudeness, he's considered beyond the pale and is never asked to parties any more.*

beyond the shadow of a doubt completely without doubt. (Said of a fact, not a person. See also *beyond reasonable doubt*.) □ *We accepted her story as true beyond the shadow of a doubt.* □ *Please assure us that you are certain*

of the facts beyond the shadow of a doubt.

beyond words more than one can say. (Especially with *grateful* and *thankful*.) □ *Sally was thankful beyond words at being released.* □ *I don't know how to thank you. I'm grateful beyond words.*

bide one's time to wait patiently. □ *I've been biding my time for years, just waiting for a chance like this.* □ *He's not the type to just sit there and bide his time. He wants some action.*

big fish in a small pond an important person in the midst of less important people. □ *I'd rather be a big fish in a small pond than the opposite.* □ *The trouble with Tom is that he's a big fish in a small pond. He needs more competition.*

birds and the bees human reproduction. (A euphemistic way of referring to human sex and reproduction.) □ *My father tried to teach me about the birds and the bees.* □ *He's twenty years old and doesn't understand about the birds and the bees.*

bird's-eye view 1. a view seen from high above. (Refers to the height of a flying bird.) □ *We got a bird's-eye view of London as the plane began its descent.* □ *From the top of the tower you get a splendid bird's-eye view of the village.* 2. a brief survey of something; a hasty look at something. (Refers to the smallness of a bird's eye.) □ *The course provides a bird's-eye view of the works of Mozart, but it doesn't deal with them in enough detail for your purpose.* □ *All you need is a bird's-eye view of the events of World War II to pass the test.*

Birds of a feather flock together. a proverb meaning that people of the same type seem to gather together. □ *Bob and Tom are just alike. They like each other's company because birds of a feather flock together.* □ *When Mary joined a club for redheaded people, she said, "Birds of a feather flock together."*

bite off more than one can chew to take (on) more than one can deal with; to be overconfident. □ *Ann is exhausted* *again. She's always biting off more than she can chew.* □ *Peter can't cope with two jobs. He's bitten off more than he can chew.*

bite one's nails to be nervous or anxious; to bite one's nails from nervousness or anxiety. □ *I spent all afternoon biting my nails, worrying about you driving on that road.* □ *We've all been biting our nails waiting to hear the result.*

bite someone's head off to speak sharply and angrily to someone. (Informal.) □ *There was no need to bite Mary's head off just because she was five minutes late.* □ *The boss has been biting everybody's head off since his wife left him.*

bite the bullet to go ahead and endure (something). □ *I didn't want to go to the doctor, but I bit the bullet and went.* □ *John, you just have to bite the bullet and do what you're told.*

bite the dust to fail; to be defeated; to die. (Slang. Typically heard in films about the U.S. Western frontier.) □ *A bullet hit the cowboy in the chest, and he bit the dust.* □ *Our plans to move the furniture have bitten the dust.*

bite the hand that feeds one to do harm to someone who does good things for you. □ *I'm your mother! How can you bite the hand that feeds you?* □ *It's a real case of biting the hand that feeds her. She's reported her stepmother to the police for shop-lifting.*

bitter pill to swallow an unpleasant fact that has to be accepted. □ *It was a bitter pill for her brother to swallow when she married his enemy.* □ *We found his deception a bitter pill to swallow.*

black and blue bruised; showing signs of having been physically harmed. □ *The child was black and blue after having been beaten.* □ *She was black and blue all over after falling out of the tree.*

black out to faint or pass out. □ *Sally blacked out just before the crash.* □ *I was so frightened that I blacked out for a minute.*

black sheep (of the family) a member of a family or group who is unsatisfactory or not up to the standard of the rest; the worst member of the family. □ *Mary is the black sheep of the family. She's always in trouble with the police.* □ *The others are all in well-paid jobs, but John is unemployed. He's the black sheep of the family.*

blank cheque freedom or permission to act as one wishes or thinks necessary. (From a signed bank cheque with the amount left blank.) □ *He's been given a blank cheque with regard to reorganizing the work-force.* □ *The manager has been given no instructions about how to train the staff. He's just been given a blank cheque.*

blaze a trail to lead or show the way towards something new, especially a new area of knowledge or activity. □ *The hospital is blazing a trail in medical discoveries.* □ *Professor Williams blazed a trail in the study of physics.*

bleep something out AND **bleep out something** to replace a word or phrase in a radio or television broadcast with some sort of musical noise. (Informal. This is sometimes done to prevent an obscene word or other information from being broadcast.) □ *He tried to say the word on television, but they bleeped it out.* □ *They tried to bleep out the whole sentence.*

blessing in disguise something that turns out to be fortunate and advantageous after seeming to be the opposite at first. □ *Our missing the train was a blessing in disguise. It was involved in a crash.* □ *It was a blessing in disguise that I didn't get the job. I was offered a better one the next day.*

blind leading the blind See *(a case of) the blind leading the blind.*

blow-by-blow account AND **blow-by-blow description** a detailed description (of an event) given as the event takes place. (This referred originally to boxing.) □ *I want to listen to a blow-by-blow account of the prize fight.* □ *The solicitor got the witness to give a blow-by-blow description of the argument.*

blow-by-blow description See the previous entry.

blow hot and cold to be changeable or uncertain (about something). (Informal.) □ *He keeps blowing hot and cold on the question of moving to the country.* □ *He blows hot and cold about this. I wish he'd make up his mind.*

blow off steam See *let off steam.*

blow one's own trumpet to boast or praise oneself. □ *Tom is always blowing his own trumpet. Is he really as good as he says he is?* □ *I find it hard to blow my own trumpet, and so no one takes any notice of me.*

blow one's top to become very angry; to lose one's temper. (Informal.) □ *His rudeness was just too much for her. She blew her top.* □ *I was so angry I could have blown my top.*

blow over to pass and be forgotten; to die down. □ *Given time, all this controversy will blow over.* □ *No one remembers the scandal. It's all blown over.*

blow someone's brains out AND **blow out someone's brains** to kill someone with a gun. (Slang.) □ *The robber grabbed the gun and blew her brains out.* □ *He went into the garden and blew out his brains with a shot-gun.*

blow someone's cover to reveal someone's true identity or purpose. (Slang.) □ *The spy was very careful not to blow her cover.* □ *I tried to disguise myself, but my dog recognized me and blew my cover.*

blow someone's mind (Slang.) **1.** to destroy the function of someone's brain. □ *It was a terrible experience. It nearly blew his mind.* □ *She blew her mind on drugs.* **2.** to overwhelm someone; to excite someone. □ *It was so beautiful, it nearly blew my mind.* □ *Sally's music was so wild. It nearly blew Fred's mind.*

blow something out of all proportion See under *out of all proportion.*

blow the gaff to reveal something secret, sometimes to the police. (Slang.) □ *The police would never have suspected Dave of the robbery, but his accomplice blew the gaff.* □ *The teacher discovered the boys smoking behind the shed, because one of the other pupils blew the gaff.*

blow the lid off (something) to reveal something, especially wrongdoing; to make wrongdoing public. (Informal.) □ *The police blew the lid off the smuggling ring.* □ *The government is glad that they blew the lid off the opposition's activities.*

blow the whistle (on someone or something) to report someone's wrongdoing to someone (such as the police) who can stop the wrongdoing. (Slang.) □ *The citizens' group blew the whistle on the skinheads by calling the police.* □ *The gangs were getting very bad. It was definitely time to blow the whistle.*

blow up to get angry; to lose one's temper and shout (at someone). (Informal.) □ *I'm sorry. I didn't mean to blow up.* □ *You'd blow up, too, if you'd had a day like mine.*

blow up in someone's face [for something] suddenly to get ruined or destroyed while seeming to go well. □ *All my plans blew up in my face when she broke off the engagement.* □ *It is terrible for your hopes of promotion to blow up in your face.*

blue blood the blood [heredity] of a noble family; aristocratic ancestry. □ *The earl refuses to allow anyone who is not of blue blood to marry his son.* □ *Although Mary's family are poor, she has blue blood in her veins.*

boggle someone's mind to confuse someone; to overwhelm someone; to blow someone's mind. (Slang.) □ *The size of the house boggles my mind.* □ *She said that his arrogance boggled her mind.*

boil down to something to *come down to something;* to be essentially something; to mean (something) in effect. (Informal.) □ *It all boils down to* *whether you wish to buy a car.* □ *It boils down to a question of good health.*

bone of contention the subject or point of an argument; an unsettled point of disagreement. □ *We've fought for so long that we've forgotten what the bone of contention is.* □ *The question of a fence between the houses has become quite a bone of contention.*

bone up (on something) to study something thoroughly; to review the facts about something. (Slang.) □ *I have to bone up on the Highway Code because I have to take my driving test tomorrow.* □ *I take mine next month, so I'll have to bone up, too.*

boot someone or something out See *kick someone or something out.*

bore someone stiff AND **bore someone to death** to bore someone very much. (Informal. *Stiff* is an old slang word meaning "dead.") □ *The play bored me stiff.* □ *The lecture bored everyone to death.*

bore someone to death See the previous entry.

born with a silver spoon in one's mouth born with many advantages; born to a wealthy family. □ *Sally was born with a silver spoon in her mouth.* □ *I'm glad I was not born with a silver spoon in my mouth.*

boss someone around AND **boss around someone** to give orders to someone; to keep telling someone what to do. (Informal.) □ *Stop bossing me around. I'm not your employee.* □ *Captain Smith bosses around the whole crew. That's his job.*

botch something up AND **botch up something** to ruin something; to make a mess of something. (Informal.) □ *I botched the whole project up.* □ *I hope you don't botch up anything else.*

bother with someone or something to concern oneself with someone or something. □ *Please don't bother with my brother.* □ *Don't bother with the dishes. I'll do them later.*

bottle something up AND **bottle up something** to hold one's feelings within; to keep from saying something which one feels strongly about. □ *Let's talk about it, John. You shouldn't bottle it up.* □ *Don't bottle up your problems. It's better to discuss them with someone.*

bottom line (Informal.) **1.** the last figure on a financial balance sheet. □ *What's the bottom line? How much do I owe you?* □ *Don't tell me all those figures! Just tell me the bottom line.* **2.** the result; the final outcome; the crux of the matter. □ *I know about all the problems, but what is the bottom line? What will happen?* □ *The bottom line is that you have to go to the meeting because no one else can.*

bottom out to reach the lowest point. □ *The price of wheat bottomed out last week. Now it's rising again.* □ *My interest in the university bottomed out in my second year, so I resigned and got a job.*

bound for somewhere on the way to somewhere; planning to go to somewhere. □ *I'm bound for Mexico. In fact, I'm leaving this afternoon.* □ *I'm bound for the seaside. Do you want to go, too?*

bound hand and foot with hands and feet tied up. □ *The robbers left us bound hand and foot.* □ *We remained bound hand and foot until the maid found us and untied us.*

bow and scrape to be very humble and subservient. □ *Please don't bow and scrape. We are all equal here.* □ *The shop assistant came in, bowing and scraping, and asked if he could help us.*

bow out to depart; to resign; to retire. □ *I've done all that I can do. Now is the time to bow out.* □ *Most workers bow out at the normal retirement age.*

bowl someone over to surprise or overwhelm someone with emotion such as gratitude, admiration, or grief. □ *The news of my promotion bowled me over.* □ *The details of the proposed project bowled everyone over.*

Box and Cox two people who keep failing to meet. (Although they both sometimes go to the same place, they are never there at the same time. From characters in a nineteenth-century comedy, one of whom rented a room by day, the other the same room by night.) □ *Since her husband started night-shift, they are Box and Cox. She leaves for work in the morning before he gets home.* □ *The two teachers are Box and Cox. Mr. Smith takes class on Monday and Wednesday and Mr. Brown on Tuesday and Thursday.*

branch out (into something) to expand; to develop in a new direction. □ *The factory must branch out into electronics in order to survive.* □ *She branched out into a new line of work.* □ *She felt it was time to branch out.*

bread and butter [a person's] livelihood or income. □ *Selling cars is a lot of hard work, but it's my bread and butter.* □ *It was hard to give up my bread and butter, but I felt it was time to retire.*

Break a leg! Good luck! (Theatrical slang. This is said to actors before a performance instead of *Good luck.* Also used literally.) □ *Before the play, John said to Mary, "Break a leg!"* □ *Saying "Break a leg!" before a performance is an old theatrical tradition.*

break camp to close down a campsite; to pack up and move on. □ *Early this morning we broke camp and moved on northward.* □ *Okay, everyone. It's time to break camp. Take those tents down and fold them neatly.*

break down to lose control of one's emotions; to have a nervous collapse. □ *He couldn't keep going. He finally broke down and wept.* □ *I was afraid I'd break down.*

break even to have an income equal to one's expenses. (This implies that money was not earned or lost.) □ *Unfortunately my business just managed to break even last year.* □ *I made a bad investment, but I broke even.*

break in (on someone or something) to interrupt someone or something; to come in suddenly and interrupt someone or something. □ *I'm sorry. I didn't mean to break in on your conference.* □ *Tom frequently broke in on his sister and her boyfriend.* □ *I think he broke in on purpose.*

break in(to something) to enter into a place (illegally) by the use of force. □ *The robber broke into the house.* □ *If the door had been left unlocked, he wouldn't have had to break in.*

break into tears to start crying suddenly. □ *I was so sad that I broke into tears.* □ *I always break into tears at a funeral.*

break it off to end a relationship. (Informal. See also *break off with someone.*) □ *I knew she was getting ready to break it off, but Tom didn't.* □ *After a few long and bitter arguments, they broke it off.*

break loose (from someone or something) to get away from a person or a thing that is holding one. □ *The criminal broke loose from the police officer.* □ *It's hard to break loose from home.* □ *I was twenty years old before I could break loose.*

break new ground to begin to do something which no one else has done; to pioneer (in an enterprise). (See also *break ground for something.*) □ *Dr. Anderson was breaking new ground in cancer research.* □ *They were breaking new ground in consumer electronics.*

break off with someone to end a friendship or relationship with someone, especially a boyfriend or a girlfriend. (Informal.) □ *Tom has finally broken off with Mary.* □ *I knew it couldn't last. He was bound to break off with her.*

break one's duck to have one's first success at something. (From a cricketing expression meaning "to begin scoring.") □ *At last Jim's broken his duck. He's got a girl to go out with him.* □ *Jane has failed all her exams up till now, but she's broken her duck by passing French.*

break one's neck (to do something) to work very hard or fast to do something; to hurry. (Informal.) □ *I broke my neck to get here on time.* □ *That's the last time I'll break my neck to help you. You didn't need the work right away.*

break one's word not to do what one said one would; not to keep one's promise. □ *Don't say you'll visit your grandmother if you can't go. She hates people to break their word.* □ *If you break your word, she won't trust you again.*

break out in a cold sweat to perspire from fever, fear, or anxiety. □ *I was so frightened I broke out in a cold sweat.* □ *The patient broke out in a cold sweat.*

break out in something to erupt with something such as a rash, a cold sweat, or pimples. (See also the previous entry.) □ *After being in the woods, I broke out in a rash. I must be allergic to some plant.* □ *When I eat chocolate, I break out in pimples.*

break out (of something) to force one's way out of a place. □ *The criminal broke out of jail.* □ *The lion broke out of its cage and terrorized the village.* □ *I've always been afraid that the lion would break out.*

break someone or something in AND **break in someone or something 1.** [with *someone*] to train someone to do a job; to supervise a new person learning a new job. □ *I have to break in a new worker.* □ *It takes time to break a new worker in.* **2.** [with *something*] to make something fit by wearing or using it; to operate something when it is new to make it run smoothly and well. □ *I'll be glad when I've finished breaking in these shoes.* □ *Yes, it takes time to break them in.* □ *The car will run better after I break it in.*

break someone's fall to cushion a falling person; to lessen the impact of a falling person. □ *When the little boy fell out of the window, the bushes broke his fall.* □ *The old lady slipped on the ice, but a snowbank broke her fall.*

break someone's heart to cause someone emotional pain. □ *It just broke my heart when Tom ran away from home.* □ *Sally broke John's heart when she refused to marry him.*

break something away AND **break something loose; break something off; break off something** to break and dislodge a piece of something. □ *Break the glass away from the frame, and then put in the new pane of glass.* □ *I broke a tooth loose.* □ *Have some of this toffee. Break a piece off.* □ *Okay, I'll break off a piece.*

break something loose See the previous entry.

break something off See *break something away.*

break the back of something to complete the largest or most difficult part of something. (Informal.) □ *He hasn't finished the essay, but he's broken the back of it.* □ *We've broken the back of the paperwork. Leave it for today.*

break the bank to leave someone without any money. (Informal.) □ *It will hardly break the bank if we go out to dinner just once.* □ *Buying a new dress at that price won't break the bank.*

break the ice to start social communication and conversation. □ *Tom is so outgoing. He's always the first one to break the ice at parties.* □ *It's hard to break the ice at formal events.*

break the news (to someone) to tell someone some important news, usually bad news. □ *The doctor had to break the news to Jane about her husband's cancer.* □ *I hope that the doctor broke the news gently.*

break up (with someone) to end a love affair or a relationship. (Informal.) □ *Tom finally broke up with Mary.* □ *I thought they would break up. He has been so moody lately.*

breath of fresh air 1. a breath of air which is not stale; a breath of air taken outside. □ *I feel faint. I think I need a breath of fresh air.* □ *You look ill,*

John. *What you need is a breath of fresh air.* **2.** a new, fresh, and imaginative approach (to something). □ *Sally, with all her wonderful ideas, is a breath of fresh air.* □ *New furniture in this room is like a breath of fresh air.*

Breathe again! Relax! □ *Breathe again! She didn't see us.* □ *Breathe again! The bus hasn't arrived yet.*

breathe down someone's neck to keep close watch on someone; to watch someone's activities, especially in order to try to hurry something along. (Informal. Refers to standing very close behind a person.) □ *I can't work with you breathing down my neck all the time. Go away.* □ *I will get through my life without your help. Stop breathing down my neck.*

breathe one's last to die; to breathe one's last breath. □ *Mrs. Smith breathed her last this morning.* □ *I'll keep running every day until I breathe my last.*

bright and early very early. □ *Yes, I'll be there bright and early.* □ *I want to see you here on time tomorrow, bright and early, or you're sacked!*

bring down the curtain (on something) See *ring down the curtain (on something).*

bring home the bacon to earn a salary. (Informal.) □ *I've got to get to work if I'm going to bring home the bacon.* □ *Go out and get a job so you can bring home the bacon.*

bring someone or something up AND **bring up someone or something** to mention a person or a thing. □ *Please don't bring up that matter again.* □ *Please don't bring up John Jones's name again.* □ *I'm sorry. I won't bring him up again.*

bring someone round **1.** to bring someone for a visit; to bring someone for someone (else) to meet. □ *Please bring your wife round sometime. I'd love to meet her.* □ *You've just got to bring the doctor round for dinner.* **2.** to bring someone to consciousness. □ *The doctor brought Tom round with smelling-*

salts. □ *The boxer was knocked out, but the trainer brought him round.*

bring someone to to bring someone to consciousness. (See also *bring someone around; come to.*) □ *The doctor brought the patient to.* □ *She's hurt! Come on, help me bring her to.*

bring someone up to date (on someone or something) to tell someone the news about something. □ *Please bring me up to date on the Middle East situation.* □ *Please bring me up to date on John. I want to hear all the news.* □ *And bring me up to date, too.*

bring something about AND **bring about something** to make something happen. (Compare to *bring something off.*) □ *Is she clever enough to bring it about?* □ *Oh yes, she can bring about anything she wants.*

bring something crashing down (around one('s ears)) to destroy something that one has built; to destroy something that one has a special interest in. □ *Her foolish action brought her whole life crashing down around her.* □ *Bob's low marks in English brought everything crashing down around his ears.*

bring something home to someone to cause someone to realize the truth of something. □ *Seeing the starving refugees on television really brings home the tragedy of their situation.* □ *It wasn't until she failed her exam that the importance of studying was brought home to her.*

bring something into question AND **call something into question** to question something; to express suspicion about something. □ *It was necessary to bring your part in this matter into question.* □ *The city council brought the building project into question.* □ *We were forced to call Dr. Jones's qualifications into question.* □ *They called the whole project into question.*

bring something off AND **bring off something** to make something happen or succeed. □ *She managed to bring the party off with no difficulty.* □ *I didn't* *think Mary would bring off the deception, but she did.*

bring something to a close See *bring something to an end.*

bring something to a halt See *bring something to an end.*

bring something to a head to cause something to come to the point when a decision has to be made or action taken. (See also *come to a head.*) □ *The latest disagreement between management and the union has brought matters to a head. There will be an all out strike now.* □ *It's a relief that things have been brought to a head. The disputes have been going on for months.*

bring something to an end AND **bring something to a close; bring something to a halt** to make an event come to an end. □ *They brought the party to an end.* □ *We brought the evening to a close at midnight.* □ *I must bring this activity to a halt.*

bring something to light to make something known; to discover something. □ *The scientists brought their findings to light.* □ *We must bring this new evidence to light.*

bring the house down AND **bring down the house** to excite a theatrical audience to laughter or applause or both. (Informal.) □ *This is a great joke. The last time I told it, it brought the house down.* □ *It didn't bring down the house; it emptied it.*

bring up the rear to be at the end of the queue or line. (Originally referred to marching soldiers.) □ *Here comes John, bringing up the rear.* □ *Hurry up, Tom! Why are you always bringing up the rear?*

broken reed an unreliable or undependable person. □ *You can't rely on Jim's support. He's a broken reed.* □ *Mr. Smith is a broken reed. His deputy has to make all the decisions.*

brush something under the carpet See *sweep something under the carpet.*

brush up on something to learn something; to review something. (See also *bone up on something.*) □ *I think I should brush up on my Spanish before I go to Mexico.* □ *There is no time to brush up on your physics before the exam.*

buck up cheer up. (Slang.) □ *Buck up, old friend! Things can't be all that bad.* □ *I know I have to buck up. Life must go on.*

buckle down to something AND **buckle to** to settle down to something; to begin to work seriously at something. □ *If you don't buckle down to your job, you'll be sacked.* □ *You had better buckle to and get busy.*

buckle to See the previous entry.

bug someone to irritate someone; to bother someone. (Slang.) □ *Go away! Stop bugging me!* □ *Leave me alone. Go and bug someone else.*

build castles in Spain See the following entry.

build castles in the air AND **build castles in Spain** to day-dream; to make plans which can never come true. □ *Ann spends most of her time building castles in Spain.* □ *I really like to sit on the porch in the evening, just building castles in the air.*

build someone or something up AND **build up someone or something** 1. to make someone or something bigger or stronger. □ *Tom is eating lots of fresh fruits and vegetables to build himself up for soccer.* □ *After her illness, she took vitamins to build herself up.* 2. to advertise, praise, or promote someone or something. □ *Theatrical agents work very hard to build up their clients.* □ *An advertising agency can build up a product so much that everyone will want it.*

build up for something See the following entry.

build up to something AND **build up for something** to lead up to something, often by indirect means; to work up to something. □ *You could tell by the way she was talking that she was building up to something unpleasant.* □ *The clouds were building up for a storm.*

bull in a china shop a very clumsy person around breakable things; a thoughtless or tactless person. (*China* is fine crockery.) □ *Look at Bill, as awkward as a bull in a china shop.* □ *Get that big dog out of my garden. It's like a bull in a china shop.* □ *Bob is so rude, a real bull in a china shop.*

bump into someone AND **run into someone** to meet someone by chance. □ *Guess who I bumped into in town today?* □ *I ran into Bob Jones yesterday.*

bump someone off AND **bump off someone** to kill someone. (Slang, especially criminal slang.) □ *They tried to bump her off, but she was too clever and got away.* □ *The crooks bumped off the witness to the crime.*

bundle someone up AND **bundle up someone** to dress someone in warm winter clothing; to put warm bedcovers on someone. □ *Mother bundled up Tom before he went to school.* □ *Father put Mary into her cot and bundled her up well.*

burn one's boats to go so far in a course of action that one cannot turn back; to do something which makes it impossible to return to one's former position. □ *I don't want to emigrate now, but I've rather burned my boats by giving up my job and selling my house.* □ *Mary would now like to marry Peter, but she burned her boats by breaking off the engagement.*

burn one's bridges (behind one) to make decisions or adopt a course of action which cannot be changed in the future. □ *If you drop out of school now, you'll be burning your bridges behind you.* □ *You're too young to burn your bridges that way.*

burn (oneself) out to do something so long and so intensely that one gets weary, stale, and sometimes ill from doing it. (Slang.) □ *I burned myself out*

as an opera singer. I just cannot sing any more. □ *Tom burned himself out playing golf. He can't stand it any more.* □ *Tom burned out too young.*

burn the candle at both ends to work very hard and stay up very late at night. □ *No wonder Mary is ill. She has been burning the candle at both ends for a long time.* □ *You can't keep on burning the candle at both ends.*

burn the midnight oil to stay up working, especially studying, late at night. (Refers to working by the light of an oil-lamp.) □ *I have to go home and burn the midnight oil tonight.* □ *If you burn the midnight oil night after night, you'll probably become ill.*

burst at the seams to be very full; to be very crowded. (Informal.) □ *The room was so crowded that it almost burst at the seams.* □ *The hall nearly burst at the seams. We had to turn people away.* ALSO: **be bursting at the seams** to be ready to explode. □ *The hall was bursting at the seams.*

burst in (on someone or something) to rush in suddenly and interrupt someone or something. (See also *break in (on someone or something)*.) □ *I didn't mean to burst in on your discussion.* □ *It's rude to burst in like that.* □ *Tom burst in on his sister while she was doing her hair.*

burst into flames to catch fire suddenly; to ignite all at once. □ *Suddenly, the car burst into flames.* □ *It was so hot in the forest fire that a few trees literally burst into flames.*

burst into tears AND **burst out crying** suddenly to begin to cry. (See also *break into tears*.) □ *After the last notes of her song, the audience burst into tears, such was its beauty and tenderness.* □ *The brother and sister burst into tears on hearing of the death of their dog.* □ *Some people find themselves bursting out crying for no reason at all.*

burst out crying See the previous entry.

burst out laughing suddenly to begin to laugh. □ *The entire audience burst out* *laughing at exactly the wrong time, and so did the actors.* □ *Every time I think of you sitting there with a lap full of noodle soup, I burst out laughing.*

burst with joy to be full to the bursting point with happiness. □ *When I got my exam results, I could have burst with joy.* □ *Joe was not exactly bursting with joy when he got the news.* ALSO: **be bursting with joy** □ *She was bursting with joy as she explained her success.*

burst with pride to be full to the bursting point with pride. □ *My parents almost burst with pride when I graduated from college.* □ *I almost burst with pride when I was chosen to go up in the space shuttle.* ALSO: **be bursting with pride** □ *Sam was bursting with pride as he displayed his trophy.*

bury one's head in the sand AND **hide one's head in the sand** to ignore or hide from obvious signs of danger or trouble. (Refers to an ostrich which we picture with its head stuck into the sand or the ground.) □ *Stop burying your head in the sand. Look at the statistics on smoking and cancer.* □ *And stop hiding your head in the sand. All of us will die somehow whether we smoke or not.*

bury the hatchet to stop fighting or arguing; to end old resentments. □ *All right, you two. Calm down and bury the hatchet.* □ *I wish Mr. and Mrs. Franklin would bury the hatchet. They argue all the time.*

bush telegraph the informal, usually rapid spreading of news or information by word of mouth. □ *The bush telegraph tells me that the manager is leaving.* □ *How did John know that Kate was divorced? He must have heard it on the bush telegraph.*

business end of something the part or end of something that actually does the work or carries out the procedure. □ *Keep away from the business end of the electric drill in case you get hurt.* □ *Don't point the business end of that gun at anyone. It might go off.*

busman's holiday leisure time spent doing something similar to what one does at work. □ *Tutoring pupils in the evening is too much of a busman's holiday for our English teacher.* □ *It's a bit of a busman's holiday to ask her to be wardrobe mistress for our amateur production in the summer. She's a professional dressmaker.*

butt in (on something) to interrupt someone or something. (Slang. See also *break in (on someone or something); burst in (on someone or something).*) □ *Pardon me for butting in on your conversation, but this is important.* □ *I don't like to butt in, but you're wanted on the phone.*

butter someone up AND **butter up someone** to flatter someone. (Informal.) □ *If I butter up the landlady, she allows me to be a few days late with my rent.* □ *I believe she prefers me to butter her up to getting the rent on time.*

button one's lip to get quiet and stay quiet. (Slang.) □ *The new neighbour is very rude. He told Jane to button her lip.* □ *Button your lip, Tom! I'll tell you when you can talk.*

buy a pig in a poke to purchase or accept something without having seen or examined it. (*Poke* means "bag.") □ *Buying a car without test driving it is like buying a pig in a poke.* □ *He bought a pig in a poke when he ordered a diamond ring by mail order.*

buy someone off AND **buy off someone** to bribe someone; to win someone over by gifts or favours. □ *They tried to buy off the whole city council with expensive lunches.* □ *It's not hard to buy politicians off.*

buy someone or something out AND **buy out someone or something 1.** [with *someone*] to buy all of something that someone has. □ *He didn't have much ice-cream, and he wouldn't let us buy him out, so we had to go elsewhere to get as much as we wanted.* □ *We bought each merchant out of ice-cream.* **2.** [with *something*] to buy all of something that someone has. □ *We bought out all the ice-cream that he had.* □ *We bought it* *all out.* **3.** to buy the controlling interest in a business; to purchase the controlling interest in a business from someone. □ *I owned a small shop for a number of years until a syndicate bought me out.* □ *The investors bought out the largest shop in town.*

buy something to believe someone; to accept something to be a fact. (Slang.) □ *It may be true, but I don't buy it.* □ *I just don't buy the idea that you can swim that far.*

buy something for a song to buy something cheaply. □ *No one else wanted it, so I bought it for a song.* □ *I could buy this house for a song, because it's so ugly.*

buy something on credit to purchase something now and pay for it later (plus interest). □ *Almost everyone who buys a house buys it on credit.* □ *I didn't have any cash with me, so I used my credit card and bought a new coat on credit.*

buy something up AND **buy up something** to buy a lot of or most of something. □ *We bought up a lot of land in Florida many years ago.* □ *Now we wish we had bought more up.*

by a hair's breadth AND **by a whisker** just barely; by a very small distance. □ *I just missed getting on the plane by a hair's breadth.* □ *The arrow missed the deer by a whisker.*

by a mile by a great distance. □ *You missed the target by a mile.* □ *Your estimate of the budget deficit was off by a mile.*

by a whisker See *by a hair's breadth.*

by all accounts See *according to all accounts.*

by all appearances apparently; according to what one sees. □ *She is, by all appearances, ready to resume work.* □ *By all appearances, we ought to be approaching the airport.*

by all means certainly; yes; absolutely. □ BOB: *Will you help?* JANE: *By all means.* □ BOB: *Can you come to din-*

ner tomorrow? JANE: *By all means, I'd love to.*

by and by after a period of time has passed. □ *By and by we found the truth.* □ *And by and by the little boy became a tall and handsome prince.*

by and large generally; usually. (Originally a nautical expression.) □ *I find that, by and large, people tend to do what they are told to do.* □ *By and large, rose-bushes need lots of care.*

by chance by accident; without cause; randomly. □ *The contestants were chosen by chance.* □ *We met only by chance, and now we are the closest of friends.*

by choice owing to conscious choice; on purpose. □ *I do this kind of thing by choice. No one makes me do it.* □ *I didn't go to this college by choice. It was the closest one to home.*

by dint of something because of something; owing to the efforts of something. (*Dint* is an old word meaning "force," and it is never used except in this phrase.) □ *They got the building finished on time by dint of hard work and good organization.* □ *By dint of much studying, John got through college.*

by fits and starts irregularly; unevenly; with much stopping and starting. (Informal.) □ *Somehow, they got the job done by fits and starts.* □ *By fits and starts, the old car finally got us to town.*

by hook or by crook by any means, legal or illegal. □ *I'll get the job done by hook or by crook.* □ *I must have that house. I intend to get it by hook or by crook.*

by leaps and bounds rapidly; by large movements forward. □ *Our garden is growing by leaps and bounds.* □ *The profits of my company are increasing by leaps and bounds.*

by no means absolutely not; certainly not. □ *I'm by no means angry with you.* □ BOB: *Did you put this box here?* TOM: *By no means. I didn't do it, I'm sure.*

by return post by a subsequent immediate posting (back to the sender). (A phrase indicating that an answer is expected soon, by mail.) □ *Since this bill is overdue, would you kindly send us your cheque by return post?* □ *I answered your request by return post over a year ago. Please check your records.*

by shank's mare AND **by shank's pony** by foot; on foot. (Informal. *Shank* refers to the shank of the leg.) □ *My car isn't working, so I'll have to travel by shank's mare.* □ *I'm aching because I've been getting around by shank's pony.*

by shank's pony See the previous entry.

by the book according to the rules. □ *We always go by the book in matters like this.* □ *In official tournaments, we always go by the book.*

by the day one day at a time. □ *I don't know when I'll have to leave town, so I rent this room by the day.* □ *Do you have tools for hire by the day?*

by the dozen twelve at a time; in a group of twelve; in some large, indefinite number. □ *Eggs are usually sold by the dozen.* □ *Around here we have problems by the dozen.*

by the hour at each hour; after each hour. □ *It kept growing darker by the hour.* □ *The illness is getting worse by the hour.*

by the month one month at a time. □ *Not many flats are rented by the month.* □ *I needed a car for a short while, so I rented one by the month.*

by the same token in the same way; reciprocally. □ *Tom must be good when he comes here, and, by the same token, I expect you to behave properly when you go to his house.* □ *The mayor votes for* his friend's causes. *By the same token, the friend votes for the mayor's causes.*

by the seat of one's pants by sheer luck and very little skill. (Informal. Especially with *fly.*) □ *I got through school by the seat of my pants.* □ *The jungle pilot spent most of his days flying by the seat of his pants.*

by the skin of one's teeth just barely; by an amount equal to the thickness of the (imaginary) skin on one's teeth. (Informal.) □ *I got through that exam by the skin of my teeth.* □ *I got to the airport late and caught the plane by the skin of my teeth.*

by the sweat of one's brow by one's efforts; by one's hard work. □ *Tom raised these vegetables by the sweat of his brow.* □ *Sally made her fortune by the sweat of her brow.*

by the way incidentally; in addition; while I think of it. □ *By the way, I'm not going to the bank today.* □ *Oh, by the way, your shoes need polishing.*

by the week one week at a time. □ *I plan my schedule by the week.* □ *Where can I rent a room by the week?*

by the year one year at a time. □ *Most flats are available by the year.* □ *We budget by the year.*

by virtue of something because of something; owing to something. □ *She's permitted to vote by virtue of her age.* □ *They are members of the club by virtue of their great wealth.*

by way of something in illustration; as an example. □ *By way of illustration, the professor drew a picture on the board.* □ *He read them a passage from Shakespeare by way of example.*

by word of mouth by speaking rather than writing. □ *I learned about it by word of mouth.* □ *I need it in writing. I don't trust things I hear about by word of mouth.*

C

call a halt (to something) to bring something to an end; to request or demand that something be stopped. (Never used to refer to stopping a moving object.) □ *The town council called a halt to the building project.* □ *The umpire called a halt to the game while the injured player was removed.* □ *I've lent him enough money. It's time to call a halt.*

call a meeting to ask that people assemble for a meeting; to request that a meeting be held. □ *The mayor called a meeting to discuss the problem.* □ *I'll be calling a meeting of the town council to discuss the new building project.*

call a spade a spade to call something by its right name; to speak frankly about something, even if it is unpleasant. □ *Well, I believe it's time to call a spade a spade. We are just avoiding the issue.* □ *Let's call a spade a spade. The man is a liar.*

call it a day to leave work and go home; to say that a day's work has been completed; to bring something to an end; to stop doing something. (Informal.) □ *I'm tired. Let's call it a day even though it's only three o'clock.* □ *They're not engaged any more. They called it a day.* □ *I haven't finished this essay, but I'm calling it a day.*

call it quits to bring something to an end on the understanding that both sides involved have an equal advantage and that neither owes the other anything. (Informal.) □ *I've won one game, and you've won one. Let's call it quits.* □ *He paid for the meal, and she paid for the wine. They called it quits.*

call of nature the need to go to the lavatory. (Humorous.) □ *Stop the car here! I have to answer the call of nature.* □ *There was no interval in the meeting to take account of the call of nature.*

call (someone) back to return someone's telephone call. □ *I'll call the doctor back in the morning.* □ *Do I have to return her call? I don't want to call back.*

call someone in AND **call in someone** to summon or send for someone, especially someone who has special talents, abilities, or power. □ *They had to call a new doctor in.* □ *Yes, they had to call in a specialist.*

call someone names to call a person unpleasant or insulting names. (Usually viewed as a childish act.) □ *Mummy! John is calling me names again!* □ *We'll never get anywhere by calling one another names.*

call someone or something off AND **call off someone or something** to cancel an event or someone's arrival. □ *Because of rain, they called off the game.* □ *It's too late to call the party off. The first guests have already arrived.* □ *You'll have to call off Mary. We have no room for her.*

call someone or something up AND **call up someone or something 1.** to call a person, business, or office on the telephone. □ *Mary called the firm up and ordered a new supply of stationery.* □ *John picked up the telephone and called his girlfriend up.* □ *Tom called up Mary.* **2.** to summon information from a computer. □ *John used a computer to* *call up the information.* □ *With a few strokes on the computer keyboard, Sally called up the figures she was looking for.*

call someone to account to demand an account or an explanation from someone. □ *Tom was called to account because of his horrible behaviour.* □ *He thought that he had got away with the crime, but they called him to account eventually.*

call someone's attention to something to make someone aware of something; to cause someone to take notice of something. □ *May I call your attention to the paragraph at the bottom of the page?* □ *He called my attention to the car parked by the birch tree.*

call someone's bluff to demand that someone prove a claim; to demonstrate that a person is or is not being deceptive. □ *All right, I'll call your bluff. Show me you can do it!* □ *Tom said, "I've got a gun here in my pocket, and I'll shoot if you come any closer!" "Go ahead," said Bill, calling his bluff.*

call something into question See *bring something into question.*

call the dogs off AND **call off the dogs** to stop threatening, chasing, or hounding (a person); literally, to order dogs away from the chase. □ *All right, I surrender. You can call your dogs off.* □ *Please call off your dogs! I plan to resign anyway.*

call the meeting to order formally to ask the members of a group to be silent and orderly so that a meeting may start or continue. □ *The president called the meeting to order shortly after midday.* □ *We cannot do anything until the president calls the meeting to order.*

call the shots AND **call the tune** to make the decisions; to decide what is to be done. (Informal.) □ *Sally always wants to call the shots, and Mary doesn't like to be told what to do. They don't get along well.* □ *The bride's father should call the tune about the number of wedding guests to be invited. He's paying for the reception.* □ *Look here,*

friend, I'm calling the shots. You just be quiet.

call the tune See the previous entry.

cancel something out AND **cancel out something** to reduce something to nothing; to wipe something out; to balance something. □ *This last payment cancels out my debt.* □ *Yes, your last payment cancels it out.* □ *Bob's two good scores cancelled out his two bad ones.* □ *His present generosity more than cancels out his past meanness.*

[can't] See the expressions listed at *not able,* as well as those listed below.

can't do anything with someone or something not able to manage or control someone or something. (Also with *cannot.*) □ *Our new dog is such a problem. I can't do anything with him.* □ *My hair is such a mess. I just can't do anything with it.*

can't hold a candle to someone not equal to someone; unable to measure up to someone. (Also with *cannot.*) □ *Mary can't hold a candle to Ann when it comes to playing the piano.* □ *As for singing, John can't hold a candle to Jane.*

can't make head or tail of someone or something unable to understand someone or something. (Also with *cannot.*) □ *John is so strange. I can't make head or tail of him.* □ *Do this report again. I can't make head or tail of it.*

can't see beyond the end of one's nose unaware of and uncaring for the things which might happen in the future; not far-sighted. (Also with *cannot.*) □ *John is a very poor planner. He can't see beyond the end of his nose.* □ *Ann can't see beyond the end of her nose. She's taken a job without finding out if the firm is financially secure.*

can't see one's hand in front of one's face unable to see very far, usually owing to darkness or fog. (Also with *cannot.*) □ *It was so dark that I couldn't see my hand in front of my face.* □ *Bob said that the fog was so thick he couldn't see his hand in front of his face.*

can't stand (the sight of) someone or something AND **can't stomach someone or something** unable to tolerate someone or something. (Also with *cannot*.) □ *I can't stand the sight of cooked carrots.* □ *Mr. Jones can't stand the sight of blood.* □ *None of us can stand this place.* □ *Nobody can stand Tom when he shows off.* □ *I can't stomach your foul language.* □ *I just can't stomach Mr. Smith.*

can't stomach someone or something See the previous entry.

cap in hand with humility. □ *She stormed off but came back cap in hand when she ran out of money.* □ *We had to go cap in hand to the council to get a grant for our proposal.*

care about someone or something to have warm feelings for someone or something; to love or respect someone or something. (See also the following entry.) □ *It's hard to believe, but Bill cares about Jane.* □ *Bob really cares about the welfare of the town.* □ *Yes, Bob cares about our welfare.*

care for someone or something **1.** to attend to the needs of someone or something. □ *Tom cares for his dog and keeps it healthy.* □ *The mother is busy caring for her child.* **2.** to care about someone or something. □ *I really care for you.* □ *I don't think he cares for cats as much as his wife does.*

care nothing about someone or something AND **care nothing for someone or something** to have no feelings at all about someone or something. □ *Jane cares nothing about Tom.* □ *Bill cares nothing for the welfare of the community.* □ *The father cared nothing for his own children.*

care nothing for someone or something See the previous entry.

care of someone [to be delivered to someone] through someone or by way of someone. (Indicates that mail is to be delivered to a person at some other person's address. Often written *c/o*.) □ *Bill Jones is living at his father's house.*

Address the letter to Bill care of Mr. John Jones. □ *Bill said, "Please send me my mail care of my father at his address."*

carried away excited or moved to (extreme) action (by someone or something). □ *The crowd got carried away by the political speech and started shouting abuse.* □ *I know that planning a party is fun but don't get carried away.*

carry a torch (for someone) to be in love with someone who does not return love; to brood over a hopeless love affair. □ *John is carrying a torch for Jane.* □ *Is John still carrying a torch?*

carry all before one to be exceptionally successful. □ *He carried all before him on school prize day.* □ *In the sports event Mary just carried all before her.*

carry coals to Newcastle AND **take coals to Newcastle** to do something unnecessary; to do something which is redundant or duplicative. □ *Taking food to a farmer is like taking coals to Newcastle.* □ *Mr. Smith is so rich he doesn't need any more money. Giving him money is like carrying coals to Newcastle.*

carry on to behave badly or mischievously. (Informal.) □ *The children always carry on when the teacher's out of the room.* □ *Stop carrying on and go to sleep!*

carry on about someone or something to make a great fuss over someone or something. (Informal.) □ *Billy, stop carrying on about your tummy ache like that.* □ *He carried on about her being late for hours.*

carry on (with someone) to have a love affair, often an illicit one, with someone. (Informal.) □ *She got the sack for carrying on with her supervisor.* □ *Look at Jane carrying on with Tom. They ought to be ashamed.* □ *Jane is said to be carrying on with Mary's husband.* □ *How long have they been carrying on?*

carry one's cross See *bear one's cross*.

carry one's (own) weight AND **pull one's weight** to do one's share; to earn one's keep. □ *Tom, you must be more helpful around the house. We all have to carry our own weight.* □ *Bill, I'm afraid that you can't work here any more. You just haven't been carrying your weight.* □ *If you would just pull your weight, we would finish this by midday.*

carry over See under *carry something over.*

carry something off AND **carry off something** to make a planned event work out successfully. (Especially **carry it off**. See also *bring something off.*) □ *The magician carried off the trick with great skill.* □ *It was a huge affair, but the hostess carried it off beautifully.* □ *Do you think you can carry it off?*

carry something over AND **carry over something** to let something like a sum of money or item of business extend into another period of time; to extend to another location. □ *We'll carry the amount of money due over into the next month.* □ *Yes, please carry over the balance.* □ *You cannot carry any of this year's holiday allowance over to next year.* □ *We'll have to carry this paragraph over to the next page.* ALSO: **carry over** to extend into another time period or location. □ *I don't like bills to carry over into the next month.* □ *Please do not let the paragraph carry over.*

carry the day See *win the day.*

carry the weight of the world on one's shoulders to appear to be burdened by many problems. □ *Look at Tom. He seems to be carrying the weight of the world on his shoulders.* □ *Cheer up, Tom! You don't need to carry the weight of the world on your shoulders.*

carry weight (with someone) [for someone] to have influence with someone; [for something] to have significance for someone. (Often in the negative.) □ *Everything Mary says carries weight with me.* □ *Don't pay any attention to John. What he says carries no weight around here.* □ *Your proposal is quite*

good, *but since you're not a member of the club, it carries no weight.*

carte blanche complete freedom to act or proceed as one pleases. (Literally, a blank card.) □ *We were given carte blanche to choose the colour scheme.* □ *They were not instructed where to shop. It was a case of carte blanche.*

case in point an example of what one is talking about; a relevant example. □ *Now, as a case in point, let's look at nineteenth-century England.* □ *Fireworks can be dangerous. For a case in point, look what happened to Bob Smith last week.*

cash and carry having to do with a sale of goods or a way of selling that requires payment at the time of sale and requires that one take the goods with one. □ *I'm sorry. We don't deliver. It's strictly cash and carry.* □ *You cannot get credit at the chemists. They are all cash and carry.*

cash in on something to earn a lot of money at something; to make a profit at something. (Informal. See also *cash something in.*) □ *This is a good year for farming, and you can cash in on it if you're clever.* □ *It's too late to cash in on that particular clothing fad.*

cash in one's chips to die. (Slang. From an expression in the card-game poker.) □ *Bob cashed in his chips yesterday.* □ *I'm too young to cash in my chips.*

cash something in AND **cash in something** to exchange something with cash value for the amount of money it is worth. □ *I need to cash in an insurance policy.* □ *I should have cashed the bonds in years ago.*

cast about for someone or something See the following entry.

cast around for someone or something AND **cast about for someone or something** to try to find someone or something, often hurriedly; to seek a thought or an idea. □ *John is casting around for a new cook. The old one left.* □ *Bob is casting about for a new car.*

43

☐ *Mary cast about for a way to win the contest.*

cast doubt (on someone or something) AND **cast doubts** to cause someone or something to be doubted. ☐ *The police cast doubt on my story.* ☐ *How can they cast doubt? They haven't looked into it yet.* ☐ *The city council cast doubt on John and his plan.* ☐ *They are always casting doubts.*

cast in the same mould very similar. ☐ *The two sisters are cast in the same mould—equally mean.* ☐ *All the family are cast in the same mould and end up in prison.*

cast one's lot in with someone AND **cast in one's lot with someone** to join in with someone and accept whatever happens. (Also with *in*.) ☐ *You might as well cast your lot in with the majority.* ☐ *Mary cast in her lot with the group going to Spain. They had a wonderful time.*

Cast (one's) pearls before swine. a proverb meaning to waste something good on someone who does not appreciate it. (It is insulting to refer to people as swine.) ☐ *To sing operatic arias for them is to cast pearls before swine.* ☐ *Serving them French cuisine is like casting one's pearls before swine.*

cast the first stone to be the first to attack; to make the first criticism. (From a biblical quotation.) ☐ *Well, I don't want to be the one to cast the first stone, but she sang horribly.* ☐ *John always casts the first stone. He's so aggressive.*

Cat got your tongue? Why don't you speak?; Speak up and answer my question! (Informal.) ☐ *Answer me! What's the matter, cat got your tongue?* ☐ *Why don't you speak up? Cat got your tongue?*

catch-as-catch-can the best one can do with whatever is available. ☐ *We went hitch-hiking for a week and lived catch-as-catch-can.* ☐ *There were ten children in our family, and every meal was catch-as-catch-can.*

catch cold to contract a cold (the disease). ☐ *Please close the window, or we'll all catch cold.* ☐ *I catch cold every year at this time.*

catch fire to ignite and burn with flames. ☐ *Keep your coat away from the flames, or it will catch fire.* ☐ *Lightning struck the forest, and the trees caught fire.*

catch forty winks AND **have forty winks** to take a nap; to have a short sleep. (Informal.) ☐ *I'll just catch forty winks before getting ready for the party.* ☐ *Tom always tries to have forty winks before going out for a late evening.*

catch hold of someone or something to grasp someone or something. ☐ *She caught hold of Billy just as he slipped and fell.* ☐ *Here, catch hold of this rope.*

catch it to get into trouble and receive punishment. (Informal.) ☐ *I know I'm going to catch it when I get home.* ☐ *Bob hit Billy in the face. He really caught it from the teacher.*

catch on (to someone or something) to figure someone or something out; to solve a puzzle; to see through a person or an act of deception. ☐ *Mary finally caught on to Bob and his tricks.* ☐ *Ann soon caught on to the woman's dishonest plan.* ☐ *The woman thought that Ann wouldn't catch on.*

catch one off one's guard See *catch someone off guard*

catch one with one's pants down See the following entry.

catch one with one's trousers down AND **catch one with one's pants down** to catch someone unprepared or off guard; to find someone in an embarrassing position. (Informal. This probably refers indirectly to having one's trousers down when one is in the toilet.) ☐ *The enemy attacked very early in the morning. They caught our army with their trousers down.* ☐ *The first guests arrived at the Smiths' party before the caterers. Talk about being caught with one's pants down!*

catch one's breath to resume one's normal breathing after exertion; to return to normal after being busy or very active. □ *I ran so fast that it took ten minutes to catch my breath.* □ *I don't have time to catch my breath. I have to start work immediately.*

catch one's death (of cold) to contract a cold; to catch a serious cold. (Informal. See *catch cold*.) □ *Dress up warmly or you'll catch your death of cold.* □ *Put on your raincoat, or you'll catch your death.*

catch sight of someone or something to see someone or something briefly; to get a glimpse of someone or something. □ *I caught sight of the rocket just before it flew out of sight.* □ *Ann caught sight of the robber as he ran out of the bank.*

catch someone in the act (of doing something) to find a person doing something illegal or private. (See also *in the act of doing something.*) □ *They know who set the fire. They caught someone in the act.* □ *I caught Tom in the act of stealing a car.* ALSO: **caught in the act** seen doing something illegal or private. □ *Tom was caught in the act.* □ *She's guilty. She was caught in the act.*

catch someone napping to find someone unprepared. (Informal. Literally, to catch someone asleep.) □ *The enemy caught our army napping.* □ *The thieves caught the security staff napping.*

catch someone off guard AND **catch one off one's guard** to catch a person unprepared or careless. □ *Tom caught Ann off guard, and she confessed to everything.* □ *She caught me off my guard, and I told her where the jewels were hidden.*

catch someone on the hop to find someone unprepared or defenceless. (Informal.) □ *The unexpected exam caught some of the pupils on the hop.* □ *The police caught the suspect on the hop without an alibi.*

catch someone red-handed to catch a person in the act of doing something wrong. (Compare to *catch someone in the act of doing something.*) □ *Tom was stealing the car when the police drove by and caught him red-handed.* □ *Mary tried to cash a forged cheque at the bank, and the teller caught her red-handed.* ALSO: **caught red-handed** caught in the act of doing something wrong. □ *Tom was caught red-handed breaking into the house.* □ *Many car thieves are caught red-handed.*

catch someone's eye to establish eye contact with someone; to attract someone's attention. □ *Try and catch the barman's eye.* □ *The shiny red car caught Mary's eye.*

catch the sun to become sunburnt. (Informal.) □ *The baby's face is red—she's caught the sun.* □ *Fair-skinned people catch the sun easily.*

catch up (with someone or something) to reach someone or something who is moving in the same direction; to draw level with someone or something. □ *The red car caught up with the blue one.* □ *Bill caught up with Ann, and they walked to the bank together.* □ *He had to run to catch up to her.*

caught in the act See under *catch someone in the act (of doing something).*

caught in the cross-fire See the following entry.

caught in the middle AND **caught in the cross-fire** caught between two arguing or fighting people or groups. □ *Mr. and Mrs. Smith tried to draw me into their argument. I don't like being caught in the middle.* □ *In Westerns, innocent people are always getting caught in the cross-fire.*

caught red-handed See under *catch someone red-handed.*

caught short 1. being without something that is needed, especially money. □ *I needed eggs for my cake, but I was caught short.* □ *Bob had to borrow money from John to pay for the meal. Bob is caught short quite often.* 2. AND **taken short** needing to go to the toilet at an inconvenient time or place. (Informal.) □ *Plan your day's hiking so you won't be caught short out in the* *meadow.* □ *There I was on the bus, taken short and no hope of rescue.*

cause a commotion See the following entry.

cause a stir AND **cause a commotion** to cause people to become agitated; to cause trouble in a group of people; to shock or alarm people. □ *When Bob appeared without his evening jacket, it caused quite a stir in the dining-room.* □ *The dog ran through the church and caused a real commotion.*

cause eyebrows to raise AND **cause raised eyebrows** to shock people; to surprise and dismay people. (See also *raise a few eyebrows.*) □ *John caused eyebrows to raise when he married a poor girl without a penny to her name.* □ *The managing director's behaviour at the party caused a few raised eyebrows.*

cause raised eyebrows See the previous entry.

cause tongues to wag to cause people to gossip; to give people something to gossip about. □ *The way John was looking at Mary will surely cause tongues to wag.* □ *The way Mary was dressed will also cause tongues to wag.*

cave in (to something) for someone to give in to something. □ *Tom caved in to the pressure of work.* □ *It's easier to cave in than to go on fighting.*

chalk something up AND **chalk up something** to add something to the record, score, or total. □ *We chalked up 500 miles today.* □ *The local football team have chalked up another victory.*

chalk something up to someone or something AND **chalk up something to someone or something** to charge something to the account of someone; to place the cost on the account of someone. □ *The barman chalked up the round of drinks to Mr. Smith.* □ *I haven't enough money on me to pay for the drinks. Could you chalk them up to me?*

chalk something up to something to ascribe something to something. □ *You cannot do anything about the mistake.*

Just chalk it up to experience. □ *The performance was poor, and the audience probably chalked it up to stage-fright.*

champ at the bit to be ready and anxious to do something; to be impatient. (Originally said about horses.) □ *The children were champing at the bit to get into the swimming-pool.* □ *The hounds were champing at the bit to begin the hunt.*

chance one's arm to do something risky or dangerous. □ *He certainly chanced his arm when he was rude to the boss's wife.* □ *Don't chance your arm by asking for yet another day off.*

chance something to risk doing something; to try doing something. □ *I don't usually ride horses, but this time I will chance it.* □ *Bob didn't have reservations, but he went to the airport anyway, chancing losing a whole day.*

chance (up)on someone or something to find someone or something by chance. □ *I just happened to chance upon this excellent restaurant down by the river. The food is superb.* □ *We were exploring a small Welsh town when we chanced on an old man who turned out to be an old friend.*

change colour to have one's face change colour; either to become pale from fear or shock, or red from embarrassment or anger. □ *She changed colour when she saw the ghostly shape.* □ *The young man changed colour when the girls laughed at him.*

change hands [for something] to be sold. (Refers to the changing of owners.) □ *How many times has this house changed hands in the last ten years?* □ *We built this house in 1920, and it has never changed hands.*

change horses in mid-stream to make major changes in an activity which has already begun; to choose someone or something else after it is too late. □ *I'm already baking a cherry pie. I can't bake an apple pie. It's too late to change horses in mid-stream.* □ *The house is half built. It's too late to employ a dif-*

ferent architect. You can't change horses in mid-stream.

change someone's mind to cause a person to think differently (about someone or something). □ *Tom thought Mary was unkind, but an evening out with her changed his mind.* □ *I can change my mind if I want to. I don't have to stick to an idea.*

change someone's tune to change the manner, attitude, or behaviour of a person, usually from bad to good, or from rude to pleasant. □ *The teller was most unpleasant until she learned that I'm a bank director. Then she changed her tune.* □ *"I will help change your tune by fining you £150," said the judge to the rude defendant.*

change the subject to begin talking about something different. □ *They changed the subject suddenly when the person whom they had been discussing entered the room.* □ *We'll change the subject if we are embarrassing you.*

chapter and verse detailed sources of information. (A reference to the method of referring to biblical texts.) □ *He gave chapter and verse for his reasons for disputing that Shakespeare had written the play.* □ *The suspect gave chapter and verse of his associate's activities.*

chapter of accidents a series of misfortunes. □ *Yesterday was just a chapter of accidents—nothing went right.* □ *The play rehearsal consisted of a chapter of accidents, but the opening performance was perfect.*

charge off to leave rapidly and with a sense of purpose, or in anger. □ *"Oh Bob," cried Mary, "why do you always get angry and charge off when I talk to you?"* □ *The knight said goodbye to the king and charged off into the forest.*

charge something to someone or something to buy something and place the cost on the account of someone or something (such as a business). (See also *chalk something up to someone or something.*) □ *He charged his new suit to his mother.* □ *Mary tried to charge*

her holiday to the company she worked for.

Charity begins at home. a proverb meaning that one should be kind to one's own family, friends, or fellow citizens before trying to help others. □ *"Mother, may I please have a pie?" asked Mary. "I know you baked them for the church fête, but charity begins at home."* □ *At church, the minister reminded us that charity begins at home, but we must remember others also.*

chase after someone or something AND **chase around (after someone or something) 1.** to pursue someone or something speedily or determinedly. □ *The dog chased after the car.* □ *I've been chasing around after your birthday present all day. I finally found the right thing.* □ *I've given up looking for a flat. I'm tired of chasing around.* **2.** [with *someone*] to flirt with someone; to follow someone around to ask for a date. □ *Tom is still chasing after Jane. Can't he see that she doesn't care for him?* □ *Jane's chasing after a married man.*

chase around (after someone or something) See the previous entry.

check in(to something) to register or sign into a place, such as a hotel. □ *I'll call you just after I check into the hotel.* □ *I can't get to a telephone until I check in.*

check on someone or something to examine or investigate someone or something. □ *I'll have to check on your facts.* □ *I'll check on the baby and make certain she's asleep.*

check out (of something) to sign out of a place and leave. □ *What time do you have to check out?* □ *I have to check out of the hotel by 2:00 P.M.*

check someone in AND **check in someone** to make a record of someone's arrival; in a hotel, to assign a person to a room. □ *The receptionist was waiting to check me in.* □ *She had just checked in another gentleman named Smith.*

check someone or something off AND **check off someone or something** to record some fact about someone or something on a list. (The *someone* refers to someone's name on a list, not a person.) □ *I have the books for the course right here. You can check them off.* □ *Look at your list of the people who can't come to the party. Have you checked off the Smiths?*

check someone or something out AND **check out someone or something 1.** [with *someone*] to make a record of someone's departure. □ *The receptionist checked out the guests when they left the hotel.* □ *I'm leaving the building now. Please check me out.* **2.** [with *something*] to record the lending of something. □ *I checked out a library book.* □ *The librarian found the book I wanted and checked it out so I could read it at home.*

check up on someone or something to investigate someone or something. □ *The police are checking up on my story.* □ *When they want to check up on someone, they don't waste any time.*

check with someone to ask someone (about something); to get permission from someone (to do something). □ *Yes, I think I can drive us to the party. I'll have to check with my parents, though.* □ *Please check with Mr. Brown, the hotel manager, about that problem.*

cheek by jowl side by side; close together. □ *The walkers had to walk cheek by jowl along the narrow streets.* □ *The two families lived cheek by jowl in one house.*

cheer someone on to give words or shouts of encouragement to someone who is trying to do something. □ *John was leading in the race, and the whole crowd was cheering him on.* □ *Sally was doing so well in her performance that I wanted to cheer her on.*

cheer someone up AND **cheer up someone** to make a sad or miserable person happy. □ *When Bill was sick, Ann tried to cheer him up by reading to him.*

□ *Interest rates went up, and that cheered up all the bankers.* ALSO: **cheer up** to become more happy. □ *Things are bad for you now, but you'll cheer up when they get better.* □ *Cheer up, Tom! Things can't be that bad.*

cheer up See under *cheer someone up.*

cheese-paring mean; niggardly. □ *He was too cheese-paring to eat properly.* □ *The cheese-paring old woman will not give to the poor.* ALSO: **cheese-paring** meanness. □ *I am disgusted at his cheese-paring.*

cheesed off bored; depressed; annoyed. □ *He was cheesed off with his job.* □ *She was cheesed off when she missed the bus.*

chew the cud to think deeply. (Informal. From the cow's habit of bringing food back from the first stomach into the mouth to chew it, called chewing the cud.) □ *I can't decide where to go on holiday. I'll have to chew the cud.* □ *He's chewing the cud about what to do next.*

chew the fat AND **chew the rag** to have an informal chat, sometimes of a complaining or argumentative nature, with someone. (Slang.) □ *The factory workers just sat around and chewed the fat. They never did make a formal complaint.* □ *We spent some time chewing the rag and decided that nothing could be done.*

chew the rag See the previous entry.

chicken out (of something) to withdraw from something because of fear or cowardice. (Informal.) □ *Jane was going to go parachuting with us, but she chickened out at the last minute.* □ *I'd never chicken out of parachute jumping, because I'd never agree to do it in the first place!*

child's play something very easy to do. (Informal.) □ *The exam was child's play to her.* □ *Finding the right street was child's play with a map.*

chilled to the bone See the following entry.

chilled to the marrow AND **chilled to the bone** very cold. □ *I was chilled to the marrow in that snowstorm.* □ *The children were chilled to the bone in that unheated room.*

chime in to add something to a discussion, usually by interrupting. (Informal.) □ *Billy chimed in by reminding us to come to dinner.* □ *We had just agreed on a suitable restaurant when Jane chimed in to tell us it had closed.*

chink in one's armour something that provides a means for attacking or impressing someone otherwise invulnerable. (See also *Achilles' heel.*) □ *His love for his child is the chink in his armour.* □ *Jane's insecurity is the chink in her armour.*

chip in (something) **1.** to contribute an amount of money to a fund which will be used to buy something. □ *Would you care to chip in some money towards a gift for the teacher?* □ *Yes, I'd be happy to chip in.* **2.** to add something to a discussion, usually by interrupting; to chime in. (Informal.) □ *Suddenly Jane chipped in that she would have to leave.* □ *Mother turned and whispered, "Children, please stop chipping in!"*

chip off the old block a person (usually a male) who behaves in the same way as his father or resembles his father. (Usually informal.) □ *John looks like his father—a real chip off the old block.* □ *Bill Jones is a chip off the old block. He's a banker just like his father.*

choke someone off AND **choke off someone** to interrupt or stop someone, usually rudely or suddenly. (Informal.) □ *She tried to sell me a book, but I choked her off.* □ *They tried to come in, but I choked off all three of them.*

choose sides to form into two opposing teams by having a leader or captain take turns choosing players. □ *Let's choose sides and play ball.* □ *When I choose sides, all the best players don't end up on the same team.*

chop and change to keep changing or altering something. □ *The shop is al-ways chopping and changing staff.* □ *The firm is constantly chopping and changing their plans.*

chop someone or something up AND **cut up someone or something** to cut someone or something into pieces. □ *The murderer chopped the body up and hid the pieces in the forest.* □ *The food processor cut up the carrots quickly and neatly.*

clam up to become silent; to refuse to talk; to close one's mouth (as tightly as a clam closes its shell). (Informal.) □ *When they tried to question her, she clammed up.* □ *The child clams up if you ask him about his father.*

clamp down (on someone or something) to become strict with someone; to become strict about something; to prevent or restrict someone or something. □ *Because Bob's marks were getting worse, his parents clamped down on his free time.* □ *The police have clamped down on speeding drivers in this town.* □ *Things have already gone too far. It's too late to clamp down.*

clap eyes on someone or something to see someone or something, perhaps for the first time; to *set eyes on someone or something.* (Informal.) □ *I wish she had never clapped eyes on her fiancé.* □ *I haven't clapped eyes on a red squirrel for years.*

clean out of something just now having sold or used up the last of something. (Informal.) □ *Sorry, I can't serve you scrambled eggs. We are clean out of eggs.* □ *We are clean out of nails. I sold the last box just ten minutes ago.* □ *Sorry. We are clean out of dried beans.*

clean someone out AND **clean out someone** to take everything—especially the money—that a person has. (Informal.) □ *I'm sorry I don't have any change. My children cleaned me out this morning.* □ *The robber cleaned the man out without hurting him.*

clean something up AND **clean up something; clean up** **1.** to make something clean. □ *This house is a mess. Let's clean it up.* □ *After you finish cooking, you must clean up.* **2.** to make something free of something, especially vice or corruption. (Slang.) □ *This town was full of drug pushers, but it's been cleaned up.* □ *The police are trying to clean up the area. The criminals are moving out.*

clean up **1.** to make a great profit. (Informal.) □ *John won at the races and really cleaned up.* □ *Ann cleaned up by taking a job selling encyclopaedias.* **2.** See *clean something up.*

clean up one's act AND **clean one's act up** to reform one's conduct. (Slang.) □ *If you don't clean up your act, you'll be sent home.* □ *Since Sally cleaned up her act, she has become very productive.*

clear out to get out (of somewhere); to leave. □ *All right, you people, clear out of here, now!* □ *I knew right then that it was time to clear out.*

clear someone's name to prove that someone is not guilty of a crime or misdeed. □ *I was accused of theft, but I cleared my name.* □ *The pupil was accused of cheating, but her name was cleared.*

clear something up AND **clear up something** **1.** to explain something; to solve a mystery. □ *I think that we can clear this matter up without calling in the police.* □ *First we have to clear up the problem of the missing jewels.* **2.** to cure a disease or a medical condition. □ *The doctor will give you something to clear up your cold.* □ *There is no medicine which will clear pimples up.*

clear the air to get rid of doubts or hostile feelings. (Sometimes this is said about an argument or other unpleasantness. The literal meaning is also used.) □ *All right, let's discuss this frankly. It'll be better if we clear the air.* □ *Mr. and Mrs. Brown always seem to have to clear the air with a big argument before they can be sociable.*

clear the table to remove the dishes and other eating utensils from the table after a meal. □ *Will you please help clear the table?* □ *After you clear the table, we'll play cards.*

clear up **1.** [for the weather] to become clear. □ *Look! It's beginning to clear up already.* □ *It usually clears up by midday.* **2.** [for a disease] to cure itself or run its course. □ *I told you your pimples would clear up without special medicine.* □ *My rash cleared up in a week.*

climb down to admit that one is wrong; to admit defeat. □ *They were sure they were in the right, but they climbed down when we proved them wrong.* □ *The teacher was forced to climb down and admit she had made a mistake.*

climb on the bandwagon See *jump on the bandwagon.*

climb the wall to become extremely anxious, bored, or angry. (Informal.) □ *The meeting was so long and the speaker so boring that most of the audience were climbing the wall.* □ *Thank goodness you've got here safely. I was climbing the wall.*

clip someone's wings to restrain someone; to reduce or put an end to someone's privileges or freedom. □ *You had better learn to get home on time, or your father will clip your wings.* □ *My mother threatened to clip my wings if I kept staying out late.*

cloak-and-dagger involving secrecy and plotting. □ *A great deal of cloak-and-dagger stuff goes on in political circles.* □ *A lot of cloak-and-dagger activity was involved in the appointment of the director.*

close at hand within easy reach; handy. □ *I'm sorry, but your letter isn't close at hand. Please remind me what you said in it.* □ *When you're cooking, you should keep all the ingredients close at hand.*

close in (on someone or something) to overwhelm or surround someone or something. □ *My problems are closing in on me.* □ *The wolves closed in on their prey.* □ *They howled as they closed in.*

close one's eyes to something to ignore something; to pretend that something is not really happening. □ *You can't close your eyes to the hunger in the world.* □ *His mother closed her eyes to the fact that he was being beaten by his father.*

close ranks to join (with someone), especially as a defensive measure. □ *We can fight this menace only if we close ranks.* □ *Let's all close ranks to support Ann against the opposition.*

close something down AND **close down something; shut down something; shut something down** to make something stop operating; to put something out of business. □ *The city council closed down the amusement park.* □ *The police closed the factory down.* □ *The manager shut down the factory for the holidays.*

close the door on something See *shut the door on something.*

close to home **1.** affecting one personally and intimately; to affect and be relevant to one personally. (Informal.) □ *Her remarks were a bit too close to home. I was afraid she was discussing me!* □ *The criticism was close to home, and my feelings were hurt a bit.* ALSO: **come too close to home** □ *She was talking about someone else, not us, but the criticisms came too close to home.* **2.** close to one's personal situation and concerns, such as in one's family or neighbourhood. □ *When those things happen close to home, we are always surprised.* □ *We never expect tragedy to strike close to home.*

close to someone fond of someone; very good friends with someone. □ *Tom is very close to Mary. They may get married.* □ *Mr. Smith isn't exactly close to Mrs. Smith.*

close up shop to stop working or operating, for the day or forever. (Informal.) □ *It's five o'clock. Time to close up shop.* □ *I can't make any money in this town. The time has come to close up shop and move to another town.*

Cloud-cuckoo-land an imaginary perfect world. □ *He thinks that he will be able to buy a house easily, but he is living in Cloud-cuckoo-land.* □ *She hopes to get a job travelling abroad— she believes in Cloud-cuckoo-land.*

clutch at straws to seek something which is useless or unattainable; to make a futile attempt at something. □ *I really didn't think that I would get the job. I was clutching at straws.* □ *She won't accept he was lost at sea. She's still clutching at straws.*

cock a snook at someone to show or express defiance or scorn at someone. □ *He cocked a snook at the traffic warden and tore up the ticket.* □ *The boy cocked a snook at the park attendant and walked on the grass.*

cock-and-bull story a silly, made-up story; a story which is untrue. □ *Don't give me that cock-and-bull story.* □ *I asked for an explanation, and all I got was your ridiculous cock-and-bull story!*

cock of the walk someone who acts in a more important manner than others in a group. □ *The deputy manager was cock of the walk until the new manager arrived.* □ *He loved acting cock of the walk and ordering everyone about.*

cold comfort no comfort or consolation at all. □ *She knows there are others worse off than her, but that's cold comfort.* □ *It was cold comfort to the student that others had failed as well as him.*

cold turkey immediately; without tapering off or cutting down gradually. (Slang. Originally drug slang. Now concerned with breaking any habit.) □ *Tom stopped smoking cold turkey.* □ *She ceased taking her sleeping-pills cold turkey and had no ill effects.* ALSO: **go cold turkey** to stop (doing something) without tapering off. □ *I had to stop smoking, so I went cold turkey. It's awful!* □ *When heroin addicts go cold turkey, they get terribly sick.*

come a cropper to have a misfortune; to fail. (Literally, to fall off one's horse.)

□ *Bob invested all his money in the shares market just before it fell. Did he come a cropper!* □ *Jane was out all night before she took her exams. She really came a cropper.*

come about to happen. □ *How did this come about?* □ *This came about because of the severe weather.*

come across someone or something AND **run across someone or something** to find someone or something by accident. □ *In Scotland, I came across this beautiful little stream full of fish.* □ *Guess who I ran across on the high street this afternoon?*

Come again? Say it again. I did not hear you. (Slang.) □ TOM: *Hello, Grandfather.* GRANDFATHER: *Come again? You'll have to talk louder.* □ *The farmer looked at me when I asked why and said, "Come again?"*

come along (with someone) to accompany someone to somewhere. □ *Come along with me, young man. We are going to see the headmaster.* □ *All right. I'll come along.*

Come and get it! The meal is ready. Come and eat it! (Informal.) □ *A shout was heard from the kitchen, "Come and get it!"* □ *No one says "Come and get it!" at a formal dinner.*

come apart at the seams suddenly to lose one's emotional or mental self-control; to be ruined. (From the literal sense referring to a garment falling apart.) □ *Bill was so upset after his broken engagement that he almost came apart at the seams.* □ *The firm came apart at the seams after the founder died.*

come at someone or something to threaten or attack someone or something. □ *The dog snarled and came at me, but I didn't get bitten.* □ *The bull turned and came at the matador's cape.*

come away empty-handed to return without anything. (See also *go away empty-handed*.) □ *All right, go gambling if you must. Don't come away empty-handed, though.* □ *Go to the*

bank and ask for the loan again. This time try not to come away empty-handed.

come between someone and someone else to interfere with the relationship between two people. □ *Mary Jones is coming between Mr. and Mrs. Franklin.* □ *I'll stay at home. I don't want to come between Tom and his brother.*

come by something to find or get something. □ *How did you come by that haircut?* □ *Where did you come by that new shirt?*

come clean (with someone) to be completely honest with someone; to confess (everything) to someone. (Slang.) □ *The solicitor said, "I can help you only if you come clean with me."* □ *All right, I'll come clean. Here is the whole story.*

come down hard on someone or something to attack vigorously; to scold someone severely. □ *Tom's parents really came down hard on him for coming home late.* □ *Yes, they came down on him hard.*

come down in the world to lose one's social position or financial standing. □ *Mr. Jones has really come down in the world since he lost his job.* □ *If I were unemployed, I'm certain I'd come down in the world, too.*

come down to earth to become realistic or practical, especially after a period of day-dreaming; to become alert to what is going on around one. (Informal.) □ *You have very good ideas, John, but you must come down to earth. We can't possibly afford any of your suggestions.* □ *Pay attention to what is going on. Come down to earth and join the discussion.*

come down to something to be reduced to something; to amount to no more than something. (Informal. Similar to *boil down to something*.) □ *It comes down to whether you want to go to the cinema or stay at home and watch television.* □ *It came down to either finding work or going back to college.*

come down with something to become ill with some disease. □ *I'm afraid I'm coming down with a cold.* □ *I'll probably come down with pneumonia.*

come from far and wide to come from many different places. □ *Everyone was there. They came from far and wide.* □ *We have foods that come from far and wide.*

come full circle to return to the original position or state of affairs. □ *The family sold the house generations ago, but the wheel has come full circle and one of their descendants lives there now.* □ *The employers' power was reduced by the unions at one point, but the wheel has come full circle again.*

come hell or high water no matter what happens. (Informal.) □ *I'll be there tomorrow, come hell or high water.* □ *Come hell or high water, I intend to have my own home.*

come home to roost to return to cause trouble (for someone). □ *As I feared, all my problems came home to roost.* □ *His lies finally came home to roost. His wife discovered his adultery.*

come in for something to receive something; to acquire something. □ *Mary came in for a tremendous amount of money when her aunt died.* □ *Her new play has come in for a lot of criticism.*

come in handy to be useful or convenient. (Informal.) □ *A small television set in the bedroom would come in handy.* □ *A good reference book comes in handy.*

come into one's or its own 1. [for one] to achieve one's proper recognition. □ *Sally finally came into her own when she started taking art lessons.* □ *After years of trying, she finally came into her own.* 2. [for something] to achieve its proper recognition. □ *The idea of an electric car finally came into its own.* □ *Film as an art medium finally came into its own.*

come into something to inherit something. □ *Jane came into a small fortune when her aunt died.* □ *Mary does*

not come into her inheritance until she comes of age.

come of age to reach an age when one is old enough to own property, get married, and sign legal contracts. □ *When Jane comes of age, she will buy her own car.* □ *Sally, who came of age last month, entered into an agreement to purchase a house.*

come off to happen; to take place. (Informal.) □ *I was very surprised when the marriage came off.* □ *Do you think the redevelopment of the area will come off?*

Come off it! Tell the truth!; Don't try to mislead!; Be serious! (Slang.) □ *Come off it, Bill! I don't believe you!* □ *Come on, Jane. Come off it! That can't be true.*

come off second-best to be in second place or worse; to be the loser. □ *You can fight with your brother if you like, but you'll come off second-best.* □ *Why do I always come off second-best in an argument with you?*

come on to hurry up; to follow (someone). □ *Come on! I'm in a hurry.* □ *If you don't come on, we'll miss the train.*

come out 1. to be presented to the public or society; to be released to the public. □ *My new book came out last month.* □ *Fewer debutantes come out nowadays.* 2. See *come out (of the closet).*

come out in the wash to work out all right. (Informal. This means that problems or difficulties will go away as dirt goes away in the process of washing.) □ *Don't worry about their accusation. It'll all come out in the wash.* □ *This trouble will go away. It'll come out in the wash.*

come out of nowhere to appear suddenly. □ *Suddenly, a container lorry came out of nowhere.* □ *Without warning, the storm came out of nowhere.*

come out of one's shell to become more friendly; to be more sociable. □ *Ann, you should come out of your shell and* *spend more time with your friends.* □ *Come out of your shell, Tom. Go out and make some friends.*

come out (of the closet) 1. to reveal one's secret interests, sometimes thought shameful. (Slang.) □ *Tom Brown came out of the closet and admitted that he likes to knit.* □ *The teacher came out of the closet and admitted playing with his model cars.* □ *I thought he would never come out.* **2.** to reveal that one is a homosexual. (Slang.) □ *Tom surprised his parents when he came out of the closet.* □ *It was difficult for him to come out of the closet because he was married.*

come out with something to say something, often suddenly or expectedly; to announce something. □ *Sometimes Jane comes out with the most interesting comments.* □ *Jane came out with a long string of swear words.*

come round 1. finally to agree or consent (to something). □ *I thought he'd never agree, but in the end he came round.* □ *She came round only after we argued for an hour.* **2.** to return to consciousness; to wake up. □ *He came round after we threw cold water in his face.* □ *The boxer was knocked out, but came round in a few seconds.* **3.** to come for a visit; to stop by (somewhere). □ *Why don't you come round about eight? I'll be home then.* □ *Come round some week-end when you aren't busy.*

come someone's way to come to someone, often by chance; to come into someone's possession; to become available to someone. □ *I wish a large sum of money would come my way.* □ *I hope that no bad luck comes my way.*

come to to become conscious; to wake up. □ *We threw a little cold water in his face, and he came to immediately.* □ *It always takes John ten minutes to come to in the mornings.*

come to a bad end to have a disaster, perhaps one which is deserved or expected; to die an unfortunate death. □ *I just know that the young man will* come to a bad end. □ *The miserly shopkeeper came to a bad end and was declared bankrupt.*

come to a head to come to a crucial point; to come to a point when a problem must be solved. (See also *bring something to a head.*) □ *Remember my problem with my neighbours? Well, last night the whole thing came to a head.* □ *The battle between the two factions of the town council came to a head yesterday.*

come to a pretty pass to develop into a bad, unfortunate, or difficult situation. □ *Things have come to a pretty pass when people have to beg in the streets.* □ *When parents are afraid of their children, things have come to a pretty pass.*

come to a standstill to stop, temporarily or permanently. □ *The building project came to a standstill because the workers went on strike.* □ *The party came to a standstill until the lights were turned on again.*

come to an end to stop; to finish. □ *The party came to an end at midnight.* □ *Her life came to an end late yesterday.*

come to an understanding (with someone) to reach a compromise with someone; [for people] to discuss something until they understand one another. □ *I spent an hour trying to come to an understanding with Tom.* □ *We argued for a long time, but we were unable to come to an understanding.*

come to an untimely end to come to an early death. □ *Poor Mr. Jones came to an untimely end in a car accident.* □ *The older brother came to an untimely end, but the twin boys lived to a ripe old age.*

come to blows (over something) to fight or quarrel about something, usually by exchanging blows or harsh or abusive words. □ *They got excited about the accident, but they never actually came to blows over it.* □ *Yes, they aren't the kind of people who come to blows.*

come to grief to fail or be unsuccessful; to have trouble or grief. □ *The artist wept when her canvas came to grief.* □

The wedding party came to grief when the bride passed out.

come to grips with something to face something; to deal or cope with something. □ *He found it difficult to come to grips with his grandmother's death.* □ *Many pupils have a hard time coming to grips with algebra.*

come to life to become alive or lively. (Usually used in a figurative sense.) □ *The party came to life about midnight.* □ *The child comes to life only when she is listening to music.*

come to light to become known; to be discovered. □ *Some interesting facts about your past have just come to light.* □ *If too many bad things come to light, you may lose your job.*

come to mind [for a thought or idea] to enter one's mind. □ *Do I know a good barber? No one comes to mind right now.* □ *Another idea comes to mind. Why not cut your own hair?*

come to naught See the following entry.

come to nothing AND **come to naught** to amount to nothing; to fail; to be worthless. □ *So all my hard work comes to nothing.* □ *Yes, the whole project comes to naught.*

come to one's senses to wake up; to become conscious; to start thinking clearly or sensibly. □ *John, come to your senses. You're being quite stupid.* □ *I hope Mary comes to her senses and breaks off her engagement.*

come to pass to happen. (Formal.) □ *When did all of this come to pass?* □ *When will this event come to pass?*

come to rest to stop moving. □ *When the car comes to rest, you can get in.* □ *The leaf fell and came to rest at my feet.*

come to terms with something to learn to accept something. □ *She had to come to terms with the loss of her sight.* □ *He was devastated by the death of his wife, but he finally came to terms with it.*

come to the fore to become obvious or prominent; to become important. □ *The question of salary has now come to the fore.* □ *Since his great showing in court, my solicitor has really come to the fore in his profession.*

come to the point AND **get to the point** to reach the important part (of something). □ *He has been talking a long time. I wish he would come to the point.* □ *Stop wasting time! Get to the point!* □ *We are talking about money, Bob! Come on, get to the point.*

come to think of it I just remembered. □ *Come to think of it, I know someone who can help.* □ *I have a screwdriver in the boot of my car, come to think of it.*

come too close to home See under *close to home.*

come true to become real; [for a dream or a wish] actually to happen. □ *When I got married, all my dreams came true.* □ *Coming to the big city was like having my wish come true.*

come up to happen unexpectedly. (Also used literally.) □ *I'm sorry, I cannot come to your party. Something has come up.* □ *The storm came up so quickly that I almost got blown away.*

come up from behind to approach someone or something from the rear; to move from a poor position to a better one. □ *As the horses came to the finishing line, my horse came up from behind and won.* □ *In my maths class, I worked and worked and finally came up from behind.*

come up in the world to improve one's status or situation in life. □ *Since Mary got her new job, she has really come up in the world.* □ *A good education certainly helped my brother come up in the world.*

come up with someone or something to find or supply someone or something. □ *I came up with a suitable date at the last minute.* □ *My mum is always able to come up with a snack for me in the afternoon.* □ *I don't have the tool you* *need, but I'll see if I can come up with something.*

come (up) on someone or something to find someone or something by accident. □ *I came upon an interesting fact in my reading last week.* □ *It is unusual for a teacher to come on a pupil who is so bright and yet so lazy.*

come what may no matter what might happen. □ *I'll be home for the holidays, come what may.* □ *Come what may, the mail will get delivered.*

come within an ace of doing something See the following entry.

come within an inch of doing something AND **come within an ace of doing something** to come very close to doing or accomplishing something. (The reference to distance is usually metaphorical.) □ *I came within an inch of going into the army.* □ *I came within an inch of falling off the roof.* □ *She came within an ace of buying the house.*

commit something to memory to memorize something. □ *We all committed the Lord's Prayer to memory.* □ *I committed your telephone number to memory.*

confide in someone to tell secrets or personal matters to someone. □ *Sally always confided in her sister Ann.* □ *She didn't feel that she could confide in her mother.*

conk out to pass out; to go to sleep. (Slang.) □ *Bob bumped his head on a tree branch and conked out.* □ *I usually conk out just after the late news at 11:00 P.M.*

conspicuous by one's absence having one's absence noticed (at an event). □ *We missed you last night. You were conspicuous by your absence.* □ *How could the bride's father miss the wedding party? He was certainly conspicuous by his absence.*

contend with someone or something to endure someone or something; to argue with someone; to struggle with something. □ *I cannot contend with John*

for another instant. □ *I prefer not to contend with this old television set any more. I want a new one.*

contradiction in terms a seeming contradiction in the wording of something. □ *A wealthy pauper is a contradiction in terms.* □ *A straight-talking politician may seem a contradiction in terms.*

control the purse-strings to be in charge of the money in a business or a household. (The purse can opened only when the purse-strings are loosened.) □ *I control the purse-strings at our house.* □ *Mr. Williams is the treasurer. He controls the purse-strings.*

cook someone's goose to damage or ruin someone. (Informal.) □ *I cooked my own goose by not showing up on time.* □ *Sally cooked Bob's goose for treating her the way he did.*

cook something up AND **cook up something** to plot something; to improvise something. (Also used literally.) □ *Mary cooked an interesting party meal up at the last minute.* □ *Let me see if I can cook up a way to get you some money.*

cook the books to cheat in bookkeeping; to make the accounts appear to balance when they do not. □ *Jane was sent to jail for cooking the books of her mother's shop.* □ *It's hard to tell whether she really cooked the books or just didn't know how to add.*

cool down See *cool off.*

Cool it! Calm down!; Take it easy! (Slang.) □ *Don't get angry, Bob. Cool it!* □ *Cool it! No fighting around here.*

cool off AND **cool down** **1.** to let one's anger die away. □ *I'm sorry I got angry. I'll cool off in a minute.* □ *Cool off, Tom. There is no sense getting so excited.* **2.** to let one's passion or love die away. □ TED: *Is Bob still in love with Jane?* BILL: *No, he's cooled off a lot.* □ TED: *I thought that they were both cooling down.*

cool one's heels to wait impatiently (for someone). (Informal.) □ *I spent all afternoon cooling my heels in the wait-*

ing room while the doctor talked on the telephone. □ *All right. If you can't behave properly, just sit down here and cool your heels until I call you.*

cool someone or something down AND **cool down someone or something; cool off someone or something; cool someone or something off 1.** to reduce the heat of someone or something. (See *cool off.*) □ *A cold drink is what I need to cool me down.* □ *She took a shower to cool herself off.* □ *She cooled down her tea by putting an ice cube in it.* **2.** [with *someone*] to reduce someone's anger. □ *I just stared at him while he was shouting. I knew that would cool him down.* □ *The coach talked to them for a long time. That cooled them off.* **3.** [with *someone*] to reduce someone's passion or love. □ *When she slapped him, that really cooled him down.* □ *Mary's indifference eventually cooled Bob off.*

cool someone or something off See the previous entry.

cop it to be punished. (Slang.) □ *You'll cop it when your mother sees your dirty clothes.* □ *The boy copped it when his father found him smoking.*

cop out to cease to be involved or take part; to get out of a difficult situation; to sneak out of a difficult situation. (Slang.) □ *Mary was on our team but at the last minute she copped out on us.* □ *Things were going badly for Mr. Phillips, so he copped out by resigning.*

cost a pretty penny to cost a lot of money. □ *I'll bet that diamond cost a pretty penny.* □ *You can be sure that house cost a pretty penny.*

cost an arm and a leg See under *pay an arm and a leg (for something).*

cost the earth to cost an enormous sum of money. (Compare to *pay the earth.*) □ *That huge car must have cost the earth!* □ *Do I look as though I can afford a house that costs the earth?*

cough something up AND **cough up something** to produce something (which someone has requested). (Slang.) □ *All right, Bill. Cough up the stolen dia-*

monds or else. □ *Okay, okay. I'll cough them up.* □ *Bill had to cough up forty pounds to pay for the broken window.*

could do with someone or something to want or need someone or something; to benefit from someone or something. (Compare to *go for someone or something.*) □ *I could do with a nice cool drink right now.* □ *I could do with some help on this project.* □ *This house could do with some cleaning up.* □ *They said they could do with John to help them finish faster.* □ *My car could do with a bigger engine.*

couldn't care less unable to care at all. (Informal.) □ *John couldn't care less whether he goes to the party or not.* □ *So she won first place. I couldn't care less.* □ *I couldn't care less if I live or die.*

count heads to count people. □ *I'll tell you how many people are here after I count heads.* □ *Everyone is here. Let's count heads so we can order the drinks.*

count off See *count someone or something off.*

count on someone or something to rely on someone or something. □ *Can I count on you to be there at twelve o'clock?* □ *I want to buy a car I can count on in winter weather.*

count one's chickens before they are hatched to plan how to make use of the good results of something before those results have occurred. (Frequently used in the negative.) □ *You're away ahead of yourself. Don't count your chickens before they are hatched.* □ *You may be disappointed if you count your chickens before they are hatched.*

count someone (in for something) AND **count in someone (for something); count someone in (on something); count in someone (on something)** to include someone in something. (Compare to *count someone out for something.*) □ *If you're looking for a group to go mountain climbing, count me in on it.* □ *I would like to count in your entire family, but there* *isn't enough room.* □ *Please count me in.*

count someone or something off AND **count off something or something** to count or enumerate someone or something. □ *He went down the road counting the houses off, one by one.* □ *They counted off the people who were waiting to get in to see the film.*

count someone out (for something) to exclude someone from something. (Compare to *count someone in for something.*) □ *Please count me out for the party next Saturday. I have other plans.* □ *You should count the whole family out. We are going to the beach for the week-end.*

count something up AND **count up something** to total something; to count something. (Also without *up.*) □ *Please count your packages up and make certain you have them all.* □ *Count up your change before you leave the cashier.*

cover a lot of ground 1. to travel over a great distance; to investigate a wide expanse of land. □ *The prospectors covered a lot of ground looking for gold.* □ *My car can cover a lot of ground in one day.* **2.** to deal with much information and many facts. □ *The history lecture covered a lot of ground today.* □ *Mr. and Mrs. Franklin always cover a lot of ground when they argue.*

cover for someone 1. to make excuses for someone; to conceal someone's errors. □ *If I miss class, please cover for me.* □ *If you're late, I'll cover for you.* **2.** to handle someone else's work. □ *Dr. Johnson's partner agreed to cover for him during his holiday.* □ *I'm on duty this afternoon. Will you please cover for me? I have a doctor's appointment.*

cover someone's tracks (up) AND **cover up someone's tracks** to conceal one's trail; to conceal one's past activities. □ *She was able to cover her tracks up so that they couldn't find her.* □ *It's easy to cover up your tracks if you aren't well known.*

cover something up AND **cover up something** to conceal something. □ *They covered up the truth about the crime.* □ *We'll cover up this little matter and make up a story for the press.*

crack a bottle to open a bottle. (Informal.) □ *Let's crack a bottle of champagne to celebrate.* □ *We always crack a bottle of port at Christmas.*

crack a joke to tell a joke. (Informal.) □ *She's never serious. She's always cracking jokes.* □ *As long as she's cracking jokes, she's okay.*

crack down (on someone or something) to be hard on someone or something; to enforce a rule or law more strenuously. □ *They are cracking down on speeding around here.* □ *It's about time they cracked down.*

crack something wide open to expose and reveal some great wrongdoing. □ *The police cracked the drug ring wide open.* □ *The newspaper story cracked the trouble at city hall wide open.*

crack up 1. to go crazy. (Slang.) □ *The mayor cracked up after only a year in office.* □ *I was afraid the boss would crack up because of too much work.* **2.** to break out in laughter. □ *The audience really cracked up during the second act.* □ *The class cracked up when I told my joke, but the teacher didn't like it.*

cradle-snatch to marry or go out with someone who is much younger than oneself. (Informal.) □ *I hear that Bill is dating Ann. Isn't that sort of cradle-snatching? She's much younger than he is.* □ *Uncle Bill—who is nearly eighty—married a thirty-year-old woman. That is really cradle-snatching.*

cramp someone's style to limit someone in some way. □ *I hope this doesn't cramp your style, but could you please not hum while you work?* □ *To ask him to keep regular hours would really be cramping his style.*

crazy about someone or something AND **mad about someone or something; nuts about someone or**

something very fond of someone or something. (Slang.) □ *Ann is crazy about John.* □ *He's crazy about her, too.* □ *I'm mad about their new song.* □ *Our whole family is nuts about home-made ice-cream.*

create a scene See *make a scene.*

create a stink (about some-thing) AND **make a stink (about some-thing); raise a stink (about something)** to make a major issue out of something; to make much over some-thing; to make a lot of complaints and criticisms about something. (Slang.) □ *Tom really created a stink about Bob's remarks.* □ *Why did he make a stink about that?* □ *Tom is always trying to raise a stink about something.*

create an uproar to cause an outburst or sensation. □ *The dog got into church and created an uproar.* □ *Her terrier created an uproar in the restaurant.*

creep up on someone or something to move up quietly and slowly on someone or something. □ *Age creeps up on all of us.* □ *The cat crept up on the bird.*

Crime doesn't pay. a proverb meaning that crime will not benefit a person. □ *At the end of the radio programme, a voice said, "Remember, crime doesn't pay."* □ *No matter how tempting it may appear, crime doesn't pay.*

crop up to appear without warning. □ *Bad luck will often crop up when you aren't ready for it.* □ *We are waiting for something good to crop up.*

cross a bridge before one comes to it to worry excessively about something be-fore it happens. □ *There is no sense in crossing that bridge before you come to it.* □ *She's always crossing bridges be-fore coming to them. She needs to learn to relax.*

cross a bridge when one comes to it to deal with a problem only when one is faced with it. □ *Please wait and cross that bridge when you come to it.* □ *He shouldn't worry about it now. He can cross that bridge when he comes to it.*

cross-examine someone to ask someone questions in great detail; to question a suspect or a witness at great length. □ *The police cross-examined the suspect for three hours.* □ *The solicitor plans to cross-examine the witness tomorrow morning.*

cross one's fingers See *keep one's fingers crossed (for someone or something).*

cross one's heart (and hope to die) to pledge or vow that the truth is being told. □ *It's true, cross my heart and hope to die.* □ *It's really true—cross my heart.*

cross someone or something off AND **cross off someone or some-thing** to take the name of someone or something off a list; to disregard or elim-inate someone or something. (Compare to the following entry.) □ *We had to cross the Franklins off our guest list.* □ *They crossed off ice-cream from the gro-cery list. It's just too cold for ice-cream.*

cross someone or something out AND **cross out someone or some-thing** to draw a line through the name of someone or something on a list. (Al-most the same as the previous entry, but more specific about physically drawing a line.) □ *We crossed out the Franklins and wrote in the Smiths instead.* □ *They crossed the ice-cream out and put cake on the list instead.*

cross someone's mind See *pass through someone's mind.*

cross swords (with someone) to enter into an argument with someone. □ *I don't want to cross swords with Tom.* □ *The last time we crossed swords, we had a terrible time.*

cross the Rubicon to do something which inevitably commits one to a fol-lowing course of action. (The crossing of the River Rubicon by Julius Caesar inev-itably involved him in a war with the Senate in 49 B.C.) □ *Jane crossed the Rubicon by signing the contract.* □ *Find another job before you cross the Rubicon by resigning from this one.*

crushed by something demoralized; with hurt feelings. (Also used literally.) □ *The whole family was completely crushed by the news.* □ *I was just crushed by your attitude. I thought we were friends.*

crux of the matter the central issue of the matter. (*Crux* is an old word meaning "cross.") □ *All right, this is the crux of the matter.* □ *It's about time that we looked at the crux of the matter.*

cry before one is hurt to cry or complain before one is injured. □ *Bill always cries before he's hurt.* □ *There is no point in crying before one is hurt.*

cry blue murder See under *scream blue murder.*

cry for the moon See *ask for the moon.*

cry one's eyes out to cry very hard. □ *When we heard the news, we cried our eyes out with joy.* □ *She cried her eyes out after his death.*

cry over spilled milk to be unhappy about having done something which cannot be undone. (*Spilled* can also be spelled *spilt.*) □ *I'm sorry that you broke your bicycle, Tom. But there is nothing that can be done now. Don't cry over spilled milk.* □ *Ann is always crying over spilt milk.*

cry wolf to cry or complain about something when nothing is really wrong. □ *Pay no attention. She's just crying wolf again.* □ *Don't cry wolf too often. No one will come.*

cue someone in AND **cue in someone 1.** to give someone a cue; to indicate to someone that the time has come. □ *All right, cue in the news-reader.* □ *Now, cue the orchestra director in.* **2.** to tell someone what is going on. (Informal.) □ *I want to know what's going on. Cue me in.* □ *Cue in the general about the troop movement.*

culture vulture someone whom one considers to be excessively interested in the (classical) arts. □ *She won't go to a funny film. She's a real culture vulture.*

□ *They watch only highbrow television. They're culture vultures.*

cupboard love affection shown to someone just because of the things, such as food or clothes, they supply. □ *She doesn't love her husband. It's just cupboard love.* □ *Her affection for her foster-parents is a pretence—simply cupboard love.*

Curiosity killed the cat. a proverb meaning that it is dangerous or unwise to be curious. □ *Don't ask so many questions, Billy. Curiosity killed the cat.* □ *Curiosity killed the cat. Mind your own business.*

curl someone's hair AND **make someone's hair curl** to really frighten or alarm someone; to shock someone with sight, sound, or taste. (Also used literally.) □ *It's enough to make your hair curl the way traffic speeds along.* □ *The horror film curled my hair.*

curl up (and die) to retreat and die; to be very embarrassed. □ *When I heard you say that, I could have curled up and died.* □ *Her mother's praises made her want to curl up.*

curry favour (with someone) to try to win favour from someone. □ *The solicitor tried to curry favour with the judge.* □ *It's silly to curry favour. Just act yourself.*

cut a fine figure to look good; to look elegant. □ *Tom really cuts a fine figure on the dance-floor.* □ *Bill cuts a fine figure since he bought some new clothes.*

cut above someone or something a measure or degree better than someone or something else. (Especially with *the average*, as in the example.) □ *Your shirt is beautiful, but mine is a cut above yours.* □ *John isn't the best mechanic in town, but he's a cut above the average.*

cut across something to reach beyond something; to embrace a wide variety; to slice across a figurative boundary or barrier. □ *His teaching cut across all human cultures and races.* □ *This rule cuts across all social barriers.*

cut and dried fixed; determined beforehand; usual and uninteresting. □ *I find your writing quite boring. It's too cut and dried.* □ *The lecture was, as usual, cut and dried. It was the same thing we've heard for years.* □ *Our plans are all cut and dried; you can't contribute anything now.*

cut and thrust intense competition. (From sword-fighting.) □ *Peter tired of the cut and thrust of business.* □ *The cut and thrust of the stock-market is not for John.*

cut back 1. to turn back; to reverse direction. □ *Suddenly, the bull cut back in our direction and began chasing us.* □ *The road cuts back about a mile ahead, and it goes west again.* **2.** See the following entry.

cut back (on something) to reduce something; to use less of something. □ *The government has to cut back on its spending.* □ *It's very difficult for the government to cut back.*

cut both ways to affect both sides of an issue equally. □ *Remember your suggestion that costs should be shared cuts both ways. You will have to pay as well.* □ *If our side cannot take along supporters to the game, then yours cannot either. The rule has to cut both ways.*

cut corners to reduce efforts or expenditures; to do things poorly or incompletely. (From the phrase *cut the corner,* meaning to avoid going to an intersection to make a turn.) □ *You cannot cut corners when you are dealing with public safety.* □ *Don't cut corners, Sally. Let's do the thing properly.*

cut down (on something) to reduce or limit use or consumption. □ *The doctor told Jane to cut down on sweets.* □ *It's very hard to cut down.*

cut in (on someone or something) 1. to interrupt someone or something. (See also the following entry.) □ *The telephone operator cut in on our call.* □ *I wish the operator hadn't cut in on us.* □ *May I cut in on your conversation?* □ *You have just cut in.* **2.** [with *someone*] to signal, by tapping on the shoulder, one member of a dancing couple to indicate that you wish to dance with the other member of the pair. □ *Tom cut in on Bob and Jane.* □ *Jane was sorry that Tom cut in.*

cut in(to something) to interrupt; to break into something. □ *We can't have a private conversation. John is always cutting in.* □ *The operator cut in on our call.*

Cut it out! See under *cut someone or something out.*

cut it (too) fine to allow scarcely enough time, money, etc., in order to accomplish something. □ *You're cutting it too fine if you want to catch the bus. It leaves in five minutes.* □ *Joan had to search her pockets for money for bus fare. She really cut it fine.*

cut loose (from someone or something) to break away from someone or something; to break ties with someone or something. □ *Jane is finding it hard to cut loose from her family.* □ *Cutting loose is part of growing up.* □ *When those farm boys get to town, they really cut loose from convention.*

cut no ice to have no effect; to make no sense; to have no influence. □ *That idea cuts no ice. It won't help at all.* □ *It cuts no ice that your mother is the director.*

cut off to stop by itself or oneself. (Informal. See also *cut someone or something off.*) □ *The machine got hot and cut off.* □ *Bob cut off in mid-sentence.*

cut off one's nose to spite one's face AND **cut one's nose off to spite one's face** to harm oneself in trying to punish another person. (The phrase is variable in form.) □ *Billy loves the zoo, but he refused to go with his mother because he was angry at her. He cut off his nose to spite his face.* □ *Jane cut off her nose to spite her face when she wouldn't go to the cinema with us.*

cut one's coat according to one's cloth AND **cut one's coat to suit one's cloth** to plan one's aims and activities in line with one's resources and circumstances. □ *We would like a bigger house, but we must cut our coat according to our cloth.* □ *They can't afford a holiday abroad—they have to cut their coat according to their cloth.*

cut one's coat to suit one's cloth See the previous entry.

cut one's eye-teeth on something to have done something since one was very young; to have much experience at something. □ *Do I know about cars? I cut my eye-teeth on cars.* □ *I cut my eye-teeth on Bach. I can whistle everything he wrote.*

cut one's teeth on something to gain one's early experiences on something. □ *You can cut your teeth on this project before getting involved in a more major one.* □ *The young police officers cut their teeth on minor crimes.*

cut out for something well-suited for something; with a talent for something. (See the following entry. Often in the negative.) □ *Tom was not cut out for banking.* □ *Sally was certainly cut out for the medical profession.*

cut out to be something well-suited for a particular role or a particular occupation. (See the previous entry. Often in the negative.) □ *Tom was not cut out to be a banker.* □ *Sally was cut out to be a doctor.*

cut someone dead to ignore someone totally. □ *Joan was just about to speak to James when he cut her dead.* □ *Jean cut her former husband dead.*

cut someone down to size to make a person more humble. □ *John's remarks really cut me down to size.* □ *Jane is too conceited. I think her new managing director will cut her down to size.*

cut someone in AND **cut in someone** to give someone a share of something. (Informal.) □ *Shall we cut Bill in on this deal?* □ *I don't think we should cut anybody in.*

cut someone or something off AND **cut off someone or something** to cut or

sever a connection to someone or something. □ *The telephone operator cut us off because we had talked too long.* □ *Someone cut me off!*

cut someone or something (off) short to end something before it is finished; to end one's speaking before one is finished. □ *We cut the picnic short because of the storm.* □ *I'm sorry to cut you off short, but I must go now.*

cut someone or something out AND **cut out someone or something** to eliminate someone or something; to remove someone or something. □ *We had to cut Bob out. There was no more room.* □ *Uncle Bob left Sally nothing in his will. He cut her out years ago.* ALSO: **Cut it out!** Stop it! □ *Stop that noise! Cut it out!*

cut someone or something to pieces to cut someone or something severely. (Informal.) □ *Ann just cut herself to pieces on the broken glass.* □ *My tie went into the mincer, which cut it to pieces.*

cut someone to the quick to hurt someone's feelings very badly. (Can be used literally when *quick* refers to the tender flesh at the base of finger- and toenails.) □ *Your criticism cut me to the quick.* □ *Tom's sharp words to Mary cut her to the quick.*

cut someone's losses to reduce someone's losses of money, goods, or other things of value. □ *I sold the shares as the market went down, thus cutting my losses.* □ *The mayor's reputation suffered because of the scandal. He finally resigned to cut his losses.*

cut someone's throat [for someone] to experience certain failure; to do damage to someone. (Informal. Also used literally.) □ *If I were to run for office, I'd just be cutting my throat.* □ *Judges who take bribes are cutting their own throats.*

cut something to the bone to cut down severely (on something). □ *We cut our expenses to the bone and are still losing* money. □ *The council had to cut the budget to the bone in order to balance it.*

cut teeth [for a baby or young person] to grow teeth. □ *Billy is cross because he's cutting teeth.* □ *Ann cut her first tooth this week.*

cut the ground out from under someone AND **cut out the ground from under someone** to destroy the foundation of someone's plans or someone's argument. □ *The politician cut the ground out from under his opponent.* □ *The committee cut out the ground from under the treasurer.*

cut up rough to act in a nasty, angry, or threatening way. (Slang.) □ *The man cut up rough when he was accused of shop-lifting.* □ *The thief cut up rough when he was caught.*

cut up someone or something See *chop someone or something up.*

D

daddy of them all the best or most extreme example of someone or something. (Informal.) □ *I've met many dishonest men, but he was the daddy of them all.* □ *Last night's thunderstorm was the daddy of them all.*

daily dozen physical exercises done every day. (Informal.) □ *My brother always feels better after his daily dozen.* □ *She would rather do a daily dozen than go on a diet.*

daily grind the everyday work routine. (Informal.) □ *I'm getting very tired of the daily grind.* □ *When my holiday was over, I had to go back to the daily grind.*

damn someone or something with faint praise to criticize someone or something indirectly by not praising enthusiastically. □ *The critic did not say that he disliked the play, but he damned it with faint praise.* □ *Mrs. Brown is very proud of her son's achievements, but damns her daughter's with faint praise.*

damp squib something which fails to be as successful or exciting as it promised to be. (Informal.) □ *The charity ball was a bit of a damp squib.* □ *The much-publicized protest turned out to be a damp squib.*

dance attendance on someone to be always ready to tend to someone's wishes or needs. □ *That young woman has three men dancing attendance on her.* □ *Her father expects her to dance attendance on him day and night.*

dance to another tune AND **dance to a different tune** to change one's behaviour or attitude. (See also *change someone's tune.*)

□ *After failing the exam, Ann danced to another tune.* □ *A stern talking-to will make her dance to a different tune.*

Darby and Joan an old married couple living happily together. (From a couple so-called in eighteenth-century ballads.) □ *Her parents are divorced, but her grandparents are like Darby and Joan.* □ *It's good to see so many Darby and Joans at the party, but it needs some young couples to liven it up.*

dark horse someone whose abilities, plans, or feelings are little known to others. (From horse-racing.) □ *It's difficult to predict who will win the prize—there are two or three dark horses in the tournament.* □ *Dave is a dark horse in this matter as far as we are concerned.*

dash something off AND **dash off something 1.** to send something off, usually quickly. (Often with *to.*) □ *I'll dash a quick note off to Aunt Mary.* □ *Ann just dashed off a message to her parents.* **2.** to compose something very rapidly. □ *He dashed off some lyrics to go with the tune.* □ *She dashed off a few sketches.*

date back (to sometime) to extend back to a particular time. □ *This record dates back to the sixties.* □ *How far does your friendship date back?*

Davy Jones's locker the bottom of the sea, especially when it is the final resting place for someone or something. (From seamen's name for the evil spirit of the sea.) □ *They were going to sail around the world, but ended up in Davy Jones's locker.* □ *Most of the gold from that trading ship is in Davy Jones's locker.*

dawn on someone to occur to someone; suddenly to become clear to someone; to *pass through someone's mind.* □ *It just dawned on me that I forgot my books.* □ *When will it dawn on him that his audience is bored?*

day after day every day without a break; daily. □ *He wears the same clothes day after day.* □ *She visits her husband in the hospital day after day.*

day and night AND **night and day** all the time; around the clock. □ *The doctor was with her day and night.* □ *The house is guarded night and day.*

day in and day out AND **day in, day out** on every day; for each day. □ *She smokes day in and day out.* □ *They eat nothing but vegetables, day in, day out.*

day-to-day daily; everyday; ordinary. □ *They update their accounts on a day-to-day basis.* □ *Just wear your ordinary day-to-day clothing.*

daylight robbery the practice of blatantly or grossly overcharging. (Informal.) □ *It's daylight robbery to charge that amount of money for a hotel room!* □ *The cost of renting a car at that place is daylight robbery.*

dead and buried gone forever. (Refers literally to persons and figuratively to ideas and other things.) □ *Now that Uncle Bill is dead and buried, we can read his will.* □ *That way of thinking is dead and buried.*

dead centre at the exact centre of something. □ *The arrow hit the target dead centre.* □ *When you put the flowers on the table, put them dead centre.*

dead loss a total loss; someone or something that is completely useless or unsuccessful. (Informal.) □ *This car is a dead loss. It was a waste of money.* □ *She is a dead loss as a teacher.*

dead on one's or its feet exhausted; worn out; no longer effective or successful. (Informal.) □ *Ann is so tired. She's really dead on her feet.* □ *He can't teach well any more. He's dead on his feet.* □ *This inefficient company is dead on its feet.*

dead set against someone or something totally opposed to someone or something. □ *I'm dead set against the new rates proposal.* □ *Everyone is dead set against the MP.*

dead to the world sleeping very soundly. (Informal. Compare to *dead on one's feet.*) □ *He spent the whole plane journey dead to the world.* □ *Look at her sleep. She's dead to the world.*

death to something having a harmful effect on something; liable to ruin something. □ *This road is terribly bumpy. It's death to tyres.* □ *Stiletto heels are death to those tiles.*

desert a sinking ship AND **leave a sinking ship** to leave a place, a person, or a situation when things become difficult or unpleasant. (Rats are said to be the first to leave a ship which is sinking.) □ *I hate to be the one to desert a sinking ship, but I can't stand it around here any more.* □ *There goes Tom. Wouldn't you know he'd leave a sinking ship rather than stay around and try to help?*

devil-may-care attitude AND **devil-may-care manner** a very casual attitude; a carefree attitude. □ *You must get rid of your devil-may-care attitude if you want to succeed.* □ *She acts so thoughtlessly with her devil-may-care manner.*

devil-may-care manner See the previous entry.

devil of a job AND **devil's own job** the most difficult task. (Informal.) □ *We had the devil of a job fixing the car.* □ *It was the devil's own job finding a hotel with vacancies.*

devil's own job See the previous entry.

die a natural death [for something] to fade away or die down. □ *I expect that all this excitement about computers will die a natural death.* □ *Most fads die a natural death.*

die away See *die out.*

die down See *die out.*

die laughing to laugh very long and hard. (Informal.) □ *The joke was so* *funny that I almost died laughing.* □ *The play was meant to be funny, but the audience didn't exactly die laughing.*

die of a broken heart to die of emotional distress. □ *I was not surprised to hear of her death. They say she died of a broken heart.* □ *In the film, the heroine appeared to die of a broken heart, but the audience knew she was poisoned.*

die of boredom to suffer from boredom; to be very bored. □ *No one has ever really died of boredom.* □ *We sat there and listened politely, even though we almost died of boredom.*

die off See the following entry.

die out AND **die away; die off 1.** AND **die down** to come slowly to an end; to subside. □ *All this talk about war will eventually die out.* □ *This trouble will die down soon.* **2.** [for a group of living things] to die one by one until all are dead. □ *The dinosaurs died out millions of years ago.* □ *Some scientists think that a change in climate caused them to die off.*

die with one's boots on to *go down fighting;* to die in some fashion other than in bed; to die fighting. (Informal. Popularized by U.S. Western films. The villains of these films said they preferred death by gunshot or hanging to dying in bed. See also *go down fighting.*) □ *I won't let him get me. I'll die with my boots on.* □ *He may give me a hard time, but I won't be overcome. I'll fight him and die with my boots on.*

dig in 1. to get ready for a very long job or session. (Informal. Refers to soldiers preparing for battle by digging trenches and getting into them.) □ *There is a long agenda today. We better dig in for a long meeting.* □ *The delegates arrived on Monday and began to dig in for a long convention.* **2.** to eat a meal; to begin eating a meal. (Slang. See also *Come and get it!*) □ *Dinner's ready, Tom. Sit down and dig in.* □ *The cowboy helped himself to some beans and dug in.*

dig in one's heels AND **dig one's heels in** to refuse to alter one's course of action or opinions; to be obstinate or determined. □ *The student dug her heels in and refused to sit the exam.* □ *I'm digging in my heels. I'm not going back.*

dig one's own grave to be responsible for one's own downfall or ruin. □ *The manager tried to get rid of his assistant, but he dug his own grave. He got the sack himself.* □ *The government have dug their own grave with their new taxation bill. They won't be re-elected.*

dig some dirt up on someone AND **dig up some dirt on someone** to find out something bad about someone. (Slang.) □ *If you don't stop trying to dig some dirt up on me, I'll get my solicitor to sue you.* □ *The citizens' group dug up some dirt on the MP and used it against her at election time.*

dig someone or something to understand something; to like someone or something; to relate to a person or a thing. (Dated slang.) □ *I really dig Tom. He's a special friend.* □ *I really dig rock music.*

dig someone or something up AND **dig up someone or something** to go to great effort to find someone or something. (Informal. There is often an implication that the thing or person dug up is not the most desirable, but it is all that could be found.) □ *Mary dug a partner up for the dance next Friday.* □ *I dug up a recipe for roast pork with pineapple.* □ *I dug up a carpenter who doesn't charge very much.*

dig something out AND **dig out something** to work hard to locate something and bring it forth. (Informal.) □ *They dug the contract out of the file cabinet.* □ *I dug this old suit out of a box in the attic.*

dine out See *eat out.*

dine out on something to be asked to social gatherings because of the information one has. □ *She's been dining out on the story of her promotion for months.* □ *The journalist dines out on all the gossip he acquires.*

dip into something to take or borrow from a supply of something, especially a supply of money. (Also used literally.) □ *I had to dip into my savings account to pay for the car.* □ *She put out her hand and dipped into the tin of sweets.* □ *The boss accused Mike of dipping into the till.*

dirt cheap extremely cheap. (Informal.) □ *Buy some more of those plums. They're dirt cheap.* □ *In Italy, the peaches are dirt cheap.*

dirty look a look or glance expressing disapproval or dislike. (Especially with *get, give, receive.*) □ *I stopped whistling when I saw the dirty look on her face.* □ *The child who sneaked received dirty looks from the other children.* □ *Ann gave me a dirty look.* □ *I gave her a dirty look back.*

dirty old man an older man who is excessively interested in sex. (Informal.) □ *Tell your daughter to stay away from him. He's a dirty old man and might attack her.* □ *There were several dirty old men reading pornographic magazines.*

dirty one's hands AND **soil one's hands** to become involved with something illegal; to do a shameful thing; to do something which is beneath one. □ *The mayor would not dirty his hands by accepting bribes.* □ *I will not dirty my hands by breaking the law.* □ *Sally felt that to talk to the tramp was to soil her hands.*

dirty word 1. a swear-word; an obscene or blasphemous word; a four-letter word. □ *You are not allowed to use dirty words in your school essays.* □ *My aunt is offended by the use of dirty words.* **2.** something that is disliked or disapproved of. □ *Since Tom broke off his engagement, his name is a dirty word in the village.* □ *Socialism is a dirty word in that house.*

dirty work 1. unpleasant or uninteresting work. □ *My boss does all the travelling. I get all the dirty work to do.* □ *She's tired of doing all the dirty work at the office.* **2.** dishonest or underhanded actions; treachery. □ *She knew there was some dirty work going on when she saw her opponents whispering together.*

□ *The firm seems respectable enough, but there's a lot of dirty work going on.*

dish something out AND **dish out something** to give something out, such as food or punishment. (Often informal.) □ *The cook dished out the stew as if he were feeding pigs.* □ *The teacher dished punishment out whenever things got too noisy.* □ *Only the wealthy dish money out like that.*

divide something fifty-fifty AND **split something fifty-fifty** to divide something into two equal parts. (Informal. The *fifty* means 50 percent.) □ *Tommy and Billy divided the sweets fifty-fifty.* □ *The thieves split the money fifty-fifty.*

do a bunk to go away unexpectedly; to run away. (Slang.) □ *The burglar did a bunk before the police could question him.* □ *The Robinson family have done a bunk without paying their bills.*

do a double take to react with surprise; to have to look twice to make sure that one really saw correctly. (Informal.) □ *When the boy led a goat into the park, everyone did a double take.* □ *When the doctor saw that the man had six toes, she did a double take.*

do an about-face to make a total reversal of opinion or action. □ *Without warning, the government did an about-face on taxation.* □ *It had done an about-face on the question of rates last year.*

do away with someone to kill someone. □ *The crooks did away with the witness.* □ *I was there, too. I hope they don't try to do away with me.*

do credit to someone AND **do someone credit** to add to the reputation of someone. (See also *do someone proud.*) □ *Your new style of dressing really does credit to you.* □ *Yes, it really does you credit.*

do justice to something 1. to do something well; to represent or portray something accurately. □ *Sally really did justice to the contract negotiations.* □ *This photograph doesn't do justice to the beauty of the mountains.* **2.** to eat or

67

drink a great deal. (Informal.) □ *Bill always does justice to the evening meal.* □ *The guests didn't do justice to the roast pig. There were nearly ten pounds of it left over.*

do one's best to do (something) as well as one can. □ *Just do your best. That's all we can ask of you.* □ *Tom isn't doing his best. We may have to replace him.*

do one's bit to do one's share of the work; to do whatever one can do to help. □ *Everybody must do their bit to help get things under control.* □ *I always try to do my bit. How can I help this time?*

do one's duty to do one's job; to do what is expected of one. □ *Please don't thank me. I'm just doing my duty.* □ *He didn't want to report the child, but he felt he had to do his duty.*

do one's nut to be very angry. (Slang.) □ *Robert's father will do his nut when he hears his exam results.* □ *The customer did his nut when his car was not ready on time.*

do one's (own) thing to do what one likes or what one pleases. (Slang.) □ *Tom doesn't like being told what to do. He prefers to do his own thing.* □ *When you do your thing, you have no one but yourself to blame if things don't work out.*

do so See *do too*.

do somehow by someone to treat someone in a particular manner. (Informal. Do not confuse this with a passive construction. The *someone* is not the subject but the object.) □ *Tom did all right by Ann when he brought her red roses.* □ *I did badly by Tom when I left him to fight alone.*

do someone a good turn to do something that is helpful to someone. □ *My neighbour did me a good turn by lending me his car.* □ *The teacher did me a good turn when he told me to work harder.*

do someone credit See *do credit to someone*.

do someone down to do something to someone's disadvantage. □ *He really did me down when he applied for the same job.* □ *Don't expect Mr. Black to help you. He enjoys doing people down.*

do someone good to benefit someone. □ *A nice hot bath really does me good.* □ *A few years in the army would do you good.*

do someone in AND **do in someone** 1. to make someone tired. (Slang.) □ *That tennis match really did me in.* □ *Yes, hard activity will do you in.* 2. to kill someone. (Slang.) □ *The crooks did in the bank guard.* □ *They'll probably do in the witnesses soon.*

do someone or something over AND **do over someone or something** 1. [with *something*] to rebuild, redesign, or redecorate something. □ *We did over our living-room for the celebration.* □ *We had to do over the sitting-room because it was looking shabby.* 2. [with *someone*] to give someone a severe beating; to beat someone up. □ *They certainly did the police spy over.* □ *He was done over so badly that he's crippled.*

do someone out of something to cheat someone out of something. (Informal.) □ *They did the widow out of her life savings.* □ *I won't let anyone do me out of anything. I'm a very cautious and suspicious person.*

do someone proud to treat someone generously. (Informal.) □ *What a good hotel. The conference has done us proud.* □ *He certainly did his daughter proud. The wedding reception cost a fortune.*

do someone's heart good to make someone feel good emotionally. (Informal.) □ *It does my heart good to hear you talk that way.* □ *When she sent me a get-well card, it really did my heart good.*

do something by hand to do something with one's hands rather than with a machine. □ *The computer was broken so I had to type the document by hand.* □ *All this tiny stitching was done by hand. Machines cannot do this kind of work.*

do something in person to appear somewhere and do something oneself rather than sending someone or doing something over the telephone or by mail. □ *I know the money should be in his account. I saw him put it there in person.* □ *The famous actor came to the hospital and greeted each patient in person.*

do something on the hoof See the following entry.

do something on the run AND **do something on the hoof** to do something while one is moving hurriedly; to do something while one is going rapidly from one place to another. (Informal.) □ *I was very busy today and had to eat on the run.* □ *I didn't have time to meet with Bill, but I was able to talk to him on the run.* □ *We always have breakfast on the hoof.*

do something over (again) to redo something; to repeat the doing of something. □ *This sewing isn't right. You'll have to do it over again.* □ *The teacher made me do my essay over.*

do something the hard way See under *learn something the hard way.*

do something up AND **do up something** to dress up something; to repair, redecorate, or refurbish something. □ *The shop assistant did up the present in beautiful silver paper.* □ *I'll have to do this room up before I sell the house.*

do the dishes to wash the dishes; to wash and dry the dishes. □ *Bill, you cannot go out and play until you've done the dishes.* □ *Why am I always the one who has to do the dishes?*

do the honours to act as host or hostess and serve one's guests by pouring drinks, serving food, etc. □ *All the guests were seated, and a huge joint sat on the table. Jane Thomas turned to her husband and said, "Bob, will you do the honours?" Mr. Thomas smiled and began carving.* □ *The president stood up and addressed the people at the dinner: "I'm delighted to do the honours this evening and propose a toast to your friend and mine, Bill Jones."*

do the trick to do exactly what needs to be done. (Informal.) □ *Push the car just a little more to the left. There, that does the trick.* □ *If you give me two pounds, I'll have enough to do the trick.*

do too AND **do so** to do something (despite anything to the contrary). (An emphatic way of saying *do*. See *be too, have too.*) □ BOB: *You don't have your money with you.* BILL: *I do too!* □ *He does so! I saw him put it in his pocket.* □ *She did too. I saw her do it.*

do without (someone or something) to manage to get through life without someone or something which you want or need. □ *I suppose I'll just have to do without a car.* □ *Poor people learn to do without.* □ *The managing director can't do without a secretary.*

dog-eat-dog a situation in which one has to act ruthlessly in order to survive or succeed; ruthless competition. □ *It is dog-eat-dog in the world of business these days.* □ *Universities are not quiet, peaceful places. It's a case of dog-eat-dog for promotion.*

dog in the manger one who prevents other people from doing or having what one does not wish them to do or have. (From one of Aesop's fables in which a dog—which cannot eat hay—lay in the hay-rack [manger] and prevented the other animals from eating the hay.) □ *Jane is a real dog in the manger. She cannot drive, but she will not lend anyone her car.* □ *If Martin were not such a dog in the manger, he would let his brother have that evening suit he never wears.*

done to a turn cooked just right. □ *Yummy! This meat is done to a turn.* □ *I like it done to a turn, not too well done and not too raw.*

donkey-work hard or boring work. (Informal.) □ *His wife picks flowers, but he does all the donkey-work in the garden.* □ *I don't only baby-sit. I do all the donkey-work around the house.*

donkey's ages AND **donkey's years** a very long time. (Informal.) □ *The woman hasn't been seen for donkey's ages.* □

Our family haven't had a holiday in donkey's years.

donkey's years See the previous entry.

Don't hold your breath. Do not stop breathing (while waiting for something to happen).; Do not expect something to happen (quickly). (Informal.) □ *You think he'll get a job? Ha! Don't hold your breath.* □ *I'll finish building the fence as soon as I have time, but don't hold your breath.*

Don't look a gift horse in the mouth. a proverb meaning that one should not expect perfect gifts. (Usually stated in the negative. Note the variation in the examples. The age of a horse and, therefore, its usefulness can be determined by looking at its teeth. It would be greedy to inspect the teeth of a horse given as a gift to make certain the horse is of the best quality.) □ *Don't complain about the type of car your father gave you. You shouldn't look a gift horse in the mouth.* □ *John complained that the television set he got for his birthday was black and white rather than colour. He was told, "Don't look a gift horse in the mouth."*

dose of one's own medicine the same kind of, usually bad, treatment which one gives to other people. (Often with *get* or *have.*) □ *Sally never is very friendly. Someone is going to give her a dose of her own medicine someday and ignore her.* □ *The thief didn't like getting a dose of his own medicine when his car was stolen.*

double back (on one's tracks) [for a person or animal] to go in the reverse direction. (Refers primarily to a person or animal that is being pursued by someone or something.) □ *The deer doubled back on on its tracks and evaded the hunter.* □ *The police lost him. He must have doubled back and gone home.*

double-cross someone to betray someone by doing the opposite of what was promised; to betray a person by not doing what was promised; to deceive someone. (Originally criminal slang.) □ *If you double-cross me again, I'll kill you.* □ *Tom is angry at Jane because she*

double-crossed him and went out with someone else.

double Dutch language or speech that is difficult or impossible to understand. □ *This book on English grammar is written in double Dutch. I can't understand a word.* □ *Try to find a lecturer who speaks slowly, not one who speaks double Dutch.*

double up (with someone) to share something with someone. □ *We don't have enough books. Tom, will you double up with Jane?* □ *We'll share hotel rooms to save money. Tom and Bill will double up in room twenty.*

doubting Thomas someone who will not easily believe something without strong proof or evidence. (From the biblical account of the apostle Thomas, who would not believe that Christ had risen from the grave until he had touched Him.) □ *Mary won't believe that I have a dog until she sees him. She's such a doubting Thomas.* □ *This school is full of doubting Thomases. They want to see his new bike with their own eyes.*

down and out having no money or means of support. □ *There are many young people down and out in London just now.* □ *John gambled away all his fortune and is now completely down and out.* ALSO: **down-and-out** someone who is very poor with no prospects of obtaining work or money. □ *London is filled with down-and-outs.* □ *Once wealthy, John is now counted among the down-and-outs.*

down at heel shabby; poorly dressed. □ *The tramp was really down at heel.* □ *Tom's house needs paint. It looks down at heel.* ALSO: **down-at-heel** rundown. □ *Look at that down-at-heel tramp.*

down in the dumps sad or depressed. (Informal.) □ *I've been down in the dumps for the past few days.* □ *Try to cheer Jane up. She's down in the dumps for some reason.*

down in the mouth sad-faced; depressed and unsmiling. □ *Ever since the party was cancelled, Barbara has been looking* *down in the mouth.* □ *Bob has been down in the mouth since his girlfriend left.*

down on one's luck without any money; unlucky. (Euphemistic for *poor* or *penniless*.) □ *Can you loan me twenty pounds? I've been down on my luck lately.* □ *The gambler had to get a job because he had been down on his luck and didn't earn enough money to live on.*

down South to or at the South of England. (See also *up North.*) □ *I used to live down South, but I moved to Scotland.* □ *We are going down South for the winter now that we have retired.*

down the drain lost forever; wasted. (Slang.) □ *I just hate to see all that money go down the drain.* □ *Well, there goes the whole project, right down the drain.*

Down the hatch! an exclamation said when swallowing something, often an alcoholic drink. (Slang.) □ *Come on, Billy. Eat your dinner. Down the hatch!* □ *John raised his glass of beer and said, "Down the hatch."*

down the tube ruined; wasted. (Slang.) □ *His political career went down the tube after the scandal. He's lost his job.* □ *The business went down the tube.*

down to earth practical; not theoretical; not fanciful. □ *Her ideas for the boutique are always very down to earth.* □ *The committee's plans for the village are anything but down to earth.* ALSO: **down-to-earth** practical; realistic. □ *She's far too dreamy. We want a more down-to-earth person.* □ *A down-to-earth businessman will not accept that financial forecast.*

down with a disease ill; sick at home. (Can be said about many diseases.) □ *Tom isn't here. He's down with a cold.* □ *Sally is down with the flu.* □ *The whole office has come down with something.*

doze off AND **drift off (to sleep)** to go slowly and gently to sleep. (Informal.) □ *When the room gets warm, I usually doze off.* □ *I hate to doze off like that.* □ *The baby drifted off to sleep.* □ *It's easy to drift off when you're a baby.*

drag on See under *drag something out.*

drag one's feet to act very slowly, often deliberately. □ *The government are dragging their feet on this bill because it will lose votes.* □ *If the planning department hadn't dragged their feet, the building would have been built by now.*

drag out See under *drag something out.*

drag something out AND **drag out something** to make something last longer than it should. □ *Why do lawyers have to drag trials out like this?* □ *They are really dragging out the negotiations.* ALSO: **drag on; drag out** to last too long; to last long and be boring. □ *Winter always seems to drag on too long.* □ *Why do operas drag on for hours?* □ *I don't know what makes them drag out like that.*

draw a blank to get no response; to find nothing. (Informal.) □ *I asked him about Tom's financial problems, and I just drew a blank.* □ *We looked in the files for an hour, but we drew a blank.*

draw a line between something and something else to separate two things; to distinguish or differentiate between two things. (The *a* can be replaced with *the.* See also *draw the line (at something).*) □ *It's necessary to draw a line between bumping into people and striking them.* □ *It's very hard to draw the line between slamming a door and just closing it loudly.*

draw a red herring to introduce information which diverts attention from the main issue. (See *red herring.*) □ *The accountant drew several red herrings to prevent people from discovering that he had embezzled the money.* □ *The government, as always, will draw a red herring whenever there is a monetary crisis.*

draw blood to hit or bite (a person or an animal) and make a wound that bleeds. □ *The dog chased me and bit me hard, but it didn't draw blood.* □ *The boxer landed just one punch and drew blood immediately.*

draw someone or something out AND **draw out someone or something 1.** [with *someone*] to coax someone to speak or answer; to bring someone into a conversation or other social interaction. □ *Jane is usually very shy with older men, but Tom really drew her out last evening.* □ *John drew out Mr. Smith on the question of rate increases.* **2.** [with *something*] to make something longer. □ *Jane drew the conversation out for more than twenty minutes.* □ *I could not draw the speech out any longer.*

draw something up AND **draw up something** to put something into writing; to prepare a written document; to put plans on paper. (Used especially with legal documents prepared by a solicitor.) □ *I went to see my solicitor this morning about drawing up a will.* □ *You should draw a will up as soon as you can.* □ *The architect is drawing up plans for the new city hall.*

draw the fire away from someone or something AND **draw someone's fire (away from someone or something)** to make oneself a target in order to protect someone or something. (Refers literally to gun-fire or figuratively to any kind of attack.) □ *The mother bird drew the fire away from her chicks.* □ *The hen drew the hunter's fire away from her nest.* □ *The former owner drew the fire away from Sally by proposing a compromise.* □ *The aeroplanes drew the soldier's fire away from the ships in the harbour.*

draw the line (at something) to set a limit at something; to decide when a limit has been reached. □ *You can make as much noise as you want, but I draw the line at fighting.* □ *It's hard to keep young people under control, but you have to draw the line somewhere.* □ *The room will seat fifty, but I think you should draw the line at forty.*

dream come true a wish or a dream which has become real. □ *Going to Hawaii is like having a dream come true.* □ *Having you for a friend is a dream come true.*

dream something up AND **dream up something** to think of something; to

invent something, often useless or fanciful; to make up something. □ *That's a great idea. Did you dream it up yourself?* □ *I like to dream up ways to make money.*

dress someone or something up AND **dress up someone or something 1.** [with *someone*] to provide fancy or better clothing for someone. □ *Sally's mother dressed her up for the party.* □ *Sally's mother likes to dress up her daughter.* **2.** [with *something*] to make something look or seem better. □ *I think we can dress this car up with some new paint and sell it.* □ *Mary is good at dressing up old ideas to make them sound new.* ALSO: **dress up** to dress in fancy or better clothing. □ *Sally knew she had to dress up for the affair.* □ *The children dressed up as fairies.*

dress up See under *dress someone or something up.*

dressed to kill dressed in fancy or stylish clothes, often showily or gaudily. (Slang.) □ *I hope my aunt doesn't come dressed to kill to the concert.* □ *Margaret was there dressed to kill in taffeta and sequins.*

dressed (up) to the nines dressed in one's best clothes. (Informal. Very high on a scale of one to ten.) □ *The applicants for the job were all dressed up to the nines.* □ *The wedding party were dressed to the nines.*

dressing down a scolding. □ *After that dressing down I won't be late again.* □ *The boss gave Fred a real dressing down for breaking the machine.*

dribs and drabs in small irregular quantities. (Especially with *in* and *by*.) □ *The cheques for the charity are coming in in dribs and drabs.* □ *The members of the orchestra arrived by dribs and drabs.*

drift off (to sleep) See *doze off.*

drink something up AND **drink up something** to drink all of something. □ *Who drank all the orange juice up?* □ *Come on, Billy. Drink up your milk.* ALSO: **drink up** to drink quickly; to take a drink. (Often said of alcoholic drinks.) □ *The barman said, "Drink up. I have to close the bar."* □ *When the hostess had served punch to all the guests, she said, "Drink up!"*

drink to excess to drink too much alcohol; to drink alcohol continually. □ *Mr. Franklin drinks to excess.* □ *Some people drink to excess only at parties.*

drink up See under *drink something up.*

drive a coach and horses through something to expose weak points or "holes" in an argument, alibi, or criminal case by [figuratively] driving a horse and carriage through them. (Formal. Emphasizes the large size of the holes or gaps in the argument.) □ *The barrister drove a coach and horses through the witness's defence.* □ *The opposition will drive a coach and horses through the wording of that government bill.*

drive a hard bargain to work hard to negotiate prices or agreements in one's own favour. □ *All right, sir, you drive a hard bargain. I'll sell you this car for £12,450.* □ *You drive a hard bargain, Jane, but I'll sign the contract.*

drive someone crazy AND **drive someone mad** to annoy or irritate someone. (Informal.) □ *This itch is driving me crazy.* □ *All these telephone calls are driving me mad.*

drive someone mad See the previous entry.

drive someone to the wall See *push someone to the wall.*

drive someone up the wall to annoy or irritate someone. (Informal.) □ *Stop whistling that tune. You're driving me up the wall.* □ *All his talk about moving to London nearly drove me up the wall.*

drive something home AND **drive home something** to make something clearly understood. □ *Why do I always have to shout at you to drive something home?* □ *Sometimes you have to be forceful to drive home a point.*

driving force (behind someone or something) a person or a thing that motivates or directs someone or something.

□ *Money is the driving force behind most businesses.* □ *Ambition is the driving force behind Tom.* □ *Love can also be a driving force.*

drop a bombshell to announce shocking or startling news. (Informal.) □ *They really dropped a bombshell when they announced that the president had cancer.* □ *Friday is a good day to drop a bombshell like that. It gives the business world the week-end to recover.*

drop a brick AND **drop a clanger** to mention something that causes embarrassment. (Informal) □ *You certainly dropped a brick when you mentioned that her ex-boyfriend had married.* □ *I could tell from her expression that I had dropped a clanger.*

drop a clanger See the previous entry.

drop back to go back or remain back; to fall behind. □ *As the crowd moved forward, the weaker ones dropped back.* □ *She was winning the race at first, but soon dropped back.*

drop dead Go away and stop bothering me. (Rude slang.) □ *If you think I'm going to put up with your rudeness all afternoon, you can just drop dead!* □ *Drop dead! I'm not your slave!*

drop in (on someone) to pay someone a casual visit, perhaps a surprise visit. (Informal.) □ *I hate to drop in on people when they aren't expecting me.* □ *You're welcome to drop in at any time.*

drop in one's tracks to stop or collapse from exhaustion; to die suddenly. □ *If I keep working this way, I'll drop in my tracks.* □ *Uncle Bob was working in the garden and dropped in his tracks. We are all sorry that he's dead.*

drop in the bucket See the following entry.

drop in the ocean AND **drop in the bucket** a very small amount; just a little bit; not enough of something to make a difference. □ *But £1 isn't enough! That's just a drop in the ocean.* □ *At this point your help is nothing more than a drop in the ocean. I need far more help than twenty people could give.* □ *I* won't accept your offer. It's just a drop in the bucket.

drop off (to sleep) to go to sleep without difficulty; to fall asleep. (See also *doze off*.) □ *I sat in the warm room for five minutes, and then I dropped off to sleep.* □ *After I've eaten dinner, I can drop off with no trouble at all.*

drop out (of something) to stop being a member of something; to stop attending or participating in something. (Informal.) □ *I'm working part-time so that I won't have to drop out of college.* □ *I don't want to drop out at this time.*

drop someone to stop being friends with someone, especially with one's boyfriend or girlfriend. (Informal.) □ *Bob finally dropped Jane. I don't know what he saw in her.* □ *I'm surprised that she didn't drop him first.*

drop someone a line AND **drop someone a few lines** to write a letter or a note to someone. (Informal. The *line* refers to lines of writing.) □ *I dropped Aunt Jane a line last week.* □ *She usually drops me a few lines around the first of the year.*

drop someone or something off AND **drop off someone or something** to deliver someone or something to a place which is part way to one's final destination. □ *If you're going to the bank, please drop off my cheque on the way.* □ *Please drop Mary off at her office.*

drop someone's name AND **drop the name of someone** to mention the name of important or famous people as if they were personal friends. □ *Mary always tries to impress people by dropping the names of well-known film stars.* □ *Joan's such a snob. Leave it to her to drop the names of all the local gentry.* ALSO: **name-dropping** □ *Mary always tries to impress people by name-dropping.* □ *Joan's such a snob. She's always name-dropping.*

drop the name of someone See the previous entry.

drown one's sorrows to try to forget one's problems by drinking a lot of alcohol. (Informal.) □ *Bill is in the bar drowning his*

sorrows. □ *Jane is at home drowning her sorrows after losing her job.*

drown someone or something out AND **drown out someone or something** to make so much noise that someone or something cannot be heard. □ *I couldn't hear what you said. The radio drowned you out.* □ *We couldn't hear all the concert because the noise of the planes drowned out the quiet parts.*

drug on the market something on the market in great abundance; a glut on the market. □ *Right now, small computers are a drug on the market.* □ *Ten years ago, small transistor radios were a drug on the market.*

drum someone out of something to expel or send someone away from something, especially in a formal or public fashion. (From the military use of drums on such occasions.) □ *The officer was drummed out of the regiment for misconduct.* □ *I heard that he was drummed out of school for cheating.*

drum something into someone to make someone learn something through persistent repetition. □ *Yes, I know that. They drummed it into me as a child.* □ *Now I'm drumming it into my own children.*

drum something up AND **drum up something** to obtain something by attracting people's attention to one's need or cause. □ *I shall try to drum up support for the party.* □ *You shall have to drum up new business by advertising.*

dry run an attempt; a rehearsal. □ *We had better have a dry run for the official ceremony tomorrow.* □ *The children will need a dry run before their procession in the pageant.*

dry someone out to cause someone to become sober; to cause someone to stop drinking alcohol to excess. (Informal.) □ *If the doctor at the clinic can't dry him out no one can.* □ *Mary's having to be dried out. She's been drinking heavily since her divorce.*

dry up 1. to become silent; to stop talking. (Informal.) □ *The young lecturer was so nervous that he forgot what he* was going to say and dried up. □ *Actors have a fear of drying up on stage.* **2.** to shut up and go away; to *drop dead.* (Rude slang. Usually a command.) □ *Quit bothering me! Dry up!* □ *Dry up! I'm tired of listening to you.*

dust someone or something down to remove the dust from someone or something; to freshen or renew someone or something, originally by removing dust. □ *Bob got up from the ground and dusted himself down.* □ *She found the book on the bottom shelf. She took it from its place and dusted it down.*

Dutch auction an auction or sale which starts off with a high asking price which is then reduced until a buyer is found. □ *Dutch auctions are rare—most auctioneers start with a lower price than they hope to obtain.* □ *My house-agent advised me to ask a reasonable price for my house rather than get involved with a Dutch auction.*

Dutch courage unusual or artificial courage arising from the influence of alcohol. □ *It was Dutch courage that made the football supporter attack the policeman.* □ *It will take a bit of Dutch courage to make an after-dinner speech.*

Dutch treat a social occasion where one pays for oneself. (See also *go Dutch.*) □ *"It's nice of you to ask me out to dinner,"* she said, *"but could we make it a Dutch treat?"* □ *The office outing is always a Dutch treat.*

Dutch uncle a man who gives frank and direct advice to someone in the manner of a parent or relative. □ *I would not have to lecture you like a Dutch uncle if you were not so extravagant.* □ *He acts more like a Dutch uncle than a husband. He's forever telling her what to do in public.*

duty-bound (to do something) forced by a sense of duty and honour to do something. □ *Good evening, madam. I'm duty-bound to inform you that we have arrested your husband.* □ *No one made me say that. I was duty-bound.*

dwell (up)on something to linger overly long on a thought, sight, or sound; to concentrate on something. □ *I wish you wouldn't dwell upon death so much.* □ *Don't spend so much of your time dwelling on your mistakes.*

dyed-in-the-wool permanent; indelible; stubborn. (Usually said of a person.) □ *My uncle was a dyed-in-the-wool farmer. He wouldn't change for anything.* □ *Sally is a dyed-in-the-wool socialist.*

dying to do something very anxious to do something; very anxious to have something. (Informal.) □ *I'm just dying to go sailing in your new boat.* □ *After a long hot day like this one, I'm just dying to drink some cool water.*

E

eager beaver someone who is very enthusiastic; someone who works very hard. □ *New volunteers are always eager beavers.* □ *The young assistant gets to work very early. She's a real eager beaver.*

eagle eye careful attention; an intently watchful eye. (From the sharp eyesight of the eagle.) □ *The pupils wrote their essays under the eagle eye of the headmaster.* □ *The umpire kept his eagle eye on the tennis match.*

early bird someone who gets up or arrives early or starts something very promptly, especially someone who gains an advantage of some kind by so doing. (See also *The early bird catches the worm.*) □ *The Smith family are early birds. They caught the first ferry.* □ *I was an early bird and got the best selection of flowers.*

Early to bed, early to rise, (makes a man healthy, wealthy, and wise). a proverb which claims that going to bed and getting up early is good for you. (Sometimes said to explain why a person is going to bed early. The last part of the saying is sometimes left out.) □ *Tom left the party at midnight saying, "Early to bed, early to rise, makes a man healthy, wealthy, and wise."* □ *I always get up at dawn. After all, early to bed, early to rise.*

earn one's keep to help out with chores in return for food and a place to live; to earn one's pay by doing what is expected. □ *I earn my keep at college by shovelling snow in the winter.* □ *Tom hardly earns his keep around here. He should be sacked.*

ease someone out AND **ease out someone** to remove a person from a job or an office gently and quietly. □ *They eased out the chairman without a scandal.* □ *It is very difficult to ease an MP out of office.*

easier said than done said of a task which is easier to talk about than to do. □ *Yes, we must find a cure for cancer, but it's easier said than done.* □ *Finding good employment is easier said than done.*

easy come, easy go said to explain the loss of something which required only a small amount of effort to get in the first place. □ *Ann found twenty pounds in the morning and spent it foolishly at lunch-time. "Easy come, easy go," she said.* □ *John spends his money as fast as he can earn it. With John it's easy come, easy go.*

Easy does it. act with care. (Informal.) □ *Be careful with that glass vase. Easy does it!* □ *Now, now, Tom. Don't get angry. Easy does it.*

easy to come by easily found; easily purchased; readily available. □ *Please be careful with that gramophone record. It was not easy to come by.* □ *A good dictionary is very easy to come by.*

eat away at someone [for something] to bother or worry someone. □ *Her failure to pass the exam was eating away at her.* □ *Fear of appearing in court was eating away at Tom.*

eat humble pie to act very humbly, especially when one is shown to be wrong. □ *I think I'm right, but if I'm wrong, I'll eat humble pie.* □ *You think you're so smart. I hope you have to eat humble pie.*

eat like a bird to eat only small amounts of food; to peck at one's food. □ *Jane is very slim because she eats like a bird.* □ *Bill is trying to lose weight by eating like a bird.*

eat like a horse to eat large amounts of food. (Informal.) □ *No wonder he's so fat. He eats like a horse.* □ *John works like a horse and eats like a horse, so he never gets fat.*

eat one's cake and have it too See *have one's cake and eat it too.*

eat one's hat a phrase telling the kind of thing that one would do if a very unlikely event really happens. □ *I'll eat my hat if you get a rise.* □ *He said he'd eat his hat if she got elected.*

eat one's heart out **1.** to be very sad (about someone or something). □ *Bill spent a lot of time eating his heart out after his divorce.* □ *Sally ate her heart out when she had to sell her house.* **2.** to be envious (of someone or something). (Informal.) □ *Do you like my new watch? Well, eat your heart out. It was the last one in the shop.* □ *Eat your heart out, Jane! I've got a new girlfriend now.*

eat one's words to have to take back one's statements; to confess that one's predictions were wrong. □ *You shouldn't say that to me. I'll make you eat your words.* □ *John was wrong about the election and had to eat his words.*

eat out AND **dine out** to eat a meal at a restaurant. □ *Yes, it's good to eat out and try different kinds of food.* □ *It costs a lot of money to dine out often.*

eat out of someone's hands to do what someone else wants; to obey someone eagerly. (Often with *have.*) □ *Just wait! I'll have everyone eating out of my hands. They'll do whatever I ask.* □

The treasurer has everyone eating out of his hands. □ *A lot of people are eating out of his hands.*

eat someone out of house and home to eat a lot of food (in someone's home); to eat all the food in the house. (Informal.) □ *Billy has a huge appetite. He almost eats us out of house and home.* □ *When the young people come home from college, they always eat us out of house and home.*

edge someone or something out AND **edge out someone or something** to remove a person or other creature from a position, usually by beating the person or creature in competition. □ *The brown horse edged the others out just before the finishing line.* □ *Tom edged out Bob as the new cook at the restaurant.*

egg someone on to encourage, urge, or dare someone to continue doing something, usually something unwise. □ *John wouldn't have done the dangerous experiment if his brother hadn't egged him on.* □ *The two boys kept throwing stones because the other children were egging them on.*

either feast or famine either too much (of something) or not enough (of something). (Also without *either.*) □ *This month is very dry, and last month it rained almost every day. Our weather is either feast or famine.* □ *Sometimes we are busy, and sometimes we have nothing to do. It's feast or famine.*

elbow-grease physical exertion; hard work. (As if lubricating one's elbow would make one more efficient.) □ *It'll take some elbow-grease to clean this car.* □ *Expensive polishes are all very well, but this floor needs elbow-grease.*

eleventh-hour decision a decision made at the last possible minute. (See also *at the eleventh hour.*) □ *Eleventh-hour decisions are seldom satisfactory.* □ *The treasurer's eleventh-hour decision was made in a great hurry, but it turned out to be correct.*

Empty vessels make the most noise. a saying meaning that it is usually the least intelligent and the least well-informed people who are quick to state their opinions. □ *James was telling everyone his views on the Russian situation, but he knows very little about it. Empty vessels make the most noise.* □ *It is a case of empty vessels make the most noise when Jack starts talking about education. He talks a lot of nonsense.*

en passant See *in passing.*

end of the line See the following entry.

end of the road AND **end of the line** the end; the end of the whole process; death. (*Line* originally referred to railway tracks.) □ *When we reach the end of the road on this project, we'll get paid.* □ *You've come to the end of the line. I'll not lend you another penny.* □ *When I reach the end of the road, I wish to be buried in a quiet place, near some trees.*

end up (by) doing something AND **wind up (by) doing something** to conclude something by doing something. □ *We ended up by going back to my house.* □ *After playing in the rain, we all wound up catching colds.*

end up somewhere AND **wind up somewhere** to finish at a certain place. (See also *land up somehow or somewhere.*) □ *If you don't get straightened out, you'll end up in jail.* □ *I fell and hurt myself. I wound up in the hospital.*

end up with the short end of the stick See *get the short end of the stick.*

enlarge on something AND **expand on something** to make a more detailed explanation of something; to explain one's previous comments. □ *Mary was asked to enlarge on her remarks.* □ *I'd now like to enlarge on my earlier statement about the growth of the economy.* □ *I would be happy to expand on my remarks.*

enough is as good as a feast a saying that one should be satisfied if one has enough of something to meet one's needs and not seek great unnecessary quantities. □ *We have enough money to live on and enough is as good as a feast.* □ *I cannot understand why they want a larger house. Enough is as good as a feast.*

Enough is enough. That is enough, and there should be no more. □ *Stop asking for money! Enough is enough!* □ *I've heard all the complaining from you that I can take. Stop! Enough is enough!*

enough to go (a)round a supply adequate to serve everyone. (Informal.) □ *Don't take too much. There's not enough to go around.* □ *I cooked some extra potatoes, so there should be enough to go round.*

enter one's mind to come to one's mind; [for an idea or memory] to come into one's consciousness. □ *Leave you behind? The thought never even entered my mind.* □ *A very interesting idea just entered my mind. What if I ran for office?*

enter the lists to begin to take part in a contest or argument. □ *He had decided not to stand election for Parliament, but entered the lists at the last minute.* □ *The family disagreement had almost been resolved when the grandfather entered the lists.*

equal to someone or something able to handle or deal with someone or something. □ *I'm afraid that I'm not equal to Mrs. Smith's problem right now. Please ask her to come back later.* □ *That's a very difficult task, but I'm sure Bill is equal to it.*

escape someone's notice to go unnoticed; not to have been noticed. (Usually a way to point out that someone has failed to see or respond to something.) □ *I suppose my earlier request escaped your notice, so I'm writing again.* □ *I'm sorry. Your letter escaped my notice.*

eternal triangle a sexual or emotional relationship involving two women and one man or two men and one woman. (Typically, a couple [man and woman] and another man or woman.) □ *Henry can't choose between his wife and his mistress. It's the eternal triangle.* □ *I'm surprised Jane doesn't get tired of* *the eternal triangle. She goes out with Peter at the week-end and Jim during the week.*

Every cloud has a silver lining. a proverb meaning that there is something good in every bad thing. □ *Jane was upset when she saw that all her flowers had died from the frost. But when she saw that the weeds had died, too, she said, "Every cloud has a silver lining." □ Sally had a sore throat and had to stay home from school. When she learned she missed a maths test, she said, "Every cloud has a silver lining."*

Every dog has its day. AND **Every dog has his day.** a proverb meaning that everyone will get a chance. □ *Don't worry, you'll get chosen for the team. Sooner or later, every dog has its day. □ You may become famous some day. Every dog has his day.*

every inch a something AND **every inch the something** completely; in every way. (With the force of an attributive adjective.) □ *Mary is every inch the schoolteacher. □ Her father is every inch a gentleman.*

every last one every one without exception; every single one. (Informal.) □ *You must eat all your peas! Every last one! □ Each of you—every last one—has to take some medicine.*

every living soul every person. □ *Every living soul has a right to have enough food to eat. □ This is the kind of problem that affects every living soul.*

every man jack (of someone) AND **every mother's son (of someone)** absolutely everyone. (*Jack* can also be capitalized.) □ *I'll sack every man jack of you if you don't finish on time. □ It'll need every man jack of them to complete the job. □ The boss said he wanted every mother's son of them to work on Saturday.*

every minute counts AND **every moment counts** time is very important. □ *Doctor, please try to get here quickly. Every minute counts. □ When you take a test, you must work rapidly because every moment counts.*

every moment counts See the previous entry.

every mother's son (of someone) See *every man jack (of someone).*

every now and again See the following entry.

every now and then AND **every now and again; every once in a while** occasionally; once in a while. □ *We eat lamb every now and then. □ I read a novel every now and again. □ We don't go to the cinema except maybe every now and then. □ I drink coffee every once in a while.*

every once in a while See the previous entry.

every time one turns around frequently; at every turn; with annoying frequency. □ *Somebody asks me for money every time I turn around. □ Something goes wrong with Bill's car every time he turns around.*

(every) Tom, Dick, and Harry everyone without discrimination; ordinary people. (Not necessarily males.) □ *The golf-club is very exclusive. They don't let any Tom, Dick, or Harry join. □ Mary's sending out very few invitations. She doesn't want every Tom, Dick, and Harry turning up.*

everything but the kitchen sink almost everything one can think of. □ *When Sally went off to college, she took everything but the kitchen sink. □ When you take a baby on holiday, you have to pack everything but the kitchen sink.*

everything from A to Z almost everything one can think of. □ *She knows everything from A to Z about decorating. □ The biology exam covered everything from A to Z.*

exception that proves the rule a saying claiming that when an exception has to be made to a particular rule or guideline, this simply emphasizes the existence of the rule. (The exception tests for the existence of a rule. Usually with *the*.) □ *Sixth-formers do not have to wear school uniforms, but they're the excep-*

tion that proves the rule. □ *The youngest dog is allowed in the house. He's the exception that proves the rule.*

expand on something See *enlarge on something.*

expecting (a child) pregnant. (A euphemism.) □ *Tommy's mother is expecting a child.* □ *Oh, I didn't know she was expecting.*

expense is no object See *money is no object.*

explain oneself to explain what one has said or done. □ *Please take a moment to explain yourself. I'm sure we are interested in your ideas.* □ *Yes, if you give me a moment to explain myself, I think you'll agree with my idea.*

explain something away AND **explain away something** to give a good explanation for something; to explain something so that it seems less important; to make excuses for something. □ *John couldn't explain away his low marks on the test.* □ *This is a very serious matter, and you cannot just explain it away.*

extend credit (to someone) to allow someone to purchase something on credit. □ *I'm sorry, Mr. Smith, but because of your poor record of payment, we are no longer able to extend credit to you.* □ *Look at this letter, Jane. The store won't extend credit any more.*

extend one's sympathy (to someone) to express sympathy to someone. (A very polite and formal way to tell someone that you are sorry about a misfortune.) □ *Please permit me to extend my sympathy to you and your children. I'm very sorry to hear of the death of your husband.* □ *Let's extend our sympathy to Bill Jones, who is in the hospital with a broken leg. We should send him some flowers.*

extenuating circumstances special circumstances which account for an irregular or improper way of doing something. □ *Mary was permitted to arrive late because of extenuating circumstances.* □ *Due to extenuating circumstances, the teacher will not meet class today. Her mother had to go to the hospital.*

eyeball to eyeball person to person; face to face. (Informal.) □ *The discussions will have to be eyeball to eyeball to be effective.* □ *Telephone conversations are a waste of time. We need to talk eyeball to eyeball.*

F

face someone down AND **face down someone** to overcome someone by being bold; to disconcert someone by displaying great confidence. □ *The teacher faced the angry pupil down without saying anything.* □ *The mayor couldn't face down the entire city council.*

face the music to receive punishment; to accept the unpleasant results of one's actions. (Informal.) □ *Mary broke a dining-room window and had to face the music when her father got home.* □ *After failing a maths test, Tom had to go home and face the music.*

face to face in person; in the same location. (Said only of people. An adverb.) □ *Let's talk about this face to face. I don't like talking over the telephone.* □ *Many people prefer to talk face to face.* ALSO: **face-to-face** facing one another; in the same location. □ *I prefer to have a face-to-face meeting.* □ *They work better on a face-to-face basis.*

face up to someone or something to confront something bravely. □ *Tom had to face up to going to the dentist.* □ *Bill doesn't want to face up to his problems.*

face value outward appearance; what something first appears to be. (From the value printed on the "face" of a coin or banknote.) □ *Don't just accept her offer at face value. Think of the implications.* □ *Joan tends to take people at face value and so she is always getting hurt.*

facts of life 1. the facts of sex and reproduction, especially human reproduction. (See also *birds and the bees*.) □ *My parents told me the facts of life when I was nine years old.* □ *Bill learned the facts of life from his classmates.* **2.** the truth about the unpleasant ways that the world works. □ *Mary really learned the facts of life when she got her first job.* □ *Tom couldn't accept the facts of life in business, so he resigned.*

fair crack of the whip a fair share of something; a fair opportunity of doing something. □ *He doesn't want to do all the overtime. He only wants a fair crack of the whip.* □ *They were supposed to share the driving equally, but James refused to give Anne a fair crack of the whip.*

fair do's fair and just treatment [done to someone]. (Informal.) □ *It's hardly fair do's to treat her like that.* □ *It's not a question of fair do's. He treats everyone in the same way.* ALSO: **Fair do's!** Be fair!; Be reasonable! □ *Fair do's! You said you would lend me your bike if I took your books home.* □ *I know I said I'd baby-sit tonight, but fair do's—I hate to work late.*

fair game someone or something that it is quite permissible to attack. □ *I don't like seeing articles exposing people's private lives, but politicians are fair game.* □ *Journalists always regard film-stars as fair game.*

fair-to-middling only fair or okay; a little better than acceptable. □ *I don't feel ill, just fair-to-middling.* □ *The play wasn't really good. It was just fair-to-middling.*

fair-weather friend someone who is one's friend only when things are going well. (This person will desert one when things go badly. Compare to *A friend in need is a friend indeed*.) □ *Bill wouldn't help me with my homework. He's just a fair-weather friend.* □ *A fair-weather friend isn't much help in an emergency.*

fall about to laugh heartily. (Informal.) □ *We fell about at the antics of the clown.* □ *The audience were falling about during the last act of the comedy.*

fall apart AND **fall to pieces** to break into pieces; to cease to function; to become disorganized. (Compare to *go to pieces*.) □ *This old car is about ready to fall apart.* □ *She just fell apart when her husband died.* □ *All my plans fell to pieces.*

fall apart at the seams to break into pieces; to *fall apart*. □ *This old car is about ready to fall apart at the seams.* □ *The plan won't succeed. It's falling apart at the seams already.*

fall asleep to go to sleep. □ *The baby cried and cried and finally fell asleep.* □ *Tom fell asleep in class yesterday.*

fall back (from something) to move back from something; to back away from something. □ *Suddenly the opposing team fell back from the end of the field.* □ *On orders from the officer, the crowd fell back.*

fall back on someone or something to turn to someone or something for help. □ *Bill can always fall back on his brother for help.* □ *John ran out of ink and had to fall back on his pencil.*

fall behind (with something) AND **get behind (with something)** to fail to do a task on time; to fail to do enough of something; to move more slowly than others, letting them move ahead of you. □ *I fell behind with my car payments, so the bank took my car back.* □ *Ann fell behind with her work and had to explain to the manager.* □ *Try not to get behind.* □ *When we were hiking, I fell behind and got lost.*

fall between two stools to come somewhere between two possibilities and so fail to meet the requirements of either. □ *The material is not suitable for an academic book or for a popular one. It falls between two stools.* □ *He tries to be both teacher and friend, but falls between two stools.*

fall by the wayside to give up and quit before the end (of something); not to succeed. (As if one became exhausted and couldn't finish a foot-race.) □ *John fell by the wayside and didn't finish college.* □ *Many people start out to train for a career in medicine, but some of them fall by the wayside.*

fall down on the job to fail to do something properly; to fail to do one's job adequately. (Informal.) □ *The team kept losing because the coach was falling down on the job.* □ *Tom was sacked because he fell down on the job.*

fall flat (on one's face) AND **fall flat (on its face)** to be completely unsuccessful. (Informal.) □ *I fell flat on my face when I tried to give my speech.* □ *The play fell flat on its face.* □ *My jokes fall flat most of the time.*

fall for someone or something (Informal.) 1. [with *someone*] to fall in love with someone. □ *Tom fell for Ann after only two dates. He wants to marry her.* □ *Some men always fall for women with blond hair.* 2. [with *something*] to be deceived by something. □ *I can't believe you fell for that old trick.* □ *Jane didn't fall for Ann's story.*

fall foul of someone or something to do something that annoys or offends someone or something; to do something that is contrary to the rules. □ *He has fallen foul of the police more than once.* □ *The political activists fell foul of the authorities.* □ *I hope I don't fall foul of your sister. She doesn't like me.* □ *John fell foul of the law.*

fall from grace to cease to be held in favour, especially because of some wrong or foolish action. □ *He was the teacher's prize pupil until he fell from grace by failing the history exam.* □ *Mary* *was the favourite grandchild until she fell from grace by running away from home.*

fall in to queue up in a row, standing shoulder to shoulder. (Usually refers to people in scouting or the armed services. Compare to *fall out*.) □ *The boy scouts were told to fall in behind the scoutmaster.* □ *The soldiers fell in quickly.*

fall in love (with someone) to develop the emotion of love for someone. □ *Tom fell in love with Mary, but she only wanted to be friends.* □ *John is too young to fall in love.*

fall in with someone or something 1. [with *someone*] to meet someone by accident; to join with someone. □ *John has fallen in with a strange group of people.* □ *We fell in with some people from our home town when we went on holiday.* **2.** [with *something*] to agree with something; to accept something. □ *Bill was not able to fall in with our ideas about painting the house red.* □ *Bob fell in with Mary's plans to move to Texas.*

fall into line to conform. □ *If you are going to work here, you will have to fall into line.* □ *He likes to do as he pleases. He hates having to fall into line.*

fall in(to) place to fit together; to be seen in its proper relationship or order and so be understood. □ *After we heard the whole story, things began to fall in place.* □ *All the clues began to fall into place and I knew who the culprit was.*

fall into the trap of doing something to be deceived or tricked into doing something. □ *We fell into the trap of thinking he was honest.* □ *Don't fall into the trap of sympathizing with her. There's nothing wrong with her.*

fall off to decline or diminish. □ *Business falls off during the summer months.* □ *If trade falls off any further, the factory will close.*

fall out 1. to happen; to result. □ *As things fell out, we had a wonderful trip.*

□ *It so fell out that we all left together.* **2.** to leave one's place in a formation, when dismissed. (Usually in scouting or the armed services. The opposite of *fall in*.) □ *The scouts fell out and ran to the camp-fire.* □ *All the soldiers fell out and talked among themselves.* **3.** See the following entry.

fall out (with someone) (over something) AND **fall out (with someone) (about something)** to quarrel or disagree with someone about something. □ *Bill fell out with Sally over the question of buying a new car.* □ *Bill fell out with John about who would sleep on the bottom bunk.* □ *They are always arguing. They fall out about once a week.* ALSO: **have a falling-out (with someone) (over something)** to have a disagreement with someone about something. □ *Bill had a falling-out with Sally over buying a new car.* □ *They had a falling-out over a car.*

fall over backwards to do something AND **bend over backwards to do something; lean over backwards to do something** to do everything possible to please someone. (Informal. See also the following entry.) □ *The taxi-driver fell over backwards to be helpful.* □ *The teacher bent over backwards to help the pupils understand.* □ *You don't have to lean over backwards to get me to help. Just ask.*

fall over oneself to try very hard and eagerly. (See also the previous entry.) □ *Tom fell over himself trying to make Jane feel at home.* □ *We fell over ourselves to make her welcome, but she left.*

fall short (of something) to fail to achieve a goal; to be less or of a lower standard than what is required or demanded. □ *We fell well short of our goal of collecting a thousand pounds.* □ *Ann ran a fast race, but fell short of the record.*

fall through to fail to happen; to come to nothing. (Informal.) □ *Our plans fell through, and we won't be going to France after all.* □ *The entire affair fell through at the last minute.*

fall to to begin (to do something), often enthusiastically. (Compare to *turn to.*) □ *The hungry children took their knives and forks and fell to.* □ *John fell to and cleaned up his room after he got shouted at.*

fall to pieces See *fall apart; go to pieces.*

fall to someone See under *fall (up)on someone or something.*

fall (up)on someone or something 1. to attack someone or something. □ *The cat fell upon the mouse and killed it.* □ *The children fell on the birthday cake and ate it all.* **2.** [with *someone*] AND **fall to someone** [for a task] to become the duty of someone. □ *The task of telling Mother about the broken vase fell upon Jane.* □ *It fell to Tom to clean up the spilt oil.*

Familiarity breeds contempt. a proverb meaning that knowing a person closely for a long time leads to bad feelings. □ *Bill and his brothers are always fighting. Like they say: "Familiarity breeds contempt."* □ *Mary and John were good friends for many years. Finally they got into a fierce argument and became enemies. That just shows that familiarity breeds contempt.*

fan the flames (of something) to make something more intense; to make a situation worse. □ *The riot fanned the flames of racial hatred even more.* □ *The hostility in the school is bad enough without anyone fanning the flames.*

fancy someone's chances to have confidence in someone's [including one's own] ability to be successful. (Informal.) □ *We all think she will refuse to go out with him, but he certainly fancies his chances.* □ *The other contestants are so talented that I don't fancy his chances at all.*

far and away by a great amount; unquestionably; absolutely. □ *This soap is far and away the best.* □ *Sally is good, but Ann is far and away the fastest.* □ *Peter is far and away the cleverest boy in the school.*

far be it from me to do something it is not really my place to do something. (Always with *but,* as in the examples.) □ *Far be it from me to tell you what to do, but I think you should buy the book.* □ *Far be it from me to attempt to advise you, but you're making a big mistake.*

far cry from something a thing which is very different from something else. □ *What you did was a far cry from what you said you were going to do.* □ *The song they played was a far cry from what I call music.*

far from it not it at all; not at all. □ *Do I think you need a new car? Far from it. The old one is fine.* □ BILL: *Does this hat look strange?* TOM: *Far from it. It looks good.*

far into the night late into the night; late. □ *She sat up and read far into the night.* □ *The party went on far into the night.*

far out 1. far from the centre of things; far from town. □ *The Smiths live very far out.* □ *The restaurant is nice, but too far out.* **2.** strange. (Slang.) □ *Ann acts pretty far out sometimes.* □ *The whole group of people seemed pretty far out.*

farm someone or something out AND **farm out someone or something 1.** [with *someone*] to send someone (somewhere) for care or development. □ *When my mother died, they farmed me out to my aunt and uncle.* □ *The team manager farmed out the player to the minor leagues until he improved.* **2.** [with *something*] to send something (elsewhere) to be dealt with. □ *I farmed out various parts of the work to different people.* □ *Bill farmed his chores out to his brothers and sisters and went to a film.*

fat chance very little likelihood. (Informal.) □ *Fat chance he has of getting promotion.* □ *You think she'll lend you the money? Fat chance!*

feast one's eyes (on someone or something) to look at someone or some-

thing with pleasure, envy, or admiration. □ *Just feast your eyes on that beautiful juicy steak!* □ *Yes, feast your eyes. You won't see one like that again for a long time.*

feather in one's cap an honour; something of which one can be proud. □ *Getting a new client was really a feather in my cap.* □ *It was certainly a feather in the journalist's cap to get an interview with the president.*

feather one's (own) nest to use power and prestige selfishly to provide for oneself, often immorally or illegally. □ *The mayor seemed to be helping people, but was really feathering her own nest.* □ *The building contractor used a lot of public money to feather his nest.*

fed up to somewhere with someone or something See the following entry.

fed up (with someone or something) AND **fed up to somewhere with someone or something** bored with or disgusted with someone or something. (Informal. The *somewhere* can be *here, the teeth, the gills,* or other places.) □ *I'm fed up with Tom and his silly tricks.* □ *I'm fed up to here with high rates.* □ *They are fed up to the teeth with screaming children.* □ *I'm really fed up!*

feed one's face to eat. (Slang.) □ *Come on, everyone. It's time to feed your faces.* □ *Bill, if you keep feeding your face all the time, you'll get fat.*

feel fit to feel well and healthy. □ *If you want to feel fit, you must eat the proper food and get enough rest.* □ *I hope I still feel fit when I get old.*

feel free to do something to feel as if one is permitted to do something or take something. □ *Please feel free to stay for dinner.* □ *If you see something you want in the refrigerator, please feel free to help yourself.*

feel it beneath one (to do something) to feel that one would be humbling oneself or reducing one's status to do something. □ *Tom feels it beneath him to scrub the floor.* □ *Ann feels it beneath her to*

carry her own luggage. □ *I would do it, but I feel it beneath me.*

feel like a million dollars to feel well and healthy, both physically and mentally. □ *A quick swim in the morning makes me feel like a million dollars.* □ *What a beautiful day! It makes you feel like a million dollars.*

feel like a new person to feel refreshed and renewed, especially after getting well or getting dressed up. □ *I bought a new suit, and now I feel like a new person.* □ *Bob felt like a new person when he got out of the hospital.*

feel like something 1. to wish to do something; to be in the mood to do something. □ *I believe I'm getting well. I feel like getting out of bed.* □ *I don't feel like going to the party. I didn't care for the last party they gave.* **2.** to want to have something; to be in the mood to have something. □ *I feel like a nice cool drink.* □ *The children feel like a swim.*

feel out of place to feel that one does not belong in a place; to feel awkward. □ *I feel out of place at formal dances.* □ *Bob and Ann felt out of place at the picnic, so they went home.*

feel put upon to feel taken advantage of or exploited. □ *Bill refused to help because he felt put upon.* □ *Sally's mother felt put upon, but she took each of the children home after the birthday party.*

feel something in one's bones to sense something; to have an intuition about something. (Informal.) □ *The train will be late. I feel it in my bones.* □ *I failed the test. I feel it in my bones.*

feel the draught See the following entry.

feel the pinch AND **feel the draught** to have money problems; to experience hardship because of having too little money. (Informal.) □ *The Smiths used to go abroad every year, but they're feeling the pinch since he retired.* □ *You're bound to feel the pinch a bit when you're a student.* □ *Henry needs someone to share the expenses of the flat. He's feeling the* *draught since Mike left.* □ *Anne's feeling the draught a bit now since she's divorced.*

feel up to something to feel well enough or prepared enough to do something. (Often in the negative.) □ *I don't feel up to jogging today.* □ *Aunt Mary didn't feel up to making the visit.* □ *Do you feel up to going out today?*

fence someone in to restrict someone in some way. (Informal. See also *hem someone or something in*.) □ *I don't want to fence you in, but you have to get home earlier at night.* □ *Don't try to fence me in. I need a lot of freedom.* ALSO: **fenced in** restricted or restrained. □ *I don't like to be fenced in.* □ *I need lots of space and lots of freedom. I can't stand being fenced in.*

fenced in See under *fence someone in.*

fend for oneself See *shift for oneself.*

ferret something out of someone or something AND **ferret out something from someone or something** to remove or retrieve something from someone or something, usually with cunning and persistence. □ *I tried very hard, but I couldn't ferret the information out of the young lady at reception.* □ *I had to ferret out the answer from a book in the library.*

few and far between very few; few and widely scattered. (Informal.) □ *Get some petrol now. Petrol stations on this motorway are few and far between.* □ *Some people think that good films are few and far between.*

fiddle around (with something) AND **fiddle about (with something)** (Informal. See also *mess around (with someone or something)*.) **1.** to idle away one's time by doing trivial things; to waste someone's time. □ *Stop fiddling around and clean your room.* □ *Now it's time for all of you to stop fiddling about with things and get to work.* **2.** to play with something; to tinker with something ineptly. □ *My brother is outside fiddling around with his car en-*

gine. □ *Stop fiddling about with that stick. You're going to hurt someone.*

fiddle while Rome burns to do nothing or something trivial while something disastrous happens. (From a legend that the emperor Nero played the lyre while Rome was burning.) □ *The Opposition don't seem to be doing anything to stop this terrible parliamentary bill. They're fiddling while Rome burns.* □ *The doctor should have sent for an ambulance right away instead of examining her. In fact, he was just fiddling while Rome burned.*

fight shy of something to avoid something; to keep from doing something. □ *She fought shy of borrowing money from her father, but had to in the end.* □ *He's always fought shy of marrying.*

fight someone or something hammer and tongs AND **fight someone or something tooth and nail; go at it hammer and tongs; go at it tooth and nail** to fight against someone or something energetically and with great determination. □ *The dogs were fighting each other hammer and tongs.* □ *The mayor fought the new law hammer and tongs.* □ *We'll fight the building of a new road tooth and nail.* □ *They fought the robber tooth and nail.*

fight someone or something tooth and nail See the previous entry.

fight to the death a bitter struggle to the end. □ *The wolf and the elk were in a fight to the death.* □ *They both wanted the top job. It was a fight to the death.*

fighting chance a good possibility of success, especially if every effort is made. □ *They have at least a fighting chance of winning the race.* □ *The patient could die, but he has a fighting chance since the operation.*

figure in something [for a person] to play a role in something. □ *Tom figures in our plans for a new building.* □ *I don't wish to figure in your future.*

fill dead men's shoes See *step into dead men's shoes.*

fill in (for someone) to take the place of another person. □ *Bob had to fill in for Tom in the play.* □ *Who filled in when the secretary was sick?*

fill out to grow fuller or fatter. (See also *fill something out.*) □ *The tree we planted two years ago is beginning to fill out.* □ *John was very thin, but now he's beginning to fill out.* □ *Mary is beginning to fill out and look like a young lady.*

fill someone in (on someone or something) AND **fill in someone (on someone or something)** to inform someone about someone or something. (Informal.) □ *Please fill me in on what is happening in Manchester.* □ *Please fill me in on Ann. How is she doing?* □ *Sit down, and I'll fill you in.* □ *Later, I'll fill in everyone else.*

fill someone or something in AND **fill in someone or something** 1. [with *something*] to write or type information into blank places on a form or application. (The same as *fill something out.*) □ *Please fill in this application.* □ *You must fill all the blanks in.* □ *Take this home and fill it in.* 2. [with *someone*] See the previous entry.

fill someone's shoes to take the place of some other person and do that person's work satisfactorily. (As if you were wearing the other person's shoes.) □ *I don't know how we'll be able to do without you. No one can fill your shoes.* □ *It'll be difficult to fill Jane's shoes. She did her job very well.*

fill something out AND **fill out something** to write or type information into blank places on a form or application; to complete an application form. (See also *fill someone or something in.*) □ *Take this form home and fill it out, please.* □ *Please fill out this application when you have a chance.*

fill the bill to be exactly the thing that is needed. □ *Ah, this steak is great. It really fills the bill.* □ *This new pair of shoes fills the bill nicely.*

final fling the last act or period of enjoyment before a change in one's circumstances or life-style. □ *You might as well have a final fling before the baby's born.* □ *Mary's going out with her girlfriends for a final fling. She's getting married next week.*

find fault (with someone or something) to find things wrong with someone or something. □ *We were unable to find fault with the meal.* □ *Sally's father was always finding fault with her.* □ *Some people are always finding fault.*

find it in one's heart to do something to have the courage or compassion to do something; to persuade oneself to do something. □ *She couldn't find it in her heart to refuse to come home to him.* □ *Could you really find it in your heart to send her away?*

find one's feet to become used to a new situation or experience. □ *She was lonely at first when she left home, but she is finding her feet now.* □ *It takes time to learn the office routine, but you will gradually find your feet.*

find one's own level to find the position or rank to which one is best suited. (As water "seeks its own level.") □ *You cannot force junior staff to be ambitious. They will all find their own level.* □ *The new pupil is happier in the lower class. It was just a question of letting her find her own level.*

find one's tongue to be able to talk. (Informal.) □ *Tom was speechless for a moment. Then he found his tongue.* □ *Ann was unable to find her tongue. She sat there in silence.*

find oneself to discover what one's talents and preferences are. □ *He doesn't really know what he wants to do when he leaves school. He hasn't found himself yet.* □ *John tried a number of different jobs. He finally found himself when he became a cook.*

find someone out to discover something bad about someone. □ *John thought he could get away with smoking, but his* *mother found him out.* □ *Jane was taking a two-hour lunch period until the manager found her out.*

find something out the hard way See *learn something the hard way.*

find time for someone or something to set aside or make time for someone or something. □ *I can't find time for it today. I'll try to find time tomorrow.* □ *I'll find time for you tomorrow.*

Finders keepers(, losers weepers). a phrase said when something is found. (The person who finds something gets to keep it. The person who loses it can only weep.) □ *John lost a pound in the dining-room yesterday. Ann found the pound there today. Ann claimed that since she found it, it was hers. She said, "Finders keepers, losers weepers."* □ *John said, "I'll say finders keepers when I find something of yours!"*

Fine feathers make fine birds. a saying indicating that people can appear to be attractive or important simply by wearing fine clothes. □ *Jean Black is not really beautiful. It is just a question of fine feathers making fine birds.* □ *Even the most junior lecturer looks important in his university gown and hood. Fine feathers make fine birds.*

fine kettle of fish a real mess; an unsatisfactory situation. □ *The dog has eaten the steak we were going to have for dinner. This is a fine kettle of fish!* □ *This is a fine kettle of fish. It's below freezing outside, and the boiler won't work.*

fine state of affairs an unpleasant state of affairs. (See also the previous entry.) □ *This is a fine state of affairs, and it's all your fault.* □ *What a fine state of affairs you've got us into.*

Fine words butter no parsnips. a proverb indicating that mere words do not help a situation. □ *Promises are all very well, but I want the work finished now. Fine words butter no parsnips.* □ *I am tired of your excuses for being late. Fine words butter no parsnips.*

Fire away! to begin to do something, often speaking or asking questions. □

Fire away! I'm ready to take dictation. □ *If you want me to hear your complaints, fire away!*

firing on all cylinders working at full strength; making every possible effort. (From an internal combustion engine.) □ *The team is firing on all cylinders under the new coach.* □ *The factory is firing on all cylinders to finish the orders on time.*

first and foremost first and most important. □ *First and foremost, I think you should work harder on your biology.* □ *Have this in mind first and foremost: Keep smiling!*

First come, first served. The first people to arrive will be served first. □ *They ran out of tickets before we got there. It was first come, first served, but we didn't know that.* □ *Please queue up and take your turn. It's first come, first served.*

first off first; the first thing. (Informal.) □ *He ordered soup first off.* □ *First off, we'll find a place to live.*

first thing (in the morning) before anything else in the morning. □ *Please call me first thing in the morning. I can't help you now.* □ *I'll do that first thing.*

first things first the most important things must be attended to first. □ *It's more important to get a job than to buy new clothes. First things first!* □ *Do your homework now. Go out and play later. First things first.*

fish for compliments to try to get someone to pay you a compliment. (Informal.) □ *When she showed me her new dress, I could tell that she was fishing for a compliment.* □ *Tom was certainly fishing for compliments when he modelled his new haircut for his friends.*

fish for something to try to get information (from someone), often by indirect methods. □ *The solicitor was fishing for evidence.* □ *The salesman was just fishing for information about his competition.*

fish in troubled waters to involve oneself in a difficult, confused, or dangerous situation, especially with a view to gaining an advantage. □ *Frank is fishing in troubled waters by buying more shares in that firm. They are supposed to be in financial difficulties.* □ *The firm could make more money by selling armaments abroad, but they would be fishing in troubled waters.*

fit for a king splendid; of a very high standard. □ *What a delicious meal. It was fit for a king.* □ *Our room at the hotel was fit for a king.*

fit in (with someone or something) to be comfortable with someone or something; to be in accord or harmony with someone or something. □ *I really feel that I fit in with that group of people.* □ *It's good that you fit in.* □ *This chair doesn't fit in with the style of furniture in my house.* □ *I won't buy it if it doesn't fit in.*

fit like a glove to fit very well; to fit tightly or snugly. □ *My new shoes fit like a glove.* □ *My new coat is a little tight. It fits like a glove.*

fit someone in(to something) to succeed with difficulty in putting someone into a schedule. □ *The doctor is busy, but I can try to fit you into the appointment book.* □ *Yes, here's a free appointment. I can fit you in.*

fit someone or something out (with something) AND **fit out someone or something (with something)** to provide or furnish someone or something with something. □ *They fitted the camper out with everything they needed.* □ *They fitted them out for only £140.* □ *He fitted his car out with lots of chrome.*

fit to be tied very angry and excited. (Informal. To be so angry that one has to be restrained with ropes.) □ *If I'm not home on time, my parents will be fit to be tied.* □ *When Ann saw the bill, she was fit to be tied.*

fix someone up (with something) to arrange to provide someone with something. (Informal.) □ *We fixed John up with a room for the night.* □ *The usher fixed us up with seats at the front of the theatre.* □ *We thanked the usher for fixing us up.*

fix something up (for someone) to arrange something for someone. □ *John couldn't get an appointment, but James fixed it up for him.* □ *I got the travel department to fix the trip up.*

flare up to grow intense for a brief period, as a flame does. □ *Just when we thought we had solved the problem, it flared up again.* □ *Mr. Jones always flares up whenever anyone mentions the cost of petrol.* □ *My hay fever usually flares up in August.*

flash in the pan something that draws a lot of attention for a very brief time. (Informal.) □ *I'm afraid that my success as a painter was just a flash in the pan.* □ *Tom had hoped to be a singer, but his career was only a flash in the pan.*

flat out at top speed; as energetically as possible. □ *How fast will this car go flat out?* □ *If we work flat out, we should finish in time.*

flea in one's ear a severe scolding. (Informal.) □ *I got a flea in my ear when I tried to give Pat some advice.* □ *Margaret was only trying to help the old lady, but she came away with a flea in her ear.*

flesh and blood 1. a living human body, especially with reference to its natural limitations; a human being. □ *This cold weather is more than flesh and blood can stand.* □ *Carrying £300 is beyond mere flesh and blood.* 2. one's own relations; one's own kin. □ *That's no way to treat one's own flesh and blood.* □ *I want to leave my money to my own flesh and blood.*

flesh something out AND **flesh out something** to make something more detailed, bigger, or fuller. (As if one were adding flesh to a skeleton.) □ *This is basically a good outline. Now you'll have to flesh it out.* □ *The play was good, except that the author needed to flesh out the third act. It was too short.*

flight of fancy an idea or suggestion that is out of touch with reality or possibility. □ *What is the point in indulging in flights of fancy about foreign holidays when you cannot even afford the rent?* □ *We are tired of her flights of fancy about marrying a millionaire.*

fling oneself at someone See *throw oneself at someone.*

flip one's lid suddenly to become angry or crazy. (Slang.) □ *Whenever anyone mentions the dole, Mr. Jones absolutely flips his lid.* □ *Stop whistling. You're going to make me flip my lid.*

flog a dead horse to try to continue discussing or arousing interest in something that already has been fully discussed or that is no longer of interest. □ *Stop arguing! You have won your point. You are just flogging a dead horse.* □ *There's no point in putting job-sharing on the agenda. We've already voted against it four times. Why flog a dead horse?*

fluff one's lines AND **muff one's lines** to say one's speech badly or forget one's lines when one is in a play. (Informal.) □ *The actress fluffed her lines badly in the last act.* □ *I was in a play once, and I muffed my lines over and over.*

fly a kite to spread rumours or suggestions about something, such as a new project, in order to find out people's attitudes to it. □ *The government is flying a kite with these stories of a new airport.* □ *No official proposal has been made about redundancies. The management is flying a kite by dropping hints.*

fly-by-night irresponsible; untrustworthy. (Refers to a person who sneaks away secretly in the night.) □ *The carpenter we employed was a fly-by-night worker who did a very bad job of work.* □ *You shouldn't deal with a fly-by-night merchant.*

fly high AND **be flying high** to be very successful in one's ambitions; to obtain an important or powerful position. (Often with the implication that this will not last very long.) □ *The government is flying high just now, but wait until the budget is announced.* □ *He's flying high these days, but he comes from a very poor family.*

fly in the face of someone or something to disregard, defy, or show disrespect for someone or something. □ *John loves to fly in the face of tradition.* □ *Ann made it a practice to fly in the face of standard procedures.*

fly in the ointment a small, unpleasant matter which spoils something; a drawback. □ *We enjoyed the play, but the fly in the ointment was not being able to find our car afterwards.* □ *It sounds like a good idea, but there must be a fly in the ointment somewhere.*

fly off the handle to lose one's temper. (Informal.) □ *Every time anyone mentions war, Mrs. Brown flies off the handle.* □ *If she keeps flying off the handle like that, she'll have a heart attack.*

fly the coop to escape; to get out or get away. (Informal. Refers to a chicken escaping from a chicken coop.) □ *I couldn't stand living with my parents, so I flew the coop.* □ *The prisoner flew the coop at the first opportunity.*

flying visit a very short, often unexpected visit. □ *She paid us a flying visit before leaving town.* □ *Very few people saw her in the office. It was just a flying visit.*

foam at the mouth to be very angry. (Informal. Related to a "mad dog"—a dog with rabies—which foams at the mouth.) □ *Bob was furious—foaming at the mouth. I've never seen anyone so angry.* □ *Bill foamed at the mouth in sheer rage.*

fob something off (on someone) AND **fob off something (on someone)** to trick someone into accepting something which is worthless. □ *The car dealer fobbed a stolen car off on Tom.* □ *He also fobbed off another on Jane.* □ *Some car dealers are always trying to fob something off.*

follow in someone's footsteps to follow someone's example; to assume someone else's role or occupation. □ *The younger MP was following in her uncle's footsteps when she called for budget cuts.* □ *She followed in her father's footsteps and went into medicine.*

follow one's heart to act according to one's feelings; to obey one's sympathetic or compassionate inclinations. □ *I couldn't decide what to do, so I just followed my heart.* □ *I trust that you will follow your heart in this matter.*

follow one's nose 1. to go straight ahead, the direction in which one's nose is pointing. (Informal.) □ *The town that you want is straight ahead on this motorway. Just follow your nose.* □ *The chief's office is right around the corner. Turn left and follow your nose.* **2.** to follow a smell to its source. (Informal.) □ *The kitchen is at the back of the building. Just follow your nose.* □ *There was a bad smell in the basement—probably a dead mouse. I followed my nose until I found it.*

follow something through to continue doing something until it is complete. □ *She started the project, but failed to follow it through.* □ *I can do the groundwork on the plan, but I can't follow it through.* ALSO: **follow-through** an act of bringing a task to a conclusion. □ *The original medical investigations were all right, but they lacked follow-through.*

follow something up AND **follow up something** to add more information or detail to something; to follow something through. □ *Bill had to follow my suggestion up.* □ *The police followed up my story.*

follow suit to follow in the same pattern; to follow someone else's example. (From card-games.) □ *Mary went to work for a bank, and Jane followed suit. Now they are both head cashiers.* □ *The Smiths went out to dinner, but the Browns didn't follow suit. They ate at home.*

follow-through See under *follow something through.*

food for thought something to think about. □ *I don't like your idea very much, but it's food for thought.* □ *Your lecture was very good. It contained much food for thought.*

fool around (with someone or something) to fiddle or play with someone or something; to waste time with someone or something. (Informal.) □ *John is out fooling around with his friends again.* □ *That child spends most of his time fooling around.* □ *Please don't fool around with the light switch. You'll break it.* □ *There are lots of interesting things in here, but you must leave them alone. Don't fool around.*

fool's paradise a condition of seeming happiness that is based on false assumptions and will not last. (Treated as a place grammatically.) □ *They think they can live on love alone, but they are living in a fool's paradise.* □ *The inhabitants of the island feel politically secure, but they are living in a fool's paradise. They could be invaded at any time.*

fools rush in (where angels fear to tread) people with little experience or knowledge often get involved in difficult or delicate situations which wiser people would avoid. □ *I wouldn't ask Jean about her divorce, but Kate did. Fools rush in, as they say.* □ *Only the newest member of the committee questioned the chairman's decision. Fools rush in where angels fear to tread.*

foot the bill to pay the bill; to pay (for something). □ *Let's go out and eat. I'll foot the bill.* □ *If the insurance firm goes bankrupt, don't worry. The government will foot the bill.*

footloose and fancy-free without responsibilities or commitments. □ *All the rest of them have wives, but John is footloose and fancy-free.* □ *Mary never stays long in any job. She likes being footloose and fancy-free.*

for all I care I don't care if (something happens). (Informal.) □ *For all I care, the whole city council can go to the devil.* □ *They can all starve for all I care.*

for all it's worth AND **for what it's worth** if it has any value. □ *My idea—for all it's worth—is to offer them only £300.* □ *Here is my thinking, for what it's worth.* □ *Ask her to give us her opinion, for what it's worth.*

for all the world 1. exactly; precisely. (Especially with *look*.) □ *She sat there looking for all the world as though she was going to cry.* □ *It started out seeming for all the world like a beautiful day. Then a storm came up.* 2. everything. (Usually in the negative.) □ *I wouldn't give up my baby for all the world.* □ *They wouldn't sell their property for all the world.*

for better or for worse under any conditions; no matter what happens. □ *I married you for better or for worse.* □ *For better or for worse, I'm going to leave my job.*

for chicken-feed AND **for peanuts** for nearly nothing; for very little money. (Informal. Also used without *for*.) □ *Bob doesn't get paid much. He works for chicken-feed.* □ *You can buy an old car for chicken-feed.* □ *I won't do that kind of work for peanuts!*

for days on end for many days without a break. (See also *for hours on end*.) □ *We kept on travelling for days on end.* □ *Doctor, I've had this pain for days on end.*

for good forever; permanently. □ *I finally left home for good.* □ *They tried to repair it many times before they fixed it for good.*

for good measure as extra; [adding] a little more to make certain there is enough. □ *He gave me some extra encouragement for good measure.* □ *I always put a little extra salt in the soup for good measure.*

for hours on end for many hours without a break. (See also *for days on end*.) □ *We sat and waited for the doctor for hours on end.* □ *We listened to the speaker for hours on end.*

for keeps forever; permanently. (Informal. Compare to *for good*.) □ *When I get married, it'll be for keeps.* □ *We've moved around a lot. Now I think we'll stay here for keeps.*

for kicks for fun; just for entertainment; for no good reason. (Slang.) □ *They didn't mean any harm. They just did it for kicks.* □ *We drove over to the next town for kicks.*

for one's (own) part as far as one is concerned; from one's point of view. □ *For my own part, I wish to stay here.* □ *For her part, she prefers chocolate.*

for one's (own) sake for one's good or benefit; in honour of someone. □ *I have to earn a living for my family's sake.* □ *I did it for my mother's sake.* □ *I didn't do it for my own sake.*

for openers AND **for starters** to start with. (Informal.) □ *For openers, they played a song everyone knows.* □ *For starters, you could come home on time!*

for peanuts See *for chicken-feed*.

for sale See *on sale*.

For shame! See under *Shame on someone.*

for short in a short form. (Usually refers to names.) □ *My name is William. They call me Bill for short.* □ *Almost everyone who is named Robert is called Bob for short.*

for starters See *for openers*.

for sure without a doubt; certainly. □ *I don't know for sure, but I think I'll be there.* □ *I'm not going alone and that's for sure.*

for that matter besides; in addition. □ *If you're hungry, take one of my doughnuts. For that matter, take two.* □ *I don't like this house. The roof leaks. For that matter, the whole place is falling apart.* □ *Tom is quite arrogant. So is his sister, for that matter.*

for the asking if one just asks (for something); simply by asking; on request. □ *Do you want to use my car? It's yours for the asking.* □ *I have an extra winter coat that's yours for the asking.*

for the birds worthless; undesirable. (Slang.) □ *This television programme is strictly for the birds.* □ *Winter weather is for the birds.*

for the hell of it just for fun; for no good reason. (Informal. Use *hell* with caution.) □ *We filled their garage with leaves just for the hell of it.* □ *John picked a fight with Tom just for the hell of it.*

for the life of one even if one's life were threatened; even in exchange for one's life. (Informal. Always with a negative, and usually having to do with one's memory.) □ *For the life of me, I don't remember your name.* □ *She couldn't recall the correct numbers for the life of her.* □ *For the life of them, they couldn't remember the way home.*

for the record so that (one's own version of) the facts will be known; so there will be a record of a particular fact. □ *I'd like to say—for the record—that at no time have I ever accepted a bribe from anyone.* □ *For the record, I've never been able to get anything done around city hall without bribing someone.*

for the sake of someone or something for the good of someone or something; for the honour or recognition of someone or something. (Compare to *for one's (own) sake.*) □ *I did it for the sake of all those people who helped me get through school.* □ *I'm investing in a house for the sake of my children.* □ *For the sake of honesty, Bill shared all the information he had.*

for the time being for the present; for now; temporarily. □ *This is all right for the time being. It'll have to be improved next week, however.* □ *This good feeling will last only for the time being.*

for what it's worth See *for all it's worth.*

forbidden fruit someone or something that one finds attractive or desirable partly because the person or thing is unobtainable. (From the fruit in the garden of Eden that was forbidden to Adam by God.) □ *Jim is in love with his sister-in-law only because she's forbidden fruit.* □ *The boy watches that programme only when his parents are out. It's forbidden fruit.*

force someone's hand to force one to do something that one is unwilling to do or sooner than one wants to do it. (Refers to a handful of cards in card-playing.) □ *We didn't know what she was doing until Tom forced her hand.* □ *The committee didn't want to reveal their plans so soon, but we forced their hand.*

forever and a day See the following entry.

forever and ever AND **forever and a day** forever. □ *I will love you forever and ever.* □ *This car won't keep running forever and ever. We'll have to get a new one sometime.* □ *When we were children, the summer seemed to last forever and a day.*

forget oneself to forget one's manners or training. (Said in formal situations in reference to bad table manners or bad taste.) □ *Sorry, Mother, I forgot myself. I didn't mean to use a four-letter word.* □ *John, we are going out to dinner tonight. Please don't forget yourself and gulp down your food.*

forgive and forget to forgive someone (for something) and forget that it ever happened. □ *I'm sorry we quarrelled, John. Let's forgive and forget. What do you say?* □ *It was nothing. We'll just have to forgive and forget.*

fork money out (for something) AND **fork out money (for something); fork out (money)** to pay (perhaps unwillingly) for something. (Informal. Often mention is made about the amount of money. See the examples.) □ *I like that stereo, but I don't want to fork out a lot of money.* □ *Do you think I'm going to fork twenty pounds out for that book?* □ *I hate having to fork out* *money day after day.* □ *Why is it always me who has to fork out?*

form an opinion to think up or decide on an opinion. (Note the variations in the examples.) □ *I don't know enough about the issue to form an opinion.* □ *Don't tell me how to think! I can form my own opinion.* □ *I don't form opinions without careful consideration.*

forty winks a short sleep; a nap. (Informal.) □ *I had forty winks on the plane.* □ *If you're lucky you'll get forty winks while the children are out.*

foul one's own nest to harm one's own interests; to bring disadvantage upon oneself. □ *He tried to discredit a fellow MP with the prime minister, but just succeeded in fouling his own nest.* □ *The boss really dislikes Mary. She certainly fouled her own nest when she spread those rumours about him.*

foul play illegal activity; a criminal act. □ *The police investigating the death suspect foul play.* □ *Foul play cannot be ruled out.*

foul someone or something up AND **foul up someone or something 1.** [with *someone*] to bring disorder and confusion to someone or something; to inconvenience someone. (Informal.) □ *They really fouled my plans up.* □ *You've fouled up my whole day!* **2.** to entangle someone or something □ *Watch out! You're going to foul up my kite strings.* □ *I fouled up my feet in the lines coiled on deck.* ALSO: **foul up** to do (something) badly; to cause things to go wrong. (Slang.) □ *At the last minute, he fouled up and failed the course.* □ *Take your time. Plan your moves, and don't foul up.* ALSO: **foul-up** an act of fouling up or messing up. (Slang.) □ *You've created a real foul-up.* □ *Look at this paper. I've never seen such a foul-up.* □ *Your foul-up took me three hours to straighten out.*

foul up See under *foul someone or something up.*

free and easy casual. □ *John is so free and easy. How can anyone be so relaxed?*

□ *Now, take it easy. Just act free and easy. No one will know you're nervous.*

free-for-all a disorganized fight or contest involving everyone; a brawl. (Informal.) □ *The picnic turned into a free-for-all after midnight.* □ *The race started out in an organized manner, but ended up being a free-for-all.*

fresh blood AND **new blood** new personnel; new members brought into a group to revive it. □ *This firm needs some fresh blood on its board to bring new ideas.* □ *We're trying to get some new blood in the club. Our membership is falling.*

(fresh fields and) pastures new new places; new activities. (From a line in Milton's poem *Lycidas*.) □ *I used to like living here, but it's fresh fields and pastures new for me now.* □ *Peter has decided to leave teaching. He's looking for fresh fields and pastures new.* □ *It's all very well to seek pastures new, but think of the unemployment situation.*

frighten one out of one's wits See *frighten the wits out of someone.*

frighten someone to death AND **scare someone to death** to frighten someone severely. (Also used literally.) □ *The dentist always frightens me to death.* □ *She scared me to death when she screamed.*

frighten the wits out of someone AND **frighten one out of one's wits; frighten the (living) daylights out of someone; scare one out of one's wits; scare the (living) daylights out of someone; scare the wits out of someone** to frighten someone very badly. □ *We nearly had an accident. It frightened the living daylights out of me.* □ *The incident scared the wits out of me.* □ *Oh! That loud noise scared me out of my wits.* □ *I'll give him a good scolding and frighten him out of his wits.*

frog in one's throat a feeling of hoarseness. (Especially with *get* or *have*.) □ *I cannot speak more clearly. I have a frog in my throat.* □ *I had a frog in my* *throat and the telephone receptionist couldn't understand me.*

from day to day on a daily basis; one day at a time. □ *He never makes plans. He just survives from day to day.* □ *When you're very poor, you live from day to day.*

from pillar to post from one place to another or to a series of other places. □ *My father was in the army, and we moved from pillar to post year after year.* □ *I went from pillar to post trying to find a telephone.*

from rags to riches from poverty to wealth. □ *The princess used to be quite poor. She certainly moved from rags to riches when she married.* □ *After I inherited the money, I went from rags to riches.*

from stem to stern from one end to another. (Refers to the front and back ends of a ship. Also used literally in reference to ships.) □ *Now, I have to clean the house from stem to stern.* □ *I polished my car carefully from stem to stern.*

from the bottom of one's heart sincerely. (Compare to *with all one's heart and soul.*) □ *When I returned the lost kitten to Mrs. Brown, she thanked me from the bottom of her heart.* □ *Don't complain! You should give thanks from the bottom of your heart for being well again.*

from the ground up from the beginning; from start to finish. (Used literally in reference to building a house or other building.) □ *We must plan our sales campaign carefully from the ground up.* □ *Sorry, but you'll have to start all over again from the ground up.*

from the heart from a deep and sincere emotional source. □ *I know that your kind words come from the heart.* □ *We don't want your gift unless it comes from the heart.*

from the word go from the beginning. (Informal.) □ *I knew about the problem from the word go.* □ *She was doing badly in the class from the word go.*

from the year dot AND **since the year dot** for a very long time; since very far back in time. (Informal.) □ *Mr. Jones worked there from the year dot.* □ *I've known Mike since the year dot.*

from this day forward See the following entry.

from this day on AND **from this day forward** from today into the future. (Formal.) □ *We shall live in love and peace from this day on.* □ *I'll treasure your gift from this day forward.*

from time to time occasionally. □ *We have pizza from time to time.* □ *From time to time, a visitor comes to our door.*

from top to bottom from the highest point to the lowest point; throughout. (Compare to *from stem to stern.*) □ *I have to clean the house from top to bottom today.* □ *We need to replace our elected officials from top to bottom.*

full of beans very lively and cheerful; healthy and energetic. (Informal.) □ *The children tire their granny out. They're always so full of beans.* □ *Joan was ill last year, but she's full of beans now.*

full of hot air full of nonsense; talking nonsense. (Slang.) □ *Oh, shut up, Mary. You're full of hot air.* □ *My English professor is full of hot air.*

full of oneself conceited; self-important. □ *Mary's very unpopular because she's so full of herself.* □ *She doesn't care about other people's feelings. She's too full of herself.*

full of the devil always making mischief. (Informal.) □ *Tom is a lot of fun, but he's certainly full of the devil.* □ *I've never seen a child get into so much mischief. He's really full of the devil.*

full steam ahead forward at the greatest speed possible; with as much energy and enthusiasm as possible. (From an instruction given to steamships.) □ *It will have to be full steam ahead for everybody if the factory gets this order.* □ *It's going to be full steam ahead for me this year. I take my final exams.*

fun and games 1. playing around; someone's lively behaviour. (Informal.) □ *All right, Bill, the fun and games are over. It's time to get down to work.* □ *I'm tired of your fun and games. Go away and read a book.* 2. difficulties; trouble. □ *There will be fun and games when her father sees the broken window.* □ *There will be fun and games if the children are home late.*

funny business trickery or deception; illegal activity. (Informal.) □ *From the silence as she entered the room, the teacher knew there was some funny business going on.* □ *There's some funny business going on at the warehouse. Stock keeps getting lost.*

funny ha-ha amusing; comic. (Informal. Compare to *funny peculiar*.) □ *I didn't mean that Mrs. Peters is funny ha-ha. She's weird—funny peculiar in fact.* □ *Mike thinks his jokes are funny ha-ha, but we laugh because they are so weird.*

funny peculiar odd; eccentric. (Informal. Compare to *funny ha-ha*.) □ *I didn't mean that Mrs. Peters is funny ha-ha. She's weird—funny peculiar in fact.* □ *His face is sort of funny— funny peculiar, not funny ha-ha.*

fuss over someone or something See *make a fuss (over someone or something).*

G

gain ground to make progress; to advance; to become more important or popular. □ *Our new product is gaining ground against that of our competitor.* □ *Since the government announced their new policies, the Opposition is gaining ground.*

gain on someone or something to draw nearer to someone or something; to move towards a goal faster than someone or something. □ *In the race, Tom kept gaining on Bob.* □ *The speeding lorry was gaining on the car.*

game at which two can play a manner of competing which two competitors can use; a strategy that competing sides can both use. □ *The mayor shouted at the town council, "Politics is a game at which two can play."* □ *"Flattery is a game at which two can play," said John as he returned Mary's compliment.* ALSO: **two can play at that game** two players can compete, using the same strategy. □ *I'm sorry you're being so hard to deal with. Two can play at that game.*

gang up (on someone) to form into a group and attack someone. (It can be either a physical attack or a verbal attack.) □ *We can't win against the enemy unless we gang up on him.* □ *All right, you lot, don't gang up on me. Play fair!*

generous to a fault too generous. □ *My favourite uncle is generous to a fault.* □ *Sally—always generous to a fault—gave away her sandwiches.*

get a big hand for something (Informal.) to receive applause for something. □ *She got a big hand for singing so well.* □ *That kind of performance always gets a big hand.* ALSO: **give someone a big hand for something** to applaud someone for something. □ *After she sang, they gave her a big hand.* □ *Come on, give them a big hand. They did very well.* ALSO: **have a big hand for someone or something** to please applaud for someone or something. (Informal. Usually a request. Always with *let's*, as in the example.) □ *Let's have a big hand for Sally and her lovely voice.*

get a big send-off AND **be given a big send-off** to receive or enjoy a happy celebration before departing. □ *I was given a wonderful send-off before I left.* □ *John got a fine send-off as he left for Australia.* ALSO: **give someone a big send-off** to see someone off on a journey with celebration and encouragement. □ *When I left for college, all my brothers and sisters came to the station to give me a big send-off.* □ *When the sailors left, everyone went down to the docks and gave them a big send-off.*

get a black eye to get a bruise near the eye from being struck. (Note: *Get* can be replaced with *have.* See the variations in the examples. *Get* usually means to become, to acquire, or to cause. *Have* usually means to possess, to be, or to have resulted in.) □ *I got a black eye from walking into a door.* □ *I have a black eye where John hit me.* ALSO: **give someone a black eye** to hit someone near the eye so that a dark bruise appears. □ *John became angry and gave me a black eye.*

get a bright idea for a clever thought or idea to occur (to someone). (Ironic in the plural. Also with *have*. See the explanation at *get a black eye*.) □ *I was about to give up. Then I got a bright idea.* □ *Listen! I have a bright idea.* □ *Don't get any bright ideas! You can't borrow my car.*

get a check-up to have a physical examination by a doctor. (Also with *have*. See the note at *get a black eye*.) □ *She got a check-up yesterday.* □ *I am going to have a check-up in the morning. I hope I'm okay.* ALSO: **give someone a check-up** [for a doctor] to give someone a physical examination. □ *The doctor gave her a check-up.*

get a clean bill of health [for someone] to be pronounced healthy by a doctor. (Also with *have*. See the note at *get a black eye*. From the fact that ships were given a clean bill of health before sailing only after the absence of infectious disease was certified.) □ *Sally got a clean bill of health from the doctor.* □ *Now that Sally has a clean bill of health, she can go back to work.* ALSO: **give someone a clean bill of health** [for a doctor] to pronounce someone well and healthy. □ *The doctor gave Sally a clean bill of health.*

get a crush on someone to become infatuated with someone. (Informal. Also with *have*. See the note at *get a black eye*.) □ *Mary thinks she's getting a crush on Bill.* □ *Sally says she'll never get a crush on anyone again.* □ *John has a crush on Mary.*

get a good run for one's money (Informal.) **1.** to receive what one deserves, expects, or wants; to be well compensated for effort, money, etc., spent. □ *We can't complain about having to stop playing. We've had a good run for our money.* □ *Even if she does get the sack now, she's had a good run for her money. She's been there for years.* **2.** to receive challenging competition or opposition from someone. □ *Bob got a good run for his money when he challenged his father to a race.* □ *Bill got a good run for his money when he played*

cards with John. ALSO: **give one a run for one's money** to provide challenging competition or opposition to someone. □ *That was some argument. Bill gave John a run for his money.* □ *Tom likes to play cards with Mary because she always gives him a run for his money.*

get a hand with something to receive assistance with something. (Also with *have*. See the note at *get a black eye*.) □ *Mary would really like to get a hand with that. It's too much for one person.* □ *I'd like to have a hand with this.* ALSO: **give someone a hand (with something)** to help someone; to give help to someone, often with the hands. □ *Will somebody please give me a hand with this?*

get a head start (on someone or something) 1. [with *someone*] to start (something) earlier than someone else. (Also with *have*. See the note at *get a black eye*.) □ *Bill always gets there first because he gets a head start on everybody else.* □ *I'm doing well in my class because I have a head start.* **2.** [with *something*] to start something earlier (than someone else). □ *I was able to get a head start on my reading during the holidays.* □ *If I hadn't had a head start, I'd be behind in my reading.* ALSO: **give someone a head start (on someone or something) 1.** [with *someone*] to allow someone to start (something) earlier than someone else. □ *Getting there early gave Bill a head start on everyone else.* **2.** [with *something*] to allow someone to start something earlier (than someone else). □ *We'll give you a head start on the project.*

get a kick out of someone or something to receive a special pleasure from someone or something. (Informal.) □ *Tom is really funny. I always get a kick out of his jokes.* □ *Bill really got a kick out of playing Santa Claus.* ALSO: **give someone a kick** to give someone a bit of excitement. (Informal.) □ *It will really give John a kick to see his old friend again.*

get a licking AND **take a licking** to get a spanking; to get beaten in a fight. □

Billy, you had better get in here if you don't want to get a licking. □ *Bob took a real licking in the shares market.* □ *Tom took a licking in the fight he was in.* ALSO: **give someone a licking** □ *Bill give Tom a licking in a fight.*

get a load of someone or something look at someone or something. (Slang.) □ *Get a load of that hairstyle!* □ *Get a load of that car. It must have cost a fortune.*

get a lucky break to have good fortune; to receive a bit of luck. (Informal. Also with *have.* See the note at *get a black eye.*) □ *Mary really got a lucky break when she got that job.* □ *After losing three times, John finally had a lucky break.*

get a lump in one's throat to have the feeling of something in one's throat—as if one were going to cry. (Also with *have.* See the note at *get a black eye.*) □ *Whenever they play the national anthem, I get a lump in my throat.* □ *I have a lump in my throat because my friends are going away.*

get a move on to start to hurry. (Informal.) □ *If we don't get a move on, we'll be late.* □ *Mary! Get a move on! We can't wait all day.*

get a pat on the back See under *pat someone on the back.*

get a raw deal to receive unfair or bad treatment. (Informal.) □ *The junior staff got a raw deal, poor pay and long hours.* □ *John really got a raw deal. He lost his job for complaining.* ALSO: **give someone a raw deal** to treat someone unfairly or badly. □ *The jury gave Mary a raw deal by declaring her guilty and the rest innocent.* □ *The pupils think that the teacher gave them a raw deal by giving them holiday essays.*

get a red face to blush from embarrassment. □ *When I'm embarrassed, I really get a red face.* □ *He got a red face when he was caught stealing.* ALSO: **give someone a red face** to embarrass someone. □ *We really gave him a red face when we caught him eavesdropping.*

get a reputation (as a something) to acquire notoriety for being something. (Also with *have.* See the note at *get a black eye.*) □ *You'll get a reputation as a cheat.* □ *He's got a reputation as a womanizer.* □ *Behave yourself, or you'll get a reputation.* □ *Unfortunately, Tom's got a reputation.* ALSO: **give someone a reputation (as a something)** to cause someone to be notorious for being something. □ *That evening gave him a reputation as a flirt.* □ *Her wild behaviour in her youth gave her a reputation.*

get a reputation (for doing something) to acquire notoriety for doing something. (Also with *have.* See the note at *get a black eye.*) □ *You'll get a reputation for cheating.* □ *I do not have a reputation for being mean.* ALSO: **give someone a reputation for doing something** to cause someone to be notorious for doing something. □ *Her wild parties gave Jane a reputation for being a bad neighbour.*

get a rise out of someone See *take a rise out of someone.*

get a rough idea (about something) AND **get a rough idea (of something)** to receive a general idea; to receive an estimate. (Also with *have.* See the note at *get a black eye.*) □ *I need to get a rough idea of how many people will be there.* □ *I don't need to know exactly. Just get a rough idea.* □ *Judy's got a rough idea about who'll be there.* □ *I have a rough idea. That's good enough.* ALSO: **give someone a rough idea (about something); give someone a rough idea (of something)** to give someone a general idea or an estimate about something. □ *I don't need to know exactly. Just give me a rough idea about how big it should be.*

get a slap on the wrist to get a light punishment (for doing something wrong). (Informal.) □ *He created quite a disturbance, but he only got a slap on the wrist.* □ *I thought I'd just get a slap on the wrist for speeding, but I got fined £200.* ALSO: **give someone a slap on the wrist; slap someone on the wrist; slap**

someone's **wrist** to give someone a light punishment (for doing something wrong). □ *The judge only gave her a slap on the wrist for speeding.* □ *The judge should have done more than slap her wrist.* □ *The legal system only slaps them on the wrist.*

get a start to receive training or a big opportunity in beginning one's career. □ *She got a start in show business in Manchester.* □ *She got a start in modelling when she was only four.* ALSO: **give someone a start** to give one training or a big opportunity in beginning one's career. □ *My career began when my father gave me a start in his act.*

get a swelled head to become conceited. (Informal. Also with *have.* See the note at *get a black eye.*) □ *Now that she's famous, she's getting a swelled head.* □ *She's trying not to get a swelled head.* ALSO: **give someone a swelled head** to make someone conceited. □ *Fame gave John a swelled head.*

get a tongue-lashing to receive a severe scolding. □ *I really got a tongue-lashing when I got home.* □ *She got a terrible tongue-lashing from her mother.* ALSO: **give someone a tongue-lashing** to give someone a severe scolding. □ *I gave Bill a real tongue-lashing when he got home late.*

get a word in (edgeways) to succeed in saying something when other people are talking and ignoring you. (Often in the negative.) □ *It was such an exciting conversation that I could hardly get a word in edgeways.* □ *Mary talks so fast that nobody can get a word in edgeways.*

get about AND **get around** to move around; to go from place to place. □ *I can't get about without a car.* □ *Aunt Mary cannot get about when her arthritis is troubling her.* □ *It's very hard for some older people to get around.*

get above oneself to behave as though one is better or more important than one is. □ *John is getting a bit above himself since he was promoted. He never goes for a drink with his old colleagues.*

□ *There was no need for her to get above herself just because she married a wealthy man.*

get after someone to remind, scold, or nag someone (to do something). (Informal.) □ *John hasn't taken out the rubbish. I'll have to get after him.* □ *Mary's mother will get after her if she doesn't do the dishes.* ALSO: **keep after someone; keep at someone** to remind or nag someone over and over to do something. □ *I'll keep after you until you do it!* □ *Mother kept at Bill until he did the dishes.*

get ahead (of someone or something) to advance; to move in front (of someone or something). □ *I had to run hard to get ahead of everyone else.* □ *Most people have to work hard to get ahead.* ALSO: **be ahead (of someone or something); keep ahead (of someone or something); stay ahead (of someone or something)** to maintain a position in front of someone or something. □ *I kept ahead of everyone by running hard.* □ *We have to work hard to keep ahead of inflation.* □ *It takes a lot of energy to be ahead.* □ *I struggle to stay ahead of my competition.*

get (all) dolled up to dress (oneself) up. (Informal. Usually refers to females.) □ *I have to get all dolled up for the dance tonight.* □ *I just love to get dolled up in my best clothes.*

get along to move along. □ *All right, everybody. Get along! The excitement is over.* □ *I think I had better get along home now.*

get along (without (someone or something)) to manage without someone or something; to do without someone or something. □ *I don't think I can get along without my secretary.* □ *My secretary just left, and I don't think I will be able to get along.* □ *I like steak, but I can't afford it. I suppose I'll have to get along without.*

get around 1. to be experienced; to know a lot about life. (Informal. Use with caution—especially with females—since this can also refer to sexual experience. See also *have been around*.) □ *That's a hard question. I'll ask Jane. She gets around.* □ *John knows a lot about London. He gets around.* **2.** See *get about*.

get around to something to find time to do something; to do something after a long delay. □ *I finally got around to buying a new coat.* □ *It takes Sally years to get around to visiting her aunt.*

get at someone or something **1.** to attack or strike someone or something. □ *The cat jumped over the wall to get at the mouse.* □ *The gang got at the boy on his way home.* **2.** [with *something*] to eat food; to gobble up food. (Informal.) □ *I can't wait to get at that cake.* □ *The dog has got at the meat.* **3.** [with *someone*] to find a way to irritate someone; to manage to wound someone, physically or emotionally. (Informal.) □ *Mr. Smith found a way to get at his wife.* □ *John kept trying to get at his teacher.* **4.** [with *something*] to explain or try to explain something; to hint at something. □ *We spent a long time trying to get at the answer.* □ *I can't understand what you're trying to get at.* **5.** [with *something*] to begin to do something; to *get around to something*. □ *I won't be able to get at it until the weekend.* □ *I'll get at it first thing in the morning.*

get away (from it all) to get away from one's work or daily routine; to go on a holiday. □ *I just love the summer when I can take time off and get away from it all.* □ *Yes, that's the best time to get away.*

get away (from someone or something) to move away or escape from someone or something; to remove (oneself) from the influence of someone or something. □ *I need to get away from my shop for a few days.* □ *Yes, getting away from it would do you good.* □ *Mary needs to get away from her mother.* □ *Yes, at a certain age, one must get away.* ALSO: **keep away (from someone or something); stay away (from someone or something)** to remain distant from someone or something. □ *I*

stayed away from my job for a week. □ *Was it all right to stay away?* □ *You should keep away from your uncle until you're over your cold.*

get away with something to do something bad and not get punished or found out. (Informal when the *something* refers figuratively to murder.) □ *Tom did it again and didn't get punished. He's always getting away with murder.* □ *Just because she's so popular, she thinks she can get away with anything.* □ *You'll never get away with it.*

get back (at someone) to repay one for a bad deed; to *get even with someone*. □ *Tom called me a wally, but I'll get back at him.* □ *In the end, I got back at him for his disloyalty.*

get back on one's feet to become independent again; to become able to *get around* again. (Note the variations with *own* and *two* in the examples.) □ *He was sick for a while, but now he's getting back on his feet.* □ *My parents helped a lot when I lost my job. I'm glad I'm back on my own feet now.* □ *It feels great to be back on my own two feet again.*

get back to someone to continue talking with someone (at a later time); to find out information and tell it to a person (at a later time). □ *I don't have the answer to that question right now. Let me find out and get back to you.* □ *I'll get back to you when I have the details.*

get behind (with something) See *fall behind (with something)*.

get better to improve. □ *I had a bad cold, but it's getting better.* □ *Business was bad last week, but it's getting better.* □ *I'm sorry you're ill. I hope you get better.*

get bogged down to become stuck; to be prevented from making progress. (Informal.) □ *The pupil has got bogged down with his maths project.* □ *The Smiths have really got bogged down in decorating their house.*

get butterflies in one's stomach to get a nervous feeling in one's stomach. (Informal. Also with *have*. See the note at *get a black eye*.) □ *Whenever I have to go on stage, I get butterflies in my stomach.* □ *She always has butterflies in her stomach before a test.* ALSO: **give one butterflies in one's stomach** to cause someone to have a nervous stomach. □ *Exams give me butterflies in my stomach.*

get by (on a shoe-string) to manage to live on very little money. □ *For the last two years, we have had to get by on a shoe-string.* □ *With so little money, it's hard to get by.*

get by (on something) to manage on the least amount. (Compare to *get by (on a shoe-string)*.) □ *We don't have much money. Can we get by on love?* □ *I'll get by as long as I have you.* □ *We don't have very much money, but we'll get by.*

get carried away to be overcome by emotion or enthusiasm (in one's thinking or actions). □ *Calm down, Jane. Don't get carried away.* □ *Here, Bill. Take this money and go to the sweet-shop, but don't get carried away.*

get close (to someone or something) 1. [with *someone*] to become close friends with someone; to get to know someone well. □ *I would really like to get close to Jane, but she's so unfriendly.* □ *We talked for hours and hours, but I never felt that we were getting close.* **2.** [with *something*] almost to equal something; to be almost as good as something. (Often in the negative.) □ *I practiced and practiced, but my bowling couldn't get close to Mary's.* □ *Her performance was so good that I couldn't get close.*

get cold feet to become timid or frightened. (Also with *have*. See the note at *get a black eye*.) □ *I usually get cold feet when I have to speak in public.* □ *John got cold feet and wouldn't run in the race.* □ *I can't give my speech now. I have cold feet.*

get cracking to get moving; to get busy. (Informal.) □ *Let's go. Come on, get cracking!* □ *We don't have all day. Let's get cracking!* □ *We'll never get finished if you don't get cracking.*

get credit (for something) to receive praise or recognition for one's role in something. (Especially with *a lot of*, *much*, etc., as in the examples.) □ *Mary should get a lot of credit for the team's success.* □ *Each of the team captains should get credit.* ALSO: **give someone credit (for something)** to praise or recognize someone for doing something. □ *The coach gave Mary a lot of credit.* □ *The director gave John much credit for his fine performance.*

get down to brass tacks to begin to talk about important things; to *get down to business*. (Informal.) □ *Let's get down to brass tacks. We've wasted too much time chatting.* □ *Don't you think that it's about time to get down to brass tacks?*

get down to business to begin to get serious; to begin to negotiate or conduct business. □ *All right, everyone. Let's get down to business. There has been enough playing around.* □ *When the president and vice-president arrive, we can get down to business.*

get down to something to begin doing some kind of work in earnest. □ *I have to get down to my typing.* □ *John, you get in here this minute and get down to that homework!*

get down to the nitty-gritty AND **get down to the nuts and bolts** to get down to the basic facts. (Informal.) □ *Stop fooling around. Get down to the nitty-gritty.* □ *Let's stop wasting time. We have to get down to the nuts and bolts.*

get down to the nuts and bolts See the previous entry.

get even (with someone) to repay someone's bad deed; to *get back at someone*. □ *Bill hit Bob, and Bob got even with Bill by hitting him back.* □ *Some people always have to get even.*

get fresh (with someone) to become overly bold or impertinent. (Informal.) □ *When I tried to kiss Mary, she slapped me and shouted, "Don't get fresh with me!"* □ *I can't stand people who get fresh.*

get goose-pimples [for one's skin] to begin to feel prickly or become bumpy owing to fear, cold, or excitement. (Also with *have*. See the note at *get a black eye*.) □ *Where's my sweater? I've got goose-pimples.* □ *That really scared her. Now she's got goose-pimples.*

get grey hair(s) to have one's hair turn grey from stress or frustration. □ *I'm getting grey hair because I have three teen-age boys.* □ *Oh, Tom, don't drive so fast! I'm going to get grey hairs.* ALSO: **give someone grey hair(s)** *My three teen-age boys are going to give me grey hairs.* □ *Tom has been giving me grey hair for months now with his fast driving.*

get hell to receive a severe scolding. (Informal. Use *hell* with caution.) □ *Bill is always getting hell about something.* □ *I'm late. If I don't get home soon, I'll get hell!* ALSO: **give someone hell** to scold someone severely. (Informal. Use *hell* with caution.) □ *I'm going to give Bill hell when he gets home. He's late again.* □ *Bill, why do I always have to give you hell?*

get hold of someone or something AND **get a hold of someone or something** (See also *get one's hands on someone or something; get in touch (with someone)*. Also with *have*. See the note at *get a black eye*.) **1.** [with *someone*] to make contact with someone; to call someone on the telephone. □ *I'll try to get hold of you in the morning.* □ *It's very hard to get a hold of John. He's so busy.* **2.** [with *something*] to obtain something. □ *I'm trying to get hold of a glass jar. I need it for school.* □ *Does anyone know where I can get a hold of a spare tyre?* □ *I have hold of a very large piece of land.* **3.** See *take hold of someone or something*.

get in on something to become associated with something, such as an organization or an idea; to find out or be told about special plans. (Also with *be,* as in the last two examples.) □ *There is a party upstairs, and I want to get in on it.* □ *I want to get in on your club's activities.* □ *Mary and Jane know a secret,*

and I want to get in on it. □ *I'm happy to be in on your celebration.* □ *There is going to be a surprise party, and I'm in on it.*

get in on the ground floor to become associated with something at its start. □ *If you move fast, you can still get in on the ground floor.* □ *A new business is starting up, and I want to get in on the ground floor.*

get in someone's hair to bother or irritate someone. (Informal.) □ *Billy is always getting in his mother's hair.* □ *I wish you'd stop getting in my hair.*

get in someone's way to interfere with someone's movement or intentions. □ *Tom is going to reverse the car out. Please don't get in his way.* □ *I intend to stand election for parliament. You had better not get in my way.*

get in touch (with someone) to make contact with someone; to telephone or write to someone. □ *I have to get in touch with John and ask him to come over for a visit.* □ *Yes, you must try to get in touch.* ALSO: **keep in touch (with someone)** to retain friendly contact with someone. □ *I try to keep in touch with my cousins.* □ *All our family tries to keep in touch.*

get into a mess to get into difficulty or confusion. (Informal. Compare to *get out of a mess*.) □ *Try to keep from getting into a mess.* □ *"Hello, Mom," said John on the telephone. "I've got into a bit of a mess down at the police station."*

get into an argument (with someone) to begin to argue with someone. □ *Let's try to discuss this calmly. I don't want to get into an argument with you.* □ *Tom got into an argument with John.* □ *Tom and John got into an argument.* □ *Let's not get into an argument.* ALSO: **have an argument (with someone)** to argue with someone. □ *Tom and John had an argument.* □ *Let's not have an argument.*

get into full swing to move into the peak of activity; to start moving fast or efficiently. (Informal.) □ *In the summer months, things really get into full swing around here.* □ *We go skiing in the mountains each winter. Things get into full swing there in November.*

get into something to get involved in something; to join something. (See also *be into something.*) □ *I'd like to get into your club.* □ *If I could run faster, I'd get into racing.*

get into the swing of things to join in the routine or the activities. (Informal.) □ *Come on, Bill. Try to get into the swing of things.* □ *John just couldn't seem to get into the swing of things.*

get involved (with someone or something) 1. to become concerned or associated with someone or something. □ *Why not try to get involved with a sport?* □ *Be careful and don't get involved with the wrong kind of people.* □ *When it comes to drugs, just don't get involved.* 2. [with *someone*] to become romantically associated with someone. □ *Sally is getting involved with Bill. They've been seeing a lot of each other.* □ *I hope they don't get too involved.* ALSO: **be involved with someone or something** 1. to have established an association with someone or something. □ *Bill is involved with swimming and rugby.* □ *Mary is very much involved with her friends.* 2. [with *someone*] to be romantically attached to someone; to be in love with someone. □ *Tom and Ann are very much involved.* □ *Tom is also involved with Sally.*

get it 1. to receive punishment. (Informal.) □ *Bill broke the window, and he's really going to get it.* □ *John got it for arriving late at school.* 2. to receive the meaning of a joke; to understand a joke. (Informal.) □ *John told a joke, but I didn't get it.* □ *Bob laughed very hard, but Mary didn't get it.*

get it (all) together to become fit or organized; to organize one's thinking; to become relaxed and rational. (Slang. Also with *have.* See the note at *get a black eye.*) □ *Bill seems to be behaving*

more normally now. I think he's getting it all together. □ *I hope he gets it together soon. His life is a mess.* □ *When Jane has it all together, she really makes sense.* □ *Sally is a lovely person. She really has it together.*

get it in the neck to receive something bad, such as punishment or criticism. (Slang. Compare to *get it.*) □ *I don't know why I should get it in the neck. I didn't break the window.* □ *Bill got it in the neck for being late.*

get lost 1. to become lost; to lose one's way. □ *We got lost on the way home.* □ *Follow the path, or you might get lost.* 2. Go away!; Stop being an annoyance! (Slang. Always a command.) □ *Stop bothering me. Get lost!* □ *Get lost! I don't need your help.* □ *Stop following me. Get lost!*

get mixed up to get confused. (Informal.) □ *I get mixed up easily whenever I take a test.* □ *Sorry, I didn't say the right thing. I got mixed up.*

get moving to get busy; to get started; to work harder or faster. (Informal.) □ *Come on, everybody. Get moving!* □ *The director is coming. You had better get moving.*

get nowhere fast not to make progress; to get nowhere. (Informal.) □ *I can't seem to make any progress. No matter what I do, I'm just getting nowhere fast.* □ *Come on. Speed up this car. We're getting nowhere fast.*

get off (See also *get something off.*) 1. to climb down from; to disembark. □ *Be careful as you get off the bus.* □ *Get off the roof and come down here this minute!* □ *Stop this train! This is where I get off!* 2. to depart. □ *Our flight got off on time.* □ *We hope to get off about four o'clock in the morning.* 3. to escape or avoid punishment (for doing something wrong). □ *It was a serious crime, but Mary got off with a light sentence.* □ *I was afraid that the robber was going to get off completely.*

get off lightly to receive very little punishment (for doing something wrong).

(See also *get a slap on the wrist.*) □ *It was a serious crime, but Mary got off lightly.* □ *Billy's punishment was very light. Considering what he did, he got off lightly.*

get off on the wrong foot AND **get off to a bad start** to start something (such as a friendship) in an unfortunate manner or with negative factors. (See also *get off.*) □ *Bill and Tom got off on the wrong foot. They had a minor car accident just before they were introduced.* □ *Let's work hard to be friends. I hate to get off on the wrong foot.* □ *Bill is getting off to a bad start in geometry. He failed the first test.* ALSO: **be off on the wrong foot; be off to a bad start** to have started something with negative factors. □ *I'm sorry we are off to a bad start. I tried to be friendly.*

get off scot-free See *go scot-free.*

Get off someone's back! Leave someone alone!; Stop picking on someone! (Slang. Usually a command.) □ *I'm tired of your criticism, Bill. Get off my back!* □ *Stop picking on her. Get off her back!*

get off the hook See under *get someone off the hook.*

get off to a bad start See *get off on the wrong foot.*

get off to a flying start to have a very successful beginning to something. □ *The new business got off to a flying start with those export orders.* □ *We shall need a large donation from the local council if the charity is to get off to a flying start.*

get on to make progress. □ *How are you getting on?* □ *They have got on in life.*

get on (in years) to grow older. □ *Grandfather is getting on in years.* □ *Yes, he's really getting on.*

get on someone's nerves to irritate someone. □ *Please stop whistling. It's getting on my nerves.* □ *All this arguing is getting on their nerves.*

get on (something) to enter a conveyance; to get aboard something; to climb onto something. □ *They just announced that it's time to get on the aeroplane.* □ *The bus stopped, and I got on.* □ *The child was afraid to get on the train.* □ *Where did you get on?*

get on the good side of someone to get into someone's favour. □ *You had better behave properly if you want to get on the good side of Mary.* □ *If you want to get on the good side of your teacher, you must do your homework.* ALSO: **keep on the good side of someone** to stay in someone's favour. □ *You have to work hard to keep on the good side of the manager.*

get on (with someone or something) 1. [with *someone*] to be friends with someone; to co-operate with someone. □ *I just can't seem to get on with you.* □ *We must try harder to get on.* □ *How do you get on with John?* □ *Oh, we get on.* **2.** [with *something*] to progress with something. □ *How are you getting on with your work?* □ *She is not getting on with her project in a timely manner.*

get on with something to continue with something. □ *I must get on with my work.* □ *Now that the crisis is over, I'll get on with my life.*

get one's act together to get oneself organized, especially mentally. (Slang. Originally from theatrical use. Also with have. See the note at *get a black eye.*) □ *I'm so confused about life. I have to get my act together.* □ *Bill Smith had a hard time getting his act together after his mother's death.* □ *Mary really has her act together. She copes very well.*

get one's come-uppance to get a reprimand; to get the punishment one deserves. □ *Tom is always insulting people, but he finally got his come-uppance. Bill hit him.* □ *I hope I don't get my come-uppance like that.*

get one's fill of someone or something to receive enough of someone or something. (Also with have. See the note at *get a black eye.*) □ *You'll soon get your* *fill of Tom. He can be quite a pest.* □ *I can never get my fill of shrimps. I love them.* □ *Three weeks of visiting grandchildren is enough. I've had my fill of them.*

get one's fingers burned to have a bad experience. (Also used literally.) □ *I tried that once before and got my fingers burned. I won't try it again.* □ *If you buy shares and get your fingers burned, you then tend to leave your money in the bank.*

get one's foot in the door to achieve a favourable position (for further action); to take the first step in a process. (People selling things from door to door used to block the door with a foot, so it could not be closed on them. Also with *have.* See the note at *get a black eye.*) □ *I think I could get the position if I could only get my foot in the door.* □ *It pays to get your foot in the door. Try to get an appointment with the managing director.* □ *I have a better chance now that I have my foot in the door.*

get one's hands off (someone or something) AND **take one's hands off (someone or something)** to release someone or something; to stop touching someone or something. (Also with *have.* See the note at *get a black eye.*) □ *Get your hands off my bicycle!* □ *Take your hands off me! Come on! Take them off!* □ *Please ask John to get his hands off the window pane.* ALSO: **keep one's hands off (someone or something)** to refrain from touching or handling something. □ *I'm going to put these biscuits here. You keep your hands off them.* □ *Get your hands off my book, and keep them off.*

get one's hands on someone or something AND **lay one's hands on someone or something** to *get hold of someone or something;* to get someone or something in one's grasp. (Informal. Sometimes said in anger, as if one may wish to do harm.) □ *Just wait until I get my hands on Tom. I'll really give him something to think about.* □ *When I lay my hands on my book again, I'll never lend it to anyone.*

get one's head above water to get ahead of one's problems; to catch up with one's work or responsibilities. (Also used literally. Also with *have.* See the note at *get a black eye.*) □ *I can't seem to get my head above water. Work just keeps piling up.* □ *I'll be glad when I have my head above water.* ALSO: **keep one's head above water** to stay ahead of one's responsibilities. □ *Now that I have more space to work in, I can easily keep my head above water.*

get one's just desserts to get what one deserves. □ *I feel better now that Jane got her just desserts. She really insulted me.* □ *Bill got back exactly the treatment which he gave out. He got his just desserts.*

get one's knuckles rapped See under *rap someone's knuckles.*

get one's marching orders See under *give one one's marching orders.*

get one's marching papers See under *give one one's marching orders.*

get one's money's worth to get everything which has been paid for; to get the best quality for the money paid. □ *Weigh that package of meat before you buy it. Be sure you're getting your money's worth.* □ *The show was so bad we felt we hadn't got our money's worth.*

get one's nose out of someone's business to stop interfering in someone else's business; to mind one's own business. (Informal.) □ *Go away! Get your nose out of my business!* □ *Bob just can't seem to get his nose out of other people's business.* ALSO: **keep one's nose out of someone's business** to refrain from interfering in someone else's business. □ *Let John have his privacy, and keep your nose out of my business, too!*

get one's say AND **have one's say** to be able to state one's position; to be able to say what one thinks. □ *I want to have my say on this matter.* □ *He got his say, and then he was happy.*

get one's second wind (Also with *have.* See the note at *get a black eye.*) **1.** for one's breathing to become stabilized after exerting oneself for a short time. □ *John was having a hard time running until he got his second wind.* □ *"At last," thought Ann, "I have my second wind. Now I can really swim fast."* **2.** to become more active or productive (after becoming tired for a time.) □ *I usually get my second wind early in the afternoon.* □ *Mary is a better worker now that she has her second wind.*

get one's start to receive the first major opportunity of one's career. □ *I got my start in painting when I was thirty.* □ *She helped me get my start by recommending me to the manager.* ALSO: **give someone a start** to give one one's first opportunity. □ *A teacher gave me my start in woodworking.*

get one's teeth into something to start on something seriously, especially a difficult task. (Informal.) □ *Come on, Bill. You have to get your teeth into your biology.* □ *I can't wait to get my teeth into this problem.*

get one's walking papers See under *give one one's marching orders.*

get one's way (with someone or something) to have someone or something follow one's plans; to control someone or something. (Also with *have.* See the note at *get a black eye.*) □ *The mayor finally got his way with the town council.* □ *He seldom gets his way.* □ *Parents usually have their way with their children.*

get out 1. See *get out of something.* **2.** to go away or leave a place. (Impolite. A command.) □ *Get out! You're a pest.* □ *That's enough from you. Get out!*

get out from under someone or something 1. [with *someone*] to get free of someone's control. □ *Mary wanted to get out from under her mother.* □ *We started our own business because we needed to get out from under our employer.* **2.** [with *something*] to get free of a burdensome problem. □ *I can't go out tonight until I get out from under this pile of homework.* □ *There is so much work to do! I don't know when I'll ever get out from under it.*

get out of a jam See under *get someone out of a jam.*

get out of a mess to get free of a bad situation. (Informal. Also with *this, such a,* etc. See the examples. Compare to *get into a mess.*) □ *How can anyone get out of a mess like this?* □ *Please help me get out of this mess!*

get out of someone's way to remove oneself from someone's path. □ *Here I come. Please get out of my way.* □ *He intends to go in. Please get out of his way.*

get out of something 1. AND **get out** to leave; to go (out of a place). □ *We didn't get out of the meeting on time.* □ *I got in, but I couldn't get out.* **2.** not to have to do something. □ *I was supposed to go to a wedding, but I got out of it.* □ *Jane had an appointment, but she got out of it.*

get out of the wrong side of the bed to get up in the morning in a bad mood. □ *What's wrong with you? Did you get out of the wrong side of the bed today?* □ *Excuse me for being cross. I got out of the wrong side of the bed.*

get over someone or something 1. to climb over someone or something. □ *Stay still. I think I can get over you. Then I'll help you up.* □ *Somehow, I managed to get over the pile of stones.* **2.** to recover from someone or something. □ *Now that Bob has left me, I have to learn to get over him.* □ *It was a horrible shock. I don't know when I'll get over it.* □ *It was a serious illness. It took two weeks to get over it.*

get physical (with someone) to use physical force against someone. (Informal.) □ *The coach got in trouble for getting physical with some members of the team.* □ *When the suspect wouldn't co-operate, the police were forced to get physical.*

get ready (to do something) to prepare to do something. □ *Get ready to* *jump!* □ *It's time to get ready to go to work.* □ *It's time to get ready.*

get religion to develop a strong religious belief. □ *When I was very ill, I really got religion.* □ *Soldiers often say they got religion in the midst of a battle.*

get rid of someone or something to get free of someone or something; to dispose of or destroy someone or something. (Also with *be,* as in the example.) □ *I'm trying to get rid of Mr. Smith. He's bothering me.* □ *I'll be happy when I'm rid of my old car.*

get second thoughts about someone or something to have doubts about someone or something. (Also with *have.* See the note at *get a black eye.*) □ *I'm beginning to get second thoughts about Tom.* □ *Tom is getting second thoughts about it, too.* □ *We now have second thoughts about going to Canada.*

get set get ready; get organized. (Also with *be,* as in the example.) □ *We are going to start. Please get set.* □ *We are set. Let's go.* □ *Hurry up and get set!*

get sick to become ill (often with vomiting). □ *I got sick and couldn't go to school.* □ *My whole family got sick after eating the meal.*

get someone off the hook to free someone from an obligation. (Informal.) □ *Thanks for getting me off the hook. I didn't want to attend that meeting.* □ *I couldn't get Tom off the hook by myself.* ALSO: **get off the hook** to get free from an obligation. □ *She did everything she could to get off the hook.* □ *I couldn't get off the hook by myself.*

get someone or something across See *put someone or something across.*

get someone or something down 1. to manage to lower someone or something. □ *After a long struggle, we got the flag down and put it away.* □ *Bill was stuck up in the tree until Sally got him down.* 2. [with *something*] to manage to swallow something, especially something large or unpleasant. □ *The pill was huge, but I got it down.* □ *It was the worst food I have ever had, but I got it*

down somehow. 3. [with *someone*] to depress a person; to make a person very sad. □ *My dog ran away, and it really got me down.* □ *Oh, that's too bad. Don't let it get you down.* ALSO: **keep someone or something down** 1. to make someone or something stay down or lowered for a period of time. □ *We had to keep the flag down for a month.* □ *Bobby loves to climb trees. We don't know how we are going to keep him down.* 2. [with *something*] to keep food in one's stomach (without vomiting it up). □ *I don't know how I managed to keep the pill down.* □ *The food must have been spoiled. I couldn't keep it down.* □ *Sally is ill. She can't keep solid food down.* 3. [with *someone*] to keep someone depressed for a period of time. □ *It's upsetting, but it shouldn't keep you down for days.* □ *Nothing is too upsetting to keep me down very long.*

get someone or something out of one's mind AND **get someone or something out of one's head** to manage to forget someone or something; to stop thinking about or wanting someone or something. (Almost the same as *put someone or something out of one's mind.*) □ *I can't get him out of my mind.* □ *Mary couldn't get the song out of her mind.* □ *Get that silly idea out of your head!*

get someone or something out of the way to move a person or a thing out of a pathway or away. □ *Get that car out of the way.* □ *Please get your children out of the way.* ALSO: **keep someone or something out of the way** to prevent someone or something from getting in the way. □ *Please keep your children out of the way.*

get someone out of a jam to free someone from a problem or a bad situation. (Informal. Compare to *in a jam.*) □ *I like John. He got me out of a jam once.* □ *I would be glad to help get you out of a jam.* ALSO: **get out of a jam** to get free from a problem or a bad situation. □ *Would you lend me five pounds? I need it to get out of a jam.*

get someone over a barrel for someone to be put *at the mercy of someone;* to get control over someone. (Informal. Also with *have.* See the note at *get a black eye.*) □ *He got me over a barrel, and I had to do what he said.* □ *Ann will do exactly what I say. I've got her over a barrel.*

get someone under one's thumb to get control over someone; to dominate someone. (Also with *have.* See the note at *get a black eye.*) □ *His wife got him under her thumb.* □ *The younger child has the family under her thumb.*

get someone's back up See the following entry.

get someone's dander up AND **get someone's back up; get someone's goat; get someone's hackles up** to make someone get angry. (Informal. Also with *have.* See the note at *get a black eye.*) □ *Now, don't get your dander up. Calm down.* □ *I insulted him and really got his hackles up.* □ *She really got her back up when I asked her for money.* □ *Now, now, don't get your hackles up. I didn't mean any harm.*

get someone's ear to get someone to listen (to you). (Also with *have.* Compare to *bend someone's ear.*) □ *He succeeded in getting my ear and talked for an hour.* □ *While I have your ear, I'd like to tell you about something I'm selling.*

get someone's eye See *catch someone's eye.*

get someone's goat See *get someone's dander up.*

get someone's hackles up See *get someone's dander up.*

get someone's number to find out about a person; to learn the key to understanding a person. (Informal. Also with *have.* See the note at *get a black eye.*) □ *I'm going to get your number if I can. You're a real puzzle.* □ *I've got Tom's number. He's ambitious.*

get something across (to someone) to convey information to someone; to teach someone. □ *I'm trying to get this across to you. Please pay attention.* □ *I'll keep trying until I get it across.*

get something back to receive something (which was already yours). □ *I lent her my algebra book. I don't know when I'll get it back.* □ *I got my watch back from the jeweller today.*

get something in order See *put something in order.*

get something into someone's thick head See the following entry.

get something into someone's thick skull AND **get something into someone's thick head** to understand something. (Informal.) □ *He can't seem to get it through his thick skull.* □ *If I could get this into my thick head once, I'd remember it.*

get something off AND **get off something** to remove an article of clothing. □ *Bill, hurry and get off your coat and come to dinner.* □ *Mummy! I can't get my boots off.*

get something off one's chest to tell something that has been bothering you. (Also with *have.* See the note at *get a black eye.*) □ *I have to get this off my chest. I broke your window with a stone.* □ *I knew I'd feel better when I had that off my chest.*

get something off the ground to get something started. □ *I can relax after I get this project off the ground.* □ *You'll have a lot of free time when you get the new business off the ground.*

get something on someone to learn something potentially damaging about a person. (Informal. Also with *have.* See the note at *get a black eye.*) □ *Tom is always trying to get something on me. I can't imagine why.* □ *If he has something on you, he'll have you over a barrel.* □ *If he gets something on you, you ought to get something on him.*

get something out in the open to make something public; to stop hiding a fact or a secret. □ *We had better get this out in the open before the press gets wind of it.* □ *I'll feel better when it's* *out in the open. I can't stand all of this secrecy.*

get something out of one's system to be rid of the desire to do something; to do something that you have been wanting to do so that you are not bothered by wanting to do it any more. □ *I bought a new car. I've been wanting to for a long time. I'm glad I finally got that out of my system.* □ *I can't get it out of my system! I want to go back to school and get a degree.*

get something out of something to get some kind of benefit from something. □ *I didn't get anything out of the lecture.* □ *I'm always able to get something helpful out of our conversations.*

get something over with AND **get something over** to complete something, especially something you have dreaded. (Also with *have.* See the note at *get a black eye.*) □ *Oh, please hurry and get it over with. It hurts.* □ *Please get it over.* □ *When I have this over with, I can relax.*

get something sewn up AND **get something wrapped up** to have something settled or finished. (Informal. See also *sew something up.* Also with *have.* See the note at *get a black eye.*) □ *I'll take the contract to the managing director tomorrow morning. I'll get the whole deal sewn up by midday.* □ *Don't worry about the car loan. I'll have it sewn up in time to make the purchase.* □ *I'll get the loan wrapped up, and you'll have the car this week.*

get something straight to understand something clearly. (Informal. Also with *have.* See the note at *get a black eye.*) □ *Now get this straight. You're going to fail history if you don't work.* □ *Let me get this straight. I'm supposed to go there in the morning?* □ *Let me make sure I have this straight.*

get something under one's belt (Informal. Also with *have.* See the note at *get a black eye.*) 1. to eat or drink something. □ *I'd feel a lot better if I had a cool drink under my belt.* □ *Come in out of the cold and get a nice warm meal*

under your belt. 2. to learn something well; to assimilate some information; to get work done. □ *I have to study tonight. I have to get a lot of algebra under my belt.* □ *I have to get all these reports under my belt before I go home.*

get something under-way to get something started. (Also with *have.* See the note at *get a black eye.*) □ *The time has come to get this meeting under-way.* □ *Now that the chairman has the meeting under-way, I can relax.*

get something wrapped up See *get something sewn up.*

get stars in one's eyes (Also with *have.* See the note at *get a black eye.*) 1. to be happy and optimistic. □ *She gets stars in her eyes when she thinks about her birthday.* □ *The lovers had stars in their eyes.* 2. to be obsessed with show business; to be stage-struck. □ *Many young people get stars in their eyes at this age.* □ *Ann has stars in her eyes. She wants to go to Hollywood.*

get the advantage of someone AND **get the advantage over someone; get the edge on someone; get the edge over someone** to achieve a position superior to someone else. (The word *the* can be replaced with *an.* See also the special sense at *have the advantage of someone.* Also with *have.* See the note at *get a black eye.* See also *take advantage of someone or something.*) □ *Toward the end of the race, I got the advantage over Mary.* □ *She'd had an advantage over me since the start of the race.* □ *He has the edge on the rest of the class in maths.* □ *It's speed that counts. You can have the edge over everyone, but if you don't have speed, you lose.*

get the axe See *get the sack.*

get the ball rolling See *start the ball rolling.*

get the benefit of the doubt to receive a judgement in your favour when the evidence is neither for you or against you. (Also with *have.* See the note at *get a black eye.*) □ *I was right between a B and an A. I got the benefit of the doubt—an A.* □ *I thought I should* *have had the benefit of the doubt, but the judge made me pay a fine.* ALSO: **give someone the benefit of the doubt** □ *I'm glad the teacher gave me the benefit of the doubt.* □ *I asked the judge to give me the benefit of the doubt.*

get the best of someone See the following entry.

get the better of someone AND **get the best of someone** to win over someone in a competition or bargain; to defeat someone. (Also with *have*. See the note at *get a black eye*.) □ *I tried to get the better of John, but he won anyway.* □ *I set out to have the better of Sally, but I didn't have enough skill.* □ *Bill got the best of John in the boxing match.*

get the blues to become sad or depressed. (Also with *have*. See the note at *get a black eye*.) □ *You'll have to excuse Bill. He has the blues tonight.* □ *I get the blues every time I hear that song.*

get the boot to be sent away (from somewhere); to be dismissed from one's employment; to be kicked out (of a place). (Slang. See also *get the sack*.) □ *I suppose I wasn't dressed well enough to go in there. I got the boot.* □ *I'll work harder at my job today. I nearly got the boot yesterday.* ALSO: **give someone the boot** to dismiss someone; to kick someone out (of a place). (Slang.) □ *You had better behave, or they'll give you the boot.*

get the brush-off to be ignored or sent away; to be rejected. (Informal.) □ *Don't talk to Tom. You'll just get the brush-off.* □ *I went up to her and asked for a date, but I got the brush-off.* ALSO: **give someone the brush-off** to send someone away; to reject someone. (Informal.) □ *Tom wouldn't talk to her. He just gave her the brush-off.*

get the cold shoulder to be ignored; to be rejected. (Informal.) □ *If you invite her to a party, you'll just get the cold shoulder.* □ *I thought that Sally and I were friends, but lately I've been getting the cold shoulder.* ALSO: **give somcone the cold shoulder** to ignore someone; to reject someone. (Informal.) □ *She*

gave me the cold shoulder when I asked her to the party. □ *Sally has been giving me the cold shoulder.*

get the creeps AND **get the willies** to become frightened; to become uneasy. (Slang.) (Also with *have*. See the note at *get a black eye*.) □ *I get the creeps when I see that old house.* □ *I really had the willies when I went down into the basement.* ALSO: **give someone the creeps; give someone the willies** to make someone uneasy; to frighten someone. (Informal.) □ *That old house gives me the creeps.* □ *That strange old man gives him the willies.*

get the day off AND **get a day off** to have a day free from working. (Also with *have*. See the note at *get a black eye*. See also *take the day off*.) □ *The next time I get a day off, we'll go to the zoo.* □ *I have the day off. Let's go to the zoo.*

get the edge on someone See *get the advantage of someone*.

get the feel of something [for someone] to learn the way something feels (when it is used). (Also with *have*. See the note at *get a black eye*. See also the special sense at *have the feel of something*.) □ *I haven't yet got the feel of this bat. I hope I don't miss the ball.* □ *I can drive better now that I have the feel of this car's steering.*

get the final word See *get the last word*.

get the go-ahead AND **get the green light** to receive a signal to start or continue. □ *We have to wait here until we get the go-ahead.* □ *I hope we get the green light on our project soon.* ALSO: **give someone the go-ahead; give someone the green light** to give someone the signal to start or continue. □ *It's time to start work. Give everybody the go-ahead.* □ *They gave us the green light to start.*

get the go-by to be ignored or passed by. (Slang.) □ *It was my turn for promotion, but I got the go-by.* □ *Tom stood on the road for fifteen minutes trying to get a ride, but he kept getting the go-by.* ALSO: **give someone the go-by** to pass by or ignore someone or something.

(Slang.) □ *I'll give the cinema the go-by tonight.*

get the green light See *get the go-ahead.*

get the hang of something to learn how to do something; to learn how something works. (Informal. Also with *have.* See the note at *get a black eye.*) □ *As soon as I get the hang of this computer, I'll be able to work faster.* □ *Now that I have the hang of starting the car in cold weather, I won't have to get up so early.*

get the hard sell to receive considerable pressure to buy or accept (something). (Slang.) □ *I won't go to that shop again. I really got the hard sell.* □ *You'll probably get the hard sell if you go to a used car dealer.* ALSO: **give someone the hard sell** to put pressure on someone to buy or accept (something). (Slang.) □ *They gave me the hard sell, but I still wouldn't buy the car.*

get the last laugh to laugh at or ridicule someone who has laughed at or ridiculed you; to put someone in the same bad position that you were once in; to *turn the tables on someone.* (Also with *have.* See the note at *get a black eye.*) □ *John laughed when I got a D on the final exam. I got the last laugh, though. He failed the course.* □ *Mr. Smith said I was foolish when I bought an old building. I had the last laugh when I sold it a month later for twice what I paid for it.*

get the last word AND **get the final word** to get to make the final point (in an argument); to get to make the final decision (in some matter). (Also with *have.* See the note at *get a black eye.*) □ *The managing director gets the last word in taking on staff.* □ *Why do you always have to have the final word in an argument?*

get the low-down (on someone or something) to receive the full story about someone or something; to get to know the details about someone or something. (Slang.) □ *I need to get the low-down on John. Is he still an accountant?* □ *Sally wants to get the low-down on the new motorway. Please tell her all about it.* □ *The police have the low-down on*

the crooked car salesman. ALSO: **give someone the low-down on someone or something** to tell someone the full story about someone or something. (Slang.) □ *Please give Sally the low-down on the new expressway.*

get the message to understand what is meant. (Informal.) □ *I get the message. You want me to go.* □ *He still doesn't seem to understand. When do you think he'll get the message?*

get the (old) heave ho to get thrown out (of a place); to get dismissed (from one's employment). (Informal. From nautical use where sailors used *heave ho* to coordinate hard physical labour. One sailor called *Heave ho,* and all the sailors would pull at the same time on the *ho.* Also with *have.* See the note at *get a black eye.*) □ *They sacked a number of people today, but I didn't get the heave ho.* □ *John had the old heave ho last week. Now he's unemployed.* □ *Jane has given her fiancé the heave ho.* ALSO: **give someone the (old) heave ho** to throw someone out (of a place); to sack someone. (Informal.) □ *John was behaving badly at our party, so my father gave him the heave ho.* □ *Jane gave Jim the old heave ho today.*

get the once-over (Informal.) to receive a quick visual examination. □ *Every time John walks by I get the once-over. Does he like me?* □ *I went to the doctor yesterday, but I only got the once-over.* □ *I wanted the mechanic to give the car the once-over.* ALSO: **give someone the once-over** to examine someone visually quickly. □ *John gives me the once-over every time he walks by me.* □ *Why does he just give me the once-over? Why doesn't he say hello?*

get the picture to understand the whole situation. (Informal or slang.) □ *Okay, Bob. That's the whole explanation. You get the picture?* □ *Yes, I got the picture.*

get the red carpet treatment to receive very special treatment; to receive royal treatment. (This refers—sometimes literally—to the rolling out of a clean red carpet for someone to walk on.) □ *I love to go to expensive shops where I get the red carpet treatment.* □ *The queen gets the red carpet treatment wherever she goes.* ALSO: **give someone the red carpet treatment** to give someone very special treatment; to give someone royal treatment. □ *We always give the queen the red carpet treatment when she comes to visit.* ALSO: **roll out the red carpet for someone** to provide special treatment for someone. □ *There's no need to roll out the red carpet for me.* □ *We rolled out the red carpet for the king and queen.*

get the runaround to receive a series of excuses, delays, and referrals. (Informal.) □ *You'll get the runaround if you ask to see the manager.* □ *I hate it when I get the runaround.* ALSO: **give someone the runaround** to give someone a series of excuses, delays, and referrals. □ *If you ask to see the manager, they'll give you the runaround.*

get the sack AND **get the axe** to get sacked; to be dismissed (from one's employment). (Slang.) □ *I got the sack yesterday. Now I have to find new employment.* □ *I tried to work harder, but I got the axe anyway.* ALSO: **give someone the sack; give someone the axe** to sack someone; to terminate someone's employment. □ *I gave Tom the sack, and he has to find a new job.* □ *I had to give three people the axe yesterday. We are having to reduce our office staff.*

get the shock of one's life to receive a serious (emotional) shock. (Also with *have*. See the note at *get a black eye*.) □ *I opened the telegram and got the shock of my life.* □ *I had the shock of my life when I won £5,000.*

get the short end of the stick AND **end up with the short end of the stick** to end up with less (than someone else); to end up cheated or deceived. (Also with *have*. See the note at *get a black eye*.) □ *Why do I always get the short end of the stick? I want my fair share!* □ *She's unhappy because she has the short end of the stick again.* □ *I hate to end up with the short end of the stick.*

get the show on the road to get (something) started. (Informal.) □ *Hurry up! Let's get the show on the road.* □ *If you don't get the show on the road right now, we'll never finish today.*

get the slip [for someone] to elude or escape (someone). (Informal.) □ *We followed her for a short distance, and then got the slip.* □ *The police got the slip, and the criminal got away.* ALSO: **give someone the slip** to escape from or elude someone. (Informal.) □ *We followed her for a short distance, and then she gave us the slip.*

get the third degree to be questioned in great detail for a long period. (Slang.) □ *Why is it I get the third degree from you every time I come home late?* □ *Poor Sally spent all night at the police station getting the third degree.* ALSO: **give someone the third degree** to question someone in great detail for a long period. (Slang.) □ *The police gave Sally the third degree.*

get the upper hand (over someone) to get into a position superior to someone; to *get the advantage of someone*. (Also with *have*. See the note at *get a black eye*.) □ *John is always trying to get the upper hand over someone.* □ *He never ends up having the upper hand, though.*

get the willies See *get the creeps*.

get the works to receive a lot of something. (Slang. The *works* can be a lot of food, good treatment, bad treatment, etc.) □ BILL: *Shall we order a snack or a big meal?* JANE: *I'm hungry. Let's get the works.* □ *She went to the beautician and had the works.* ALSO: **give someone the works** to give someone the full amount or the full treatment. (Slang.) □ *The teacher gave him the works for being late.*

get the worst of something to experience the worst aspects of something. (Also with *have*. See the note at *get a black eye*.) □ *No matter what happens at the office, I seem to get the worst of it.* □ *He always gets the worst of the bargain.* □ *I got to choose which one I wanted, but I still got the worst of the lot.*

get through something 1. to finish something; to work one's way through something. □ *If I read fast, I can get through this book in an hour.* □ *I don't think I can get through all this work by finishing time.* **2.** to survive something; to *go through something.* □ *This is a busy day. I don't know how I'll get through it.* □ *Somehow she got through the divorce.*

get through (to someone) 1. to reach someone; to manage to communicate to someone. □ *I called her on the telephone time after time, but I couldn't get through to her.* □ *I tried every kind of communication, but I couldn't get through.* **2.** to pass through (something). □ *The crowd was so thick that I couldn't get through to him.* □ *I tried, but I couldn't get through. The crowd was too heavy.* **3.** to make someone understand something; to *get something into someone's thick skull.* □ *Why don't you try to understand me? What do I have to do to get through to you?* □ *Can anybody get through, or are you just stubborn?* □ *Ann is still too sick to understand what I'm saying. Maybe I can get through to her tomorrow.*

get time off to receive a period of time which is free from employment. (Compare to *get the day off.* See *take time off.* Also with *have.* See the note at *get a black eye.*) □ *I got time off to go shopping.* □ *I don't have time off from work very often.* ALSO: **get time off for good behaviour** to have one's prison sentence shortened because of good behaviour. □ *Bob will get out of jail tomorrow rather than next week. He got time off for good behaviour.*

get time off for good behaviour See under *get time off.*

get time to catch one's breath to find enough time to relax or behave normally. (Also with *have.* See the note at *get a black eye.*) □ *When things slow down around here, I'll get time to catch my breath.* □ *Sally was so busy she didn't even have time to catch her breath.*

get to one's feet to stand up, sometimes in order to address the audience. □ *On a signal from the director, the singers got to their feet.* □ *I was so weak, I could hardly get to my feet.*

get to the bottom of something to get an understanding of the causes of something. □ *We must get to the bottom of this problem immediately.* □ *There is clearly something wrong here, and I want to get to the bottom of it.*

get to the heart of the matter AND **get at the heart of the matter** to get to the essentials of a matter. □ *We have to stop wasting time and get to the heart of the matter.* □ *You've been very helpful. You really seem to be able to get at the heart of the matter.*

get to the point See *come to the point.*

get together (with someone) to meet with someone; to come together for a social occasion. □ *We are going to get together with the Smiths for bridge next Thursday.* □ *It's good to see you, Bill. We'll have to get together again soon.* ALSO: **get-together** a gathering. □ *We were at an informal get-together at Tom's house last night.*

get tough (with someone) to become firm with someone; to use physical force against someone. (Slang.) □ *The teacher had to get tough with the class because the pupils were acting badly.* □ *I've tried to get you to behave, but it looks like I'll have to get tough.*

get under someone's skin to bother or irritate someone. (Informal.) □ *John is so annoying. He really gets under my skin.* □ *I know he's a nuisance, but don't let him get under your skin.*

get under-way to start going; to start. (The word *get* can be replaced with *be.* Compare to *get something under-way.*) □ *The ship is leaving soon. It's about to get under-way.* □ *Let us get our journey under-way.* □ *I'm glad our project is under-way.*

get up to wake up and get out of bed. □ *What time do you usually get up?* □ *I get up when I have to.*

get-up-and-go energy; motivation. (Informal.) □ *I must be getting old. I just don't have my old get-up-and-go.* □ *A good breakfast will give you lots of get-up-and-go.*

get up enough nerve (to do something) to get brave enough to do something. □ *I could never get up enough nerve to sing in public.* □ *I'd do it if I could get up enough nerve, but I'm shy.*

get used to someone or something to become accustomed to someone or something. □ *I got used to being small many years ago.* □ *John is nice, but I really can't get used to him. He talks too much.*

get well to become healthy again. □ *Ann had a cold for a week, and then she got well.* □ *Hurry up and get well!*

get wet to become soaked with water. □ *Get out of the rain or you'll get wet.* □ *Don't get wet, or you'll catch a cold.*

get what for to get scolded. (Informal.) □ *If I don't get home on time, I'm really going to get what for.* □ *Billy, if you don't want to get what for, you had better get in this house now.* ALSO: **give someone what for** to scold someone. (Informal.) □ *Billy's mother gave him what for because he didn't get home on time.*

get what is coming to one to get what one deserves, usually something bad. □ *If you cheat, you'll get into trouble. You'll get what's coming to you.* □ *Bill got what was coming to him when Anne left him.* ALSO: **give one what is coming to one** to give one what one deserves. □ *Jim gave Bill what was coming to him.*

get wind of something to hear about something; to receive information about something. (Informal.) □ *I just got wind of the job vacancy and have applied.* □ *Wait until the treasurer gets wind of this. Somebody is going to get in trouble.*

get wise to someone or something to find out about someone or something; to see through the deception of someone or something. (Slang.) □ *Watch out, John. Your friends are getting wise to your tricks.* □ *John's friends are getting wise to him. He had better watch out.*

get worked up (over something) AND **get worked up (about something)** to get excited or emotionally distressed about something. □ *Please don't get worked up over this matter.* □ *They get worked up about these things very easily.* □ *I try not to get worked up.*

ghost of a chance even the slightest chance. (Slang.) □ *She can't do it. She doesn't have a ghost of a chance.* □ *There is just a ghost of a chance that I'll be there on time.*

gild the lily to add ornament or decoration to something which is pleasing in its original state; to attempt to improve something which is already fine the way it is. (Often refers to flattery or exaggeration.) □ *Your house has lovely brickwork. Don't paint it. That would be gilding the lily.* □ *Oh, Sally, you're beautiful the way you are. You don't need make-up. You would be gilding the lily.*

gird (up) one's loins to get ready; to prepare oneself (for something). (Jocular.) □ *Well, I suppose I had better gird up my loins and go to work.* □ *Somebody has to do something about the problem. Why don't you gird your loins and do something?*

give a free rein to someone AND **give someone a free rein** to allow someone to be completely in charge (of something). (See also give someone a free hand (with something).) □ *The delegates gave the manager a free rein with the new project.* □ *The headmistress gave a free rein to Mrs. Brown in her classes.*

give a good account of oneself to do (something) well or thoroughly. □ *John gave a good account of himself when he gave his speech last night.* □ *Mary was not hungry, and she didn't give a good account of herself at dinner.*

give an account of someone or something AND **give someone an account of someone or something** to tell (someone) about someone or something. □ *Mary gave an account of Bill's trip to town.* □ *She gave Ann an account of Bill's trip.* □ *We gave them an account of the new teacher.*

give as good as one gets to give as much as one receives; to pay someone back *in kind.* □ *John can hold his own in a fight. He can give as good as he gets.* □ *Sally usually wins a formal debate. She gives as good as she gets.*

give away something See *give someone or something away.*

give birth to someone or something **1.** AND **give birth** [with *someone*] to bear a child. □ *The mother gave birth to her second child last week.* □ *She gave birth last week.* **2.** [with *something*] to give rise to or start something. □ *The composer gave birth to a new kind of music.* □ *They gave birth to a new view of language.*

give chase (to someone or something) to chase someone or something. □ *The dogs gave chase to the fox.* □ *A mouse ran by, but the cat was too tired to give chase.* □ *The police gave chase to the robber.*

give credence to something **1.** to believe something. □ *He tells lies. Don't give credence to what he says.* □ *Please don't give credence to Mary. She doesn't know what she's talking about.* **2.** to support or back up something. □ *Her untidy appearance gave credence to her statement that she had been attacked.* □ *The fact that he ran away gives credence to the suggestion that he is guilty.*

give credit where credit is due to give credit to someone who deserves it; to acknowledge or thank someone who deserves it. □ *We must give credit where credit is due. Thank you very much, Sally.* □ *Let's give credit where credit is due. Mary is the one who wrote the report, not Jane.*

give ground to retreat (literally or figuratively). □ *When I argue with Mary, she never gives ground.* □ *I approached the barking dog, but it wouldn't give ground.*

give in (to someone or something) to yield to someone or something; to give up to someone or something. □ *He argued and argued and finally gave in to my demands.* □ *I thought he'd never give in.*

give it to someone straight to tell something to someone clearly and directly. (Informal.) □ *Come on, give it to me straight. I want to know exactly what happened.* □ *Quit wasting time, and tell me. Give it to me straight!*

give of oneself to be generous with one's time and concern. □ *Tom is very good with children because he gives of himself.* □ *If you want to have more friends, you have to learn to give of yourself.*

give off something to release light, a sound, or an odour. □ *This flower gives off a lovely perfume.* □ *The machine gave off a soft hum.* □ *The crystal lamp gave off a rosy glow.*

give one a run for one's money See under *get a good run for one's money.*

Give one an inch, and one will take a mile. AND **If you give one an inch, one will take a mile.** a proverb meaning that a person who is granted a little of something (such as a reprieve or lenience) will want more. □ *I told John he could hand in his essay one day late, but he handed it in three days late. Give him an inch, and he'll take a mile.* □ *First we let Jane borrow our car for a day. Now she wants to go on a two-week holiday. If you give her an inch, she'll take a mile.*

give one butterflies in one's stomach See *get butterflies in one's stomach.*

give one one's freedom to set someone free; to divorce someone. □ *Mrs. Brown wanted to give her husband his freedom.* □ *Well, Tom, I hate to break it to you this way, but I have decided to give you your freedom.*

give one one's marching orders AND **give one one's walking papers** to sack someone; to *give someone the sack.* (Informal.) □ *Tom has proved unsatisfactory. I decided to give him his marching orders.* □ *We might even give Sally her walking papers, too.* ALSO: **get one's marching orders; get one's walking papers** to get sacked. (Informal.) □ *Well, I'm through. I got my walking papers today.* □ *They are closing down my department. I suppose I'll get my marching orders soon.*

give one what's coming to one See under *get what's coming to one.*

give one's right arm (for someone or something) to be willing to give something of great value for someone or something. □ *I'd give my right arm for a nice cool drink.* □ *I'd give my right arm to be there.* □ *Tom really admires John. He would give his right arm for John.*

give oneself airs to act in a conceited or superior way. □ *Sally is always giving herself airs. You'd think she had royal blood.* □ *Come on, John. Don't act so haughty. Stop giving yourself airs.*

give oneself up (to someone or something) to surrender or yield to someone or something. □ *The suspect gave himself up to the police.* □ *She was innocent, but she gave herself up.* □ *The painter gave himself up to his work.*

give out to wear out; to become exhausted and stop. □ *The old lady's heart finally gave out.* □ *Our television set gave out right in the middle of my favourite programme.* □ *Bill gave out in the middle of the race.*

give rise to something to cause something. □ *The bad performance gave rise to many complaints.* □ *The new law gave rise to violence in the cities.*

give someone a big hand for something See under *get a big hand for something.*

give someone a big send-off See under *get a big send-off.*

give someone a black eye See under *get a black eye.*

Give someone a break! to give someone a chance. □ *Give me a break! I got here as fast as I could.* □ *Peter's trying his best. Give him a break.*

give someone a buzz See *give someone a ring.*

give someone a check-up See *get a check-up.*

give someone a clean bill of health See *get a clean bill of health.*

give someone a dig to insult someone; to say something which will irritate a person. (Slang.) □ *Jane gave Bob a dig about his carelessness with money.* □ *The headmaster's daughter gets tired of people giving her digs about favouritism.*

give someone a free hand (with something) See under *be given a free hand (with something).*

give someone a hand (with something) See under *get a hand with something.*

give someone a hard time See under *be given a hard time.*

give someone a head start (on someone or something) See under *get a head start (on someone or something).*

give someone a kick See under *get a kick out of someone or something.*

give someone a licking See under *get a licking.*

give someone a pain to annoy or bother someone. (Slang.) □ *Here comes Sally. Oh, she gives me a pain.* □ *She's such a pest. She really gives me a pain.*

give someone a pat on the back See *pat someone on the back.*

give someone a piece of one's mind to reprimand or scold someone; to *tell someone off.* □ *I've had enough from John. I'm going to give him a piece of my mind.* □ *Sally, stop it, or I'll give you a piece of my mind.*

117

give someone a raw deal See under *get a raw deal.*

give someone a red face See under *get a red face.*

give someone a reputation (as a something) See under *get a reputation (as a something).*

give someone a reputation for doing something See under *get a reputation (for doing something).*

give someone a ring AND **give someone a buzz** to call someone on the telephone. (Informal.) □ *Nice talking to you. Give me a ring sometime.* □ *Give me a buzz when you're in town.*

give someone a rough idea (about something) See under *get a rough idea (about something).*

give someone a slap on the wrist See under *get a slap on the wrist.*

give someone a start See under *get a start; get one's start.*

give someone a swelled head See under *get a swelled head.*

give someone a ticking-off See under *tick someone off.*

give someone a tongue-lashing See under *get a tongue-lashing.*

give someone credit (for something) See under *get credit (for something).*

give someone grey hair(s) See under *get grey hair(s).*

give someone hell See under *get hell.*

give someone or something a wide berth to keep a reasonable distance from someone or something; to *steer clear of someone or something.* (Originally referred to sailing ships.) □ *The dog we are approaching is very bad-tempered. Better give it a wide berth.* □ *Give Mary a wide berth. She's in a very bad mood.*

give someone or something away 1. to reveal a secret about someone or something. □ *I thought no one knew where I was, but my loud breathing gave me away.* □ *We know that Billy ate the cherry pie. The cherry juice on his shirt gave him away.* □ *I had planned a surprise, but John gave it away.* **2.** AND **give away something** [with *something*] to make a gift of something. (See also *give the bride away.*) □ *Mary gave away the cherry pie.* □ *Mary gave it away.*

give someone or something the once-over See *get the once-over.*

give someone or something up AND **give up someone or something** to release or relinquish someone or something; to give someone or something (to someone else). □ *Tom loved Ann very much, but he had to give her up.* □ *John was forced to give up smoking.*

give someone pause to cause someone to stop and think. □ *When I see a golden sunrise, it gives me pause for thought.* □ *Witnessing an accident is likely to give all of us pause.*

give someone the axe See under *get the sack.*

give someone the benefit of the doubt See under *get the benefit of the doubt.*

give someone the boot See under *get the boot.*

give someone the brushoff See under *get the brushoff.*

give someone the cold shoulder See under *get the cold shoulder.*

give someone the creeps See under *get the creeps.*

give someone the eye to look at someone in a way that communicates romantic interest. (Informal. See also *catch someone's eye.*) □ *Ann gave John the eye. It really surprised him.* □ *Tom kept giving Sally the eye. She finally left.*

give someone the go-ahead See under *get the go-ahead.*

give someone the go-by See under *get the go-by.*

give someone the green light See under *get the go-ahead.*

give someone the hard sell See under *get the hard sell.*

give someone the low-down on someone or something See under *get the low-down (on someone or something).*

give someone the (old) heave ho See under *get the (old) heave ho.*

give someone the once-over See under *get the once-over.*

give someone the red carpet treatment- See under *get the red carpet treatment.*

give someone the runaround See under *get the runaround.*

give someone the sack See under *get the sack.*

give someone the shirt off one's back to be very generous or solicitous to someone. □ *Tom really likes Bill. He'd give Bill the shirt off his back.* □ *John is so friendly that he'd give anyone the shirt off his back.*

give someone the slip See under *get the slip.*

give someone the third degree See under *get the third degree.*

give someone the willies See under *get the creeps.*

give someone the works See under *get the works.*

give someone tit for tat to give someone something equal to what was given you; to exchange a series of things, one by one with someone. (Informal.) □ *They took my car after I took theirs. It was tit for tat.* □ *He punched me, so I punched him. Every time he hit me, I hit him. I just gave him tit for tat.*

give someone to understand something to explain something to someone; to imply something to someone. (This may mislead someone, accidentally or intentionally.) □ *Mr. Smith gave Sally to understand that she should be home by midnight.* □ *The prime minister gave the electorate to understand that there would be no tax rate increase.*

He didn't promise, though. ALSO: **be given to understand** made to believe. □ *They were given to understand that there would be no tax rate increase, but after the election rates went up.* □ *She was given to understand that she had to be home by midnight.*

give someone what for See under *get what for.*

give something a lick and a promise to do something poorly—quickly and carelessly. (Informal.) □ *John! You didn't clean your room! You just gave it a lick and a promise.* □ *This time, Tom, comb your hair. It looks like you just gave it a lick and a promise.*

give something a miss not to go to something; not to bother with something; to leave something alone. (Informal.) □ *Betty decided to give the fair a miss this year.* □ *I regretted having to give Monday's lecture a miss, but I was just too busy to attend.*

give something one's best shot to give a task one's best effort. (Informal. Often with *it.*) □ *I gave the project my best shot.* □ *Sure, try it. Give it your best shot!*

give something out AND **give out something** to release something; to distribute something. (See also *have something out (with someone).*) □ *The teacher gave the papers out.* □ *The dog gave out a loud growl.*

give the bride away [for a bride's father] to accompany the bride to the groom in a wedding ceremony. □ *Mr. Brown is ill. Who'll give the bride away?* □ *In the traditional wedding ceremony, the bride's father gives the bride away.*

give the devil his due AND **give the devil her due** to give your foe proper credit (for something). (This usually refers to a person who has acted in an evil way—like the devil.) □ *She's generally impossible, but I have to give the devil her due. She's always honest.* □ *John may squander money, but give the devil his due. He makes sure his family are well taken care of.*

give the game away to reveal a plan or strategy. (Informal.) □ *Now, all of you have to keep quiet. Please don't give the game away.* □ *If you keep giving out hints, you'll give the game away.*

give the glad eye to someone to look at someone in such as way as to indicate romantic or sexual interest. (Informal.) □ *John was giving Mary the glad eye during the dinner party.* □ *I saw Sally giving the glad eye to a man on the bus.*

give up to surrender; to yield. □ *Even though things get hard, don't give up.* □ *The soldiers were surrounded, but they wouldn't give up.*

give up the ghost to die; to release one's spirit. (Considered formal or humorous.) □ *The old man sighed, rolled over, and gave up the ghost.* □ *I'm too young to give up the ghost.*

give vent to something to express anger. (The *something* is usually *anger, ire, irritation,* etc.) □ *John gave vent to his anger by shouting at Sally.* □ *Bill couldn't give vent to his frustration because he had been warned to keep quiet.*

give voice to something to express a feeling or an opinion in words; to speak out about something. □ *The bird gave voice to its joy in the golden sunshine.* □ *All the people gave voice to their anger at the government.*

give way (to someone or something) to yield to someone or something; to get out of the way of someone or something. □ *All the cars gave way to the fire engine.* □ *The law requires them to give way.* □ *The children gave way to the teen-agers. They didn't want to argue with them.*

given to understand See *give someone to understand something.*

gloss over something to cover up or conceal an error; to make something appear right by minimizing or concealing the flaws. □ *When Mr. Brown was selling me the car, he tried to gloss over its defects.* □ *When I asked the teacher not to gloss over the flaws of the school, he got angry.*

glutton for punishment someone who seems to like doing or seeking out difficult, unpleasant, or badly paid tasks. □ *If you work for this charity, you'll have to be a glutton for punishment and work long hours for nothing.* □ *Jane must be a real glutton for punishment. She's typing Bill's manuscript free of charge and he doesn't even thank her.*

go a long way in doing something See the following entry.

go a long way towards doing something AND **go a long way in doing something** to satisfy specific conditions almost completely; to be almost right. □ *This machine goes a long way towards meeting our needs.* □ *Your plan went a long way in helping us with our problem.*

go about doing something AND **set about doing something** to do something (in a particular manner); to approach the doing of something. □ *I don't know how to go about painting the house.* □ *That isn't the proper way to set about baking a cake.*

go about one's business to mind one's business; to move elsewhere and mind one's own business. □ *Leave me alone! Just go about your business!* □ *I have no more to say. I would be pleased if you would go about your business.*

go after someone or something to pursue someone or something; to chase someone or something. □ *The entire sales staff is out going after new business.* □ *In the race, Tom is the one to beat. Why not go after him?*

go against the grain to go against the natural direction or inclination. □ *You can't expect me to help you cheat. That goes against the grain.* □ *Would it go against the grain for you to lend her money?*

go ahead (with something) to start something; to continue with something. □ *I hope we can go ahead with this project soon.* □ *If we cannot go ahead, we'll have to make new plans.*

go all out to use all one's resources; to be very thorough. (Informal.) □ *Whenever they have a party, they really go all out.* □ *My cousin is coming for a visit, and she expects us to go all out.*

go all the way (to somewhere) to travel the total distance to a place. □ *I don't want to go all the way to Wales.* □ *All right. You don't have to go all the way.*

go all the way (with someone) to have sexual intercourse with someone. (Euphemistic. Use with caution.) □ *If you go all the way, you stand a chance of getting pregnant.* □ *He tried to persuade her to go all the way with him.*

go along for the ride to accompany (someone) for the pleasure of being in a car, etc. □ *Join us. You can go along for the ride.* □ *I don't really need to visit the shops, but I'll go along for the ride.*

go along (with someone or something) 1. to move or travel along with someone or something. □ *John is going to California. I think I'll go along with him.* □ *When I go sailing, I love to go along with the wind.* 2. to agree to something. □ *All right. I'll go along with your plan.* □ *I'm sure that John won't want to go along with it.* 3. to agree with someone. □ *I go along with Sally. I'm sure she's right.* □ *I can't go along with John. He doesn't know what he's talking about.*

go ape (over someone or something) to become very excited and enthusiastic about someone or something. (Slang.) □ *I really go ape over chocolate ice-cream.* □ *Tom really goes ape over Mary.*

go (a)round in circles to be or act confused. (Informal.) □ *I'm so busy I'm going around in circles.* □ *I can't work any more. I'm so tired that I'm going round in circles.*

go (a)round the bend to go crazy; to lose one's mind. (Slang.) □ *If I don't get some rest, I'll go round the bend.* □ *Poor Bob. He has been having trouble for a long time. He finally went around the bend.*

go around with someone See *hang around (with someone); run around with someone.*

go astray 1. to leave the proper path (literally or figuratively). □ *Stay right on the road. Don't go astray and get lost.* □ *Follow the rules I've given you and don't go astray. That'll keep you out of trouble.* 2. to get lost or mislaid. □ *The parcel has gone astray.* □ *One of the papers you need went astray.*

go at it hammer and tongs See *fight someone or something hammer and tongs.*

go at it tooth and nail See *fight someone or something hammer and tongs.*

go at someone or something to attack someone or something; to move or lunge towards someone or something. □ *The dog went at the visitor and almost bit him.* □ *He went at the door and tried to break it down.*

go away empty-handed to depart with nothing. (Compare to *come away empty-handed.*) □ *I'm sorry that you're going away empty-handed, but I cannot afford to contribute any money.* □ *They came hoping for some food, but they had to go away empty-handed.*

go AWOL See under *absent without leave.*

go back on one's word to break a promise which one has made. □ *I hate to go back on my word, but I won't pay you £100 after all.* □ *Going back on your word makes you a liar.*

go bad to become rotten. □ *I'm afraid that this apple has gone bad.* □ *Fish goes bad quickly in hot weather.*

go bananas to go crazy or become silly. (Slang.) □ *Whenever I see Sally, I just go bananas! She's fantastic.* □ *This was a horrible day! I almost went bananas.*

go begging AND **go (a-)begging** to be unwanted or unused. (As if a thing were begging for an owner or a user.) □ *There is still food left. A whole lobster is going begging. Please eat some more.* □ *There are many excellent books in the library just going a-begging because people don't know they are there.*

go broke to run out of money and other assets. □ *This company is going to go broke if you don't stop spending money foolishly.* □ *I made some bad investments last year, and it looks as though I may go broke this year.*

go by the board to get ruined or lost. (This is a nautical expression meaning to fall or be washed overboard.) □ *I hate to see good food go by the board. Please eat up so we won't have to throw it out.* □ *Your plan has gone by the board. The entire project has been cancelled.*

go chase oneself to go away (and stop being a nuisance). (Slang.) □ *He was bothering me, so I told him to go chase himself.* □ *Get out, you pest! Go chase yourself!*

go cold turkey See under *cold turkey.*

go down fighting to continue the struggle until one is completely defeated. □ *I won't give up easily. I'll go down fighting.* □ *Sally, who is very determined, went down fighting.*

go down in history to be remembered as historically important. □ *Wellington went down in history as a famous general.* □ *This is the greatest affair of the century. I bet it'll go down in history.*

go down like a lead balloon to fail, especially to fail to be funny. □ *Your joke went down like a lead balloon.* □ *If that play was supposed to be a comedy, it went down like a lead balloon.*

go downhill [for something] to decline and grow worse and worse. (Also used literally.) □ *This industry is going downhill. We lose money every year.* □ *As one gets older, one tends to go downhill.*

go Dutch to share the cost of a meal or some other event with someone; to participate in a *Dutch treat.* □ JANE: *Let's*

go out and eat. MARY: *Okay, but let's go Dutch.* □ *It's getting expensive to have Sally for a friend. She never wants to go Dutch.*

go easy (on someone or something) 1. to be kind or gentle with someone or something. □ *Go easy on Tom. He just got out of the hospital.* □ *Go easy on the cat. It doesn't like to be teased.* □ *Okay, I'll go easy.* 2. [with *something*] to use something sparingly. □ *Go easy on the mustard. That's all there is.* □ *Please go easy on the onions. I don't like them very much.*

go for it to make a try for something; to decide to do something. (Slang.) □ *I have an offer of a new job. I think I'm going to go for it.* □ *That's great. Go for it!*

go for someone or something 1. to move towards someone or something; to reach for someone or something. □ *John was very close to the edge. Bill went for John and caught him just in time.* □ *John went for the door, but turned and came back without opening it.* 2. to go out and find someone or something. □ *Who went for pizza?* □ *I went for Mary, but she wasn't ready. I'll go back for her later.* 3. to go at someone or something; to attack someone or something. □ *The dog went for the robber and drove him back.* □ *The robber started to go for the guard, but stopped suddenly.* 4. [with *someone*] to desire someone. (Informal. Usually with *could,* as in the examples. Compare to *fall for someone or something* and *could do with someone or something.*) □ *Look at that attractive boy. I could really go for him.* □ *He said he could really go for her sister.*

go from bad to worse to progress from a bad state to a worse state. □ *This is a terrible day. Things are going from bad to worse.* □ *My cold is awful. It went from bad to worse in just an hour.*

go great guns to go fast or energetically. (Informal.) □ *I'm over my cold and going great guns.* □ *Business is great. We are going great guns selling ice-cream.*

go hand in hand See under *hand in hand.*

go haywire to go wrong; to malfunction; to break down. (Informal.) □ *We were all organized, but our plans suddenly went haywire.* □ *There we were, driving along, when the engine went haywire. It was two hours before the breakdown lorry came.*

go in a body to move in a group. □ *The whole team went in a body to talk to the coach.* □ *Each of us was afraid to go alone, so we went in a body.*

go in for something to take part in something; to enjoy (doing) something. □ *John doesn't go in for sports.* □ *None of them seems to go in for swimming.*

go in one ear and out the other [for something] to be heard and then forgotten. (Informal.) □ *Everything I say to you seems to go in one ear and out the other. Why don't you pay attention?* □ *I can't concentrate. Things people say to me just go in one ear and out the other.*

go into a nosedive AND **take a nosedive** **1.** [for a plane] suddenly to dive towards the ground, nose first. □ *It was a bad day for flying, and I was afraid we'd go into a nosedive.* □ *The small plane took a nosedive. The pilot was able to bring it out at the last minute, so the plane didn't crash.* **2.** to go into a rapid emotional or financial decline, or a decline in health. (Informal.) □ *Our profits took a nosedive last year.* □ *After breaking his hip, Mr. Brown's health went into a nosedive, and he never recovered.*

go into a tail-spin **1.** [for a plane] to lose control and spin to the earth, nose first. □ *The plane shook and then suddenly went into a tail-spin.* □ *The pilot was not able to bring the plane out of the tail-spin, and it crashed into the sea.* **2.** [for someone] to become disoriented or panicked; [for someone's life] to fall apart. (Informal.) □ *Although John was a great success, his personal life went into a tail-spin. It took him a year to get straightened out.* □ *After her fa-*

ther died, Mary's world fell apart, and she went into a tail-spin.

go into action AND **swing into action** to start doing something. □ *I usually get to work at 7:45, and I go into action at 8:00.* □ *When the ball comes in my direction, you should see me swing into action.*

go into effect AND **take effect** [for a law or a rule] to become effective. □ *When does this new law go into effect?* □ *The new tax laws won't go into effect until next year.* □ *This law takes effect almost immediately.*

go into orbit to get very excited; to be in ecstasy. (Slang. Also used literally.) □ *When I got a letter from my boyfriend in Australia, I almost went into orbit.* □ *Tom goes into orbit every time his team scores.*

go into something to start something new. (Especially a new career, project, product line, etc.) □ *I may give up selling and go into management.* □ *We are shifting production away from glass bottles, and we are going into vases and other decorative containers.* □ *After she graduated, she went into law.*

go it alone to do something by oneself. (Informal.) □ *Do you need help, or will you go it alone?* □ *I think I need a little more experience before I go it alone.*

go like clockwork to progress with regularity and dependability. □ *The building project is progressing nicely. Everything is going like clockwork.* □ *The elaborate pageant was a great success. It went like clockwork from start to finish.*

go off **1.** [for someone] to go away (from other people). □ *It was a very busy day. At lunch-time, I went off to think.* □ *You need to go off by yourself and do some hard thinking.* **2.** [for something] to explode. □ *The fireworks didn't go off when they were supposed to.* □ *There was a bomb in the building, but it didn't go off.*

go off at a tangent to go off suddenly in another direction; suddenly to change one's line of thought, course of action, etc. (A reference to geometry. Plural: **go off at tangents**.) □ *Please stick to one subject and don't go off at a tangent.* □ *If Mary would settle down and deal with one subject she would be all right, but she keeps going off at tangents.*

go off at half cock to proceed without proper preparation; to speak (about something) without adequate knowledge. (Informal.) □ *Their plans are always going off at halfcock.* □ *Get your facts straight before you make your presentation. There is nothing worse than going off at half cock.*

go off the deep end to become angry or hysterical; to lose one's temper. (Informal. Refers to going into a swimming-pool at the deep end—rather than the shallow end—and finding oneself *in deep water.*) □ *Her father went off the deep end when she came in late.* □ *The teacher went off the deep end when she saw his work.*

go on **1.** See *go on (doing something).* **2.** (Usually **Go on!**) Stop saying those things!; Not so!; I don't believe you! □ *Go on! You don't know what you're talking about!* □ *Oh, go on! You're just trying to flatter me.*

go on a binge to do too much of something; to do something excessively. (Slang. Especially to drink too much.) □ *Jane went on a binge last night and is very sick this morning.* □ *Bill loves to spend money on clothes. He's out on a binge right now—buying everything in sight.*

go on an errand See *run an errand.*

go on and on to (seem to) last or go forever. □ *You talk too much, Bob. You just go on and on.* □ *The road to their house is very boring. It goes on and on with nothing interesting to look at.*

go on (doing something) AND **go on (with something)** to continue doing something. □ *How long can that man go on talking?* □ *Please go on with your* reading. *I'm finished talking now.* □ *This play is really boring. How long can it go on?* □ *It's safe to cross the street now, so go on and cross.*

go on (with something) See the previous entry.

go one better to do something superior to that which someone else has done; to top someone. □ *That was a great joke, but I can go one better.* □ *He may have travelled a lot, but I can go one better.*

go out (for something) to leave one's home to do something. (Usually refers to food or entertainment.) □ *Let's go out for dinner.* □ *Mother likes to go out.* □ *Do you want to go out for a walk?*

go out of one's way (to do something) **1.** to travel an indirect route in order to do something. □ *I'll have to go out of my way to give you a lift home.* □ *I'll give you a lift even though I have to go out of my way.* **2.** to make the effort to do something; to accept the bother of doing something. □ *We went out of our way to please the visitor.* □ *We appreciate anything you can do, but don't go out of your way.*

go (out) on strike [for a group of people] to stop working at their jobs until certain demands are met. □ *If we don't have a contract by midday tomorrow, we'll go out on strike.* □ *The entire work-force went on strike at midday.*

go out (with someone) **1.** to go out with someone for entertainment. □ *The Smiths went out with the Franklins to the cinema.* □ *Those chaps don't have much time to go out.* **2.** to go on a date with someone; to date someone regularly; to be someone's girlfriend or boy-friend. □ *Is Bob still going out with Sally?* □ *No, they've stopped going out.*

go over someone's head [for the intellectual content of something] to be too difficult for someone to understand. □ *All that talk about computers went over my head.* □ *I hope my lecture didn't go over the pupils' heads.*

go over something to review or explain something. □ *The teacher went over the lesson.* □ *Will you please go over this form? I don't understand it.*

go over something with a fine-tooth comb AND **search something with a fine-tooth comb** to search through something very carefully. (As if one were searching for something very tiny lost in some kind of fibre.) □ *I can't find my calculus book. I went over the whole place with a fine-tooth comb.* □ *I searched this place with a fine-tooth comb and didn't find my ring.*

go over the top See under *over the top.*

go overboard **1.** to fall off of or out of a boat or ship. □ *Don't stand near the side of the boat. You'll go overboard.* □ *That man just went overboard. I think he jumped.* **2.** to do too much; to be extravagant. □ *Look, Sally, let's have a nice party, but don't go overboard. It doesn't need to be elaborate.* □ *Okay, you can buy a big comfortable car, but don't go overboard.*

go places to have a good future. (Informal.) □ *Sally shows great promise as a scholar. She's really going to go places.* □ *Tom is as good as we thought. He's certainly going places now.*

go round in circles to keep going over the same ideas or repeating the same actions, often resulting in confusion, without reaching a satisfactory decision or conclusion. □ *We're just going round in circles discussing the problems of the feête. We need to consult someone else to get a new point of view.* □ *Fred's trying to find out what's happened but he's going round in circles. No one will tell him anything useful.*

go scot-free AND **get off scot-free** to go unpunished; to be acquitted of a crime. (This *scot* is an old word meaning "tax" or "tax burden.") □ *The thief went scot-free.* □ *Jane cheated in the test and got caught, but she got off scot-free.*

go sky-high to go very high. (Informal.) □ *Prices go sky-high whenever there is*

inflation. □ *Oh, it's so hot. The temperature went sky-high about midday.*

go so far as to say something to put something into words; to risk saying something. □ *I think that Bob is dishonest, but I wouldn't go so far as to say he's a thief.* □ *Red meat may be harmful in some cases, but I can't go so far as to say it causes cancer.*

go steady (with someone) to date someone on a regular basis. □ *Mary is going steady with John.* □ *Bill went steady for two years before he got married.*

go straight to begin to obey the law; to become law-abiding. (Slang. Primarily criminal slang.) □ *When John got out of prison, he decided to go straight.* □ *I promised the teacher that I would go straight and that I would never cheat again.*

go the distance AND **stay the distance** to do the whole amount; to play the entire game; to run the whole race. (Informal. Originally sports use.) □ *That horse runs fast. I hope it can go the distance.* □ *This is going to be a long, hard project. I hope I can go the distance.* □ *Jim changes jobs a lot. He never stays the distance.*

go the whole hog to do everything possible; to be extravagant. (Informal.) □ *Let's go the whole hog. Order steak and lobster.* □ *Show some restraint. Don't go the whole hog and leave yourself penniless.*

go through to be approved; to succeed in getting through the approval process. (See also *go through something.*) □ *I sent the board of directors a proposal. I hope it goes through.* □ *We all hope that the new law goes through.*

go through something **1.** to pass through something. □ *The speeding car went through the traffic lights.* □ *The visitor said goodbye and went through the door to the hallway.* **2.** to examine something. □ *Give me a day or two to go through this contract, and then I'll call you with advice.* □ *Don't go through it* too fast. *Read it carefully, or you might miss something.* **3.** to experience something; to endure something unpleasant; to *get through something.* □ *It was a terrible thing. I don't know how I went through it.* □ *It'll take four years to go through college.*

go through the motions to make a feeble effort to do something; to pretend to do something. □ *Jane isn't doing her best. She's just going through the motions.* □ *Bill was supposed to be raking the garden, but he was just going through the motions.*

go through the proper channels to proceed by consulting the proper persons or offices. □ *If you want an answer to your question, you'll have to go through the proper channels.* □ *Your application will have to go through the proper channels.*

go through the roof **1.** to go very high; to reach a very high degree (of something). (Informal.) □ *It's so hot! The temperature is going through the roof.* □ *Prices are going through the roof.* **2.** AND **hit the roof** to become very angry. □ *Mr. Brown went through the roof when his son crashed the car.* □ *She hit the roof when she saw the mess.*

go through with something to decide to do something; to finish something. □ *We decided to go through with the new motorway.* □ *I can't do it. I just can't go through with it.*

go to See *go to hell.*

go to any lengths to do whatever is necessary. □ *I'll go to any lengths to secure this contract.* □ *I want to get a college degree, but I won't go to any lengths to get one.*

go to bed (with someone) to have sexual intercourse with someone. (Euphemism.) □ *He tries to get all the girls to go to bed with him.* □ *They didn't go to bed together before they were married.*

go to Davy Jones's locker to go to the bottom of the sea; to drown. (Thought of as a nautical expression.) □ *My un-*

cle was a sailor. *He went to Davy Jones's locker during a terrible storm.* □ *My camera fell overboard and went to Davy Jones's locker.*

go to hell AND **go to; go to the devil** to go away and stop bothering (someone). (Informal. Use caution with *hell.*) □ *He told her to go to hell, that he didn't want her.* □ *Leave me alone! Go to the devil!*

go to hell in a handbasket to become totally worthless; to *go to hell.* (Informal. Use caution with *hell.* Not used as a command.) □ *The whole country is going to hell in a handbasket.* □ *Look at my lawn—full of weeds. It's going to hell in a handbasket.*

go to pieces AND **fall to pieces** **1.** to break into pieces; to *fall apart.* □ *The fabric just fell to pieces.* □ *The furniture fell to pieces.* **2.** to break out in tears; to break down mentally. □ *On hearing of the death, we just went to pieces.* □ *I couldn't talk about it any longer. I went to pieces.*

go to pot AND **go to the dogs** to go to ruin; to deteriorate. (Slang.) □ *My whole life seems to be going to pot.* □ *My lawn is going to pot. I had better weed it.* □ *The government is going to the dogs.*

go to rack and ruin AND **go to wrack and ruin** to go to ruin. (The words *rack* and *wrack* mean "wreckage" and are found only in this expression.) □ *That lovely old house on the corner is going to go to rack and ruin.* □ *My lawn is going to wrack and ruin.*

go to seed See *run to seed.*

go to someone's head to make someone conceited; to make someone overly proud. □ *You did a fine job, but don't let it go to your head.* □ *He let his success go to his head, and soon he became a complete failure.*

go to the devil See *go to hell.*

go to the dogs See *go to pot.*

go to the expense of doing something to pay the (large) cost of doing something.

□ *I hate to have to go to the expense of painting the house.* □ *Don't go to the expense of taking us out to a meal.*

go to the limit to do as much as is possible to do. □ *Okay, we can't afford it, but we'll go to the limit.* □ *How far shall I go? Shall I go to the limit?*

go to the toilet to eliminate bodily wastes through defecation and urination. □ *The child needed to go to the toilet.* □ *After drinking so much he wanted to go to the toilet.*

go to the trouble (of doing something) AND **go to the trouble (to do something)** to endure the bother of doing something. □ *I really don't want to go to the trouble to cook.* □ *Should I go to the trouble of cooking something for her to eat?* □ *Don't go to the trouble. She can eat a sandwich.*

go to the trouble (to do something) See the previous entry.

go to the wall to be defeated; to fail in business. (Informal.) □ *During the recession, many small companies went to the wall.* □ *The company went to the wall because of that contract. Now it's broke and the employees are redundant.*

go to town to make a great effort; to work with energy or enthusiasm. (Informal.) □ *They really went to town on cleaning the house. It's spotless.* □ *You've really gone to town with the food for the party.*

go to waste to be wasted; to be unused (and therefore thrown away). □ *Eat your potatoes! Don't let them go to waste.* □ *He never practices on the piano. It's sad to see talent going to waste.*

go to wrack and ruin See *go to rack and ruin.*

go together 1. [for two things] to look, sound, or taste well together. □ *Do you think that this pink one and this purple one go together?* □ *Milk and grapefruit don't go together.* 2. [for two people] to date each other regularly. □ *Bob and Ann have been going together*

for months. □ *Tom and Jane want to go together, but they live too far apart.*

go too far to do more than is acceptable. □ *I didn't mind at first, but now you've gone too far.* □ *If you go too far, I'll slap you.*

go under 1. to pass underneath (something). □ *I couldn't get over it, so I went under.* □ *It was too tall to climb, so we went under.* 2. to fail. (Informal.) □ *The company was weak from the start, and it finally went under.* □ *Tom had a lot of trouble in school, and finally he went under.*

go under the knife to have a surgical operation. (Informal.) □ *Mary didn't want to go under the knife, but the doctor insisted.* □ *If I go under the knife, I want to be completely asleep.*

go up in flames AND **go up in smoke** to burn up. □ *The whole museum went up in flames.* □ *My paintings—my whole life's work—went up in flames.* □ *What a shame for all that to go up in smoke.*

go up in smoke See the previous entry.

go with someone or something 1. [with *someone*] to accompany someone. □ *Daddy is leaving now. Why don't you go with him?* □ *Sally is going with him in the car.* 2. [with *something*] to go well with something. □ *That hat goes well with that dress.* □ *Pink doesn't go with orange.*

go without (something) to manage to get along without something. (Compare to *do without (someone or something).)* □ *I went without food for three days.* □ *Some people have to go without a lot longer than that.*

go wrong to fail; [for something bad] to happen. □ *The project failed. I don't know what went wrong.* □ *I'm afraid that everything will go wrong.*

goes to show (someone) [something] serves to prove [something] to someone. □ *His teeth are rotten. It just goes to show you that too much sugar is bad for you.* □ *Of course you shouldn't have* married her. *It goes to show you that your parents are always right.* □ *Look at what happened. It just goes to show that you can't be too careful.*

goes without saying [something] is so obvious that it need not be said. □ *It goes without saying that you must keep the place clean.* □ *Of course. That goes without saying.*

gone died. (Euphemistic.) □ *Both her parents are gone now.* □ *Let us remember those who have gone before.*

good and something very something. (The *something* can be *ready, angry, tired, worn out,* etc.) □ *Now I'm good and angry, and I'm going to fight back.* □ *I'll be there when I'm good and ready.* □ *He'll go to bed when he's good and tired.*

good enough for someone or something adequate or fine for someone or something. □ *This seat is good enough for me. I don't want to move.* □ *That table isn't good enough for my office.*

good-for-nothing a worthless person. □ *Tell that good-for-nothing to go home at once.* □ *Bob can't get a job. He's such a good-for-nothing.*

good riddance (to bad rubbish) [it is] good to be rid (of worthless persons or things). □ *She slammed the door behind me and said, "Good riddance to bad rubbish!"* □ *"Good riddance to you, madam," thought I.*

grasp the nettle to tackle a difficult or unpleasant task with firmness and determination. □ *We must grasp the nettle and do something about our overspending.* □ *The education committee is reluctant to grasp the nettle of lack of textbooks.*

grease someone's palm to bribe someone. (Slang.) □ *If you want to get something done around here, you have to grease someone's palm.* □ *I'd never try to grease a policemen's palm. That's illegal.*

Greek to me unintelligible to me. (Usually with some form of *be*.) □ *I can't*

understand it. *It's Greek to me.* □ *It's Greek to me. Maybe Sally knows what it means.*

green around the gills See *pale around the gills.*

green with envy envious; jealous. □ *When Sally saw me with Tom, she turned green with envy. She likes him a lot.* □ *I feel green with envy whenever I see you in your new car.*

grey area an area of a subject, etc., which is difficult to put into a particular category as it is not clearly defined and may have connections or associations with more than one category. □ *The responsibility for social studies in the college is a grey area. Several departments are involved.* □ *Publicity is a grey area in that firm. It is shared between the marketing and design divisions.*

grey matter intelligence; brains; power of thought. (Informal.) □ *Use your grey matter and think what will happen if the committee resigns.* □ *Surely they'll come up with an acceptable solution if they use a bit of grey matter.*

grin and bear it to endure something unpleasant with good humour. □ *There is nothing you can do but grin and bear it.* □ *I hate having to work for rude people, but I suppose I have to grin and bear it.*

grind to a halt to slow to a stop. □ *By the end of the day, the factory had ground to a halt.* □ *The train ground to a halt, and we got out to stretch our legs.*

grist to the mill something which can be put to good use or which can bring advantage or profit. (Grist was corn brought to a mill to be ground and so kept the mill operating.) □ *Some of the jobs that we are offered are more interesting than others, but all is grist to the mill.* □ *The firm is having to sell rather ugly souvenirs, but they are grist to the mill and keep the firm in business.*

grit one's teeth to grind one's teeth together in anger or determination; to show determination. □ *I was so angry that all I could do was stand there and grit my teeth.* □ *All through the race, Sally was gritting her teeth. She was really determined.*

ground someone to take away someone's privileges. (Informal. Usually said of a teen-ager.) □ *My father said that if I didn't get at least Cs, he'd ground me.* □ *Guess what! He grounded me!*

grow on someone [for something] to become commonplace to a person. (The *someone* is usually *one, someone, a person,* etc., not a specific person.) □ *That music is strange, but it grows on you.* □ *I didn't think I could ever get used to this town, but after a while it grows on one.*

grow out of something 1. to grow too big for something. □ *Tommy has grown out of all his trousers.* □ *I grew out of my shirts, too.* 2. to abandon something as one matures. □ *I used to have a lot of allergies, but I grew out of them.* □ *She grew out of the habit of biting her nails.* ALSO: **outgrow something** 1. to get too big for something. □ *Tom outgrew all his clothes in two months.* □ *The plant outgrew its pot.* 2. to abandon something as one matures; to become too mature for something. □ *I outgrew my allergies.* □ *The boys will outgrow their toys.*

grow up 1. to become adult or mature. □ *When I grow up, I want to be a*

banker. □ *The children all left the village as they grew up.* 2. [for a person] to become physically and mentally mature. □ *Oh, grow up, Tom! You act like a child.* □ *When Bill grows up a little more, he'll be a better pupil.*

guard against someone or something to take care to avoid someone or something. □ *Try to guard against getting a cold.* □ *You should guard against pickpockets.*

guess at something to guess at the answer to something. (The *something* is a question, riddle, etc.) □ *Guess at the answer if you don't know it.* □ *Try to guess at what I have in my hand.*

gum something up AND **gum up the works; gum up something** to make something inoperable; to ruin someone's plans. (Informal.) □ *Please, Bill, be careful and don't gum up the works.* □ *Tom gummed the whole plan up.*

gum up the works See the previous entry.

gun for someone to be looking for someone, presumably to harm the person. (Informal. Originally from Western and gangster films.) □ *The coach is gunning for you. I think he's going to drop you from the team.* □ *I've heard that Tom is gunning for me for going out with his girlfriend, so I'm getting out of town.*

H

had as soon do something AND **would as soon do something** prefer to do something else; to be content to do something. (The *would* or *had* is usually *'d.* Also with *just,* as in the examples.) □ *They want me to go into town. I'd as soon stay at home.* □ *Since that restaurant is not always good, we'd as soon eat somewhere else.* □ *I would just as soon stay at home as see a bad film.* □ *If that's what we're having for dinner, I'd just as soon starve.*

had best do something ought to do something. (Informal. Almost the same as the following entry.) □ *You had best get that fixed right away.* □ *You had best be at school on time every day.*

had better do something ought to do something (or face the consequences). (Almost the same as the previous entry.) □ *I had better get home for dinner, or I'll get shouted at.* □ *You had better do your homework right now.*

had rather do something AND **had sooner do something** prefer to do something. □ *I'd rather go to town than sit here all evening.* □ *They'd rather not.* □ *I'd sooner not make the trip.*

had sooner do something See the previous entry.

hail-fellow-well-met friendly to everyone; falsely friendly to everyone. (Usually said of males.) □ *Yes, he's friendly, sort of hail-fellow-well-met.* □ *He's not a very sincere person. Hail-fellow-well-met—you know the type.* □ *He's one of those hail-fellow-well-met people that you don't quite trust.*

hail from somewhere [for someone] to come originally from somewhere. (Informal.) □ *I'm from Edinburgh. Where do you hail from?* □ *I hail from the Southwest.*

hair of the dog that bit one an alcoholic drink taken when one has a hangover; an alcoholic drink taken when one is recovering from drinking too much alcohol. (Informal.) □ *Oh, I have a terrible headache. I need some of the hair of the dog that bit me.* □ *That's some hangover you've got there, Bob. Here, drink this. It's some of the hair of the dog that bit you.*

hale and hearty well and healthy. □ *Doesn't Ann look hale and hearty after the baby's birth?* □ *I don't feel hale and hearty. I'm really tired.*

Half a loaf is better than none. a proverb meaning that having part of something is better than having nothing. □ *When her rise was smaller than she expected, Sally said, "Half a loaf is better than none."* □ *People who keep saying "Half a loaf is better than none" usually have as much as they need.*

ham something up AND **ham up something** to make a performance seem silly by showing off or exaggerating one's part; to exaggerate actions, a role, etc. (Informal. A show-off actor is known as a *ham.*) □ *The play was going fine until Bob got out there and hammed up his part.* □ *Come on, Bob. Don't ham it up!*

hammer away (at someone or something) to keep trying to accomplish something with someone or something.

□ *John, you've got to keep hammering away at your geometry.* □ *They hammered away at questioning the prisoner until he confessed.* □ *They kept hammering away.*

hammer something home AND **hammer home something** to try extremely hard to make someone understand or realize something. □ *I tried to hammer home to Anne the fact that she would have to get a job.* □ *The boss hopes to hammer home the firm's precarious financial position to the staff.*

hammer something out AND **hammer out something 1.** to flatten something by hammering it. □ *The mechanic hammered out the dent in the car's bumper.* □ *The mechanic hammered the dent out.* **2.** to work hard at writing up an agreement; to work hard at writing something, sometimes without creativity. (As if one were hammering at the keys of a typewriter.) □ *The solicitors sat down to hammer out a contract.* □ *I'm busy hammering my latest novel out.* **3.** to play something on the piano with energy and enthusiasm, sometimes without creativity. □ *Listen to John hammer out that song on the piano.* □ *The soloist did little more than hammer the concerto out.*

hand in glove (with someone) very close to someone. □ *John is really hand in glove with Sally, although they pretend to be on different sides.* □ *The teacher and the headmaster work hand in glove.*

hand in hand holding hands. □ *They walked down the street hand in hand.* □ *Bob and Mary sat there quietly, hand in hand.* ALSO: **go hand in hand** together, one with the other. (Said of two things, the presence of either of which implies the other.) □ *Biscuits and milk seem to go hand in hand.* □ *Teenagers and arguing often go hand in hand.*

hand it to someone give credit to someone, often with some reluctance. (Informal. Often with *have to* or *must*.) □ *I must hand it to you. You did a fine job.* □ *We must hand it to Sally. She helped us a lot.*

hand-me-down something, such as an article of used clothing, which has been handed down from someone. (Informal. See *hand something down to someone*.) □ *Why do I always have to wear my brother's hand-me-downs? I want some new clothes.* □ *This is a nice shirt. It doesn't look like a hand-me-down at all.*

hand over fist [for money and merchandise to be exchanged] very rapidly. □ *What a busy day. We took in money hand over fist.* □ *They were buying things hand over fist.*

hand over hand [moving] one hand after the other (again and again). □ *Sally pulled in the rope hand over hand.* □ *The man climbed the rope hand over hand.*

hand something down to someone AND **hand down something to someone** to give something to a younger person. (Either at death or during life. See also *hand-me-down*.) □ *John handed his old shirts down to his younger brother.* □ *I hope my uncle will hand down his golf-clubs to me when he dies.*

hand something in AND **hand in something** to submit something by hand. □ *Did you hand your application form in?* □ *I forgot to hand in my test paper.*

hand something on (to someone) AND **hand on something (to someone)** to pass something on to someone. □ *This watch was given to me by my grandfather. I'll hand it on to my grandson.* □ *Would you please hand the tray of food on to the next person?* □ *Yes, please hand on the tray. I'm hungry.*

hand something out (to someone) AND **hand out something (to someone)** to distribute something; to pass something out to someone. □ *Please hand out these papers to everyone.* □ *I'll hand them out.* □ *Look! They are handing sweets out! Get some!*

hand something over AND **hand over something** to give something (to someone); to relinquish something (to someone); to turn something over (to someone). □ *Come* *on, John! Hand over my wallet.* □ *Please hand this over to the guard.*

handle someone with kid gloves to be very careful with a sensitive or touchy person. □ *Bill has become so sensitive. You really have to handle him with kid gloves.* □ *You don't have to handle me with kid gloves. I can take what you have to tell me.*

Hands off! Do not touch (someone or something). □ *Careful! Don't touch that wire. Hands off!* □ *The sign says, "Hands off!" and you had better do what it says.*

Hands up! AND **Stick 'em up!** Put your hands in the air. (Slang. Said by robbers and police officers.) □ *All right, you, hands up!* □ *Stick 'em up! I got you covered.*

Handsome is as handsome does. a proverb meaning that it is all very well to be good-looking, but good looks have their limitations and one really needs other qualities. □ *Handsome is as handsome does. Jack is good-looking, but he will need to convince Sally's father that he can support a wife.* □ *Sam may look like a film-star, but his manners are horrible. Handsome is as handsome does.*

hang around (with someone) AND **go around with someone** to spend a lot of time with someone; to waste away time with someone. (Informal. See also *run around with someone.*) □ *John hangs around with Bill a lot.* □ *They've been going around with the Smiths.* □ *I've asked them all to stop hanging around.*

hang back to stay behind (the others); to hold back (from the others). □ *Walk with the group, Bob. Don't hang back. You'll get left behind.* □ *Three of the marchers hung back and talked to each other.*

hang by a hair AND **hang by a thread** to be in an uncertain position; to depend on something very insubstantial; to *hang in the balance.* (Informal.) □ *Your whole argument is hanging by a thread.* □ *John hasn't yet failed geometry, but his fate is hanging by a hair.*

hang fire to delay or wait; to be delayed. □ *I think we should hang fire and wait for other information.* □ *Our plans have to hang fire until we get planning permission.*

hang in the balance to be in an undecided state; to be between two equal possibilities. (See also *in the balance.*) □ *The prisoner stood before the judge with his life hanging in the balance.* □ *The fate of the entire project is hanging in the balance.*

hang in there to keep trying; to persevere. (Slang.) □ *I know things are tough, John, but hang in there.* □ *I know if I hang in there, things will come out okay.*

hang loose to relax; to remain calm. (Slang.) □ *I know I can pass this test if I just hang loose.* □ *Hang loose, Bob. Everything is going to be all right.*

hang on 1. be prepared for fast or rough movement. (Usually a command.) □ *Hang on! The train is going very fast.* □ *Hang on! We're going to crash!* 2. to continue; to persevere. □ *If you can hang on, we'll rescue you as soon as possible.* □ *He hung on as long as he could.* 3. to wait for a short time. □ *Hang on, I won't be a minute.* □ *Could you hang on until I run home?* 4. to pause in a telephone conversation. □ *Please hang on until I get a pen.* □ *If you'll hang on, I'll get her.*

hang on someone's coat-tails to make one's good fortune or success depend on another person. (Also with *else,* as in the examples.) □ *Bill isn't very creative, so he hangs on John's coat-tails.* □ *Some people just have to hang on somebody else's coat-tails.*

hang on someone's every word to listen carefully and obsequiously to everything someone says. □ *He gave a great lecture. We hung on his every word.* □ *Look at the way John hangs on Mary's every word. He must be in love with her.*

hang on to someone or something AND **hold on to someone or something** 1. to keep someone or something in one's grasp; to hold someone or something tightly. □ *The child hung on to her mother and cried and cried.* □ *Please hang on to your purse. It might get stolen.* **2.** to remember someone or something for a long time; to be affected very much by someone or something in the past. □ *That's a nice thought, Bob. Hang on to it.* □ *You've been holding on to those bad memories for too long. It's time to let them go.*

Hang on to your hat! AND **Hold on to your hat!** Prepare for a sudden surprise or shock. (Informal.) □ *Are you ready to hear the final score? Hang on to your hat! We won ten nothing!* □ *Guess who got married. Hold on to your hat!*

hang one's hat up somewhere to take up residence somewhere. (Informal.) □ *George loves London. He's decided to buy a flat and hang his hat up there.* □ *Bill moves from place to place and never hangs his hat up anywhere.*

hang out (somewhere) to spend time somewhere; to waste time somewhere. (Informal.) □ *I wish you boys wouldn't hang out around the bowling lanes.* □ *Why do you have to hang out near our house?*

hang out with someone frequently to be in the company of someone. (Informal.) □ *I hope Bob isn't hanging out with the wrong people.* □ *He needs to spend more time studying and less time hanging out with his friends.*

hang together to be or stay (figuratively or literally) united. □ *If our group hangs together, we can accomplish a lot.* □ *Your argument doesn't hang together.*

hang up to replace the telephone receiver. □ *If you have called a wrong number, you should apologize before you hang up.* □ *When you hear the engaged signal, you're supposed to hang up.* ALSO: **hang-up** a personal problem; an obsession. (Slang. See also *hung up (on someone or something).*) □ *John has a lot of hang-ups he's going to have*

to get over before he can relax. □ *I'm tired of hearing about your hang-ups.*

happen on someone or something to find someone or something unexpectedly. □ *I happened on this nice little restaurant in Pine Street yesterday.* □ *Mr. Simpson and I happened on one another in the bank last week.*

hard-and-fast rule a strict rule. □ *It's a hard-and-fast rule that you must be home by midnight.* □ *You should have your project completed by the end of the month, but it's not a hard-and-fast rule.*

hard cash cash, not cheques or credit. (Informal.) □ *I want to be paid in hard cash, and I want to be paid now!* □ *No plastic money for me. I want hard cash.*

hard nut to crack AND **tough nut to crack** difficult person or thing to deal with. (Informal.) □ *This problem is getting me down. It's a hard nut to crack.* □ *Tom sure is a hard nut to crack. I can't make him out.* □ *He certainly is a tough nut to crack.*

hard on someone's heels following someone very closely. (Informal.) □ *I ran as fast as I could, but the dog was still hard on my heels.* □ *Here comes Sally, and John is hard on her heels.*

hard on the heels of something soon after something. (Informal.) □ *There was a rainstorm hard on the heels of the high winds.* □ *They had a child hard on the heels of getting married.*

hard pressed (to do something) See the following entry.

hard put (to do something) AND **hard pressed (to do something)** able to do something only with great difficulty. □ *I'm hard put to come up with enough money to pay the rent.* □ *We'll be hard pressed to get there on time.* □ *I can't pay you just now. I'm a bit hard pressed.*

hard up for something greatly in need of something, usually money. (Informal.) □ *Ann was hard up for the cash to pay the bills.* □ *I was so hard up, I couldn't* *afford to buy food.* □ *The press were hard up for news.*

hardly have time to breathe to be very busy. □ *This was such a busy day. I hardly had time to breathe.* □ *They made him work so hard that he hardly had time to breathe.*

hark(en) back to something (*Harken* is an old form of *hark*, which is an old word meaning "listen.") **1.** to have originated as something; to have started out as something. □ *The word icebox harks back to refrigerators which were cooled by ice.* □ *Our modern breakfast cereals hark back to the porridge and gruel of our ancestors.* **2.** to remind one of something. □ *Seeing a horse and buggy in the park harks back to the time when horses drew milk wagons.* □ *Sally says it harkens back to the time when everything was delivered by horse-drawn wagon.*

harp on about something to keep talking about something; to refer to something again and again. (Informal.) □ *Mary's always harping on about being poor, but she has more than enough money.* □ *Jack has been harping on about looking for a new job for years.*

Haste makes waste. a proverb meaning that time gained in doing something rapidly and carelessly will be lost when one has to do the thing over again correctly. □ *Now, take your time. Haste makes waste.* □ *Haste makes waste, so be careful as you work.*

hate someone's guts to hate someone very much. (Informal.) □ *Oh, Bob is terrible. I hate his guts!* □ *You may hate my guts for saying so, but I think you're getting grey hairs.*

haul someone in AND **haul in someone** to arrest someone; [for a police officer] to take someone to the police station. (Slang.) □ *The police hauled the crook in.* □ *The policeman said, "Do you want me to haul you in?"*

haul someone over the coals to give someone a severe scolding. □ *My mother hauled me over the coals for*

coming in late last night. □ *The manager hauled me over the coals for being late again.*

have a ball to have a really enjoyable time. (Slang. This *ball* is a formal social dancing affair.) □ *The picnic was fantastic. We had a ball!* □ *Have a ball at the party tonight!*

have a bee in one's bonnet to have an idea or a thought remain in one's mind; to have an obsession. □ *She has a bee in her bonnet about table manners.* □ *I had a bee in my bonnet about swimming. I couldn't stop wanting to go swimming.*

have a big mouth to be a gossiper; to be a person who tells secrets. (Informal.) □ *Mary has a big mouth. She told Bob what I was getting him for his birthday.* □ *You shouldn't say things like that about people all the time. Everyone will say you have a big mouth.*

have a blow-out (Informal.) **1.** to have one of one's car tyres burst. □ *I had a blow-out on the way here. I nearly lost control of the car.* □ *If you have a blow-out in one tyre, you should check the other tyres.* **2.** to have a celebration or party. □ *We had a real blow-out when Jane and Bob married.* □ *The office has an annual blow-out at Christmas.*

have a bone to pick (with someone) to have a matter to discuss with someone; to have something to argue about with someone. □ *Look, Bill. I've got a bone to pick with you. Where is the money you owe me?* □ *I had a bone to pick with her, but she was so sweet that I forgot about it.* □ *Ted and Alice have a bone to pick.*

have a bright idea See *get a bright idea.*

have a brush with something to have a brief contact with something; to have a brief experience of something, especially with the law. (Sometimes a *close* brush.) □ *Ann had a close brush with the law. She was nearly arrested for speeding.* □ *When I was younger, I had a brush with death in a car accident, but I recovered.*

have a case (against someone) to have much evidence which can be used against someone in court. (*Have* can be replaced with *build, gather, assemble,* etc.) □ *Do the police have a case against John?* □ *No, they don't have a case.* □ *They are trying to build a case against him.* □ *My solicitor is busy assembling a case against the other driver.*

have a chip on one's shoulder to feel resentful; to bear resentment. □ *What are you angry at? You always seem to have a chip on your shoulder.* □ *John has had a chip on his shoulder about the police ever since he got his speeding ticket.*

have a clean conscience (about someone or something) See the following entry.

have a clear conscience (about someone or something) AND **have a clean conscience (about someone or something)** to be free of guilt about someone or something. □ *I'm sorry that John got the blame. I have a clear conscience about the whole affair.* □ *I have a clear conscience about John and his problems.* □ *I didn't do it. I have a clean conscience.* □ *She can't sleep at nights because she doesn't have a clear conscience.*

have a close call See the following entry.

have a close shave AND **have a close call** to have a narrow escape from something dangerous. (See also *have a brush with something.*) □ *What a close shave I had! I nearly fell off the roof when I was working there.* □ *I almost got struck by a speeding car. It was a close call.*

have a crack at something to give something a try; to make an attempt to do something. (Informal.) □ *I don't think I can persuade her to leave, but I'll have a crack at it.* □ *Someone had to try to rescue the child. Bill said he'd have a crack at it.*

have a crush on someone See *get a crush on someone.*

have a down on someone to treat someone in an unfair or hostile way; to have hostile feelings towards someone; to re-

sent and oppose someone. □ *That teacher's had a down on me ever since I was expelled from another school.* □ *The supervisor has a down on anyone who refuses to work overtime.*

have a falling-out (with someone) (over something) See under *fall out (with someone) (over something).*

have a familiar ring [for a story or an explanation] to sound familiar. □ *Your excuse has a familiar ring. Have you done this before?* □ *This term paper has a familiar ring. I think it has been copied.*

have a fit to be very angry. (Informal.) □ *The teacher had a fit when the dog ran through the classroom.* □ *John had a fit when he found his car had been damaged.*

have a foot in both camps to have an interest in or to support each of two opposing groups of people. □ *The shop steward had been promised promotion and so had a foot in both camps during the strike—workers and management.* □ *Mr. Smith has a foot in both camps in the parents/teachers dispute. He teaches maths, but he has a son at the school.*

have a go (at something) to have a try at something. (Informal. See also *take a stab at something.*) □ *I've never fished before, but I'd like to have a go at it.* □ *Great, have a go right now. Take my fishing rod and give it a try.*

have a good command of something to know something well. □ *Bill has a good command of French.* □ *Jane has a good command of economic theory.*

have a good head on one's shoulders to have common sense; to be sensible and intelligent. □ *Mary doesn't do well in school, but she's got a good head on her shoulders.* □ *John has a good head on his shoulders and can be depended on to give good advice.*

have a good thing going to have something arranged that is to one's benefit or advantage. (Informal.) □ *Sally paints pictures and sells them at art fairs. She* *has a good thing going.* □ *John inherited a fortune and doesn't have to work for a living any more. He's got a good thing going.*

have a grasp of something to understand something. (Also with *good, solid, sound,* as in the examples.) □ *She has been in that job for years but still doesn't have a solid grasp of the industry.* □ *You don't have a good grasp of the principles yet.* □ *John started out having a solid grasp of the methods used in his work.*

have a grudge against someone See *bear a grudge (against someone).*

have a hand for someone or something See under *get a big hand for something.*

have a hand in something See under *take a hand in something.*

have a head start on someone or something See *get a head start (on someone or something).*

have a heart to be compassionate; to be generous and forgiving. □ *Oh, have a heart! Give me some help!* □ *If Ann had a heart, she'd have made us feel more welcome.*

have a heart of gold to be generous, sincere, and friendly. □ *Mary is such a lovely person. She has a heart of gold.* □ *You think Tom stole your watch? Impossible! He has a heart of gold.*

have a heart of stone to be cold and unfriendly. □ *Sally has a heart of stone. She never even smiles.* □ *The villain in the play had a heart of stone. He was an ideal villain.*

have a heart-to-heart (talk) to have a sincere and intimate talk. □ *I had a heart-to-heart talk with my father before I went off to college.* □ *I have a problem, John. Let's sit down and have a heart-to-heart.*

have a lot going for one to have many things working to one's benefit. (Informal.) □ *Jane is so lucky. She has a lot going for her.* □ *He's made a mess of his life although he had a lot going for him.*

have a lot of promise AND **show promise** to be very promising; to have a good future ahead. □ *Sally is quite young, but she has a lot of promise.* □ *The building is in its early stages, but it has a lot of promise.* □ *The young singer shows promise.*

have a lot on one's mind to have many things to worry about; to be preoccupied. □ *I'm sorry that I'm so cross. I have a lot on my mind.* □ *He forgot to go to his appointment because he had a lot on his mind.*

have a low boiling-point to get angry easily. (Informal.) □ *Be nice to John. He's upset and has a low boiling-point.* □ *Mr. Jones certainly has a low boiling-point. I hardly said anything, and he got angry.*

have a lump in one's throat See *get a lump in one's throat.*

have a near miss nearly to crash or collide. □ *The planes—flying much too close—had a near miss.* □ *I had a near miss while driving over here.*

have a penchant for doing something to have a taste, desire, or inclination for doing something. □ *John has a penchant for eating fattening foods.* □ *Ann has a penchant for buying clothes.*

have a pick-me-up to eat or drink something stimulating. (The *have* can be replaced with *need, want,* etc. The *me* does not change.) □ *I'd like to have a pick-me-up. I think I'll have a bottle of lemonade.* □ *You look tired. You need a pick-me-up.*

have a price on one's head to be wanted by the authorities, who have offered a reward for one's capture. (Informal.) □ *We captured a thief who had a price on his head, and the police gave us the reward.* □ *The crook was so mean, he turned in his own brother, who had a price on his head.*

have a red face See *get a red face.*

have a reputation as a something See *get a reputation as a something.*

have a reputation for doing something See *get a reputation for doing something*.

have a right to do something AND **have the right to do something** to have the freedom to do something; to possess the legal or moral permission or licence to do something. □ *You don't have the right to enter my home without my permission.* □ *I have a right to grow anything I want on my farm land.*

have a rough idea about something See *get a rough idea about something*.

have a rough time (of it) to experience a difficult period. (Informal.) □ *Since his wife died, Mr. Brown has been having a rough time of it.* □ *Be nice to Bob. He's been having a rough time.*

have a say (in something) AND **have a voice (in something)** to have a part in making a decision. □ *I'd like to have a say in choosing the carpet.* □ *John wanted to have a voice in deciding on the result also.* □ *He says he seldom gets to have a say.*

have a score to settle with someone See under *settle a score (with someone)*.

have a screw loose to act silly or crazy. (Slang.) □ *John's such a clown. He acts as though he has a screw loose.* □ *What's the matter with you? Do you have a screw loose or something?*

have a shot at something See *have a try at something*.

have a smoke to smoke a cigarette, cigar, or pipe. (Informal. The *have* can be replaced with *need, want,* etc.) □ *Can I have a smoke? I'm very nervous.* □ *Do you have a cigarette? I need a smoke.*

have a snowball's chance in hell to have no chance at all. (A snowball would melt in hell. Use *hell* with caution.) □ *He has a snowball's chance in hell of passing the test.* □ *You don't have a snowball's chance in hell of her agreeing to marry you.*

have a soft spot for someone or something to be fond of someone or some-

thing. □ *John has a soft spot for Mary.* □ *I have soft spot for the countryside.*

have a stab at something See *take a stab at something*.

have a stroke to experience sudden unconsciousness or paralysis owing to an interruption in the blood supply to the brain. (Also used as an exaggeration. See the last two examples.) □ *The patient who received an artificial heart had a stroke two days after the operation.* □ *My uncle Bill—who is very old—had a stroke last May.* □ *Calm down, Bob. You're going to have a stroke.* □ *My father almost had a stroke when I came home at three o'clock this morning.*

have a sweet tooth to have the desire to eat many sweet foods—especially candy and pastries. □ *I have a sweet tooth, and if I don't watch it, I'll really get fat.* □ *John eats sweets all the time. He must have a sweet tooth.*

have a swelled head See *get a swelled head*.

have a thin time (of it) to experience a difficult or unfortunate time, especially because of a shortage of money. □ *Jack had a thin time of it when he was a student. He didn't have enough to eat.* □ *The Browns had a thin time of it when the children were small and he was badly paid.*

have a thing about someone or something to have strong likes or dislikes about someone or something. (Informal.) □ *I have a thing about celery. I can't stand it.* □ *John can't get enough celery. He has a thing about it.* □ *John has a thing about Mary. He thinks he's in love.*

have a thing going (with someone) AND **have something going (with someone)** to have a romance or a love affair with someone. (Slang.) □ *John and Mary have a thing going.* □ *Bill has a thing going with Ann.* □ *They have something going.*

have a try at something AND **have a shot at something** to give something a try. (The expression with *shot* is informal.)

□ *I don't know if I can eat a whole pizza, but I'll be happy to have a shot at it.* □ *I can't seem to get this computer to work right. Would you like to have a try at it?* □ *I like your new bike. Can I have a try at riding it?*

have a vested interest in something to have a personal or biased interest, often financial, in something. □ *Margaret has a vested interest in wanting her father to sell the family firm. She has shares in it and would make a large profit.* □ *Jack has a vested interest in keeping the village traffic-free. He has a holiday house there.*

have a voice (in something) See *have a say in something*.

have a way with someone or something to handle or deal well with someone or something. (Informal.) □ *John has a way with sauces. They're always delicious.* □ *Mother has a way with Father. She'll get him to paint the house.*

have a weakness for someone or something to be unable to resist someone or something; to be fond of someone or something; to be (figuratively) powerless against someone or something. (Compare to *have a soft spot for someone or something.*) □ *I have a weakness for chocolate.* □ *John has a weakness for Mary. I think he's in love.*

have a whale of a time to have an exciting or enjoyable time. (Slang. *Whale* is a way of saying *big*.) □ *We had a whale of a time at Sally's birthday party.* □ *Enjoy your holiday! I hope you have a whale of a time.*

have a word with someone to speak to someone, usually privately. □ *The manager asked to have a word with me when I was not busy.* □ *John, could I have a word with you? We need to discuss something.*

have an accident 1. to experience something which was not foreseen or intended. □ *Traffic is very bad. I almost had an accident.* □ *Drive carefully. Try to avoid having an accident.* **2.** to lose control of the bowels or the bladder.

(Euphemistic. Usually said of a young child.) □ *"Oh, Ann," cried Mother. "It looks like you've had an accident!"* □ *Mother asked Billy to go to the toilet before they left so that he wouldn't have an accident in the car.*

have an argument (with someone) See under *get into an argument (with someone)*.

have an axe to grind (with someone) to have something to complain about or discuss with someone. (Informal.) □ *Tom, I need to talk to you. I have an axe to grind with you.* □ *Bill and Bob went into the other room to discuss the matter. They each had an axe to grind.*

have an eye for someone or something to have a taste or an inclination for someone or something. □ *Bob has an eye for beauty.* □ *He has an eye for colour.* □ *Ann has an eye for well-dressed men.*

have an eye on someone or something AND **keep an eye on someone or something** to keep watch on someone or something; to keep track of someone or something. (The *an* can be replaced by various pronouns.) □ *I have my eye on the Chinese vase in the auction. I'll bid for it.* □ *Please keep an eye on the baby.* □ *Will you please keep your eye on my house while I'm on holiday?*

have an itchy palm AND **have an itching palm** to be in need of a tip; to tend to ask for tips. (Informal. As if placing money in the palm would stop its itching.) □ *All the waiters at that restaurant have itchy palms.* □ *The taxi-driver was troubled by an itching palm. Since he refused to carry my bags, I gave him nothing.*

have an out to have an excuse; to have a (literal or figurative) means of escape or avoiding something. (Informal.) □ *He's very clever. No matter what happens, he always has an out.* □ *I agreed to go to a party which I don't want to go to now. I'm looking for an out.*

have another think coming to have to re-think something because one was wrong the first time. (Informal.) □ *She's quite wrong. She's got another think* coming if she wants to walk in here like that. □ *You've got another think coming if you think you can treat me like that!*

have ants in one's pants to become restless; to fidget. (Informal.) □ *Sit still! Have you got ants in your pants?* □ *The children have ants in their pants. It's time to go home.*

have bats in one's belfry to be slightly crazy. □ *Poor old Tom has bats in his belfry.* □ *Don't act so silly, John. People will think you have bats in your belfry.*

have been around to be experienced in life. (Informal. Use with caution—especially with females—since this can also refer to sexual experience. See also *get around.*) □ *Ask Sally about how the government works. She's been around.* □ *They all know a lot about life. They've been around.*

have been had to have been mistreated; to have been cheated or dealt with badly. (Slang.) □ *They were cheated out of a thousand pounds. They've really been had.* □ *Look what they did to my car. Boy, have I been had!*

have been through the mill to have been badly treated; to have suffered hardship or difficulties. (Informal.) □ *This has been a rough day. I've really been through the mill.* □ *She's quite well now, but she's been really through the mill with her illness.*

have butterflies in one's stomach See *get butterflies in one's stomach.*

have charge (of someone or something) See *in charge (of someone or something).*

have clean hands to be guiltless. (As if the guilty person would have bloody hands.) □ *Don't look at me. I have clean hands.* □ *The police took him in, but let him go again because he had clean hands.*

have cold feet See *get cold feet.*

have come a long way to have accomplished much; to have advanced much.

□ *My, how famous you are. You've come a long way.* □ *Tom has come a long way in a short time.*

have designs on someone or something to have plans for someone or something. (When referring to a person, the plans are often romantic or matrimonial.) □ *Mrs. Brown has designs on my apple tree. I think she's going to cut off the part that hangs over her fence.* □ *Mary has designs on Bill. I think she'll try to date him.*

have egg on one's face to be embarrassed because of an error which is obvious to everyone. (Informal.) □ *Bob has egg on his face because he wore jeans to the affair and everyone else wore formal clothing.* □ *John was completely wrong about the weather for the picnic. It snowed! Now he has egg on his face.*

have eyes bigger than one's stomach See under *one's eyes are bigger than one's stomach.*

have eyes in the back of one's head to seem to be able to sense what is going on outside of one's vision. □ *My teacher seems to have eyes in the back of her head.* □ *My teacher doesn't need to have eyes in the back of his head. He watches us very carefully.*

have feet of clay to have a defect of character. □ *All human beings have feet of clay. No one is perfect.* □ *Sally prided herself on her complete honesty. She was nearly fifty before she learned that she, too, had feet of clay.*

have forty winks See *catch forty winks.*

have green fingers to have the ability to grow plants well. □ *Just look at Mr. Simpson's garden. He has green fingers.* □ *My mother has green fingers when it comes to house-plants.*

have growing pains [for an organization] to have difficulties in its growth. □ *The banker apologized for losing my cheque and said the bank was having growing pains.* □ *Governments have terrible growing pains.*

have had enough to have had as much of something as is needed or will be tolerated. □ *Stop shouting at me. I've had enough.* □ *No more potatoes, please. I've had enough.* □ *I'm leaving you, Bill. I've had enough!*

have had it (up to here) to have reached the end of one's endurance or tolerance. (Informal. The *up to here* is often accompanied with a gesture showing how high up on one's body the amount of offence has reached—typically, up to one's neck.) □ *Okay, I've had it. You children go to bed this instant.* □ *We've all had it, John. Get out!* □ *I've had it. I've got to go to bed before I drop dead.* □ *Tom is disgusted. He said that he has had it up to here.*

have had its day to be no longer useful or successful. □ *Trams have had their day in Britain.* □ *Some people think that radio has had its day, but others prefer it to television.*

have half a mind to do something to have almost decided to do something, especially something unpleasant. (Informal.) □ *I have half a mind to go off and leave you here.* □ *The cook had half a mind to serve cold chicken.*

have hell to pay See *have the devil to pay.*

have (high) hopes of something to be expecting something. (Also with *high*, as in the examples.) □ *I have hopes of getting there early.* □ *We have high hopes that John and Mary will have a girl.*

have hold of someone or something See *get hold of someone or something.*

have it both ways to have both of two seemingly incompatible things. (See also *have one's cake and eat it too.*) □ *John wants the security of marriage and the freedom of being single. He wants to have it both ways.* □ *John thinks he can have it both ways—the wisdom of age and the vigour of youth.*

have it in for someone to have something against someone; to plan to scold or punish someone. □ *Don't go near Bob. He has it in for you.* □ *Billy! You had better go home. Your mum really has it in for you.*

have mixed feelings (about someone or something) to be uncertain about someone or something. □ *I have mixed feelings about Bob. Sometimes I think I like him; other times I think I don't.* □ *I have mixed feelings about my trip to England. I love the people, but the climate upsets me.* □ *Yes, I also have mixed feelings.*

have money to burn to have lots of money; to have more money than one needs. (Informal. See also *Money burns a hole in someone's pocket.*) □ *Look at the way Tom buys things. You'd think he had money to burn.* □ *If I had money to burn, I'd just put it in the bank.*

have no business doing something to be wrong to do something; to be extremely unwise to do something. □ *You have no business bursting in on me like that!* □ *You have no business spending money like that!*

have no staying-power to lack endurance; not to be able to last. □ *Sally can swim fast for a short distance, but she has no staying-power.* □ *That horse can race fairly well, but it has no staying-power.*

have no time for someone or something See the following entry.

have no use for someone or something AND **have no time for someone or something** to dislike someone. □ *I have no use for John. I can't see why Mary likes him.* □ *We have no time for the Smiths. We don't get along.*

have none of something to tolerate or endure no amount of something. □ *I'll have none of your talk about leaving school.* □ *We'll have none of your gossip.*

have nothing on someone or something (Informal.) **1.** [with *someone*] to lack evidence against someone. □ *The police had nothing on Bob, so they let him loose.* □ *You've got nothing on me! Let me go!* **2.** not to be a match for someone or something; to have no advantage over someone or something. □ *She's got nothing on him when it comes to cunning.* □ *He's got nothing on his brother with regard to womanizing.*

have nothing to do with someone or something to ignore or avoid someone or something. (Also with *anything,* as in the example. See also *have something to do with someone or something.*) □ *I will have nothing to do with Ann.* □ *I won't have anything to do with Ann.* □ *Billy would have nothing to do with the clown.*

have one's back to the wall to be in a defensive position; to be in (financial) difficulties. (Informal.) □ *He'll have to give in. He has his back to the wall.* □ *How can I bargain when I've got my back to the wall?*

have one's cake and eat it too AND **eat one's cake and have it too** to enjoy both having something and using it up; to *have it both ways.* □ *Tom wants to have his cake and eat it too. It can't be done.* □ *Don't buy a car if you want to walk and stay healthy. You can't eat your cake and have it too.*

have one's ear to the ground AND **keep one's ear to the ground** to listen carefully, hoping to get advance warning of something. □ *John had his ear to the ground, hoping to find out about new ideas in computers.* □ *Keep your ear to the ground for news of possible jobs.*

have one's eye on someone or something See *have an eye on someone or something.*

have one's feet on the ground AND **keep one's feet on the ground** to be or remain realistic or practical. □ *Sally will have no trouble keeping her feet on the ground even when she is famous.* □ *They are ambitious but have their feet firmly on the ground.*

have one's fill of someone or something See *get one's fill of someone or something.*

have one's finger in the pie to be involved in something. □ *I like to have my finger in the pie so I can make sure things go my way.* □ *As long as John has his finger in the pie, things will happen slowly.*

have one's foot in the door See *get one's foot in the door.*

have one's hand in the till to be stealing money from a company or an organization. (Informal. The *till* is a cash box or drawer.) □ *Mr. Jones had his hand in the till for years before he was caught.* □ *I think that the new shop assistant has her hand in the till. There is cash missing every morning.*

have one's hands full (with someone or something) to be busy or totally occupied with someone or something. □ *I have my hands full with my three children.* □ *You have your hands full with the shop.* □ *We both have our hands full.*

have one's hands tied AND **one's hands are tied** to be prevented from doing something. □ *I can't help you. I was told not to, so I have my hands tied.* □ *My hands are tied. My boss says I cannot employ you.*

have one's head in the clouds to be unaware of what is going on. □ *"Bob, do you have your head in the clouds?" said the teacher.* □ *She walks around all day with her head in the clouds. She must be in love.*

have one's heart in one's boots to be very depressed; to have little or no hope. □ *My heart's in my boots when I think of going back to work.* □ *Jack's heart was in his boots when he thought of leaving home.*

have one's heart in the right place to have good intentions, even if there are bad results. □ *I don't always do what is right, but my heart is in the right place.* □ *Good old Tom. His heart's in the right place.* □ *It doesn't matter if she did not succeed. She has her heart in the right place.* ALSO: **one's heart is in the right place** [for one] to have good intentions, even if the results are bad. □

She gave it a good try. Her heart was in the right place.

have one's heart on one's sleeve See *wear one's heart on one's sleeve.*

have one's heart set against something to be totally against something. (Also with *dead,* as in the example.) □ *Jane has her heart dead set against going to Australia.* □ *John has his heart set against going to college.* ALSO: **set one's heart against something** to turn against something; to become totally against something. (Cannot be used with *dead* as can the phrase above.) □ *Jane has set her heart against going to Australia.* ALSO: **one's heart is set against something** one is totally against something. □ *Jane's heart is set against going there.*

have one's heart set on something to be desiring and expecting something. □ *Jane has her heart set on going to London.* □ *Bob will be disappointed. He had his heart set on going to college this year.* ALSO: **set one's heart on something** to become determined about something. □ *Jane set her heart on going to London.* ALSO: **one's heart is set on something** to desire and expect something. □ *Jane's heart is set on going to London.* □ *His heart is set on it.*

have one's knuckles rapped See under *rap someone's knuckles.*

have one's nose in a book to be reading a book; to read books all the time. (Informal.) □ *Bob has his nose in a book every time I see him.* □ *His nose is always in a book. He never gets any exercise.*

have one's nose in the air AND **keep one's nose in the air** to be conceited or aloof. □ *Mary always seems to have her nose in the air.* □ *She keeps her nose in the air and never notices him.* ALSO: **one's nose is in the air** one is acting conceited or aloof. □ *Mary's nose is always in the air and she ignores other people.*

have one's say See *get one's say.*

have one's tail between one's legs to be frightened or cowed. (Refers to a frightened dog. Also used literally with dogs.) □ *John seems to lack courage. Whenever there is an argument, he has his tail between his legs.* □ *You can tell that the dog is frightened because it has its tail between its legs.* ALSO: **one's tail is between one's legs** one is acting frightened or cowed. □ *He should have stood up and argued, but—as usual—his tail was between his legs.*

have one's way (with someone or something) See *get one's way (with someone or something).*

have one's wits about one to concentrate; to have one's mind working. □ *You have to have your wits about you when you are dealing with John.* □ *She had to have her wits about her when living in the city.* ALSO: **keep one's wits about one** to keep one's mind operating, especially in a time of stress. □ *If Jane hadn't kept her wits about her during the fire, things should have been much worse.*

have one's work cut out (for one) to have a large and difficult task prepared for one. □ *They sure have their work cut out for them, and it's going to be hard.* □ *There is a lot for Bob to do. He has his work cut out.* ALSO: **one's work is cut out (for one)** one's task is prepared for one; one has a lot of work to do. □ *This is a big job. My work is certainly cut out for me.*

have other fish to fry to have other things to do; to have more important things to do. (Informal. *Other* can be replaced by *bigger, better, more important,* etc.) □ *I don't have time for your problems. I have other fish to fry.* □ *I won't waste time on your question. I have bigger fish to fry.*

have pull with someone to have influence with someone. (Slang. With *some, much, lots,* etc.) □ *Let's ask Ann to help us. She has a lot of pull with the mayor.* □ *Do you know anyone who has some pull with the bank manager? I need a loan.*

have reason (to do something) to have a cause or a reason to do something. (Note the variation in the examples.) □ *Tom has reason to act like that.* □ *Yes, he has good reason.* □ *We don't have any reason to do that.*

have second thoughts about someone or something See *get second thoughts about someone or something.*

have seen better days to be worn or worn out. (Informal.) □ *This coat has seen better days. I need a new one.* □ *Oh, my old legs ache. I've seen better days, but everyone has to grow old.*

have someone in one's pocket to have control over someone. (Informal.) □ *Don't worry about the mayor. She'll co-operate. I've got her in my pocket.* □ *John will do just what I tell him. I've got him and his brother in my pocket.*

have someone on a string to have someone waiting for one's decision or actions. (Informal.) □ *Sally has John on the string. He has asked her to marry him, but she hasn't replied yet.* □ *Yes, it sounds like she has him on the string.*

have someone or something in one's hands to have control of or responsibility for someone or something. (*Have* can be replaced with *leave* or *put.*) □ *You have the whole project in your hands.* □ *The managing director put the whole project in your hands.* □ *I have to leave the baby in your hands while I go to the doctor.*

have someone or something in tow **1.** [with *something*] to tow something (around). □ *We saw a breakdown lorry that had a car in tow.* □ *That car has a boat in tow.* ALSO: **with something in tow** towing something. □ *There goes a car with a boat in tow.* **2.** [with *someone*] to be accompanied by someone, often in a lowly position. □ *She has her children in tow.* □ *Mary always has a lover in tow.* ALSO: **with someone in tow** leading someone along with one. □ *Here comes Mrs. Smith with her son Billy in tow.*

have someone or something on **1.** [with *someone*] to kid or deceive someone. (Informal.) □ *You can't be serious. You're having me on!* □ *Bob is such a joker. He's always having someone on.* **2.** [with *something*] to have plans for a particular time. (Note the variation with *anything* in the examples.) □ *I can't get to your party. I have something on.* □ *I have something on almost every Saturday.* □ *Mary rarely has anything on during the week.*

have someone or something on one's mind to think often about someone or something; to be obsessed with someone or something. □ *Bill has chocolate on his mind.* □ *John has Mary on his mind every minute.*

have someone over a barrel See *get someone over a barrel.*

have someone under one's thumb See *get someone under one's thumb.*

have someone's ear See *get someone's ear.*

have someone's hide to scold or punish someone. (Informal. Refers to skinning an animal.) □ *If you ever do that again, I'll have your hide.* □ *He said he'd have my hide if I entered his garage again.*

have someone's number See *get someone's number.*

have something against someone or something to possess something (such as prejudice or knowledge) which is harmful to someone or something. (Note the variation in the examples.) □ *He seems to have something against foreigners.* □ *Do you have something against North Americans?* □ *What do you have against me?* □ *I don't have anything against eating beef.*

have something at hand to have something within (one's) reach. □ *I try to have everything I need at hand.* □ *They have medical services at hand.*

have something at one's fingertips to have all the knowledge or information one needs. □ *He has lots of gardening hints* at his fingertips. □ *They have all the tourist information at their fingertips.*

have something coming (to one) to deserve punishment (for something). (Informal.) □ *Bill broke a window, so he has a reprimand coming.* □ *You've got a lot of criticism coming to you.*

have something going to have a business deal in progress. (Informal.) □ *Sally has a new business project going. Her firm will announce a new product in the spring.* □ *John and Tom work as stockbrokers. I've heard that they have a business deal going.*

have something going (with someone) See *have a thing going (with someone).*

have something hanging over one's head to have something bothering or worrying one; to have a deadline worrying one. (Informal. Also used literally.) □ *I keep worrying about being declared redundant. I hate to have something like that hanging over my head.* □ *I have a history essay which is hanging over my head.*

have something in common (with someone or something) [for groups of people or things] to resemble one another in specific ways. □ *Bill and Bob both have red hair. They have that in common with each other.* □ *Bob and Mary have a lot in common. I can see why they like each other.*

have something in hand to be prepared to take action on something. □ *I have the matter in hand.* □ *The management has your complaint in hand.*

have something in mind to think of something; to have an idea or image (of something) in one's mind. □ BILL: *I would like to purchase some wine.* SALESPERSON: *Yes, sir. Did you have something in mind?* □ *Do you have something in mind for your mother's birthday?*

have something in stock to have merchandise available and ready for sale. □ *Do you have extra-large sizes in stock?*

□ *Of course, we have all sizes and colours in stock.*

have something in store (for someone) to have something planned for one's future. □ *Tom has a large inheritance in store for him when his uncle dies.* □ *I wish I had something like that in store.*

have something left to have some part remaining. □ *I hope you have some cake left.* □ *Is there any left?* □ *Sorry, there isn't any left.*

have something made 1. to employ someone to make something. □ *Isn't it a lovely coat? I had to have it made because I couldn't find one I liked in any of the shops.* □ *We had the cake made at the bakery. Our oven isn't big enough for a cake that size.* **2.** to have achieved a successful state. (Slang. Usually with *it*.) □ *Mary really has it made. She inherited one million pounds.* □ *I wish I had it made like that.*

have something on file to have a written record of something in storage. □ *I'm certain I have your letter on file. I'll check again.* □ *We have your application on file somewhere.*

have something on one's hands to be burdened with something. □ *I run a record shop. I sometimes have a large number of unwanted records on my hands.* □ *I have too much time on my hands.*

have something on someone See *get something on someone.*

have something on the brain to be obsessed with something. (Informal.) □ *They have good manners on the brain.* □ *Mary has money on the brain. She wants to earn as much as possible.*

have something out (with someone) to settle a disagreement or a complaint. (Informal.) □ *John has been angry at Mary for a week. He finally had it out with her today.* □ *I'm glad we are having this out today.*

have something sewn up See *get something sewn up.*

have something to do with someone or something to be related to or associated with someone or something. (See *have nothing to do with someone or something*.) □ *Does Waterloo have something to do with water?* □ *No, Waterloo has something to do with Napoleon Bonaparte.*

have something to spare to have more than enough of something. (Informal.) □ *Ask John for some firewood. He has plenty to spare.* □ *Do you have any sweets to spare?*

have something up one's sleeve to have a secret or surprise plan or solution (to a problem). (Refers to one's cheating at cards by having a card hidden in one's sleeve.) □ *He hasn't lost yet. He has something up his sleeve.* □ *The manager has something up her sleeve. She'll surprise us with it later.*

have something wrapped up See *get something sewn up.*

have stars in one's eyes See *get stars in one's eyes.*

have sticky fingers to have a tendency to steal. (Slang.) □ *The shop assistant— who had sticky fingers—got sacked.* □ *The little boy had sticky fingers and was always taking his father's small change.*

have the advantage of someone (over someone) to know more about a person than the person knows about you; to know the name of a person to whom you have not been formally introduced. (Formal. Sometimes used as a way of asking to be introduced to someone. *The* can be replaced with *an.*) □ *I'm sorry, but I'm afraid you have the advantage of me.* □ *You have an advantage over me, sir. I regret that I have never had the pleasure of making your acquaintance.*

have the blues See *get the blues.*

have the boot on the other foot See under *The boot is on the other foot.*

have the cards stacked against one to have luck against one. (Informal.) □ *You can't get very far in life if the cards are stacked against you.* □ *I can't seem*

to get ahead. *I always have the cards stacked against me.* ALSO: **The cards are stacked against one.** luck is against one. (Informal.) □ *I have the worst luck. The cards are stacked against me all the time.*

have the courage of one's convictions to have enough courage and determination to carry out one's aims. □ *It's fine to have noble goals in life and to believe in great things. If you don't have the courage of your convictions, you'll never succeed.* □ *Others don't trust him, but I do. I have the courage of my convictions.*

have the day off See *get the day off.*

have the devil to pay AND **have hell to pay** to have a great deal of trouble. (Informal. Use *hell* with caution.) □ *If you're late for dinner, you'll have the devil to pay.* □ *I came home after three o'clock in the morning and had hell to pay from my parents.* ALSO: **There will be the devil to pay.** One will have to face a lot of trouble. □ *If the pupils fail the exam again, there will be the devil to pay.*

have the edge on someone See *get the advantage of someone.*

have the feel of something 1. [for something] to feel like something (else). □ *This plastic has the feel of fine leather.* □ *The little car has the feel of a much larger one.* **2.** See *get the feel of something.*

have the gift of gab to have a great facility with language; to be able to use language very effectively. (Slang.) □ *My brother really has the gift of gab. He can convince anyone of anything.* □ *If I had the gift of gab like you do, I'd achieve more in life.*

have the last laugh See *get the last laugh.*

have the last word See *get the last word.*

have the Midas touch to have the ability to be successful, especially the ability to make money easily. (From the name of a legendary king whose touch turned everything to gold.) □ *Bob is a merchant banker and really has the Midas touch.* □ *The poverty-stricken boy turned out* to have the Midas touch and was a millionaire by the time he was twenty-five.

have the right of way to possess the legal right to occupy a particular space on a public roadway. □ *I had a traffic accident yesterday, but it wasn't my fault. I had the right of way.* □ *Don't pull out onto a motorway if you don't have the right of way.*

have the time of one's life to have a very good or entertaining time; to have the most exciting time in one's life. (Informal.) □ *What a great party! I had the time of my life.* □ *We went to Florida last winter and had the time of our lives.*

have the upper hand on someone See *get the upper hand (over someone).*

have the wherewithal (to do something) to have the means to do something, especially money. □ *He has good ideas, but he doesn't have the wherewithal to carry them out.* □ *I could do a lot if I only had the wherewithal.*

have them rolling in the aisles to make an audience roll in the aisles with laughter. (Informal.) □ *I'll tell the best jokes you've ever heard. I'll have them rolling in the aisles.* □ *What a great performance. We had them rolling in the aisles.*

have time off See *get time off.*

have time to catch one's breath See *get time to catch one's breath.*

have to do something for it to be necessary to do something. □ *I have to go to the doctor today.* □ *We have to pay our bills this week.*

have to live with something to have to endure something. □ *I have a slight limp in the leg which I broke last year. The doctor says I'll have to live with it.* □ *We don't like the new carpeting in the living-room, but we'll have to live with it.*

have too AND **have so** to have done something (despite appearances to the contrary). (This is an emphatic way of affirming that something has happened.) □ BILL: *You haven't made your bed.* BOB: *I have too!* □ *I have so*

handed in my paper! If you don't have it, you lost it!

have too many irons in the fire to be doing too many things at once. □ *Tom had too many irons in the fire and missed some important deadlines.* □ *It's better if you don't have too many irons in the fire.*

have turned the corner to have passed a critical point in a process. □ *The patient has turned the corner. She should begin to show improvement now.* □ *The project has turned the corner. The rest should be easy.*

have what it takes to have the courage, stamina, or ability (to do something). □ *Bill has what it takes. He can swim for miles.* □ *Tom won't succeed. He doesn't have what it takes.*

He who laughs last laughs longest. a proverb meaning that whoever succeeds in making the last move or pulling the last trick has the most enjoyment or success. □ *Bill had pulled many silly tricks on Tom. Finally Tom pulled a very funny trick on Bill and said, "He who laughs last laughs longest."* □ *Mary told a joke at Tom's expense, getting even for something he had said about her. She grinned and said, "He who laughs last laughs longest."*

He who pays the piper calls the tune. a saying meaning that the person who is paying for something should have some control over how the money is used. □ *Fred's father is paying him through university, and wants to help him choose his course. He says that he who pays the piper calls the tune.* □ *The bride's parents should have a say in where the wedding is held since they're paying for it. He who pays the piper calls the tune.*

head and shoulders above someone or something clearly superior to someone. (Often with *stand,* as in the example.) □ *This wine is head and shoulders above that one.* □ *John stands head and shoulders above Bob.*

head for someone or something to aim for or move towards someone or something. □ *She waved goodbye as she headed for the door.* □ *Ann came in and headed for her mother.*

head over heels in love (with someone) very much in love with someone. □ *John is head over heels in love with Mary.* □ *They are head over heels in love with each other.* □ *They are head over heels in love.*

head someone or something off AND **head off someone or something** to prevent someone or something from arriving. □ *The farmer headed off the herd of sheep before it ruined our picnic.* □ *The doctors worked round the clock to head the epidemic off.* □ *Bill headed his mother off so that we had time to clean up the mess before she saw it.*

head something up AND **head up something** to serve as leader or head of something. (Informal.) □ *They asked me to head up the meeting.* □ *I had already agreed to head the fund-raising campaign up.*

heads will roll some people will get into trouble. (Informal. From the use of the guillotine to execute people.) □ *When company's end-of-year results are known, heads will roll.* □ *Heads will roll when the headmaster sees the damaged classroom.*

hear from someone to get a message from someone. □ *I haven't heard from my cousin in ten years.* □ *I just heard from Tom. He's in California.*

hear of someone or something 1. to know of the existence of someone or something. □ *I have heard of banana ice-cream, but I have never eaten any.* □ *I've heard of Mr. Smith, but I've never met him.* **2.** [with *something*] to tolerate something; to permit something. (Usually negative.) □ *No, you cannot go to the cinema! I won't hear of it!* □ *My mother wouldn't hear of my marrying Bill.*

heavy going difficult to do, understand, or make progress with. (Informal.) □ *Jim finds maths heavy going.* □ *Talk-*

ing to Mary is heavy going. She has nothing to say.

hedge one's bets to reduce one's loss on a bet or on an investment or action by counterbalancing possible loss in some way. (Slang.) □ *Bob bet Ann that the plane would be late. He usually hedges his bets. This time he called the airline and asked about the plane before he made the bet.* □ *Jim asked Jane to go to the dance, but he hedged his bets by asking Joan also in case Jane refused.*

hell for leather moving or behaving recklessly. (Informal.) □ *They took off after the horse thief, riding hell for leather.* □ *They ran hell for leather for the train.*

help oneself to take whatever one wants or needs. □ *Please have some sweets. Help yourself.* □ *When you go to a cafeteria, you help yourself to the food.* □ *Bill helped himself to dessert.*

help someone or something out (with someone or something) AND **help out someone or something (with someone or something)** to assist someone or something with a person or a thing. □ *Can you help me out with my geometry?* □ *Yes, I can help you out.* □ *Please help out my son with his geometry.* □ *Please help me out around the house.* □ *We helped the school out with its fund raising.*

hem and haw AND **hum and haw** to be uncertain about something; to be evasive; to say "ah" and "eh" when speaking—avoiding saying something meaningful. □ *Stop hemming and hawing. I want an answer.* □ *Don't just hem and haw. Speak up. We want to hear what you think.* □ *Stop humming and hawing and say whether you are coming or not.* □ *Jean hummed and hawed for a long time before deciding to marry Henry.*

hem someone or something in AND **hem in someone or something** to trap or enclose someone or something. □ *Don't hem the bird in. Let it have a way to escape.* □ *The large city buildings hem me in.* ALSO: **hemmed in** enclosed;

trapped. □ *I hate to feel hemmed in.*
□ *The high wall makes our garden seem hemmed in.*

hemmed in See under *hem someone or something in.*

here and now the present, as opposed to the past or the future. □ *I don't care what's happening tomorrow or next week! I care about the here and now.* □ *The past is dead. Let's worry about the here and now.*

here and there at this place and that; from place to place. □ *We find rare books in used-bookshops here and there.* □ *She didn't make a systematic search. She just looked here and there.*

here's to someone or something an expression used as a toast to someone or something to wish someone or something well. □ *Here's to Jim and Mary! May they be very happy!* □ *Here's to your new job!*

hide one's face in shame to cover one's face because of shame or embarrassment. □ *Mary was so embarrassed. She could only hide her face in shame.* □ *When Tom broke Ann's crystal vase, he wanted to hide his face in shame.*

hide one's head in the sand See *bury one's head in the sand.*

hide one's light under a bushel to conceal one's good ideas or talents. (A biblical theme.) □ *Jane has some good ideas, but she doesn't speak very often. She hides her light under a bushel.* □ *Don't hide your light under a bushel. Share your gifts with other people.*

high and mighty proud and powerful. (Informal. Especially with *be* or *act*.) □ *Why does the doctor always have to act so high and mighty?* □ *If Sally wouldn't act so high and mighty, she'd have more friends.* □ *Don't be so high and mighty!*

high-flyer a person who is ambitious or who is very likely to be successful. (Informal.) □ *Jack was one of the high-flyers of our university year, and he is now in the foreign office.* □ *Tom is a*

high-flyer and has applied for the post of managing director.

high on something (Slang.) **1.** intoxicated with some drug. □ *He got thrown out of the cinema because he was high on something.* □ *Bill was high on marijuana and was singing loudly.* **2.** enthusiastic about something. □ *Jane stopped eating red meat. She's really high on fish, however.* □ *Bob is high on meditation. He sits and meditates for an hour each day.*

high spot an exceptionally good or enjoyable part of something. (Informal. See also *hit the high spots.*) □ *One of the high spots of the evening was the children's singing.* □ *The closing talk was the high spot of the conference.*

high-tail it out of somewhere to get away from somewhere fast. (Informal.) □ *Here come the police. We'd better high-tail it out of here.* □ *Look at that boy go! He really high-tailed it out of town.*

hinge on something to depend on something. □ *This all hinges on how much risk you're willing to take.* □ *Whether we have the picnic hinges on the weather.*

hit a snag to run into a problem. (Informal.) □ *We've hit a snag with the building project.* □ *I stopped working on the project when I hit a snag.*

hit and miss AND **hit or miss** carelessly; aimlessly; without plan or direction. □ *There was no planning. It was just hit and miss.* □ *We handed out the free tickets hit or miss. Some people got one; others got five or six.* ALSO: **hit-and-miss; hit-or-miss** careless; aimless; directionless. □ *They did it in a hit-and-miss fashion.* □ *This isn't a hit-or-miss operation. We are well organized.*

hit bottom to reach the lowest or worst point. (Informal.) □ *Our profits have hit bottom. This is our worst year ever.* □ *When my life hit bottom, I gradually began to feel much better. I knew that if there was going to be any change, it would be for the better.*

hit it off (with someone) to quickly become good friends with someone. (Informal.) □ *Look how John hit it off with Mary.* □ *Yes, they really hit it off.*

hit on something See *hit (up)on something.*

hit or miss See *hit and miss.*

hit (someone) below the belt to do something unfair or unsporting to someone. (Informal. From boxing, where a blow below the belt line is not permitted. Also used literally.) □ *You really hit me below the belt when you told my sister about my health problems.* □ *In business Bill is difficult to deal with. He hits below the belt.*

hit someone between the eyes to become completely apparent; to surprise or impress someone. (Informal. Also with *right,* as in the examples. Also used literally.) □ *Suddenly, it hit me right between the eyes. John and Mary were in love.* □ *Then—as he was talking—the exact nature of the evil plan hit me between the eyes.*

hit (someone or something) like a ton of bricks to surprise, startle, or shock someone. (Informal.) □ *Suddenly, the truth hit me like a ton of bricks.* □ *The sudden tax rate increase hit like a ton of bricks. Everyone became angry.*

hit the bull's-eye 1. to hit the centre area of a circular target. □ *The archer hit the bull's-eye three times in a row.* □ *I didn't hit the bull's-eye even once.* 2. to achieve the goal perfectly. (Informal.) □ *Your idea really hit the bull's-eye. Thank you!* □ *Jill has a lot of insight. She hit the bull's-eye in her choice of flowers for my mother.*

hit the ceiling AND **hit the roof** to become very angry. (Informal.) □ *My father hit the ceiling when I damaged the car.* □ *Our employer hit the ceiling when we lost an important contract.* □ *His wife hit the roof when he was late home.*

hit the hay to go to bed and get some sleep. (Slang.) □ *Look at the clock. It's time to hit the hay.* □ *I like to hit the hay before midnight.*

hit the high spots to reach a high level. (Informal. See also *high spot.*) □ *The band is good, but it never hits the high spots.* □ *She'll get into college although her work never hits the high spots.*

hit the jackpot (Slang.) 1. to win at gambling. (Refers to the "jack" in playing cards.) □ *Bob hit the jackpot three times in one night.* □ *I've never hit the jackpot even once.* 2. to have a success. □ *I hit the jackpot on a business deal.* □ *I really hit the jackpot in the library. I found just what I needed.*

hit the nail on the head to be absolutely right; to do exactly the right thing; to do something in the most effective and efficient way. (Also with *right,* as in the examples.) □ *You've spotted the flaw, Sally. You hit the nail on the head.* □ *Bob doesn't say much, but every now and then he hits the nail right on the head.*

hit the roof See under *go through the roof; hit the ceiling.*

hit the spot to be exactly right; to be just what is needed; to be refreshing. (Informal.) □ *This cool drink really hits the spot.* □ *That was a delicious meal, dear. It hit the spot.*

hit (up)on something to discover or think up something. (Informal.) □ *Ann hit on the idea of baking lots of bread and freezing it.* □ *John hit upon a new way of getting to work.*

hitch a lift See *thumb a lift.*

Hobson's choice the choice between taking what is offered and getting nothing at all. (From the name of a stable owner in the seventeenth century who offered customers the hire of the horse nearest the door.) □ *We didn't really want that holiday cottage, but it was a case of Hobson's choice. We booked very late and there was nothing else left.* □ *If you want a yellow car, it's Hobson's choice. The garage has only one.*

hoist with one's own petard to be harmed or disadvantaged by an action of one's own which was meant to harm someone else. (From a line in Shakespeare's *Hamlet*.) □ *She intended to murder her brother but was hoist with her own petard when she ate the poisoned food intended for him.* □ *The vandals were hoist with their own petard when they wanted to make an emergency call from the phone-box they had broken.*

hold a grudge (against someone) See *bear a grudge (against someone)*.

hold a meeting to meet; to have a meeting (of an organization). □ *We'll have to hold a meeting to make a decision.* □ *Our club held a meeting to talk about future projects.*

hold all the cards to be in a favourable position; to be in a controlling position. (Slang. Refers to having possession of the highest-scoring cards in a card-game.) □ *How can I beat him when he holds all the cards?* □ *If I held all the cards, I'd trounce him.*

hold forth to speak, usually at length. (Informal.) □ *The guide held forth about the city.* □ *I've never seen anyone who could hold forth so long.* □ *The professor held forth about economic theory for nearly an hour.*

Hold it! Stop!; Stop moving! □ *Hold it, Tom! You're going the wrong way.* □ *You're speaking out of turn. Hold it!*

hold no brief for someone or something not to care about someone or something; not to support someone or something; to dislike someone or something. □ *I hold no brief for people who cheat the company.* □ *My father says he holds no brief for the new plans.*

hold off (doing something) to refrain from doing something; to wait until later to do something. □ *Please hold off going inside until I get there.* □ *I can't hold off very long. It'll be too cold pretty soon.*

hold on 1. See *hang on to someone or something*. **2.** stop; wait. □ *Hold on for a minute.* □ *Now, hold on. You're talking too fast.*

hold (on) tight to grasp (someone or something) tightly. □ *Here we go on the roundabout! Hold on tight!* □ *The children were told to hold tight on the swings.*

hold on to someone or something See *hang on to someone or something*.

Hold on to your hat! See *Hang on to your hat!*

hold one's breath 1. to stop breathing for a short period, on purpose. □ *Do you hold your breath when you dive into the water?* □ *I can't hold my breath for very long.* **2.** (almost) to stop breathing in surprise, admiration, or horror. □ *The children held their breath at the conjurer's tricks.* □ *The crowd held their breath at the tightrope walker.* **3.** (figuratively) to stop breathing until something special happens. (Informal. Usually in the negative.) □ BOB: *The bus is going to come soon.* BILL: *Don't hold your breath until it does.* □ *I expect the mail to be delivered soon, but I'm not holding my breath.*

hold one's fire 1. to refrain from shooting (a gun, etc.). □ *The sergeant told the soldiers to hold their fire.* □ *Please hold your fire until I get out of the way.* **2.** to postpone one's criticism or commentary. (Informal.) □ *Now, now, hold your fire until I've had a chance to explain.* □ *Hold your fire, Bill. You're too quick to complain.*

hold one's head up AND **hold up one's head** to have one's self-respect; to retain or display one's dignity. □ *I've done nothing wrong. I can hold my head up in public.* □ *I'm so embarrassed and ashamed. I'll never be able to hold up my head again.*

hold one's own 1. to do as well as anyone else. □ *I can hold my own in a foot-race any day.* □ *She was unable to hold her own, and she had to leave.* **2.** [for someone] to remain on a stable physical condition. □ *Mary is still seriously ill, but she is holding her own.* □ *We thought Jim was holding his own after the accident, but he died suddenly.*

hold one's peace to remain silent. □ *Bill was unable to hold his peace any longer. "Don't do it!" he cried.* □ *Quiet, John. Hold your peace for a little while longer.*

hold one's temper See *keep one's temper.*

hold one's tongue to refrain from speaking; to refrain from saying something unpleasant. □ *I felt like scolding her, but I held my tongue.* □ *Hold your tongue, John. You can't talk to me that way.*

hold out 1. to last or endure. (Compare to *hold up.*) □ *I need to eat something now. I can't hold out much longer.* □ *How long can a human being hold out without water?* **2.** See the following entry.

hold out (for someone or something) to wait for someone or something; to forego everything for someone or something. □ *The employers are holding out for a better deal.* □ BOB: *Would you like some of this chocolate ice-cream?* BILL: *No, I'll hold out for the vanilla.* □ *How long will you hold out?*

hold out the olive branch to offer to end a dispute and be friendly; to offer reconciliation. (The olive branch is a symbol of peace and reconciliation. A biblical reference.) □ *Jill was the first to hold out the olive branch after our argument.* □ *I always try to hold out the olive branch to someone I have hurt. Life is too short for a person to bear grudges for very long.*

hold someone accountable (for something) to consider someone responsible for something; to blame something on someone. (The *something* can be replaced with *someone* meaning "someone's welfare.") □ *I hold you accountable for John's well-being.* □ *Yes, you may hold me accountable for John.* □ *I must hold you accountable for the missing money.* □ *No! Please don't hold me accountable.*

hold someone down AND **hold down someone** to try to keep someone from succeeding. □ *I'm not trying to hold down my brother.* □ *I still think you're trying to hold him down.*

hold someone or something at bay See *keep someone or something at bay.*

hold someone or something back See *keep someone or something back.*

hold someone or something in check See *keep someone or something in check.*

hold someone or something off See *keep someone or something off.*

hold someone or something up AND **hold up someone or something 1.** to support someone or something. (Compare to *keep someone or something up.*) □ *I don't think those nails will hold those shelves up.* □ *It took both of us to hold up the old man.* **2.** [with *someone*] to rob someone. □ *That's the thief who held me up at gunpoint.* □ *The shop owner was held up twice in one month.* **3.** to detain someone or something; to make someone or something late. □ *A storm in Scotland held up our plane.* □ *The traffic on the motorway held me up.*

hold someone or something up as an example AND **hold up someone or something as an example** to point out someone or something as a good example. □ *I was embarrassed when the supervisor held me up as an example of good time-keeping.* □ *The teacher held up the leaf as an example of a typical compound leaf.*

hold something against someone to blame something on someone; to *bear a grudge against someone;* to resent someone. □ *Your brother is nasty to me, but I can't hold it against you.* □ *You're holding something against me. What is it?*

hold still See *keep still.*

hold still (for someone or something) See *stand still (for someone or something).*

hold the fort to oversee and look after a place, such as a shop or one's home. (Informal. From Western films.) □ *I'm going next door to visit Mrs. Jones. You stay here and hold the fort.* □ *You should open the shop at eight o'clock* *and hold the fort until I get there at ten o'clock.*

hold true [for something] to be true; [for something] to remain true. □ *Does this rule hold true all the time?* □ *Yes, it holds true no matter what.*

hold up to endure; to last. □ *How long will his strength hold up?* □ *Our stores are holding up well.*

hold water to be able to be proved; to be correct or true. □ *Jack's story doesn't hold water. It sounds too unlikely.* □ *The police's theory will not hold water. The suspect has an alibi.*

hold with something to accept or agree with something. (Usually in the negative.) □ *My father doesn't hold with fancy clothes.* □ *I don't hold with too many X-rays.*

Hold your horses! wait a minute and be reasonable; do not run off wildly. (From Western films.) □ *Now, hold your horses, John. Be reasonable for a change.* □ *Don't get so angry. Just hold your horses!*

hole-and-corner AND **hole-in-the-corner** secretive; secret and dishonourable. □ *Jane is tired of the hole-and-corner affair with Tom. She wants him to marry her.* □ *The wedding was a hole-in-the-corner occasion because the bride's parents refused to have anything to do with it.*

hole in one (Informal.) **1.** an instance of hitting a golf ball into a hole in only one try. □ *John made a hole in one yesterday.* □ *I've never got a hole in one.* **2.** an instance of succeeding the first time. □ *It worked the first time I tried it—a hole in one.* □ *Bob got a hole in one on that sale. A lady walked in the door, and he sold her a car in five minutes.*

hole-in-the-corner See *hole-and-corner.*

hole up (somewhere) to hide somewhere; to live in hiding somewhere. (Slang. Typically in Western or gangster films.) □ *The old man is holed up in the mountains, waiting for the war to end.* □ *If we are going to hole up for the winter, we'll need lots of food.*

holier-than-thou excessively pious; acting as though one is more virtuous than other people. □ *Jack always adopts a holier-than-thou attitude to other people, but people say he has been in prison.* □ *Jane used to be holier-than-thou, but she is marrying Tom, who is a crook.*

home and dry having been successful in one's aims. □ *There is the cottage we are looking for. We are home and dry.* □ *We need £100 to reach our target. Then we are home and dry.*

home in (on someone or something) to aim exactly at something and move towards it. □ *The plane homed in on the beacon at the airport.* □ *First, you must set your goal and then home in.* □ *The teacher immediately homed in on the reasons for failure.*

honest to goodness I speak the truth. (The *goodness* can be replaced with *God*. Some people may object to the use of *God* in this phrase.) □ *Did he really say that? Honest to goodness?* □ *Honest to goodness, I've been to the moon.* □ *I've been there, too—honest to God.*

honour someone's cheque to accept someone's personal cheque. □ *The bank didn't honour your cheque when I tried to deposit it. Please give me cash.* □ *The foreign bank refused to honour the cheque.*

hook something up AND **hook up something** to attach something; to install something electrical or mechanical. □ *Have they hooked up the new heating system yet?* □ *I bought a computer, but I can't hook it up.*

hooked on something (Slang.) **1.** addicted to a drug or something similar. □ *Jenny is hooked on cocaine.* □ *She was not hooked on anything before that.* □ *John is hooked on coffee.* **2.** enthusiastic about something; supportive of something. □ *Mary is hooked on cricket. She never misses a match.* □ *Jane is so happy! She's hooked on life.*

Hop it! Go away! (Slang.) □ *Hop it! I'm busy.* □ *The children were told to hop it.*

hope against hope to have hope even when the situation appears to be hopeless. □ *We hope against hope that she'll see the right thing to do and do it.* □ *There is little point in hoping against hope, except that it makes you feel better.*

horn in (on something) to intrude on something. (Informal.) □ *I'm going to ask Sally to the party. Don't you dare try to horn in on our date!* □ *I wouldn't think of horning in.*

horse around to play around; to waste time in frivolous activities. (Informal.) □ *Stop horsing around and get to work.* □ *The children were on the playground horsing around when the bell rang.*

horse of a different colour See the following entry.

horse of another colour AND **horse of a different colour** another matter altogether. □ *I was talking about trees, not bushes. Bushes are a horse of another colour.* □ *Gambling is not the same as investing in the shares market. It's a horse of a different colour.*

horse-play physically active and frivolous play. (Informal. See also *horse around*.) □ *Stop that horse-play and get to work.* □ *I won't tolerate horse-play in my living-room.*

horse sense common sense; practical thinking. □ *Jack is no scholar but he has a lot of horse sense.* □ *Horse sense tells me I should not be involved in that project.*

hot and bothered excited; anxious. (Informal.) □ *Now don't get hot and bothered. Take it easy.* □ *John is hot and bothered about the tax rate increase.*

Hot enough for you? What do you think about this heat?; Do you like this hot weather? (Said only in very hot weather.) □ *Well, hello, Sally. Hot enough for*

you? □ *Some weather, huh? Hot enough for you?*

hot on something enthusiastic about something; very much interested in something; knowledgeable about something. (Informal.) □ *Meg's hot on animal rights.* □ *Jean is hot on modern ballet just now.*

hot under the collar very angry. (Informal.) □ *The solicitor was really hot under the collar when you told him you lost the contract.* □ *I get hot under the collar every time I think about it.*

hotfoot it out of somewhere to run away from a place. (Compare to *hightail it out of somewhere*.) □ *Did you see Tom hotfoot it out of the office when the boss came in?* □ *Things are looking bad. I think we had better hotfoot it out of here.*

house-proud extremely or excessively concerned about the appearance of one's house. □ *Mrs. Smith is so house-proud that she makes her guests take their shoes off at the front door.* □ *Mrs. Brown keeps plastic covers over her chairs. She's much too house-proud.*

hover over someone or something **1.** to remain close to or above someone or something. □ *Vultures hovered over the corpse.* □ *The hawk hovered over the rabbit for a second and then attacked.* **2.** to watch over or supervise someone or something; to remain too close to someone. □ *I can't work when he's hovering over me.* □ *Hovering over them won't get the work finished earlier.*

hue and cry a loud public protest or opposition. □ *There was a hue and cry when the council wanted to build houses in the playing-field.* □ *The decision to close the local school started a real hue and cry.*

hum and haw See *hem and haw*.

hung up (on someone or something) AND **hung up (about someone or something)** obsessed with someone or something. (Slang. See also *hang-up* under *hang up*.) □ *John is really hung up* on Mary. □ *She's hung up, too. See how she smiles at him.* □ *Jane's hung up about her appearance.*

hunt high and low for someone or something AND **search high and low for someone or something** to look carefully in every possible place for someone or something. □ *We looked high and low for the right teacher.* □ *The Smiths are searching high and low for the country cottage of their dreams.*

hurry back come back again. (A friendly way of inviting someone to return.) □ *Thank you for shopping here. Hurry back.* □ *I'm glad you could come to my house for a visit. Hurry back.*

hurt someone's feelings to cause someone emotional pain. □ *It hurts my feelings when you talk that way.* □ *I'm sorry. I didn't mean to hurt your feelings.*

hush-money money paid as a bribe to persuade someone to remain silent and not reveal certain information. (Informal.) □ *Bob gave his younger sister hush-money so that she wouldn't tell Jane that he had gone to the cinema with Sue.* □ *The crooks paid Fred hush-money to keep their whereabouts secret.*

hush someone or something up AND **hush up someone or something** 1. [with *someone*] to make someone be quiet. □ *Watching television hushes the children up.* □ *Even constant rocking won't hush the baby up.* 2. [with *something*] to keep something a secret; to try to stop a rumour from spreading. □ *Please try to hush up the rumour about my uncle.* □ *Okay, I'll try to hush it up.*

I

If the cap fits, wear it. a proverb meaning that you should pay attention to something if it applies to you. □ *Some people here constantly arrive late. If the cap fits, wear it.* □ *This doesn't apply to everyone. If the cap fits, wear it.*

if the worst comes to the worst in the worst possible situation; if things really get bad. □ *If the worst comes to the worst, we'll employ someone to help you.* □ *If the worst comes to the worst, I'll have to borrow some money.*

If you give one an inch, one will take a mile. See *Give one an inch, and one will take a mile.*

ill at ease uneasy; anxious. □ *I feel ill at ease about the interview.* □ *You look ill at ease. Please relax.*

ill-gotten gains money or other possessions acquired in a dishonest or illegal fashion. □ *Fred cheated at cards and is now living on his ill-gotten gains.* □ *Mary is also enjoying her ill-gotten gains. She deceived an old lady into leaving her money in her will.*

impose on someone to use someone for one's own benefit; to take advantage of someone. □ *I don't want to impose on you, but could I have a lift to the library?* □ *Jane imposes on her friends too often by asking them to stand in for her.*

impose something on someone to force something on someone; to make someone accept something. □ *I wish you wouldn't impose your will on all of us.* □ *She said she'd impose a solution on*

them *if they couldn't agree among themselves.*

improve (up)on something to make something better; to improve something. □ *It's very good the way it is, but I can improve on it.* □ *It's so beautiful that it cannot be improved upon.*

in a bad mood sad; depressed; cross; with low spirits. □ *He's in a bad mood. He may shout at you.* □ *Please try to cheer me up. I'm in a bad mood.*

in a bad way in a critical or bad state. (Can refer to health, finances, mood, etc.) □ *Mr. Smith is in a bad way. He may have to go to the hospital.* □ *My bank account is in a bad way. It needs some help from a millionaire.* □ *My life is in a bad way, and I'm depressed about it.*

in a body as a group (of people). □ *All the guests left in a body.* □ *Things become very busy when everyone arrives in a body.*

in a dead heat [finishing a race] at exactly the same time; tied. □ *The two horses finished the race in a dead heat.* □ *They ended the contest in a dead heat.*

in a fix in a bad situation. (Informal. *In* can be replaced with *into*. See comment at *in a jam* and the examples below.) □ *I really got myself into a fix. I owe a lot of money on my car.* □ *John is in a fix because he lost his wallet.* □ *John certainly has got into a fix.*

in a flash quickly; immediately. □ *I'll be there in a flash.* □ *It happened in a flash. Suddenly my wallet was gone.*

in a hole in trouble. (Informal.) □ *I'm in a hole. I have a large overdraft.* □ *He's in a hole. The police suspect him.*

in a huff in an angry or offended manner or state. (Informal. *In* can be replaced with *into*. See comment at *in a jam* and the examples below.) □ *He heard what we had to say, then left in a huff.* □ *She came in a huff and ordered us to bring her something to eat.* □ *She gets into a huff very easily.*

in a jam in a tight or difficult situation. (*In* can be replaced with *into* to show movement towards or into the state described by *jam*. Especially *get into*.) □ *I'm in a jam. I owe a lot of money.* □ *Whenever I get into a jam, I ask my supervisor for help.*

in a jiffy very fast; very soon. (Informal.) □ *Just wait a minute. I'll be there in a jiffy.* □ *I'll be finished in a jiffy.*

in a lather flustered; excited and agitated. (Slang. *In* can be replaced with *into*.) □ *Now, calm down. Don't be in a lather.* □ *I always get in a lather when I'm late.* □ *I get into a lather easily.*

in a mad rush in a hurry. □ *I ran around all day today in a mad rush looking for a present for Bill.* □ *Why are you always in a mad rush?*

in a month of Sundays in a very long time. □ *How are you? I haven't seen you in a month of Sundays.* □ *John hasn't seen a film in a month of Sundays.*

in a nutshell in a few words; briefly; concisely. □ *I don't have time for the whole explanation. Please give it to me in a nutshell.* □ *Well, in a nutshell, we have to work late.*

in a (pretty) pickle in a mess; in trouble. (Informal. *In* can be replaced with *into*. See comment at *in a jam* and the examples below.) □ *John has got himself into a pickle. He has two dates for the party.* □ *Now we are in a pretty pickle. We are out of petrol.*

in a quandary uncertain about what to do; confused. (*In* can be replaced with *into*. See comment at *in a jam* and the examples below.) □ *Mary was in a quandary about what college to go to.* □ *I couldn't decide what to do. I was in such a quandary.* □ *I got myself into a quandary about where to go on holiday.*

in a sense in a way. □ *In a sense, cars make life better.* □ *But, in a sense, they also make life worse.*

in a split second in just an instant. □ *The lightning struck, and in a split second the house burst into flames.* □ *Just wait. I'll be there in a split second.*

in a spot See *in a (tight) spot.*

in a stage whisper in a loud whisper which everyone can hear. □ *John said in a stage whisper, "This play is boring."* □ *"When do we eat?" asked Billy in a stage whisper.*

in a stew (about someone or something) upset or bothered about someone or something. (Informal. *In* can be replaced with *into*. See comment at *in a jam* and the examples below.) □ *I'm in such a stew about my dog. She ran away last night.* □ *Now, now. Don't be in a stew. She'll be back when she gets hungry.* □ *I hate to get into a stew worrying about my children.*

in a (tight) spot caught in a problem; *in a jam*. (Informal. *In* can be replaced with *into*. See comment at *in a jam* and the examples below.) □ *Look, John, I'm in a tight spot. Can you lend me £20?* □ *I'm in a spot too. I need £300.* □ *He's always getting into a tight spot financially.*

in a word said simply; concisely said. □ *Mrs. Smith is—in a word—haughty.* □ *In a word, the play flopped.*

in a world of one's own aloof; detached. □ *John lives in a world of his own. He has very few friends.* □ *Mary walks* *around in a world of her own, but she's very intelligent.*

in accordance with something following the rules of something; according to the directions. □ *I've filled out the form in accordance with your instructions.* □ *We always play the game in accordance with the rules.*

in addition (to someone or something) added to someone or something. □ *In addition to the roast beef, I would like to have a baked potato.* □ *I invited Tom in addition to John and Ann.* □ *I think I'll invite Jane in addition.*

in advance (of someone or something) before someone or something. (Refers to both time and space.) □ *They reached the station in advance of the seven o'clock train.* □ *It's good to be there in advance.* □ *The infantry went in advance of the cavalry.*

in all one's born days ever; in all one's life. □ *I've never been so angry in all my born days.* □ *Have you ever heard such a thing in all your born days?*

in all probability very likely; almost certainly. □ *He'll be here on time in all probability.* □ *In all probability, they'll finish the work today.*

in an interesting condition pregnant. (Humorous.) □ *Joan has resigned because she is in an interesting condition.* □ *We suspect that Mary is in an interesting condition.*

in any case AND **in any event** no matter what happens. □ *I intend to be home by suppertime, but in any case by eight o'clock.* □ *In any event, I'll see you this evening.*

in any event See the previous entry.

in apple-pie order in very good order; very well organized. (*In* can be replaced with *into.* See comment at *in a jam* and the examples below.) □ *Please put everything in apple-pie order before you leave.* □ *I always put my desk in apple-pie order every evening.* □ *How*

long will it take to get everything into apple-pie order?

in arrears overdue; late, especially in reference to bills and money. □ *This bill is three months in arrears. It must be paid immediately.* □ *I was in arrears on my car payments, so the bank threatened to take my car away.*

in at the kill present at the end of some activity, usually an activity with negative results. (Literally, present when a hunted animal is put to death. Informal when used about any other activity.) □ *I went to the final hearing on the proposed ring-road. I knew it would be shouted down strongly, and I wanted to be in at the kill.* □ *The judge will sentence the criminal today, and I'm going to be in at the kill.*

in awe (of someone or something) fearful and respectful of someone or something. □ *Everyone in the country was in awe of the king and queen.* □ *I love my new car. In fact, I'm in awe of it.* □ *When I first saw the house, I just stood there in awe.*

in bad faith without sincerity; with bad or dishonest intent; with duplicity. (Compare to *in good faith.*) □ *It appears that you acted in bad faith and didn't live up to the terms of our agreement.* □ *If you do things in bad faith, you'll get a bad reputation.*

in bad taste AND **in poor taste** rude; vulgar; obscene. □ *Mrs. Franklin felt that your joke was in bad taste.* □ *We found the play to be in poor taste, so we walked out in the middle of the second act.*

in black and white official, in writing or printing. (Said of something, such as an agreement or a statement, which has been recorded in writing. *In* can be replaced with *into.* See comment at *in a jam* and the examples below.) □ *I have it in black and white that I'm entitled to three weeks' holiday each year.* □ *It says right here in black and white that oak trees produce acorns.* □ *Please put the agreement into black and white.*

in brief briefly; concisely. □ *The whole story, in brief, is that Bob failed algebra because he did not study.* □ *In brief, you must leave immediately.*

in broad daylight publicly visible in the daytime. □ *The thief stole the car in broad daylight.* □ *There they were, selling drugs in broad daylight.*

in cahoots (with someone) in conspiracy with someone; in league with someone. (Informal.) □ *The mayor is in cahoots with the construction company which got the contract for the new building.* □ *Those two have been in cahoots before.*

in case of something in the event of something; if something happens. (Compare to *in the case of someone or something.*) □ *Please leave the building at once in case of fire.* □ *Please take your raincoat in case of rain.* ALSO: **just in case** if (something happens). □ *All right. I'll take it just in case.* □ *I'll take along some aspirin, just in case.*

in character typical of someone's behaviour. □ *For Tom to shout that way wasn't at all in character. He's usually quite pleasant.* □ *It was quite in character for Sally to walk away angry.*

in charge (of someone or something) AND **have charge (of someone or something)** to be in control of someone or something; to have the responsibility for someone or something. □ *Who is in charge of this office?* □ *How long have you had charge of this office?* □ *Do you like being in charge?*

in clover with good fortune; in a very good situation, especially financially. (Informal.) □ *If I get this contract, I'll be in clover for the rest of my life.* □ *I have very little money saved, so when I retire I won't exactly be in clover.*

in cold blood without feeling; with cruel intent. (Informal or slang. Frequently said of a crime, especially murder.) □ *The killer walked up and shot the woman in cold blood.* □ *How insulting! For a person to say something like that in cold blood is just horrible.*

in concert (with someone) in co-operation with someone; with the aid of someone. □ *Mrs. Smith planned the affair in concert with her sister.* □ *The conspirators plotted the scheme in concert.*

in condition AND **in shape** in good health; strong and healthy. (Used only with people. Compare to *in good shape. In* can be replaced with *into.* See comment at *in a jam* and the examples below.) □ *Bob exercises frequently, so he's in condition.* □ *If I were in shape, I could run faster and farther.* □ *I'm not healthy. I have to try to get into shape.*

in conformity with something being in agreement or accordance with something. (*In* can be replaced with *into.* See comment at *in a jam* and the examples below.) □ *Your actions aren't in conformity with our contract.* □ *Please make sure your accountancy system is in conformity with our agreement.* □ *Your new garage isn't in conformity with the planning laws of this community.*

in consequence (of something) as a result of something; because of something. □ *In consequence of the storm, there was no electricity.* □ *The wind blew down the wires. In consequence, we had no electricity.*

in consideration of something in return for something; as a result of something. (Compare to *out of consideration for someone or something.*) □ *In consideration of your many years of service, we are pleased to present you with this gold watch.* □ *In consideration of your efforts, here is a cheque for £3,000.*

in creation See *on earth.*

in deep deeply involved. (Slang.) □ *John and Peter are both in deep in the embezzlement scheme.* □ *Jane and Mary aren't involved in the controversy, but Kate is in deep.*

in deep water in a dangerous or vulnerable situation; in a serious situation; in trouble. (As if one were swimming in or had fallen into water which is over one's head. See also *go off the deep end. In* can be replaced with *into.* See comment at *in a jam* and the examples below.) □ *John is having trouble with his wife. He's in deep water.* □ *Bill is in deep water in algebra class. He's almost failing.* □ *He really got himself into deep water when he ran away from school.*

in defiance of someone or something against someone's will or against instructions; in bold resistance to someone or someone's orders. □ *Jane spent the afternoon in the park in defiance of her mother's instructions.* □ *She did it in defiance of her mother.*

in due course AND **in due time; in good time; in the course of time; in time** in a normal or expected amount of time. □ *The roses will bloom in due course.* □ *The vice-president will become president in due course.* □ *I'll retire in due time.* □ *Just wait, my dear. All in good time.* □ *It'll all work out in the course of time.* □ *In time, things will improve.*

in due time See the previous entry.

in earnest sincerely. □ *This time I'll try in earnest.* □ *She spoke in earnest, and many people believed her.*

in exchange (for someone or something) in return for someone or something. □ *They gave us two of our prisoners in exchange for two of theirs.* □ *I gave him chocolate in exchange for some liquorice.* □ *John gave Mary a book and got a sweater in exchange.*

in favour of someone See under *in someone's favour.*

in favour (of someone or something) **1.** approving, supporting, or endorsing someone or something. □ *Are you in favour of lower tax rates?* □ *Of course, I'm in favour.* **2.** [with *someone*] See *in someone's favour* (sense 3).

in fear and trembling with anxiety or fear; with dread. □ *In fear and trembling, I went into the room to take the exam.* □ *The witness left the courtroom in fear and trembling.*

in fine feather in good humour; in good health. (*In* can be replaced with *into.* See comment at *in a jam* and the examples below.) □ *Hello, John. You appear to be in fine feather.* □ *Of course I'm in fine feather. I get lots of sleep.* □ *Good food and lots of sleep put me into fine feather.*

in for something due to receive a surprise; due to receive punishment. (Informal. When the *something* is *it*, the *it* usually means punishment.) □ *I hope I'm not in for any surprises when I get home.* □ *Tommy, you broke my bat. You're really in for it!*

in force in a very large group. (See also *out in force.*) □ *The entire group arrived in force.* □ *The mosquitoes will attack in force this evening.*

in front (of someone or something) before someone or something; ahead of someone or something. □ *We waited quietly in front of the house.* □ *John said, "Who is in front of me?"* □ *Ann said, "I'm in front."*

in full swing in progress; operating or running without restraint. (Informal. *In* can be replaced with *into.* See comment at *in a jam* and the examples below.) □ *We can't leave now! The party is in full swing.* □ *Our programme to help the starving people is in full swing. You should see results soon.* □ *Just wait until our project gets into full swing.*

in good condition See *in good shape.*

in good faith with good and honest intent; with sincerity. (Compare to *in bad faith.*) □ *We are convinced you were acting in good faith, even though you made a serious error.* □ *I think you didn't sign the contract in good faith. You never intended to carry out our agreement.* ALSO: **show good faith** to demonstrate good intentions or good will. □ *I'm certain that you showed good faith when you signed the contract.*

in good shape AND **in good condition** physically and functionally sound and sturdy. (Used for both people and things. Compare to *in condition. In* can be replaced with *into*. See comment at *in a jam* and the examples below.) □ *This car isn't in good shape.* □ *I'd like to have one that's in better condition.* □ *Mary is in good condition. She works hard to keep healthy.* □ *You have to make an effort to get into good shape.*

in good time 1. quickly; in a short amount of time. □ *We travelled from London to Edinburgh in good time.* □ *I've never been able to make that trip in good time.* **2.** See *in due course*.

in great haste very fast; in a big hurry. □ *John always did his homework in great haste.* □ *Why not take time and do it properly? Don't do everything in great haste.*

in heat in a period of sexual excitement; in oestrus. (*Oestrus* is the period of time in which females are most willing to breed. This expression is usually used for animals. It has been used for humans in a joking sense. *In* can be replaced with *into*. See comment at *in a jam* and the examples below.) □ *Our dog is in heat.* □ *She goes into heat every year at this time.* □ *When my dog is in heat, I have to keep her locked in the house.*

in high gear (*In* can be replaced with *into*. See comment at *in a jam* and the examples below.) **1.** [for a machine, such as a car] to be set in its highest gear, giving the greatest speed. □ *When my car is in high gear, it goes very fast.* □ *You can't start out in high gear. You must work up through the low ones.* □ *You don't go into high gear soon enough.* **2.** very fast and active. (Informal.) □ *When Jane is in high gear, she's a superb athlete.* □ *When Jane moved into high gear, I knew she'd win the race.*

in honour of someone or something showing respect or admiration for someone or something. □ *Our club gave a party in honour of the club's president.* □ *I wrote a poem in honour of John and Mary's marriage.*

in hot water in trouble. (Slang. *In* can be replaced with *into*. See comment at *in a jam* and the examples below.) □ *John got himself into hot water by being late.*

□ *I'm in hot water at home for coming in late last night.* □ *I get into hot water a lot.*

in (just) a second in a very short period of time. □ *I'll be there in a second.* □ *I'll be with you in just a second. I'm on the phone.*

in keeping (with something) AND **in line with something** in accord or harmony with something; following the rules of something. □ *In keeping with your instructions, I've cancelled your order.* □ *I'm disappointed with your behaviour. It really wasn't in keeping.* □ *It was not in line with the kind of behaviour we expect here.*

in kind 1. in goods rather than in money. □ *The country doctor was sometimes paid in kind. He accepted two pigs as payment for an operation.* □ *Do you have to pay VAT tax on payments made in kind?* **2.** similarly; [giving] something similar to what was received. □ *John punched Bill, and Bill gave it back in kind.* □ *She spoke rudely to me, so I spoke to her in kind.*

in league (with someone) in co-operation with someone; in a conspiracy with someone. □ *The mayor is in league with the council treasurer. They are misusing public money.* □ *Those two have been in league for years.*

in less than no time very quickly. □ *I'll be there in less than no time.* □ *Don't worry. This won't take long. It'll be over with in less than no time.*

in lieu of something in place of something; instead of something. (The word *lieu* occurs only in this phrase.) □ *They gave me roast beef in lieu of steak.* □ *We gave money to charity in lieu of sending flowers to the funeral.*

in limbo (*In* can be replaced with *into*. See comment at *in a jam* and the examples below.) **1.** a region on the border of hell. (In some Christian religions, there is a *limbo* set aside for souls which do not go to either heaven or hell. This sense is used only in this religious context.) □ *The baby's soul was in limbo* *because she had not been baptized.* **2.** in a state of neglect; in a state of oblivion; in an indefinite state. □ *We'll have to leave the project in limbo for a month or two.* □ *Our plans are in limbo until I hear about the job.*

in line with something See *in keeping with something.*

in love (with someone or something) feeling love for someone or something; experiencing a strong affectionate emotion for someone or something. □ *John is deeply in love with Mary.* □ *Those two are really in love.* □ *Mary was in love with her new car! It was perfect for her.*

in luck fortunate; lucky. □ *You want a red one? You're in luck. There is one red one left.* □ *I had an accident, but I was in luck. It was not serious.*

in mint condition in perfect condition. (Refers to the perfect state of a coin which has just been minted. *In* can be replaced with *into.* See comment at *in a jam* and the examples below.) □ *This is a fine car. It runs well and is in mint condition.* □ *We found a first edition in mint condition and decided to buy it.* □ *We put our house into mint condition before we sold it.*

in name only nominally; not actual, only by terminology. □ *The president is head of the country in name only.* □ *Mr. Smith is the managing director of the Smith Company in name only. Mrs. Smith handles all the business affairs.*

in no mood to do something not to feel like doing something; to wish not to do something. □ *I'm in no mood to cook dinner tonight.* □ *Mother is in no mood to put up with our arguing.*

in no time (at all) very quickly. (Compare to *in less than no time.*) □ *I'll be there in no time.* □ *It won't take long. I'll be finished in no time at all.*

in no uncertain terms in very specific and direct language. □ *I was so mad. I told her in no uncertain terms to leave and never come back.* □ *I told him in no uncertain terms to stop it.*

in one ear and out the other [for something to be] ignored; [for something to be] unheard or unheeded. (Informal. *In* can be replaced with *into.* See the explanation at *in a jam* and the examples below.) □ *Everything I say to you goes into one ear and out the other!* □ *Bill just doesn't pay attention. Everything is in one ear and out the other.*

in one fell swoop See *at one fell swoop.*

in one's birthday suit naked; nude. (Informal. In the "clothes" in which one was born.) □ *I've heard that John sleeps in his birthday suit.* □ *We used to go down to the river and swim in our birthday suits.*

in one's blood See *in the blood.*

in one's book in one's opinion. (Informal.) □ *He's okay in my book.* □ *In my book, this is the best that money can buy.*

in one's cups drunk. □ *She doesn't make much sense when she's in her cups.* □ *The speaker—who was in his cups—could hardly be understood.*

in one's element in a natural or comfortable situation or environment. (Compare to *out of one's element.*) □ *Sally is in her element when she's working with algebra or calculus.* □ *Bob loves to work with colour and texture. When he's painting, he's in his element.*

in one's glory at one's happiest or best. □ *When I go to the seaside on holiday, I'm in my glory.* □ *Sally is a good teacher. She's in her glory in the classroom.*

in one's mind's eye in one's mind. (Refers to visualizing something in one's mind.) □ *In my mind's eye, I can see trouble ahead.* □ *In her mind's eye, she could see a beautiful building beside the river. She decided to design such a building.*

in one's opinion according to one's belief or judgement. □ *In my opinion, that is a very ugly picture.* □ *That isn't a good idea in my opinion.*

in one's or its prime at one's or its peak or best time. (Compare to *in the prime* *of life.*) □ *Our dog—which is in its prime—is very active.* □ *The programme ended in its prime when we ran out of money.* □ *I could work long hours when I was in my prime.*

in one's (own) backyard (figuratively) very close to one. (Informal.) □ *That kind of thing is quite rare. Imagine it happening right in your backyard.* □ *You always think of something like that happening to someone else. You never expect to find it in your own backyard.*

in one's (own) (best) interests to one's advantage; as a benefit to oneself. □ *It is not in your own interests to share your ideas with Jack. He will say that they are his.* □ *Jane thought it was in the best interests of her friend to tell her mother about her illness.*

in one's own time not while one is at work. □ *My employer made me write the report in my own time. That's not fair.* □ *Please make your personal telephone calls in your own time.*

in one's own way **1.** as the best one can do; using a personal and individual strategy. □ *I don't know the answer to the problem, but perhaps I can help in my own way.* □ *She couldn't go to war and carry a gun, but she helped in her own way.* **2.** in the special way that one wishes or demands. □ *I don't like doing it your way. I want to do it in my own way.* □ *I prefer to do it in my own way.*

in one's right mind sane; rational and sensible. (Often in the negative.) □ *That was a stupid thing to do. You're not in your right mind.* □ *You can't be in your right mind! That sounds crazy!*

in one's second childhood being interested in things or people which normally interest children. □ *My father bought himself a toy train, and my mother said he was in his second childhood.* □ *Whenever I go to the river and throw stones, I feel as though I'm in my second childhood.*

in one's spare time in one's leisure time; in the time not reserved for doing something else. □ *I write novels in my spare*

time. □ *I'll try to paint the house in my spare time.*

in one's Sunday best in one's best Sunday clothes; in the clothes one wears to church. (*In* can be replaced with *into*. See comment at *in a jam* and the examples below.) □ *All the children were dressed up in their Sunday best.* □ *I like to be in my Sunday best whenever I go out.* □ *Let's get into our Sunday best and go out for dinner.*

in opposition (to someone or something) against someone or something; opposing someone or something. □ *You'll find that I'm firmly in opposition to any further expenditures.* □ *The mayor stands in direct opposition to the entire town council.* □ *The council and the mayor are usually in opposition.*

in orbit (*In* can be replaced with *into*. See comment at *in a jam* and the examples below.) **1.** [for something] to circle a heavenly body. (Planets, moons, and stars are heavenly bodies.) □ *The moon is in orbit around the earth.* □ *They put the satellite into orbit.* **2.** ecstatic; thrilled; emotionally high; very angry. (Slang.) □ *She went into orbit when she saw the damage.* □ *John went into orbit when he got the cheque in the mail.*

in order to do something for the purpose of doing something; as a means of doing something. □ *I went to college in order to further my education.* □ *I gave John three pounds in order to buy lunch.*

in other words said in another, simpler way. □ BOB: *Cease! Desist!* BILL: *In other words you want me to stop?* □ *Our cash flow is negative, and our assets are worthless. In other words, we are broke.*

in over one's head with more difficulties than one can manage. (Informal. See also *in deep; in deep water.*) □ *Calculus is very hard for me. I'm in over my head.* □ *Ann is too busy. She's really in over her head.*

in part partly; to a lesser degree or extent. □ *I was not there, in part because* *of my disagreement about the purpose of the meeting, but I also had a previous appointment.* □ *I hope to win, in part because I want the prize money.*

in passing AND **en passant** casually; as an aside. □ *I just mentioned your name in passing. I didn't say more than that.* □ *The lecturer referred to Oliver Cromwell in passing.* □ *He alluded to the matter en passant.*

in place in the proper place or location. (See also *out of place.*) □ *Everything was in place for the ceremony.* □ *It's good to see everything in place again.*

in place of someone or something instead of someone or something. □ *John went in place of Mary.* □ *We had vegetables in place of meat.*

in plain English in simple, clear, and straightforward language. (*In* can be replaced with *into*. See comment at *in a jam* and the examples below.) □ *That's too confusing. Please say it again in plain English.* □ *Tell me again in plain English.* □ *Please put it into plain English.*

in poor taste See *in bad taste.*

in practice **1.** in an application (of a principle, etc.); in the actual doing of something. □ *Our official policy is to be very particular, but in practice we don't care that much.* □ *The instructions say not to set it too high. In practice I always set it as high as possible.* **2.** well rehearsed; well practised; well exercised. □ *The swimmer was not in practice and almost drowned.* □ *I play the piano for a living, and I have to keep in practice.*

in print available in printed form. (Compare to *out of print.*) □ *I think I can get that book for you. It's still in print.* □ *This is the only book in print on this subject.*

in progress happening now; taking place at this time. □ *You can't go into that room. There is a meeting in progress.* □ *Please tell me about the work you have in progress.*

in pursuit of something chasing after something. □ *Bill spends most of his time in pursuit of money.* □ *Every year Bob goes into the countryside in pursuit of butterflies.*

in Queer Street in a difficult situation, especially because of lack of money. (Informal.) □ *We're in Queer Street. We've no money to pay the rent.* □ *No wonder Jack's in Queer Street. He spends more than he earns.*

in quest of someone or something AND **in search of someone or something** seeking or hunting something; trying to find something. □ *They went into town in quest of a reasonably priced restaurant.* □ *On Monday morning I'll go out in search of a job.*

in rags in worn-out and torn clothing. □ *The beggars were in rags.* □ *I think the new casual fashions make you look as though you're in rags.*

in reference to someone or something AND **in regard to someone or something; in relation to someone or something; with respect to someone or something** concerning or about someone or something; in connection with someone or something. (*In* can be replaced with *with,* as in the examples.) □ *What shall we do in reference to Bill and his problem?* □ *With reference to what problem?* □ *I'm writing this letter in regard to your recent telephone call.* □ *I mention this fact with respect to your proposed trip.* □ *With respect to my trip, I have nothing to say.* □ *Let's discuss Bill in relation to his future with this company.*

in regard to someone or something See the previous entry.

in relation to someone or something See *in reference to someone or something.*

in return (for someone or something) in exchange for someone or something; in trade for someone or something. □ *What do they ask in return for their hostages?* □ *I'll give you four chocolate truffles in return for eight chocolate mints.* □ *I ask nothing in return.*

in round figures See the following entry.

in round numbers AND **in round figures** as an estimated number; a figure which has been rounded off. (*In* can be replaced with *into*. See comment at *in a jam*.) □ *Please tell me in round numbers what it'll cost.* □ *I don't need the exact amount. Just give it to me in round figures.*

in search of someone or something See *in quest of someone or something*.

in season 1. currently available for selling. (Some foods and other things are available only at certain seasons. Compare to *out of season*. *In* can be replaced with *into*, especially when used with *come*. See *in a jam* and the examples below.) □ *Oysters are available in season.* □ *Strawberries aren't in season in January.* □ *When do strawberries come into season?* **2.** legally able to be caught or hunted. □ *Catfish are in season all year round.* □ *When are salmon in season?*

in seventh heaven in a very happy state. □ *Ann was really in seventh heaven when she got a car of her own.* □ *I'd be in seventh heaven if I had a million pounds.*

in shape See *in condition*.

in short stated briefly. □ *At the end of the financial report, the treasurer said, "In short, we are okay."* □ *My remarks, in short, indicate that we are in good financial shape.*

in short supply scarce. □ *Fresh vegetables are in short supply in the winter.* □ *Yellow cars are in short supply because everyone likes them and buys them.*

(in) single file queued up, one behind the other; in a queue, one person or one thing wide. (*In* can be replaced with *into*. See comment at *in a jam* and the examples below.) □ *Have you ever seen ducks walking in single file?* □ *No, do they usually walk single file?* □ *Please march in single file.* □ *Please get into single file.*

in so many words exactly; explicitly; literally. □ *I told her in so many words to leave me alone.* □ *He said yes, but not in so many words.*

in some neck of the woods in a particular area or neighborhood. (The *some* is usually *this, that, your, their*, etc.) □ *I think that the Smiths live in your neck of the woods.* □ *I don't know what's happening in our neck of the woods.*

in someone else's place See the following entry.

in someone else's shoes AND **in someone else's place** seeing or experiencing something from someone else's point of view. □ *You might feel different if you were in her shoes.* □ *Pretend you're in Tom's place, and then try to think why he acts the way he does.* ALSO: **put oneself in someone else's place** to allow oneself to see or experience something from someone else's point of view. □ *Put yourself in Jane's place, and see how it feels.*

in someone's favour 1. to someone's advantage or credit. (Especially in sports scores, as in the examples.) □ *The score was ten to twelve in our favour.* □ *At the end of the second half, the score was forty to three in the other team's favour.* **2.** liked by someone; approved of by someone. (*In* can be replaced with *into*. See comment at *in a jam* and the examples below.) □ *John might be able to help me. I hope I'm currently in his favour.* □ *My mother is angry at me. I'm certainly not in her favour.* □ *I'll try to get into her favour.* **3.** AND **in favour of someone** to someone, as when writing a cheque. (See also *honour someone's cheque*.) □ *Please make out a cheque for £300 in Tom's favour.* □ *I'm making out the cheque in favour of Mr. Brown.*

in someone's name 1. See *on behalf of someone*. **2.** in someone's ownership; as someone's property. (*In* can be replaced with *into*. See comment at *in a jam* and the examples below.) □ *The house is in my name. I own all of it.* □ *I put the* *house into my husband's name.* □ *The car is in both our names.*

in someone's or something's way See under *in the way of someone or something.*

in spite of someone or something regardless of someone or something; in defiance of someone or something. □ *In spite of what you said, I still like you.* □ *He went to the concert in spite of his parents.*

in step (with someone or something) (*In* can be replaced with *into.* See comment at *in a jam* and the examples below.) **1.** [with *someone*] [marching or dancing] in time with another person. □ *Please keep in step with Jane.* □ *You two, back there. You aren't in step.* □ *Get into step!* **2.** AND **in time (with someone or something)** [with *something*] keeping in time with music. □ *John, your violin isn't in step with the beat. Sit up straight and try it again.* □ *I'm trying to play in time.* **3.** as up to date as someone or something. □ *Bob is not in step with the times.* □ *We try to keep in step with the fashion of the day.*

in stock readily available, as with goods in a shop. □ *I'm sorry, I don't have that in stock. I'll have to order it for you.* □ *We have all our Christmas merchandise in stock now.*

in style 1. in fashion; fashionable. (*In* can be replaced with *into,* especially with *come.* See comment at *in a jam* and the examples below.) □ *This old coat isn't in style any more.* □ *I don't care if it's not in style. It's warm.* □ *I hope this coat comes into style again.* **2.** in elegance; in luxury. (Informal.) □ *If I had a million pounds, I could really live in style.* □ *If he saves his money, someday he'll be able to live in style.*

in terms of something regarding something; concerning something. □ *I don't know what to do in terms of John's problem.* □ *Now, in terms of your proposal, don't you think you're asking for too much?*

in the absence of someone or something while someone or something isn't

here; without someone or something. □ *In the absence of the cook, I'll prepare dinner.* □ *In the absence of opposition, she won easily.*

in the act (of doing something) while doing something. (See also *catch someone in the act (of doing something).*) □ *There he was, in the act of opening the door.* □ *I tripped while in the act of climbing.* □ *It happened in the act, not before or after.*

in the air everywhere; all about. (Also used literally.) □ *There is such a feeling of joy in the air.* □ *We felt a sense of tension in the air.*

in the altogether AND **in the buff; in the raw** naked; nude. (Informal.) □ *We often went swimming in the altogether down at the lake.* □ *The museum has a painting of some ladies in the buff.* □ *Bill says he sleeps in the raw.*

in the back in the back part of a building; in the rear garden. □ *I don't have your size here, but perhaps I can find it in the back.* □ *They have a very nice house with a garage in the back.*

in the bag assured; certain. (Slang.) □ *I've got the election in the bag. Everyone is going to vote for me.* □ *I've got the contract in the bag. They are going to sign it tomorrow.*

in the balance in an undecided state. (See also *hang in the balance.*) □ *He is waiting for the operation. His life is in the balance.* □ *With his fortune in the balance, John rolled the dice.*

in the bargain in addition to what was agreed on. (*In* can be replaced with *into.* See comment at *in a jam* and the examples below.) □ *I bought a car, and they threw a trailer into the bargain.* □ *When I bought the house, I asked the seller to include the furniture in the bargain.*

in the best of health very healthy. □ *Bill is in the best of health. He eats well and exercises.* □ *I haven't been in the best of health. I think I have the flu.*

in the black not in debt; in a financially profitable condition. (Compare to *in the red*. *In* can be replaced with *into*. See comment at *in a jam* and the examples below.) □ *I wish my accounts were in the black.* □ *Sally moved the company into the black.*

in the blood AND **in one's blood** built into one's personality or character. □ *John's a great runner. It's in his blood.* □ *The whole family is very athletic. It's in the blood.*

in the buff See *in the altogether*.

in the care of someone AND **in the charge of someone** in the keeping of someone. □ *I left the baby in the care of my mother.* □ *I placed the house in the care of my friend.* □ *Bill left the office in the charge of his assistant.*

in the case of someone or something 1. in the matter of someone or something; in the instance of someone or something. (See also *in case of something*. Compare to *in the event of something*.) □ *In the case of John, I think we had better allow his request.* □ *In the case of this woman, we'll not grant permission.* **2.** [with *someone*] in the legal proceedings relating to someone. (The *someone* may be contained in the official name of a legal case.) □ *I recall a similar situation in the case of* The Crown *vs.* Jane Smith. □ *Have they found any new facts in the case against Bill Wilson?*

in the charge of someone See *in the care of someone*.

in the clear innocent; not guilty. (Informal.) □ *Don't worry, Tom. I'm certain you're in the clear.* □ *He's in the clear. He has an alibi.*

in the course of time See *in due course*.

in the dark (about someone or something) uninformed about someone or something; ignorant about someone or something. □ *I'm in the dark about who is in charge around here.* □ *I can't imagine why they are keeping me in the dark.* □ *You won't be in the dark long.*

I'm in charge. □ *She's in the dark about how this machine works.*

in the doghouse in trouble; in (someone's) disfavour. (Informal.) □ *I'm really in the doghouse. I was late for an appointment.* □ *I hate being in the doghouse all the time. I don't know why I can't stay out of trouble.*

in the doldrums sluggish; inactive; in low spirits. □ *He's usually in the doldrums in the winter.* □ *I had some bad news yesterday which put me in the doldrums.*

in the event of something if something happens. (Compare to *in the case of someone or something*.) □ *In the event of fire, please leave quickly and quietly.* □ *The picnic will be cancelled in the event of rain.*

in the family restricted to one's own family, as with private or embarrassing information. (Especially with *keep*.) □ *Don't tell anyone else about the bankruptcy. Please keep it in the family.* □ *He told only his brother because he wanted it to remain in the family.*

in the family way pregnant. (Informal.) □ *I've heard that Mrs. Smith is in the family way.* □ *Our daughter is in the family way.*

in the first instance as a beginning; to begin with. (Formal.) □ *If you want a visa, you must fill out a form in the first instance.* □ *Before you can build a house, you must apply for planning permission in the first instance.*

in the first place initially; to begin with. (Compare to *in the second place*.) □ *In the first place, you don't have enough money to buy a car. In the second place, you don't need one.* □ *In the first place, I don't have the time. In the second place, I'm not interested.*

in the flesh really present; in person. □ *I've heard that the queen is coming here in the flesh.* □ *Is she really here? In the flesh?* □ *The old man wanted to see the pope in the flesh.*

in the gutter [for a person to be] in a low state; depraved. (*In* can be replaced with *into*. See *in a jam* and the examples below.) □ *You had better straighten out your life, or you'll end up in the gutter.* □ *His bad habits put him into the gutter.*

in the hot seat See *on the hot seat.*

in the interest(s) of someone or something as an advantage or benefit to someone or something; in order to advance or improve someone or something. (Formal.) □ *In the interest of health, people are asked not to smoke.* □ *The police imprisoned the suspects in the interests of the safety of the public.*

in the know knowledgeable. (Informal.) □ *Let's ask Bob. He's in the know.* □ *I have no knowledge of how to work this machine. Find someone in the know.*

in the lap of luxury in luxurious surroundings. □ *John lives in the lap of luxury because his family is very wealthy.* □ *When I retire, I'd like to live in the lap of luxury.*

in the light of something because of certain knowledge; considering something. (As if knowledge or information shed light on something.) □ *In the light of what you have told us, I think we must abandon the project.* □ *In the light of the shop assistant's rudeness, we didn't return to that shop.*

in the limelight at the centre of attention. (*In* can be replaced with *into*. See comment at *in a jam* and the examples below. *Limelight* is an obsolete form of *spotlight,* and the word occurs only in this phrase.) □ *John will do almost anything to get himself into the limelight.* □ *All elected officials spend a lot of time in the limelight.*

in the line of duty as part of the expected (military, police, or other) duties. □ *When soldiers fight people in a war, it's in the line of duty.* □ *Police officers have to do things they may not like in the line of duty.*

in the long run over a long period of time; ultimately. □ *We'd be better off in the long run buying a car instead of renting one.* □ *In the long run we'd be happier in the South.*

in the market (for something) wanting to buy something. □ *I'm in the market for a video recorder.* □ *If you have a boat for sale, we're in the market.*

in the middle of nowhere in a very remote place. (Informal. *In* can be replaced with *into*. See comment at *in a jam* and the examples below.) □ *We found a nice place to eat, but it's out in the middle of nowhere.* □ *To get to my house, you have to drive into the middle of nowhere.*

in the money wealthy. (Informal.) □ *John is really in the money. He's worth millions.* □ *If I am ever in the money, I'll be generous to others.*

in the mood (for something) in an appropriate state of mind for something. (*In* can be replaced with *into*. See comment at *in a jam* and the examples below.) □ *I'm not in the mood for joking.* □ *I can't get into the mood for dancing.* □ *Sorry, I'm just not in the mood.*

in the near future in the time immediately ahead. □ *I don't plan to go to Florida in the near future.* □ *What do you intend to do in the near future?*

in the nick of time just in time; at the last possible instant; just before it is too late. □ *The doctor arrived in the nick of time. The patient's life was saved.* □ *I reached the airport in the nick of time.*

in the offing happening at some time in the future. (*In* can be replaced with *into*. See comment at *in a jam*.) □ *There is a big investigation in the offing, but I don't know when.* □ *It's hard to tell what's in the offing if you don't keep track of things.*

in the pink (of condition) in very good health; in very good condition, physically and emotionally. (Informal. *In* can be replaced with *into*. See comment at *in a jam* and the examples below.) □ *The* *garden is lovely. All the flowers are in the pink of condition.* □ *Jane has to exercise hard to get into the pink of condition.* □ *She's been ill, but she's in the pink now.*

in the prime of life in the best and most productive period of one's life. (See also *in one's* or *its prime. In* can be replaced with *into.* See comment at *in a jam* and the examples below.) □ *He was struck down by a heart attack in the prime of life.* □ *The good health of one's youth can carry over into the prime of life.*

in the public eye publicly; visible to all; conspicuous. (*In* can be replaced with *into.* See comment at *in a jam* and the examples below.) □ *Elected officials find themselves constantly in the public eye.* □ *The mayor made it a practice to get into the public eye as much as possible.*

in the raw See *in the altogether.*

in the red in debt. (Compare to *in the black. In* can be replaced with *into.* See comment at *in a jam* and the examples below.) □ *My accounts are in the red at the end of every month.* □ *It's easy to get into the red if you don't pay close attention to the amount of money you spend.*

in the right on the moral or legal side of an issue; on the right side of an issue. (Compare to *in the wrong.*) □ *I felt I was in the right, but the judge ruled against me.* □ *It's hard to argue with Jane. She always believes that she's in the right.*

in the running in competition; competing and having a chance to win. (Compare to *out of the running. In* can be replaced with *into.* See comment at *in a jam* and the examples below.) □ *Is Tom still in the running? Does he still have a chance to be elected?* □ *I'm glad I didn't get into the running.*

in the same boat in the same situation; having the same problem. □ TOM: *I'm broke. Can you lend me twenty pounds?* BILL: *Sorry. I'm in the same boat.* □ *Jane and Mary are both in the same*

boat. They both have been called to the boss's office.

in the same breath [stated or said] almost at the same time. □ *He told me I was lazy, but then in the same breath he said I was doing a good job of work.* □ *The teacher said that the pupils were working hard and, in the same breath, that they were not working hard enough.*

in the second place secondly; in addition. (Usually said after one has said *in the first place.*) □ *In the first place, you don't have enough money to buy a car. In the second place, you don't need one.* □ *In the first place, I don't have the time. In the second place, I'm not interested.*

in the short run for the immediate future. (Compare to *in the long run.*) □ *In the short run, we'd be better off saving our money.* □ *We decided to rent a flat in the short run. We can buy a house later.*

in the soup in a bad situation. (Informal.) □ *Now I'm really in the soup. I broke Mrs. Franklin's window.* □ *The child's always in the soup. He attracts trouble.*

in the swim (of things) involved in or participating in events or happenings. (The *in* can be replaced with *into.* See the explanation at *in a jam* and the examples below.) □ *I've been ill, but soon I'll be back in the swim of things.* □ *He can't wait to grow up and get into the swim of things.* □ *Mary loves to be in the swim socially.*

in the twinkling of an eye very quickly. (A biblical reference.) □ *In the twinkling of an eye, the deer had disappeared into the forest.* □ *I gave Bill ten pounds and, in the twinkling of an eye, he spent it.*

in the unlikely event of something if something—which probably will not happen—actually happens. (Compare to *in the event of something.*) □ *In the unlikely event of my getting the job, I'll have to buy a car to get there every day.*

□ *In the unlikely event of a fire, please walk quickly to an exit.*

in the wake of something 1. in the waves and turbulence which follow a boat or a ship. (*In* can be replaced with *into*. See comment at *in a jam* and the examples below.) □ *The small boat followed in the wake of the big boat.* □ *It's dangerous to steer into the wake of a large ship or a barge.* 2. after something; as a result of some event. □ *In the wake of the fire, we had no place to live.* □ *In the wake of the storm, there were many broken branches.*

in the way See the following entry.

in the way of someone or something 1. AND **in someone's or something's way; in the way** blocking someone or something; obstructing someone or something. □ *Please don't get in the way of progress.* □ *You're in the way of the mayor. Make room!* □ *Please leave! You're in the way.* 2. [with *something*] kind of something; style of something. □ *What do you have in the way of leather shoes?* □ *We have nothing in the way of raincoats.*

in the wind about to happen. (Also used literally.) □ *There are some major changes in the wind. Expect these changes to happen soon.* □ *There is something in the wind. We'll find out what it is soon.*

in the world See *on earth*.

in the wrong on the wrong or illegal side of an issue; guilty or in error. (Compare to *in the right*.) □ *I felt she was in the wrong, but the judge ruled in her favour.* □ *It's hard to argue with Jane. She always believes that everyone else is in the wrong.*

in thing (to do) the fashionable thing to do. (Informal.) □ *Eating low-fat food is the in thing to do.* □ *Bob is very old-fashioned. He never does the in thing.*

in this day and age presently; currently; nowadays. □ *You don't expect people to be polite in this day and age.* □ *Young people don't care for their parents in this day and age.*

in time 1. See *in due course*. 2. See *in step (with someone or something)*. 3. before the deadline; before the last minute. □ *Did you hand in your essay on time?* □ *I didn't go to Florida. I didn't get to the airport in time.*

in time (with someone or something) See under *in step (with someone or something)*.

in tune (with someone or something) 1. at the same or a harmonizing musical pitch. □ *The violin isn't in tune with the piano.* □ *Bill is in tune with the others.* 2. [with *something*] keeping up with something. □ *Tom, your clothes are old-fashioned. You aren't in tune with the times.* □ *Come on, Sally. Get in tune with what's going on around you.* 3. in agreement or harmony with someone or something. □ *The two sisters are in tune with each other.* □ *Our ideas are in tune.*

in turn 1. one at a time in sequence. □ *Each of us can read the book in turn.* □ *We cut the hair of every child in turn.* 2. in return (for something). □ *I took Sally out to lunch, and she took me out in turn.* □ *They invited us to their house in turn.*

in two shakes of a lamb's tail in a very short time. □ *Jane returned in two shakes of a lamb's tail.* □ *Fred was able to solve the problem in two shakes of a lamb's tail.*

in vain for no purpose; with no success. □ *They rushed her to the hospital, but they did it in vain.* □ *We tried in vain to get her there on time.* □ *They tried and tried, but their efforts were in vain.*

in view of something in consideration of something; because of something. □ *In view of the high cost of petrol, I sold my car.* □ *I won't invite John to the meeting in view of his attitude.*

in with someone friends with someone; having influence with someone. (Informal.) □ *She's in with management. She'll get promotion.* □ *The politician is in with the prime minister.*

inch along (something) to move slowly along something little by little. □ *The cat inched along the carpet towards the mouse.* □ *Traffic was inching along.*

inch by inch one inch at a time; little by little. □ *Traffic moved along inch by inch.* □ *Inch by inch, the snail moved across the stone.*

incumbent upon someone to do something necessary for someone to do something. (*Upon* can be replaced with *on.*) □ *It's incumbent upon you to do the work.* □ *It was incumbent on me to make the presentation of the first prize.*

inquire after someone to ask about someone. □ *Mary inquired after you. I told her you were well and looked forward to seeing her.* □ *Please inquire after Mary's father the next time you see her.*

ins and outs of something the details that one needs to know in order to do or understand something. (Informal.) □ *I don't understand the ins and outs of politics.* □ *Jane knows the ins and outs of working with computers.*

instrumental in doing something playing an important part in doing something. □ *John was instrumental in getting the contract to build the new building.* □ *Our MP was instrumental in defeating the proposal.*

into something See *be into something.*

iron hand in the velvet glove a strong, ruthless type of control that gives the appearance of being gentle and liberal. □ *In that family, it is a case of the iron hand in the velvet glove. The father looks gentle and loving, but he is a tyrant.* □ *It is a case of the iron hand in the velvet glove in that country. The president pretends to be liberal, but his people have little freedom.*

iron something out AND **iron out something** to solve a problem; to straighten out a problem; to smooth out a difficulty. □ *I just have to iron out this little problem; then I'll be able to see you.* □ *The headmaster had to iron a classroom problem out.*

it behoves one to do something it is necessary for one to do something; it is *incumbent upon someone to do something.* (Formal.) □ *It behoves me to report the crime.* □ *It behoves you to pay for the window which you broke.*

It figures. It makes sense.; It confirms what one might have guessed.; I'm not surprised. (Informal.) □ BOB: *Tom was the one who broke the window.* BILL: *It figures. He's very careless.* □ ANN: *Mary was the last one to arrive.* SALLY: *It figures. She's always late.*

It never rains but it pours. a proverb meaning that a lot of bad things tend to happen at the same time. □ *The car won't start, the stairs broke, and the dog died. It never rains but it pours.* □ *Everything seems to be going wrong. It never rains but it pours.*

It's a deal. Okay.; It is agreed. (Informal.) □ *You want to sell me your stereo for £100? It's a deal.* □ BILL: *Let's go to dinner together tonight.* MARY: *It's a deal.*

It's about time! It is almost too late!; I've been waiting a long time! (Informal.) □ *So you finally got here! It's about time!* □ *They finally paid me my money. It's about time!*

it's high time it is past time (for something); [something] is overdue. (Informal.) □ *It's high time that you got recognition for what you do.* □ *They sent me my cheque, and it's high time, too.*

it's no use (doing something) it is hopeless to do something; it is pointless to do something. □ *It's no use trying to call on the telephone. The line is always engaged.* □ *They tried and tried, but it was no use.*

J

jack of all trades someone who can do several different jobs instead of specializing in one. □ *John can do plumbing, joinery, and roofing—a real jack of all trades. He isn't very good at any of them.* □ *Take your car to a trained mechanic, not a jack of all trades.*

jack something in AND **jack in something** to stop doing something; to abandon something. (Slang.) □ *I'd jack in working tomorrow.* □ *He's jacked his job in for good.*

jack something up AND **jack up something 1.** to raise something with a jack. □ *Ann jacked up the car to change the tyre.* □ *The workers jacked the house up, put logs under it, and rolled it away.* **2.** to raise the price. (Informal.) □ *The electric company jacked up the price of electricity.* □ *The butcher jacks the price of meat up at the week-end.*

jam tomorrow good things in the future. (It is suggested that the future never comes. From Lewis Carroll's *Through the Looking-Glass* in which the Red Queen offers Alice "jam every other day . . . jam yesterday and jam tomorrow but never jam today.") □ *The politicians promised the people jam tomorrow during the hard times.* □ *Jack was tired of working for a firm that kept promising him a large salary in the future—jam tomorrow.*

jazz something up AND **jazz up something** to make something more exciting, colourful, or lively. (Slang. Said originally of music.) □ *I think we need to jazz up this room. It looks so drab.*

□ *When we play the music this time, let's jazz it up a bit.*

Jekyll and Hyde someone with both an evil and a good personality. (From *The Strange Case of Dr. Jekyll and Mr. Hyde* by Robert Louis Stevenson.) □ *Bill thinks Mary is so soft and gentle, but she can be very cruel—she is a real Jekyll and Hyde.* □ *Jane doesn't know that Fred is a Jekyll and Hyde. She sees him only when he is being kind and generous, but he can be very mean and miserly.*

job lot a mixed collection of varying quality. (Informal.) □ *Mike found a valuable vase in that job lot he bought at the auction.* □ *There was nothing but junk in the job lot that I bought.*

Job's comforter someone who makes matters worse when trying to comfort or console someone. □ *Jane is a Job's comforter. She told me how many other people were looking for jobs when I lost my job.* □ *John's a Job's comforter, too. He told Mary that there were lots of other unattached girls in the district when her engagement was broken off.*

jockey for position to try to push or manoeuvre one's way into an advantageous position at the expense of others. □ *All the staff in that firm are jockeying for position. They all want the manager's job.* □ *It is unpleasant working for a firm where people are always jockeying for position.*

johnny-come-lately someone who joins in (something) after it is under way. □ *Don't pay any attention to Sally. She's just a johnny-come-lately and doesn't* *know what she's talking about.* □ *We've been here for thirty years. Why should some johnny-come-lately tell us what to do?*

join forces (with someone) to join with someone. □ *We joined forces with the police to search for the lost child.* □ *The choirs joined forces to sing the song.*

Join the club! an expression indicating that the person spoken to is in the same, or a similar, unfortunate state as the speaker. (Informal.) □ *You've got nowhere to stay? Join the club! Neither have we.* □ *Did you get the sack, too? Join the club!*

joking apart being serious for a moment; in all seriousness. □ *I know I laugh at him but, joking apart, he's a very clever scientist.* □ *I know I threatened to leave and go round the world, but, joking apart, I need a holiday.*

jolly someone along to keep someone happy and satisfied in order to obtain compliance with one's wishes. □ *If you jolly Jim along, he will help you with the garden.* □ *You'll have to jolly Bert along if you want his help. If he's in a bad mood, he'll refuse.*

judge one on one's own merit(s) AND **judge something on its own merit(s)** to judge or evaluate one on one's own achievements and virtues, not someone else's; to judge or evaluate a thing on its own good points and usefulness. □ *Please judge me on my own merits, not on those of my family.* □ *You should judge Sally on her own merit. Forget that her mother is a famous opera star.* □ *You have to judge each painting on its own merits. Not every painting by a famous painter is superior.* □ *Each rose must be judged on its own merit.*

judge something on its own merit(s) See the previous entry.

judging by something considering something; using something as an indication (of something else). □ *Judging by your wet clothing, it must be raining.* □ *Judging by the looks of this house, I would guess there has been a party here.*

jump at something to seize the opportunity to do something. (Usually with *it*. See *jump at the chance (to do something)* from which this phrase comes.) □ *When I heard about John's chance to go to England, I knew he'd jump at it.* □ *If something you really want to do comes your way, jump at it.*

jump at the chance (to do something) AND **jump at the opportunity (to do something); leap at the opportunity (to do something)** to take advantage of a chance to do something. □ *John jumped at the chance to go to England.* □ *I don't know why I didn't jump at the opportunity myself.* □ *I should have leapt at the chance.*

jump at the opportunity (to do something) See the previous entry.

jump bail AND **skip bail** to fail to appear in court for trial and forfeit one's bail bond. (Slang.) □ *Not only was Bob arrested for theft, he skipped bail and left town. He's in a lot of trouble.* □ *I thought only criminals jumped bail.*

jump down someone's throat AND **jump on someone** to scold someone severely. (Informal.) □ *If I disagree with them, my parents will jump down my throat.* □ *Don't jump on me! I didn't do it!*

jump off the deep end See *go off the deep end.*

jump on someone See *jump down someone's throat.*

jump on the bandwagon AND **climb on the bandwagon** to join others in doing something; to join the popular side (of an issue); to take a popular position. □ *Everyone's jumping on the bandwagon and criticizing the government.* □ *The workers are all climbing on the bandwagon and buying shares in the company.*

jump out of one's skin to react strongly to shock or surprise. (Informal. Usually with *nearly, almost,* etc.) □ *Oh! You really scared me. I nearly jumped out of* *my skin.* □ *Bill was so startled he almost jumped out of his skin.*

jump the gun to start before the starting signal. (Informal. Originally used in sports contests which are started by firing a gun.) □ *We all had to start the race again because Jane jumped the gun.* □ *When we took the test, Tom jumped the gun and started early.*

jump through a hoop AND **jump through hoops** to do everything possible to obey or please someone; to *bend over backwards to do something.* (Informal. Trained animals jump through hoops.) □ *She expects us to jump through hoops for her.* □ *What do you want me to do—jump through a hoop?*

jump to conclusions AND **leap to conclusions** to judge or decide something without having all the facts; to reach unwarranted conclusions. □ *Now don't jump to conclusions. Wait until you hear what I have to say.* □ *Please find out all the facts so you won't leap to conclusions.*

jump to it to hurry up; to get moving. (Slang.) □ *Jump to it and load that lorry!* □ *You had better jump to it if you want to catch that bus.*

jumping-off point a point or place from which to begin a venture. □ *The local library is a good jumping-off point for your research.* □ *The office job in that*

firm would be a good jumping-off point for a job in advertising.

just as soon do something See *had as soon do something.*

just in case See under *in case of something.*

just one of those things something which couldn't have been prevented; something caused by fate. □ *I'm sorry, too. It's not your fault. It's just one of those things.* □ *I feel terrible that I didn't pass the bar exam. I suppose it was just one of those things.*

just so 1. in perfect order; neat and tidy. □ *Her hair is always just so.* □ *Their front garden is just so.* 2. (Usually **Just so!**) Precisely right!; Quite right! □ BILL: *The letter should arrive tomorrow.* TOM: *Just so!* □ JANE: *We must always try our best.* MARTIN: *Just so!*

just the job exactly what is required. (Informal.) □ *Those pills were just the job for Jean's headache.* □ *That jacket was just the job for wet weather.*

just the same See *all the same.*

just what the doctor ordered exactly what is required, especially for health or comfort. □ *That meal was delicious, Bob. Just what the doctor ordered.* □ BOB: *Would you like something to drink?* MARY: *Yes, a glass of cold water would be just what the doctor ordered.*

K

keel over [for a person] to fall over or fall down in a faint or in death. □ *Suddenly, Mr. Franklin keeled over. He had had a heart attack.* □ *It was so hot in the room that two people just keeled over.*

keen on someone or something enthusiastic about someone or something. □ *I'm not too keen on going to London.* □ *Sally is fairly keen on getting a new job.* □ *Mary isn't keen on her new assignment.*

keep a civil tongue (in one's head) to speak decently and politely. □ *Please, John. Don't talk like that. Keep a civil tongue in your head.* □ *John seems unable to keep a civil tongue.*

keep a stiff upper lip to be cool and unmoved by unsettling events. □ *John always keeps a stiff upper lip.* □ *Now, Billy, don't cry. Keep a stiff upper lip.*

keep a straight face to make one's face stay free from laughter or smiling. □ *It's hard to keep a straight face when someone tells a funny joke.* □ *I knew it was John who played the trick. He couldn't keep a straight face.*

keep abreast (of something) AND **be abreast (of something)** to keep informed about something; to keep up (with the times). □ *I try to keep abreast of the financial markets.* □ *I believe that I'm abreast of foreign events.* □ *Yes, I try to keep abreast by reading the papers every day.*

keep after someone See under *get after someone.*

keep ahead (of someone or something) See under *get ahead (of someone or something).*

keep an eye on someone or something See *have an eye on someone or something.*

keep an eye out (for someone or something) to watch for the arrival or appearance of someone or something. (The *an* can be replaced by *one's.*) □ *Please keep an eye out for the bus.* □ *Keep an eye out for rain.* □ *Keep your eye out for a raincoat on sale.* □ *Okay. I'll keep my eye out.*

keep at someone See under *get after someone.*

keep at someone or something **1.** [with *someone*] See *get after someone.* **2.** [with *something*] to continue doing something; to continue trying to do something. □ *Keep at the project if you want to get it finished.* □ *Don't give up now. Keep at it!*

keep away (from someone or something) See under *get away (from someone or something).*

keep body and soul together to feed, clothe, and house oneself. □ *I hardly have enough money to keep body and soul together.* □ *How the old man was able to keep body and soul together is beyond me.*

keep company with someone to spend much time with someone; to associate or consort with someone. (Compare to *keep someone company.*) □ *Bill has been keeping company with Ann for* *three months.* □ *Bob has been keeping company with a tough-looking bunch of boys.*

keep cool to keep calm and undisturbed. (Slang.) □ *Relax, man, keep cool!* □ *If Sally could just keep cool before a race, she could probably win.*

keep good time [for a watch or clock] to be accurate. □ *I have to return my watch to the shop because it doesn't keep good time.* □ *Mine keeps good time.*

keep house to manage a household. □ *I hate to keep house. I'd rather live in a tent than keep house.* □ *My grandmother kept house for nearly sixty years.*

keep in touch (with someone) See under *get in touch (with someone).*

keep in with someone to remain friendly with a person, especially a person who might be useful. (Informal.) □ *Jack keeps in with Jane because he likes to borrow her car.* □ *The children keep in with Peter because his father has a sweet-shop.*

keep late hours to stay up or stay out until very late. □ *I'm always tired because I keep late hours.* □ *If I didn't keep late hours, I wouldn't sleep so late in the morning.*

keep off (something) to stay off something; not to trespass. (See also *keep someone or something off.*) □ *You had better keep off my property.* □ *The sign says "Keep off."*

keep on an even keel to remain cool and calm. (Originally nautical.) □ *If Jane can keep on an even keel and not panic, she will be all right.* □ *Try to keep on an even keel and not get upset so easily.*

keep on (doing something) to continue to do something. □ *I have to keep on painting the house until I'm finished.* □ *Please keep on working until the bell rings.* □ *I just have to keep on.*

keep on someone See *get after someone.*

keep on the good side of someone See under *get on the good side of someone.*

keep on (with something) to continue to do something; to pursue the doing of something. (See also *get on (with someone or something).*) □ *I have to keep on with my studies.* □ *I can't stop now. I have to keep on.*

keep one's chin up to keep one's spirits high; to act brave and confident. (Informal.) □ *Keep your chin up, John. Things will get better.* □ *Just keep your chin up and tell the judge exactly what happened.*

keep one's distance (from someone or something) to maintain a respectful or cautious distance from someone or something. (The distance can be figurative or literal.) □ *Keep your distance from John. He's in a bad mood.* □ *Keep your distance from the fire.* □ *Okay. I'll tell Sally to keep her distance, too.*

keep one's ear to the ground See *have one's ear to the ground.*

keep one's end of the bargain See *keep one's side of the bargain.*

keep one's eye on someone or something See *have an eye on someone or something.*

keep one's eye on the ball to remain alert to the events occurring around one. (Informal.) □ *If you want to get along in this office, you're going to have to keep your eye on the ball.* □ *Bill would do better in his classes if he would just keep his eye on the ball.*

keep one's eyes open (for someone or something) AND **keep one's eyes peeled (for someone or something)** to remain alert and watchful for someone or something. (The entries with *peeled* are informal. *Peel* refers to moving the eyelids back.) □ *I'm keeping my eyes open for a sale on winter coats.* □ *Please keep your eyes peeled for Mary. She's due to arrive here any time.* □ *Okay. I'll keep my eyes open.*

keep one's eyes peeled (for someone or something) See the previous entry.

keep one's feet on the ground See *have one's feet on the ground.*

keep one's fingers crossed (for someone or something) AND **cross one's fingers** to wish for luck for someone or something, often by crossing one's fingers; to hope for a good outcome for someone or something. □ *I hope you win the race Saturday. I'm keeping my fingers crossed for you.* □ *I'm auditioning for a play. Keep your fingers crossed!*

keep one's hand in (something) to retain one's control of something. (See also *take a hand in something.*) □ *I want to keep my hand in the business.* □ *Mrs. Johnson has retired from the library, but she still wants to keep her hand in. She works part-time.*

keep one's hands off (someone or something) See under *get one's hands off (someone or something).*

keep one's head above water See under *get one's head above water.*

keep one's mouth shut (about someone or something) to keep quiet about someone or something; to keep a secret about someone or something. (Informal.) □ *They told me to keep my mouth shut about the problem or I'd be in big trouble.* □ *I think I'll keep my mouth shut.*

keep one's nose clean to keep out of trouble, especially trouble with the law. (Slang.) □ *I'm trying to keep my nose clean by staying away from those rough blokes.* □ *John, if you don't learn how to keep your nose clean, you're going to end up in jail.*

keep one's nose in the air See *have one's nose in the air.*

keep one's nose out of someone's business See under *get one's nose out of someone's business.*

keep one's nose to the grindstone to keep busy doing one's work. (Also with *have* and *get,* as in the examples.) □ *The manager told me to keep my nose to the grindstone or be sacked.* □ *I've had my nose to the grindstone ever since I started working here.* □ *If the other*

people in this office would get their noses to the grindstone, more work would get done.

keep one's own counsel to keep one's thoughts and plans to oneself; not to tell other people about one's thoughts and plans. □ *Jane is very quiet. She tends to keep her own counsel.* □ *I advise you to keep your own counsel.*

keep one's side of the bargain AND **keep one's end of the bargain** to do one's part as agreed; to attend to one's responsibilities as agreed. □ *Tom has to learn to co-operate. He must keep his side of the bargain.* □ *If you don't keep your side of the bargain, the whole project will fail.*

keep one's temper AND **hold one's temper** not to become angry; to hold back an expression of anger. □ *She should have learned to keep her temper when she was a child.* □ *Sally got thrown off the team because she couldn't hold her temper.*

keep one's weather eye open to watch for something (to happen); to be on the alert (for something); to be on guard. □ *Some trouble is brewing. Keep your weather eye open.* □ *Try to be more alert. Learn to keep your weather eye open.*

keep one's wits about one See under *have one's wits about one.*

keep one's word to uphold one's promise. □ *I told her I'd be there to collect her, and I intend to keep my word.* □ *Keeping one's word is necessary in the legal profession.*

keep oneself to oneself to remain private; not to mix with other people very much. □ *We never see our neighbours. They keep themselves to themselves.* □ *Jean used to go out a lot, but she has kept herself to herself since her husband died.*

keep out (of something or somewhere) AND **stay out (of something or somewhere)** not to enter something or somewhere; to refrain from entering something or somewhere. □ *Keep out* *of here!* □ *Don't you hear me? Stay out!* □ *Stay out of the school building.*

keep pace (with someone or something) to move at the same speed as someone or something; to keep up with someone or something. □ *The black horse was having a hard time keeping pace with the brown one.* □ *Bill can't keep pace with the geometry class.* □ *You've just got to keep pace.*

keep quiet (about someone or something) not to reveal something about someone or something; to keep a secret about someone or something. □ *Please keep quiet about the missing money.* □ *Please keep quiet about Mr. Smith's illness.*

keep someone company to sit or stay with someone, especially one who is on one's own. □ *I kept my uncle company for a few hours.* □ *He was very grateful for someone to keep him company. He gets very lonely.*

keep someone from doing something to prevent someone from doing something. □ *My good sense kept me from making a total fool of myself.* □ *Her father kept her from going to the party.*

keep someone in line to make certain that someone behaves properly. (Informal.) □ *It's very hard to keep Bill in line. He's sort of rowdy.* □ *The teacher had to struggle to keep the class in line.*

keep someone in stitches to cause someone to laugh loud and hard, over and over. (Informal. Also with *have*. See the examples.) □ *The comedian kept us in stitches for nearly an hour.* □ *The teacher kept the class in stitches, but the pupils didn't learn anything.* □ *The clown had the crowd in stitches.*

keep someone on tenterhooks to keep someone anxious or in suspense. (Also with *have*. See the examples.) □ *Please tell me now. Don't keep me on tenterhooks any longer!* □ *Now that we have her on tenterhooks, shall we let her worry, or shall we tell her?*

keep someone or something at a distance AND **keep someone or something at arm's length** to keep someone or something away from one; to keep from getting acquainted with someone or something. (See also *keep one's distance (from someone or something).*) □ *I used a stick to keep the angry dog at a distance.* □ *John is in a bad mood and that tends to keep people at arm's length.*

keep someone or something at arm's length See the previous entry.

keep someone or something at bay AND **hold someone or something at bay** to keep someone or something unable either to advance or to escape. □ *The dogs managed to keep the wild-cat at bay.* □ *The bear held the hunters at bay.* □ *The secretary held the reporters at bay while the mayor left by the side door.*

keep someone or something back AND **keep back someone or something; hold someone or something back; hold back someone or something** 1. to keep someone or something from moving forward. □ *Hurry! We must set sail now. I can't keep back the tide.* □ *Run away! John is angry at you, and I can't hold him back any longer.* 2. [with *someone*] to fail a pupil who then must remain another year in the same form. □ *We decided it would be best if we kept your child back for a year.* □ *The decision held back nearly half the pupils.* 3. [with *something*] to hold something in reserve. □ *We'll hold back some money for emergencies.* □ *Yes, it's a good idea to keep some back.*

keep someone or something down See under *get someone or something down.*

keep someone or something hanging in mid-air See under *leave someone or something hanging in mid-air.*

keep someone or something in check AND **hold someone or something in check** to keep someone or something under control; to restrain someone or something. □ *Hang on to this rope to keep the dog in check.* □ *I was so angry I could hardly hold myself in check.*

keep someone or something in mind AND **bear someone or something in mind** to remember and think about someone or something. □ *When you're driving a car, you must bear this in mind at all times: Keep your eyes on the road.* □ *As you leave home, bear in mind that your family need you.*

keep someone or something off AND **keep off someone or something; hold off someone or something; hold someone or something off** to make someone or something keep or stay away (from someone). (See also *keep off something.*) □ *How did you keep off the wild-cat?* □ *I used a pole to hold the wild-cat off.*

keep someone or something out of the way See under *get someone or something out of the way.*

keep someone or something quiet 1. to make someone or something silent or less noisy. □ *Can you please keep the baby quiet?* □ *Keep that stereo quiet!* **2.** [with *something*] to keep something a secret. (See also *keep quiet (about someone or something).*) □ *I'm leaving my job, but my husband doesn't know yet. Please keep it quiet.* □ *Okay. I'll keep it quiet.*

keep someone or something up AND **keep up someone or something 1.** to support someone or something; to *hold someone or something up.* □ *The flagpole I was carrying was so heavy, I could hardly keep it up.* □ *I could barely stand up myself, but I managed to keep up Ann until we got out of the smoke-filled room.* **2.** to prevent someone from going to bed; to keep someone awake. □ *Their party kept me up all night.* □ *The noise kept up the entire household.* **3.** [with *something*] to continue doing something. □ *I don't know how long I can keep this up.* □ *I can't keep up working this way much longer.*

keep someone out in the cold See under *leave someone out in the cold.*

keep someone posted to keep someone informed (of what is happening); to keep someone up to date. □ *If the price of corn goes up, I need to know. Please keep me posted.* □ *Keep her posted about the patient's condition.*

keep something for another occasion See *leave something for another occasion.*

keep something on an even keel to keep something in a steady and untroubled state. □ *The manager cannot keep the firm on an even keel any longer.* □ *When the workers are unhappy, it is difficult to keep the factory on an even keel.*

keep something to oneself to keep something a secret. □ *I'm leaving my job, but please keep that to yourself.* □ *Keep it to yourself, but I'm leaving my job.* □ *John is always gossiping. He can't keep anything to himself.*

keep something under one's hat to keep something a secret; to keep something in one's mind (only). (Informal. If the secret stays under your hat, it stays in your mind.) □ *Keep this under your hat, but I'm getting married.* □ *I'm getting married, but keep it under your hat.*

keep something under wraps to keep something concealed (until some future time). □ *We kept the plan under wraps until after the election.* □ *The car company kept the new model under wraps until most of the old models had been sold.*

keep still AND **hold still** do not move. □ *Stop wiggling. Keep still!* □ *"Hold still. I can't examine your ear if you're moving," said the doctor.*

keep still about someone or something See *keep quiet (about someone or something).*

keep tab(s) (on someone or something) AND **keep track (of someone or something)** to monitor someone or something; to follow the activities of someone or something. (The entries with *tab(s)* are informal.) □ *I'm supposed to keep track of my books.* □ *Try to keep tabs on everyone who works for you.* □ *It's hard to keep tabs when you have a lot of other work to do.* □ *I* *can't keep track of the money I earn. Maybe someone else is spending it.*

keep the ball rolling See under *start the ball rolling.*

keep the home fires burning to keep things going at one's home or other central location. □ *My uncle kept the home fires burning when my sister and I went to school.* □ *The manager stays at the office and keeps the home fires burning while I'm out selling our products.*

keep the lid on something to restrain something; to keep something quiet or under control. (Informal.) □ *The politician worked hard to keep the lid on the scandal.* □ *Try to keep the lid on the situation. Don't let it get out of hand.*

keep the wolf from the door to maintain oneself at a minimal level; to keep from starving, freezing, etc. □ *I don't make a lot of money, just enough to keep the wolf from the door.* □ *We have a small amount of money saved, hardly enough to keep the wolf from the door.*

keep time 1. to maintain a musical rhythm. □ *Bob had to drop out of the band because he couldn't keep time.* □ *Since he can't keep time, he can't march, and he can't play the drums.* **2.** [for a clock or watch] to keep track of time accurately. (See also *keep good time.*) □ *This watch doesn't keep time.* □ *My other watch kept time better.*

keep to oneself to be solitary; to stay away from other people. □ *Ann tends to keep to herself. She doesn't have many friends.* □ *I try to keep to myself each morning so I can get some work done.*

keep track (of someone or something) See *keep tabs (on someone or something).*

keep up an act AND **keep up the act** to maintain a false front; to act in a special way which is different from one's natural behaviour. □ *Most of the time John kept up an act. He was really not a friendly person.* □ *James works hard*

to keep up the act of being generous. In fact, he's mean.

keep up (with someone or something) to keep pace with someone or something; to advance at the same rate as someone or something. (See also the following two entries.) □ *You're running so fast that I cannot keep up with you.* □ *I don't make enough money to keep up with your spending.* □ *You don't even try to keep up.*

keep up (with the Joneses) to stay financially even with one's peers or associates; to work hard to get the same amount of material goods that one's friends and neighbours have. □ *Mr. and Mrs. Brown bought a new car simply to keep up with the Joneses.* □ *Keeping up with the Joneses can take all your money.*

keep up (with the times) to stay in fashion; to keep up with the news; to be contemporary or modern. □ *I try to keep up with the times. I want to know what's going on.* □ *I bought a whole new wardrobe because I want to keep up with the times.* □ *Sally learns all the new dances. She likes to keep up.*

keep watch (on someone or something) to monitor someone or something; to observe someone or something. □ *Keep watch on Bill. I think he's taking too much time off.* □ *Okay. I'll keep watch, but I think he's a good worker.*

keep watch (over someone or something) to guard or care for someone or something. (Also with *close.*) □ *I'm keeping watch over my children to make certain they have the things they need.* □ *I think that an angel is keeping watch over her to make certain nothing bad happens to her.* □ *Angels don't have much to do except to keep watch.*

Keep your shirt on! Wait a minute!; Don't get angry! (Slang.) □ *Look here, now. Keep your shirt on! I'll be with you in a minute.* □ *I'll bring you your hamburger when it's cooked. Just keep your shirt on, friend.*

keyed up anxious; tense and expectant. (Informal.) □ *I don't know why I'm so keyed up all the time. I can't even sleep.* □ *Ann gets keyed up before a test.*

kick a habit AND **kick the habit 1.** (Slang.) to break a habit. □ *It's hard to kick a habit, but it can be done. I stopped biting my nails.* □ *I used to drink coffee every morning, but I kicked the habit.* **2.** [with *kick the habit* only] to put an end to one's drug addiction. (Slang.) □ *John had to go to a treatment centre to get help with kicking the habit.* □ *If you can kick the habit, there are other problems you have to face.*

kick off to start a football game by kicking the ball a great distance. □ *Tom kicked off in the last game. Now it's my turn.* □ *John tripped when he was kicking off.*

kick one's heels to be kept waiting for someone or something; to have nothing to do. (Informal.) □ *They left me kicking my heels while they had lunch.* □ *Mary is just kicking her heels until the university re-opens.*

kick oneself (for doing something) to regret doing something. (Informal.) □ *I could just kick myself for going off and not locking the car door. Now the car is stolen.* □ *James felt like kicking himself when he missed the train.*

kick over See under *turn over.*

kick someone or something around AND **kick around someone or something** (Slang.) **1.** to treat someone or something badly. (Also used literally.) □ *I finally left my job. My co-workers wouldn't stop kicking me around.* □ *Stop kicking my car around. It does everything I ask it.* **2.** [with *something*] to discuss an idea or a proposal. □ *We kicked around John's idea for a while.* □ *That sounds like a good idea to me. Let's kick it around in our meeting tomorrow.*

kick someone or something out AND **boot someone or something out; boot out someone or something; kick out some-**one or something** to throw someone or something out; to insist that someone leaves. (Slang.) □ *I lived at home until I was eighteen and my father kicked me out.* □ *He kicked out his own child?* □ *Yes. He booted out my brother when he was twenty.*

kick something in AND **kick in something** to break in something by kicking. □ *John was so angry that he kicked the door in.* □ *Did he kick in a glass door?*

kick the bucket to die. (Slang.) □ *James inherited a fine house when his aunt kicked the bucket.* □ *When James kicks the bucket, his daughter gets the estate.*

kick the habit See *kick a habit.*

kick up a fuss AND **kick up a row** to become a nuisance; to misbehave and disturb (someone). (Informal. *Row* rhymes with *cow.*) □ *The customer kicked up such a fuss about the food that the manager came to apologize.* □ *I kicked up such a row that they kicked me out.*

kick up a row See the previous entry.

kick up one's heels to act in a frisky way; to be lively and have fun. (Informal.) □ *I like to go to an old-fashioned dance and really kick up my heels.* □ *For an old man, your uncle is really kicking up his heels by going on a cruise.*

kid's stuff a very easy task. (Informal.) □ *Climbing that hill is kid's stuff.* □ *Driving an automatic car is kid's stuff.*

kill someone or something off AND **kill off someone or something** to put an end to someone or something. □ *We are going to have to kill off that idea very soon.* □ *The criminals tried to kill the witnesses off.*

kill the fatted calf to prepare an elaborate banquet (in someone's honour). (From the biblical story recounting the return of the prodigal son.) □ *When Bob got back from college, his parents killed the fatted calf and threw a great party.* □ *Sorry this meal isn't much, John. We didn't have time to kill the fatted calf.*

kill the goose that laid the golden egg a proverbial phrase concerning the destruction of the source of one's good fortune. □ *If you sack your best office worker, you'll be killing the goose that laid the golden egg.* □ *He sold his computer, which was like killing the goose that laid the golden egg.*

kill time to waste time. (Informal.) □ *Stop killing time. Get to work!* □ *We went over to the record shop just to kill time.*

kill two birds with one stone to solve two problems with one solution. □ *John learned the words to his part in the play while peeling potatoes. He was killing two birds with one stone.* □ *I have to cash a cheque and make a payment on my bank loan. I'll kill two birds with one stone by doing them both in one trip to the bank.*

kind of (something) See *sort of (something)*.

kiss and make up to forgive (someone) and be friends again. □ *They were very angry, but in the end they kissed and made up.* □ *I'm sorry. Let's kiss and make up.*

kiss of death an act that puts an end to someone or something. (Informal.) □ *The mayor's veto was the kiss of death for the new law.* □ *Fainting on stage was the kiss of death for my acting career.*

kiss something goodbye to anticipate or experience the loss of something. (Informal.) □ *If you leave your camera on a park bench, you can kiss it goodbye.* □ *You kissed your wallet goodbye when you left it in the shop.*

knee-high to a grasshopper not very tall; short and small, as a child. (Informal.) □ *Hello, Billy. I haven't seen you since you were knee-high to a grasshopper.* □ *I have two grandchildren, both knee-high to a grasshopper.*

knit one's brow to wrinkle one's brow, especially by frowning. □ *The woman knit her brow and asked us what we wanted from her.* □ *While he read his book, John knitted his brow occasionally. He must not have agreed with what he was reading.*

knock about (somewhere) to travel around; to act as a vagabond. (Informal.) □ *I'd like to take off a year and knock about Europe.* □ *If you're going to knock about, you should do it when you're young.*

knock it off to stop something; to cease something. (Slang.) □ *Shut up, you lot. Knock it off!* □ *Knock it off. I've heard enough of your music.*

knock off work to stop work (for the day). (Slang.) □ *It's time to knock off work.* □ *It's too early to knock off work.*

knock on wood AND **touch wood** a phrase said to cancel out imaginary bad luck. □ *My stereo has never given me any trouble—knock on wood.* □ *We plan to be in London by tomorrow evening—touch wood.*

knock one off one's feet See *sweep one off one's feet*.

knock people's heads together to scold some people; to get some people to do what they are supposed to be doing. (Informal.) □ *If you children don't quiet down and go to sleep, I'm going to come up there and knock your heads together.* □ *The government is in a mess. We need to go down to London and knock their heads together.*

knock someone cold 1. to knock someone out. (Informal.) □ *The blow knocked the boxer cold.* □ *The attacker knocked the old man cold.* **2.** to stun someone; to shock someone. □ *The news of his death knocked me cold.* □ *Pat was knocked cold by the imprisonment of her son.*

knock someone dead to put on a stunning performance or display for someone. (Informal. *Someone* is often replaced by *'em* from *them*.) □ *This band is going to do great tonight. We're going to knock them dead.* □ *"See how your sister is all dressed up!" said Bill. "She's going to knock 'em dead."*

knock someone down with a feather to push over a person who is stunned, surprised, or awed by something extraordinary. □ *I was so surprised you could have knocked me down with a feather.* □ *When she heard the news, you could have knocked her down with a feather.*

knock someone or something about See the following entry.

knock someone or something around AND **knock someone or something about** to mistreat someone or something physically. □ *They fairly knocked my baggage around on the flight to Mexico.* □ *The tough blokes knocked me around a little.* □ *They knocked my brother about a bit also.*

knock someone or something down AND **knock down someone or something** to knock someone or something to the floor or to the ground. □ *The toughs knocked the old lady down and took her purse.* □ *The cat knocked the flowers down.*

knock someone or something off AND **knock off someone or something** (Slang.) **1.** [with *something*] to finish something, especially in haste or carelessly. □ *I knocked off the last chapter of my book in four hours.* □ *I knocked it off with the help of Bob.* **2.** [with *someone*] See *bump someone off.*

knock someone or something out AND **knock out someone or something** · **1.** [with *someone*] to strike someone unconscious. □ *I knocked out the champ.* □ *He accidentally knocked the guard out.* **2.** [with *something*] to hammer something out; to remove something from inside something. □ *Bill knocked out the glass.* □ *John knocked a tooth out.*

knock someone's block off to strike someone hard, especially in the head. (Slang. Used in threats.) □ *If you touch me again, I'll knock your block off.* □ *John punched Bob so hard that he almost knocked his block off.*

knock something back AND **knock back something** to drink down a drink of something, especially something alcoholic. (Slang.) □ *John knocked back two beers in ten minutes.* □ *I don't see how he can knock that stuff back.*

know a thing or two (about someone or something) to be well informed about someone or something; to know something, often something unpleasant, about someone or something. (Informal.) □ *I know a thing or two about cars.* □ *I know a thing or two about Mary that would really shock you.*

know all the tricks of the trade to possess the skills and knowledge necessary to do something. (Also without *all.*) □ *Tom can repair car engines. He knows the tricks of the trade.* □ *If I knew all the tricks of the trade, I could be a better plumber.*

know better to be wise, experienced, or well taught. □ *Mary should have known better than to accept a lift from a stranger.* □ *Children should know better than to play in the road.*

know-how knowledge and skill. (Informal.) □ *Peter doesn't have the know-how to mend that car.* □ *Mary hasn't the know-how to work the computer.*

know one's ABC to know the alphabet; to know the most basic things (about something). (Informal.) □ *Bill can't do it. He doesn't even know his ABC.* □ *You can't expect to write novels when you don't know your ABC.*

know one's onions See *know one's stuff.*

know one's place to know and accept the behaviour appropriate to one's position or status in life. (See also *put one in one's place.*) □ *I know my place. I won't speak unless spoken to.* □ *People around here are expected to know their place. You have to follow all the rules.*

know one's stuff AND **know one's onions** to know what one is expected or required to know. (Slang. See also *know what's what.*) □ *I know my stuff. I can do the work.* □ *She can't handle the job. She doesn't know her onions.*

know one's way about See the following entry.

know one's way around AND **know one's way about** 1. to know how to get from one place to another. □ *John won't get lost. He knows his way about.* □ *Don't let John go into the city. He doesn't know his way around.* 2. to know the techniques of getting something done, especially in a bureaucracy. □ *Sally can get the job done. She knows her way around.* □ *Since Sally worked at the head office for a year, she really knows her way about.*

know someone by sight to know the name and recognize the face of someone. □ *I've never met the man, but I know him by sight.* □ BOB: *Have you ever met Mary?* JANE: *No, but I know her by sight.*

know someone or something like a book See *know someone or something like the palm of one's hand.*

know someone or something like the back of one's hand See the following entry.

know someone or something like the palm of one's hand AND **know someone or something like the back of one's hand; know someone or something like a book** to know someone or something very well. □ *Of course I know John. I know him like the back of my hand.* □ *I know him like a book.*

know something by heart See under *learn something by heart.*

know something from memory to have memorized something so that one does not have to consult a written version; to know something very well from seeing it very often. □ *Mary didn't need the script because she knew the play from memory.* □ *The conductor went through the entire concert without music. He knew it from memory.*

know something inside out to know something thoroughly; to know about something thoroughly. (Informal.) □ *I know my geometry inside out.* □ *I studied and studied for my driver's test until I knew the rules inside out.*

know something only too well to know something very well; to know something from unpleasant experience. (Note the variation in the examples.) □ *I know the problem only too well.* □ *I know only too well the kind of problem you must face.*

know the ropes to know how to do something. (Informal.) □ *I can't do the job because I don't know the ropes.* □ *Ask Sally to do it. She knows the ropes.* ALSO: **show someone the ropes** to tell or show someone how something is to be done. □ *Since this was my first day on the job, the manager spent a lot of time showing me the ropes.*

know the score AND **know what's what** to know the facts; to know the facts about life and its difficulties. (Informal.) □ *Bob is so naive. He just doesn't know the score.* □ *I know what you're trying to do. Oh yes, I know what's what.*

know what's what See the previous entry.

know where someone stands (on someone or something) to know what someone thinks or feels about something. □ *I don't know where John stands on this issue.* □ *I don't even know where I stand.*

know which is which AND **tell which is which** to be able to distinguish one person or thing from another person or thing. □ *I have an old one and a new one, but I don't know which is which.* □ *I know that Bill and Bob are twins, but I can't tell which is which.*

know which side one's bread is buttered on to know what is most advantageous for one. □ *He'll do it if his mother tells him to. He knows which side his bread is buttered on.* □ *Since John knows which side his bread is buttered on, he'll be there on time.*

knuckle down (to something) to get busy doing something; to get serious about one's work. (Informal.) □ *It's time you knuckled down to your studies.* □ *You must knuckle down if you want to succeed.*

knuckle under (to someone or something) to submit to someone or something; to yield or give in to someone or something. (Informal.) □ *You have to knuckle under to your bosses if you expect to keep your job.* □ *I'm too stubborn to knuckle under.*

L

labour of love a task which is either unpaid or badly paid and which one does simply for one's own satisfaction or pleasure or to please someone whom one likes or loves. □ *Jane made no money out of the biography she wrote. She was writing about the life of a friend and the book was a labour of love.* □ *Mary hates knitting, but she made a sweater for her boyfriend. What a labour of love.*

lace into someone or something AND **light into someone or something** to attack or scold someone or something. (Slang.) □ *The bully punched John once, and then John really laced into him.* □ *John lit into him with both fists.* □ *My father really lit into me when I came in late. He shouted at me for ten minutes.*

ladies' man a man who likes the company of women and whose company is liked by women, the suggestion being that he likes to flirt with them. □ *John is a real ladies' man. He hates all-male parties.* □ *The new boss is always flirting with the office girls. He's a bit of a ladies' man.*

lady-killer a man who likes to flirt and make love with women and who is popular with them. □ *Fred used to be a real lady-killer, but now women laugh at him.* □ *Jack's wife doesn't know that he's a lady-killer, but he goes out with other women.*

lag behind (someone or something) to fall behind someone or something; to linger behind someone or something. □ *John always lags behind the marcher in front of him.* □ *"Don't lag behind!" shouted the leader.*

laid back relaxed and at ease. (Slang.) □ *John is so laid back. Nothing seems to disturb him.* □ *I wish I could be more laid back. I get so tense.*

laid up immobilized for recuperation or repairs; unable to get around or function. (Informal. Said of people and things.) □ *I was laid up for two weeks after my accident.* □ *My car is laid up for repairs.*

lame duck someone or something that is helpless, useless, or inefficient. □ *Jack is always having to help his brother, who is a lame duck.* □ *The best firms will survive, but the lame ducks will not.*

land a blow (somewhere) to strike someone or something with the hand or fist. □ *Bill landed a blow on Tom's chin.* □ *When Bill wasn't looking, Tom landed a blow.*

land of Nod sleep. (Humorous. From the fact that people sometimes nod when they are falling asleep.) □ *The baby is in the land of Nod.* □ *Look at the clock! It's time we were all in the land of Nod.*

land on both feet See the following entry.

land on one's feet AND **land on both feet** to recover satisfactorily from a trying situation or a setback. (Informal.) □ *Her first year was terrible, but she landed on both feet.* □ *It's going to be a hard day. I only hope I land on my feet.*

land someone with someone or something to give or hand on someone or something unpleasant or unwanted to someone else. (Informal.) □ *John has landed his horrible little sister on me.* □ *No one wanted to judge the competition so they landed Jean with the job.*

land up somehow or somewhere to finish somehow or somewhere; to come to be in a certain state or place at the end. (Usually in the wrong place or in a bad situation. See also *end up somewhere.*) □ *We set out for London but landed up in Leeds.* □ *He's so extravagant that he landed up in debt.*

landslide victory a victory by a large margin; a very substantial victory, particularly in an election. □ *The Conservatives won a landslide victory in the general election.* □ *The younger man won a landslide victory in the presidential contest.*

lap something up AND **lap up something 1.** [for an animal] to drink up something. □ *The cat lapped up all the spilled milk.* □ *I watched the cat lap it up.* **2.** to accept or believe something. (Informal.) □ *Did she believe it? She just lapped it up.* □ *I can't imagine why she lapped up that ridiculous story.*

lash out (at someone or something) to threaten or attack someone or something, physically or verbally. □ *The snake lashed out at the bird, but the bird escaped.* □ *It lashed out so fast that I hardly saw it.* □ *She has such a temper. She always lashes out at whoever is close by.*

last but not least last in sequence, but not last in importance. (Often said in introductions.) □ *The speaker said, "And now, last but not least, I'd like to present Bill Smith, who will give us some final words."* □ *And last but not least, here is the owner of the firm.*

last-ditch effort a final effort; the last possible attempt. □ *I made one last-ditch effort to get her to stay.* □ *It was a last-ditch effort. I didn't expect it to work.*

last something out AND **last out something** to endure something. □ *I hope I can last out the day. I'm so awfully tired.* □ *Yes, I hope you can last it out.*

late in life when one is old. □ *She injured her hip running. She's taken to exercising rather late in life.* □ *Isn't it rather late in life to buy a house?*

late in the day far on in a project or activity; too late in a project or activity for action, decisions, etc., to be taken. □ *It was a bit late in the day for him to apologize.* □ *It's late in the day to change the plans.*

laugh out of the other side of one's mouth to change sharply from happiness to sadness. □ *Now that you know the truth, you'll laugh out of the other side of your mouth.* □ *He was so proud that he won the election. He's laughing out of the other side of his mouth since they re-counted the ballots and found out that he lost.*

laugh something off AND **laugh off something** to avoid or reject a serious problem by laughing at it. □ *Tom suffered an injury to his leg, but he laughed it off and kept playing ball.* □ *Mary just laughed off her bad experience.*

laugh something out of court to dismiss something as ridiculous. □ *The committee laughed the suggestion out of court.* □ *Jack's request for a large salary increase was laughed out of court.*

laugh up one's sleeve to laugh secretly; to laugh quietly to oneself. (Informal.) □ *Jane looked very serious, but I knew she was laughing up her sleeve.* □ *They pretended to admire her singing voice, but they were laughing up their sleeves at her. She screeches.*

launch forth (into something) AND **launch into something** to begin to speak; to begin one's speech on a particular topic. □ *James launched into a long explanation.* □ *When does the next speaker launch forth?*

launch forth (on something) to start out a lecture on something; to begin a discussion of something. □ *My uncle is* *always launching forth on the state of the economy.* □ *When he launches forth, I leave the room.*

launch into something See *launch forth (into something).*

law unto oneself one who makes one's own laws or rules; one who sets one's own standards of behaviour. □ *You can't get Bill to follow the rules. He's a law unto himself.* □ *Jane is a law unto herself. She's totally unwilling to co-operate.*

lay a finger on someone or something to touch someone or something, even slightly. (Usually in the negative. Compare to *put one's finger on something.*) □ *Don't you dare lay a finger on my pencil. Go and get your own!* □ *If you lay a finger on me, I'll scream.*

lay about one to strike at people and things in all directions around one; to hit everyone and everything near one. □ *When the police tried to capture the robber, he laid about him wildly.* □ *In trying to escape, the prisoner laid about him and injured several people.*

lay an egg to give a bad performance. (Informal.) □ *The cast of the play really laid an egg last night.* □ *I hope I don't lay an egg when it's my turn to sing.*

lay down one's life (for someone or something) AND **lay one's life down (for someone or something)** to sacrifice one's life for someone or something. □ *Would you lay down your life for your country?* □ *There aren't many things for which I'd lay down my life.*

lay down the law 1. to state firmly what the rules are (for something). □ *Before the meeting, the managing director laid down the law. We all knew exactly what to do.* □ *The way she laid down the law means that I'll remember her rules.* 2. to express one's opinions with force. □ *When the teacher caught us, he really laid down the law.* □ *Poor Bob. He really got it when his mother laid down the law.*

lay eyes on someone or something See *set eyes on someone or something.*

lay hold of someone or something to grasp someone or something with the hands. (Compare to *get hold of someone or something.*) □ *Just wait till I lay hold of Bill!* □ *I can't wait to lay hold of that fishing-rod. I'm ready to catch a huge fish.*

lay into someone or something to attack or scold someone or something. (Informal.) □ *The bear laid into the hunter.* □ *My father really laid into me when I got home.*

lay it on thick AND **pour it on thick; spread it on thick** to exaggerate praise, excuses, or blame. (Informal.) □ *Sally was laying it on thick when she said that Tom was the best singer she had ever heard.* □ *After Bob finished making his excuses, Sally said that he was pouring it on thick.* □ *Bob always spreads it on thick.*

lay off (someone or something) to leave someone or something alone; to stop bothering someone or something; to *take it easy on someone or something.* (Informal. See also *lay someone off.*) □ *Lay off Bill. He didn't mean any harm!* □ *Now, look! I said lay off!* □ *Lay off the butter. Don't use it all up.*

lay one's cards on the table See *put one's cards on the table.*

lay one's hands on someone or something See *get one's hands on someone or something.*

lay someone off AND **lay off someone** to put an employee out of work, possibly temporarily. □ *The computer factory laid off 2,000 workers.* □ *They even laid the managing director off.*

lay someone or something out AND **lay out someone or something** 1. [with *someone*] to prepare a corpse for burial or for a wake. □ *They laid out their uncle for the wake.* □ *The women of the community used to lay their dead out.* 2. [with *someone*] to knock someone down with a punch; to knock someone unconscious. (Slang.) □ *Tom laid* out Bill with one punch to the chin. □ *The policeman laid the thief out.* **3.** [with *something*] to spend an amount of money. (Informal.) □ *I had to lay out twenty pounds for that book.* □ *I laid thirty pounds out for this one.* **4.** [with *something*] to explain or present a plan of action or a set of events. □ *The farmer laid out the plan for cleaning up the barn.* □ *If you wait until I lay the plan out, you'll know what to do.* **5.** [with *something*] to spread something out. □ *The theatre nurse laid out the instruments necessary for the operation.* □ *The valet laid out the clothing for his master.*

lay someone up AND **lay up someone** to cause someone to be ill in bed. (Informal.) □ *A broken leg laid me up for two months.* □ *Flu laid up everyone at work for a week or more.* ALSO: **laid up** sick in bed. □ *I was laid up with the flu for a week.*

lay something aside See under *set something aside.*

lay something by See *put something by.*

lay something down AND **lay down something** to place something down (on something), especially when one is finished using it. (See also *lay down one's life (for someone or something); lay down the law.*) □ *I laid down my pencil when I finished writing.* □ *The workers laid their tools down and went on strike.*

lay something in AND **lay in something** to get something and store it for future use. □ *We always lay in a large supply of firewood each November.* □ *They laid a lot of food in for the holidays.*

lay something on the line to speak very firmly and directly about something. □ *She was very angry. She laid it on the line, and we had no doubt about what she meant.* □ *All right, you lot! I'm going to lay it on the line. Don't ever do that again if you know what's good for you.*

lay something to rest See *put something to rest.*

lay something to waste AND **lay waste to something** to destroy something. □ *The invaders laid the village to waste.* □ *The party of tourists laid waste to the park.*

lay something up AND **lay up something** **1.** to store something for future use; to lay something in. □ *We laid up some potatoes for use in the winter months.* □ *I laid some extra pencils up for your department.* **2.** to put a ship in a shipyard for repairs or maintenance. □ *We laid our boat up for a month to repair the mast.* □ *The storm laid up our boat by causing severe damage.*

lay the blame on someone or something See *put the blame on someone or something.*

lay the finger on someone See *put the finger on someone.*

lead a dog's life AND **live a dog's life** to lead a miserable life. □ *Poor Jane really leads a dog's life.* □ *I've been working so hard. I'm tired of living a dog's life.*

lead off to begin; to start (assuming that others will follow). □ *We were waiting for someone to start dancing. Finally, Bob and Jane led off.* □ *The hunter led off, and the dogs followed.* □ *Fred will lead off as our first speaker.*

lead someone a merry dance See *lead someone on a merry chase.*

lead someone by the nose to force someone to go somewhere (with you); to lead someone by coercion. (Informal.) □ *John had to lead Tom by the nose to get him to the opera.* □ *I'll go, but you'll have to lead me by the nose.*

lead someone on to tempt someone (to do something); to lure someone (into something); to deceive someone by providing false hopes. □ *I didn't want to do it, but he kept leading me on.* □ *I knew she really wanted me to buy the car by the way she was leading me on.* □ *Mary thought Bob would marry her, but he was only leading her on.*

lead someone on a merry chase AND **lead someone a merry dance** to lead someone in a purposeless pursuit. □ *What a waste of time. You really led me on a merry chase.* □ *Jane led Bill a merry dance trying to find an antique lamp.*

lead someone to believe something to imply something to someone; to cause someone to believe something untrue, without lying. □ *But you led me to believe that this watch was guaranteed!* □ *Did you lead her to believe that she was employed as a cook?*

lead someone to do something to cause someone to do something. □ *This agent led me to purchase a worthless piece of land.* □ *My illness led me to resign.*

lead someone up the garden path to deceive someone. □ *Now, be honest with me. Don't lead me up the garden path.* □ *That swindler really led her up the garden path.*

lead the life of Riley to live in luxury. (Informal. No one knows who Riley is.) □ *If I had a million pounds, I could live the life of Riley.* □ *The treasurer took our money to Mexico, where he lived the life of Riley until the police caught him.*

lead the way to lead (someone) along the proper pathway. □ *You lead the way, and we'll follow.* □ *I feel better when you're leading the way. I get lost easily.*

lead up to something to prepare the way for something; to have as a consequence. □ *His compliments were his way of leading up to asking for money.* □ *What were his actions leading up to?*

leaf through something See *thumb through something.*

leak something (out) AND **let something get out** to disclose special information to the press so that the resulting publicity will accomplish something. (Usually said of government disclosures. Also used for accidental disclosures.) □ *Don't leak that information out.* □ *The education department were accused of leaking the attendance figures.* □ *They let the data get out on purpose.*

lean on someone to try to make someone do something; to coerce someone to do something. (Slang.) □ *If she refuses to do it, lean on her a bit.* □ *Don't lean on me! I don't have to do it if I don't want to.*

lean over backwards to do something See *fall over backwards to do something.*

leap at the opportunity (to do something) See *jump at the chance (to do something).*

leap to conclusions See *jump to conclusions.*

learn something by heart to learn something so well that it can be written or recited without thinking; to memorize something. □ *The director told me to learn my speech by heart.* □ *I had to go over it many times before I learned it by heart.* ALSO: **know something by heart** to know something perfectly; to have memorized something perfectly. □ *I know my speech by heart.* □ *I went over and over it until I knew it by heart.*

learn something by rote to learn something without giving any thought to what is being learned. □ *I learned history by rote; then I couldn't pass the test which required me to think.* □ *If you learn things by rote, you'll never understand them.*

learn something from the bottom up to learn something thoroughly, from the very beginning; to learn all aspects of something, even the most lowly. (Informal.) □ *I learned my business from the bottom up.* □ *I started out sweeping the floors and learned everything from the bottom up.*

learn something the hard way AND **find something out the hard way; find out something the hard way** to learn something by experience, especially by an unpleasant experience; to learn something by a more difficult process than necessary; to learn something by one's own experience rather than from the advice of others. □ *She learned how to make investments the hard way.* □ *I wish I didn't have to learn things the hard way.* □ *I found out the hard way that it's difficult to work and go to college at the same time.* □ *Investing in property is tricky. I found that out the hard way.* ALSO: **do something the hard way** to accomplish something in the most difficult manner, rather than by an easier manner. □ *Mary is doing the course the hard way—by correspondence.* □ *There is an easy way to climb the hill, but she did it the hard way.*

learn the ropes to learn how to do something; to learn how to work something. (Informal.) □ *I'll be able to do my job very well as soon as I learn the ropes.* □ *John is very slow to learn the ropes.*

least of all least; of smallest importance. (Informal. Compare to *most of all*.) □ *There were many things wrong with the new house. Least of all, the water taps leaked.* □ *No one has done well, least of all Jack.*

Least said soonest mended. a proverb meaning the less one says the less harm one does. □ *Don't criticize James for his behaviour in case you offend him. Least said soonest mended, I always say.* □ *I did not comment on his actions. Least said soonest mended.*

leave a bad taste in someone's mouth [for something] to leave a bad feeling or memory with someone. (Informal.) □ *The whole business about the missing money left a bad taste in his mouth.* □ *It was a very nice affair, but something about it left a bad taste in my mouth.*

leave a lot to be desired to be lacking something important; to be inadequate. (A polite way of saying that something is bad.) □ *This report leaves a lot to be desired.* □ *I'm sorry to have to sack you, Mary, but your work leaves a lot to be desired.*

leave a sinking ship See *desert a sinking ship.*

leave no stone unturned to search in all possible places. (As if one might find something under a rock.) □ *Don't worry. We'll find your stolen car. We'll leave no stone unturned.* □ *In searching for a nice place to live, we left no stone unturned.*

leave off (doing something) to stop doing something, usually temporarily. □ *Tom had to leave off work for a few hours to go to the dentist.* □ *Can't you leave off smoking for even a few days?* □ *No, I can't leave off, not even for a day.*

leave one to one's fate to abandon someone to whatever may happen—possibly death or some other unpleasant event. □ *We couldn't rescue the miners and were forced to leave them to their fate.* □ *Please don't try to help. Just go away and leave me to my fate.*

leave oneself wide open for something AND **leave oneself wide open to something** to invite criticism or joking about oneself; to fail to protect oneself from criticism or ridicule. □ *Yes, that was a harsh remark, Jane, but you left yourself wide open to it.* □ *I can't complain about your joke. I left myself wide open for it.*

leave someone flat to fail to entertain or stimulate someone. (Informal.) □ *Your joke left me flat.* □ *We listened carefully to his lecture, but it left us flat.*

leave someone for dead to abandon someone as being dead. (The abandoned person may actually be alive.) □ *He looked so bad that they almost left him for dead.* □ *As the soldiers turned, leaving the enemy captain for dead, the captain fired at them.*

leave someone high and dry to leave someone unsupported and unable to manoeuvre; to leave someone helpless. (Informal.) □ *All my workers resigned and left me high and dry.* □ *All the children ran away and left Billy high and dry to take the blame for the broken window.*

leave someone holding the baby to leave someone with the responsibility for something, especially something difficult or unpleasant, often when it was originally someone else's responsibility. (Informal. Note passive use in the examples.) □ *We all promised to look after the house when the owner was away, but I was left holding the baby on my own.* □ *It was her brother who promised to finish the work, and it was he who left her holding the baby also.*

leave someone in peace to stop bothering someone; to go away and leave someone in peace. □ *Please go—leave me in peace.* □ *Can't you see that you're upsetting her? Leave her in peace.*

leave someone in the lurch to leave someone waiting on or anticipating your actions. □ *Where were you, John? You really left me in the lurch.* □ *I didn't mean to leave you in the lurch. I thought we had cancelled our meeting.*

leave someone or something alone AND **let someone or something alone; leave someone or something be; let someone or something be** to stop bothering someone or something. □ *Don't torment the cat. Leave it alone.* □ *I don't want your help. Let me alone.* □ *Don't argue about it. Let it be!*

leave someone or something behind to fail or forget to bring someone or something along. □ *John was sick, so we had to leave him behind.* □ *Oh, I left my money behind.*

leave someone or something hanging in mid-air to leave off dealing with someone or something; to leave someone or something waiting to be finished or continued. □ *She left her sentence hanging in mid-air.* □ *She left us hanging in mid-air when she paused.* □ *Tell me the rest of the story. Don't leave me hanging in mid-air.* □ *Don't leave the story hanging in mid-air.* ALSO: **keep someone or something hanging in mid-air** to leave someone or something waiting to be dealt with, completed, or continued with. □ *Please don't keep us hanging in mid-air.*

leave someone or something out to exclude someone or something; to ignore someone or something. (See also the following entry.) □ *If you decide to go out to eat after the play, please don't leave me out.* □ *They left out the last paragraph.*

leave someone out in the cold to exclude someone. (Informal. Compare to the previous entry. Also used literally.) □ *Jack wasn't at the union meeting. The bosses left him out in the cold.* □ *Tom wasn't invited. They left him out in the cold.* ALSO: **keep someone out in the cold** to prevent someone from coming in; to prevent someone from being invited. □ *Please don't keep Jane out in the cold. Invite her to the wedding.*

leave something for another occasion AND **keep something for another occasion** to hold back something for later. (*Occasion* can be replaced with *time, day, person*, etc.) □ *Please leave some cake for another day.* □ *Don't eat all the cheese. Leave some for another time.* □ *I have to leave some of my earnings for next month.*

leave something on to leave something running or operating. (Also used literally in reference to wearing clothes.) □ *Please don't leave the light on.* □ *Ann went to school and left her radio on.*

leave well alone See *let well alone*.

leave word (with someone) to leave a message with someone (who will pass the message on to someone else). □ *If you decide to go to the convention, please leave word with my secretary.* □ *Leave word before you go.* □ *I left word with your brother. Didn't he give you the message?*

left, right, and centre everywhere; to an excessive extent. (Informal.) □ *John lent money left, right, and centre.* □ *Mary spent her money on clothes, left, right, and centre.*

lend a hand See *lend (someone) a hand*.

lend an ear (to someone) to listen to someone. (Formal or literary.) □ *Lend an ear to John. Hear what he has to say.*

□ *I'd be delighted to lend an ear. I find great wisdom in everything John has to say.*

lend oneself or itself to something [for someone or something] to be adaptable to something; [for someone or something] to be useful for something. □ *This room doesn't lend itself to bright colours.* □ *John doesn't lend himself to casual conversation.*

lend (someone) a hand to give someone some help, not necessarily with the hands. □ *Could you lend me a hand with this piano? I need to move it across the room.* □ *Could you lend a hand with this maths problem?* □ *I'd be happy to lend a hand.*

less than pleased displeased. □ *We were less than pleased to learn of your comments.* □ *Bill was less than pleased at the outcome of the election.*

let alone someone or something not to mention or think of someone or something; not even to take someone or something into account. □ *Do I have a pound? I don't even have a penny, let alone a pound.* □ *I didn't invite John, let alone the rest of his family.*

Let bygones be bygones. a proverb meaning that one should forget the problems of the past. □ *Okay, Sally, let bygones be bygones. Let's forgive and forget.* □ *Jane was unwilling to let bygones be bygones. She still won't speak to me.*

let go (of someone or something) AND **let someone or something go** to release someone or something (figuratively and literally). (Figuratively, *something* can be *guilt, horror, tension, fear,* etc.) □ *Please let go of me!* □ *I can't let go of those horrible memories.*

let her rip AND **let it rip** to go ahead and start something; let something begin. (Informal or slang. *Her* is usually *'er.*) □ *When Bill was ready for John to start the engine, he said, "Okay, John, let 'er rip."* □ *When Sally heard Bob say "Let 'er rip," she let the anchor go to*

the bottom of the lake. □ *Let's go, Bill. Let it rip! Tell us about the meeting.*

let it all hang out to tell or reveal everything and hold back nothing (because one is relaxed or carefree). (Slang.) □ *Sally has no secrets. She lets it all hang out all the time.* □ *Relax, John. Let it all hang out.*

let it rip See *let her rip.*

let off steam AND **blow off steam** to release excess energy or anger. (Informal.) □ *Whenever John gets a little angry, he blows off steam by jogging.* □ *Don't worry about John. He's just letting off steam. He won't sack you.*

let on **1.** to admit to knowing something. □ *Bill knew about the surprise, but he didn't let on.* □ *He had been told exactly what would happen, but he didn't let on.* **2.** to imply; to act like. (Informal.) □ *Ann let on that she was a famous writer.* □ *She let on that she was better known than she really is.*

let one's hair down AND **let down one's hair** to become more intimate and begin to speak frankly. (Informal.) □ *Come on, Jane, let your hair down and tell me all about it.* □ *I have a problem. Do you mind if I let down my hair?*

let oneself go to become less constrained; to get excited and have a good time. □ *I love to dance and just let myself go.* □ *Let yourself go, John. Learn to enjoy life.*

Let sleeping dogs lie. a proverb meaning that one should not search for trouble or that one should leave well enough alone. □ *Don't mention that problem with Tom again. It's almost forgotten. Let sleeping dogs lie.* □ *You'll never be able to reform Bill. Leave him alone. Let sleeping dogs lie.*

let someone down to disappoint someone; to fail someone. □ *I'm sorry I let you down. Something came up, and I couldn't meet you.* □ *I don't want to let you down, but I can't support you in the election.*

let someone have it to strike someone or attack someone verbally. (Informal.) □ *I really let Tom have it. I told him he had better not do that again if he knows what's good for him.* □ *Bob let John have it—right on the chin.*

let someone in for something to cause someone to be involved in something, usually something unpleasant. □ *Fred had no idea what his brother had let him in for when he agreed to take his place in the race.* □ *Jack didn't know what he was letting himself in for when he married that dreadful woman.*

let someone in on something to tell someone the secret. (Informal. The *something* can be a *plan, arrangements, scheme, trick,* or anything else which might be kept a secret.) □ *Should we let John in on the secret?* □ *Please let me in on the plan.*

let someone off (the hook) to release someone from a responsibility. (Informal.) □ *Please let me off the hook for Saturday. I have other plans.* □ *Okay, I'll let you off.*

let someone or something alone See *leave someone or something alone.*

let someone or something be See *leave someone or something alone.*

let someone or something go See *let go (of someone or something).*

let someone or something in AND **let in someone or something** to permit or help someone or something to enter. □ *Please let in the dog.* □ *I hope they'll let me in without a ticket.*

let someone or something loose See *let go (of someone or something).*

let someone or something off AND **let off someone or something** 1. [with *someone*] to release or dismiss someone without punishment. □ *The judge let off Mary with a warning.* □ *The judge didn't let me off.* 2. [with *someone*] to permit someone to disembark or leave a means of transportation. □ *The driver let Mary off the bus.* □ *"I can't let you off at this corner," said the driver.* 3.

[with *something*] to release something; to *give off something.* □ *The engine was letting off some kind of smoke.* □ *The chemical let off a horrible smell.*

let someone or something out AND **let out someone or something** 1. to permit or help someone or something to exit. □ *Please let out the dog.* □ *I was locked in the room, and no one would let me out.* 2. [with *something*] to reveal something which is a secret. □ *Please don't let this out, but I'm leaving my job.* □ *John let out the secret by accident.*

let something get out See *leak something (out).*

let something ride to allow something to continue or remain as it is. (Informal.) □ *It isn't the best plan, but we'll let it ride.* □ *I disagree with you, but I'll let it ride.*

let something slide to neglect something. (Informal.) □ *John let his lessons slide.* □ *Jane doesn't let her work slide.*

let something slip by AND **let something slide by** 1. to forget or miss an important time or date. □ *I'm sorry I just let your birthday slip by.* □ *I let it slide by accidentally.* 2. to waste a period of time. □ *You wasted the whole day by letting it slip by.* □ *We were having fun, and we let the time slide by.*

let something slip (out) to tell a secret by accident. □ *I didn't let it slip out on purpose. It was an accident.* □ *John let the plans slip when he was talking to Bill.*

let the cat out of the bag AND **spill the beans** to reveal a secret or a surprise by accident. (Informal.) □ *When Bill glanced at the door, he let the cat out of the bag. We knew then that he was expecting someone to arrive.* □ *We are planning a surprise party for Jane. Don't let the cat out of the bag.* □ *It's a secret. Try not to spill the beans.*

let the chance slip by to lose the opportunity (to do something). □ *When I was younger, I wanted to become a* *doctor, but I let the chance slip by.* □ *Don't let the chance slip by. Do it now!*

let the grass grow under one's feet to do nothing; to stand still. □ *Mary doesn't let the grass grow under her feet. She's always busy.* □ *Bob is too lazy. He's letting the grass grow under his feet.*

let up (on someone or something) to take the pressure off someone or something; to *take it easy on someone or something.* □ *Please let up on me. I can't work any faster, and you're making me nervous.* □ *Let up on the project. You're working too hard.* □ *Yes, I had better let up.*

let well alone AND **leave well alone** to leave things as they are (and not try to improve them). □ *There isn't much more you can accomplish here. Why don't you just let well alone?* □ *This is as good as I can do. I'll stop and leave well alone.*

level off to even out; to move up or down to an average level. □ *After the holidays, business will level off.* □ *As soon as things level off around here, I can talk to you.*

level something off AND **level off something** to make something level or even. □ *They used machines to level off the road.* □ *I have to level the soil off in the garden before I plant seeds.*

level with someone to be honest with someone. (Slang.) □ *Come on, Bill. Level with me. Did you do it?* □ *I'm levelling with you. I wasn't even in town. I couldn't have done it.*

lick one's lips to show eagerness or pleasure about a future event. (Informal. From the habit of people licking their lips when they are about to enjoy eating something.) □ *The children licked their lips at the sight of the cake.* □ *The author's readers were licking their lips in anticipation of her new novel.* □ *The journalist was licking his lips when he went off to interview the disgraced politician.*

lick something into shape AND **whip something into shape** to put something into

good condition, usually with difficulty. (Informal.) □ *I have to lick this report into shape this morning.* □ *Let's all lend a hand and whip this house into shape. It's a mess.*

lie down on the job to do one's job poorly or not at all. (Informal.) □ *Tom was sacked because he was lying down on the job.* □ *The telephonist was not answering the phone. She was lying down on the job.*

lie in state [for a corpse] to be on display in a public place. □ *The dead leader lay in state for three days in the country's main city.* □ *While the king lay in state, many people walked by and paid their respects.*

lie in wait for someone or something to wait quietly in ambush for someone or something. □ *The lion lay in wait for the zebra.* □ *The robber was lying in wait for a victim.*

lie low to keep quiet and not be noticed; to avoid being conspicuous. □ *I suggest you lie low for a few days.* □ *The robber said that he would lie low for a short time after the robbery.*

lie through one's teeth to lie boldly. (Informal.) □ *I knew she was lying through her teeth, but I didn't want to say so just then.* □ *I'm not lying through my teeth! I never do!*

life (and soul) of the party the type of person who is lively and helps make a party fun and exciting. □ *Bill is always the life and soul of the party. Be sure to invite him.* □ *Bob isn't exactly the life of the party, but he's polite.*

light into someone or something See *lace into someone or something.*

light out (for somewhere) to depart in haste for somewhere. (Slang.) □ *It's time I lit out for home.* □ *I should have lit out ten minutes ago.*

light out (of somewhere) to depart from somewhere in haste. (Slang.) □ *It's time I lit out of here. I'm late for my next appointment.* □ *Look at that* *horse go. He really lit out of the starting-gate.*

Lightning never strikes twice (in the same place). a saying meaning that it is extremely unlikely that the same misfortune will occur again in the same set of circumstances or to the same people. □ *Ever since the fire, Jean has been afraid that her house will go on fire again, but they say that lightning never strikes twice.* □ *Supposedly lightning never strikes twice, but the Smiths' house has been burgled twice this year.*

like a bat out of hell with great speed and force. (Informal. Use caution with the word *hell*.) □ *Did you see her leave? She left like a bat out of hell.* □ *The car sped down the street like a bat out of hell.*

like a bolt out of the blue suddenly and without warning. (Refers to a bolt of lightning coming out of a clear blue sky.) □ *The news came to us like a bolt out of the blue.* □ *Like a bolt out of the blue, the managing director came and sacked us all.*

like a fish out of water awkward; in a foreign or unaccustomed environment. □ *At a formal dance, John is like a fish out of water.* □ *Mary was like a fish out of water at the bowling tournament.*

like a house on fire 1. very rapidly. (Informal.) □ *Mary's typing like a house on fire.* □ *Jane's getting through the work like a house on fire.* 2. very well. (Informal.) □ *The families get on like a house on fire.* □ *We hope that the children get on like a house on fire.*

like a lamb to the slaughter quietly and without seeming to realize or complain about the likely difficulties or dangers of a situation. (Also plural and sometimes without *like a*. From the expression, "lead someone like a lamb to the slaughter.") □ *Young men fighting in World War I were simply lambs to the slaughter.* □ *Out team went on the football field like lambs to the slaughter to meet the league-leaders.*

like a sitting duck AND **like sitting ducks** unguarded; unsuspecting and unaware. □ *He was waiting there like a sitting duck—a perfect target for a mugger.* □ *The soldiers were standing at the top of the hill like sitting ducks. It's a wonder they weren't all killed.*

like a three-ring circus chaotic; exciting and busy. □ *Our household is like a three-ring circus on Monday mornings.* □ *This meeting is like a three-ring circus. Quiet down and listen!*

like crazy AND **like mad** furiously; very much, fast, many, or actively. (Informal.) □ *We sold ice-cream like crazy. It was a very hot day.* □ *When she stubbed her toe, she started screaming like mad.* □ *He's working like crazy these days.*

like it or lump it either accept it or *drop dead*. (Slang and fairly rude.) □ *I don't care whether you care for my attitude or not. You can just like it or lump it.* □ *This is all the food you get. Like it or lump it!*

like looking for a needle in a haystack engaged in a hopeless search. □ *Trying to find a white dog in the snow is like looking for a needle in a haystack.* □ *I tried to find my lost contact lens on the beach, but it was like looking for a needle in a haystack.*

like mad See *like crazy.*

like nothing on earth to be very untidy or very unattractive. (Informal.) □ *Joan arrived at the office looking like nothing on earth. She'd fallen in the mud.* □ *Alice was like nothing on earth in that electric yellow dress.*

like one of the family as if someone (or a pet) were a member of one's family. (Informal.) □ *We treat our dog like one of the family.* □ *We are very happy to have you stay with us, Bill. I hope you don't mind if we treat you like one of the family.*

like sitting ducks See *like a sitting duck.*

like water off a duck's back without any apparent effect. □ *Insults rolled off*

John like water off a duck's back. □
There's no point in scolding the children. It's like water off a duck's back.

likes of someone the type of person that someone is; anyone like someone. (Informal. Almost always in a negative sense.) □ *I don't like Bob. I wouldn't do anything for the likes of him.* □ *Nobody wants the likes of him around.*

line of least resistance the course of action that will cause least trouble or effort. □ *Jane won't stand up for her rights. She always takes the line of least resistance.* □ *Joan never states her point of view. She takes the line of least resistance and agrees with everyone else.*

line one's own pockets to make money for oneself in a greedy or dishonest fashion. (Slang.) □ *When it was discovered that the sales manager was lining her own pockets, she was sacked.* □ *If you line your pockets while in public office, you'll get into serious trouble.*

line someone or something up with something AND **line up someone or something with something** to position someone or something (or a group) in reference to other things. □ *Line up this brick with the bricks below and at both sides. That's the way you lay bricks.* □ *Please line the chairs up with the floor tiles.* □ *Line up the flowers with the row of trees.* ALSO: **line up (with something)** to be in line with something. □ *That brick doesn't line up with the others. Please move it.* □ *The books line up with the edge of the bookshelf and look really nice.* □ *Yes, they line up nicely.*

line someone up for something AND **line up someone for something** to schedule someone for something; to arrange for someone to do or be something. □ *I lined up four of my best friends to serve as ushers at my wedding.* □ *I lined gardeners up for the summer work on the gardens.*

line up (with something) See under *line someone or something up with something.*

lion's share (of something) the larger share of something. □ *The elder boy always takes the lion's share of the food.* □ *Jim was supposed to divide the cake in two equal pieces, but he took the lion's share.*

listen in (on someone or something) to eavesdrop on someone or something. □ *I hope you weren't listening in on their conversation.* □ *Were you listening in on John and Tom?* □ *No, I'd never listen in.*

listen to reason to yield to a reasonable argument; to take the reasonable course. □ *Please listen to reason, and don't do something you'll regret.* □ *She got into trouble because she wouldn't listen to reason and was always late.*

little by little slowly, a bit at a time. □ *Little by little, he began to understand what we were talking about.* □ *The snail crossed the stone little by little.*

live a dog's life See *lead a dog's life.*

live and let live not to interfere with other people's business or preferences. □ *I don't care what they do! Live and let live, I always say.* □ *Your parents are strict. Mine prefer to live and let live.*

live beyond one's means to spend more money than one can afford. (Compare to *live within one's means.*) □ *The Browns are deeply in debt because they are living beyond their means.* □ *I stick to a budget so that I don't live beyond my means.*

live by one's wits to survive by being clever. □ *When you're in the kind of business I'm in, you have to live by your wits.* □ *John was orphaned at the age of ten and grew up living by his wits.*

live for the moment to live without planning for the future. □ *John has no health or life insurance. He lives only for the moment.* □ *When you're young, you tend to live for the moment and not plan for your future security.*

live from hand to mouth to live in poor circumstances; to be able to get only what one needs for the present, not save for the future. (Informal.) ☐ *When both my parents were out of work, we lived from hand to mouth.* ☐ *We lived from hand to mouth during the war. Things were very difficult.*

live in to live at the residence at which one works. ☐ *In order to be here early enough to prepare breakfast, the cook has to live in.* ☐ *Mr. Simpson has a valet, but he doesn't live in.*

live in an ivory tower to be aloof or separated from the realities of living. (*Live* can be replaced by a number of expressions meaning to dwell or spend time, as in the examples.) ☐ *If you didn't spend so much time in your ivory tower, you'd know what people really think!* ☐ *Many professors are said to live in ivory towers. They don't know what the real world is like.*

live it up to have an exciting time; to do what one pleases—regardless of cost—to please oneself. (Informal.) ☐ *At the party, John was really living it up.* ☐ *Come on! Have fun! Live it up!* ☐ *They spent a week in Mexico living it up and then came home broke.*

live next door (to someone) to live in the house or dwelling next to someone. ☐ *I live next door to John.* ☐ *John lives next door to me.* ☐ *John lives next door.*

live off someone or something to get one's income from or be supported by someone or something. ☐ *John is thirty years old and still lives off his parents.* ☐ *I live off my investments.* ☐ *James lives off his wife. She works and he doesn't.*

live off the fat of the land to live in a very affluent or luxurious way. (From the Bible.) ☐ *If I had a million pounds, I'd invest it and live off the fat of the land.* ☐ *Jean married a wealthy man and lived off the fat of the land.*

live on borrowed time to live longer than circumstances warrant; to live longer than expected; to remain in a situation longer than circumstances warrant. ☐ *John has a terminal disease, and he's living on borrowed time.* ☐ *The student's living on borrowed time. If he doesn't pass this exam, he will be asked to go.*

live on something to depend on something for sustenance. (Compare to *live off someone or something.*) ☐ *I can't live on bread and water.* ☐ *We can hardly live on £300 a week.*

live out of a suitcase to live briefly in a place, never unpacking one's luggage. ☐ *I hate living out of a suitcase. For my next holiday, I want to go to just one place and stay there the whole time.* ☐ *We were living out of suitcases in a hotel while they repaired the damage the fire caused to our house.*

live something down AND **live down something** to overcome the shame or embarrassment of something. ☐ *I'll never be able to live down what happened at the party last night.* ☐ *Oh, you'll live it down someday.*

live through something to endure something. ☐ *I thought I'd never be able to live through the lecture. It was so boring.* ☐ *I just can't live through another day like this.*

live up to something to fulfil expectations; to satisfy a set of aims. (Often with *one's reputation, standards,* etc.) ☐ *I hope I can live up to my reputation.* ☐ *The class lives up to its reputation of being exciting and interesting.* ☐ *She was unable to live up to her own high standards.*

live within one's means to spend no more money than one has. (Compare to *live beyond one's means.*) ☐ *We have to struggle to live within our means, but we manage.* ☐ *John is unable to live within his means.*

load off one's mind relief from something which has been worrying one. (Informal.) ☐ *It will be a load off Jane's mind when her mother leaves hospital.* ☐ *You aren't going to like what I'm going to say, but it will be a load off my mind.*

197

lock horns (with someone) to get into an argument with someone. (Informal.) □ *Let's settle this peacefully. I don't want to lock horns with your lawyer.* □ *The judge doesn't want to lock horns either.*

lock someone or something in something to cause someone or something to be locked within a room, car, etc., possibly accidentally. (Compare to *lock someone or something up.*) □ *I locked my keys in the car, and I can't get them out.* □ *The robber locked us in the vault and took all our valuables.*

lock someone or something up AND **lock up someone or something** to lock someone or something (in a place) deliberately. □ *The police locked Bob up in jail.* □ *We locked up the dog in the basement during the party.*

lock, stock, and barrel everything. □ *We had to move everything out of the house—lock, stock, and barrel.* □ *We lost everything—lock, stock, and barrel—in the fire.*

Long time no see. not to have seen someone for a long time. (Informal.) □ *Hello, John. Long time no see.* □ *When John and Mary met on the street, they both said, "Long time no see."*

look after someone or something to watch over and care for someone or something. □ *Please look after my cat while I'm on holiday.* □ *I'd be happy to look after your baby while you go shopping.*

look as if butter wouldn't melt in one's mouth to appear to be very innocent, respectable, honest, etc. □ *Sally looks as if butter wouldn't melt in her mouth, but she is going out with a married man.* □ *The child looks as though butter wouldn't melt in his mouth, but he bullies the other children.*

look back on someone or something to review one's memories of someone or something. □ *When I look back on Tom and the good times we had, I realize what good friends we were.* □ *I get upset when I look back on the car accident.*

look daggers at someone to give someone an unpleasant or nasty look. □ *Tom must have been angry at Ann from the way he was looking daggers at her.* □ *Don't you dare look daggers at me! I haven't done anything.*

look down on someone or something AND **look down one's nose at someone or something** to regard someone or something with contempt or displeasure. (Informal.) □ *I think that John liked Mary, although he did seem to look down on her.* □ *Don't look down your nose at my car just because it's rusty and noisy.*

look down one's nose at someone or something See the previous entry.

look for someone or something to hunt or search for someone or something. □ *I'm looking for someone to give me a lift home.* □ *I'm looking for a lift home.*

look for someone or something high and low AND **look high and low (for someone or something)** to look everywhere for someone or something. □ *I've looked for our dog high and low, and I can't find him.* □ *I've looked high and low for a red jacket.* □ *I don't know where my glasses are. I've looked high and low.*

look for trouble to behave in such a way as to invite trouble. (Informal. Usually *be looking for.*) □ *The club bouncer asked me to leave unless I was looking for trouble.* □ *The football fans were looking for trouble when they booed the other team.*

look forward to something to anticipate something with pleasure. □ *I'm really looking forward to your visit next week.* □ *We all look forward to your new book on gardening.*

look high and low (for someone or something) See *look for someone or something high and low.*

look in (on someone or something) to visit and check on someone or something. □ *I'll look in on your house while you're on holiday.* □ *Yes, just look in and make sure nothing is wrong.*

□ *Would you please look in on the baby?*

look into something AND **see into something** to investigate something. □ *I'll have to look into that matter.* □ *Don't worry about your problem. I'll see into it.*

look like a million dollars to look very good. □ *Oh, Sally, you look like a million dollars.* □ *Your new hair-do looks like a million dollars.*

look like someone or something **1.** to resemble someone or something. □ *I look like my father.* □ *This box looks like my box.* **2.** to give the appearance of predicting (something). □ *The sky looks like rain.* □ *No, it looks like snow.* □ *Oh, oh. This looks like trouble. Let's go.*

look like the cat that swallowed the canary AND **look like the cat that swallowed the cream** to appear as if one had just had a great success. □ *After the meeting John looked like the cat that swallowed the canary. I knew he must have been a success.* □ *What happened? You look like the cat that swallowed the canary.* □ *Jean must have won. She looks like the cat that swallowed the cream.*

look on (at something) to be an observer of something (rather than a participant). □ *There was nothing to do but stand there and look on at the disaster.* □ *I don't like to stand there and look on.*

look on someone as something to view or think of someone as something. □ *I look on you as a very thoughtful person.* □ *Mary looked on Jane as a good friend.*

look out for someone or something See *watch out for someone or something.*

look someone in the eye See the following entry.

look someone in the face AND **look someone in the eye; stare someone in the face** to face someone directly. (Facing someone this way should assure sincerity.) □ *I don't believe you. Look me in the eye*

and say that. □ *She looked him in the face and said she never wanted to see him again.* □ *I dare you to stare him in the face and say that!*

look someone or something over AND **look over someone or something** to examine someone or something carefully. □ *Please look over this report.* □ *She looked him over and decided to employ him.*

look someone or something up AND **look up someone or something** to search for and find someone or something. □ *Would you please look up John? I need to talk to him.* □ *Ann looked the word up in the dictionary.* □ *Look up Fred's number in the telephone book.*

look the other way to ignore (something) on purpose. □ *John could have prevented the problem, but he looked the other way.* □ *By looking the other way, he actually made the problem worse.*

look to one's laurels to take care not to lower or diminish one's reputation or position, especially in relation to that of someone else potentially better. □ *With the arrival of the new member of the football team, James will have to look to his laurels to remain as the highest scorer.* □ *The older members of the team will have to look to their laurels when young people join.*

look to someone or something (for something) to expect someone to supply something. □ *Children look to their parents for help.* □ *Tom looked to the bank for a loan.* □ *Most people who need to borrow money look to a bank.*

look up and down something to examine something from end to end. □ *The dog looked up and down the street, and then it went across.* □ *The man looked up and down the railway tracks, but he didn't see a train.*

look up to someone to view someone with respect and admiration. □ *Bill really looks up to his father.* □ *Everyone in the class looked up to the teacher.*

loom large to be of great importance, especially when referring to a possible problem, danger, or threat. □ *The exams were looming large.* □ *Eviction was looming large when the students could not pay their rent.*

lord it over someone to dominate someone; to direct and control someone. □ *Mr. Smith seems to lord it over his wife.* □ *The old man lords it over everyone in the office.*

lose face to lose status; to become less respectable. □ *John is more afraid of losing face than losing money.* □ *Things will go better if you can explain to him where he was wrong without making him lose face.*

lose ground to fall behind; to fall back. □ *She was recovering nicely yesterday, but she lost ground last night.* □ *We are losing ground in our fight against mosquitoes.*

lose heart to lose one's courage or confidence. □ *Now, don't lose heart. Keep trying.* □ *What a disappointment! It's enough to make one lose heart.*

lose one's cool to lose one's temper; to lose one's nerve. (Slang.) □ *Wow, he really lost his cool! What a tantrum!* □ *Whatever you do, don't lose your cool.*

lose one's grip to lose control (over something). □ *I can't seem to run things like I used to. I'm losing my grip.* □ *They replaced the board of directors because it was losing its grip.*

lose one's head (over someone or something) 1. [with *someone*] to become foolishly emotionally attached to someone. □ *Don't lose your head over John. He isn't worth it.* □ *She is at the age that she loses her head over every other boy she meets.* **2.** [with *something*] to become confused about something. □ *Fred lost his head over the whole business.* □ *I'm sorry. I got upset and lost my head.*

lose one's marbles AND **lose one's mind** to go crazy; to go out of one's mind. (The first phrase is slang.) □ *What a silly thing to say! Have you lost your marbles?*

□ *I can't seem to remember anything. I think I'm losing my mind.*

lose one's mind See the previous entry.

lose one's reason to lose one's power of reasoning, possibly in anger. □ *I was so confused that I almost lost my reason.* □ *Bob seems to have lost his reason when he struck John.*

lose one's shirt to lose all of one's assets (including one's shirt). (Slang.) □ *I almost lost my shirt on that deal. I have to invest more wisely.* □ *No, I can't loan you £200. I just lost my shirt at the racetrack.*

lose one's temper to become angry. □ *Please don't lose your temper. It's not good for you.* □ *I'm sorry that I lost my temper.*

lose one's touch (with someone or something) to lose one's ability to handle someone or something. □ *I seem to have lost my touch with my children. They don't pay any attention to me any more.* □ *We've both lost our touch as far as managing people goes.* □ *Tom said that he had lost his touch with the shares market.*

lose one's train of thought to forget what one was talking or thinking about. □ *Excuse me, I lost my train of thought. What was I talking about?* □ *You made the speaker lose her train of thought.*

lose oneself in something to become deeply involved in something (so that everything else is forgotten). □ *Jane has a tendency to lose herself in her work.* □ *I often lose myself in thought.*

lose oneself in something to have all one's attention taken up by something. □ *I can lose myself in a book any time.* □ *The children lose themselves in their favourite TV programme on Saturdays.*

lose out (on something) See *miss out (on something).*

lose out to someone or something to lose a competition to someone or something.

☐ *Our team lost out to the other team.* ☐ *Bill lost out to Sally in the contest.*

lose sight of someone or something to forget about the importance of someone or something. ☐ *We lost sight of you when we planned the party.* ☐ *You lose sight of the important things too often.*

lose sleep over someone or something to worry about someone or something. (Usually negative.) ☐ *Your job's not worth losing sleep over.* ☐ *Fred's not losing any sleep over his broken engagement.*

lose touch (with someone or something) to lose contact with someone or something. (Compare to *keep in touch (with someone).*) ☐ *Poor Sally has lost touch with reality.* ☐ *I've lost touch with all my relations.* ☐ *Jane didn't mean to lose touch, but she did.*

lose track (of someone or something) to forget where someone or something is; to lose or misplace someone or something. ☐ *I've lost track of the time.* ☐ *The mother lost track of her child and started calling her.*

lost in thought busy thinking. ☐ *I'm sorry, I didn't hear what you said. I was lost in thought.* ☐ *Bill—lost in thought as always—went into the wrong room.*

lost on someone having no effect on someone; wasted on someone. (Informal.) ☐ *The joke was lost on Jean. She didn't understand it.* ☐ *The humour of the situation was lost on Mary. She was too upset to see it.*

lost to something no longer having or feeling something. ☐ *Mary was lost to all sense of reason when she fell in love with John.* ☐ *Bob was lost to any finer feelings after he joined the army.*

louse something up AND **louse up something** to mess up or ruin something. (Slang.) ☐ *I've worked hard on this. Please don't louse it up.* ☐ *You've loused up all my plans.*

lousy with something with something in abundance. (Slang.) ☐ *This place is lousy with policemen.* ☐ *Our picnic table was lousy with ants.*

love at first sight love established when two people first see one another. ☐ *Bill was standing at the door when Ann opened it. It was love at first sight.* ☐ *It was love at first sight when they met, but it didn't last long.*

lovely weather for ducks rainy weather. ☐ BOB: *Not very nice out today, is it?* BILL: *It's lovely weather for ducks.* ☐ *I don't like this weather, but it's lovely weather for ducks.*

lower one's sights to set one's goals or aims lower. ☐ *Even though you get frustrated, don't lower your sights.* ☐ *I shouldn't lower my sights. If I work hard, I can do what I want.*

lower one's voice to speak more softly. ☐ *Please lower your voice, or you'll disturb the people who are working.* ☐ *He wouldn't lower his voice, so everyone heard what he said.*

luck out to get lucky (about something). (Slang.) ☐ *I won £100 in the lottery. I really lucked out.* ☐ *Bob lucked out when he got such a good teacher for geometry.*

lucky dip a situation in which one is given no choice in what one is given, what happens, etc. (From the name of a fairground side-show in which children choose a parcel at random from a tub of bran.) ☐ *The allocation of jobs is a lucky dip. You can't choose.* ☐ *Which coach you go back to school on is a lucky dip.*

lull someone into a false sense of security to lead someone into believing that all is well before attacking or doing something bad. ☐ *We lulled the enemy into a false sense of security by pretending to retreat. Then we launched an attack.* ☐ *The boss lulled us into a false sense of security by saying that our jobs were safe and then sacked half the staff.*

M

mad about someone or something See *crazy about someone or something.*

made for doing something well suited for doing a specific task. □ *This tool is made for turning this kind of screw.* □ *Jane is very talented. She's just made for designing furniture.*

made for each other [for two people] to be very well suited romantically. □ *Bill and Jane were made for each other.* □ *Mr. and Mrs. Smith were not exactly made for each other. They really don't get along.*

made to measure [of clothing] made especially to fit the measurements of a particular person. □ *Jack has his suits made to measure because he's rather large.* □ *Having clothes made to measure is rather expensive.*

made to order See *make something to order.*

maiden speech a first public speech, especially a British Member of Parliament's first speech to the House of Commons. □ *The new MP makes his maiden speech tonight.* □ *Our professor made her maiden speech to the conference yesterday.*

maiden voyage the first voyage of a ship or boat. □ *The liner sank on its maiden voyage.* □ *Jim is taking his yacht on its maiden voyage.*

make a bee-line for someone or something to head straight towards someone or something. (Informal.) □ *Billy came into the kitchen and made a bee-line for the biscuits.* □ *After the game,*

we all made a bee-line for John, who was serving cold drinks.

make a big deal about something to exaggerate the seriousness of something. (Slang.) □ *Come on. It was nothing! Don't make a big deal about it.* □ *I only stepped on your toe. Don't make a big deal about it.*

make a break for something or somewhere to move or run quickly to something or somewhere. (Informal.) □ *Before we could stop her, she made a break for the door and got away.* □ *The mouse got frightened and made a break for a hole in the wall.*

make a cheque out (to someone) AND **make out a cheque (to someone)** to write a cheque naming someone as payee. □ *Please make a cheque out to John Jones.* □ *Do you want cash, or should I make out a cheque?*

make a clean breast of something to confess something; to *get something off one's chest.* □ *You'll feel better if you make a clean breast of it. Now tell us what happened.* □ *I was forced to make a clean breast of the whole affair.*

make a clean sweep to do something completely or thoroughly, with no exceptions. (Informal.) □ *The managing director decided to sack everybody, so he made a clean sweep.* □ *The council decided to make a clean sweep and repair all the roads in the district.*

make a come-back to return to one's former (successful) career. (Informal.) □ *After ten years in retirement, the* *singer made a come-back.* □ *You're never too old to make a come-back.*

make a day of doing something AND **make a day of it** to spend the whole day doing something. □ *We went to the museum to see the new exhibit and then decided to make a day of it.* □ *They made a day of cleaning the attic.*

make a dent in something to begin to consume or accomplish something. (Informal.) □ *Bob, you've hardly made a dent in your dinner!* □ *There is a lot of rice left. We hardly made a dent in it all week.* □ *Get busy! You haven't even made a dent in your work.*

make a face See *pull a face.*

make a face (at someone) **1.** to alter or screw up one's facial features at someone in ridicule. □ *Mother, Billy made a face at me!* □ *The teacher sent Jane to the headmistress for making a face in class.* **2.** to attempt to communicate to someone through facial gestures, usually an attempt to say "no" or "stop." □ *I started to tell John where I was last night, but Bill made a face so I didn't.* □ *John made a face at me as I was testifying, so I avoided telling everything.*

make a fast buck to make money with little effort. (Slang. Originally American.) □ *Tom is always ready to make a fast buck.* □ *I made a fast buck selling used cars.*

make a fool out of someone AND **make a monkey out of someone; make an ass of someone** to make someone look foolish. (The second and third phrases are informal.) □ *John made a fool out of himself at the party.* □ *Are you trying to make a monkey out of me?* □ *Don't make an ass of yourself!*

make a fuss (over someone or something) AND **fuss over someone or something; make over someone or something** **1.** to worry about or complain about someone or something. □ *Why do you fuss over a problem like that?* □ *Stop fussing over your hair. It's fine.* **2.** to be very caring and helpful towards a person or a pet. □ *How can*

anyone make a fuss over a cat? □ *Billy was embarrassed when his mother made a fuss over him.* □ *Please stop making over me.* **3.** to argue about someone or something. □ *Please don't make a fuss over who gets the last sweet.* □ *Please discuss it. Don't fuss about it!*

make a go of it to make something work out all right. (Informal.) □ *It's a tough situation, but Ann is trying to make a go of it.* □ *We don't like living here, but we have to make a go of it.*

make a great show of something to make something obvious; to do something in a showy fashion. □ *Ann made a great show of wiping up the drink that John spilled.* □ *Jane displayed her irritation at our late arrival by making a great show of serving the overcooked dinner.*

make a hit (with someone or something) to please someone. (Informal.) □ *The singer made a hit with the audience.* □ *She was afraid she wouldn't make a hit.* □ *John made a hit with my parents last evening.*

make a killing to have a great success, especially in making money. (Slang.) □ *John's got a job selling insurance. He's not exactly making a killing.* □ *Bill made a killing at the race-track yesterday.*

make a living to earn enough money to live on. □ *Mary made a living selling second-hand clothes.* □ *I can hardly make a living with the skills I have.*

make a long story short to bring a story to an end. (A formula which introduces a summary of a story or a joke.) □ *And—to make a long story short—I never got back the money that I lent him.* □ *If I can make a long story short, let me say that everything worked out fine.*

make a meal of something to take much more time or trouble over something than is usually required; to make something out to be more complicated than it actually is. □ *Don't make such a meal out of having a baby. Millions of women* have had them before you. □ *That boy made a meal of weeding the garden. It took him hours!*

make a mess (of something) to do something badly; to mess up something. □ *You certainly have made a mess of your life!* □ *Oh, how could I make a mess like this?*

make a monkey out of someone See *make a fool out of someone.*

make a mountain out of a molehill to make a major issue out of a minor one; to exaggerate the importance of something. □ *Come on, don't make a mountain out of a molehill. It's not that important.* □ *Mary is always making mountains out of molehills.*

make a muck of something to make a mess of something; to do something badly. (Slang.) □ *You made a real muck of baking that cake.* □ *Bob made a muck of parking the car.*

make a name for oneself to make oneself famous; to become famous. □ *Sally wants to work hard and make a name for herself.* □ *It's hard to make a name for oneself without a lot of talent and hard work.*

make a night of doing something to do something for the entire night. □ *We partied until three in the morning and then decided to make a night of it.* □ *Once or twice in the early spring we make a night of fishing.*

make a note of something to write something down. □ *Please make a note of this address.* □ *This is important. Make a note of it.*

make a nuisance of oneself to become a constant source of annoyance. □ *I'm sorry to make a nuisance of myself, but I do need an answer to my question.* □ *Stop making a nuisance of yourself and wait your turn.*

make a packet AND **make a pile** to make a lot of money. (Slang.) □ *John really made a packet on that deal.* □ *I'd like to make a pile and retire.*

make a pass at someone to flirt with someone; to make a romantic advance at someone. (This often has sexual implications.) □ *I was shocked when Ann made a pass at me.* □ *I think Bob was making a pass at me, but he did it very subtly.*

make a pile See *make a packet.*

make a pitch for someone or something to say something in support of someone or something; to attempt to promote or advance someone or something. (Informal.) □ *Bill is making a pitch for his friend's new product again.* □ *The theatrical agent came in and made a pitch for her client.*

make a play for someone to attempt to attract the romantic interest of someone. (Informal. Compare to *make a pass at someone.*) □ *Ann made a play for Bill, but he wasn't interested in her.* □ *I knew he liked me, but I never thought he'd make a play for me so obviously.*

make a point to state an item of importance. □ *You made a point which we all should remember.* □ *He spoke for an hour without making a point.*

make a point of (doing) something to make an effort to do something. □ *Please make a point of posting this letter. It's very important.* □ *The hostess made a point of thanking me for bringing flowers.*

make a practice of something AND **make something a practice** to turn something into a habitual activity. □ *Jane makes a practice of planting daisies every summer.* □ *Her mother also made it a practice.*

make a run for it to run fast to get away or get somewhere. (Informal. Compare to *make a break for something or somewhere.*) □ *When the guard wasn't looking, the prisoner made a run for it.* □ *The police have spotted you. You'll have to make a run for it.*

make a scene AND **create a scene** to make a public display or disturbance. □ *When John found a fly in his drink, he started to create a scene.* □ *Oh,*

John, please don't make a scene. Just forget about it.

Make a silk purse out of a sow's ear. to create something of value out of something of no value. (Often in the negative.) □ *Don't bother trying to fix up this old bicycle. You can't make a silk purse out of a sow's ear.* □ *My mother made a lovely jacket out of an old coat. She succeeded in making a silk purse out of a sow's ear.*

make a stink (about something) See *create a stink (about something).*

make allowances (for someone or something) to judge someone less severely than others by taking into consideration certain negative effects or aspects. □ *You must make allowances for Mary's poor reading. She was taught badly.* □ *The teacher made allowances for the fact that Jean was nervous.* □ *Not everyone is as clever as you. You must learn to make allowances.*

make an all out effort See *all out effort.*

make an appearance to appear; to appear in a performance. (Compare to *put in an appearance.*) □ *We waited for thirty minutes for the professor to make an appearance, then we went home.* □ *The famous singing star made an appearance in Birmingham last August.*

make an appointment (with someone) to schedule a meeting with someone. □ *I made an appointment with the doctor for late today.* □ *The professor wouldn't see me unless I made an appointment.*

make an arrangement (with someone) to make plans with someone; to fix an appointment with someone. □ *I made an arrangement with John to come to his house and collect him.* □ *Have you made an arrangement with Jack to borrow his house?*

make an ass of someone See *make a fool out of someone.*

make an example of someone to punish someone as a public warning to others. □ *The judge decided to make an* example of John, so he fined him the full amount. □ *The teacher made an example of Mary, who disturbed the class constantly with her whispering. She sent her out of the room.*

make an exception (for someone) to suspend a rule or practice for someone in a single instance. □ *Please make an exception just this once.* □ *The rule is a good one, and I will not make an exception for anyone.*

make an impression (on someone) to produce a memorable effect on someone. (Often with *good, bad,* or some other adjective.) □ *Tom made a bad impression on the banker.* □ *I'm afraid that you haven't made a very good impression on our visitors.* □ *You made quite an impression on my father.*

make an issue of something to draw attention to something and turn it into an important matter. □ *Please don't make an issue of John's comment. He didn't mean to be rude.* □ *Tom has a lot of problems. Please don't make an issue of them.*

make an uproar See *create an uproar.*

make arrangements (to do something) to make plans to do something. □ *I'm making arrangements to sell my car.* □ *Pat is making arrangements to work abroad.*

make as if to do something to act as if one were about to do something. □ *The thief made as if to run away but changed his mind.* □ *Jane made as if to smack the child.*

make book on something to make or accept bets on something. (Slang.) □ *It looks like it will rain, but I wouldn't make book on it.* □ *John's making book on the test this Saturday.*

make (both) ends meet to manage to live on a small amount of money. □ *It's hard these days to make ends meet.* □ *I have to work overtime to make both ends meet.*

make cracks (about someone or something) to ridicule or make jokes about someone or something. (Informal.) □ *Please stop making cracks about my haircut. It's the new style.* □ *Some people can't help making cracks. They are just rude.*

make do (with someone or something) to do as well as possible with someone or something. □ *You'll have to make do with less money next year. The economy is very weak.* □ *We'll have to make do with John even though he's a slow worker.* □ *Yes, we'll have to make do.*

make eyes (at someone) to flirt with someone. □ *Tom spent all afternoon making eyes at Ann.* □ *How could they sit there in class making eyes?*

make fast work of someone or something See *make short work of someone or something.*

make for somewhere to run or travel to somewhere. □ *When I got out of class, I made for the gym.* □ *When he got out of jail, he made for Brighton.*

make free (with someone or something) 1. [with *someone*] See *take liberties with someone or something.* 2. [with *something*] to take advantage of or use something as if it were one's own. (Compare to *take liberties with someone or something.*) □ *I wish you wouldn't come into my house and make free with my food and drink.* □ *Please do not make free with my car while I'm gone.*

make friends (with someone) to become a friend of someone. □ *I tried to make friends with John, but he didn't seem to like me.* □ *I find it hard to make friends.*

make fun of someone or something to ridicule someone or something. □ *Please stop making fun of me. It hurts my feelings.* □ *Billy teases and makes fun of people a lot, but he means no harm.*

make good to succeed in one's career; to be successful. □ *All the members of the family made good.* □ *Jane was determined to make good.*

make good as something to succeed in a particular role. □ *I hope I make good as a teacher.* □ *John made good as a soccer player.*

make good money to earn a large amount of money. (Informal.) □ *Ann makes good money at her job.* □ *I don't know what she does, but she makes good money.*

make good time to proceed at a fast or reasonable rate. (Informal.) □ *On our trip to Brighton, we made good time.* □ *I'm making good time, but I have a long way to go.*

Make hay while the sun shines. a proverb meaning that you should make the most of good times. □ *There are lots of people here now. You should try to sell them your cold lemonade. Make hay while the sun shines.* □ *Go to school and get a good education while you're young. Make hay while the sun shines.*

make it hot for someone to make things difficult for someone; to put someone under pressure. (Slang.) □ *Maybe if we make it hot for them, they'll leave.* □ *John likes making it hot for people. He's sort of a nasty person.*

Make it snappy! Hurry up! (Slang.) □ *Come on. Make it snappy! I can't wait all day.* □ *Make it snappy! We have to leave now!*

make it worth someone's while to make something profitable enough for someone to do. □ *If you deliver this parcel for me, I'll make it worth your while.* □ *The boss said he'd make it worth our while if we worked late.*

make life miserable for someone to make someone unhappy over a long period of time. □ *My shoes are tight, and they are making life miserable for me.* □ *Jane's mother is making life miserable for her.*

make light of something to treat something as if it were unimportant or humorous. □ *I wish you wouldn't make light of his problems. They're quite serious.* □ *I make light of my problems, and that makes me feel better.*

make little of someone or something 1. to treat someone or something as unimportant; not to appreciate the good points or success of someone or something; to *play someone or something down.* □ *John made little of my efforts to collect money for charity.* □ *The neighbours made little of John and thought he would amount to nothing.* **2.** not to understand someone or something. □ *I could make little of his lecture.* □ *Jean is odd. I can make little of her.*

make love (to someone) to share physical or emotional love (or both) with someone. (This phrase usually has a sexual meaning.) □ *Tom and Ann turned out the lights and made love to each other.* □ *The actress refused to make love on stage.*

make merry to have fun; to have an enjoyable time. □ *The guests certainly made merry at the wedding.* □ *The children were making merry in the garden.*

make mincemeat of someone 1. to defeat someone completely. (Informal.) □ *Our football team made mincemeat of theirs.* □ *Bob made mincemeat of John in the tennis finals.* **2.** to scold or punish someone severely. □ *Jack's mother will make mincemeat of him when she sees the broken window.* □ *The teacher made mincemeat of Mike when he played truant.*

make mischief to cause trouble. □ *Bob loves to make mischief and get other people into trouble.* □ *Don't believe what Mary says. She's just trying to make mischief.*

make no bones about something to have no hesitation in saying or doing something; to be open about something. (*Something* is often *it*.) □ *Fred made no bones about his dislike of games.* □ *Make no bones about it, Mary is a great singer.*

make no difference (to someone) [for something] not to matter to someone. □ *It makes no difference to me what you do.* □ *Do whatever you want. It really makes no difference.*

make no mistake about it without a doubt; certainly. (Compare to *make no bones about it.* Also used literally.) □ *This car is a great buy. Make no mistake about it.* □ *We support your candidacy—make no mistake about it.*

make nothing of it not to understand something; not to get the significance of something. □ *I could make nothing of his statement.* □ *I saw him leave, but I made nothing of it.*

make off with someone or something to take someone or something away. □ *The robber made off with the jewellery.* □ *The kidnapper made off with the child.*

make one's way (through something) to work or travel through something. □ *Slowly, she made her way through the forest.* □ *The speaker made his way through the speech very slowly.*

make oneself at home to make oneself comfortable as if one were in one's own home. □ *Please come in and make yourself at home.* □ *I'm glad you're here. During your visit, just make yourself at home.*

make oneself conspicuous to attract attention to oneself. □ *Please don't make yourself conspicuous by weeping. It embarrasses me.* □ *Ann makes herself conspicuous by wearing brightly coloured clothing.*

make oneself miserable to do things which cause one to be unhappy. □ *You're just making yourself miserable by trying to do something you aren't qualified to do.* □ *I'm not making myself miserable! You're making me miserable.*

make oneself scarce to go away. (Slang.) □ *Look, chum, go away. Make yourself scarce.* □ *When there is work to be done, I make myself scarce.*

make or break someone to improve or ruin someone. (Informal.) □ *The army will either make or break him.* □ *It's a tough assignment, and it will either make or break her.*

make over someone or something See *make a fuss (over someone or something).*

make peace (with someone) to end a quarrel with someone. (Compare to *kiss and make up.*) □ *Don't you think it's time to make peace with your brother? There is no point in arguing any more.* □ *Yes, it's time we made peace.*

make sense out of someone or something to understand or interpret someone or something. (Also with *some,* as in the examples.) □ *I can hardly make sense out of John.* □ *I'm trying to make some sense out of what John is saying.* ALSO: **make sense** to be understandable. □ *John doesn't make sense.* □ *What John says makes sense.*

make short work of someone or something AND **make fast work of someone or something** to finish with someone or something quickly. □ *I made short work of Tom so I could leave the office to play golf.* □ *Billy made fast work of his dinner so he could go out and play.*

make someone eat crow to cause someone to retract a statement or admit an error. (Informal.) □ *Because Mary was completely wrong, we made her eat crow.* □ *They won't make me eat crow. They don't know I was wrong.*

make someone look good to cause someone to appear successful or competent (especially when this is not the case). □ *John arranges all his affairs to make himself look good.* □ *The manager didn't like the quarterly report because it didn't make her look good.*

make someone look ridiculous to make someone look foolish. □ *This hat makes me look ridiculous.* □ *Please make me look good. Don't make me look ridiculous!*

make someone or something available to someone to supply someone with someone or something. □ *I made my car available to Bob.* □ *They made their maid available to us.*

make someone or something tick to cause someone or something to run or function. (Informal. Usually with *what.*) □ *I don't know what makes this firm tick.* □ *What makes John tick? I just don't understand him.* □ *I took apart the radio to find out what made it tick.*

make someone or something up AND **make up someone or something** **1.** [with *something*] to repay or redo something. □ *Can I make up the work I missed?* □ *Please make up the payment you missed.* **2.** [with *something*] to think up something; to make and tell a lie. □ *That's not true! You just made that up!* □ *I didn't make it up!* **3.** to prepare something; to assemble something. (The *up* can be left out.) □ JOHN: *Is my prescription ready?* CHEMIST: *No, I haven't made it up yet. I'll make up your prescription in a minute.* □ *How long does it take to make up a cheese sandwich?* **4.** [with *someone*] to put make-up on someone. □ *She made herself up before leaving the house.* □ *The crew made up the cast before the play.* ALSO: **make up** to put make-up on oneself. □ *I have to make up now. I go on stage in ten minutes.*

make someone's bed See *make the bed.*

make someone's blood boil to make someone very angry. (Informal.) □ *It just makes my blood boil to think of the amount of food that gets wasted in this house.* □ *Whenever I think of that dishonest man, it makes my blood boil.*

make someone's blood run cold to shock or horrify someone. □ *The terrible story in the newspaper made my blood run cold.* □ *I could tell you things about prisons which would make your blood run cold.*

make someone's hair curl See *curl someone's hair.*

make someone's hair stand on end to cause someone to be very frightened. (Informal.) □ *The horrible scream made my hair stand on end.* □ *The ghost story made our hair stand on end.*

make someone's head spin See the following entry.

make someone's head swim AND **make someone's head spin** **1.** to make someone dizzy or disoriented. □ *Riding in your car so fast makes my head spin.* □

Breathing the gas made my head swim.
2. to confuse or overwhelm someone.
□ *All these numbers make my head swim.* □ *The physics lecture made my head spin.*

make someone's mind up AND **make up someone's mind** to make someone decide. □ *Please make your mind up. Which do you want?* □ *Would you help me make my mind up? I can't decide which dress to buy.*

make someone's mouth water to make someone hungry (for something); to make someone desirous of something. (Informal.) □ *That beautiful salad makes my mouth water.* □ *Talking about food makes my mouth water.* □ *Seeing those holiday brochures makes my mouth water.*

make someone's position clear to clarify where someone stands on an issue. □ *I don't think you understand what I said. Let me make my position clear.* □ *I can't tell whether you are in favour or against the proposal. Please make your position clear.*

make something from scratch to make something by starting with the basic ingredients. (Informal.) □ *We made the cake from scratch, not using a cake mix.* □ *I didn't have a ladder, so I made one from scratch.*

make something out AND **make out something** to read something (which is not written or printed clearly); to decipher something. □ *What does this say? I can hardly make it out.* □ *Can you make out what this says?*

make something out of nothing to make an issue of something of little importance. (See also *make a mountain out of a molehill*.) □ *Relax, John, you're making a problem out of nothing.* □ *You have no evidence. You're making a case out of nothing.*

make something to order to put something together only when someone requests it. (Usually said about clothing.) □ *This shop only makes suits to order.*

□ *Our shirts fit perfectly because each one is made to order.*

make something up to someone to repay someone; to make amends to someone. (The *something* is usually *it*.) □ *I'm so sorry I've insulted you. How can I make it up to you?* □ *I'm sorry I broke our date. I'll make it up to you, I promise.*

make the arrangements (for someone or something) to make plans for someone or something; to organize someone or something. □ *I'm making the arrangements for the convention.* □ *It starts next week, and I hardly have time to make the arrangements.* □ *Peter is making the arrangements for his father's funeral.*

make the bed AND **make someone's bed** to restore a bed to an unslept-in condition. □ *I make my bed every morning.* □ *The maid goes to all the rooms to make the beds.*

make the best of something to try to make a bad situation work out well. (Compare to *make the most of something*.) □ *It's not good, but we'll have to make the best of it.* □ *Ann is clever enough to make the best of a bad situation.*

make the feathers fly See the following entry.

make the fur fly AND **make the feathers fly** to cause a fight or an argument; to *create an uproar* (about something). (Informal.) □ *When your mother gets home and sees what you've done, she'll really make the fur fly.* □ *When those two get together, they'll make the feathers fly. They hate each other.*

make the grade to be satisfactory; to be what is expected. (Informal.) □ *I'm sorry, but your work doesn't exactly make the grade.* □ *Jack will never make the grade as a teacher.*

make the most of something to make something appear as good as possible; to exploit something; to get as much out of something as is possible. (Compare to *make the best of something*.) □ *Mary knows how to make the most of her* *talents.* □ *They designed the advertisements to make the most of the product's features.*

make tracks (somewhere) to leave and travel (by foot or horse) to somewhere. (Informal.) □ *Come on, partner. It's time to make tracks home.* □ *Yes, let's make tracks.*

make up See *make up (with someone)* and under *make someone or something up.*

make up for lost time to do much of something; to make up for not doing much before; to do something fast. □ *At the age of sixty, Bill learned to play golf. Now he plays it all the time. He's making up for lost time.* □ *Because we spent too much time eating lunch, we have to drive faster to make up for lost time. Otherwise we won't arrive when we should.*

make up for something to give (something) as compensation for something. □ *This money will make up for your loss of earnings.* □ *Take a week's holiday to make up for the extra hours worked.*

make up (with someone) to apologize and become friends with someone. □ *I'm sorry. I was wrong. I want to make up with you.* □ *I want to make up, too.*

make use of someone or something to utilize someone or something (for a specific purpose). □ *Can you make use of an extra helper?* □ *I could make use of a lot of help.* □ *I could make use of John to help me.*

make waves to make trouble or difficulties. (Informal. Compare to *rock the boat.*) □ *I don't want to make waves, but this just isn't right.* □ *Why do you always have to make waves? Can't you be constructive?*

make way 1. to make progress; to move ahead. (Originally nautical.) □ *Is this project making any way?* □ *A sailing-boat can't make way if there is no wind.* 2. See the following entry.

make way (for someone or something) to clear a path for someone or something. □ *Make way for the stretcher.* □ *Please make way for the Chancellor.* □ *Here comes the doctor—make way!*

man about town a fashionable man who leads a sophisticated life. □ *He prefers wine bars to pubs—quite a man about town.* □ *Jack's too much of a man about town to go to a football match.*

man in the street the ordinary person. □ *Politicians rarely care what the man in the street thinks.* □ *The man in the street has little interest in literature.*

man to man AND **woman to woman** speaking frankly and directly, one person to another. □ *Let's discuss this man to man so we know what each other thinks.* □ *The two mothers discussed their child-minding problems woman to woman.*

manna from heaven unexpected help or comfort; an unlooked-for benefit or advantage. (A biblical reference.) □ *The arrival of the rescue team was like manna from heaven to the injured climber. He thought he would have been on the mountain all night.* □ *The offer of a new job just as she had been sacked was manna from heaven to Joan.*

Many hands make light work. a proverb meaning that the more people that are involved in a job, the quicker the job will get done. (The opposite of *Too many cooks spoil the broth.*) □ *Our neighbours helped us dig the garden and many hands made light work.* □ *Let's all help clear this stuff away. Many hands make light work.*

many is the time on many occasions. □ *Many is the time I wanted to complain, but I just kept quiet.* □ *Many is the time that we don't have enough to eat.*

mark my word(s) remember what I'm telling you. □ *Mark my word, you'll regret this.* □ *This whole project will fail—mark my words.*

mark someone or something down AND **mark down someone or something** 1. [with *someone*] to make a note about someone; to note a fact about someone. □ *I'm going to the party. Please mark me down as attending.* □ *Mark me down, too.* **2.** [with *something*] to lower the price of something. □ *Let's mark down this butter so it'll sell faster.* □ *Okay, we'll mark it down.*

mark something up AND **mark up something** to raise the price of something. □ *They mark up the price of beef at the week-end.* □ *The shopkeeper seems to mark the price of food up every week.*

marked man someone who is in danger from harm by someone else. (Usually with males.) □ *Bob's a marked man. His tutor found out that he's missing lectures.* □ *Fred's a marked man, too. Jack is looking for him to get his money back from him.*

matter-of-fact businesslike; unfeeling. (See also *as a matter of fact.*) □ *Don't expect a lot of sympathy from Ann. She's very matter-of-fact.* □ *Don't be so matter-of-fact. It hurts my feelings.*

matter of life and death a matter of great urgency; an issue that will decide between living and dying. (Usually an exaggeration; sometimes humorous.) □ *We must find a doctor. It's a matter of life and death.* □ *I must have some water. It's a matter of life and death.*

matter of opinion the question of how good or bad someone or something is. □ *It's a matter of opinion how good the company is. John thinks it's great and Fred thinks it's poor.* □ *How efficient the committee is is a matter of opinion.*

mealy-mouthed not frank or direct. (Informal.) □ *Jane's too mealy-mouthed to tell Frank she dislikes him. She just avoids him.* □ *Don't be so mealy-mouthed. It's better to speak plainly.*

mean nothing (to someone) **1.** not to make sense to someone. (See also the following entry.) □ *This sentence means nothing to me. It isn't clearly written.* □ *I'm sorry. This message means nothing.* **2.** [for someone] not to have feeling for (someone or some-

thing). □ *Do I mean nothing to you after all these years?* □ *Do all those years mean nothing?*

mean something (to someone) **1.** to make sense to someone. (See also the preceding entry. This *something* is used literally in this expression.) □ *Does this line mean something to you?* □ *Yes, it means something.* **2.** for someone to have feeling for (someone or something). □ *Yes, Jean means something to him.* □ *This job certainly means something to Ann.*

mean to (do something) to intend to do something. □ *Did you mean to do that?* □ *No, it was an accident. I didn't mean to.*

measure up (to someone or something) to be equal to someone or something. □ *Ann is good, but she doesn't measure up to Mary.* □ *This measures up to my standards quite nicely.* □ *Yes, it measures up.*

measure up (to someone's expectations) to be as good as one expects. □ *This meal doesn't measure up to my expectations.* □ *Why doesn't it measure up?*

Mecca for someone a place which is frequently visited by a particular group of people because it is important to them for some reason. (From the city of Mecca, the centre of Islam.) □ *Liverpool was a Mecca for fans of the Beatles.* □ *St. Andrews is a Mecca for golf enthusiasts because of its famous course.*

meet one's end to die. □ *The dog met his end under the wheels of a car.* □ *I don't intend to meet my end until I'm one hundred years old.*

meet one's match to meet one's equal. □ *John played tennis with Bill yesterday, and it looks like John has finally met his match.* □ *Listen to Jane and Mary argue. I always thought that Jane was aggressive, but she has finally met her match.*

meet one's Waterloo to meet one's final and insurmountable challenge. (Refers to Napoleon at Waterloo.) □ *This teacher is being very hard on Bill, unlike* the previous one. *It seems that Bill has met his Waterloo.* □ *John was more than Sally could handle. She had finally met her Waterloo.*

meet someone half-way to offer to compromise with someone. □ *No, I won't give in, but I'll meet you half-way.* □ *They settled the argument by agreeing to meet each other half-way.*

meet the requirements (for something) to fulfil the requirements for something. □ *Sally was unable to meet the requirements for the job.* □ *Jane met the requirements and was told to report to work the next day.*

melt in one's mouth to taste very good. (Informal.) □ *This cake is so good it'll melt in your mouth.* □ *John said that the food didn't exactly melt in his mouth.*

mend (one's) fences to restore good relations (with someone). (Also used literally.) □ *I think I had better get home and mend my fences. I had an argument with my daughter this morning.* □ *Sally called up her uncle to apologize and try to mend fences.*

mend one's ways to improve one's behaviour. □ *John used to be very wild, but he's mended his ways.* □ *You'll have to mend your ways if you go out with Mary. She hates people to be late.*

mention something in passing to mention something casually; to mention something while talking about something else. □ *He just happened to mention in passing that the mayor had resigned.* □ *John mentioned in passing that he was nearly eighty years old.*

mess about (with someone or something) See the following entry.

mess around (with someone or something) AND **mess about (with someone or something); monkey around (with someone or something)** to play with or waste time with someone or something. (Slang.) □ *Will you please stop messing around with that old car!* □ *Stop messing about! Get busy!* □ *Tom wastes a lot of time messing around with*

Bill. □ *Don't monkey around with my computer!* □ *Fred is always monkeying around.*

mess something up AND **mess up something** to make something disorderly. (Informal.) □ *You really messed this place up!* □ *Who messed up my bed?*

method in one's madness [for there to be] purpose in what one is doing. (From Shakespeare's *Hamlet*.) □ *What I'm doing may look strange, but there is method in my madness.* □ *Wait until she finishes; then you'll see that there is method in her madness.*

middle-of-the-road half-way between two extremes, especially political extremes. □ *Jane is very left-wing, but her husband is politically middle-of-the-road.* □ *I don't want to vote for either the left-wing or the right-wing candidate. I prefer someone with more middle-of-the-road views.*

milestone in someone's life a very important event or point in one's life. (From the stone at the side of a road showing the distance to or from a place.) □ *Joan's wedding was a milestone in her mother's life.* □ *The birth of a child is a milestone in every parent's life.*

milk of human kindness natural kindness and sympathy shown to others. (From Shakespeare's play *Macbeth*.) □ *Mary is completely hard and selfish—she has no milk of human kindness in her.* □ *Roger is too full of the milk of human kindness and people take advantage of him.*

millstone about one's neck a continual burden or handicap. □ *This huge and expensive house is a millstone about my neck.* □ *Bill's huge family is a millstone about his neck.*

mince (one's) words to lessen the force of one's statement by choosing weak or polite words; to be euphemistic. (Formal.) □ *I won't mince words. You made a bloody mess of it.* □ *I'm not one to mince words, so I have to say that you behaved very badly.*

mind one's own business to attend only to the things which personally concern one. □ *Leave me alone, Bill. Mind your own business.* □ *I'd be fine if John would mind his own business.*

mind one's P's and Q's to mind one's manners. □ *When we go to the mayor's reception, please mind your P's and Q's.* □ *I always mind my P's and Q's when I eat at formal restaurants.*

mind you you must also take into consideration the fact that.... □ *He's very well dressed, but mind you he's got plenty of money to buy clothes.* □ *Jean is unfriendly to me, but mind you she's never very nice to anyone.*

mine of information someone or something that is full of information. □ *Grandfather is a mine of information about World War I.* □ *The new encyclopaedia is a positive mine of useful information.*

miscarriage of justice a wrong or mistaken decision, especially one taken in a lawcourt. □ *Sentencing the old man on a charge of murder proved to be a miscarriage of justice.* □ *Punishing the pupil for cheating was a miscarriage of justice. He was innocent.*

miss out (on something) AND **lose out (on something)** to fail to participate in something; to fail to take part in something. (Informal.) □ *I'm sorry I missed out on the party.* □ *I lost out on it, too.* □ *We both missed out.*

miss (something) by a mile to fail to hit something by a great distance; to land wide of the mark. □ *Ann shot the arrow and missed the target by a mile.* □ *"Good grief, you missed by a mile,"* shouted Sally.

miss the boat to miss an opportunity. (Informal.) □ *Tom really missed the boat when it came to gaining promotion.* □ *Jane should have married when she was younger. I think she's missed the boat now.*

miss the point to fail to understand the point. □ *I'm afraid you missed the point. Let me explain it again.* □ *You keep explaining, and I keep missing the point.*

mistake someone for someone else AND **mix someone up with someone else** to confuse someone with someone else; to think that one person is another person. □ *I'm sorry. I mistook you for John.* □ *Tom is always mistaking Bill for me. We don't look alike at all, though.* □ *Try not to mix Bill up with Bob.*

mistake something for something else AND **mix something up with something else** to confuse something with something else; to think that one thing is another thing. □ *I mistook the roast chicken for turkey.* □ *How can anyone mix chicken up with turkey?* □ *Tom will probably mistake your house for mine.*

mix it to cause trouble. (Slang.) □ *John is always mixing it. There's trouble wherever he is.* □ *Our family used to be friends until our cousin started mixing it.*

mix someone or something up AND **mix up someone or something** 1. to confuse two things or two people with each other. □ *Please don't mix these ideas up. They are quite distinct.* □ *I always mix up Bill and Bob.* □ *Why do you mix them up?* 2. [with *someone*] to cause someone to be confused or puzzled. (Informal.) □ *I'm confused as it is. Don't mix me up any more.* □ *They mixed up my uncle by giving him too many things to remember.* 3. [with *something*] to blend the ingredients of something; to assemble and mix the parts of something. (Usually refers to fluid matter such as paint, petrol, or milk.) □ *Now, mix up the eggs, water, and salt; then add the mixture to the flour and sugar.* □ *The glue will be ready to use as soon as I mix it up.*

mix someone up with someone else See *mistake someone for someone else.*

mix something up with something else See *mistake something for something else.*

213

mixed bag a varied collection of people or things. (Refers to a bag of game brought home after a day's hunting.) □ *The new pupils are a mixed bag—some bright, some positively stupid.* □ *The furniture I bought is a mixed bag. Some of it is valuable and the rest is worthless.*

moment of truth the point at which someone has to face the reality or facts of a situation. □ *The moment of truth is here. Turn over your exam papers and begin.* □ *Now for the moment of truth when we find out whether we have got planning permission or not.*

Money burns a hole in someone's pocket. someone spends as much money as possible. (Informal. See also *have money to burn.*) □ *Sally can't seem to save anything. Money burns a hole in her pocket.* □ *If money burns a hole in your pocket, you never have any for emergencies.*

money for jam AND **money for old rope** payment for very little; money very easily obtained. (Informal.) □ *Baby-sitting is money for jam if the child does not wake up.* □ *Jack finds getting paid to caretake the house money for old rope.*

money for old rope See the previous entry.

money is no object AND **expense is no object** it does not matter how much something costs. □ *Please show me your finest car. Money is no object.* □ *I want the finest earrings you have. Don't worry about how much they cost because expense is no object.*

Money is the root of all evil. a proverb meaning that money is the basic cause of all wrongdoing. (From the biblical quotation, "The love of money is the root of all evil.") □ *Why do you work so hard to make money? It will just cause you trouble. Money is the root of all evil.* □ *Any thief in prison can tell you that money is the root of all evil.*

money talks money gives one power and influence to help get things done or get one's own way. (Informal.) □ *Don't worry, I have a way of getting things done. Money talks.* □ *I can't compete against rich old Mrs. Jones. She'll get her way because money talks.*

monkey around with someone or something See *mess around with someone or something.*

monkey business peculiar or out of the ordinary activities, especially mischievous or illegal ones. □ *There's been some monkey business in connection with the firm's accounts.* □ *Bob left the firm quite suddenly. I think there was some funny business between him and the boss's wife.*

mope around to go about in a depressed state. (Informal.) □ *Since her dog ran away, Sally mopes around all day.* □ *Don't mope around. Cheer up!*

More fool you! You are extremely foolish! □ *More fool you for agreeing to lend John money.* □ *You've offered to work for nothing. More fool you!*

more fun than a barrel of monkeys a great deal of fun and excitement. □ *At the fair, everyone had more fun than a barrel of monkeys.* □ *Fred is more fun than a barrel of monkeys.*

more often than not usually. □ *These flowers will live through the winter more often than not.* □ *This kind of dog will grow up to be a good watch-dog more often than not.*

more or less to some extent; approximately; sort of. □ *This one will do all right, more or less.* □ *We'll be there at eight, more or less.*

more (to something) than meets the eye [there are] hidden facts or information in something. □ *There is more to that problem than meets the eye.* □ *What makes you think that there is more than meets the eye?*

more's the pity it is a great pity or shame; it is sad. □ *Jack can't come, more's the pity.* □ *Jane had to leave early, more's the pity.*

morning after (the night before) the morning after a night spent drinking, when one has a hangover. □ *Oh, I've got a headache. Talk about the morning after the night before!* □ *It looked like a case of the morning after the night before, and Frank asked for some aspirin.*

most of all of greatest importance; more than any other. (Compare to *least of all.*) □ *I wanted to go to that museum most of all. Why can't I go?* □ *There are many reasons why I didn't use my car today. Most of all, it's a lovely day for walking.*

move heaven and earth to do something to make a major effort to do something. □ *"I'll move heaven and earth to be with you, Mary," said Bill.* □ *I had to move heaven and earth to get there on time.*

move in(to something) to move into a living or working space. □ *I hear you have a new place to live. When did you move in?* □ *We moved into our new offices last week.*

move on to keep moving; to move away. □ *Okay, everyone, move on now. The excitement is over.* □ *I've done all that I can do in this town. It's time to move on.*

move out to move out of a living or working space. □ *We didn't like our flat, so we moved out.* □ *We have a lease. We can't move out.*

move up (in the world) to advance (oneself) and become successful. □ *The harder I work, the more I move up in the world.* □ *Keep your eye on John. He's really moving up.*

much ado about nothing a lot of excitement about nothing. (This is the title of a play by Shakespeare.) □ *All the commotion about the new law turned out to be much ado about nothing.* □ *Your complaints always turn out to be much ado about nothing.*

much in evidence very visible or evident. □ *John was much in evidence during the conference.* □ *Your influence is much in evidence. I appreciate your efforts.*

much of a muchness very alike or similar; not much different. □ *I don't mind whether we go to the restaurant in the high street or the one by the cinema. They're much of a muchness.* □ *We can go via Edinburgh or Glasgow. The two journeys are much of a muchness.*

much sought after wanted or desired very much. □ *This kind of crystal is much sought after. It's very rare.* □ *Sally is a great singer. She's much sought after.*

muck in (with someone) to co-operate or work with someone. (Slang.) □ *If John mucks in with Mike to clear the garden, the work will be finished in no time.* □ *You'll have to help me prepare this meal. Muck in!*

muff one's lines See *fluff one's lines.*

mug's game a thing which only foolish people would become involved in. (Slang.) □ *Jean enjoys teaching, but Mary thinks it's a mug's game—it's so badly paid.* □ *Child-minding is even more of a mug's game if you're just thinking of money.*

mull something over AND **mull over something** to think about something; to ponder or worry about something. □ *That's an interesting idea, but I'll have to mull it over.* □ *I'll mull over your suggestions and report to you next week.*

mum's the word don't spread the secret. (Informal.) □ *Don't tell anyone what I told you. Remember, mum's the word.* □ *Okay, mum's the word. Your secret is safe with me.*

muscle in (on something) to try forcefully to displace someone or take over someone's property, interests, or relationships. (Slang.) □ *Are you trying to muscle in on my scheme?* □ *If you try to muscle in, you'll be facing big trouble.*

N

nail in someone's or something's coffin something which will harm or destroy someone or something. □ *Every word of criticism that Bob said about the firm was a nail in his coffin. I knew the boss would sack him.* □ *Losing the export order was the final nail in the company's coffin.*

nail one's colours to the mast to commit oneself to a particular course of action or to a particular point of view. (A ship's flag—its colours—could not be lowered to indicate surrender when it was nailed to the mast.) □ *Fred nailed his colours to the mast by publicly declaring for strike action.* □ *Mary really believes in socialism, but she refuses to nail her colours to the mast and join the Labour Party.*

nail someone or something down AND **nail down someone or something 1.** [with *someone*] to get a firm and final decision from someone (on something). (Informal.) □ *I want you to find Bob and get an answer from him. Nail him down one way or the other.* □ *Please nail down John on the question of signing the contract.* **2.** [with *something*] to nail (with a hammer) something which is loose. □ *Nail down this loose floor-board.* □ *Please nail this thing down.*

naked eye the human eye, unassisted by optics such as a telescope, microscope, or spectacles. □ *I can't see the bird's markings with the naked eye.* □ *The scientist could see nothing in the liquid with the naked eye, but with the aid of a microscope, she identified the bacteria.*

name-dropping See under *drop someone's name.*

name of the game the goal or purpose; the important or central thing. (Informal.) □ *The name of the game is sell. You must sell, sell, sell if you want to make a living.* □ *Around here, the name of the game is look out for yourself.*

name someone after someone else AND **name someone for someone else** to give someone (usually a baby) the name of another person. □ *We named our baby after my aunt.* □ *My parents named me for my grandfather.*

near at hand close or handy (to someone). □ *Do you have a car near at hand?* □ *How near at hand is the railway station?*

near the bone AND **near the knuckle** (Informal.) **1.** coming too close to mentioning something which should not be mentioned, for example because it might hurt or offend someone. □ *Jack's remark about prisons was a bit near the bone. Jane's father is on trial just now.* □ *Mike's speech about traffic safety was near the knuckle. Joan—who just had a serious car crash—was in the first row of the audience.* **2.** rather indecent. □ *The comedian's jokes were a bit near the bone.* □ *Uncle Fred's stories are always near the knuckle.*

near the knuckle See the previous entry.

neck and neck exactly even, especially in a race or a contest. (Informal.) □ *John and Tom finished the race neck and neck.* □ *Mary and Ann were neck and neck in the spelling contest.*

needs must if it is absolutely necessary for something to be done, then it must be done. □ *I don't want to sell the car, but needs must. I can't afford to run it.* □ *Needs must. Mary'll have to go out to work now her husband's died.*

neither fish nor fowl not any recognizable thing. □ *The car that they drove up in was neither fish nor fowl. It must have been made out of spare parts.* □ *This proposal is neither fish nor fowl. I can't tell what you're proposing.*

neither here nor there of no consequence or meaning; irrelevant and immaterial. □ *Whether you go to the cinema or stay at home is neither here nor there.* □ *Your comment—though interesting—is neither here nor there.*

neither hide nor hair no sign or indication (of someone or something). □ *We could find neither hide nor hair of him. I don't know where he is.* □ *I could see neither hide nor hair of the children.*

never darken my door again See *not to darken someone's door.*

never fear do not worry; have confidence. □ *I'll be there on time—never fear.* □ *I'll help you, never fear.*

never had it so good [have] never had so much good fortune. (Informal.) □ *No, I'm not complaining. I've never had it so good.* □ *Mary is pleased with her new job. She's never had it so good.*

never in one's life not in one's experience. □ *Never in my life have I been so insulted!* □ *He said that never in his life had he seen such an ugly painting.*

never mind forget it; pay no more attention (to something). □ *I wanted to talk to you, but never mind. It wasn't important.* □ *Never mind. I'm sorry to bother you.*

new ball game a new set of circumstances. (Slang. Originally from sports. Often with *whole.*) □ *It's a whole new ball game since Jane took over the office.* □ *You can't do the things you used to do around here. It's a new ball game.*

new blood See *fresh blood.*

new lease on life a renewed and revitalized outlook on life. □ *Getting the offer of employment gave James a new lease on life.* □ *When I got out of the hospital, I felt like I had a new lease on life.*

new one on someone something one has not heard before and that one is not ready to believe. (Informal. The *someone* is often *me.*) □ *Jack's poverty is a new one on me. He always seems to have plenty of money.* □ *The firm's difficulties are a new one on me. I thought that they were doing very well.*

next to nothing hardly anything; almost nothing. □ *This car's worth next to nothing. It's full of rust.* □ *I bought this antique chair for next to nothing.*

night and day See *day and night.*

night on the town a night of celebrating (at one or more places in a town). (Informal.) □ *Did you enjoy your night on the town?* □ *After we got the contract signed, we celebrated with a night on the town.*

night-owl someone who usually stays up very late. (Informal.) □ *Anne's a real night-owl. She never goes to bed before 2 a.m. and sleeps till midday.* □ *Jack's a night-owl and is at his best after midnight.*

nine days' wonder something that is of interest to people only for a short time. □ *Don't worry about the story about you in the newspaper. It'll be a nine days' wonder and then people will forget.* □ *The elopement of Jack and Anne was a nine days' wonder. Now people never mention it.*

nine-to-five job a job with regular and normal hours. □ *I wouldn't want a nine-to-five job. I like the freedom I have as my own employer.* □ *I used to work night-shift, but now I have a nine-to-five job.*

nip something in the bud to put an end to something at an early stage. □ *John is getting into bad habits, and it's best to* *nip them in the bud.* □ *There was trouble in the classroom, but the teacher nipped it in the bud.*

no buts about it See *no ifs about it.*

no can do cannot do (something). (Slang.) □ *Sorry, John. No can do. I can't sell you this one. I've promised it to Mrs. Smith.* □ BILL: *Please fix this clock today.* BOB: *No can do. It'll take a week to get the parts.*

No dice. No.; Absolutely not. (Slang.) □ *As John hung up the telephone, he said, "No dice. She says she won't co-operate."* □ *No dice! I won't lie in court!*

no doubt surely; without a doubt; undoubtedly. □ *He will be here again tomorrow, no doubt.* □ *No doubt you will require a ride home?*

no end of something lots of something. (Informal.) □ *It was a wonderful banquet. They had no end of good food.* □ *Tom is a real problem. He's no end of trouble.*

no great shakes nothing important or worth noticing. (Slang.) □ *It's okay, but it's no great shakes.* □ *I like John, but he's no great shakes when it comes to sports.*

no hard feelings no anger or resentment. (Informal. *No* can be replaced with *any.*) □ *I hope you don't have any hard feelings.* □ *No, I have no hard feelings.*

no holds barred with no restraints. (Informal. From wrestling.) □ *I intend to argue it out with Mary, no holds barred.* □ *When Ann negotiates a contract, she goes in with no holds barred and comes out with a good contract.*

no ifs about it AND **no buts about it** absolutely no discussion, dissension, or doubt about something. □ *I want you there exactly at eight, no ifs about it.* □ *This is the best television set available for the money, no buts about it.*

no joke a serious matter. (Informal.) □ *It's no joke when you miss the last train.* □ *It's certainly no joke when you have to walk home.*

no kidding honestly; [someone is] not joking or lying. (Informal.) □ *No kidding, you really got an A in geometry?* □ *I really did, no kidding.*

no laughing matter a serious matter. □ *Be serious. This is no laughing matter.* □ *This disease is no laughing matter. It's quite deadly.*

no love lost (between someone and someone else) no friendship wasted between someone and someone else (because they are enemies). □ *Ever since their big argument, there has been no love lost between Tom and Bill.* □ *You can tell by the way that Jane is acting towards Ann that there is no love lost.*

no matter what (happens) in any event; without regard to what happens (in the future). □ *We'll be there on time, no matter what.* □ *No matter what happens, we'll still be friends.*

No news is good news. a saying meaning if one has not had any information about someone or something for some time, it means that all is well, as one would have heard if anything bad or unfortunate had occurred. □ *I haven't heard from my son since he left for London, but I suppose no news is good news.* □ *I think Joan would have heard by now if she had failed. No news is good news.*

no problem See *no sweat.*

no skin off someone's nose no difficulty for someone; no concern of someone. □ *It's no skin off my nose if she wants to act that way.* □ *She said it was no skin off her nose if we wanted to sell the house.*

no sooner said than done done quickly and obediently. (Informal.) □ *When Sally asked for someone to open the window, it was no sooner said than done.* □ *As Jane opened the window, she said, "No sooner said than done."*

no spring chicken not young (any more). (Informal.) □ *I don't get around very well any more. I'm no spring chicken, you know.* □ *Even though John is no* *spring chicken, he still plays tennis twice a week.*

no sweat AND **no problem** no difficulty; do not worry. (Slang.) □ *Of course I can have your car repaired by midday. No sweat.* □ *You'd like a red one? No problem.*

no trespassing do not enter. (Usually seen on a sign. Not usually spoken.) □ *The sign on the tree said "No Trespassing." So we didn't go in.* □ *The angry farmer chased us out of the field, shouting, "Get out! Don't you see the no trespassing sign?"*

no two ways about it no choice about it; no other interpretation of it. (Informal.) □ *You have to go to the doctor whether you like it or not. There's no two ways about it.* □ *This letter means you're in trouble with Inland Revenue. There's no two ways about it.*

no way not any means (to do something). (Slang.) □ *You think I'm going to sit around here while you're having fun at the picnic? No way!* □ BOB: *Will you please take this to the post office for me?* BILL: *No way.*

no wonder [something is] not surprising. □ *No wonder the baby is crying. She's wet.* □ *It's no wonder that plant died. You watered it too much.*

nobody's fool a sensible and wise person who is not easily deceived. □ *Mary's nobody's fool. She knows Jack would try to cheat her.* □ *Anne looks as though she's not very bright, but she's nobody's fool.*

nod off to fall asleep. (Informal.) □ *Jack nodded off during the minister's sermon.* □ *Father always nods off after Sunday lunch.*

none other than the very person. □ *The new building was opened by none other than the prime minister.* □ *Jack's wife turned out to be none other than my cousin.*

none the wiser not knowing any more. □ *I was none the wiser about the project after the lecture. It was a complete waste of time.* □ *Anne tried to explain the situation tactfully to Jack, but in the end, he was none the wiser.*

none the worse for wear no worse because of use or effort. □ *I lent my car to John. When I got it back, it was none the worse for wear.* □ *I had a hard day today, but I'm none the worse for wear.*

none to speak of See *nothing to speak of.*

none too something not very; not at all. □ *The towels in the bathroom were none too clean.* □ *It was none too warm in their house.*

nose about See the following entry.

nose around AND **nose about** to investigate; to check (into something). (Slang.) □ *I don't have an answer to your question, but I'll nose around and see what I can find out.* □ *I'll nose about, too. Who knows what we'll find out?*

nose in(to something) to move into something, front end first. (See also *nose something in(to something).)* □ *Slowly the car nosed into its parking place.* □ *You must nose in very carefully.*

nose something in(to something) AND **nose in something** to move, drive, or steer something into something, front end first. (See also *nose in(to something).)* □ *The skipper nosed the boat into the harbour.* □ *James nosed in the boat with great skill.*

Not a bit (of it). Not at all. □ *Am I unhappy? Not a bit.* □ *She said she was not disappointed. Not a bit, in fact.* □ *You needn't apologize—not a bit of it.*

not a living soul nobody. (Informal.) □ *I won't tell anybody—not a living soul.* □ *I won't tell a living soul.* □ *They wouldn't think of telling a living soul.*

not able See the expressions listed at *can't* as well as those listed below.

not able to call one's time one's own too busy; so busy as not to be in charge of one's own schedule. (Informal. *Not able to* is often expressed as *can't.)* □ *It's* *been so busy around here that I haven't been able to call my time my own.* □ *She can't call her time her own these days.*

not able to go on unable to continue (doing something—even living). (*Not able to* is often expressed as *can't.*) □ *I just can't go on this way.* □ *Before her death, she left a note saying she was not able to go on.*

not able to help something unable to prevent or control something. (*Not able to* is often expressed as *can't.*) □ *I'm sorry about being late. I wasn't able to help it.* □ *Bob can't help being boring.*

not able to make anything out of someone or something unable to understand someone or something. (*Not able to* is often expressed as *can't.* The *anything* may refer to something specific, as in the first example.) □ *I couldn't make anything out of what you just said.* □ *We were not able to make anything out of the message.*

not able to see the wood for the trees allowing many details of a problem to obscure the problem as a whole. (*Not able to* is often expressed as *can't.*) □ *The solution is obvious. You missed it because you can't see the wood for the trees.* □ *She suddenly realized that she hadn't been able to see the wood for the trees.*

not able to wait **1.** too anxious to wait; excited (about something in the future.) (*Not able to* is often expressed as *can't.*) □ *I'm so excited. I can't wait.* □ *Billy couldn't wait for his birthday.* **2.** to have to *go to the toilet* urgently. (Informal.) □ *Mom, I can't wait.* □ *Driver, stop the bus! My little boy can't wait.*

not all it is cracked up to be AND **not what it is cracked up to be** not as good as something is supposed to be. (Informal.) □ *This isn't a very good pen. It's not all it's cracked up to be.* □ *Is this one all it's cracked up to be?* □ *This restaurant isn't what it's cracked up to be.*

not all there mentally deficient; crazy or silly. (Informal.) □ *Sometimes I think*

you're not all there. □ *Be nice to Sally. She's not all there.* ALSO: **not have all one's marbles** to be mentally deficient. (Slang.) □ *John acts as though he doesn't have all his marbles.*

not at all certainly not; absolutely not. □ *No, it doesn't bother me—not at all.* □ *I'm not complaining. Not me. Not at all.* ALSO: **not in the least** not even a little bit. □ *You've been no trouble at all, no sir, not in the least.*

not born yesterday experienced; knowledgeable in the ways of the world. (Informal.) □ *I know what's going on. I wasn't born yesterday.* □ *Sally knows the score. She wasn't born yesterday.*

not breathe a word (about someone or something) to keep a secret about someone or something. □ *Don't worry. I won't breathe a word about it.* □ *Please don't breathe a word about Bob and his problems.* ALSO: **not breathe a word (of something)** not to tell something (to anyone). □ *Don't worry. I won't breathe a word of it.* □ *Tom won't breathe a word.*

not buy something not accept something (to be true). (Slang.) □ *You may believe what she says, but I don't buy it.* □ *The police wouldn't buy his story.*

not by a long shot not by a great amount; not at all. □ *Did I win the race? Not by a long shot.* □ *Not by a long shot did she complete the task.*

not care two hoots about someone or something AND **not give two hoots about someone or something; not give a hang about someone or something; not give a hoot about someone or something** not to care at all about someone or something. (Informal.) □ *He doesn't care two hoots about his children.* □ *She doesn't give a hoot about me. Why should I care?* □ *I don't give a hang about it.*

not enough room to swing a cat not very much space. (Informal.) □ *Their living-room was very small. There wasn't enough room to swing a cat.* □ *How can you work in a small room like* *this? There's not enough room to swing a cat.*

not for anything in the world   See *not for the world.*

not for love nor money   See the following entry.

not for the world AND **not for anything in the world; not for love nor money; not on your life**   not for anything (no matter what its value). □ *I won't do it for love nor money.* □ *He said he wouldn't do it—not for the world.* □ *She said no, not for anything in the world.* □ *Me, go there? Not on your life!*

not give a hang about anyone or anything   See *not care two hoots about someone or something.*

not give a hoot about anyone or anything   See *not care two hoots about someone or something.*

not give someone the time of day   to ignore someone (usually out of dislike). (Informal.) □ *Mary won't speak to Sally. She won't give her the time of day.* □ *I couldn't get an appointment with Mr. Smith. He wouldn't even give me the time of day.*

not give two hoots about someone or something   See *not care two hoots about someone or something.*

not half bad   okay; pretty good. (Informal.) □ *Say, this roast beef isn't half bad.* □ *Well, Sally! You're not half bad!*

not have a care in the world   free and casual; unworried and carefree. □ *I really feel good today—as if I didn't have a care in the world.* □ *Ann always acts as though she doesn't have a care in the world.*

not have a leg to stand on   [for an argument or a case] to have no support. (Informal.) □ *You may think you're in the right, but you don't have a leg to stand on.* □ *My solicitor said I didn't have a leg to stand on, and that I shouldn't sue the company.*

not have all one's marbles   See under *not all there.*

not hold water   to make no sense; to be illogical. (Said of ideas or arguments. It means that the idea has holes in it.) □ *Your argument doesn't hold water.* □ *This scheme won't work because it won't hold water.*

not in the least   See under *not at all.*

not in the same league as someone or something   not nearly as good as someone or something. □ *John isn't in the same league as Bob and his friends. He is not nearly as talented.* □ *This house isn't in the same league as our old one.*

not know if one is coming or going   See *not know whether one is coming or going.*

not know someone from Adam   not to know someone at all. □ *I wouldn't recognize John if I saw him. I don't know him from Adam.* □ *What does she look like? I don't know her from Adam.*

not know the first thing about someone or something   not to know anything about someone or something. □ *I don't know the first thing about flying an aeroplane.* □ *She doesn't know the first thing about John.*

not know where to turn AND **not know which way to turn**   to have no idea about what to do (about something). □ *I was so confused I didn't know where to turn.* □ *We needed help, but we didn't know which way to turn.*

not know whether one is coming or going AND **not know if one is coming or going**   to be very confused. □ *I'm so busy that I don't know if I'm coming or going.* □ *You look as if you don't know whether you're coming or going.*

not know which way to turn   See *not know where to turn.*

not lift a finger (to help someone)   to do nothing to help someone. □ *They wouldn't lift a finger to help us.* □ *Can you imagine that they wouldn't lift a finger?*

not long for this world about to die. □ *Our dog is nearly twelve years old and not long for this world.* □ *I'm so tired. I think I'm not long for this world.*

not move a muscle to remain perfectly motionless. □ *Be quiet. Sit there and don't move a muscle.* □ *I was so tired I couldn't move a muscle.*

not on any account See *on no account.*

not on your life See *not for the world.*

Not on your Nelly! Certainly not!; Not likely! (Slang.) □ *Can you borrow my car? Not on your Nelly!* □ *Did Bob ask Mary out? Not on your Nelly! He hates her!*

not open one's mouth AND **not utter a word** not to say anything at all; not to tell something (to anyone). □ *Don't worry, I'll keep your secret. I won't even open my mouth.* □ *Have no fear. I won't utter a word.* □ *I don't know how they found out. I didn't even open my mouth.*

not see further than the end of one's nose not to care about what is not actually present or obvious; not to care about the future or about what is happening elsewhere or to other people. □ *Mary can't see further than the end of her nose. She doesn't care about what will happen to the environment in the future as long as she's comfortable now.* □ *Jack's been accused of not seeing further than the end of his nose. He refuses to expand the firm and look for new markets.*

not set foot somewhere not to go somewhere. □ *I wouldn't set foot in John's room. I'm very angry at him.* □ *He never set foot here.*

not show one's face not to appear (somewhere). □ *After what she said, she had better not show her face around here again.* □ *If I don't say I'm sorry, I'll never be able to show my face again.*

not sleep a wink not to sleep at all. (Informal.) □ *I couldn't sleep a wink last night.* □ *Ann hasn't been able to sleep a wink for a week.*

not someone's cup of tea not something one likes or prefers. (Informal.) □ *Playing cards isn't her cup of tea.* □ *Sorry, that's not my cup of tea.*

not take no for an answer not to accept someone's refusal. (A polite way of being insistent.) □ *Now, you must drop over and see us tomorrow. We won't take no for an answer.* □ *I had to go. They just wouldn't take no for an answer.*

not to darken someone's door AND **never darken my door again** to go away and not come back. □ *The heroine of the drama told the villain never to darken her door again.* □ *She touched the back of her hand to her forehead and said, "Get out and never darken my door again!"*

not up to scratch not adequate. (Informal.) □ *Sorry, your essay isn't up to scratch. Please do it over again.* □ *The performance was not up to scratch.*

not utter a word See *not open one's mouth.*

not what it is cracked up to be See *not all it is cracked up to be.*

not worth a button See *not worth a penny.*

not worth a cent See the following entry.

not worth a penny AND **not worth a cent; not worth a button** worthless. (Informal.) □ *This land is all swampy. It's not worth a penny.* □ *This pen I bought isn't worth a cent. It has no ink.* □ *This vase is not worth a button.*

nothing but only; just. □ *Joan drinks nothing but milk.* □ *Fred buys nothing but expensive clothes.*

nothing but skin and bones AND **all skin and bones** very thin or emaciated. (Informal.) □ *Bill has lost so much weight. He's nothing but skin and bones.* □ *That old horse is all skin and bones. I won't ride it.*

nothing doing no. (Slang.) □ *No, I won't do that. Nothing doing.* □ BOB: *Will you help me with this?* BILL: *Nothing doing.*

nothing of the kind no; absolutely not. □ *I didn't insult him—nothing of the kind!* □ *Were we rude? Nothing of the kind!*

nothing short of something more or less the same as something bad; as bad as something. □ *His behaviour was nothing short of criminal.* □ *Climbing those mountains alone is nothing short of suicide.*

nothing to complain about all right. (Said in answer to the question "How are you?") □ *Bob said he has nothing to complain about.* □ BILL: *How're you doing, Bob?* BOB: *Nothing to complain about, Bill. Yourself?*

nothing to it it is easy; no difficulty involved. □ *Driving a car is easy. There's nothing to it.* □ *Geometry is fun to learn. There's nothing to it.*

nothing to sneeze at nothing small or unimportant. (Informal.) □ *It's not a lot of money, but it's nothing to sneeze at.* □ *Our house isn't a mansion, but it's nothing to sneeze at.*

nothing to speak of AND **none to speak of** not many; not much. (Informal.) □ JOHN: *What's happening around here?* BILL: *Nothing to speak of.* □ MARY: *Has there been any rain in the last week?* SALLY: *None to speak of.*

nothing to write home about nothing exciting or interesting. (Informal.) □ *I've been busy, but nothing to write home about.* □ *I had a dull week—nothing to write home about.*

Nothing ventured, nothing gained. a proverb meaning that you cannot achieve anything if you do not try. □ *Come on, John. Give it a try. Nothing ventured, nothing gained.* □ *I felt like I had to take the chance. Nothing ventured, nothing gained.*

now and again See the following entry.

now and then AND **now and again** occasionally. □ *I like to smoke a cigar now and then.* □ *Now and again we go out to dinner and a show.*

now or never at this time and no other, if it is to happen at all. □ *This is your only chance, John. It's now or never.* □ *I decided that it was now or never and jumped.*

nowhere near not nearly. □ *We have nowhere near enough coal for the winter.* □ *They're nowhere near ready for the match.*

null and void cancelled; worthless. □ *I tore the contract up, and the entire agreement became null and void.* □ *The judge declared the whole business null and void.*

nurse a grudge (against someone) to keep resenting and disliking someone. □ *Sally is still nursing a grudge against Mary.* □ *How long can anyone nurse a grudge?*

nuts about someone or something See *crazy about someone or something.*

nuts and bolts (of something) the basic facts about something; the practical details of something. □ *Tom knows all about the nuts and bolts of the chemical process.* □ *Ann is familiar with the nuts and bolts of public relations.*

O

obligated to someone owing someone a favour. □ *I'll help John with his homework because I'm obligated to him.* □ *Just because I gave you some advice, it doesn't mean you're obligated to me.*

occur to someone [for an idea or thought] to come into someone's mind. □ *It occurred to me that you might be hungry after your long journey.* □ *Would it ever occur to you that I want to be left alone?*

odd man out an unusual or atypical person or thing. □ *I'm odd man out because I'm not wearing a tie.* □ *You had better learn to work a computer unless you want to be odd man out.*

odour of sanctity an atmosphere of excessive holiness or piety. (Derogatory.) □ *I hate their house. There's such an odour of sanctity with Bibles and holy pictures everywhere.* □ *People are nervous of Jane's odour of sanctity. She's always praying for people or doing good works and never has any fun.*

of all the nerve how shocking; how dare (someone). (Informal.) □ *How dare you talk to me that way! Of all the nerve!* □ *Imagine anyone coming to a formal dance in jeans. Of all the nerve!*

Of all things! Can you imagine?; Imagine that! (Informal.) □ *She wore jeans to the dance. Of all things!* □ *Of all things, she was rude to the headmaster!*

of benefit (to someone) serving someone well; to the good or advantage of someone. □ *I can't believe that this proposal is of benefit to anyone.* □ *Oh, I'm sure it's of benefit.*

of late lately. □ *Have you seen Sally of late?* □ *We haven't had an opportunity to eat out of late.*

of no avail See *to no avail.*

of one's own accord AND **of one's own free will** by one's own choice, without coercion. □ *I wish that Sally would choose to do it of her own accord.* □ *I'll have to order her to do it because she won't do it of her own free will.*

of one's own free will See the previous entry.

of the first water of the finest quality. □ *This is a very fine pearl—a pearl of the first water.* □ *Tom is a musician of the first water.*

of the old school holding attitudes and ideas that were popular and important in the past, but which are no longer considered relevant or in line with modern trends. □ *Grammar was not much taught in my son's school, but fortunately he had a teacher of the old school.* □ *Aunt Jane is of the old school. She never goes out without wearing a hat and gloves.*

off again, on again AND **on again, off again** uncertain; indecisive. □ *I don't know about the picnic. It's off again, on again. It depends on the weather.* □ *Tom and Jane's engagement is on again, off again.*

off and on See *on and off.*

off-centre not exactly in the centre or middle. □ *The arrow hit the target a little off-centre.* □ *The picture hanging over the chair is a little off-centre.*

off colour 1. not very well; slightly ill. □ *Mary is a bit off colour after the long journey.* □ *Fred went to the doctor when he was feeling off colour.* **2.** in bad taste; rude, vulgar, or impolite. □ *That joke you told was off colour and embarrassed me.* □ *The night-club act was a bit off colour.*

off duty not working at one's regular employment. (The opposite of *on duty.*) □ *I'm sorry, I can't talk to you until I'm off duty.* □ *The police officer couldn't help me because he was off duty.*

off limits AND **out of bounds** [an area that is] forbidden; [a place] where people are not allowed to go freely. □ *This area is off limits. You can't go in there.* □ *The playing-fields are out of bounds at night.* □ *Don't go there. It's out of bounds.* □ *The village is out of bounds for the younger boarding-school pupils.*

off one's nut See *off one's rocker.*

off one's oats not eating much; having lost one's appetite, often because of not feeling well. (Slang.) □ *Bob's been off his oats since he's been in hospital.* □ *It's not like Fred to be off his oats. He must be ill.*

off one's rocker AND **off one's nut; off one's trolley** mad; crazy. (Slang.) □ *Sometimes, Bob, I think you're off your rocker.* □ *Good grief, John. You're off your nut.* □ *About this time of the day I almost go off my trolley. I get so bored with my work.*

off one's trolley See the previous entry.

off someone or something goes someone or something is leaving. (Said on the departure of someone or something.) □ *It's time to leave. Off I go.* □ *Sally looked at the aeroplane taking off and said, "Off it goes."*

off the air not broadcasting (a radio or television programme). □ *The radio audience won't hear what you say when you're off the air.* □ *When the performers were off the air, the director told them how well they had done.*

off the beaten track in an unfamiliar place; on a route which is not often travelled. □ *Their home is in a quiet neighbourhood, off the beaten track.* □ *We like to stop there and admire the scenery. It's off the beaten track, but it's worth the trip.*

off the cuff spontaneous; without preparation or rehearsal. (Informal.) □ *Her remarks were off the cuff, but very sensible.* □ *I'm not very good at making speeches off the cuff.* ALSO: **off-the-cuff** without any preparation; spontaneous. □ *Her off-the-cuff remarks were quite sensible.*

off the record unofficial; informal. □ *This is off the record, but I disagree with the mayor on this matter.* □ *Although her comments were made off the record, the newspaper published them anyway.*

off the top of one's head without much thought or preparation. (Informal.) □ *I can't think of the answer off the top of my head.* □ *Jane can tell you the correct amount off the top of her head.*

off the wall odd; unusual; weird. (Slang.) □ *His humour is really off the wall.* □ *This book is strange. It's really off the wall.*

off to a running start with a good, fast beginning, possibly a head start. □ *I got off to a running start in maths this year.* □ *The horses got off to a running start.*

oil someone's palm to bribe someone. (Slang.) □ *The way to get things done around there is to oil someone's palm.* □ *No sense oiling her palm. She's totally honest.*

oil the wheels to make something easier to do or obtain. □ *It would have taken me ages to get a visa, but a friend at the embassy was able to oil the wheels.* □ *Usually it is difficult to get a place in that college, but Mary's father is a lecturer there and oiled the wheels for her.*

old enough to be someone's father See the following entry.

old enough to be someone's mother AND **old enough to be someone's father** as old as someone's parents. (Usually a way of saying that a person is too old.) □ *You can't go out with Bill. He's old enough to be your father!* □ *He married a woman who is old enough to be his mother.*

old hand at doing something someone who is experienced at doing something. (Informal.) □ *I'm an old hand at fixing clocks.* □ *With four children, he's an old hand at changing nappies.*

on a diet trying to lose weight by eating less food or less of specific foods. □ *I didn't eat any cake because I'm on a diet.* □ *I'm getting too heavy. I'll have to go on a diet.*

on a first-name basis (with someone) AND **on first-name terms (with someone)** knowing someone very well; good friends with someone. □ *I'm on a first-name basis with John.* □ *John and I are on first-name terms.*

on a fool's errand involved in a useless journey or task. □ *Bill went for an interview, but he was on a fool's errand. The job had already been filled.* □ *I was sent on a fool's errand to buy some flowers. I knew the shop would be shut by then.*

on a par with someone or something equal to someone or something. □ *Your effort is simply not on a par with what's expected from you.* □ *John's work is not on a par with Bob's.*

on account [money paid or owed] on a debt. □ *I paid £12 on account last month. Wasn't that enough?* □ *I still have £100 due on account.*

on account of someone or something because of someone or something. □ *We can't go on a picnic on account of the rain.* □ *I was late on account of John.*

on active duty in battle or ready to go into battle. (Military.) □ *The soldier was on active duty for ten months.* □ *That was a long time to be on active duty.*

on again, off again See *off again, on again.*

on all fours on one's hands and knees. □ *I dropped a contact lens and spent an hour on all fours looking for it.* □ *The baby can walk, but is on all fours most of the time anyway.*

on and off AND **off and on** occasionally; erratically; *now and again.* □ *I feel better off and on, but I'm not well yet.* □ *He only came to class on and off.*

on approval AND **on appro** for examination, with the privilege of return if not suitable. □ *I ordered the merchandise on approval so I could send it back if I didn't like it.* □ *Sorry, you can't buy this on approval. All sales are final.* □ *Why don't you take the dress on appro?*

on average generally; usually. □ *On average, you can expect about a 10 percent failure.* □ *On average, we see about ten people a day.*

on behalf of someone AND **on someone's behalf** [doing something] as someone's agent; [doing something] in place of someone; for the benefit of someone. □ *I'm writing on behalf of Mr. Smith, who has applied for a position with your company.* □ *I'm calling on behalf of my client, who wishes to complain about your actions.* □ *I'm acting on your behalf.*

on board 1. aboard (on or in) a ship, bus, aeroplane, etc. □ *Is there a doctor on board? We have a sick passenger.* □ *When everyone is on board, we will leave.* 2. employed by (someone); working with (someone). (Informal.) □ *Our firm has a computer specialist on board to advise us about automation.* □ *Welcome to the company, Tom. We're all glad you're on board now.*

on call ready to serve when called. □ *Junior hospital doctors live a very hard life. They're sometimes on call twenty hours a day.* □ *I'm sorry, but I can't go out tonight. I'm on call at the hospital.*

on cloud nine very happy. (Informal.) □ *When I got my promotion, I was on cloud nine.* □ *When the cheque came, I was on cloud nine for days.*

on deck on the deck of a boat or a ship. □ *Everyone except the cook was on deck when the storm hit.* □ *Just pull up the anchor and leave it on deck.*

on deposit deposited or stored in a safe place. □ *I have £10,000 on deposit in that bank.* □ *We have some gold coins on deposit in the bank's vault.*

on duty at work; currently doing one's work. (The opposite of *off duty*.) □ *I can't help you now, but I'll be on duty in about an hour.* □ *Who is on duty here? I need some help.*

on earth AND **in creation; in the world** how amazing!; *of all things!* (Used as an intensifier after the interrogative pronouns *who, what, when, where, how, which*.) □ *What on earth do you mean?* □ *How in creation do you expect me to do that?* □ *Who in the world do you think you are?* □ *When on earth do you expect me to do this?*

on Easy Street in luxury. (Slang.) □ *If I had a million pounds, I'd be on Easy Street.* □ *Everyone has problems, even people who live on Easy Street.*

on edge nervous. □ *I have really been on edge lately.* □ *Why are you so on edge?*

on first-name terms (with someone) See *on a first-name basis with someone.*

on foot by walking. □ *My bicycle is broken, so I'll have to travel on foot.* □ *You can't expect me to get there on foot! It's twelve miles!*

on good terms (with someone) friendly with someone. □ *I'm on good terms with Ann. I'll ask her to help.* □ *We're on good terms now. Last week we were not.*

on hold (See also *put someone or something on hold.*) **1.** waiting; temporarily halted. □ *The building project is on hold while we try to find money to complete it.* □ *We put our plans on hold until we finished school.* **2.** left waiting during a telephone call. □ *I hate to call up someone and then end up on hold.* □ *I waited on hold for ten minutes when I called town hall.*

on holiday away, having a holiday; on holiday. □ *Where are you going on holiday this year?* □ *I'll be away on holiday for three weeks.*

on in years See *up in years.*

on no account AND **not on any account** for no reason; absolutely not. □ *On no account will I lend you the money.* □ *Will I say I'm sorry? Not on any account.*

on occasions occasionally. □ *We go out for dinner on occasions.* □ *I enjoy going to a film on occasions.*

on one's best behaviour being as polite or well-mannered as possible. □ *When we went out, the children were on their best behaviour.* □ *I try to be on my best behaviour all the time.*

on one's feet **1.** standing up. □ *Get on your feet. They are playing the national anthem.* □ *I've been on my feet all day, and they hurt.* **2.** well and healthy, especially after an illness. □ *I hope to be back on my feet next week.* □ *I can help out as soon as I'm back on my feet.*

on one's guard cautious; watchful. □ *Be on your guard. There are pickpockets around here.* □ *You had better be on your guard.*

on one's honour on one's solemn oath; promised sincerely. □ *On my honour, I'll be there on time.* □ *He promised on his honour that he'd pay me back next week.*

on one's mind occupying one's thoughts; currently being thought about. □ *You've been on my mind all day.* □ *Do you have something on your mind? You look so serious.*

on one's own by oneself. □ *Did you do this on your own, or did you have help?* □ *I have to learn to do this kind of thing on my own.*

on one's (own) head be it one must take the responsibility for one's actions. □ *On your head be it if you set fire to the* *house.* □ *James insisted on going to the party uninvited. On his head be it if the host is annoyed.*

on one's toes alert. (Informal. See also *step on someone's toes.*) □ *You have to be on your toes if you want to be in this business.* □ *My job keeps me on my toes.*

on one's way (somewhere) See *on the way (somewhere).*

on one's way (to doing something) See *on the way (to doing something).*

on order ordered with delivery expected. □ *Your car is on order. It'll be here in a few weeks.* □ *I don't have the part in stock, but it's on order.*

on pins and needles anxious; in suspense. (Informal.) □ *I've been on pins and needles all day waiting for you to call with the news.* □ *We were on pins and needles until we heard that your plane landed safely.*

on record recorded for future reference. □ *We had the coldest winter on record last year.* □ *This is the fastest race on record.*

on sale AND **for sale** offered for sale; able to be bought. □ *There are antiques on sale at the market.* □ *There is a wide range of fruit for sale.*

on schedule at the expected or desired time. □ *The plane came in right on schedule.* □ *Things have to happen on schedule in a theatrical performance.*

on second thoughts having given something more thought; having reconsidered something. □ *On second thoughts, maybe you should sell your house and move into a flat.* □ *On second thoughts, let's not go to a film.*

on someone's account because of someone. □ *Don't do it on my account.* □ *They were late on Jane's account.*

on someone's back constantly criticizing someone. (Slang.) □ *I'm tired of your being on my back all the time.* □ *It seems as though someone is always on his back.*

on someone's behalf See *on behalf of someone.*

on someone's doorstep See *at someone's doorstep.*

on someone's or something's last legs [for someone or something] to be almost finished or near to collapse. (Informal.) □ *This building is on its last legs. It should be torn down.* □ *I feel like I'm on my last legs. I'm really tired.*

on someone's say-so on someone's authority; with someone's permission. (Informal.) □ *I can't do it on your say-so. I'll have to get a written request.* □ BILL: *I cancelled the contract with the ABC Company.* BOB: *On whose say-so?*

on someone's shoulders on someone's own self. (Usually with *responsibility. On* can be replaced with *upon.*) □ *Why should all the responsibility fall on my shoulders?* □ *She carries a tremendous amount of responsibility on her shoulders.*

on speaking terms (with someone) on friendly terms with someone. (Often in the negative. Compare to *on good terms with someone.*) □ *I'm not on speaking terms with Mary. We had a serious disagreement.* □ *We're not on speaking terms.*

on target on schedule; exactly as predicted. □ *Your estimate of the cost was right on target.* □ *My prediction was not on target.*

on the air broadcasting (a radio or television programme). □ *The radio station came back on the air shortly after the storm.* □ *We were on the air for two hours.*

on the alert (for someone or something) watchful and attentive for someone or something. □ *Be on the alert for pickpockets.* □ *You should be on the alert when you cross the street in heavy traffic.*

on the ball alert, effective, and efficient. (Slang.) □ *Sally was really on the ball when she spotted the error.* □ *You've* *got to be on the ball if you want to succeed in this business.*

on the beam exactly right; thinking along the correct lines. (Slang.) □ *That's the right idea. Now you're on the beam!* □ *She's not on the beam yet. Explain it to her again.*

on the bench **1.** directing a session of court. (Said of a judge.) □ *I have to go to court tomorrow. Who's on the bench?* □ *It doesn't matter who's on the bench. You'll get a fair hearing.* **2.** sitting, waiting for a chance to play in a game. (In sports, such as basketball, football, soccer, etc.) □ *Bill is on the bench now. I hope he gets to play.* □ *John played during the first half, but now he's on the bench.*

on the blink not operating; not operating correctly. (Slang.) □ *This vacuum cleaner is on the blink. Let's get it fixed.* □ *How long has the TV been on the blink?*

on the button exactly right; in exactly the right place; at exactly the right time. (Informal.) □ *That's it! You're right on the button.* □ *He got here at one o'clock on the button.*

on the cards in the future. (Informal.) □ *Well, what do you think is on the cards for tomorrow?* □ *I asked the managing director if there was a raise on the cards for me.*

on the contrary [as the] opposite. (Compare to *to the contrary.*) □ *I'm not ill. On the contrary, I'm very healthy.* □ *She's not in a bad mood. On the contrary, she's as happy as a lark.*

on the dot at exactly the right time. (Informal. Compare to *at sometime sharp.*) □ *I'll be there at three o'clock on the dot.* □ *I expect to see you here at eight o'clock on the dot.*

on the double very fast. (Slang.) □ *Get over here on the double.* □ *Get yourself into this house on the double.*

on the eve of something just before something, possibly the evening before something. □ *John decided to leave*

school on the eve of his graduation. □ *The team held a party on the eve of the tournament.*

on the face of it superficially; from the way it looks. □ *This looks like a serious problem on the face of it. It probably is minor, however.* □ *On the face of it, it seems worthless.*

on the go busy; moving about busily. (Informal.) □ *I'm usually on the go all day long.* □ *I hate being on the go all the time.*

on the horizon soon to happen. (Informal. See also *in the offing.*) □ *Do you think there are any jobs on the horizon?* □ *Is there a wedding on the horizon?*

on the horns of a dilemma having to decide between two things, people, etc. □ *Mary found herself on the horns of a dilemma. She didn't know which dress to choose.* □ *I make up my mind easily. I'm not on the horns of a dilemma very often.*

on the hot seat AND **in the hot seat** in a difficult or uncomfortable position; subject to much criticism. (Slang.) □ *The MP was really in the hot seat for a while.* □ *Now that John is on the hot seat, no one is paying any attention to what I do.*

on the hour at each hour; on the hour mark. □ *I have to take this medicine every hour on the hour.* □ *I expect to see you there on the hour, not one minute before and not one minute after.*

on the house given away free. (Informal.) □ *"Here," said the barman, "have a pint on the house."* □ *I went to a restaurant last night. I was the ten thousandth customer, so my dinner was on the house.*

on the job working; doing what one is expected to do. (Informal.) □ *I'm always on the job when I should be.* □ *The policeman was not on the job when he should have been.*

on the level honest; dependably open and fair; not crooked. (Slang.) □ *How* *can I be sure you're on the level?* □ *You can trust Sally. She's on the level.*

on the look-out (for someone or something) watchful for someone or something. □ *Be on the look-out for signs of a storm.* □ *I'm on the look-out for John, who is due here any minute.* □ *Okay, you remain on the look-out for another hour.*

on the loose running around free. (Informal.) □ *Look out! There is a bear on the loose from the zoo.* □ *Most young people enjoy being on the loose when they go to college.*

on the make 1. trying to make a profit for oneself; trying to turn something to one's advantage. (Slang.) □ *Fred won't do anything for nothing. He's always on the make.* □ *Bob's on the make as well. He wants to be a millionaire.* 2. making sexual advances; seeking sexual activities. (Slang.) □ *It seems like Bill is always on the make.* □ *He should meet Sally, who is also on the make.*

on the market available for sale; offered for sale. □ *I had to put my car on the market.* □ *This is the finest home computer on the market.*

on the mend getting well; healing. (Informal.) □ *My cold was terrible, but I'm on the mend now.* □ *What you need is some hot chicken soup. Then you'll really be on the mend.*

on the move moving; happening busily. □ *What a busy day. Things are really on the move at the shop.* □ *When all the buffalo were on the move across the plains, it must have been very exciting.*

on the nose exactly; precisely. (Slang.) □ *I paid £20 on the nose.* □ *They got six pounds of apples on the nose.*

on the off chance because of a slight possibility that something may happen, might be the case, etc.; just in case. □ *I went to the theatre on the off chance that there were tickets for the show left.* □ *We didn't think we would get into the football ground, but we went on the off chance.*

on the one hand from one point of view; as one side (of an issue). □ *On the one hand, I really ought to support my team. On the other hand, I don't have to time to attend all the games.* □ *On the one hand, I need Ann's help. On the other hand, she and I don't get along very well.* ALSO: **on the other hand** from another point of view; as the other side (of an issue). See the examples above.

on the other hand See the previous entry.

on the point of doing something AND **at the point of doing something** ready to start doing something. (Compare to *on the verge of (doing) something.*) □ *I was just on the point of going out the door.* □ *We were almost at the point of buying a new car.*

on the q.t. quietly; secretly. (Informal.) □ *The managing director was making payments to his wife on the q.t.* □ *The mayor accepted a bribe on the q.t.*

on the sly slyly or sneakily. (Informal.) □ *He was seeing Mrs. Smith on the sly.* □ *She was supposed to be losing weight, but she was eating chocolate on the sly.*

on the spot (Informal.) 1. at exactly the right place; in the place where one is needed. □ *Fortunately the ambulance men were on the spot when the accident happened at the football match.* □ *I expect the police to be on the spot when and where trouble arises.* 2. at once; then and there. □ *She liked the house so much that she bought it on the spot.* □ *He was fined on the spot for parking illegally.*

on the spur of the moment suddenly; spontaneously. □ *We decided to go on the spur of the moment.* □ *I went on holiday on the spur of the moment.*

on the strength of something because of the support of something, such as a promise or evidence; owing to something. □ *On the strength of your comment, I decided to give John another chance.* □ *On the strength of my neighbour's testimony, my case was dismissed.*

on the telephone connected to the telephone system; having a telephone installed in one's home. □ *Mrs. Johnson isn't on the telephone. You'll have to send her a letter.* □ *We will be on the telephone in a fortnight at the latest.*

on the tip of one's tongue about to be said; almost remembered. □ *I have his name right on the tip of my tongue. I'll think of it in a second.* □ *John had the answer on the tip of his tongue, but Ann said it first.*

on the track of someone or something See the following entry.

on the trail of someone or something AND **on the track of someone or something** seeking someone or something; about to find someone or something. (See also *track someone or something down.*) □ *I'm on the trail of a new tin-opener which is supposed to be easier to use.* □ *The police are on the track of the murderer.*

on the verge of (doing) something just about to do something, usually something important. (Compare to *on the point of doing something.*) □ *I'm on the verge of opening a shoe-shop.* □ *Tom was on the verge of leaving school when he became interested in physics.* □ *The teacher is on the verge of a nervous breakdown.*

on the wagon not drinking alcohol; no longer drinking alcohol. (Slang.) □ *No wine for me, thanks. I'm on the wagon.* □ *Look at John with that huge glass of whisky. I don't think he's on the wagon any more!*

on the waiting-list [with one's name] on a list of people waiting for an opportunity to do something. □ *I couldn't get a seat on the plane, but I got on the waiting-list.* □ *There is no room for you, but we can put your name on the waiting-list.*

on the war-path angry and upset (at someone). (Informal.) □ *Oh, oh. Here comes Mrs. Smith. She's on the war-path again.* □ *Why are you always on the war-path? What's wrong?*

on the watch for someone or something alert and watching for someone or something. □ *Please stay on the watch for trouble.* □ *I'm always on the watch for Ann. I want to know when she's around.*

on the way (somewhere) AND **on one's way (somewhere)** along the route to somewhere. □ *She's now on her way to London.* □ *Yes, she's on her way.*

on the way (to doing something) AND **on one's way (to doing something)** in the process of doing something. □ *You're on the way to becoming a very good carpenter.* □ *She's on her way to becoming a first-class sculptor.*

on the whole generally; considering everything. □ *On the whole, this was a very good day.* □ *Your work—on the whole—is quite good.*

on the wing while flying; while in flight. (Formal. Usually refers to birds, fowl, etc.) □ *There is nothing as pretty as a bird on the wing.* □ *The hawk caught the sparrow on the wing.*

on the wrong track going the wrong way; following the wrong set of assumptions or clues. (Also used literally.) □ *You'll never get the right answer. You're on the wrong track.* □ *They won't catch the culprit because they are on the wrong track.*

on time at the scheduled time; at the predicted time. □ *The plane landed right on time.* □ *We'll have to hurry to get there on time.*

on tiptoe standing or walking on the front part of the feet (the balls of the feet) with no weight put on the heels. (This is done to gain height or to walk quietly.) □ *I had to stand on tiptoe in order to see over the fence.* □ *I came in late and walked on tiptoe so I wouldn't wake anybody up.*

on top 1. victorious over something. □ *I have to study day and night to be on top.* □ *People tried to get the manager dismissed, but he stayed on top.* **2.** See the following entry.

on top of something 1. AND **on top** resting on the upper surface of something. □ *Please put this book on top of the piano.* □ *Where do you want it? On top?* **2.** AND **on top** up to date on something; knowing about the current state of something. (Informal.) □ *Ask Mary. She's on top of this issue.* □ *This issue is constantly changing. She has to pay attention to it to stay on top.* **3.** in addition to something. □ *Jane told Bill he was dull. On top of that, she said he was unfriendly.* □ *On top of being dull, he's unfriendly.* **4.** AND **on top** dealing satisfactorily with something. □ *I really don't think that Joan is on top of this matter.* □ *She has to work very hard to keep on top of all the things that she must deal with.*

on top of the world See *(sitting) on top of the world.*

on trial being tried in court. □ *My sister is on trial today, so I have to go to court.* □ *They placed the suspected thief on trial.*

on view visible; on public display. □ *The painting will be on view at the museum.* □ *I'll pull the curtains so that we won't be on view to everyone.*

once and for all finally and irreversibly. □ *I want to get this problem settled once and for all.* □ *I told him once and for all that he has to start studying.*

once in a blue moon very rarely. □ *I seldom go to the cinema—maybe once in a blue moon.* □ *I don't go into the city except once in a blue moon.*

once-in-a-lifetime chance a chance that will never occur again in one's lifetime. □ *This is a once-in-a-lifetime chance. Don't miss it.* □ *She offered me a once-in-a-lifetime chance, but I turned it down.*

once in a while occasionally; *every now and then.* □ *I go to see a film once in a while.* □ *Once in a while we have lamb, but not very often.*

once upon a time once in the past. (A formula used to begin a fairy-tale.) □ *Once upon a time, there were three*

bears. □ *Once upon a time, I had a puppy of my own.*

one and all everyone. □ *"Good morning to one and all," said Jane as she walked through the outer office.* □ *Let's hope that this turns out to be a wonderful party for one and all.*

one and only 1. the famous and talented (person). (Used in theatrical introductions.) □ *And now—the one and only—Jane Smith!* □ *Let's have a big hand for the one and only Bob Jones!* **2.** one alone. (Used for emphasis.) □ *This is my one and only trophy.* □ *She lost her one and only son, but has several daughters.*

one and the same the very same person or thing. □ *John Jones and J. Jones are one and the same.* □ *Adultery and affair are almost one and the same.*

one at a time See the following entry.

one by one AND **one at a time** the first one, then the next one, then the next one, etc. □ *I have to deal with problems one by one. I can't handle them all at once.* □ *Okay, just take things one at a time.*

one for the record (books) a record-breaking act. □ *What a dive! That's one for the record books.* □ *I've never heard such a funny joke. That's really one for the record.*

One good turn deserves another. a proverb meaning that a good deed should be repaid with another good deed. □ *If he does you a favour, you should do him a favour. One good turn deserves another.* □ *Glad to help you out. One good turn deserves another.*

one in a hundred See *one in a thousand.*

one in a million See the following entry.

one in a thousand AND **one in a hundred; one in a million** unique; one of a very few. □ *He's a great friend. He's one in million.* □ *Mary's one in a hundred—such a hard worker.*

one in the eye for someone something unpleasant that is considered just punishment or treatment for someone. (Slang.) □ *Anne's getting engaged was one in the eye for Bob, who was taking her for granted.* □ *Mike's getting into university was one in the eye for the teacher who called him stupid.*

one jump ahead (of someone or something) AND **one move ahead (of someone or something)** one step in advance of someone or something. □ *Try to stay one jump ahead of the customer.* □ *If you're one move ahead, you're well prepared to deal with problems. Then, nothing is a surprise.*

One man's meat is another man's poison. a proverb meaning that one person's preference may be disliked by another person. □ *John just loves his new fur hat, but I think it is horrible. Oh well, one man's meat is another man's poison.* □ *The neighbours are very fond of their dog even though it's ugly, loud, and smelly. I suppose that one man's meat is another man's poison.*

one means business one is very serious. (Informal.) □ *Billy, get into this house and do your homework, and I mean business.* □ *We mean business when we say you must stop all this nonsense.*

one move ahead (of someone or something) See *one jump ahead (of someone or something)*.

one-night stand 1. an activity lasting one night. (Informal. Often refers to a musical performance.) □ *Our band has played a lot of one-night stands.* □ *What we want is an engagement for a week, not just a one-night stand.* 2. a sexual liaison lasting only one night. (Slang.) □ *Bob won't marry. He spends his life having one-night stands.* □ *He regarded Mary as simply a one-night stand.*

one of these days some day; in some situation like this one. □ *One of these days, someone is going to steal your purse if you don't watch out.* □ *You're going to get in trouble one of these days.*

one-off something that is intended for one occasion or use only. □ *The design of the plate is a one-off. It was produced for the coronation.* □ *Jane stated she didn't want a mass-produced engagement ring. She would have to have a one-off or nothing.* ALSO: **one-off** singular; once only. □ *The concert was a one-off thing. The singer doesn't give public performances any more.*

one-track mind a mind which thinks entirely or almost entirely about one subject, often sex. □ *Adolescent boys often have one-track minds. All they're interested in is the opposite sex.* □ *Bob has a one-track mind. He can only talk about football.*

one-up (on someone) ahead of someone; with an advantage over someone. (Informal.) □ *Tom is one-up on Sally because he got a job and she didn't.* □ *Yes, it sounds like Tom is one-up.*

one way or another somehow. □ *I'll get to Spain one way or another.* □ *One way or another, I'll get through school.*

One's bark is worse than one's bite. a proverb meaning that one may threaten, but not do much damage. □ *Don't worry about Bob. He won't hurt you. His bark is worse than his bite.* □ *She may scream and shout, but have no fear. Her bark is worse than her bite.*

one's better half one's spouse. (Informal.) □ *I think we'd like to come for dinner, but I'll have to ask my better half.* □ *I have to go home now to my better half. We are going out tonight.*

one's days are numbered [for someone] to face death, dismissal, or ruin. (Informal.) □ *If I don't get this contract, my days are numbered at this firm.* □ *His days as a member of the club are numbered.* □ *Uncle Tom has a terminal disease. His days are numbered.*

one's eyes are bigger than one's stomach (Informal.) [for one] to take more food than one can eat. □ *I can't eat all this. I'm afraid that my eyes were bigger than my stomach when I ordered.* □ *Try to take less food. Your eyes are bigger than* *your stomach at every meal.* ALSO: **have eyes bigger than one's stomach** to have a desire for more food than one could possibly eat. □ *I know I have eyes bigger than my stomach, so I won't take a lot of food.*

one's hands are tied See *have one's hands tied.*

One's heart goes out to someone. One feels compassion for someone. □ *My heart goes out to those starving children I see on television.* □ *His heart goes out to his widowed sister.*

one's heart is in one's mouth one feels nervous or frightened. □ *My heart was in my mouth when he dived.* □ *His heart was in his mouth when she parachuted.*

one's heart is in the right place See under *have one's heart in the right place.*

one's heart is set against something See under *have one's heart set against something.*

one's heart is set on something See under *have one's heart set on something.*

one's heart misses a beat AND **one's heart skips a beat** one's heart flutters or beats unevenly because of emotion. □ *Whenever I'm near you, my heart skips a beat.* □ *When the racehorse fell, my heart missed a beat.*

one's heart skips a beat See the previous entry.

one's heart stands still one's heart (figuratively) stops beating because of strong emotions. □ *When I first saw you, my heart stood still.* □ *When he jumped, my heart stood still.*

one's luck runs out one's good luck stops. □ *My luck ran out, so I had to come home.* □ *Her luck ran out when the police caught her.*

one's name is mud for one to be in trouble or humiliated. (Slang.) □ *If I can't get this contract signed, my name will be mud.* □ *His name is mud ever since he broke the crystal vase.*

one's nose is in the air See under *have one's nose in the air.*

one's number is up one's time to die—or suffer some other unpleasantness—has come. (Informal.) □ *John is worried about his sore chest. He thinks his number is up.* □ *The manager's number is up. He's been sacked for stealing.*

one's old stamping-ground the place where one was raised or where one has spent a lot of time. (Informal.) □ *Ann should know about that place. It's near her old stamping-ground.* □ *I can't wait to get back to my old stamping-ground and see old friends.*

one's tail is between one's legs See under *have one's tail between one's legs.*

one's way of life one's life-style; one's pattern of living. □ *That kind of thing just doesn't fit into my way of life.* □ *Children change one's way of life.*

one's words stick in one's throat one finds it difficult to speak because of emotion. □ *My words stick in my throat whenever I try to say something kind or tender.* □ *I wanted to apologize, but the words stuck in my throat.*

one's work is cut out (for one) See under *have one's work cut out (for one).*

only have eyes for someone to be loyal to only one person, in the context of romance; to be interested in only one person. □ *Oh, Jane! I only have eyes for you!* □ *Don't waste any time on Tom. He only has eyes for Ann.*

onto someone or something having discovered the truth about someone or something. (Informal.) □ *The police are onto John's plot.* □ *Yes, they are onto him, and they are onto the plot.*

open a can of worms to uncover a set of problems or complications; to create unnecessary complications. (Informal.) □ *If you start asking questions about the firm's accounts, you'll open a can of worms.* □ *How about clearing up this mess before you open up a new can of worms?*

open and above-board See *above-board.*

open-and-shut case something, usually a law-case or problem, that is simple and straightforward without complications. □ *The murder trial was an open-and-shut case. The defendant was caught with the murder weapon.* □ *Jack's death was an open-and-shut case of suicide. He left a suicide note.*

open book someone or something that is easy to understand. □ *Jane's an open book. I always know what she is going to do next.* □ *The council's intentions are an open book. They want to save money.*

open fire (on someone) to start (doing something, such as asking questions or criticizing). (Informal. Also used literally.) □ *The reporters opened fire on the mayor.* □ *When the reporters opened fire, the film-star was smiling, but not for long.* □ *The soldiers opened fire on the villagers.*

open one's heart (to someone) to reveal one's most private thoughts to someone. □ *I always open my heart to my wife when I have a problem.* □ *It's a good idea to open your heart every now and then.*

open Pandora's box to uncover a lot of unsuspected problems. □ *When I asked Jane about her problems, I didn't know I had opened Pandora's box.* □ *You should be cautious with people who are upset. You don't want to open Pandora's box.*

open season for something unrestricted hunting of a particular game animal. □ *It's always open season for rabbits around here.* □ *Is it ever open season for deer?*

open secret something which is supposed to be secret, but which is known to a great many people. □ *Their engagement is an open secret. Only their friends are supposed to know, but in fact, the whole town knows.* □ *It's an open secret that Fred's looking for a new job.*

open someone's eyes (to something) **1.** to become aware of something. □ *He fi-*nally opened his eyes to what was going on.* □ *It was a long time before he opened his eyes and realized what had been happening.* **2.** to cause someone to be aware of something. □ *I opened his eyes to what was happening at the office.* □ *Why can't I make you understand? Why don't you open your eyes?*

open something up AND **open up something** **1.** to open something. □ *I can't wait to open up my presents.* □ *Yes, I want to open them up, too.* □ *Open up this door!* **2.** to begin examining or discussing something. □ *Now is the time to open up the question of taxation.* □ *Do you really want to open it up now?* **3.** to reveal the possibilities of something; to reveal an opportunity. □ *Your comments opened up a whole new train of thought.* □ *Your letter opened new possibilities up.* **4.** to start the use of something, such as land, a building, a business, etc. □ *They opened up the coastal lands to cotton planting.* □ *We opened up a new shop last March.* **5.** to make a vehicle go as fast as possible. (Informal.) □ *We took the new car out on the motorway and opened it up.* □ *I've never really opened up this truck. I don't know how fast it'll go.* ALSO: **open up** **1.** open your door. (A command.) □ *I want in. Open up!* □ *Open up! This is the police.* **2.** to become available. □ *A new job is opening up at my office.* □ *Let me know if any other opportunities open up.* **3.** to go as fast as possible. □ *I can't get this car to open up. Must be something wrong with the engine.* □ *Faster, Tom! Open up! Let's go!*

open the door to something to permit or allow something to become a possibility. (Also used literally.) □ *Your policy opens the door to cheating.* □ *Your statement opens the door to John's candidacy.*

open up See under *open something up* and the next two entries.

open up (on someone or something) to fire a gun or other weapon at someone or something. □ *The sergeant told the soldiers to open up on the enemy posi-*

235

tion. □ *"Okay, you lot," shouted the sergeant. "Open up!"*

open up (to someone) AND **open up (with someone)** to talk frankly, truthfully, or intimately. (Informal.) □ *Finally Sally opened up to her sister and told her what the problem was.* □ *Bill wouldn't open up with me. He's still keeping quiet.* □ *At last, Sally opened up and told everything.*

open up (with someone) See the previous entry.

open with something to start out with something. (Usually said of a performance of some type.) □ *We'll open with a love-song and then go on to something faster.* □ *The play opened with an exciting first act, and then it became very boring.*

opposite sex [from the point of view of a female] the male; [from the point of view of a male] the female. (Also with *member of,* as in the examples.) □ *Ann is crazy about the opposite sex.* □ *Bill is very shy when he's introduced to the opposite sex.* □ *Do members of the opposite sex make you nervous?*

order of the day something necessary or usual at a certain time. □ *Warm clothes are the order of the day when camping in the winter.* □ *Going to bed early was the order of the day when we were young.*

order someone about AND **order someone around** to give commands to someone; to boss someone. □ *I don't like people ordering me about.* □ *Don't order me around!*

order someone around See the previous entry.

other way round the reverse; the opposite. □ *No, it won't fit that way. Try it the other way round.* □ *It doesn't make any sense like that. It belongs the other way round.*

out and about able to go out and travel around; well enough to go out. □ *Beth has been ill, but now she's out and about.* □ *As soon as I feel better, I'll be able to get out and about.*

out-and-out something a complete or absolute something; an indisputable thing or type of person. (The *something* must always be a specific thing.) □ *If he said that, he told you an out-and-out lie!* □ *You're an out-and-out liar!* □ *She married an out-and-out rogue!*

out cold AND **out like a light** unconscious; fast asleep. (Informal.) □ *I fell and hit my head. I was out cold for about a minute.* □ *Tom fainted! He's out like a light!* □ *The child went out like a light when he went to bed.*

out from under (something) free and clear of something; no longer bearing a (figurative) burden. □ *I'll feel much better when I'm out from under this project.* □ *Now that I'm out from under, I can relax.*

out in force appearing in great numbers. (See also *in force.*) □ *What a night! The mosquitoes are out in force.* □ *The police were out in force over the holiday week-end.*

out like a light See *out cold.*

out of all proportion of an exaggerated proportion; of an unrealistic proportion compared to something else; [for something] to be considered more important than it really is; (figuratively) lopsided. (The *all* can be left out.) □ *This problem has grown out of all proportion.* □ *Yes, this thing has got completely out of proportion.* ALSO: **blow something out of all proportion** to cause something to be unrealistically proportioned relative to something else; to consider something to be more important than it really is. (The *all* can be left out.) □ *The press has blown this issue out of all proportion.* □ *Let's be reasonable. Don't blow this scandal out of proportion.*

out of bounds 1. outside the boundaries of the playing area. (In various sports.) □ *The ball went out of bounds, but the referee didn't notice.* □ *The play ended when Sally ran out of bounds.* **2.** See *off limits.*

out of breath breathing fast and hard. □ *I ran so much that I got out of breath.* □ *Mary gets out of breath when she climbs stairs.*

out of character unlike one's usual behaviour. □ *Ann's remark was quite out of character.* □ *It was out of character for Ann to be so stubborn.*

out of circulation 1. no longer available for use or lending. (Usually said of library materials.) □ *I'm sorry, but the book you want is temporarily out of circulation.* □ *How long will it be out of circulation?* 2. not socializing with other people. (Informal.) □ *I don't know what's happening because I've been out of circulation for a while.* □ *My cold has kept me out of circulation for a few weeks.*

out of commission 1. [for a ship] to be not currently in use or under command. □ *This vessel will remain out of commission for another month.* □ *The ship has been out of commission since repairs began.* 2. broken, unserviceable, or inoperable. □ *My watch is out of commission and is running slowly.* □ *I can't run in the marathon because my knees are out of commission.*

out of condition See *out of shape.*

out of consideration (for someone or something) with consideration or care for someone or something; with kind regard for someone or something. □ *Out of consideration for your mother's feelings, I won't sack you.* □ *They let Jane stay in the house out of consideration for her condition. She's pregnant.*

out of control AND **out of hand** uncontrollable; wild and unruly. □ *The party got out of control about midnight, and the neighbours called the police.* □ *We tried to keep things from getting out of hand.*

out of courtesy (to someone) in order to be polite to someone; out of consideration for someone. □ *We invited Mary's brother out of courtesy to her.* □ *They invited me out of courtesy.*

out of date old-fashioned; out of style; obsolete. □ *Isn't that suit sort of out of date?* □ *All my clothes are out of date.* □ *His ideas are completely out of date.* ALSO: **out-of-date** old-fashioned; in an old style. □ *Please take off that out-of-date suit.* □ *You can't go out wearing that out-of-date hat!*

out of fashion not fashionable; old-fashioned; obsolete. □ *John's clothes are really out of fashion.* □ *He doesn't care if his suits are out of fashion.* ALSO: **go out of fashion** to become unfashionable; to become obsolete. □ *That kind of furniture went out of fashion years ago.*

out of favour (with someone) no longer desirable or preferred by someone. □ *I can't ask John to help. I'm out of favour with him.* □ *That kind of thing has been out of favour for years.*

out of hand 1. See *out of control.* 2. immediately and without consulting anyone; without delay. □ *I can't answer that out of hand. I'll check with the manager and call you back.* □ *The offer was so good that I accepted it out of hand.*

out of it AND **out to lunch** not alert; giddy; uninformed. (Slang.) □ *Bill is really out of it. Why can't he pay attention?* □ *I tried to explain the situation to John, but he was completely out of it.* □ *Ann is really out to lunch these days. Is she quite well?*

out of keeping with something not following the rules of something; not appropriate to something; not in harmony with something. (Compare to *in keeping with something.*) □ *The length of this report is out of keeping with your request.* □ *Your clothes are out of keeping with the formality of the occasion.*

out of kilter out of working order; malfunctioning; *on the blink.* (Informal.) □ *My furnace is out of kilter. I have to call someone to fix it.* □ *This computer is out of kilter. It doesn't work.*

out of line 1. improper; inappropriate. □ *I'm afraid that your behaviour was* quite out of line. I do not wish to speak further about this matter. □ Bill, that remark was out of line. Please be more respectful. 2. See the following entry.

out of line (with something) 1. not properly lined up in a line of things. □ One of those books on the shelf is out of line with the others. Please fix it. □ The files are out of line also. 2. unreasonable when compared to something (else). □ The cost of this meal is out of line with what other restaurants charge. □ Your request is out of line.

out of luck without good luck; having bad fortune. (Informal.) □ If you wanted some ice-cream, you're out of luck. □ I was out of luck. I got there too late to get a seat.

out of necessity because of necessity; because it was necessary. □ I bought this hat out of necessity. I needed one, and this was all there was. □ We sold our car out of necessity.

out of one's element not in a natural or comfortable situation. (Compare to in one's element.) □ When it comes to computers, I'm out of my element. □ Sally's out of her element on the dance-floor.

out of one's head See the following entry.

out of one's mind AND **out of one's head** silly and senseless; crazy; irrational. □ Why did you do that? You must be out of your mind! □ Good grief, Tom! You have to be out of your head!

out of order 1. not in the correct order. □ This book is out of order. Please put it in the right place on the shelf. □ You're out of order, John. Please get in the queue after Jane. 2. not following correct procedure. □ My question was declared out of order by the president. □ Ann inquired, "Isn't a motion to table the question out of order at this time?"

out of place 1. not in a proper place. □ The salt was out of place in the cupboard, so I couldn't find it. □ Billy, you're out of place. Please sit next to Tom. 2. im-

proper and impertinent; out of line. □ That kind of behaviour is out of place in church. □ Your rude remark is quite out of place.

out-of-pocket expenses the actual amount of money spent. (Refers to the money one person pays while doing something on someone else's behalf. One is usually paid back this money.) □ My out-of-pocket expenses for the party were nearly £175. □ My employer usually pays all out-of-pocket expenses for a business trip.

out of practice performing poorly because of a lack of practice. □ I used to be able to play the piano extremely well, but now I'm out of practice. □ The players lost the game because they were out of practice.

out of print no longer available for sale. (Said of a book or periodical.) □ The book you want is out of print, but perhaps I can find a used copy for you. □ It was published nearly ten years ago, so it's probably out of print.

out of reach 1. not near enough to be reached or touched. □ Place the sweets out of reach, or Bob will eat them all. □ The mouse ran behind the piano, out of reach. The cat just sat and waited for it. 2. unattainable. □ I wanted to be president, but I'm afraid that such a goal is out of reach. □ Foreign holidays are out of the reach of Bill's family.

out of season (The opposite of in season.) 1. not now available for sale. □ Sorry, oysters are out of season. We don't have any. □ Watermelon is out of season in the winter. 2. not now legally able to be hunted or caught. □ Are salmon out of season? □ I caught a trout out of season and had to pay a fine.

out of service not now operating. □ Both lifts are out of service, so I had to use the stairs. □ The toilet is temporarily out of service.

out of shape AND **out of condition** not in the best physical condition. □ I get out of breath when I run because I'm out of shape. □ Keep exercising regularly, or you'll get out of condition.

out of sight not visible. (Especially with get, keep, stay.) □ The cat kept out of sight until the mouse came out. □ "Get out of sight, or they'll see you!" called John.

Out of sight, out of mind. a proverb meaning that if you do not see something, you will not think about it. □ When I go home, I put my school-books away so I won't worry about doing my homework. After all, out of sight, out of mind. □ Jane dented the side on her car. It's on the left side so she doesn't have to look at it. As they say, out of sight, out of mind.

out of sorts not feeling well; cross and irritable. □ I've been out of sorts for a day or two. I think I'm coming down with flu. □ The baby is out of sorts. Maybe she's getting a tooth.

out of step (with someone or something) (Compare to in step (with someone or something).) **1.** [with someone] [marching or dancing] out of cadence with someone else. □ You're out of step with the music. □ Pay attention, Ann. You're out of step with the other dancers. **2.** not as up to date as someone or something; not keeping up with someone or something. □ John is out of step with the times. □ Billy is out of step with the rest of the class.

out of stock not immediately available in a shop; [for goods] to be temporarily unavailable. □ Those items are out of stock, but a new supply will be delivered on Thursday. □ I'm sorry, but the red ones are out of stock. Would a blue one do?

out of the blue suddenly; without warning. (See also like a bolt out of the blue.) □ Then, out of the blue, he told me he was leaving. □ Mary appeared on my doorstep out of the blue.

out of the corner of one's eye [seeing something] at a glance; glimpsing (something). □ I saw someone do it out of the corner of my eye. It might have been Jane who did it. □ I only saw the accident out of the corner of my eye. I don't know who is at fault.

out of the frying-pan into the fire from a bad situation to a worse situation. □ When I tried to argue about my fine for a traffic violation, the judge charged me with contempt of court. I really went out of the frying-pan into the fire. □ I got deeply in debt. Then I really got out of the frying-pan into the fire when I lost my job.

out of the ordinary unusual. □ It was a good meal, but not out of the ordinary. □ Your report was nicely done, but nothing out of the ordinary.

out of the question not possible; not permitted. □ I'm sorry, but leaving early is out of the question. □ You can't go to France this spring. We can't afford it. It's out of the question.

out of the running no longer being considered; eliminated from a contest. □ After the first part of the diving competition, three of our team were out of the running. □ After the scandal was made public, I was no longer in the running. I pulled out of the election.

out of the swim of things not in the middle of activity; not involved in things. (Informal. The opposite of in the swim of things.) □ While I had my cold, I was out of the swim of things. □ I've been out of the swim of things for a few weeks. Please bring me up to date.

out of the way AND **out of one's way 1.** not blocking or impeding the way. □ Please get out of my way. □ Would you please get your foot out of the way? **2.** not along the way. □ I'm sorry, but I can't give you a ride home. It's out of the way. □ That route is out of my way. ALSO: **out-of-the-way** difficult to get to. □ They live on a quiet, out-of-the-way street.

out of the woods past a critical phase; no longer at risk. (Informal.) □ When the patient got out of the woods, everyone relaxed. □ I can give you a better *prediction for your future health when you are out of the woods.*

out of thin air out of nowhere; out of nothing. (Informal.) □ *Suddenly—out of thin air—the messenger appeared.* □ *You just made that up out of thin air.*

out of this world wonderful; extraordinary. □ *This pie is just out of this world.* □ *Look at you! How lovely you look—simply out of this world.*

out of time with no more time. □ *I was out of time before I could finish.* □ *I can't be out of time! I still have a lot to do.* ALSO: **run out of time** to use up all the available time. □ *I ran out of time and couldn't finish.*

out of touch (with someone or something) **1.** [with *someone*] no longer talking to or writing to someone; knowing no news of someone. □ *I've been out of touch with my brother for many years.* □ *We've been out of touch for quite some time.* **2.** [with *something*] not keeping up with the developments of something. □ *I've been out of touch with teaching for many years.* □ *I couldn't go back into teaching because I've been out of touch for too long.*

out of town temporarily not in one's own town. □ *I'll be out of town next week. I'm going to a conference.* □ *I care for Mary's cat when she's out of town.*

out of tune (with someone or something) **1.** in musical harmony with someone or something. □ *The oboe is out of tune with the flute.* □ *The flute is out of tune with John.* □ *They are all out of tune.* **2.** not in (figurative) harmony or agreement. □ *Your proposal is out of tune with my ideas of what we should be doing.* □ *Let's get all our efforts in tune.*

out of turn not at the proper time; not in the proper order. (See also *speak out of turn.*) □ *We were permitted to be served out of turn, because we had to leave early.* □ *Bill tried to register out of turn and was sent away.*

out of work unemployed, temporarily or permanently. □ *How long have you been out of work?* □ *My brother has been out of work for nearly a year.*

out on a limb in a dangerous or difficult position; taking a chance or a risk. □ *I don't want to go out on a limb, but I think I'd agree to your request.* □ *She really went out on a limb when she gave him permission to leave early.*

out on bail out of jail because bail bond money has been paid. (The money will be forfeited if the person who is out on bail does not appear in court at the proper time. See also *jump bail.*) □ *Bob is out on bail waiting for his trial.* □ *The robber committed another crime while out on bail.*

out on parole out of jail but still under police supervision. □ *Bob got out on parole after serving only a few years of his sentence.* □ *He was out on parole because of good behaviour.*

out on the town celebrating at one or more places in a town. (Informal. See also *night on the town.*) □ *I'm really tired. I was out on the town until dawn.* □ *We went out on the town to celebrate our wedding anniversary.*

out to lunch **1.** eating lunch away from one's place of work. □ *I'm sorry, but Sally Jones is out to lunch. May I take a message?* □ *She's been out to lunch for nearly two hours. When will she be back?* **2.** See *out of it.*

outgrow something See under *grow out of something.*

over and above something more than something; in addition to something. □ *I'll need another £20 over and above the amount you have already given me.* □ *You've been eating too much food over and above what is required for good nutrition. That's why you're gaining weight.*

over and done with finished. □ *I'm glad that's over and done with.* □ *Now that I have college over and done with, I can seek employment.*

over and over (again) repeatedly. □ *She stamped her foot over and over again.* □ *Bill whistled the same song over and over.*

over my dead body not if I can stop you. (It means that you'll have to kill me to prevent me from keeping you from doing something.) □ *Over my dead body you'll sell this house!* □ *You want to leave college? Over my dead body!*

over the hill over age; too old to do something. (Informal.) □ *Now that Mary's forty, she thinks she's over the hill.* □ *My grandfather was over eighty before he felt like he was over the hill.*

over the hump over the difficult part. (Informal.) □ *This is a difficult project, but we're over the hump now.* □ *I'm half-way through—over the hump— and it looks like I may get finished after all.*

over the odds more than one would expect to pay. (From betting in horse-racing.) □ *We had to pay over the odds for a house in the area where we wanted to live.* □ *It's a nice car, but the owner's asking well over the odds for it.*

over the top (Informal.) exaggerated; excessive. □ *Her reaction to my statement was a bit over the top. She hugged me.* □ *Everyone thought her behaviour was over the top.* ALSO: **go over the top** to do something in an exaggerated or excessive way; to overreact. □ *Jane really went over the top with the dinner she prepared for us. It took her hours to prepare.* □ *Uncle Jack went completely over the top when he bought my baby's present. It must have been incredibly expensive.*

own up (to something) to confess to something. □ *I know you broke the window. Come on and own up to it.* □ *The boy holding the bat owned up. What else could he do?*

P

pack a punch See the following entry.

pack a wallop AND **pack a punch** to provide a burst of energy, power, or excitement. (Slang.) □ *Wow, this spicy food really packs a wallop.* □ *I put a special kind of petrol in my car because I thought it would pack a punch. It didn't.*

pack it in to stop doing whatever one is doing. (Slang.) □ *Mary's complaining again. I wish she'd pack it in.* □ *Bob's not driving a taxi any more. He's packed it in.*

pack someone off (to somewhere) AND **pack off someone (to somewhere)** to send someone away to somewhere, often with the suggestion that one is glad to do so. (Compare to *send someone packing.*) □ *His parents packed him off to boarding-school as soon as possible.* □ *We packed off my aunt to York yesterday.* □ *John finally has left for France. We packed him off last week.*

pack someone or something in to leave someone or something; to have nothing more to do with someone or something. (Slang.) □ *Jack's packed in his girlfriend to go out with Mary.* □ *Jean's packed in her job.*

pack them in to draw a lot of people. (Informal.) □ *It was a good night at the theatre. The play really packed them in.* □ *The circus manager knew he could pack them in if he advertised the lion tamer.*

pack up to stop working or operating. (Slang.) □ *The car's engine packed up.* □ *The whole computer system packed up.*

packed (in) like herring in a barrel See the following entry.

packed (in) like sardines AND **packed (in) like herring in a barrel** packed very tightly. □ *It was terribly crowded there. We were packed in like sardines.* □ *The bus was full. The passengers were packed like sardines.* □ *They were packed like herring in a barrel.*

packed out very crowded; containing as many people as possible. (Informal.) □ *The theatre was packed out.* □ *The cinema was packed out twenty minutes before we arrived.*

paddle one's own canoe to do (something) by oneself; to be alone. □ *I've been left to paddle my own canoe since I was a child.* □ *Sally didn't stay with the group. She went to paddle her own canoe.*

pain in the neck a bother; an annoyance. (Informal.) □ *This assignment is a pain in the neck.* □ *Your little brother is a pain in the neck.*

paint the town red to have a wild celebration during a *night on the town.* □ *Let's all go out and paint the town red!* □ *Oh, I feel awful. I was out all last night painting the town red.*

pair off (with someone) AND **pair up (with someone)** [for two people] to form a pair for some purpose, possibly a romantic purpose. □ *All right. You two pair off and go to the right. The rest of us will go to the left.* □ *Tom paired* *off with Ann for the rest of the evening.* □ *Okay—everybody pair up and let's get this thing finished.*

pair up (with someone) See the previous entry.

pal around (with someone) to be friends with someone; to be the companion of someone. (Informal.) □ *Bill likes to pal around with Mary, but it's nothing serious.* □ *Ann and Jane still like to pal around.*

pale around the gills AND **green around the gills** looking sick. (Informal. The *around* can be replaced with *about*.) □ *John is looking a little pale around the gills. What's wrong?* □ *Oh, I feel a little green about the gills.*

palm someone or something off (on someone) AND **palm off someone or something (on someone)** to get rid of someone or something by giving or selling it to another person. (Informal.) □ *My brother palmed off his old clothes on me.* □ *Tom palmed Ann off on Bill. Both Ann and Bill were furious.*

pan out See *turn out (all right)*.

paper over the cracks (in something) to try to hide faults or difficulties, often in a hasty or not very successful way. □ *The politician tried to paper over the cracks in his party's economic policy.* □ *Tom tried to paper over the cracks in his relationship with the boss, but it was not possible.*

par for the course typical; about what one could expect. (This refers to a golf-course.) □ *So he went off and left you? Well, that's about par for the course. He's no friend.* □ *I worked for days on this project, but it was rejected. That's par for the course around here.*

parcel someone or something out AND **parcel out someone or something** to give out or hand out someone or something, often to get rid of the person or thing. (Informal.) □ *Mr. and Mrs. Smith went on holiday and parcelled out the children to various relations.* □ *We parcelled the jobs out to all the volunteers.*

parrot-fashion without understanding the meaning of what one has learnt, is saying, etc. □ *The child learnt the material by heart and repeated it in parrot-fashion.* □ *Jean never thinks for herself. She just repeats what her father says, parrot-fashion.*

part and parcel (of something) part of something; an important part of something. (See also *bag and baggage*.) □ *This point is part and parcel of my whole argument.* □ *Get every part and parcel of this machine out of my living-room.* □ *Come on! Move out—part and parcel!*

part company (with someone) to leave someone; to depart from someone, often permanently. □ *Tom finally parted company with his brother.* □ *The two families parted company after the couple's divorce.*

part with someone or something to separate from someone or something; to give up someone or something. □ *I hated to part with that old hat. I've had it for years.* □ *Tom was sad to part with Ann, but that's the way it had to be.*

partake of something to take something; to eat or drink something. (Formal.) □ *I don't usually partake of rich foods, but in this instance I'll make an exception.* □ *Good afternoon, Judge Smith, would you care to partake of some wine?*

parting of the ways a point at which people separate and go their own ways. (Often with *come to a, arrive at a, reach a*, etc.) □ *Jane and Bob finally came to a parting of the ways and divorced.* □ *Bill and his parents reached a parting of the ways, and he left home.*

party line the official ideas and attitudes which are adopted by the leaders of a particular group and which the other members are expected to accept. □ *Tom has left the club. He refused to follow the party line.* □ *Many politicians agree with the party line without thinking.*

pass as someone or something to succeed in being accepted as someone or something. □ *The spy was able to pass as a regular citizen.* □ *The thief was arrested when he tried to pass as a priest.*

pass away AND **pass on** to die. (A euphemism.) □ *My aunt passed away last month.* □ *When I pass away, I want to have lots of flowers and a big funeral.* □ *When I pass on, I won't care about the funeral.*

pass muster to measure up to the required standards. □ *I tried my best, but my efforts didn't pass muster.* □ *If you don't wear a suit, you won't pass muster at that expensive restaurant. They won't let you in.*

pass on See *pass away.*

pass out to faint; to lose consciousness. □ *Oh, look! Tom has passed out.* □ *When he got the news, he passed out.*

pass over someone or something See *pass someone or something over.*

pass someone or something by AND **pass by someone or something** to miss someone or something; to overlook someone or something. □ *The storm passed the town by.* □ *The teacher passed me by and chose the next person in the queue.* □ *Happiness passed John by. He was miserable all his life.*

pass someone or something over AND **pass over someone or something** 1. to move over without affecting someone or something. (Refers specifically to moving above.) □ *The storm passed over us.* □ *The cloud passed over the mountain.* 2. to skip over someone or something; to ignore or overlook someone or something. □ *They passed over John and chose Ann.* □ *Please don't pass me over again.*

pass someone or something up AND **pass up someone or something** to ignore or avoid someone or something; to overlook someone or something. (Informal.) □ *Yes, I'd love some chocolate cake, but I'll have to pass it up. I'm on a diet.* □ *They passed up John in favour of Mary.*

pass something off (as something) See *shrug something off (as something).*

pass something off (on someone) (as something) AND **pass off something (on someone) (as something)** to get rid of something deceptively by giving or selling it to someone as something else. □ *I passed the rhinestone off on John as a diamond.* □ *Don't try to pass that fake off on me!*

pass something on AND **pass on something** 1. to hand or give something (to another person). □ *Have a piece of toffee and pass the box on.* □ *Please pass on this book to the next person on the list.* 2. to tell someone something; to spread news or gossip. □ *Don't pass this on, but Bill isn't living at home any more.* □ *I refuse to pass on rumours.*

pass something out AND **pass out something** to distribute or hand out something. □ *Please pass out one paper to each person.* □ *Please pass these pencils out for me.*

pass the buck to pass the blame (to someone else); to give the responsibility (to someone else). (Informal.) □ *Don't try to pass the buck! It's your fault, and everybody knows it.* □ *Some people try to pass the buck whenever they can. They won't accept responsibility.*

pass the hat round to attempt to collect money for some (charitable) project. □ *Bob is passing the hat round to collect money to buy flowers for Ann.* □ *He's always passing the hat round for something.*

pass the time to fill up time (by doing something). □ *I never know how to pass the time when I'm on holiday.* □ *What do you do to pass the time in an airport?*

pass the time of day (with someone) to chat or talk informally with someone. (Informal.) □ *I saw Mr. Brown in town yesterday. I stopped and passed the time of day with him.* □ *No, we didn't have a serious talk; we just passed the time of day.*

pass through someone's mind AND **cross someone's mind** [for a thought] to come to mind briefly or to occur to someone. (Compare to *come to mind*.) □ *Let me tell you what just crossed my mind.* □ *As you were speaking, something passed through my mind which I'd like to discuss.*

past it See the following entry.

past someone's or something's best AND **past someone's or something's sell-by date; past it** less good or efficient now than someone or something was before. (*Past it* and *past someone's or something's sell-by date* are informal.) □ *Joan was a wonderful singer, but she's past her best now.* □ *This old car's past it. I'll need to get a new one.* □ *Mary feels she's past her sell-by date when she sees so many young women joining the company.* □ *This cooker's past its sell-by date. We'll have to get a new one.*

past someone's or something's sell-by date See the previous entry.

pastures new See *(fresh fields and) pastures new*.

pat someone on the back AND **give someone a pat on the back** to congratulate someone; to encourage someone. □ *We patted Ann on the back for a good performance.* □ *When people do a good job, you should give them a pat on the back.* ALSO: **get a pat on the back** to receive congratulations. □ *Ann was glad to get a pat on the back.*

patch someone or something up AND **patch up someone or something 1.** to give first aid to someone; to dress someone's wounds. (Informal.) □ *I patched up Ann's cuts with bandages and sent her home.* □ *They patched John up in the emergency room.* **2.** [with *something*] to repair something temporarily. □ *I tried to patch the lawn-mower up so I could use it for the rest of the summer.* □ *See if you can patch up this tyre for me. I can't afford a new one.* **3.** [with *something*] to (figuratively) repair the damage done by an argument or disagreement. □ *Mr. and Mrs. Smith are*

trying to patch things up. □ *We patched up our argument, then kissed and made up.*

pave the way (for someone or something) to prepare (someone or something) for someone or something. □ *The public doesn't understand the metric system. We need to pave the way for its introduction.* □ *They are paving the way in the schools for a new system of exams.*

pay a visit (to someone) See *pay someone a visit*.

pay an arm and a leg (for something) AND **pay through the nose (for something)** to pay too much money for something. (Informal.) □ *I hate to have to pay an arm and a leg for a tank of petrol.* □ *If you shop around, you won't have to pay an arm and a leg.* □ *Why should you pay through the nose?* ALSO: **cost an arm and a leg** to cost too much. □ *It cost an arm and a leg, so I didn't buy it.*

pay as you go to pay costs as they occur; to pay for goods as they are bought (rather than charging them to an account). □ *You ought to pay as you go. Then you won't be in debt.* □ *If you pay as you go, you'll never spend too much money.*

pay attention (to someone or something) to be attentive to someone or something; to give one's attention or concentration to someone or something. □ *Pay attention to me!* □ *I'm paying attention!*

pay for something to suffer punishment for doing something wrong. □ *The criminal will pay for his crimes.* □ *I don't like what you did to me, and I'm going to see that you pay for it.*

pay in advance to pay (for something) before it is received or delivered. □ *I want to make a special order. Will I have to pay in advance?* □ *Yes, please pay for all purchases in advance.*

pay lip-service (to something) to express loyalty, respect, or support for something insincerely. □ *You don't really* care about politics. You're just paying lip-service to the candidate. □ The students pay lip-service to the new rules, but they plan to ignore them in practice.

pay one's debt to society to serve a sentence for a crime, usually in prison. □ The judge said that Mr. Simpson had to pay his debt to society. □ Mr. Brown paid his debt to society in prison.

pay one's dues to pay the fees required to belong to an organization. □ If you haven't paid your dues, you can't come to the club picnic. □ How many people have paid their dues?

pay one's own way See pay someone's way.

pay someone a compliment to compliment someone. □ Sally thanked me for paying her a compliment. □ When Tom did his job well, I paid him a compliment.

pay someone a left-handed compliment to give someone a false compliment which is really an insult. □ John said that he had never seen me looking better. I think he was paying me a left-handed compliment. □ I'd prefer that someone insulted me directly. I hate it when someone pays me a left-handed compliment—unless it's a joke.

pay someone a visit AND **pay a visit (to someone)** to visit someone. □ I think I'll pay Mary a visit. □ We'd like to see you. When would be a good time to pay a visit?

pay someone or something off AND **pay off someone or something 1.** [with *someone*] to pay someone a bribe (for a favour already done). (Informal.) □ The solicitor paid off the witness for services rendered. □ The solicitor was put in prison for paying the witness off. The witness was imprisoned also. **2.** to pay a debt; to pay a debtor; to pay the final payment for something bought on credit. □ Did you pay off the plumber yet? □ This month I'll pay off the car.

pay someone's way AND **pay one's own way** to pay the costs (of something) for a person. □ I wanted to go to Italy this spring, but my parents say I have to pay my own way. □ My aunt is going to pay my way to Italy—only if I take her with me!

pay the earth to pay a great deal of money for something. (Informal. Compare to cost the earth.) □ Bob paid the earth for that ugly old sideboard. □ You have to pay the earth for property in that area.

pay the piper to provide the money for something and so have some control over how the money is spent. (From the expression, He who pays the piper calls the tune.) □ The parents at a fee-paying school pay the piper and so should have a say in how the school is run. □ Hotel guests pay the piper and should be treated politely.

pay through the nose for something See pay an arm and a leg for something.

Pay up! Pay me now! (Informal.) □ You owe me £200. Come on, pay up! □ If you don't pay up, I'll take you to court.

peg away (at something) See plug away (at something).

penny wise and pound foolish being foolish by losing a lot of money to save a little money. □ Sally shops very carefully to save a few pence on food, then charges the food to a credit card that costs a lot in annual interest. That's being penny wise and pound foolish. □ John drives thirty miles to buy petrol for three pence a gallon less than it costs here. He's really penny wise and pound foolish.

Perish the thought. Do not even consider thinking of something. (Formal.) □ If you should become ill—perish the thought—I'd look after you. □ I'm afraid that we need a new car. Perish the thought!

perk someone or something up AND **perk up someone or something** to make someone or something more cheerful or lively. (Informal.) □ Don't you think that new curtains would perk up this *room?* □ *A nice cup of tea would really perk me up.*

peter out to die away; to dwindle away; to become exhausted gradually. (Informal.) □ *When the fire petered out, I went to bed.* □ *My money finally petered out, and I had to come home.*

phase someone or something out AND **phase out someone or something** to plan the gradual removal of someone or something. □ *They are phasing out dial telephones. Only button telephones will be available.* □ *There is a new policy at my place of work of phasing out older staff. I hope they won't phase me out, too.*

pick a quarrel (with someone) to start an argument with someone. □ *Are you trying to pick a quarrel with me?* □ *No, I'm not trying to pick a quarrel.*

pick and choose to choose very carefully from a number of possibilities; to be selective. □ *You must take what you are given. You cannot pick and choose.* □ *Meg is so beautiful. She can pick and choose from a whole range of suitors.*

pick at something 1. to eat only little bits of something. □ *You're only picking at your food. Don't you feel well?* □ *Billy is only picking at his peas, and he usually eats all of them.* **2.** to pull, scratch, or pluck at something. □ *If you pick at that sore, it'll get infected.* □ *Don't pick at the label. It'll come off.*

pick holes in something to criticize something severely; to find all the flaws or fallacies in an argument. (Informal.) □ *The solicitor picked holes in the witness's story.* □ *They will pick holes in your argument.*

pick on someone (Informal.) to criticize someone or something constantly; to abuse someone or something. □ *Stop picking on me!* □ *Why are you always picking on the office junior?* ALSO: **Pick on someone your own size!** Criticize or abuse someone who is big enough to fight back! □ *Go pick on someone your own size!*

Pick on someone your own size! See under *pick on someone.*

pick one's way through something 1. to work slowly and carefully through something. □ *My teacher said he couldn't even pick his way through my report. It was just too confusing.* □ *I spent an hour picking my way through the instructions.* **2.** to move along a route full of obstacles; to make one's way through something with difficulty. □ *When the grandchildren visit, I have to pick my way through the toys on the floor.* □ *We slowly picked our way through the thorny bushes to get to the ripe raspberries.*

pick someone or something off AND **pick off someone or something 1.** [with *something*] to remove something by picking, scratching, or plucking. □ *Don't pick the scab off. You'll get an infection.* □ *Pick off all the feathers before you cook the duck.* **2.** to kill someone or something with a carefully aimed gunshot. (Informal.) □ *The hunter picked the deer off with great skill.* □ *The killer tried to pick off the police officer.*

pick someone or something out AND **pick out someone or something** to choose someone or something. □ *I don't know which one to choose. You pick one out for me.* □ *I used the telephone book to pick out a plumber.* □ *The mayor picked out John as the winner of the contest.*

pick someone or something up AND **pick up someone or something 1.** [with *someone*] to collect someone; to go to a place in a car, bus, etc., and take on a person as a passenger. □ *Please come to my office and pick me up at midday.* □ *I have to pick up Billy at school.* **2.** [with *someone*] to stop one's car, bus, etc., and offer someone a ride. □ *I picked up a hitch-hiker today, and we had a nice chat.* □ *Don't ever pick a stranger up when you're out driving!* **3.** [with *someone*] to attempt to become acquainted with someone for romantic or sexual purposes. (Informal.) □ *Who are you anyway? Are you trying to pick* me up? □ *No, I never picked up any-body in my life!* **4.** [with *someone*] [for the police] to find and bring someone to the police station for questioning or arrest. □ *Sergeant Jones, go pick up Sally Franklin and bring her in to be questioned about the jewel robbery.* □ *I tried to pick her up, but she heard me coming and got away.* **5.** [with *something*] to find or acquire something casually, without looking for it. □ *I picked up this tool at the shop.* □ *Where did you pick that gadget up?* **6.** [with *something*] to learn something. □ *I picked up a lot of knowledge about music from my brother.* □ *I picked up an interesting melody from a film.* **7.** [with *something*] to resume something. □ *I'll have to pick up my work where I left off.* □ *Pick the relationship up right where you stopped.* **8.** [with *something*] to receive radio signals; to bring something into view. □ *I can hardly pick up a signal.* □ *We can pick up a pretty good television picture where we live.* □ *I can just pick it up with a powerful telescope.* **9.** [with *something*] to find a trail or route. □ *The dogs finally picked up the scent.* □ *You should pick up the M4 in a few miles.* ALSO: **pick up 1.** to tidy up. □ *I'm not going to pick up after you.* □ *Children always expect mothers to pick up for them.* **2.** to get busier; to become more lively. (Informal.) □ *Things usually pick up in the restaurant about eight o'clock.* □ *Trade in the bar doesn't pick up until ten o'clock.*

pick something over AND **pick over something** to sort through something; to rummage through something. □ *The shoppers quickly picked over the sale goods.* □ *They picked all the records over.*

pick up See under *pick someone or something up.*

pie in the sky a supposed future reward which one is not likely to get. (From a quotation: "You'll get pie in the sky when you die" from a poem by U.S. radical labour organizer, Joe Hill.) □ *The firm have promised him a large reward,*

but I think it's just pie in the sky. □ *Don't hold out for a big reward, you know—pie in the sky.*

piece of cake something very easy. (Informal.) □ *No, it won't be any trouble. It's a piece of cake.* □ *Climbing this is easy! Look here—a piece of cake.*

piece of the action a share in a scheme or project; a degree of involvement. (Slang.) □ *If you chaps are going to bet on the soccer game, I want a piece of the action, too.* □ *My brother wants in on the building project. Give him a piece of the action.*

piece something together AND **piece together something** to assemble something from pieces, parts, or bits. □ *The police pieced together a profile of the criminal with difficulty.* □ *We pieced the puzzle together in about an hour.*

pig(gy)-in-the-middle a person who is in a position between two opposing groups. □ *Jack and Tom share a secretary who is always pig-in-the-middle because they are always disagreeing with each other.* □ *Fred's mother is piggy-in-the-middle when Fred and his father start to argue. She tries to please both of them.*

pigs might fly a saying indicating that something is extremely unlikely to happen. □ *Pam might marry Tom, but there again, pigs might fly.* □ *Do you really believe that Jack will lend us his car? Yes, and pigs might fly.*

pile in(to something) to climb in or get in roughly. (Informal.) □ *Okay, children, pile in!* □ *The children piled into the car and slammed the door.*

pile on something See *pile something on (someone or something).*

pile out (of something) to get out of something roughly. (Informal.) □ *Okay, children, pile out!* □ *The car door burst open, and the children piled out.*

pile something on (someone or something) AND **pile on something** to put a lot of something on someone or something; to provide a lot of something for someone or something. (Informal.) □ *The teacher really piled the homework on us this week.* □ *Bill piled a lot of mashed potatoes on his plate.* □ *He really piled on the potatoes.*

pile up to accumulate; to grow into a pile. □ *My work is piling up. I have to work faster and harder.* □ *The newspapers are piling up. It's time to get rid of them.* ALSO: **pile-up** a car crash, usually one involving several vehicles. (Informal.) □ *There was a bad pile-up on the motorway in the fog.* □ *Several cars and a lorry were involved in the pile-up.*

pin one's faith on someone or something to put one's hope, trust, or faith in someone or something. □ *I'm pinning my faith on your efforts.* □ *Don't pin your faith on Tom. He's not dependable.*

pin someone or something down (on something) AND **pin down someone or something (on something)** 1. to hold someone or something down on something. □ *Bob pinned down Tom on the judo mat.* □ *We pinned the calf down on the ground so it couldn't get away.* 2. [with *someone*] to force someone to explain or clarify something. (Informal.) □ *Try to pin her down on what she expects us to do.* □ *Please find out exactly how much it costs. Pin them down on the price.*

pin someone's ears back to scold someone severely; to beat someone. (Informal.) □ *Tom pinned my ears back because I insulted him.* □ *I got very angry at John and wanted to pin his ears back, but I didn't.*

pin something on someone to place the blame for something on someone. (Slang.) □ *I didn't take the money. Don't try to pin it on me. I wasn't even there.* □ *The police managed to pin the crime on Bob although he had an alibi.*

pinch and scrape to live on very little money, sometimes in order to save money. □ *Bob has to pinch and scrape all the time because of his low wages.* □ *Students have to pinch and scrape in order to buy books.*

pins and needles a tingling feeling in some part of one's body. □ *I've got pins and needles in my legs.* □ *Mary gets pins and needles if she crosses her arms for long.*

pipe down to be quiet; to get quiet. (Informal.) □ *Okay, you lot, pipe down!* □ *I've heard enough out of you. Pipe down!*

pipe-dream a wish or an idea which is impossible to achieve or carry out. (From the dreams or visions induced by the smoking of an opium pipe.) □ *Going to the West Indies is a pipe-dream. We'll never have enough money.* □ *Your hopes of winning a lot of money are just a silly pipe-dream.*

pipe up (with something) to speak up; to say something, especially with a high-pitched voice. □ *Billy piped up with a silly remark.* □ *"I saw you," the child piped up.*

pipped at the post beaten in the final stages of a race or competition; defeated in some activity at the last minute. (Informal. From horse-racing.) □ *Tom led the race for most of the time, but he was pipped at the post by his rival.* □ *Jane nearly bought that house, but she was pipped at the post by the present owner.*

pit someone or something against someone or something to set someone or something in opposition to someone or something. □ *The rules of the tournament pit their team against ours.* □ *John pitted Mary against Sally in the tennis match.* □ *In the illegal dog fight, large dogs were pitted against small ones.*

pitch in (and help) to get busy and help (with something). (Informal.) □ *Pick up a paintbrush and pitch in and help.* □ *Why don't some of you pitch in? We need all the help we can get.*

place the blame on someone or something See *put the blame on someone or something.*

plain sailing progress made without any difficulty; an easy situation. □ *Once you've passed that exam, it will be all plain sailing.* □ *Working there was not all plain sailing. The boss had a very hot temper.*

plan on something to make arrangements for something; to anticipate something. □ *I didn't plan on so much trouble.* □ *I'm planning on inviting four people for dinner.*

play about (with someone or something) See *play around (with someone or something)*.

play along with someone or something to agree to co-operate or conspire with someone or someone's plan; to pretend to agree to co-operate or conspire with someone or someone's plan. □ *I refused to play along with the treasurer when he outlined his plan.* □ *It might be wise to play along with the kidnappers, at least for a little while.* □ *I'll play along with your scheme until the others get here, but I don't like it.*

play around (with someone or something) AND **play about (with someone or something)** to engage in some idle or amusing activity with someone or something. □ *Please don't play around with that vase. You'll break it.* □ *Don't play about with the parrot. It'll bite you.* □ *Bill and I were just playing around when we heard the sound of breaking glass.*

play ball (with someone) to co-operate with someone. (Slang.) □ *Look, friend, if you play ball with me, everything will work out all right.* □ *We offered him a really good deal, but he won't play ball.*

play both ends (against the middle) [for one] to scheme in a way that pits two sides against each other (for one's own gain). (Informal.) □ *I told my brother that Mary doesn't like him. Then I told Mary that my brother doesn't like her. They broke up, so now I can have the car this week-end. I succeeded in playing both ends against the middle.* □ *If you try to play both ends against the middle,* you're likely to get in trouble with both sides.

play by ear See *play something by ear*.

play cat and mouse (with someone) to capture and release someone over and over; to treat a person in one's control in such a way that the person does not know what is going to happen next. □ *The police played cat and mouse with the suspect until they had sufficient evidence to make an arrest.* □ *Tom has been playing cat and mouse with Ann. Finally she got tired of it and broke up with him.*

play fair to do something by the rules or in a fair and just manner. □ *John won't do business with Bill any more because Bill doesn't play fair.* □ *You moved the golf ball with your foot! That's not playing fair!*

play fast and loose (with someone or something) to act carelessly, thoughtlessly, and irresponsibly (Informal.) □ *I'm tired of your playing fast and loose with me. Leave me alone.* □ *Bob played fast and loose with Sally's affections.*

play footsie (with someone) to attract someone's attention by touching feet under the table; to flirt with someone. (Slang.) □ *Bill was trying to play footsie with Sally at the dinner-table. The hostess was appalled.* □ *He shouldn't play footsie with someone else's wife.*

play gooseberry to be with two lovers who wish to be alone. (Informal.) □ *I'm not going to the cinema with Tom and Jean. I hate playing gooseberry.* □ *Come on! Let's go home! Bob and Mary don't want us playing gooseberry.*

play hard to get to be coy and excessively shy; to make it difficult for someone to talk to one or be friendly. (Usually refers to someone of the opposite sex.) □ *Why can't we go out? Why do you play hard to get?* □ *Sally annoys all the boys because she plays hard to get.*

play havoc (with someone or something) to cause a lot of damage to something; to ruin something. (*Play* can be replaced with *create*.) □ *The road-works played havoc with the traffic.* □ *A runaway horse created havoc in the high street.*

play hookey not to go to school or to some important meeting. (Slang.) □ *Why aren't you in school? Are you playing hookey?* □ *I don't have time for the sales meeting today, so I think I'll just play hookey.*

play into someone's hands to do exactly what an opponent wants one to do without one realizing it; to assist one in one's scheming without realizing it. (From card-games in which one's method of playing benefits another player.) □ *John is doing exactly what I hoped he would. He's playing into my hands.* □ *John played into my hands by taking the coins he found in my desk. I caught him and had him arrested.*

play it cool to act calm and unconcerned. (Slang.) □ *No one will suspect anything if you play it cool.* □ *Don't get angry, Bob. Play it cool.*

play it safe not to take risks; to act in a safe manner. □ *You should play it safe and take your umbrella.* □ *If you have a cold or the flu, play it safe and go to bed.*

play on something to make use of something for one's own ends; to exploit something; to manage something for a desired effect. (The *on* can be replaced by *upon*.) □ *The shop assistant played on my sense of responsibility in trying to get me to buy the book.* □ *See if you can get her to confess by playing on her sense of guilt.*

play one's cards close to one's chest to work or negotiate in a careful and private manner. □ *It's hard to figure out what John is up to because he plays his cards close to his chest.* □ *Don't let them know what you're up to. Play your cards close to your chest.*

play one's cards right to work or negotiate correctly and skilfully. (Informal.) □ *If you play your cards right, you can get whatever you want.* □ *She didn't play her cards right, so she didn't get promotion.*

play one's trump card to use one's most powerful or effective strategy or device. □ *I won't play my trump card until I have tried everything else.* □ *I thought that the whole situation was hopeless until Mary played her trump card and told us her uncle would lend us the money.*

play politics to allow politics to dominate in matters where principles should prevail. □ *Look, I came here to discuss this trial, not play politics.* □ *They're not making reasonable decisions. They're playing politics.*

play possum to pretend to be inactive, unobserved, asleep, or dead. (Informal. The *possum* is an *opossum*.) □ *I knew that Bob wasn't asleep. He was just playing possum.* □ *I can't tell if this animal is dead or just playing possum.*

play second fiddle (to someone) to be in a subordinate position to someone. □ *I'm tired of playing second fiddle to John.* □ *I'm better trained than he is, and I have more experience. I shouldn't play second fiddle.*

play someone off against someone else to scheme in a manner that sets two people against one another. □ *Bill wanted to beat me up and so did Bob. I did some fast talking, and they ended up fighting with each other. I really played Bill off against Bob.* □ *Jane's parents are separated, and she plays them off against each other.*

play someone or something down AND **play down someone or something** to try to lessen the effect or importance of someone or something. □ *They tried to play down her part in the crime.* □ *John is a famous actor, but the director tried to play him down as just another member of the cast.*

play someone or something up AND **play up someone or something** to make someone or something seem to be more important; to stress or emphasize the importance of someone or something. □

John really played up his own part in the rescue. □ *Try to play up the good qualities of our product.*

play someone up See under *play up.*

play something by ear **1.** to be able to play a piece of music after just listening to it a few times, without looking at the notes. □ *I can play* Stardust *by ear.* □ *Some people can play Chopin's music by ear.* **2.** to deal with a situation at the required time without planning in advance. (Informal.) □ *You'll have to play the situation by ear.* □ *If you don't know how they'll react, play it by ear.*

play (the) devil's advocate to put forward arguments against or objections to a proposition—which one may actually agree with—purely to test the validity of the proposition. (The devil's advocate was given the role of opposing the canonization of a saint in the medieval Church in order to prove that the grounds for canonization were sound.) □ *I agree with your plan. I'm just playing the devil's advocate so you'll know what the opposition will say.* □ *Mary offered to play devil's advocate and argue against our case so that we would find out any flaws in it.*

play the field to date many different people rather than going steady with just one. (Informal. See *go steady (with someone).*) □ *Tom wanted to play the field, so he said goodbye to Ann.* □ *He said he wanted to play the field rather than get married while he was still young.*

play the fool to act in a silly manner in order to amuse other people. □ *The teacher told Tom to stop playing the fool and sit down.* □ *Fred likes playing the fool, but we didn't find him funny last night.*

play the game to behave or act in a fair and honest way. □ *You shouldn't try to disturb your opponent's concentration. That's not playing the game.* □ *Listening to other people's phone calls is certainly not playing the game.*

play the market to invest in the shares market. (As if it were a game or as if it were gambling.) □ *Would you rather put your money in the bank or play the market?* □ *I've learned my lesson playing the market. I lost a fortune.*

play to the gallery to perform in a manner that will get the strong approval of the audience; to perform in a manner that will get the approval of the lower elements in the audience. □ *John is a competent actor, but he has a tendency to play to the gallery.* □ *When he made the rude remark, he was just playing to the gallery. He wanted others to find him amusing.*

play tricks (on someone) to trick or confuse someone. □ *I thought I saw a camel over there. I think that my eyes are playing tricks on me.* □ *Please don't play tricks on your little brother. It makes him cry.*

play up to cause trouble; to be a nuisance. (Informal.) □ *My leg is playing up. It's really sore.* □ *Her arthritis always plays up in this cold, damp weather.* ALSO: **play someone up** to annoy someone. □ *That child played me up. He was naughty all day.* □ *The pupils played the substitute teacher up the entire day.*

play up to someone to try to gain someone's favour; to flatter someone or to pretend to admire someone in order to gain favour. □ *Bill is always playing up to the teacher.* □ *Ann played up to Bill as if she wanted him to marry her.*

play with fire to do something very risky or dangerous. □ *The teacher was playing with fire by threatening a pupil.* □ *I wouldn't talk to Bob that way if I were you—unless you like playing with fire.*

played out (Informal.) **1.** exhausted. □ *I'm played out after looking after the baby.* □ *Bob's always played out after he's been gardening.* **2.** no longer of interest or influence. □ *Jane's political ideas are all played out.* □ *That particular religious sect is played out now.*

please oneself to do what one wishes. (Informal.) □ *We don't mind whether you stay or not. Please yourself!* □ *The boss preferred me to work late, but he told me to please myself.*

plough into someone or something to crash or push into someone or something. □ *The car ploughed into the ditch.* □ *The lorry ploughed into the crowd.*

pluck up (one's) courage to increase one's courage a bit; to become brave enough to do something. □ *Come on, Ann, make the dive. Pluck up your courage and do it.* □ *Fred plucked up courage and asked Jean for a date.*

plug away (at something) AND **peg away (at something)** to keep trying something; to keep working at something. (Informal.) □ *John kept pegging away at learning the trumpet until he became pretty good at it.* □ *I'm not very good at tennis, but I keep plugging away.* □ *If you keep plugging away at your biology, you can't help but succeed.*

plug something in AND **plug in something** to place the plug of an appliance into the electrical supply. (*In* can be replaced with *into*.) □ *Please plug in this lamp.* □ *This television set won't work unless you plug it in!*

plug something up AND **plug up something** to stop or fill up a hole, crack, or gap. □ *You have to plug up the cracks to keep out the cold.* □ *Take out the nail and plug the hole up with something.*

poetic justice the appropriate but chance receiving of rewards or punishments by those deserving them. □ *It was poetic justice that Jane won the race after Mary tried to get her banned.* □ *The car robbers stole a car with no petrol. That's poetic justice.*

point someone or something out AND **point out someone or something** to select or indicate someone or something (from a group). □ *She pointed out the boy who took her purse.* □ *Everyone pointed the error out.*

point the finger at someone to blame someone; to identify someone as the guilty person. □ *Don't point the finger at me! I didn't take the money.* □ *The manager refused to point the finger at anyone in particular and said the whole staff were sometimes guilty of being late.*

point up something to emphasize something; to demonstrate a fact. □ *This kind of incident points up the flaws in your system.* □ *I'd like to point up the problems by telling of my own experiences.*

poke about See the following entry.

poke around AND **poke about** to look or search around. (Informal.) □ *I've been poking around in the library looking for some statistics.* □ *I don't mind if you look in my drawer for a paperclip, but please don't poke about.*

poke fun (at someone or something) to make fun of someone; to ridicule someone. (Informal.) □ *Stop poking fun at me! It's not nice.* □ *Bob is always poking fun.*

poke one's nose in(to something) AND **stick one's nose in(to something)** to interfere with something; to be nosy about something. (Informal.) □ *I wish you'd stop poking your nose into my business.* □ *She was too upset for me to stick my nose in and ask what was wrong.* □ *Will you please stop sticking your nose into my business!*

polish something off AND **polish off something** to finish something off. (Informal.) □ *Bob polished off the rest of the pie.* □ *There is just a little bit of work left. It won't take any time to polish it off.*

pop off (Informal.) **1.** to go away. □ *I'll pop off now and come back later.* □ *Tell the maid she can pop off now.* **2.** to die. □ *The old man popped off in his sleep.* □ *The old lady is very ill. She could pop off at any time.*

pop the question to ask someone to marry you. (Informal.) □ *I was surprised when he popped the question.* □

I've been waiting for years for someone to pop the question.

pop up to arise suddenly; to appear without warning. (Informal.) □ *New problems keep popping up all the time.* □ *Billy popped up out of nowhere and scared his mother.*

possessed by something under the control of something; obsessed with something. □ *She acted as if she were possessed by evil spirits.* □ *He was possessed by a powerful sense of guilt.*

possessed of something having something. □ *Bill was possessed of an enormous sense of self-worth.* □ *The Smiths were possessed of a great deal of fine farming land.*

Possession is nine points of the law. a saying meaning that in any argument over the ownership or control of something, the person who has it at the time is in the strongest position. □ *Jim says his grandmother meant him to have her cottage when she died, but his brother Jack lives in it and possession is nine points of the law.* □ *The football team want to use the hut in the playing-field on a Saturday. However, the hockey club already uses it then, and possession is nine points of the law.*

pot calling the kettle black [the instance of] someone with a fault accusing someone else of having the same fault. □ *Ann is always late, but she was rude enough to tell everyone when I was late. Now that's the pot calling the kettle black!* □ *You're calling me thoughtless? That's really a case of the pot calling the kettle black.*

pound a beat to walk a route. (Usually said of a police officer.) □ *The constable pounded the same beat for years and years.* □ *Pounding a beat will wreck your feet.*

pound for pound considering the amount of money involved; considering the cost. (Often seen in advertising.) □ *Pound for pound, you cannot buy a better car.* □ *Pound for pound, this*

detergent washes cleaner and brighter than any other product on the market.

pound something out AND **pound out something** (Informal.) **1.** to play something loudly on the piano or organ. (Compare to *belt something out.*) □ *Listen to her pound out that song.* □ *Don't pound the music out! Just play it!* **2.** to type something on a typewriter. □ *It'll take just a few hours to pound out this letter.* □ *The journalist pounded out a new article every day.*

pound the streets to walk through the streets looking for a job. (Informal.) □ *I spent two months pounding the streets after the factory I worked for closed.* □ *Look, Bob. You'd better get on with your work unless you want to be out pounding the streets.*

pour cold water on something AND **throw cold water on something** to discourage doing something; to reduce enthusiasm for something. □ *When my father said I couldn't have the car, he poured cold water on my plans.* □ *John threw cold water on the whole project and refused to participate.*

pour it on thick See *lay it on thick.*

pour money down the drain to waste money; to throw money away. □ *What a waste! You're just pouring money down the drain.* □ *Don't buy any more of that low-quality material. That's just pouring money down the drain.*

pour oil on troubled waters to calm things down. (If oil is poured onto rough seas during a storm, the water will become more calm.) □ *That was a good thing to say to John. It helped pour oil on troubled waters. Now he looks happy.* □ *Bob is the kind of person who always pours oil on troubled waters.*

pour one's heart out (to someone) AND **pour out one's heart (to someone)** to tell all one's hopes, fears, and feelings to someone. □ *She was so upset. She poured her heart out to Sally.* □ *She sat there for over an hour talking—pouring out her heart.*

power behind the throne the person who controls the person who is apparently in charge. □ *Mr. Smith appears to run the shop, but his brother is the power behind the throne.* □ *They say that the mayor's husband is the power behind the throne.*

powers that be the people who are in authority. □ *The powers that be have decided to send back the immigrants.* □ *I have applied for a licence and the powers that be are considering my application.*

Practice makes perfect. a saying meaning that if one practices doing something often enough, one will eventually be able to do it very well. □ *You should play tennis every day even though you're not very good. Practice makes perfect, you'll see.* □ *Do your ballet exercises regularly if you want to be a ballerina. Practice makes perfect.*

practise what you preach to do what you advise other people to do. □ *If you'd practise what you preach, you'd be better off.* □ *You give good advice. Why not practise what you preach?*

praise someone or something to the skies to give someone much praise. □ *He wasn't very good, but his friends praised him to the skies.* □ *They liked your pie. Everyone praised it to the skies.*

preach to the converted to praise or recommend something to someone who is already in favour of it. □ *Mary was preaching to the converted when she tried to persuade Jean to become a feminist. She's been one for years.* □ *Bob found himself preaching to the converted when he was telling Jane the advantages of living in the country. She hates city life.*

precious few AND **precious little** very few; very little. (Informal.) □ *We get precious few tourists here in the winter.* □ *There's precious little food in the house and we've no money.*

precious little See the previous entry.

presence of mind calmness and the ability to act sensibly in an emergency or difficult situation. □ *Jane had the presence of mind to phone the police when the child disappeared.* □ *The child had the presence of mind to take a note of the car's number-plate.*

press-gang someone into doing something to force someone into doing something. (From the noun *press-gang*, a group of sailors employed to seize men and force them to join the navy.) □ *Aunt Jane press-ganged me into helping with the church fête.* □ *The boss press-ganged us all into working late.*

press one's luck See *push one's luck.*

press the panic button See *push the panic button.*

prevail (up)on someone to ask or beg someone (for a favour). □ *Can I prevail upon you to give me some help?* □ *Perhaps you could prevail on my brother for a loan.*

prey (up)on someone or something 1. [with *someone*] to make a practice of cheating or swindling someone. □ *The crooks preyed upon widows.* □ *Watch out for swindlers who prey on elderly people.* **2.** [with *something*] to exploit someone's fears or weakness. □ *They were unable to prey on our fears.* □ *Please don't prey upon the fact that they aren't well educated.* **3.** [with *something*] to use something as food; to live on something. (Said of animals.) □ *Cats prey on mice.* □ *Hawks prey upon small birds.*

prick up one's ears to listen more closely. □ *At the sound of my voice, my dog pricked up her ears.* □ *I pricked up my ears when I heard my name mentioned.*

Pride goes before a fall. a saying meaning that someone who behaves in an arrogant or vain way is likely to suffer misfortune. □ *Bert was so busy admiring his reflection in a shop-window that he stepped in a puddle. Pride goes before a fall.* □ *Jean was boasting about how well she thought she'd done in her* *exams, but she failed. You know what they say. Pride goes before a fall.*

pride of place the best or most important place or space. □ *Jack's parents gave pride of place in their living-room to his sports trophy.* □ *The art gallery promised to give pride of place to Mary's painting of the harbour.*

pride oneself on something to take special pride in something. □ *Ann prides herself on her apple pies.* □ *John prides himself on his ability to make people feel at ease.*

prime mover the force that sets something going; someone or something that starts something off. □ *The assistant manager was the prime mover in getting the manager sacked.* □ *Discontent with his job was the prime mover in John's deciding to emigrate.*

promise the moon (to someone) AND **promise someone the moon** to make extravagant promises to someone. □ *Bill will promise you the moon, but he won't live up to his promises.* □ *My employer promised the moon, but only paid the lowest possible wages.*

psych someone out AND **psych out someone** (Slang. Pronounced as if it were spelled *sike*.) **1.** to get the measure of someone psychologically. □ *I think I've psyched out my opponent so I can beat him.* □ *Don't try to psych me out. Just be my friend.* **2.** to confuse someone; to intimidate someone; to cause someone to go crazy. □ *All that bright light psyched me out. I couldn't think straight.* □ *They psyched out the enemy, causing them to jump into the river.*

psych someone up AND **psych up someone** to cause someone to be enthusiastic about doing something; to prepare someone for a contest, ordeal, etc. (Slang.) □ *The coach psyched up the team before the game.* □ *I need someone to psych me up before I go on stage.* ALSO: **psyched up** excited and enthusiastic. (Slang.) □ *I can play a great tennis game if I'm psyched up.*

psyched up See under *psych someone up*.

pull a face AND **make a face** to twist one's face into a strange expression in order to show one's dislike, ridicule, etc., or in order to make someone laugh. (Also plural: *pull faces, make faces*.) □ *The comedian pulled faces in order to amuse the children.* □ *Jane made a face when she was asked to work late.*

pull a fast one to succeed in an act of deception. (Informal.) □ *She was pulling a fast one when she said she had a headache and got to go home.* □ *Don't try to pull a fast one with me! I know what you're doing.*

pull a stunt to stage a display or perform an unusual deed in order to attract attention. (Note the variation in the examples.) □ *We pulled a stunt on the teacher.* □ *The children were told not to pull a stunt like that again after they had climbed the fountain.* □ *"Don't pull that stunt again," the warders told the prisoners who had climbed onto the roof.*

pull ahead (of someone or something) to pass someone or something. □ *The runner pulled ahead of the rest of the field.* □ *Our car pulled ahead of theirs.*

pull in (somewhere) to drive into a place and stop. □ *Please pull in at this service station.* □ *Okay, I'll pull in and get some petrol.*

pull one's punches **1.** [for a boxer] to strike with light blows to enable the other boxer to win. □ *Bill has been barred from the boxing-ring for pulling his punches.* □ *"I never pulled my punches in my life!" cried Tom.* **2.** to hold back in one's criticism or attack. (Usually in the negative. The *one's* can be replaced with *any*.) □ *I didn't pull any punches. I told her just what I thought of her.* □ *The teacher doesn't pull any punches when it comes to discipline.*

pull one's socks up to make an effort to improve one's behaviour or performance. □ *If you don't want to be expelled from school, you'll have to pull your socks up.* □ *The firm will have to pull its socks up in order to stay in business.*

pull one's weight See *carry one's (own) weight.*

pull oneself together to become calm or steady; to become emotionally stabilized; to *regain one's composure.* □ *Now, calm down. Pull yourself together.* □ *I'll be all right as soon as I can pull myself together. I just can't stop weeping.*

pull oneself up by one's bootstraps to achieve (something) through one's own efforts. (Informal.) □ *He's wealthy now, but he pulled himself up by his bootstraps.* □ *The orphan pulled himself up by his bootstraps to become a doctor.*

pull out all the stops to use all one's energy and effort in order to achieve something. (From the stops of a pipe-organ. The more that are pulled out, the louder it gets.) □ *You'll have to pull out all the stops if you're going to pass the exam.* □ *The doctors will pull out all the stops to save the child's life.*

pull out (of something) to leave or abandon a place or situation. □ *The soldiers pulled out of their dangerous position and marched on.* □ *Our team pulled out of the competition.*

pull over to drive to the side of the road and stop. □ *Okay, pull over right here. I'll get out here.* □ *I'll pull over up ahead where there is more room.*

pull rank (on someone) to assert one's rank, authority, or position over someone when making a request or giving an order. □ *Don't pull rank on me! I don't have to do what you say!* □ *When she couldn't get her way politely, she pulled rank and really got some action.*

pull someone or something down AND **pull down someone or something 1.** [with *someone*] to degrade someone; to draw someone down socially; to humiliate someone. □ *I'm afraid that your friends are pulling you down. Your manners used to be much better.* □ *Her ungrammatical speech is pulling her down.* **2.** [with *something*] to demolish something; to raze something. □ *They are going to pull down the old building today.* □ *Why do they want to pull it down? Why not remodel it?* **3.** [with *something*] to lower or reduce the amount of something. □ *Let's see if we can pull down your temperature.* □ *The low exam scores pulled down the standard generally.*

pull someone through (something) to help someone survive something. (See also *pull through.*) □ *With the help of the doctor, we pulled her through her illness.* □ *With lots of encouragement, we pulled John through.*

pull someone's leg to kid, fool, or trick someone. (Informal.) □ *You don't mean that. You're just pulling my leg.* □ *Don't believe him. He's just pulling your leg.*

pull someone's or something's teeth to reduce the power of someone or something. (Informal.) □ *The mayor tried to pull the teeth of the new law.* □ *The new government pulled the teeth of the trade unions.*

pull something off AND **pull off something** to manage to make something happen. (Informal.) □ *Do you think you can pull this project off?* □ *Yes, I can pull it off.*

pull something on someone to surprise someone with a weapon. □ *He pulled a knife on me!* □ *The robber pulled a gun on the bank teller.*

pull something out of a hat AND **pull something out of thin air** to produce something as if by magic. □ *This is a serious problem, and we just can't pull a solution out of a hat.* □ *I'm sorry, but I don't have a pen. What do you want me to do, pull one out of thin air?*

pull something out of thin air See the previous entry.

pull strings to use influence (with someone to get something done or gain an advantage). □ *I can borrow the hall easily by pulling strings.* □ *Is it possible to get anything done around here without pulling strings?*

pull the plug (on someone or something) to cause someone or something to end; to reduce the power or effectiveness of someone or something. (Slang.) □ *Jane pulled the plug on the whole project.* □ *The council were doing a fine job until the treasurer pulled the plug because there was no more money.*

pull the rug out from under someone('s feet) to do something suddenly which leaves someone in a weak position; to make someone ineffective. □ *The news that his wife had left him pulled the rug out from under him.* □ *The boss certainly pulled the rug out from under Bob's feet when he lowered his salary.*

pull the wool over someone's eyes to deceive someone. □ *You can't pull the wool over my eyes. I know what's going on.* □ *Don't try to pull the wool over her eyes. She's too smart.*

pull through to get better; to recover from a serious illness or other problem. (Informal.) □ *She's very ill, but I think she'll pull through.* □ *Oh, I hope she pulls through.*

pull up (somewhere) to stop somewhere; to come to rest somewhere. □ *The car pulled up at the garage.* □ *My hat blew away just as the bus pulled up.*

push off to go away. (Informal.) □ *We told the children to push off.* □ *Push off! We don't want you here.*

push one's luck AND **press one's luck** to expect continued good fortune; to expect to continue to escape bad luck. (Informal.) □ *You're okay so far, but don't push your luck.* □ *Bob pressed his luck once too often when he tried to flirt with the new secretary. She slapped him.*

push someone to the wall AND **drive someone to the wall** to force someone into a position of helplessness or weakness; to put someone in a defensive position; to ruin someone. (See also *have one's back to the wall*.) □ *My creditors have ruined my business. They pushed me to the wall.* □ *Lack of money pushed us to the wall eventually.* □ *The government are driving the unemployed to the wall with low social security benefits.* □ *The company is being driven to the wall by high interest rates.*

push the panic button AND **press the panic button** to panic; to become anxious or hysterical. (Informal.) □ *I do all right in exams as long as I don't push the panic button.* □ *Whatever you do in a traffic accident, don't press the panic button.*

pushing up the daisies dead. (Slang.) □ *If you don't drive safely, you'll be pushing up the daisies.* □ *We'll all be pushing up the daisies in the long run.*

put a brave face on it to try to appear happy or satisfied when faced with misfortune or danger. □ *We've lost all our money, but we must put a brave face on it for the sake of the children.* □ *Jim's lost his job and is worried, but he's putting a brave face on it.*

put a stop to something AND **put an end to something** to bring something to an end. □ *I want you to put a stop to all this bad behaviour.* □ *Please put an end to this conversation at once.*

put all one's eggs in one basket to risk everything at once; to depend entirely on one plan, venture, etc. (Often negative.) □ *Don't put all your eggs in one basket. You shouldn't invest all your money in one business.* □ *John only applied to the one college he wanted to go to. He put all his eggs in one basket.*

put an end to something See *put a stop to something*.

put ideas into someone's head to suggest something—usually something that is bad or unfortunate for someone—to someone (who would not have thought of it otherwise). □ *Jack can't afford a holiday abroad. Please don't put ideas into his head.* □ *Bob would get along* all right if his chums didn't put ideas into his head.

put in a good word for someone to say something to someone in support of someone. ☐ *I hope you get the job. I'll put in a good word for you.* ☐ *You might get the TV part if Mike puts in a good word for you.*

put in an appearance to appear somewhere, sometimes for just a little while. (Compare to *make an appearance.*) ☐ *I couldn't stay for the whole party, so I just put in an appearance and left.* ☐ *Even if you can't stay for the whole thing, at least put in an appearance.*

put in one's two halfpennies (worth) AND **put one's two halfpennies in** to add one's comments (to something). (Informal.) ☐ *Can I put in my two halfpennies worth?* ☐ *Sure, go ahead—put your two halfpennies in.*

put it on to pretend; to act as if something were true. (Informal.) ☐ *Ann wasn't really angry. She was just putting it on.* ☐ *I can't believe she was just putting it on. She really looked mad.*

put off by someone or something See *put someone or something off.*

put on airs to act superior. (Informal.) ☐ *Stop putting on airs. You're just human like the rest of us.* ☐ *Ann is always putting on airs. You'd think she was a queen.*

put on an act to pretend that one is something other than what one is; to pretend. (See also *let on.*) ☐ *Be yourself, Ann. Stop putting on an act.* ☐ *You don't have to put on an act. We accept you the way you are.* ☐ *We know you didn't break your leg. You're putting on an act.*

put on one's thinking-cap to start thinking in a serious manner. ☐ *Let's put on our thinking-caps and decide where to go on holiday.* ☐ *It's time to put on our thinking-caps, children, and choose a name for the dog.*

put on weight to gain weight; to grow fatter. ☐ *I have to go on a diet because*

I've been putting on a little weight lately. ☐ *The doctor says I need to put on some weight.*

put one across someone to deceive or trick someone. (Informal.) ☐ *He tried to put one across the old lady by pretending to be her long-lost nephew.* ☐ *Meg thought she'd put one across her parents by claiming to spend the night at her friend's house.*

put one in one's place to rebuke someone; to remind one of one's (lower) rank or station. ☐ *My employer put me in my place for criticizing her.* ☐ *Lady Jane put the butler in his place when he grew too familiar.*

put one over (on someone) to manage to trick or deceive someone. (Informal.) ☐ *They really put one over on me.* ☐ *I didn't realize that Joan was putting one over when she asked me to look after the children.*

put one through one's paces to make one demonstrate what one can do; to test someone's abilities or capacity. (See also *put something through its paces.*) ☐ *The teacher put the children through their paces before the exam.* ☐ *I tried out for a part in the play, and the director really put me through my paces.*

put one's back into something (Informal.) 1. to apply great physical effort to lift or move something. ☐ *All right, you! Put your backs into moving this piano.* ☐ *You can lift it if you put your back into it.* 2. to apply a lot of mental or creative effort to doing something. ☐ *If we put our backs into it, we can bake twelve dozen biscuits today.* ☐ *The artist put his back into finishing the picture on time.*

put one's best foot forward to prepare to do one's best; to make the best attempt possible to make a good impression. ☐ *When you apply for a position, you should always put your best foot forward.* ☐ *Since you failed last time, you must put your best foot forward now.*

put one's cards on the table AND **lay one's cards on the table** to reveal everything;

to be open and honest with someone. □ *Come on, John, lay your cards on the table. Tell me what you really think.* □ *Why don't we both put our cards on the table and make our intentions clear?*

put one's finger on something to identify something. □ *Ann put her finger on the cause of the problem.* □ *Mary put her finger on the reason for Fred's unhappiness.*

put one's foot down (about something) to be adamant about something. □ *Ann put her foot down about what kind of car she wanted.* □ *She doesn't put her foot down very often, but when she does, she really means it.*

put one's foot in it to say something which one regrets; to say something tactless, insulting, or hurtful. (Informal.) □ *When I told Ann that her hair was more beautiful than I had ever seen it, I really put my foot in it. It was a wig.* □ *I put my foot in it by mistaking John's girlfriend for his wife.*

put one's hand to the plough to begin to do a big and important task; to undertake a major effort. □ *If John would only put his hand to the plough, he could do an excellent job of work.* □ *You'll never accomplish anything if you don't put your hand to the plough.*

put one's hand(s) on something to locate and acquire something. (Compare to *get one's hands on someone or something.*) □ *I wish I could put my hands on a 1954 Morris Minor.* □ *If I could put my hands on that book, I could find the information I need.*

put one's house in order to put one's business or personal affairs into good order. □ *There was some trouble at work and the manager was told to put his house in order.* □ *Every now and then, I have to put my house in order. Then life becomes more manageable.*

put one's oar in AND **put in one's oar; stick one's oar in; stick in one's oar** to interfere by giving unasked-for advice. (Informal.) □ *You don't need to put your oar in. I don't need your advice.*

□ *I'm sorry. I shouldn't have stuck in my oar when you were arguing with your wife.*

put one's shoulder to the wheel to take up a task; to get busy. □ *You won't accomplish anything unless you put your shoulder to the wheel.* □ *I put my shoulder to the wheel and finished the task quickly.*

put oneself in someone else's place See under *in someone else's shoes.*

put out See under *put someone or something out.*

put out (some) feelers to attempt to find out something without being too obvious. □ *I wanted to get a new position, so I put out some feelers.* □ *We'd like to move house and so we've put out feelers to see what's on the market.*

put paid to something to put an end to something; to prevent someone from doing something; to prevent something from happening. (From the practice of bookkeepers of writing "paid" in the account book when a bill has been settled.) □ *Jean's father's objections put paid to John's thoughts of marrying her.* □ *Lack of money put paid to our holiday plans.*

put someone down as something to assume that someone is something. (See also *put someone or something down.*) □ *He was so rude that I put him down as someone to be avoided.* □ *If you act silly all the time, people will put you down as a fool.*

put someone down (for something) to put someone's name on a list of people who volunteer to do something or give an amount of money. □ *Can I put you down for £10?* □ *We're having a picnic, and you're invited. Everyone is bringing something. Can I put you down for potato salad?*

put someone in mind of someone or something to remind someone of someone or something. □ *Mary puts me in mind of her mother when she was that age.* □ *This place puts me in mind of the village where I was brought up.*

put someone in the picture to give someone all the necessary facts about something. (Informal.) □ *They put the police in the picture about how the accident happened.* □ *Would someone put me in the picture about what went on in my absence?*

put someone on a pedestal to respect or admire someone too much; to worship someone. □ *He has put her on a pedestal and thinks she can do no wrong.* □ *Don't put me on a pedestal. I'm only human.*

put someone on the spot to ask someone embarrassing questions; to put someone in an uncomfortable or difficult position. □ *Don't put me on the spot. I can't give you an answer.* □ *We put Bob on the spot and demanded that he do everything he had promised.*

put someone or something across AND **get someone or something across** 1. [with *someone*] to present someone in a certain way or light. □ *I don't want Tom to make the speech. He doesn't put himself across well.* □ *In fact, he puts himself across very badly.* 2. to make a clear explanation of something; to explain oneself clearly. □ *The teacher got the idea across with the help of pictures.* □ *I'm taking a course in public speaking to help put myself across better.*

put someone or something at someone's disposal to make someone or something available to someone; to offer someone or something to someone. □ *I'd be glad to help you if you need me. I put myself at your disposal.* □ *I put my car at my neighbour's disposal.*

put someone or something away AND **put away someone or something** 1. [with *something*] to put something into a safe place; to put something where it belongs. □ *Billy, please put away your toys.* □ *No! I won't put them away.* 2. [with *someone*] to kill someone. (Slang.) □ *The gangster threatened to put me away if I told the police.* □ *They've put away witnesses in the past.* 3. [with *someone*] to imprison someone. (Slang.)

□ *The judge put the robber away for five years.* □ *Instead of receiving a fine, Bob was put away for six months.* 4. [with *someone*] to have someone put into a mental institution. (Informal.) □ *My uncle became irrational, and they put him away.* □ *They put away my aunt the year before.*

put someone or something down AND **put down someone or something** 1. to belittle or degrade someone or something. (Slang.) □ *It's an old car, but that's no reason to put it down.* □ *Please stop putting me down all the time. It hurts my feelings.* 2. [with *something*] to repress or (figuratively) crush something. □ *The army was called to put down the rebellion.* □ *The police used tear-gas to put the riot down.* 3. [with *something*] to write something down. □ *I'll give you the address, and you can put it down in your diary.* □ *I'll put it down in my address book.* 4. [with *something*] to take the life of an animal, such as a pet which is suffering. (This is usually done by a vet.) □ *We had to put our dog down. She was suffering so.* □ *It's very difficult to put one's pet down.*

put someone or something off AND **put off someone or something** 1. [with *someone*] to divert or avoid someone. □ *I don't wish to see Mr. Brown now. Please put him off.* □ *I won't talk to reporters. Tell them something which will put them off.* 2. [with *someone*] to cause someone to dislike one; to upset or distress someone. (Informal.) □ *She always puts me off. She's so rude.* □ *I know I should be friendly with her, but she really puts me off.* 3. [with *something*] to delay something; to postpone something. □ *I had to put off my appointment with the doctor.* □ *It's raining, so we'll have to put the picnic off.*

put someone or something on hold (See also *on hold*.) 1. [with *someone*] to leave someone waiting on a telephone call. □ *Please don't put me on hold. I'll call back later when you aren't so busy.* □ *I'll have to put you on hold while I look up the information.* 2. [with *something*] to postpone something; to stop the progress of something. □ *They put the project on hold until they got enough money to finish it.* □ *Sorry, but we must put your plan on hold.*

put someone or something out AND **put out someone or something 1.** [with *something*] to extinguish something. □ *Put out the fire before you go to bed.* □ *My grandfather told me to put out the light and go to bed.* **2.** [with *someone*] to distress or inconvenience someone. □ *I'd like to have a ride home, but not if it puts you out.* □ *Don't worry. It won't put out anybody.* **3.** [with *something*] to publish something. □ *They are putting the book out next month.* □ *When did you put the article out?* ALSO: **put out** irritated; bothered. □ *John behaved rudely at the party, and the hostess was quite put out.*

put someone or something out of one's mind to forget someone or something; to make an effort to stop thinking about someone or something. □ *Try to put it out of your mind.* □ *I can't seem to put him out of my mind.*

put someone or something out to pasture to retire someone or something. (Informal. Originally said of a horse which was too old to work.) □ *Please don't put me out to pasture. I have lots of good years left.* □ *This car has reached the end of the line. It's time to put it out to pasture.*

put someone or something to bed 1. [with *someone*] to help someone— usually a child—get into a bed. □ *Come on, Billy, it's time for me to put you to bed.* □ *I want Grandpa to put me to bed.* **2.** [with *something*] to complete work on something and send it on to the next step in production, especially in newspapers or other publishing. □ *This edition is finished. Let's put it to bed.* □ *Finish the editing of this book and put it to bed.*

put someone or something to sleep 1. [with *something*] to kill something. (Euphemistic.) □ *We had to put our dog to sleep.* □ *The vet put the cat to sleep, and we buried it in the garden.* **2.** to

cause someone or something to sleep, perhaps through drugs or anesthesia. □ *The doctor put the patient to sleep before the operation.* □ *I put the cat to sleep by stroking its tummy.* **3.** [with *someone*] to bore someone. □ *That dull lecture put me to sleep.* □ *Her long story almost put me to sleep.*

put someone or something up AND **put up someone or something 1.** [with *something*] to raise up something; to put something up (onto something). □ *Please put the window up.* □ *It's time to put the decorations up.* **2.** [with *someone*] to provide lodging for someone. □ *They were able to put up John for the night.* □ *I hope I can find someone to put me up.* **3.** [with *something*] to offer something, such as an idea. □ *Let me put up a different idea.* □ *We need a better idea. Who'll put one up?* **4.** [with *someone*] to nominate someone as a candidate. □ *We're putting up Ann for treasurer.* □ *I think you should put someone else up.* **5.** [with *something*] to build a building, a sign, a fence, a wall, etc. □ *The city put up a fence next to our house.* □ *We'll put a garage up next month.* **6.** [with *something*] to provide the money for something. □ *Who will put up the money for my education?* □ *The government put the money up for the cost of construction.* **7.** [with *something*] to pile one's hair on the top of one's head with hairpins, etc. □ *Girls used to have to put their hair up when they reached a certain age.* □ *I usually wear my hair loose, but I put it up for the dance.* **8.** [with *something*] to make a struggle, a fight, etc. (Usually *put up something,* and not *put something up.*) □ *Did he put up a fight?* □ *No, he only put up a bit of a struggle.*

put someone through the wringer to give someone a difficult or exhausting time. (Informal.) □ *They are really putting me through the wringer at school.* □ *We all put Bob through the wringer over this contract.*

put someone to shame to show someone up; to embarrass someone; to make someone ashamed. □ *Your excellent* *efforts put us all to shame.* □ *I put him to shame by telling everyone about his bad behaviour.*

put someone to the test to test someone; to see what someone can achieve. □ *I think I can jump that far, but no one has ever put me to the test.* □ *I'm going to put you to the test right now!*

put someone up to something to cause someone to do something; to bribe someone to do something; to give someone the idea of doing something. □ *Who put you up to it?* □ *Nobody put me up to it. I thought it up myself.*

put someone wise to someone or something to inform someone about someone or something. (Informal.) □ *I put her wise to the way we do things around here.* □ *I didn't know she was taking money. Mary put me wise to her.*

put someone's nose out of joint to cause someone to feel slighted or insulted. (Informal.) □ *I'm afraid I put his nose out of joint by not inviting him to the picnic.* □ *Jane's nose was put out of joint when her baby brother was born.*

put something aside See under *set something aside.*

put something by AND **lay something by** to reserve a portion of something; to preserve and store something, such as food. □ *I put some money by for a rainy day.* □ *I laid some eggs by for our use tomorrow.*

put something down to something AND **set something down to something** to explain something as being caused by something else. □ *I put his bad humour down to his illness.* □ *We set your failure down to your emotional upset.*

put something forward to state an idea; to advance an idea. (The object is often the word *something*.) □ *Now, I'd like to put something forward.* □ *Toward the end of the meeting, Sally put an idea forward.*

put something in AND **put in something** **1.** to submit something. □ *I put in a* request for a new typewriter. □ *In fact, I put it in some time ago.* **2.** to spend an amount of time (doing something). □ *I put in four months on that project.* □ *You put how much time in?*

put something in order AND **get something in order** to make something orderly. □ *I'll put your papers in order as soon as possible.* □ *I'll be able to get my office in order only when I get free from other things.*

put something in the way (of someone or something) to put a (figurative or literal) barrier in someone's way. □ *I hate to put something in the way of your happiness, but I'm afraid that your husband is gravely ill.* □ *You certainly put something in the way of Mary's success when you took away her grant.*

put something into practice to start using a scheme or plan. □ *I hope we can put your idea into practice soon.* □ *The MP hopes to put the new plan into practice after the next election.*

put something into print to have something printed and published. □ *It's true, but I never believed you'd put it into print.* □ *This is a very interesting story. I can't wait to put it into print.*

put something into words to state or utter a thought; to find a way to express a feeling with words. □ *I can hardly put my gratitude into words.* □ *John has a hard time putting his feelings into words.*

put something on ice AND **put something on the back burner** to delay or postpone something; to put something on hold. (Informal.) □ *I'm afraid that we'll have to put your project on ice for a while.* □ *Just put your idea on ice and keep it there till we get some money.*

put something on paper to write something down. □ *You have a great idea for a novel. Now put it on paper.* □ *I'm sorry, I can't discuss your offer until I see something in writing. Put it on paper, and then we'll talk.*

put something on the back burner See *put something on ice.*

put something over to accomplish something; to put something across. □ *This is a very hard thing to explain to a large audience. I hope I can put it over.* □ *This is a big request for money. I go before the board of directors this afternoon, and I hope I can put it over.*

put something plainly to state something firmly and explicitly. □ *To put it plainly, I want you out of this house immediately.* □ *Thank you. I think you've put your feelings quite plainly.*

put something right AND **set something right** to correct something; to alter a situation to make it more fair. □ *This is a very unfortunate situation. I'll ask the people responsible to set this matter right.* □ *I'm sorry that we overcharged you. We'll try to put it right.*

put something straight AND **set something straight** to clarify something; to straighten something out. □ *He has made such a mess of this report. It'll take hours to put it straight.* □ *I'm sorry I confused you. Let me set it straight.*

put something through its paces to demonstrate how well something operates; to demonstrate all the things something can do. (Compare to *put one through one's paces*.) □ *I was down by the barn watching Sally put her horse through its paces.* □ *This is an excellent police dog. Watch me put it through its paces.*

put something to (good) use to use something. □ *This is a very nice present. I'm certain I'll put it to good use.* □ *I hope you can put these old clothes to use.*

put something to rest AND **lay something to rest** to put an end to a rumour; to finish dealing with something and forget about it. □ *I've heard enough about Ann and her illness. I'd like to put the whole matter to rest.* □ *I'm happy to lay it to rest, but will Jane?*

put something together AND **put together something** 1. to assemble something. □ *I bought a model aeroplane, but I couldn't put it together.* □ *I need some help to put this thing together.* 2. to consider some facts and arrive at a conclusion. (See also *put two and two together*.) □ *When I put together all the facts, I found the answer.* □ *I couldn't put everything together to figure out the answer in time.*

Put that in your pipe and smoke it! See how you like that!; It is final, and you have to live with it! (Informal.) □ *Well, I'm not going to do it, so put that in your pipe and smoke it!* □ *I'm sick of you, and I'm leaving. Put that in your pipe and smoke it!*

put the arm on someone to apply pressure to someone. (Slang.) □ *John's been putting the arm on Mary to get her to go out with him.* □ *John has been putting the arm on Bill to get him to cooperate.*

put the bite on someone to try to get money from someone. (Slang.) □ *Tom put the bite on me for ten pounds.* □ *Bill tried to put the bite on me, but I told him to drop dead.*

put the blame on someone or something AND **lay the blame on someone or something; place the blame on someone or something** to blame someone or something. □ *Don't put the blame on me. I didn't do it.* □ *We'll have to lay the blame for the damage on the storm.* □ *She was trying to place the blame on me.*

put the cart before the horse to have things in the wrong order; to have things confused and mixed up. □ *You're eating your dessert! You've put the cart before the horse.* □ *Slow down and get organized. Don't put the cart before the horse!* □ *John puts the cart before the horse in most of his projects.*

put the cat among the pigeons AND **set the cat among the pigeons** to cause trouble or a disturbance, especially by doing or saying something suddenly or unexpectedly. □ *Meg put the cat among the pigeons by announcing that she was leaving home.* □ *When Frank told of Bob's problems with the police, he really put the cat among the pigeons.*

put the clamps on (someone) AND **put on the clamps** to restrain or restrict someone. (Slang.) □ *Tom's parents put the clamps on him. They decided he was getting out of hand.* □ *They got angry and put the clamps on.*

put the finger on someone to accuse someone; to identify someone as the one who did something. (Slang.) □ *Tom put the finger on John, and John is really mad.* □ *He'd better not put the finger on me. I didn't do it.*

put the heat on (someone) AND **put the screws on (someone); put the screws to someone; put the squeeze on (someone)** to put pressure on someone (to do something); to coerce someone. (Slang.) □ *John wouldn't talk, so the police were putting the heat on him to confess.* □ *When they put the screws on, they can be very unpleasant.* □ *The police know how to put the squeeze on.*

put the kibosh on something to put an end to something; to veto something. (Slang.) □ *The prime minister put the kibosh on the project.* □ *It's a great idea, and I'm sorry that I had to put the kibosh on it.*

put the screws on someone See *put the heat on (someone).*

put the skids on something to cause something to fail. (Slang.) □ *They put the skids on the project when they refused to give us any more money.* □ *That's the end of our great idea! Somebody put the skids on it.*

put the squeeze on someone See *put the heat on someone.*

put two and two together to find the answer to something from the information available; to reach an understanding of something. □ *Well, I put two and two together and came up with an idea of who did it.* □ *Don't worry. John won't figure it out. He can't put two and two together.*

put up a (brave) front to appear to be brave (even if one is not). □ *Mary is frightened, but she's putting up a brave front.* □ *If she weren't putting up a front, I'd be more frightened than I am.*

put-up job something done to give a good—but false—appearance or impression of something in order to deceive or trick someone. (Slang.) □ *The award-winning ceremony was a put-up job to persuade the parents that the school was a good one.* □ *The open day at the prison was a put-up job. Conditions there are terrible and visitors were allowed to enter only certain areas.*

put up with someone or something to endure someone or something. □ *I can't put up with you any more. I'm leaving.* □ *She couldn't put up with the smell, so she opened the window.*

put upon someone to make use of someone to an unreasonable degree; to take advantage of someone for one's own benefit. (Typically passive.) □ *My mother was always put upon by her neighbours. She was too nice to refuse their requests for help.* □ *Jane feels put upon by her husband's parents. They're always coming to stay with her.*

put words into someone's mouth to speak for another person without permission. □ *Stop putting words into my mouth. I can speak for myself.* □ *The solicitor was scolded for putting words into the witness's mouth.*

Put your money where your mouth is! a command to stop talking or boasting and make a bet or to stop talking and provide money for something which one claims to support. □ *I'm tired of your bragging about your skill at betting. Put your money where your mouth is!* □ *You talk about betting, but you don't bet. Put your money where your mouth is!* □ *She keeps talking about the need for more contributions, but she doesn't put her money where her mouth is.*

putty in someone's hands [someone who is] easily influenced by someone else; excessively willing to do what someone else wishes. □ *Bob's wife is putty in his hands. She never thinks for herself.* □ *Jane's putty in her mother's hands. She always does exactly what she says.*

Q

quake in one's shoes See *shake in one's shoes.*

queer someone's pitch to upset or ruin someone's plans or arrangements. (Slang. From *pitch* in the sense of a place where a market stall is set up.) □ *Frank certainly queered John's pitch when he told his mother about John's debts.* □ *Alice tried to queer Jack's pitch by telling Mary that he was married, but Mary knew already.*

queue up to get into a queue; to form a queue. □ *Will you all please queue up?* □ *It's time to go from here to the theatre. Please queue up.*

quick on the draw (Informal.) **1.** quick to draw a gun and shoot. □ *Some of the old cowboys were known to be quick on the draw.* □ *Wyatt Earp was particularly quick on the draw.* **2.** quick to respond to anything; quick to act. □ *John gets the right answer before anyone else. He's really quick on the draw.* □ *Sally will probably win the quiz game. She's really quick on the draw.*

quick on the uptake quick to understand (something). □ *Just because I'm not quick on the uptake, it doesn't mean I'm stupid.* □ *Mary understands jokes before anyone else because she's so quick on the uptake.*

quids in with someone in an advantageous or favourable position with someone. (Informal.) □ *You'll be quids in with Jean if you can charm her mother.* □ *Fred's quids in with the boss after his successful export deal.*

quite a bit AND **quite a few; quite a lot; quite a number** much or many. □ *Do you need one? I have quite a few.* □ *I have quite a bit—enough to spare some.* □ *How many? Oh, quite a number.*

quite a lot See the previous entry.

quite a number See *quite a bit.*

quite something something very good or remarkable. (Informal. The word *something* is always used in this expression.) □ *You should see their new house. It's quite something.* □ *Meg's mother has brought a new hat for the wedding and it's quite something.*

R

race against time   to hurry to beat a deadline; to hurry to achieve something by a certain time.   □ *We had to race against time to finish the work before the deadline.*   □ *You don't need to race against time. Take all the time you want.* ALSO: **race against time** a task which must be finished within a certain time.   □ *It was a race against time to finish before the deadline.*

rack one's brains   to try very hard to think of something.   □ *I racked my brains all afternoon, but couldn't remember where I put the book.*   □ *Don't waste any more time racking your brains. Go and borrow the book from the library.*

rain cats and dogs   to rain very hard. (Informal.)   □ *It's raining cats and dogs. Look at it pour!*   □ *I'm not going out in that storm. It's raining cats and dogs.*

rain or shine   no matter whether it rains or the sun shines. (Informal.)   □ *Don't worry. I'll be there rain or shine.*   □ *We'll hold the picnic—rain or shine.*

rained off   cancelled or postponed because of rain.   □ *Oh, the weather looks awful. I hope the picnic isn't rained off.*   □ *It's starting to drizzle now. Do you think the game will be rained off?*

raise a few eyebrows   to shock or surprise people mildly by doing or saying something.   □ *What you just said may raise a few eyebrows, but it shouldn't make anyone really angry.*   □ *John's sudden marriage to Ann raised a few eyebrows.*

raise a hand (against someone or something) AND **raise a hand (to someone or something)**   to threaten (to strike) someone or something. (Often in the negative. The *a hand* can be replaced with *one's hand*.)   □ *She's very peaceful. She wouldn't raise a hand against a fly.*   □ *Would you raise your hand to your own brother?*

raise a stink about something   See *create a stink about something.*

raise an objection (to someone or something)   to mention an objection about someone or something.   □ *I hope your family won't raise an objection to my staying for dinner.*   □ *I'm certain no one will raise any objection. We are delighted to have you.*

raise Cain (with someone or something)   See the following entry.

raise hell (with someone or something) AND **raise Cain (with someone or something)**   to be very angry with someone; to scold someone severely. (Informal. Use *hell* with caution.)   □ *John raised hell with his son when he saw the car.*   □ *The children raised hell on the bus on the way home.*   □ *Father will raise Cain if you are late.*

raise one's sights   to set higher goals for oneself.   □ *When you're young, you tend to raise your sights too high.*   □ *On the other hand, some people need to raise their sights higher.*

raise one's voice (to someone)   to speak loudly or shout at someone in anger.   □ *Don't you dare raise your voice to me!*

□ *I'm sorry. I didn't mean to raise my voice.*

raise the wind for something to obtain the money for something. (Informal.) □ *I can't raise the wind for a foreign holiday.* □ *Bob's trying to raise the wind to buy a new car.*

rake something up to uncover something unpleasant and remind people about it. □ *The young journalist raked up the old scandal about the MP.* □ *The politician's opponents are trying to rake up some unpleasant details about his past.*

rally round someone or something to come together to support someone or something. □ *The family rallied round Jack when he lost his job.* □ *The former pupils rallied round their old school when it was in danger of being closed.*

ram someone or something down someone's throat See *shove someone or something down someone's throat.*

ramble on (about something) to talk aimlessly about something. □ *John is so talkative. He's always rambling on about something.* □ *You're rambling on yourself.*

rank and file 1. regular soldiers, not the officers. □ *I think there is some trouble with the rank and file, sir.* □ *The rank and file usually do exactly as they are told.* 2. the members of a group, not the leaders. □ *The rank and file will vote on the proposed contract tomorrow.* □ *The last contract was turned down by the rank and file last year.*

rant and rave to shout angrily and wildly. □ *Bob rants and raves when anything displeases him.* □ *Father rants and raves if we arrive home late.*

rap someone's knuckles to rebuke or punish someone. □ *She rapped his knuckles for whispering too much.* □ *Don't rap my knuckles. I didn't do it.* ALSO: **get one's knuckles rapped; have one's knuckles rapped** to receive punishment. □ *I got my knuckles rapped for whispering too much.* □ *You should*

have your knuckles rapped for doing that!

rarin' to go extremely keen to act or do something. (Informal.) □ *Jane can't wait to start her job. She's rarin' to go.* □ *Mary is rarin' to go and can't wait for her university term to start.*

rat on someone to report someone's bad behaviour; to tell on someone. (Slang.) □ *John ratted on me, and I got in trouble.* □ *If he rats on me, I'll hit him!*

rat race a fierce struggle for success, especially in one's career or business. □ *Bob's got tired of the rat race. He's retired and gone to live in the country.* □ *The money-market is a rat race, and many people who work in it die of the stress.*

rate someone to think highly of someone; to have a good opinion of someone. (Slang.) □ *The children don't rate the teacher.* □ *I don't rate the new director.*

rattle something off AND **rattle off something; reel something off; reel off something** to recite something quickly and accurately. □ *Listen to Mary rattle off those numbers.* □ *Joan can really reel off telephone numbers.*

rave about someone or something 1. to shout and carry on about someone or something in great anger. □ *From the way Bill was raving about his car, I knew he was angry.* □ *There is a man in the office raving about his gas bill.* 2. to praise someone or something with great enthusiasm. (Informal.) □ *The audience just raved about Mary's performance.* □ *The critics raved about her, too.*

reach an agreement (with someone) to agree on something, especially after much discussion. □ *We were unable to reach an agreement with the opposition.* □ *After three weeks of exchanging letters, we were finally able to reach an agreement.*

reach for the sky 1. to aspire to something; to set one's goals high. □ *It's a good idea to set high goals, but there is no point in reaching for the sky.* □ *Go* *ahead, you can do it! Reach for the sky!* **2.** a command to put one's hands up, as in a robbery. (Slang.) □ *Reach for the sky! This is a stick-up!* □ *The guard told the bank robbers to reach for the sky.*

read between the lines to infer something (from something). (Usually figurative. Does not necessarily refer to written or printed information.) □ *After listening to what she said, if you read between the lines, you can begin to see what she really means.* □ *Don't believe everything you hear. Learn to read between the lines.*

read someone like a book to understand someone very well. □ *I've got John figured out. I can read him like a book.* □ *Of course I understand you. I read you like a book.*

read someone the Riot Act to give someone a severe scolding. (Under the Riot Act of 1715, an assembly of people could be dispersed by magistrates reading the act to them.) □ *The manager read me the Riot Act for coming in late.* □ *The teacher read the pupils the Riot Act for their failure to do their homework.*

read someone's mind to guess what someone is thinking. □ *You'll have to tell me what you want. I can't read your mind, you know.* □ *If I could read your mind, I'd know what you expect of me.*

read something into something to attach or attribute a new or different meaning to something; to find a meaning that is not intended in something. □ *This statement means exactly what it says. Don't try to read anything else into it.* □ *Am I reading too much into your comments?*

read something through AND **read through something** to read all of something. □ *Take this home and read it through.* □ *Read through this report and see if you can find any errors.*

read up (on someone or something) to find and read some information about someone or something. □ *I don't know*

anything about that. I suppose I shall have to read up on it. □ *Please go to the library and read up on Queen Victoria.*

rear its ugly head [for something unpleasant] to appear or become obvious after lying hidden. □ *Jealousy reared its ugly head and destroyed their marriage.* □ *The question of money always rears its ugly head in matters of business.*

receive someone with open arms AND **welcome someone with open arms** to welcome someone eagerly. (Used literally or figuratively.) □ *I'm certain they wanted us to stay for dinner. They received us with open arms.* □ *When I came home from school, the whole family welcomed me with open arms.*

reckon with someone to deal with someone; to confront someone. (Informal.) □ *Eventually you will have to reckon with Mary's father.* □ *I really don't want to have to reckon with the manager when she's mad.*

red herring a piece of information or suggestion introduced to draw attention away from the truth or real facts of a situation. (A red herring is a type of strong-smelling smoked fish that was once drawn across the trail of scent to mislead hunting dogs and put them off the scent. See also *draw a red herring.*) □ *The detectives were following a red herring, but they're on the right track now.* □ *Jack and Mary were hoping their friends would confuse their parents with red herrings so that they wouldn't realize that they had eloped.*

red in the face embarrassed. □ *After we found Ann hiding in the cupboard, she became red in the face.* □ *The speaker kept making errors and became red in the face.*

red tape over-strict attention to the wording and details of rules and regulations, especially by government or public departments. (From the colour of the tape used by government departments to tie up bundles of documents.) □ *Because of red tape, Frank took weeks to get a visa.*

☐ *Red tape prevented Jack's wife from joining him abroad.*

redbrick university one of the universities built in England in the late nineteenth century, contrasted with Oxford and Cambridge Universities. (Derogatory.) ☐ *John's tutor ridicules the redbrick universities.* ☐ *Alice is a snob. She refuses to go to a redbrick university.*

reel something off See *rattle something off.*

regain one's composure to become calm and composed. ☐ *I found it difficult to regain my composure after the argument.* ☐ *Here, sit down and relax so that you can regain your composure.*

regain one's feet 1. to stand up again after falling or stumbling. ☐ *I fell on the ice and almost couldn't regain my feet.* ☐ *I helped my uncle regain his feet as he tried to get up from the chair.* 2. to become independent after financial difficulties. ☐ *I lent Bill £400 to help him regain his feet.* ☐ *I'll be able to pay my bills when I regain my feet.*

relative to someone or something 1. concerning someone or something. ☐ *I have something to say relative to Bill.* ☐ *Do you have any information relative to the situation in South America?* 2. in proportion to someone or something. ☐ *My happiness is relative to yours.* ☐ *I can spend an amount of money relative to the amount of money I earn.*

resign oneself to something to accept something reluctantly. ☐ *I finally resigned myself to working abroad even though I didn't want to.* ☐ *Mary resigned herself to her fate.*

rest assured to be assured; to be certain. ☐ *Rest assured that you'll receive the best of care.* ☐ *Please rest assured that we will do everything possible to help.*

rest on one's laurels to enjoy one's success and not try to achieve more. ☐ *Don't rest on your laurels. Try to continue to do great things!* ☐ *I think I'll rest on my laurels for a time before attempting anything new.*

rest on one's oars to take a rest after a period of work or other activity. ☐ *Now that we've won the export order we can rest on our oars.* ☐ *After working hard to get into university, you can rest on your oars for the summer.*

result in something to cause something to happen. ☐ *The storm resulted in a lot of flooding.* ☐ *Her fall resulted in a broken leg.*

return the compliment AND **return someone's compliment** to pay a compliment to someone who has paid you a compliment. (See *pay someone a compliment.*) ☐ *Mary told me that my hair looked nice, so I returned her compliment and told her that her hair was lovely.* ☐ *When someone says something nice, it is polite to return the compliment.*

return the favour to do a good deed for someone who has done a good deed for you. ☐ *You helped me last week, so I'll return the favour and help you this week.* ☐ *There is no point in helping Bill. He'll never return the favour.*

return ticket a ticket (for a plane, train, bus, etc.) which allows one to go to a destination and return. ☐ *A return ticket will usually save you some money.* ☐ *How much is a return ticket to Harrogate?*

rev something up AND **rev up something; rev up** to make an idling engine run very fast, in short bursts of speed. ☐ *I wish that Tom wouldn't sit out in front of our house in his car and rev up his engine.* ☐ *Stop revving it up!* ☐ *Will you please stop revving up!*

ride roughshod over someone or something to treat someone or something with disdain or scorn. ☐ *Tom seems to ride roughshod over his friends.* ☐ *You shouldn't have come into our town to ride roughshod over our laws and our traditions.*

ride something out AND **ride out something** to endure something unpleasant. (Originally referred to ships lasting out a storm.) ☐ *It was a nasty situation, but the mayor tried to ride it out.* ☐ *The MP decided to ride out the scandal.*

riding for a fall risking failure or an accident, usually owing to over-confidence. □ *Tom drives too fast, and he seems too sure of himself. He's riding for a fall.* □ *Bill needs to stop borrowing money. He's riding for a fall.*

rift in the lute a small flaw or fault that is likely to develop into a major flaw or fault that will ruin or destroy something. □ *I detect a rift in the lute of their relationship. They keep contradicting each other.* □ *There's a rift in the lute of industrial relations in the factory which might lead to a strike. The union leader and the works manager dislike each other.*

right and left to both sides; on all sides; everywhere. □ *I dropped the tennis balls, and they rolled right and left.* □ *There were children everywhere—running right and left.*

right away immediately. □ *Please do it right away!* □ *I'll be there right away. I'm leaving this instant.*

Right on! Exactly!; That is exactly right! (Slang.) □ *After the speaker finished, many people in the audience shouted, "Right on!"* □ *One member of the crowd called out, "Right on!"*

right on time at the correct time; no later than the specified time. □ *Bill always shows up right on time.* □ *If you get there right on time, you'll get one of the free tickets.*

right side up with the correct side upwards, as with a box or some other container. □ *Keep this box right side up, or the contents will become crushed.* □ *Please turn your coffee-cup right side up so I can fill it.*

right under someone's nose See *under someone's (very) nose.*

right up someone's street ideally suited to one's interests or abilities. (Informal.) □ *Skiing is right up my street. I love it.* □ *This kind of thing is right up John's street.*

ring a bell [for something] to cause someone to remember something or to seem familiar. (Informal.) □ *I've never met John Franklin, but his name rings a bell.* □ *The face in the photograph rang a bell. It was my cousin.*

ring down the curtain (on something) AND **bring down the curtain (on something)** to bring something to an end; to declare something to be at an end. □ *It's time to ring down the curtain on our relationship. We have nothing in common any more.* □ *We've tried our best to make this company a success, but it's time to ring down the curtain.* □ *After many years the old man brought down the curtain and closed the restaurant.*

ring in the New Year to celebrate the beginning of the New Year at midnight on December 31. □ *We are planning a big affair to ring in the New Year.* □ *How did you ring in the New Year?*

ring off to end a telephone call. □ *I must ring off now and get back to work.* □ *James rang off rather suddenly and rudely when Alice contradicted him.*

ring someone or something up AND **ring up someone or something 1.** [with *something*] to record the cost of an item on a cash register. □ *The cashier rang up each item and told me how much money I owed.* □ *Please ring this chewing-gum up first, and I'll put it in my handbag.* **2.** [with *someone*] to call someone on the telephone. □ *Please ring up Ann and ask her if she wants to come over.* □ *Just ring me up any time.*

ring the changes to do or arrange things in different ways to achieve variety. (From bell-ringing.) □ *Jane doesn't have many clothes, but she rings the changes by adding different-coloured scarves to her basic outfits.* □ *Aunt Mary rings the changes in her small flat by rearranging the furniture.*

ring true to sound or seem true or likely. (From testing the quality of metal or glass by striking it and listening to the noise made.) □ *The pupil's excuse for being late doesn't ring true.* □ *Do you* think that Mary's explanation for her absence rang true?

rip into someone or something to attack someone or something, physically or verbally. (Informal.) □ *The bear ripped into the deer.* □ *The angry teacher ripped into the pupils.*

rip someone or something off AND **rip off someone or something** (Slang.) **1.** [with *someone*] to cheat or deceive someone; to steal from someone. □ *That shopkeeper ripped me off.* □ *They shouldn't rip off people like that.* **2.** [with *something*] to steal something. □ *The crooks ripped off a car in broad daylight.* □ *I bought it! I didn't rip it off!*

ripe old age a very old age. □ *Mr. Smith died last night, but he was a ripe old age—ninety-nine.* □ *All the Smiths seem to live to a ripe old age.*

rise and shine to get out of bed and be lively and energetic. (Informal. Often a command.) □ *Come on, children! Rise and shine! We're going to the seaside.* □ *Father always calls "Rise and shine!" in the morning when we want to go on sleeping.*

rise to the occasion to meet the challenge of an event; to try extra hard to do a task. □ *John was able to rise to the occasion and make the conference a success.* □ *It was a big challenge, but he rose to the occasion.*

risk one's neck (to do something) to risk physical harm in order to accomplish something. (Informal.) □ *Look at that traffic! I refuse to risk my neck just to cross the street to buy a paper.* □ *I refuse to risk my neck at all.*

road-hog someone who drives carelessly and selfishly. (Informal.) □ *Look at that road-hog driving in the middle of the road and stopping other drivers getting past him.* □ *That road-hog nearly knocked the children over. He was driving too fast.*

rob Peter to pay Paul to take from one person in order to give to another. □ *Why borrow money to pay your bills?*

That's just robbing Peter to pay Paul. □ *There's no point in robbing Peter to pay Paul. You will still be in debt.*

rock the boat to cause trouble; to disturb a situation which is otherwise stable and satisfactory. (Often negative.) □ *Look, Tom, everything is going fine here. Don't rock the boat!* □ *You can depend on Tom to mess things up by rocking the boat.*

roll in to come in large numbers or amounts. (Informal.) □ *We didn't expect many people at the fête, but they just kept rolling in.* □ *Money is simply rolling in for our charity appeal.*

roll on something [for something, such as a time or a day] to approach rapidly. (Said by someone who wants the time or the day to arrive sooner than is possible. Usually a command.) □ *Roll on Saturday! I get the day off.* □ *Roll on spring! We hate the snow.*

roll one's sleeves up AND **roll up one's sleeves** to get ready to do some work. (Informal.) □ *Come on, you chaps, get busy. Roll up your sleeves and go to work.* □ *Roll your sleeves up and get busy. This isn't a picnic. This is work!*

roll out the red carpet for someone See under *get the red carpet treatment.*

rolling in something having large amounts of something, usually money. (Informal.) □ *That family is rolling in money.* □ *Jack doesn't need to earn money. He's rolling in it.*

Rome wasn't built in a day. important things don't happen overnight. □ *Don't expect a lot to happen right away. Rome wasn't built in a day, you know.* □ *Don't be anxious about how slowly your business is growing. Rome wasn't built in a day.*

romp home to win a race or competition easily. (Informal.) □ *Our team romped home in the relay race.* □ *Jack romped home in the election for president of the club.*

root and branch completely. □ *The legal system needs to be changed root and* branch. □ *The government altered the educational policy root and branch.*

root for someone or something to cheer and encourage someone or something; to support someone or something. (Informal.) □ *Are you rooting for anyone in particular, or are you just shouting because you're excited?* □ *I'm rooting for the home team.*

root something out to get rid of something completely; to destroy something. □ *No government will ever root out crime completely.* □ *The headmaster wants to root out truancy from the school.*

rooted to the spot unable to move because of fear or surprise. □ *Joan stood rooted to the spot when she saw the ghostly figure.* □ *Mary was rooted to the spot when the thief snatched her bag.*

rope someone into doing something to persuade or trick someone into doing something. (Informal.) □ *I don't know who roped me into this, but I don't want to do it.* □ *See if you can rope somebody into taking this to the post office.*

rough it to live in discomfort; to live in uncomfortable conditions without the usual amenities. (Informal.) □ *The students are roughing it in a shack with no running water.* □ *Bob and Jack had nowhere to live and so they had to rough it in a tent till they found somewhere.*

rough someone up AND **rough up someone** to beat or physically harass someone. (Slang.) □ *The police roughed up the suspect, and they got into trouble for it.* □ *The gangsters roughed their victim up.*

round on someone to attack someone verbally. □ *Jane suddenly rounded on Tom for arriving late.* □ *Peter rounded on Meg, asking what she'd done with the money.*

round something off AND **round off something 1.** to make something rounded or curved. □ *I rounded off the sharp corner with sandpaper.* □ *Please try to*

round off that sharp place. **2.** to finish something (in a special way; by doing something). □ *She rounded her schooling off with a trip to Europe.* □ *I like to round off the day with a period of meditation.*

round something up AND **round up something 1.** to collect something; to organize something into a group. □ *The cowboys rounded up the cattle for market.* □ *See if you can round some helpers up.* **2.** to change a number to the next higher whole number. □ *I rounded up 8.789 to 9.* □ *You should round up £65.99 to £66.*

rub along with someone to get along fairly well with someone. (Informal.) □ *Jack and Fred manage to rub along with each other although they're not best friends.* □ *Jim just about rubs along with his in-laws.*

rub off (on someone) [for a characteristic of one person] to seem to transfer to someone else. □ *I'll sit by Ann. She has been lucky all evening. Maybe it'll rub off on me.* □ *Sorry. I don't think that luck rubs off.*

rub salt in the wound deliberately to make someone's unhappiness, shame, or misfortune worse. □ *Don't rub salt in the wound by telling me how enjoyable the party was.* □ *Jim is feeling miserable about losing his job, and Fred is rubbing salt in the wound by saying how good his replacement is.*

rub shoulders (with someone) to associate with someone; to work closely with someone. □ *I don't care to rub shoulders with someone who acts like that!* □ *I rub shoulders with John every day at work. We are good friends.*

rub someone or something down AND **rub down someone or something 1.** to dry someone or something. □ *I like to rub myself down after a cold shower.* □ *The trainer rubbed down the horse after running it through the stream.* **2.** to massage or knead the muscles of someone or something. □ *The trainer rubbed down the horse after the race.* □ *The* *coach rubbed down the boxer before and after the fight.*

rub someone out AND **rub out someone** to kill someone. (Slang.) □ *The gangsters tried to rub out the witness.* □ *The crook said, "Bill is getting to be a problem. We're going to have to rub him out."*

rub someone up the wrong way to irritate someone. (Informal.) □ *I'm sorry I rubbed you up the wrong way. I didn't mean to upset you.* □ *Don't rub her up the wrong way!*

rub someone's nose in it to remind one of something one has done wrong; to remind one of something bad or unfortunate that has happened. (From a method of house-training animals.) □ *When Bob failed his exam, his brother rubbed his nose in it.* □ *Mary knows she shouldn't have broken off her engagement. Don't rub her nose in it.*

rub something in AND **rub in something** 1. to work something into something by rubbing. □ *If your sunburn hurts, take this lotion and rub it in.* □ *Should I rub in all of it?* 2. to keep reminding one of one's failures; to nag someone about something. (Especially **rub it in.** Informal.) □ *Why do you have to rub in everything I do wrong?* □ *I like to rub it in. You deserve it!*

ruffle someone's feathers to upset or annoy someone. (A bird's feathers become ruffled if it is angry or afraid.) □ *You certainly ruffled Mrs. Smith's feathers by criticizing her garden.* □ *Try to be tactful and not ruffle people's feathers.*

rule of thumb a rough or inexact guide, rather than an exact measurement, used for quick calculations. (From the use of one's thumb to make quick and rough measurements.) □ *By rule of thumb, that table is about six feet long.* □ *I haven't measured that pole, but I would think, according to rule of thumb, that it's about ten feet high.*

rule someone or something out AND **rule out someone or something** to prevent, disqualify, overrule, or cancel someone

or something. □ *John's bad temper rules him out for the appointment.* □ *The weather ruled out a picnic for the week-end.*

rule someone or something with a rod of iron to control someone or something strictly and severely. □ *Jane's father rules the family with a rod of iron.* □ *The old king ruled the country with a rod of iron.*

rule the roost to be the boss or manager, especially at home. (Informal.) □ *Who rules the roost at your house?* □ *Our new office manager really rules the roost.*

run a fever AND **run a temperature** to have a body temperature higher than normal; to have a fever. □ *I ran a fever when I had the flu.* □ *The baby is running a temperature and is cross.*

run a risk (of something) AND **run the risk (of something)** to take a chance that something (bad) will happen. □ *I don't want to run the risk of losing my job.* □ *Don't worry. You won't have to run a risk.*

run a temperature See *run a fever.*

run a tight ship to run a ship or an organization in an orderly, efficient, and disciplined manner. □ *The new office manager really runs a tight ship.* □ *The headmaster runs a tight ship.*

run across someone or something See *come across someone or something.*

run after someone to chase someone of the opposite sex hoping for a date or some attention. □ *Is John still running after Ann?* □ *No, Ann is running after John.*

run against the clock to be in a race with time; to be in a great hurry to get something done before a particular time. (See also *race against time.*) □ *Bill set a new track record running against the clock. He lost the actual race, however.* □ *The front runner was running against the clock. The others were a lap behind.*

run an errand AND **go on an errand** to take a short trip to do a specific thing.

□ *I've got to run an errand. I'll be back in a minute.* □ *John has gone on an errand. He'll be back shortly.*

run around in circles See the following entry.

run around like a chicken with its head cut off AND **run around in circles** to run around frantically and aimlessly; to be in a state of chaos. (Informal.) □ *I spent all afternoon running around like a chicken with its head cut off.* □ *If you run around in circles, you'll never get anything done.* □ *Get organized and stop running around in circles.*

run around with someone AND **go around with someone** to be friends with someone; to go places with regular friends. (Informal.) □ *John and I were great friends. We used to run around with each other all the time.* □ *Mary went around with Jane for about a year.*

run away (with someone or something) to flee (from somewhere) with someone, as in an elopement. (See *run off with someone or something*.) □ *Tom ran away with Ann and got married.* □ *They ran away because her parents opposed the marriage.*

run circles around someone AND **run rings around someone** to outrun or outdo someone. (Informal.) □ *John is a much better writer than Mary. He can run circles around her.* □ *Mary can run rings around Sally when it comes to acting.*

run counter to something to be in opposition to something; to run against something. (This has nothing to do with running.) □ *Your proposal runs counter to what is required by the manager.* □ *His idea runs counter to good sense.*

run down to run out of power or energy. (Said especially of batteries and clock springs.) □ *My watch has run down. I need new batteries.* □ *It used to be that when a watch ran down, you just wound it up again.*

run-down not very healthy; not in peak condition. □ *The teacher is feeling a bit run-down.* □ *People often feel run-down after an operation.*

run for it to try and escape by running. (Informal.) □ *The guard's not looking. Let's run for it!* □ *The convict tried to run for it, but the warder caught him.*

run for one's life to run away to save one's life. □ *The dam has burst! Run for your life!* □ *The captain told us all to run for our lives.*

run high [for feelings] to be in a state of excitement or anger. □ *Feelings were running high as the general election approached.* □ *The mood of the crowd was running high when they saw the man beat the child.*

run in the family for a characteristic to appear in all (or most) members of a family. □ *My grandparents lived well into their nineties, and longevity runs in the family.* □ *My brothers and I have red hair. It runs in the family.*

run into someone See *bump into someone*.

run of the mill common or average; typical. □ *The restaurant we went to was nothing special—just run of the mill.* □ *The service was good, but the food was run of the mill or worse.*

run off with someone or something **1.** to take something or someone away; to steal something or kidnap someone. □ *The thief ran off with the lady's purse.* □ *The kidnapper ran off with the baby.* **2.** [with *someone*] AND **run off** to run away with someone, as in an elopement. □ *Tom and Ann ran off and got married.* □ *Mary ran off with Tim to Gretna Green.*

run out of something to use up the last of something and have no more. □ *I ran out of eggs while I was baking the cakes. I had to buy more right then.* □ *We ran out of petrol on the motorway.*

run out of time See under *out of time*.

run over someone or something [for a car, bus, etc.] to drive over someone or something; to drive (a car, bus, etc.) over someone or something. □ *Be careful* *when you cross the street so that a car doesn't run over you.* □ *The car ran over the bicycle left in the driveway.*

run rings around someone See *run circles around someone.*

run riot AND **run wild** to get out of control. □ *The dandelions have run riot on our lawn.* □ *The children ran wild at the birthday party and had to be taken home.*

run short (of something) to use up almost all of something; to have too little or few of something left. □ *We are running short of milk. Please buy some on the way home.* □ *When it comes to money, we are always running short.*

run someone in AND **run in someone** to take someone to the police station and make an arrest. (Informal.) □ *The police officer got angry and ran in the motorist.* □ *"Don't run me in," cried the driver. "I'm innocent."*

run someone or something down AND **run down someone or something** 1. to run over someone or something (with a car, bus, etc.). □ *The hunters ran down the deer.* □ *The murderer ran the man down with a car.* 2. to say bad things about someone or something. □ *Why are you always running your friends down?* □ *Don't run down my paintings! You just don't understand art!*

run someone or something to earth to find something after a search. (From a fox-hunt chasing a fox into its hole.) □ *Jean finally ran her long-lost cousin to earth in Paris.* □ *After months of searching, I ran a copy of Jim's book to earth.*

run someone ragged to keep someone very busy. (Informal.) □ *This busy season is running us all ragged at the shop.* □ *What a busy day. I ran myself ragged.*

run something up AND **run up something** 1. to make something quickly and roughly, usually by sewing. (Informal. Note the indirect object in the first ex-

ample.) □ *Could you run me up a dance dress by Friday?* □ *Mary's really good at running cheap summer dresses up.* 2. to cause something to rise sharply in amount. □ *Joan's run up a huge account in her parents' name.* □ *Fred has run up a large bill at the local garage and cannot pay it.* 3. to raise a flag. □ *We run up the flag every day.* □ *I run it up every day except when it's raining.*

run through something to waste something; to use up something rapidly. (Also used literally.) □ *Have you run through all those eggs already?* □ *I ran through my allowance in one day.*

run to seed AND **go to seed** to become worn-out and uncared for. □ *The estate has gone to seed since the old man's death.* □ *Pick things up around here. This place is going to seed. What a mess!*

run to something 1. to be sufficient for something; to have enough money for something. □ *Our budget doesn't run to holidays abroad.* □ *We just can't run to a new car.* 2. to amount to a certain amount of money. □ *In the end, the bill ran to thousands of pounds.* □ *His account ran to more than I expected.*

run up against a brick wall See the following entry.

run up against a stone wall AND **run up against a brick wall** to come to a barrier against further progress. (Informal. Also used literally.) □ *We've run up against a stone wall in our investigation.* □ *We were going to build a house, but we ran up against a brick wall when we applied to the planning department.*

run wild See *run riot.*

rush one's fences to act hurriedly without enough care or thought. (From horse-riding.) □ *Jack's always rushing his fences. He should think things out first.* □ *Think carefully before you buy that expensive house. Don't rush your fences.*

rustle something up AND **rustle up something** to find and prepare some food. (Informal.) □ *Just go out into the kitchen and ask Bill to rustle up some food.* □ *I'm certain he can rustle something up.*

S

sacred cow something that is regarded by some people with such respect and veneration that they don't like it being criticized by anyone in any way. (From the fact that the cow is regarded as sacred in India.) □ *University education is a sacred cow in the Smith family. Fred is regarded as a failure because he left school at sixteen.* □ *Don't talk about eating meat to Pam. Vegetarianism is one of her sacred cows.*

saddle someone with something to give someone something undesirable, annoying, or difficult to deal with. (Informal.) □ *Mary says she doesn't want to be saddled with a baby, but her husband would love one.* □ *Jim's saddled Eddie with the most boring jobs so that he'll leave.*

safe and sound safe and whole or healthy. □ *It was a rough trip, but we got there safe and sound.* □ *I'm glad to see you here safe and sound.*

sail through something to finish something quickly and easily. (Informal.) □ *The test was not difficult. I sailed through it.* □ *Bob sailed through his homework in a short amount of time.*

sail under false colours to pretend to be something that one is not. (Originally nautical, referring to a pirate ship disguised as an innocent merchant ship.) □ *John has been sailing under false colours. He's really a spy.* □ *I thought you were wearing that uniform because you worked here. You are sailing under false colours.*

salt of the earth the most worthy of people; a very good or worthy person. (A biblical reference.) □ *Mrs. Jones is the salt of the earth. She is the first to help anyone in trouble.* □ *Frank's mother is the salt of the earth. She has five children of her own and yet fosters three others.*

salt something away AND **salt away something** to store something. (Originally referred to preserving food and storing it.) □ *I salted away about £1,000 by working overtime.* □ *Mary salted away some extra sweets for the holidays.*

same here Me too!; I agree! (Informal.) □ BOB: *I'll have chocolate ice-cream!* BILL: *Same here.* □ MARY: *I'll vote for the best candidate.* TOM: *Same here!*

same old story something that occurs or has occurred in the same way often. □ *Jim's got no money. It's the same old story. He's spent it all on clothing.* □ *The firm are getting rid of staff. It's the same old story—a shortage of orders.*

same to you the same comment applies to you. (Informal. Can be a polite or a rude comment.) □ BILL: *Have a pleasant evening.* BOB: *Thank you. The same to you.* □ MARY: *You're the most horrible person I've ever met!* JOHN: *The same to you!*

save one's breath to refrain from talking, explaining, or arguing. (Informal.) □ *There is no sense in trying to convince her. Save your breath.* □ *Tell her to save her breath. He won't listen to her.*

save (one's) face to preserve one's good standing or high position (after a failure).

□ *The ambassador was more interested in saving his face than winning the argument.* □ *Most diplomats are concerned with saving face.*

save someone's skin to save someone from injury, embarrassment, or punishment. (Informal.) □ *I saved my skin by getting the job done on time.* □ *Thanks for saving my skin. If you hadn't given me an alibi, the police would have arrested me.*

save something for a rainy day to reserve something—usually money—for some future need. (*Save something* can be replaced with *put something aside, hold something back, keep something,* etc.) □ *I've saved a little money for a rainy day.* □ *Keep some sweets for a rainy day.*

save something up AND **save up something** to save something; to accumulate something. (*Up* can also be left out.) □ *I'm saving up coupons to get a prize.* □ *If you'd only save your money up, you could buy anything you want.*

save the day to produce a good result when a bad result was expected. □ *The team was expected to lose, but Sally made many points and saved the day.* □ *Your excellent speech saved the day.*

save up (for something) to save money for something. □ *I'm saving up for a bicycle.* □ *I'll have to save up for a long time. It costs a lot of money.*

saved by the bell rescued from a difficult or dangerous situation just in time by something which brings the situation to a sudden end. (From the sounding of a bell marking the end of a round in a boxing match.) □ *James didn't know the answer to the question, but he was saved by the bell when the teacher was called away from the room.* □ *I couldn't think of anything to say to the woman at the bus-stop, but I was saved by the bell by my bus arriving.*

say a mouthful to say a lot; to say something very important or meaningful. (Informal.) □ *When you said things were busy around here, you said a mouthful.*

It is terribly busy. □ *You sure said a mouthful, Bob. Things are really busy.*

say something in a roundabout way to imply something without saying it; to say something indirectly; to speak using circumlocution. □ *Why don't you say what you mean? Why do you always say things in a roundabout way?* □ *What did she mean? Why did she say it in a roundabout way?*

say something out loud to say something so that people can hear it; to say something aloud. □ *If you know the answer, say it out loud.* □ *Don't mumble. Say it out loud.*

say something (right) to someone's face to say something (unpleasant) directly to someone. □ *She knew I thought she was rude because I said it right to her face.* □ *I thought she felt that way about me, but I never thought she'd say it to my face.*

say something under one's breath to say something so softly that almost no one can hear it. □ *John was saying something under his breath, and I don't think it was very pleasant.* □ *I'm glad he said it under his breath. If he had said it out loud, it would have caused an argument.*

say the word to give a signal to begin; to say *yes* or *okay.* (Informal.) □ *I'm ready to start anytime you say the word.* □ *We'll all shout "Happy birthday!" when I say the word.*

scale something down AND **scale down something** to make something smaller. □ *Your plan is much too grand. We'll have to scale it down.* □ *We can't afford to build a building that big. Please scale down the size and the cost.*

scare one out of one's wits See *frighten one out of one's wits.*

scare someone stiff to scare someone severely; to *frighten someone to death.* (*Stiff* means dead.) □ *That loud noise scared me stiff.* □ *The robber jumped out and scared us stiff.* ALSO: **scared stiff** badly frightened. (See also *scared to*

279

death at *frighten someone to death.*) □ *We were scared stiff by the robber.*

scare someone to death See *frighten someone to death.*

scare the (living) daylights out of someone See *frighten the wits out of someone.*

scare the wits out of someone See *frighten the wits out of someone.*

scared stiff See under *scare someone stiff.*

scared to death See *frighten someone to death.*

scrape something together AND **scrape together something** to assemble something quickly, usually from a small supply of components. (Informal.) □ *I'll try to scrape something together for dinner.* □ *We really should try to have a party to celebrate the old boy's birthday. Let's try to scrape together enough money to pay for it.*

scrape the bottom of the barrel to select from among the worst; to choose from what is left over. □ *You've bought a dreadful old car. You really scraped the bottom of the barrel to get that one.* □ *The worker you sent over was the worst I've ever seen. Send me another—and don't scrape the bottom of the barrel.*

scratch around (for something) to look here and there for something; to try with difficulty to find something. (Informal.) □ *Let me scratch around for a better bargain. Maybe I can come up with something you like.* □ *The charity workers are scratching around for more money.*

scratch someone's back to do a favour for someone in return for a favour done for you. (Informal.) □ *You scratch my back, and I'll scratch yours.* □ *We believe that the manager has been scratching the treasurer's back.*

scratch the surface just to begin to find out about something; to examine only the superficial aspects of something. □ *The investigation of the firm's books showed some inaccuracies. It is thought*

that the investigators have just scratched the surface. □ *We don't know how bad the problem is. We've only scratched the surface.*

scream blue murder 1. AND **cry blue murder** to scream very loudly. (Informal.) *The kidnapped child screamed blue murder.* □ *The baby screams blue murder all night.* □ *Now that Bill is really hurt, he's crying blue murder.* □ *The baby was crying blue murder.* **2.** to complain bitterly; to complain unduly. (Slang.) □ *When we put him in an office without a window, he screamed blue murder.* □ *She screamed blue murder when she learned about the new tax.*

screw someone or something up AND **screw up someone or something** (Slang.) **1.** to cause trouble for someone or something. □ *Your advice about making a lot of money really screwed me up. Now I'm broke.* □ *Your efforts screwed up the entire project.* **2.** [with *someone*] to drive someone crazy. □ *Bob screwed himself up with drugs.* □ *All the trouble at home really screwed up the two brothers.*

screw up one's courage to get one's courage together; to force oneself to be brave. □ *I suppose I have to screw up my courage and go to the dentist.* □ *I spent all morning screwing up my courage to take my driver's test.*

scrimp and save to be very thrifty; to live on very little money, often in order to save up for something. □ *We had to scrimp and save in order to send the children to college.* □ *The Smiths scrimp and save all year in order to go on a foreign holiday.*

seamy side of life the most unpleasant or roughest aspect of life. (Informal. A reference to the inside of a garment where the seams show.) □ *Doctors in that area really see the seamy side of life.* □ *Mary saw the seamy side of life when she worked as a home help in the housing estate.*

search high and low for someone or something See *hunt high and low for someone or something.*

Search me. I do not know.; You will not find the answer with me. (Informal.) □ BILL: *Where is the screwdriver?* BOB: *Search me.* □ *When I asked Mary what time it was, she only said, "Search me."*

search someone or something out AND **search out someone or something** to search for and find someone or something in particular. □ *I searched out John and asked him about the party.* □ *I searched the right-sized hammer out and took it with me.*

search something with a fine-tooth comb See *go over something with a fine-tooth comb.*

second nature to someone easy and natural for someone. □ *Being polite is second nature to Jane.* □ *Driving is no problem for Bob. It's second nature to him.*

second-rate not of the best quality; inferior. □ *Fred's a second-rate tennis player compared with Jim.* □ *The council are building second-rate housing.*

second sight the supposed power of seeing into the future. □ *My aunt was the seventh child of a seventh child and was said to have second sight.* □ *I don't know who'll get the job. I don't have second sight.*

second to none better than anyone or anything else. □ *This is an excellent car—second to none.* □ *Mary is an excellent teacher—second to none.*

see a man about a dog to leave for some unmentioned purpose. (Informal.) □ *I don't know where Tom went. He said he had to see a man about a dog.* □ *When John said he was going to see a man about a dog, I knew he was going somewhere in secret.*

see about something to organize or arrange something. □ *I'll have to see about your request to leave early.* □ *I must see about the arrangement for tomorrow.*

see double to see two of everything instead of one. □ *When I was driving, I saw two people on the road instead of one. I'm seeing double. There's something wrong with my eyes.* □ *Mike thought he was seeing double when he saw Mary. He didn't know she had a twin.*

see eye to eye (about something) AND **see eye to eye (on something)** to view something in the same way (as someone else). (Usually negative.) □ *John and Ann never see eye to eye about anything. They always disagree.* □ *James and Jean rarely see eye to eye either.*

see fit (to do something) See *think fit (to do something).*

see into something See *look into something.*

see no objection (to something) not to think of any objection to something. (The *no* is *any* in the affirmative.) □ *I see no objection to your idea.* □ *Do you see any objection?*

see one's way clear (to do something) to find it possible to do something. □ *I'd be happy if you could see your way clear to attend our meeting.* □ *I wanted to be there, but I couldn't see my way clear to go.*

see over something to take a close look at something. □ *We decided to buy the house after seeing over it.* □ *The visitors asked to see over the factory.*

see red to be angry. (Informal.) □ *Whenever I think of the needless destruction of trees, I see red.* □ *Bill really saw red when the tax bill arrived.*

see someone home to accompany someone home. □ *Bill agreed to see his aunt home after the film.* □ *You don't need to see me home. It's perfectly safe, and I can get there on my own.*

see someone off AND **see off someone** to bid someone goodbye at an airport, train station, bus station, etc. □ *John left for Hull, and his whole family turned out to see the coach off.* □ *We saw off the children who were going to summer camp.*

see someone out See *show someone out.*

see someone to the door See *show someone to the door.*

see something through to follow something through until it is completed. (Compare to *see through someone or something.*) □ *Mary is prepared to see the project through.* □ *It's going to be an unpleasant experience, and I hope you'll see it through.*

see something with half an eye to see or understand very easily. □ *You could see with half an eye that the children were very tired.* □ *Anyone could see with half an eye that the work was badly done.*

see stars to see flashing lights after receiving a blow to the head. □ *I saw stars when I bumped my head on the attic ceiling.* □ *The little boy saw stars when he fell head first onto the concrete.*

see the colour of someone's money to verify that someone has money or has enough money. (Slang.) □ *So, you want to make a bet? Not until I see the colour of your money.* □ *I want to see the colour of your money before we go any further with this business deal.*

see the last of someone or something to see someone or something for the last time. □ *I'm glad to see the last of that old car. It has a lot of problems.* □ *The people at my office were happy to see the last of John. He caused a lot of trouble before he left.*

see the light to understand something clearly at last. □ *After a lot of studying and asking many questions, I finally saw the light.* □ *I know that geometry is difficult. Keep working at it. You'll see the light pretty soon.*

see the light at the end of the tunnel to foresee an end to one's problems after a long period of time. (See also *begin to see daylight.*) □ *I had been horribly ill for two months before I began to see the light at the end of the tunnel.* □ *We were in debt for years, but then we saw the light at the end of the tunnel.*

see the light of day [for something] to be finished or produced. (Often negative.) □ *The product will never see the light of day.* □ *His inventions will never see the light of day. They are too impractical.*

see the sights to see the important things in a place; to see what tourists usually see. □ *We plan to visit Paris and see the sights.* □ *Everyone left the hotel early in the morning to see the sights.*

see the writing on the wall to know that something unpleasant or disastrous is certain to happen. (From a biblical reference.) □ *If you don't improve your performance, they'll sack you. Can't you see the writing on the wall?* □ *Jack saw the writing on the wall when the firm reduced his salary.*

see things to imagine one sees someone or something that is not there. □ *Jean says that she saw a ghost, but she was just seeing things.* □ *I thought I was seeing things when Bill walked into the room. Someone had told me he was dead.*

see through someone or something to understand or detect the true nature of someone or something. (Compare to *see something through.*) □ *You can't fool me any more. I can see through you and all your tricks.* □ *This plan is designed to make money for you, not to help people. I can see through it! I'm not a fool!*

see to someone or something to attend to someone or something. □ *Tom will see to the horses. Come to the house and freshen up.* □ *I hear the doorbell. Will someone please see to the door?* □ *This TV needs mending. Will you please see to it?*

seeing is believing one must believe something that one sees. □ *I never would have thought that a cow could swim, but seeing is believing.* □ *I can hardly believe we are in Paris, but there's the Eiffel Tower, and seeing is believing.*

seeing that considering; since. □ *Seeing that she has no money, Sally won't be going shopping.* □ *Seeing that it's raining, we won't go to the beach.*

seize on something (figuratively) to take hold of something and make an issue of it. (*On* can be replaced with *upon*. Also used literally.) □ *Whenever I mention money, you seize on it and turn it into an argument!* □ *The solicitor seized upon one point and asked many questions about it.*

seize the opportunity to take advantage of an opportunity. □ *My uncle offered me a trip to Europe, so I seized the opportunity.* □ *Whenever you have a chance, you should seize the opportunity.*

seize up to stop working, usually because something has stuck. □ *The car's engine has seized up.* □ *Work stopped for the day because the conveyor belt seized up.*

sell like hot cakes [for something] to be sold very fast. □ *The delicious toffee sold like hot cakes.* □ *The fancy new cars were selling like hot cakes.*

sell someone a pup to cheat someone by selling the person something that is inferior or worthless. (Informal.) □ *Jack sold me a pup when I bought a bike from him. It broke down in two days.* □ *The salesman sold Jane a pup when he persuaded her to buy the second-hand washing-machine. Water pours out of it.*

sell someone down the river to betray someone; to reveal damaging information about someone. (Slang, especially criminal slang.) □ *Bill told everything he knew about Bob, and that sold Bob down the river.* □ *They went over to the other side and sold their former allies down the river.*

sell someone or something short to underestimate someone or something; to fail to see the good qualities of someone or something. □ *This is a very good restaurant. Don't sell it short.* □ *When you say that John isn't interested in music, you're selling him short. Did you know he plays the violin quite well?*

sell someone something to convince someone of something. (Informal.) □ *You don't have to sell me the value of an education.* □ *Try to sell John the idea of emigrating.*

sell something off AND **sell off something** to sell much or all of something. □ *I sold off all my books.* □ *Please try to sell these items off. We have too many of them.*

send away for something to order or request something by mail. □ *I sent away for a record catalogue from a small company in Leeds.* □ *I can't find what I want locally, so I'll have to send away for it.*

send off for something AND **write off for something** to request something by mail, presumably from a great distance. □ *I couldn't find the one I wanted in a shop, so I had to send off for it.* □ *No one here could answer my questions, so I had to write off for more information.*

send one about one's business to send someone away, usually in an unfriendly way. □ *Is that annoying man on the telephone again? Please send him about his business.* □ *Ann, I can't clean up the house with you running around. I'm going to have to send you about your business.*

send out for someone or something to request that something be brought (to where one is). (The request can be made by telephone or in person.) □ *Let's send out for a pizza!* □ *We sent out for John because we needed his advice.* □ *We have no more food, so we'll have to send out for some.*

send someone or something up to ridicule or make fun of someone or something; to satirize someone or something. (Informal.) □ *John is always sending Jane up by mocking the way she walks.* □ *The drama group sent their lecturers up.*

send someone (out) on an errand to send someone out to do a specific task. □ *Mother sent Billy out on an errand.* □ *I'm late because Bill sent me on an errand.*

send someone packing to send someone away; to dismiss someone, possibly rudely. (Informal.) □ *I couldn't stand him any more, so I sent him packing.* □

The maid proved to be so incompetent that I had to send her packing.

send someone to Coventry to refuse to speak to or associate with someone or a group of people as a punishment. □ *The other people sent Tom to Coventry for telling tales to the teacher.* □ *Fred was sent to Coventry by his fellow workers for breaking the strike.*

send something C.O.D. to send merchandise to someone who will pay for it when it is delivered. (*C.O.D.* means "cash on delivery.") □ *I sent away for a record album and asked them to send it C.O.D.* □ *This person has ordered a copy of our record. Send the record C.O.D.*

send something off AND **send off something** to dispatch something; to send something on its way. □ *I sent off the letter yesterday.* □ *Her mother sent her luggage off last week.*

send up a trial balloon to suggest something and see how people respond to it; to test public opinion. (Informal.) □ *Mary had an excellent idea, but when we sent up a trial balloon, the response was very negative.* □ *Don't start the whole project without sending up a trial balloon.*

send word (to someone) to send a message to someone. □ *Send word to Sally that her essay won first place.* □ *If you need any help, please send word.*

separate the grain from the chaff to separate what is of value from what is useless. □ *Could you have a look at this furniture and separate the grain from the chaff?* □ *The English exam will separate the grain from the chaff among the pupils.*

separate the men from the boys to separate the competent from those who are less competent. □ *This is the kind of task that separates the men from the boys.* □ *This project requires a lot of thinking. It'll separate the men from the boys.*

separate the sheep from the goats to divide people into two groups in order to distinguish the good from the bad, etc. □ *Working in a place like this really separates the sheep from the goats.* □ *We can't go on with the game until we separate the sheep from the goats.*

serve as a guinea pig [for someone or something] to be experimented on. □ *Try it on someone else! I don't want to serve as a guinea pig!* □ *Jane agreed to serve as a guinea pig. She'll be the one to try out the new flavour of ice-cream.*

serve notice to announce something. □ *John served notice that he was leaving the company.* □ *I'm serving notice that I'll resign as secretary next month.*

serve someone right [for an act or event] to punish someone fairly (for doing something). □ *John copied off my test paper. It would serve him right if he fails the test.* □ *It'd serve John right if he got arrested.*

serve someone's purpose See *answer someone's purpose.*

serve something up AND **serve up something** 1. to serve food. □ *The cook served up a fine soup for lunch.* □ *Please don't serve so much meat up.* 2. to present an idea or an opinion; often something uninteresting or hackneyed. (Informal.) □ *You can't go on serving up nonsense if you expect people to trust you.* □ *The managing director served up the usual words of encouragement to the staff.*

set a precedent to establish a pattern; to set a policy which must be followed in future cases. □ *I'll do what you ask this time, but it doesn't set a precedent.* □ *We've already set a precedent in matters such as these.*

set about doing something See *go about doing something.*

set about someone or something 1. [with *someone*] to attack someone. □ *The thieves set about the night-watchman with knives.* □ *The older boys set about Tom on his way home.* 2. [with *something*] to begin something; to tackle something. □ *He doesn't know how to* *set about repairing the bike.* □ *She set about the task right away.*

set eyes on someone or something AND **lay eyes on someone or something** to see someone or something, often for the first time. □ *I knew when I set eyes on that car that it was the car for me.* □ *Have you ever laid eyes on such a beautiful flower?*

set fire to someone or something AND **set someone or something on fire** to ignite someone or something; to set alight to someone or something. □ *The thief set fire to the building.* □ *The poor man accidentally set himself on fire.*

set foot somewhere to go or enter somewhere. (Often in the negative.) □ *If I were you, I wouldn't set foot in that town.* □ *I wouldn't set foot in her house! Not after the way she spoke to me.*

set forth (on something) to start out on something. □ *We intend to set forth on our journey very early in the morning.* □ *What time will you set forth?*

set great store by someone or something to have positive expectations for someone or something; to have high hopes for someone or something. □ *I set great store by my computer and its ability to help me in my work.* □ *We set great store by John because of his quick mind.*

set in to begin. (Often said of weather or climatic conditions.) □ *Winter set in very early this year.* □ *We got the windows closed before the storm set in.*

set off (for somewhere) AND **set out (for somewhere)** to begin a journey to a place. (See also *set forth (on something)*.) □ *We set off for the seaside late in the afternoon.* □ *We couldn't set off then because the dog was lost.* □ *The children set out for school even though the snow was quite deep.*

set one back on one's heels to surprise, shock, or overwhelm someone. □ *Her sudden announcement set us all back on our heels.* □ *The manager scolded me, and that really set me back on my heels.*

set one's heart against something See under *have one's heart set against something*.

set one's heart on something See under *have one's heart set on something*.

set one's sights on something to select something as a goal. □ *I set my sights on a good degree.* □ *Don't set your sights on something you cannot possibly achieve.*

set out (for somewhere) See *set off (for somewhere)*.

set sail (for somewhere) to depart in a boat for somewhere. (In a sailing-boat or power boat.) □ *This ship sets sail for Japan in two days.* □ *When do you set sail?*

set someone or something back AND **set back someone or something** 1. to delay someone or something; to undo the progress of someone or something. □ *The storm set back the work on the new building.* □ *A serious illness set the brilliant pupil back in school.* 2. [with *someone*] to cost someone (an amount of money). (Informal.) □ *This coat set me back about £250.* □ *That dinner at the restaurant last night set us back a fortune.*

set someone or something free to free someone or something. □ *I found a bird caught in the fence, and I set it free.* □ *I was locked in the room for an hour before someone opened the door and set me free.*

set someone or something off AND **set off someone or something** 1. [with *someone*] to get someone very excited and angry. □ *Whenever I see someone mistreating an animal, it really sets me off.* □ *The bill set off Bob. He raved for an hour!* 2. [with *something*] to start something. □ *The question of taxation set off an argument.* □ *Don't set another discussion off, please!*

set someone or something on fire See *set fire to someone or something*.

set someone or something up AND **set up someone or something** 1. [with *some-*

285

one] to lead—by deception—a person to play a particular role in an event; to arrange an event—usually by deception—so that a specific person takes the consequences for the event; to frame someone. (Slang.) □ *John isn't the one who started the fight. Somebody set up the poor chap.* □ *I had nothing to do with the robbery! I was just standing there. Somebody must have set me up!* **2.** [with *someone*] See *set someone up (in business).* **3.** [with *something*] to put something together; to erect something. □ *My parents bought me a dollhouse, but I had to set it up myself.* □ *It took nearly an hour to set up the tent.* **4.** [with *something*] to establish or found something. □ *We set up a fund to buy food for the needy.* □ *The business owners set a bank up in the small town.* **5.** [with *something*] to make plans for something. □ *Sally and Tom set up a party for Saturday night.* □ *John and Mary are hard at work setting something up for the meeting.* **6.** [with *something*] [for a bartender] to serve drinks to a customer. (Slang. Usually *something* is *'em.*) □ *The mean-looking man walked into the bar, looked at the bartender, and said, "Set 'em up."* □ *The bartender set up a drink for the man. He wanted no trouble.*

set someone straight to explain something to someone. (See also *put something straight.*) □ *I don't think you understand about taxation. Let me set you straight.* □ *Ann was confused, so I set her straight.*

set someone up as something AND **set up someone as something** to establish someone as something. □ *Bill set himself up as a free-lance journalist.* □ *When Mary got her degree, she set herself up as a consultant.* □ *My father set up my sisters as co-owners of the family business.*

set someone up (in business) to help establish someone in business; to provide the money someone needs to start a business. (Compare to the previous entry.) □ *My father set my sisters up in*

business. □ *He helped set them up so he could keep the business in the family.*

set someone's teeth on edge **1.** [for a sour or bitter taste] to irritate one's mouth. □ *Have you ever eaten a lemon? It'll set your teeth on edge.* □ *Vinegar sets my teeth on edge.* **2.** [for a person or a noise] to be irritating or get on one's nerves. □ *Please don't scrape your finger-nails on the blackboard! It sets my teeth on edge!* □ *Here comes Bob. He's so annoying. He really sets my teeth on edge.*

set something aside **1.** to discard or reject something. □ *The judge set the ruling aside and released the prisoner.* □ *I have to set aside your opinion. I think you're wrong.* **2.** AND **lay something aside; put something aside** to put something apart or to the side. □ *Take part of the cooking juices and set it aside for later use.* □ *Lay that glass aside because it's cracked.*

set something down to something See *put something down to something.*

set something out AND **set out something** **1.** to plant small plants out of doors. □ *We set some tomatoes out early in the spring.* □ *Don't set out your plants until after the last frost.* **2.** to remove something (from something) and leave it out (of something). □ *Please set some lamb chops out to thaw.* □ *When you find the file on Tom Smith, please set it out so I can look at it later.*

set something right See *put something right.*

set something straight See *put something straight.*

set the ball rolling See *start the ball rolling.*

set the cat among the pigeons See *put the cat among the pigeons.*

set the record straight to put right a mistake or misunderstanding; to make sure that an account, etc., is correct. □ *The manager thought Jean was to blame, but she soon set the record straight.* □ *Jane's mother heard that Tom is a mar-*

ried man, but he set the record straight. He's divorced.

set the stage for something to prepare for something; to lay the groundwork for something else to happen. □ *The committee set the stage for a major discussion.* □ *That kind of talk just sets the stage for more conflict.*

set the table to place plates, glasses, napkins, etc., on the table before a meal. □ *Jane, would you please set the table?* □ *I'm tired of setting the table. Ask someone else to do it.*

set the world on fire to do exciting things that bring fame and glory. (Frequently negative.) □ *I'm not very ambitious. I don't want to set the world on fire.* □ *You don't have to set the world on fire. Just do a good job.*

set up shop somewhere to establish one's place of work somewhere. (Informal.) □ *Mary set up shop in a small office building in Oak Street.* □ *The police officer said, "You can't set up shop right here on the pavement!"*

set upon someone or something to attack someone or something violently. □ *The dogs set upon the bear and chased it up a tree.* □ *Bill set upon Tom and struck him hard in the face.*

settle a score (with someone) AND **settle the score (with someone)** to clear up a problem with someone; to get even with someone. (Slang.) □ *John wants to settle a score with his neighbour.* □ *Tom, it's time you and I settled the score.* ALSO: **have a score to settle with someone** to have a problem to clear up with someone; to have to get even with someone about something. □ *I have a score to settle with John.*

settle down 1. to calm down. □ *Now, children, it's time to settle down and start class.* □ *If you don't settle down, I'll send you all home.* 2. to settle into a stable way of life; to get married and settle into a stable way of life. □ *Tom, don't you think it's about time you settled down and stopped all of this run-*

ning around? □ *Bill and Ann decided to settle down and raise a family.*

settle for something to agree to accept something (even though something else would be better); to accept a compromise. □ *We wanted a red one, but settled for a blue one.* □ *They would have liked a larger house, but they had to settle for a two-bedroom one.*

settle on something to decide on something. □ *We've discussed the merits of all of them, and we've settled on this one.* □ *I can't settle on one or the other, so I'll buy both.*

settle someone's affairs to deal with one's business matters; to manage the business affairs of someone who cannot. □ *When my uncle died, I had to settle his affairs.* □ *I have to settle my affairs before going to Spain for a year.*

settle up with someone to pay someone what one owes; to pay one one's share of something. □ *I must settle up with Jim for the bike I bought from him.* □ *Fred paid the whole restaurant bill and we all settled up with him later.*

sew something up AND **sew up something** (See also *get something sewn up*.) 1. to sew something; to stitch closed a tear or hole. □ *I had better sew this rip up before it tears more.* □ *Please sew up this hole in my sock. My toe keeps coming out.* 2. to finalize something; to secure something. (Informal.) □ *The manager told me to sew the contract up, or else.* □ *Let's sew this contract up today.*

shack up (with someone) to cohabit with someone; to live with someone of the opposite sex with whom one is having a sexual relationship. (Slang.) □ *Jim's not married to Jane. He just shacks up with her.* □ *Mary and Tom are shacking up now.*

shades of someone or something reminders of someone or something; reminiscent of someone or something. □ *When I met Jim's mother I thought "shades of Aunt Mary."* □ *"Shades of* *school," said Jack as the university lecturer rebuked him for being late.*

shaggy-dog story a kind of funny story which relies for its humour on its length and its sudden ridiculous ending. □ *Don't let John tell a shaggy-dog story. It'll go on for hours.* □ *Mary didn't get the point of Fred's shaggy-dog story.*

shake (hands) on something to clasp and shake the hand of someone as a sign of agreement about something. □ *The two people didn't sign a contract. They just shook hands on the terms of the agreement.* □ *I think it would be better to sign an agreement than just shake on it.*

shake hands (with someone) to clasp and shake the hand of someone as a greeting. □ *His hands were full, and I didn't know whether to try to shake hands with him or not.* □ *She put down her packages, and we shook hands.*

shake in one's shoes AND **quake in one's shoes** to be afraid; to shake from fear. □ *I was shaking in my shoes because I had to go and see the manager.* □ *Stop quaking in your shoes, Bob. I'm not going to sack you.*

shake someone or something off AND **shake off someone or something 1.** [with *someone*] to get rid of someone; to get free of someone who is bothering you. (Informal.) □ *I wish I could shake off John. He's such a pest!* □ *Stop bothering me! What do I have to do to shake you off?* **2.** [with *something*] to avoid getting a disease, such as a cold; to fight something off. (Informal.) □ *I hope I can shake off this cold pretty soon.* □ *I thought I was catching a cold, but I think I shook it off.*

shake someone up AND **shake up someone** to shock or upset someone. (Informal.) □ *The sight of the injured man shook me up.* □ *Your rude remark really shook up Tom.*

shake something off See *toss something off.*

Shame on someone. What a shameful thing!; someone should be ashamed. □ *You've torn your shirt again, Billy! Shame on you!* □ *When Billy tore his shirt, his mother said, "Shame on you!"* ALSO: **For shame!** That is wicked or shameful. □ *What a terrible thing to do. For shame!*

shape up to improve one's behaviour or performance; to develop or become formed. □ *Look at this, John! What a poor job you've done! It's time you shaped up!* □ *The football team is shaping up well.*

share and share alike with equal shares. □ *I kept five and gave the other five to Mary—share and share alike.* □ *The two room-mates agreed that they would divide expenses—share and share alike.*

sharp practice dishonest or illegal methods or behaviour. □ *I'm sure that Jim's firm was guilty of sharp practice in getting that export order.* □ *The Smith brothers accused their competitors of sharp practice, but they couldn't prove it.*

shed crocodile tears to shed false tears; to pretend that one is weeping. □ *The child wasn't hurt, but shed crocodile tears anyway.* □ *He thought he could get his way if he shed crocodile tears.*

shed (some) light on something to reveal something about something; to clarify something. □ *This discussion has shed some light on the problem.* □ *Let's see if Ann can shed light on this question.*

shell something out AND **shell out something** to pay money (out). (Slang.) □ *The traffic ticket turned out to be very expensive. I had to shell out £150.* □ *You'll have to shell plenty out to settle this bill.*

shift for oneself AND **fend for oneself** to get along by oneself; to support oneself. □ *I'm sorry, I can't pay your rent any more. You'll just have to shift for yourself.* □ *When I became twenty years old, I left home and began to fend for myself.*

shift one's ground to change one's opinions or arguments, often without being challenged or opposed. □ *At first Jack and I were on opposite sides, but he suddenly shifted his ground and started agreeing with me.* □ *Jim has very fixed views. You won't find him shifting his ground.*

ships that pass in the night people who meet each other briefly by chance and who are unlikely to meet again. □ *Mary would have liked to see Jim again, but to him, they were ships that passed in the night.* □ *When you travel a lot on business, you meet many ships that pass in the night.*

shipshape (and Bristol fashion) in good order; neat and tidy. (A nautical term. Bristol was a major British port.) □ *You had better get this room shipshape before your mother gets home.* □ *Mr. Jones always keeps his garden shipshape and Bristol fashion.*

shirk one's duty to neglect one's job or task. □ *The guard was sacked for shirking his duty.* □ *You cannot expect to continue shirking your duty without someone noticing.*

shoot a line to exaggerate or boast in order to impress someone. (Slang.) □ *Fred's shooting a line about his big house so that Mary will go out with him.* □ *George is always shooting a line about how important his job is but in fact he's a caretaker.*

shoot from the hip 1. to fire a gun which is held at one's side, against one's hip. (This increases one's speed in firing a gun.) □ *When I lived at home on the farm, my father taught me to shoot from the hip.* □ *I quickly shot the snake before it bit my horse. I'm glad I learned to shoot from the hip.* 2. to speak directly and frankly. (Informal.) □ *John has a tendency to shoot from the hip, but he generally speaks the truth.* □ *Don't pay any attention to John. He means no harm. It's just his nature to shoot from the hip.*

shoot one's mouth off AND **shoot off one's mouth** to boast or talk too much; to tell someone's secrets. (Slang.) □ *Don't pay any attention to Bob. He's always shooting his mouth off.* □ *Oh, Sally! Stop shooting off your mouth! You don't know what you're talking about.*

shop around (for something) to visit different shops to find what you want at the best price. □ *I've been shopping around for a new car, but they are all priced too high.* □ *You can find a bargain, but you'll have to shop around.*

shore someone or something up AND **shore up someone or something** 1. [with *someone*] to (figuratively) prop up or support someone. □ *Everyone cooperated to shore up John when his mother died.* □ *Mary's solid character and personality helped shore her up during her recent problems with the law.* 2. [with *something*] to prop up or support something. □ *The storm weakened the foundation of our house, and we had to have workers shore up the house.* □ *The fence fell over, so we shored it up.*

short and sweet brief (and pleasant because of briefness). □ *That was a good sermon—short and sweet.* □ *I don't care what you say, as long as you make it short and sweet.*

short of something not having enough of something. □ *I wanted to bake a cake, but I was short of eggs.* □ *Usually at the end of the month, I'm short of money.*

shot across the bows something acting as a warning. (A naval term.) □ *The student was sent a letter warning him to attend lectures, but he ignored the shot across the bows.* □ *Fred's solicitor sent Bob a letter as a shot across the bows to get him to pay the money he owed Fred.*

shot-gun wedding a forced wedding. (Informal. From the bride's father having threatened the bridegroom with a shotgun to force him to marry.) □ *Mary was six months pregnant when she married Bill. It was a real shot-gun wedding.* □ *Bob would never have married Jane if she hadn't been pregnant. Jane's fa-*

ther saw to it that it was a shot-gun wedding.

shot in the arm a boost; something that gives someone energy. (Informal.) □ *Thank you for cheering me up. Your visit was a real shot in the arm.* □ *Your friendly greeting card was just what I needed—a real shot in the arm.*

shot in the dark a random or wild guess or try. (Informal.) □ *I don't know how I guessed the right answer. It was just a shot in the dark.* □ *I was lucky to take on such a good worker as Sally. When I employed her, it was just a shot in the dark.*

shot through with something containing something; interwoven, intermixed, or filled with something. □ *The rose was a lovely pink shot through with streaks of white.* □ *John's comments are often shot through with sarcasm.* □ *I want a well-marbled steak—one shot through with fat.*

shoulder to shoulder side by side; with a shared purpose. □ *The two armies fought shoulder to shoulder against the joint enemy.* □ *The strikers said they would stand shoulder to shoulder against the management.*

shout someone or something down AND **shout down someone or something** to overwhelm someone or something by shouting. □ *Mary was trying to speak, but Sally shouted her down.* □ *Ann brought up a very important suggestion, but Bob shouted it down.*

shove off to depart [for somewhere]. (Slang. As if one were pushing a boat away from the shore.) □ *Well, it's time for me to shove off home.* □ *Yes, I have to shove off, too.*

shove someone or something down someone's throat AND **ram someone or something down someone's throat** to try to force someone or something on someone; to try to force someone to accept or endure someone or something. (Informal.) □ *I don't want any more insurance, and I don't want anyone to shove any insurance down my throat.* □ *Stop trying to ram your political views down my throat.*

show good faith See under *in good faith.*

show of hands a vote expressed by people raising their hands. □ *We were asked to vote for the candidates for captain by a show of hands.* □ *Jack wanted us to vote on paper, not by a show of hands, so that we could have a secret ballot.*

show off to behave in a way that will draw attention to oneself. (Informal.) □ *Bob is always showing off. He needs lots of attention.* □ *Why do you show off so much?* ALSO: **show-off** a person who shows off. □ *Ann is such a show-off!*

show one's hand to reveal one's intentions to someone. (From card-games.) □ *I don't know whether Jim's intending to marry Jane or not. He's not one to show his hand.* □ *If you want to get a rise, don't show the boss your hand too soon.*

show one's paces to show what one can do; to demonstrate one's abilities. (From horses demonstrating their skill and speed.) □ *The runners had to show their paces for a place in the relay team.* □ *All the singers had to show their paces to be selected for the choir.*

show one's teeth to act in an angry or threatening manner. □ *We thought Bob was meek and mild, but he really showed his teeth when Jack insulted his girlfriend.* □ *The enemy forces didn't expect the country they invaded to show its teeth.*

show oneself in one's true colours to show what one is really like or what one is really thinking. □ *Jane always pretends to be sweet and gentle, but she showed herself in her true colours when she lost the match.* □ *Mary's drunken husband didn't show himself in his true colours until after they were married.*

show promise See *have a lot of promise.*

show signs of something to show hints or indications of something. □ *I let the horse run at full speed until it began to show signs of tiring.* □ *Sally is showing signs of stress.*

show someone around to give someone a tour of somewhere. □ *I'm very glad you've come to work here. Let me show you around so you'll know where things are.* □ *Welcome to our town. As soon as you unpack, I'll get someone to show you around.*

show someone into somewhere to lead or usher someone into somewhere. □ *The butler showed me into the sitting-room and asked me to wait.* □ *The car dealer showed me into the sales office and asked me to sign some papers.*

show someone or something off AND **show off someone or something** to display someone or something so that the best features are apparent; to display someone or something for others to admire. □ *Mrs. Williams was showing off her baby to the neighbours.* □ *Bill drove around all afternoon showing his new car off.*

show someone out AND **see someone out** to lead or take someone to the way out (of a place). □ *Thank you for coming. John will show you out.* □ *There is no need to show me out. I can find the way.* □ *I'm so glad you came. I'll see you out.*

show someone the door to force someone to leave; to insist that someone leave. □ *Mary showed the uninvited guest the door.* □ *As soon as Frank disagreed, his father showed him the door.*

show someone the ropes See under *know the ropes.*

show someone to the door AND **see someone to the door** to lead or take someone to the door or exit. □ *After we finished our talk, she showed me to the door.* □ *Bill and I finished our chat as he saw me to the door.*

show someone up AND **show up someone** to make someone's faults or shortcomings apparent. (Informal.) □ *John's excellent effort really showed up Bill, who didn't try very hard at all.* □ *John is always trying to show someone up to make himself look better.*

show someone up as something to reveal that someone is really something (else). □ *The investigation showed her up as a fraud.* □ *The test showed the banker up as unqualified.*

show something to advantage to display the best features of something; to display something so that its best features are apparent. □ *Put the vase in the centre of the table and show it to advantage.* □ *Having and using a large vocabulary shows your intelligence to advantage.*

show the flag to be present at a gathering just so that the organization to which one belongs will be represented or just to show others that one has attended. (From a ship flying its country's flag.) □ *The firm wants all the salesmen to attend the international conference in order to show the flag.* □ *As many as possible of the family should attend the wedding. We must show the flag.*

show the white feather to reveal fear or cowardice. (From the fact that a white tail-feather was a sign of inferior breeding in a fighting cock.) □ *Jim showed the white feather by refusing to fight with Jack.* □ *The enemy army showed the white feather by running away.*

show up to appear; to arrive. (Informal.) □ *Where is John? I hope he shows up soon.* □ *When will the bus show up?* □ *Weeds began to show up in the garden.*

shrug something off (as something) AND **pass something off (as something); pass off something (as something); shrug off something (as something)** to ignore something unpleasant or offensive as if it meant something else. □ *She shrugged off the criticism as harmless.* □ *I passed off the remark as misinformed.* □ *Bill scolded me, but I just passed it off.*

shut someone or something out AND **shut out someone or something** to exclude someone or something; to refuse entrance to someone or something. □ *We tried to get into the stadium, but they shut us out because there was no more room.* □ *She felt shut out of her parents' love for each other.*

shut someone up AND **shut up someone** to silence someone. (Slang.) □ *Will you please shut up that crying baby!* □ *Oh, shut yourself up!* ALSO: **Shut up!** Be quiet! □ *Oh, shut up!*

shut something down See *close something down.*

shut the door on something AND **close the door on something** to terminate, exclude, or obstruct something. □ *Your unhelpful attitude shuts the door on any future co-operation from me.* □ *The bad service at that shop closes the door on any more business from my company.*

Shut up! See under *shut someone up.*

shy away (from someone or something) to avoid someone or something. □ *The dog shies away from John since John kicked it.* □ *I can understand why the dog would shy away.* □ *I shy away from eating onions. I think I'm allergic to them.*

sick and tired of someone or something disgusted and annoyed with someone or something. (Informal.) □ *I'm sick and tired of Ann and her whistling.* □ *We are all sick and tired of this old car.*

sick in bed remaining in bed while (one is) ill. □ *Tom is sick in bed with the flu.* □ *He's been sick in bed for nearly a week.*

side against someone to be against someone; to take sides against someone. □ *I thought you were my friend! I never thought you would side against me!* □ *The two brothers were always siding against their sister.*

side with someone to join with someone; to take someone else's part; to be on someone's side. □ *Why is it that you always side with him when he and I argue?* □ *I never side with anybody. I form my own opinions.*

sight for sore eyes a welcome sight. (Informal.) □ *Oh, am I glad to see you here! You're a sight for sore eyes.* □ *I'm so hungry. This meal is a sight for sore eyes.*

sign in to register; to sign one's name or have one's name signed on a list which shows that one has arrived. □ *Please sign in as soon as you arrive so that we'll know you're here.* □ *Go over to that table and sign in. Then you'll be told what to do next.*

sign off to stop radio or television transmission. □ *The voice said, "This is radio station 2L0 signing off for Thursday, the nineteenth of December."* □ *This television station broadcasts from dawn until it signs off at midnight.*

sign on **1.** to begin radio or television transmission. □ *What time does the station sign on?* □ *The station broadcasts twenty-four hours a day, so it never signs on and it never signs off.* **2.** to register as unemployed and so be able to obtain social security payments. (Informal.) □ *She lost her job in the morning and had signed on by midday.* □ *Too many people would rather just sign on than take a low-paying job.*

sign on the dotted line to place one's signature on a contract or other important paper. □ *This agreement isn't properly concluded until we both sign on the dotted line.* □ *Here are the papers for the purchase of your car. As soon as you sign on the dotted line, that beautiful, shiny vehicle will be all yours!*

sign one's own death-warrant (figuratively) to sign a paper which calls for one's own death; to do something that will lead to one's own ruin or downfall. □ *I wouldn't ever gamble a large sum of money. That would be signing my own death-warrant.* □ *The killer signed his own death-warrant when he walked into the police station and gave himself up.*

sign someone in AND **sign in someone** to register someone; to write someone's name on a registration list. □ *Please go over to the table where the secretary will sign you in.* □ *The secretary is signing in everyone at that table.*

sign someone on AND **sign on someone** to employ someone; to recruit someone as an employee. □ *How many workers did the manager sign on?* □ *The construction company security signed on ten new workers.*

sign something over (to someone) to transfer ownership of something to someone. □ *The seller signed the house over to the buyer when everyone was satisfied with the sale.* □ *I'm ready to purchase your car from you anytime you're ready to sign it over.*

sign up (for something) to put one's name on a list for something. □ *I was too late to sign up for the class. I had to enrol in a different one.* □ *I should have signed up yesterday.*

signed, sealed, and delivered formally and officially signed; [for a formal document to be] executed. (Informal.) □ *Here is the deed to the property— signed, sealed, and delivered.* □ *I can't begin work on this project until I have the contract signed, sealed, and delivered.*

silly season the time of year, usually in the summer, when there is a lack of important news and newspapers contain articles about unimportant or trivial things instead. □ *It must be the silly season. There's a story here about peculiarly shaped potatoes.* □ *There's a piece on the front page about people with big feet. Talk about the silly season.*

simmer down to get quiet or calm. □ *Look, you lot! Simmer down! Stop all the noise and go to sleep!* □ *I'm very busy now. Please come back in a few hours when things have simmered down a bit.*

since the year dot See *from the year dot.*

sing a different tune See *change someone's tune.*

sing someone's praises to praise someone highly and enthusiastically. □ *The boss is singing the praises of his new secretary.* □ *The theatre critics are singing the praises of the young actor.*

single file See *in single file.*

single someone or something out AND **single out someone or something** to select or refer to a particular person or thing. □ *I'm not the only one who is late. Don't single me out!* □ *Why did you single out that book to criticize?* □ *John singled out Mary for a special award.*

sink in **1.** to submerge slowly in(to something); to soak in(to something). □ *The road was very muddy, and my car's tyres kept sinking in.* □ *I couldn't serve myself any stew because the spoon had sunk in.* **2.** [for knowledge] to be understood. (Informal.) □ *I heard what you said, but it took a while for it to sink in.* □ *I pay careful attention to everything I hear in class, but it usually doesn't sink in.*

sink into despair [for someone] to grieve or become depressed. □ *After losing all my money, I sank into despair.* □ *There is no need to sink into despair. Everything is going to be all right.*

sink one's teeth into something to take a bite of some kind of food, usually a special kind of food. □ *I can't wait to sink my teeth into a nice, juicy steak.* □ *Look at that chocolate cake! Don't you want to sink your teeth into that?*

sink or swim fail or succeed. □ *After I've studied and learned all I can, I have to take the test and sink or swim.* □ *It's too late to help John now. It's sink or swim for him.*

sink our differences AND **sink their differences** to forget or agree to set aside disagreements of opinion, attitude, etc. □ *We decided to sink our differences and try to be friends for Mary's sake.* □ *Individual members of the team must sink their differences and work for the success of the team.*

sit at someone's feet to admire someone greatly; to be influenced by someone's teaching; to be taught by someone. □ *Jack sat at the feet of Picasso when he was studying in Europe.* □ *Tom would love to sit at the feet of the musician Yehudi Menuhin.*

sit back and let something happen to relax and not interfere with something; to let something happen without playing a part in it. □ *I can't just sit back and let you waste all our money!* □ *Don't worry. Just sit back and let things happen.*

sit (idly) by to remain inactive when other people are doing something; to ignore a situation which calls for help. □ *Bob sat idly by even though everyone else was hard at work.* □ *I can't sit by while all those people need food.*

sit in for someone to take someone else's place in a specific activity. (The activity usually involves being seated.) □ *I can't be at the meeting Thursday. Will you sit in for me?* □ *Sorry, I can't sit in for you. John is also going to be absent, and I am sitting in for him.*

sit in (on something) to witness or observe something without participating. (Usually involves being seated.) □ *I can't enrol for the history class, but I have permission to sit in on it.* □ *I asked the professor if I could sit in.*

sit on one's hands to do nothing; to fail to help. □ *When we needed help from Mary, she just sat on her hands.* □ *We need the co-operation of everyone. You can't sit on your hands!*

sit on something to hold something back; to delay something. (Informal.) □ *The project cannot be finished because the city council is sitting on the final approval.* □ *Ann deserves to be promoted, but the manager is sitting on her promotion because of a disagreement.*

sit on the fence not to take sides in a dispute; not to make a clear choice between two possibilities. □ *When Jane and Tom argue it is as well to sit on the fence and then you won't offend either of them.* □ *No one knows which of the candidates Joan will vote for. She's sitting on the fence.*

sit something out AND **sit out something** not to participate in something; to wait until something is over before participating. □ *I'm tired of playing cards, so I think I'll sit out this game.* □ *Oh, please play with us. Don't sit it out.*

sit through something to witness or endure all of something. □ *The performance was so bad that I could hardly sit through it.* □ *You can't expect small children to sit through a long film.*

sit tight to wait; to wait patiently. (Informal. Does not necessarily refer to sitting.) □ *Just relax and sit tight. I'll be right with you.* □ *We were waiting in the queue for the gates to open when someone came out and told us to sit tight because it wouldn't be much longer before we could go in.*

sit up and take notice to become alert and pay attention. □ *A loud noise from the front of the room caused everyone to sit up and take notice.* □ *The firm wouldn't pay any attention to my complaints. When I had my solicitor write them a letter, they sat up and took notice.*

sit up with someone to stay with someone through the night, especially with a sick or troubled person or with someone who is waiting for something. □ *I had to sit up with my younger sister when she was ill.* □ *I sat up with Bill while he waited for an overseas telephone call.*

sit with someone 1. to stay with someone; to *sit up with someone.* □ *Sally was upset, so I sat with her for a while.* □ *My uncle sat with me my first day in the hospital.* **2.** to stay with and care for one or more children; to baby-sit someone. □ *I engaged Mrs. Wilson to sit with the children.* □ *We couldn't go out for dinner because we couldn't find anyone to sit with the children.*

sitting on a powder keg in a risky or explosive situation; in a situation where something serious or dangerous may happen at any time. □ *Things are very* *tense at work. The whole office is sitting on a powder keg.* □ *The fire at the oil-field seems to be under control for now, but all the workers there are sitting on a powder keg.*

(sitting) on top of the world feeling wonderful; glorious; ecstatic. □ *Wow, I feel on top of the world.* □ *Since he got a new job, he's on top of the world.* □ *I've been sitting on top of the world all week because I passed my exams.*

sitting pretty living in comfort or luxury; in a good situation. (Informal.) □ *My uncle died and left enough money for me to be sitting pretty for the rest of my life.* □ *Now that I have a good-paying job, I'm sitting pretty.*

sitting target someone or something that is in a position that is easily attacked. □ *The old man was a sitting target for the burglars. He lived alone and did not have a telephone.* □ *People recently taken on will be sitting targets if the firm need to reduce staff.*

six of one and half a dozen of the other about the same one way or another. □ *It doesn't matter to me which way you do it. It's six of one and half a dozen of the other.* □ *What difference does it make? They're both the same— six of one and half a dozen of the other.*

sixth sense a supposed power to know or feel things that are not perceptible by the five senses of sight, hearing, smell, taste, and touch. □ *My sixth sense told me to avoid going home by my usual route. Later I discovered there had been a fatal accident on it.* □ *Meg's sixth sense demanded that she not trust Tom, even though he seemed honest enough.*

size someone or something up AND **size up someone or something** to observe someone or something to get information. □ *The comedian sized the audience up and decided not to use his new material.* □ *I like to size up a situation before I act.*

skate over something to pass lightly over something, trying to avoid drawing attention or avoid taking something into

consideration. □ *Sally prefers to skate over her reasons for leaving her job.* □ *Meg skated over the reason for her quarrel with Dick.*

(skating) on thin ice in a risky situation. □ *If you try that you'll really be on thin ice. That's too risky.* □ *You're skating on thin ice if you criticize the lecturer. He has a hot temper.*

skeleton in the closet a hidden and shocking secret. (Often in the plural.) □ *You can ask anyone about how reliable I am. I don't mind. I don't have any skeletons in the closet.* □ *My uncle was in jail for a day once. That's our family's skeleton in the closet.*

skin someone alive to be very angry with someone; to scold someone severely. (Informal.) □ *I was so angry at Jane that I could have skinned her alive.* □ *If I don't get home on time, my parents will skin me alive.*

skip bail See *jump bail.*

Skip it! Forget it! (Informal.) □ BILL: *What did you say?* BOB: *Oh, skip it!* □ *It's not important. Just skip it!*

slack off (Informal.) **1.** to taper off; to reduce gradually. □ *Business tends to slack off during the winter months.* □ *The storms begin to slack off in April.* **2.** to become less active; to become lazy or inefficient. □ *Near the end of the school year, Sally began to slack off, and her marks showed it.* □ *John got sacked for slacking off during the busy season.*

slanging match an angry argument in which both sides are rude to each other. (Slang.) □ *Bob and the boss had a slanging match in front of the whole office.* □ *Sally and her mother-in-law are always getting into slanging matches.*

slap in the face an insult; an act that causes disappointment or discouragement. □ *Losing the election was a slap in the face for the club president.* □ *Failing to get into college was a slap in the face to Tim after his year of study.*

slap someone down to rebuke or rebuff someone. □ *You may disagree with her, but you needn't slap her down like that.* □ *I only asked you what time it was! There's no need to slap me down!*

slap someone's wrist See *get a slap on the wrist.*

slate something to criticize something severely. □ *The critics slated the place.* □ *The teacher slated the pupil's performance.*

sleep in to oversleep; to sleep late in the morning. □ *If you sleep in again, you'll get the sack.* □ *Get an alarm clock to stop you sleeping in.*

sleep like a log AND **sleep like a top** to sleep very soundly. □ *Nothing can wake me up. I usually sleep like a log.* □ *Everyone in our family sleeps like a top, so no one heard the fire engines in the middle of the night.*

sleep like a top See the previous entry.

sleep on something to think about something overnight; to weigh up a decision overnight. □ *I don't know whether I agree to do it. Let me sleep on it.* □ *I slept on it, and I've decided to accept your offer.*

sleep something off AND **sleep off something** to sleep while the effects of alcohol or drugs pass away. □ *John drank too much and went home to sleep it off.* □ *Bill is at home sleeping off the effects of the drug they gave him.*

sleep with someone to have sex with someone; to copulate with someone. (Euphemistic. This may not involve sleep.) □ *Everyone assumes that Mr. Franklin doesn't sleep with Mrs. Franklin.* □ *Jane's afraid that her mother will find out that she's sleeping with Tom.*

slice of the cake a share of something. □ *There's not much work around and so everyone must get a slice of the cake.* □ *The firm makes huge profits, and the workers want a slice of the cake.*

slip away AND **slip off; slip out** to go away or escape quietly or in secret. □ *I* slipped away when no one was looking. □ *Let's slip off somewhere and have a little talk.* □ *I'll try to slip out for an hour or two when Tom is asleep.*

slip of the tongue an error in speaking where a word is pronounced incorrectly, or where something which the speaker did not mean to say is said. □ *I didn't mean to tell her that. It was a slip of the tongue.* □ *I failed to understand the instructions because the speaker made a slip of the tongue at an important point.*

slip off See *slip away.*

slip one's mind [for something which was to be remembered] to be forgotten. □ *I meant to go to the shops on the way home, but it slipped my mind.* □ *My birthday slipped my mind. I suppose I wanted to forget it.*

slip out 1. [for secret information] to be revealed. □ *I asked her to keep our engagement secret, but she let it slip out.* □ *I didn't mean to tell. It just slipped out.* 2. See *slip away.*

slip through someone's fingers to get away from someone; [for something] to be lost or forgotten by someone. □ *I had a copy of the book you want, but somehow it slipped through my fingers.* □ *There was a detective following me, but I managed to slip through his fingers.*

slip up to make an error. (Informal. Also without *up.*) □ *Try as hard as you can to do it right and not slip up.* □ *Everything was going fine until the last minute when I slipped up.* ALSO: **slip-up** an error. (Informal.) □ *See if you can get through this match without another slip-up.*

slope off to go away, especially secretively. (Informal.) □ *Fred will slope off at the first sign of trouble.* □ *Don't slope off before we tidy up after the party.*

slough something off AND **slough off something** to shed something; to get rid of something; to throw off or repel something. (See also *shrug something off as something.*) □ *The snake spent*

---

about an hour sloughing off its old skin. □ Ann made an insulting remark to me, but I just sloughed it off.

Slow and steady wins the race. a proverb meaning that deliberateness and determination will lead to success, or (literally) a reasonable pace will win a race. □ I worked my way through college in ten years. Now I know what they mean when they say, "Slow and steady wins the race." □ Ann works slowly but diligently. Slow and steady wins the race.

slow on the uptake slow to figure something out; slow-thinking. □ Sally didn't get the joke because she's sort of slow on the uptake. □ Bill—who's slow on the uptake—didn't get the joke until it was explained to him.

smack dab in the middle right in the middle. (Informal.) □ I want a big helping of mashed potatoes with a glob of butter smack dab in the middle. □ Tom and Sally were having a terrible argument, and I was trapped smack dab in the middle.

smack in the eye something that will hurt or humiliate someone, often when it is considered deserved; an insult. (Informal.) □ Being rejected by Jane was a real smack in the eye for Tom, who thought she was fond of him. □ Meg thought she was the best-qualified candidate for the job, and not getting it was a smack in the eye.

small fry 1. unimportant people or things. □ The police have only caught the small fry. The leader of the gang is still free. □ At the moment our business is small fry, but we're planning to expand. **2.** children. (Informal.) □ Peter's taking the small fry to the zoo. □ We should take the small fry to the pantomime.

small hours the hours immediately after midnight. □ The dance went on to the small hours. □ Jim goes to bed in the small hours and gets up at lunch-time.

small print the part of a document that is not easily noticed, often because of the smallness of the print, and that often

contains important information. □ You should have read the small print before signing the contract. □ You should always read the small print in an insurance policy.

small talk talk about minor matters rather than important matters or personal matters. □ All the people at the party were engaging in small talk. □ It was just aimless small talk, not a real conversation.

small time small; on a small scale. □ Our business is small time just now, but it's growing. □ He's a small time crook.

smear campaign (against someone) a campaign aimed at damaging someone's reputation by making accusations and spreading rumours. □ His opponents are engaging in a smear campaign against the politician. □ Jack started a smear campaign against Tom in the firm so that Tom wouldn't get the manager's job.

smell a rat to suspect that something is wrong; to sense that someone has caused something wrong. (Informal.) □ I don't think this was an accident. I smell a rat. Bob had something to do with this. □ The minute I came in, I smelled a rat. Sure enough, I had been robbed.

smell of the lamp [for a book] to show signs of being revised and researched carefully and to lack spontaneity. □ I preferred her earlier spontaneous novels. The later ones smell of the lamp. □ The student has done a lot of research, but has few original ideas. His essay smells of the lamp.

smile on someone or something to be favourable to someone or something. □ Fate smiled on me and I got the job. □ Lady Luck smiled on our venture and we made a profit.

smoke someone or something out AND **smoke out someone or something** to force someone or something out (of something), perhaps with smoke. □ There was a mouse in the attic, but I smoked it out. □ The officers smoked out the bank robbers.

smooth something out AND **smooth out something 1.** to make something flat, neat, and smooth. □ *The sheet of paper was wrinkled, so I smoothed it out.* □ *The workers used a huge roller to smooth out the gravel road.* **2.** See the following entry.

smooth something over AND **smooth something out; smooth out something; smooth over something** to reduce the intensity of an argument or a misunderstanding; to try to make people feel better about something that has happened. □ *Mary and John had a terrible argument, and they are both trying to smooth it over.* □ *Let's get everyone together and try to smooth things out. We can't keep on arguing with one another.*

snake in the grass a low and deceitful person. □ *Sally said that Bob couldn't be trusted because he was a snake in the grass.* □ *"You snake in the grass!" cried Sally. "You cheated me."*

snap out of something to become suddenly freed from a state. (Informal. The state can be a depression, an illness, unconsciousness, etc.) □ *I was very depressed for a week, but this morning I snapped out of it.* □ *It isn't often that a cold gets me down. Usually I can snap out of it quickly.*

snap something up AND **snap up something** to grab and buy something. (Informal.) □ *I went to the shops, and one had soup on sale, so I snapped up plenty.* □ *I always snap bargains up whenever I go shopping.*

sneak up on someone or something to move up on someone or something quietly or secretly. (Informal.) □ *Jane sneaked up on John and startled him.* □ *The date when car payments are due sneaks up on us before we know it.*

snowed in trapped somewhere because of too much snow. □ *The snow was so deep that we were snowed in for three days.* □ *Being snowed in is no problem if you have enough food.*

snowed under having too much work to do. (Informal.) □ *I had to stay in town and work late last night because we were snowed under at the office.* □ *If I keep up with my work, I won't get snowed under.*

so-and-so 1. a despised person. (Informal. This expression is used in place of other very insulting terms.) □ *The dirty so-and-so! I can't stand him!* □ *Don't you call me a so-and-so, you creep!* **2.** an unnamed or unidentified person or thing. □ *I don't care what so-and-so thinks.* □ *He's always giving me orders to do so-and-so.*

so be it this is the way it will be. □ *If you insist on running off and marrying her, so be it. Only don't say I didn't warn you!* □ *Mary has decided that this is what she wants. So be it.*

so far as anyone knows See *(as) far as anyone knows.*

so far as possible See *as far as possible.*

so far as someone is concerned See *as far as someone is concerned.*

So far, so good. All is going well so far. □ *We are half finished with our project. So far, so good.* □ *The operation is proceeding quite nicely—so far, so good.*

so long goodbye. (Informal.) □ *So long, see you later.* □ *As John got out of the car, he said, "Thanks for the lift. So long."*

so much for someone or something that is the last of someone or something; there is no need to consider someone or something any more. □ *It just started raining. So much for our picnic this afternoon.* □ *So much for John. He just called in sick and can't come to work today.*

so much the better even better; all to the better. □ *Please come to the picnic. If you can bring a salad, so much the better.* □ *Please come. If your wife can come, so much the better.*

so-so not good and not bad; mediocre. (Informal.) □ *I didn't have a bad day.*

It was just so-so. □ *The players put on a so-so performance.*

so still you could hear a pin drop AND **so quiet you could hear a pin drop** very quiet. (Also with *can*.) □ *When I came into the room, it was so still you could hear a pin drop. Then everyone shouted, "Happy birthday!"* □ *Please be quiet. Be so quiet you can hear a pin drop.*

so to speak as one might say; said a certain way, even though the words are not exactly accurate. □ *John helps me with my accounts. He's my accountant, so to speak.* □ *I just love my little poodle. She's my baby, so to speak.*

soak something up AND **soak up something; take something up; take up something** to absorb something such as liquid, knowledge, sunshine, etc. □ *Billy spilled a glass of water and used a paper towel to soak it up.* □ *The lecture was great. I sat there and soaked up the whole thing.* □ *The sponge didn't take up all the spilled water.*

soaked to the skin with one's clothing wet clear through to the skin. □ *I was caught in the rain and got soaked to the skin.* □ *Oh, come in and dry off! You must be soaked to the skin.*

soil one's hands See *dirty one's hands.*

some new blood new members of an organization who are expected to make it more efficient or more lively. □ *Our club needs some new blood. It has become boring.* □ *The firm's management has at last got some new blood. Things should improve now.*

something about someone or something something strange or curious about someone or something. □ *There is something about Jane. I just can't figure her out.* □ *I love Mexican food. There's just something about it.*

something else **1.** something unusual or extraordinary. (Informal.) □ *Did you see her new car? That's really something else!* □ *John hit a ball yesterday that went out of the stadium and kept on going. He's something else!* **2.** See the following entry.

something else (again) something entirely different. (Informal.) □ *Borrowing is one thing, but stealing is something else.* □ *Skin-diving is easy and fun, but scuba-diving is something else again.*

something of the sort something of the kind just mentioned. □ *The tree isn't exactly a spruce tree, just something of the sort.* □ *Jane has a cold or something of the sort.*

something or other something; one thing or another. (Informal.) □ *I can't remember what Ann said—something or other.* □ *A messenger came by and dropped off something or other at the front desk.*

something sticks in one's craw something bothers one. □ *Her criticism stuck in my craw.* □ *I knew that everything I said would stick in his craw and upset him.*

something to that effect meaning something like that. (Informal.) □ *She said she wouldn't be available until after three, or something to that effect.* □ *I was told to keep out of the house—or something to that effect.*

something's up something is going to happen; something is going on. (Slang.) □ *Everybody looks very nervous. I think something's up.* □ *From the looks of all the activity around here, I think something's up.*

sooner or later eventually; in the short term or in the long term. □ *He'll have to pay the bill sooner or later.* □ *She'll get what she deserves sooner or later.*

sort of (something) AND **kind of (something)** almost something; somewhat; somehow. (Informal.) □ *Isn't it sort of cold out?* □ *Yes, sort of.* □ *He's a sort of consultant.* □ *She's a kind of caretaker.*

sort something out AND **sort out something** **1.** to arrange something in numerical or alphabetical order; to arrange or classify something according to some order. □ *I have to sort out this box of cards.* □ *As soon as I sort out these* files and put them away, I can help you. **2.** to clear up confusion; to straighten out something disorderly. □ *Now that things are settled down, I can sort out my life.* □ *This place is a mess. Let's sort things out before we do anything else.*

sound off to speak loudly and freely about something, especially when complaining. (Informal.) □ *The people at the bus-stop were sounding off about the poor transportation services.* □ *Bob was sounding off about the government's economic policies.*

sound someone out AND **sound out someone** to try to find out what someone thinks (about something). □ *I don't know what Jane thinks about your suggestion, but I'll sound her out.* □ *Please sound out everyone in your department.*

soup something up AND **soup up something** to make something (especially a car) more powerful. (Slang.) □ *Bill spent all summer souping up that old car he bought.* □ *I wish someone would soup up my car. It'll hardly run.*

sow one's wild oats to do wild and foolish things in one's youth. (Often assumed to have some sort of sexual meaning.) □ *Jack was out sowing his wild oats last night, and he's in jail this morning.* □ *Mrs. Smith told Mr. Smith that he was too old to be sowing his wild oats.*

spaced out giddy; in a daze; in another world. (Slang. From drug slang.) □ *I don't see how Sally can accomplish anything. She's so spaced out!* □ *She's not really spaced out. She acts that way on purpose.*

speak for itself AND **speak for themselves** not to need explaining; to have an obvious meaning. □ *The facts speak for themselves. Tom's guilty.* □ *Your results speak for themselves. You need to work harder.*

speak highly of someone or something to say good things about someone or something. (Note the variations in the examples.) □ *Ann speaks quite highly of Jane's work.* □ *Everyone speaks very highly of Jane.*

speak of the devil said when someone whose name has just been mentioned appears or is heard from. □ *Well, speak of the devil! Hello, Tom. We were just talking about you.* □ *I had just mentioned Sally when—speak of the devil—she walked in the door.*

speak off the cuff to speak in public without preparation. (Informal.) □ *I'm not too good at speaking off the cuff.* □ *I need to prepare a speech for Friday, although I speak off the cuff quite well.*

speak one's mind to say frankly what one thinks (about something). □ *Please let me speak my mind, and then you can do whatever you wish.* □ *You can always depend on John to speak his mind. He'll let you know what he really thinks.*

speak out (against something) AND **speak up (against something)** to say something frankly and directly. (See also speak up.) □ *This law is wrong, and I intend to speak out against it until it is repealed.* □ *You must speak out. People need to know what you think.*

speak out of turn to say something unwise or imprudent; to say something at the wrong time. □ *Excuse me if I'm speaking out of turn, but what you are proposing is quite wrong.* □ *Bob was quite honest, even if he was speaking out of turn.*

speak the same language [for people] to have similar ideas, tastes, etc. □ *Jane and Jack get along very well. They really speak the same language about almost everything.* □ *Bob and his father don't speak the same language when it comes to politics.*

speak up 1. to speak more loudly. □ *They can't hear you in the back of the room. Please speak up.* □ *What? Speak up, please. I'm hard of hearing.* **2.** See the following entry.

speak up (against something) See *speak out (against something)*.

speak up for someone or something to speak in favour of someone or something. □ *If anybody says bad things about me, I hope you speak up for me.* □ *I want to speak up for the rights of pupils.*

speak with a forked tongue to tell lies; to try to deceive someone. □ *Jean's mother sounds very charming, but she speaks with a forked tongue.* □ *People tend to believe Fred because he seems plausible, but we know he speaks with a forked tongue.*

speed someone or something up AND **speed up someone or something** to make someone or something go faster. □ *Bill is going too slowly. See if you can speed him up.* □ *We have to speed up the election process so that we can have officers by the end of the month.*

spell something out AND **spell out something 1.** to spell something (in letters). (Also without *out*.) □ *I can't understand your name. Can you spell it out?* □ *Please spell out all the strange words so I can write them down correctly.* **2.** to give all the details of something. □ *I want you to understand this completely, so I'm going to spell all this out very carefully.* □ *The instruction book for my computer spells out everything very carefully.*

spell trouble to signify future trouble; to mean trouble. (Informal.) □ *This letter that came today spells trouble.* □ *The sky looks angry and dark. That spells trouble.*

spend a penny to urinate. (Informal. From the former cost of admission to the cubicles in public lavatories.) □ *Stop the car. The little girl needs to spend a penny.* □ *The station toilets are closed and I have to spend a penny.*

spick and span very clean. (Informal.) □ *I have to clean up the house and get it spick and span for the party on Friday night.* □ *I love to have everything around me spick and span.*

spike someone's guns to spoil someone's plans; to make it impossible for someone to carry out a course of action. (From driving a metal spike into the touch-hole of an enemy gun to render it useless.) □ *The boss was going to sack Sally publicly, but she spiked his guns by resigning.* □ *Jack intended borrowing his father's car when he was away, but his father spiked his guns by locking it in the garage.*

spill the beans See *let the cat out of the bag*.

spin something out AND **spin out something** to cause something to last longer, especially longer than necessary. □ *The lecturer really spun his talk out.* □ *I don't think I can spin out my material to cover twenty pages.*

spitting image the perfect likeness (of a person). □ *Jane is the spitting image of her mother.* □ *John is his brother's spitting image.*

splash out on something to spend a lot of money on something in an extravagant way. (Informal.) □ *Jack splashed out on a new car that he couldn't afford.* □ *Let's splash out on a really good meal out.*

split hairs to quibble; to try to make petty distinctions. □ *They don't have any serious differences. They are just splitting hairs.* □ *Don't waste time splitting hairs. Accept it the way it is.*

split people up AND **split up people** to separate two or more people (from one another). (See also *split up*.) □ *If you two don't stop chattering, I'll have to split you up.* □ *The group of people grew too large, so we had to split it up.*

split something fifty-fifty See *divide something fifty-fifty*.

split the difference to divide the difference (with someone else). □ *You want to sell for £120, and I want to buy for £100. Let's split the difference and close the deal at £110.* □ *I don't want to split the difference. I want £120.*

split up [for people] to separate or leave one another. (Informal. Can refer to divorce or separation.) □ *I heard that Mr. and Mrs. Brown have split up.* □ *Our little club had to split up because everyone was too busy.*

spoil the ship for a ha'porth of tar to risk ruining something valuable by not buying something relatively inexpensive but essential for it. (*Ha'porth* is a halfpenny's worth. From the use of tar to make boats watertight.) □ *Meg spent a lot of money on a new dress but refused to buy shoes. She certainly spoilt the ship for a ha'porth of tar.* □ *Bob bought a new car but doesn't get it serviced because it's too expensive. He'll spoil the ship for a ha'porth of tar.*

spoken for taken; reserved (for someone). □ *I'm sorry, but this one is already spoken for.* □ *Pardon me. Can I sit here, or is this seat spoken for?*

spoon-feed to treat someone with too much care or help; to teach someone with methods that are too easy and do not stimulate the learner to independent thinking. □ *The teacher spoon-feeds the pupils by dictation notes on the novel instead of getting the children to read the books themselves.* □ *You mustn't spoon-feed the new recruits by telling them what to do all the time. They must use their initiative.*

sporting chance a reasonably good chance. □ *If you hurry, you have a sporting chance of catching the bus.* □ *The firm has only a sporting chance of getting the export order.*

spot on exactly right or accurate. (Informal.) □ *Jack's assessment of the state of the firm was spot on.* □ *Mary's description of the stolen car was spot on.*

spout off (about someone or something) to talk too much about someone or something. (Slang.) □ *Why do you always have to spout off about things that don't concern you?* □ *Everyone in our office spouts off about the managing director.* □ *There is no need to spout off like that. Calm down and think about what you're saying.*

spread it on thick See *lay it on thick.*

spread like wildfire to spread rapidly and without control. □ *The epidemic is spreading like wildfire. Everyone is getting ill.* □ *John told a joke that was so funny it spread like wildfire.*

spread oneself too thin to do so many things that you can do none of them well. □ *It's a good idea to get involved in a lot of activities, but don't spread yourself too thin.* □ *I'm too busy these days. I'm afraid I've spread myself too thin.*

spring something on someone to surprise someone with something. □ *I'm glad you told me now, rather than springing it on me at the last minute.* □ *I sprang the news on my parents last night. They were not glad to hear it.*

square accounts (with someone) 1. to settle one's financial accounts with someone. □ *I have to square accounts with the bank this week, or it'll take back my car.* □ *I called the bank and said I needed to come in and square accounts.* **2.** to get even with someone; to straighten out a misunderstanding with someone. (Informal.) □ *I'm going to square accounts with Tom. He insulted me in public, and he owes me an apology.* □ *Tom, you and I are going to have to square accounts.*

square deal a fair and honest transaction; fair treatment. (Informal.) □ *All the workers want is a square deal, but their boss underpays them.* □ *You always get a square deal with that travel firm.*

square meal a nourishing, filling meal. (Informal.) □ *All you've eaten today is junk food. You should sit down to a square meal.* □ *The tramp hadn't had a square meal in weeks.*

square peg in a round hole a misfit. □ *John just can't seem to get along with the people he works with. He's just a square peg in a round hole.* □ *I'm not a square peg in a round hole. It's just that no one understands me.*

square up (for something) to get ready for an argument or a fight. □ *John was angry and appeared to be squaring up for a fight.* □ *When those two square up, everyone gets out of the way.*

square up to someone or something to face someone or something bravely; to tackle someone or something. □ *You'll have to square up to the bully or he'll make your life miserable.* □ *It's time to square up to your financial problems. You can't just ignore them.*

square up with someone to pay someone what one owes; to pay one's share of something to someone; to settle an account with someone. (Informal.) □ *I'll square up with you later if you pay the whole bill now.* □ *Bob said he would square up with Tom for his share of the petrol.*

squirrel something away AND **squirrel away something** to hide or store something. (Informal.) □ *I've been squirrelling away a little money each week for years.* □ *Billy has been squirrelling candy away in his top drawer.*

stab someone in the back to betray someone. □ *I thought we were friends! Why did you stab me in the back?* □ *You don't expect a person whom you trust to stab you in the back.*

stack the cards (against someone or something) to arrange things against someone or something; to make it difficult for someone to succeed. (Informal. Originally from card-playing. Usually in the passive.) □ *I can't make any progress at my office. The cards are stacked against me.* □ *The cards seem to be stacked against me. I am having very bad luck.*

stake a claim (on something) to lay or make a claim for something. □ *The farmer has staked a claim on that field.* □ *I want to stake a claim on that last piece of pie.* □ *You don't need to stake a claim. Just ask politely.*

stamp something out AND **stamp out something** 1. to extinguish something. □ *Tom stamped out the sparks before* they started a fire. □ *Quick, stamp that fire out before it spreads.* 2. to eliminate something. □ *Many people think that they can stamp out evil.* □ *The doctors hope they can stamp out cancer.*

stand a chance to have a chance. □ *Do you think I stand a chance of winning first place?* □ *Everyone stands a chance of catching the disease.*

stand by to wait and remain ready. (Generally heard in communication, such as broadcasting, telephones, etc.) □ *Your transatlantic telephone call is almost ready. Please stand by.* □ *Is everyone ready for the telecast? Only ten seconds—stand by.*

stand by someone to support someone; to continue supporting someone even when things are bad. □ *Don't worry. I'll stand by you no matter what.* □ *I feel I have to stand by my brother even if he goes to jail.*

stand corrected to admit that one has been wrong. □ *I realize that I accused him wrongly. I stand corrected.* □ *We appreciate now that our conclusions were wrong. We stand corrected.*

stand down to withdraw from a competition or a position. □ *John has stood down from the election for president of the club.* □ *It is time our chairman stood down and made room for a younger person.*

stand for something 1. to endure something. □ *The teacher won't stand for any whispering in class.* □ *We just can't stand for that kind of behaviour.* 2. to signify something. □ *In a traffic signal, the red light stands for "stop."* □ *The abbreviation Dr. stands for "Doctor."* 3. to endorse or support an ideal; to represent a quality. □ *The mayor claims to stand for honesty in government and jobs for everyone.* □ *Every candidate for public office stands for all the good things in life.*

stand-in See under *stand in (for someone).*

stand in awe of someone or something to be overwhelmed with respect for someone or something. □ *Many*

303

people stand in awe of the queen. □ *The children stood in awe of the headmistress.*

stand in (for someone) to act as a substitute for someone; to serve in someone's place. □ *The famous opera singer was ill, and an inexperienced singer had to stand in for her.* □ *Mary is ill. Jean will have to stand in for her.* ALSO: **stand-in** a person who acts as a substitute for another person. □ *We had hoped to hear a famous opera star, but the stand-in was absolutely superb.*

stand in someone's way 1. to block someone's pathway. □ *Please don't stand in my way. I have to get out of here fast.* □ *I tried to grab her before she fell, but someone was standing in my way.* 2. to be a barrier to someone's desires or intentions. □ *I know you want a divorce so you can marry Ann. Well, I won't stand in your way. You can have the divorce.* □ *I know you want to leave home, and I don't want to stand in your way. You're free to go.*

stand on ceremony to hold rigidly to formal manners. (Often in the negative.) □ *Please help yourself to more. Don't stand on ceremony.* □ *We are very informal around here. Hardly anyone stands on ceremony.*

stand on one's own two feet to be independent and self-sufficient. □ *I'll be glad when I have a good job and can stand on my own two feet.* □ *When Jane gets out of debt, she'll be able to stand on her own two feet again.*

stand one's ground to stand up for one's rights; to resist an attack. □ *The solicitor tried to confuse me when I was giving testimony, but I managed to stand my ground.* □ *Some people were trying to crowd us off the beach, but we held our ground.*

stand out to be extremely visible or conspicuous; to be noticeable by being exceptional. □ *This computer stands out as one of the best available.* □ *Because John is so tall, he really stands out in a crowd.*

stand out a mile See *stick out a mile.*

stand out against someone or something to go on resisting someone or something; to refuse to yield to someone or something. □ *You must stand out against the enemy.* □ *We stood out against salary reductions.*

stand over someone to watch over or supervise someone. □ *You don't have to stand over me. I can do it by myself.* □ *I know from previous experience that if I don't stand over you, you'll never finish.*

stand someone in good stead to be useful or beneficial to someone. □ *This is a fine overcoat. I'm sure it'll stand you in good stead for many years.* □ *I did the managing director a favour which I'm sure will stand me in good stead.*

stand someone something to pay for a treat for someone. (Informal.) □ *We went to the zoo, and my father stood us all ice-cream and soft drinks.* □ *We went to a nice restaurant and had a fine meal. It was even better when Mr. Williams told us he was standing us it.* □ *Jane's father stood us the tickets for the opera.*

stand someone up AND **stand up someone** to fail to meet someone for a date or an appointment, without any warning. (Slang.) □ *John and Jane were supposed to go out last night, but she stood him up.* □ *If you stand up people very often, you'll find that you have no friends at all.*

stand still (for someone or something) AND **hold still (for someone or something)** to remain motionless while something is happening (to oneself). □ *Please hold still for the barber.* □ *Please keep still for the picture.* □ *If you don't stand still, you'll fall off the stool.*

stand to reason to seem reasonable; [for a fact or conclusion] to survive careful or logical evaluation. □ *It stands to reason that it'll be colder in January than it is in June.* □ *It stands to reason* *that Bill left in a hurry, because he didn't pack his clothes.*

stand up against someone or something See *stand up to someone or something.*

stand up and be counted to state publicly one's support (for someone or something). □ *If you believe in more government help for farmers, write to your MP—stand up and be counted.* □ *I'm generally in favour of what you propose, but not enough to stand up and be counted.*

stand up for someone or something to support or defend someone or something. □ *You must stand up for your own ideals!* □ *They were saying bad things about you after you left, but I stood up for you.*

stand up to someone or something AND **stand up against someone or something** to endure or resist someone or something. □ *After I learned to stand up to the manager, I found that my job was more pleasant and less threatening.* □ *I was glad that the fence I built was able to stand up against the storm.*

standing joke a subject that regularly and over a period of time causes amusement whenever it is mentioned. □ *Uncle Jim's driving was a standing joke. He used to drive incredibly slowly.* □ *Their mother's inability to make a decision was a standing joke in the Smith family all their lives.*

stare someone in the face 1. [for something] to be very obvious to someone; to be very easy for someone to see or understand. (Informal.) □ *Her child's needs for special teachers must have been staring Sally in the face, but she ignored it.* □ *It's staring Dick in the face that the boss is displeased with him.* 2. [for someone] to look into someone's face intently. □ *She stared me in the face for the longest time before she spoke.* □ *Don't stare people in the face so much. It embarrasses them.*

start from scratch to start from the beginning; to start from nothing. (Infor-

mal. Compare to *make something from scratch.*) □ *Whenever I bake a cake, I start from scratch. I never use a cake mix in a box.* □ *I built every bit of my own house. I started from scratch and did everything with my own hands.*

start (off) with a clean slate to start out again afresh; to ignore the past and start over again. □ *James started off with a clean slate when he went to a new school.* □ *When Bob got out of jail, he started off with a clean slate.*

start out (as something) to begin as something. □ *How did you start out in this business?* □ *I started out as a cook, and now I own the restaurant.*

start something to start a fight or an argument. (*Something* is *anything* or *nothing* in the negative.) □ *Better be careful unless you want to start something.* □ *I don't want to start anything. I'm just leaving.*

start something up AND **start up something** to start something, such as a car, or some procedure. (Also without *up*.) □ *It was cold, but I managed to start up the car without any difficulty.* □ *We can't start the project up until we have more money.*

start the ball rolling AND **get the ball rolling; set the ball rolling** to begin something; to get some process going; to get a discussion started. □ *If I could just get the ball rolling, then other people would help.* □ *Jack started the ball rolling by asking for volunteers.* ALSO: **keep the ball rolling** □ *Tom started the project, and we kept the ball rolling.*

stay ahead of someone or something See *get ahead of someone or something.*

stay away (from someone or something) See under *get away (from someone or something).*

stay out (of something or somewhere) See *keep out (of something or somewhere).*

stay put not to move; to stay where one is. (Informal.) □ *We've decided to stay put and not to move house.* □ *If the* children just stay put, their parents will collect them soon.

stay the distance See *go the distance.*

steal a march on someone to get some sort of an advantage over someone without being noticed. □ *I got the contract because I was able to steal a march on my competitor.* □ *You have to be clever and fast to steal a march on anyone.*

steal someone's thunder to prevent someone from receiving the public recognition expected upon the announcement of an achievement, by making the announcement in public before the intended receiver of the recognition can do so. □ *I stole Mary's thunder by telling her friends about Mary's engagement to Tom before she could do so herself.* □ *Someone stole my thunder by leaking my announcement to the press.*

steal the show to give the best or most popular performance in a show, play, or some other event; to get attention for oneself. □ *The lead in the play was very good, but the butler stole the show.* □ *Ann always tries to steal the show when she and I make a presentation.*

steamed up angry. (Slang.) □ *What Bob said really got me steamed up.* □ *Why do you get so steamed up about nothing?*

steer clear (of someone or something) to avoid someone or something. □ *John is angry at me, so I've been steering clear of him.* □ *Steer clear of that book. It has many errors in it.* □ *Good advice. I'll steer clear.*

step by step little by little, one step at a time. □ *Just follow the instructions step by step, and everything will be fine.* □ *The old man slowly moved across the lawn step by step.* ALSO: **step-by-step** [listed] one after the other; gradual and orderly. □ *Just follow the step-by-step instructions, and everything will be okay.*

step down (from something) to resign a job or a responsibility. □ *The mayor*

stepped down from office last week. □ *He stepped down for health reasons.*

step into dead men's shoes AND **fill dead men's shoes** to take over the job or position of someone who has died; to gain an advantage by someone's death. □ *The only hope of promotion in that firm is to step into dead men's shoes.* □ *Jack and Ben are both going out with rich widows. They hope to fill dead men's shoes.*

step in(to the breach) to move into a space or vacancy. □ *When Ann resigned as president, I stepped into the breach.* □ *A number of people asked me to step into the breach and take her place.*

step on it to hurry up. (Slang.) □ *I'm in a hurry, driver. Step on it!* □ *I can't step on it, mister. There's too much traffic.*

step on someone's toes AND **tread on someone's toes** to interfere with or offend someone. (Also used literally. Note example with *anyone.*) □ *When you're in public office, you have to avoid stepping on anyone's toes.* □ *Ann tread on someone's toes during the last campaign and lost the election.*

step out of line to misbehave or break the rules; to behave in an unacceptable way. □ *I'm terribly sorry. I hope I didn't step out of line.* □ *John is a lot of fun to go out with, but he has a tendency to step out of line.*

step (right) up to move forward, towards someone. □ *Step right up and get your mail when I call your name.* □ *Come on, everybody. Step right up and help yourself to supper.*

step something up AND **step up something** to cause something to go faster. □ *The factory was not making enough cars, so they stepped up production.* □ *The music was not fast enough, so the conductor told everyone to step it up.*

stew in one's own juice to be left alone to suffer one's anger or disappointment. (Informal.) □ *John has such a terrible temper. When he got angry at us, we just* *let him go away and stew in his own juice.* □ *After John stewed in his own juice for a while, he decided to come back and apologize to us.*

stick around [for a person] to remain in a place. (Slang.) □ *The children stuck around for a time after the party was over.* □ *Oh, Ann. Please stick around for a while. I want to talk to you later.*

stick by someone or something AND **stick with someone or something** to support someone or something; to continue supporting someone or something when things are bad. (Informal.) □ *Don't worry. I'll stick by you no matter what.* □ *I feel I have to stick by my brother even if he goes to jail.* □ *I'll stick by my ideas whether you like them or not.*

Stick 'em up! See *Hands up!*

stick-in-the-mud someone who is stubbornly old-fashioned. (Informal.) □ *Come on to the party with us and have some fun. Don't be an old stick-in-the-mud!* □ *Tom is no stick-in-the-mud. He's really up to date.*

stick it out to put up with or endure a situation, however difficult. (Informal.) □ *This job's boring, but we're sticking it out until we find something more interesting.* □ *I know the children are being annoying, but can you stick it out until their mother returns?*

stick one's neck out to take a risk. (Informal.) □ *Why should I stick my neck out to do something for her? What's she ever done for me?* □ *He made a risky investment. He stuck his neck out because he thought he could make some money.*

stick one's nose in(to something) See *poke one's nose in(to something).*

stick one's oar in See *put one's oar in.*

stick out a mile AND **stand out a mile** to be very obvious. (*Stick out* is informal.) □ *It stands out a mile that Tom and Jane have quarrelled.* □ *The firm's lack of good management sticks out a mile.*

stick out for something to insist on getting something; to refuse to accept less than something. (Informal.) □ *The workers are sticking out for a reasonable pay rise.* □ *The teachers are sticking out for a reduction in class size.*

stick out like a sore thumb to be very prominent or unsightly; to be very obvious. (Informal.) □ *Bob is so tall that he sticks out like a sore thumb in a crowd.* □ *The house next door needs painting. It sticks out like a sore thumb.*

stick someone or something up AND **stick up someone or something 1.** [with *something*] to affix or attach something onto a wall, post, etc. □ *This notice ought to be on the notice board. Please stick it up.* □ *I'm going to stick up this poster near the entrance.* **2.** to rob someone or something. (Slang.) □ *The robbers came in and tried to stick up the bank, but they got caught first.* □ *One robber stuck the cashier up first, but someone sounded the alarm before any money was taken.*

stick to one's guns to remain firm in one's opinions and convictions; to stand up for one's rights. (Informal.) □ *I'll stick to my guns on this matter. I'm sure I'm right.* □ *Bob can be persuaded to do it our way. He probably won't stick to his guns on this point.*

stick together to remain together as a group. (Informal.) □ *Come on, you chaps. Let's stick together. Otherwise somebody will get lost.* □ *Our group of friends has managed to stick together for almost twenty years.*

stick up for someone or something to support someone or something; to *stand up for someone or something.* (Informal.) □ *Everyone was making unpleasant remarks about John, but I stuck up for him.* □ *Our team was losing, but I stuck up for it anyway.*

stick with someone or something See *stick by someone or something.*

Still waters run deep. a proverb meaning that a quiet person is probably thinking deep or important thoughts. □ *Jane is* *so quiet. She's probably thinking. Still waters run deep, you know.* □ *It's true that still waters run deep, but I think that Jane is really half asleep.*

stir one's stumps to start acting quickly; to hurry up. (Slang. *Stumps* is a slang term for legs.) □ *Stir your stumps or you will never get to the station on time.* □ *If Paul stirs his stumps, he'll finish the work on time.*

stir up a hornets' nest to create trouble or difficulties. □ *By finding pupils copying from each other, you've really stirred up a hornets' nest.* □ *Bill stirred up a hornets' nest when he discovered the theft.*

stock up (on something) to build up a supply of something. □ *Before the first snow, we always stock up on firewood.* □ *John drinks a lot of milk, so we stock up when we know he's coming.*

stone's throw away a short distance; a relatively short distance. □ *John saw Mary across the street, just a stone's throw away.* □ *Harrogate is just a stone's throw away from Leeds.*

stoop to (doing) something to degrade oneself or condescend to do something; to do something which is supposed to be beneath one. □ *I never dreamed that Bill would stoop to stealing.* □ *Jane wants to be an executive. She would hate to stoop to being an ordinary office worker.*

stop at nothing to do everything possible (to accomplish something); to be unscrupulous. □ *Bill would stop at nothing to get his way.* □ *Bob is completely determined to get promoted. He'll stop at nothing.*

stop off (somewhere) to stop somewhere on the way to some other place. (Informal.) □ *I stopped off at a local shop to buy milk on the way home.* □ *We stopped off for a few minutes to visit my uncle.*

stop one dead in one's tracks AND **stop something dead in its tracks** to stop someone or something instantly. (This does not usually have anything to do with death.) □ *Her unkind words stopped me dead in my tracks.* □ *When I saw the adder, I stopped dead in my tracks.* □ *The van juddered to a halt dead in its tracks.*

stop over (somewhere) to break one's journey, usually overnight or even longer. (Informal.) □ *On our way to Brussels, we stopped over in Paris for the night.* □ *There's no connecting flight. We'll have to stop over at an airport hotel.* ALSO: **stopover** a place where one breaks one's journey. □ *We went to Brussels with a stopover in Paris.*

stop short of doing something not to go as far as doing something. □ *Fortunately Bob stopped short of hitting Tom.* □ *The boss criticized Jane's work, but stopped short of sacking her.*

stop something dead in its tracks See *stop one dead in one's tracks.*

stopover See under *stop over (somewhere).*

storm in a teacup an uproar about practically nothing. □ *This isn't a serious problem—just a storm in a teacup.* □ *Even a storm in a teacup can take a lot of time to get settled.*

stow away to hide away on a ship or an aeroplane in order to get free transportation. □ *I once read about a man who made a journey around the world by stowing away.* □ *You can get arrested if you stow away.* ALSO: **stowaway** someone who stows away. □ *The crew found two stowaways aboard and locked them in a cabin.*

straight away right away; immediately. □ *We'll have to go straight away.* □ *Straight away I knew something was wrong.*

straight from the horse's mouth from an authoritative or dependable source. □ *I know it's true! I heard it straight from* *the horse's mouth!* □ *This comes straight from the horse's mouth, so it has to be believed.*

straight from the shoulder sincerely; frankly; holding nothing back. □ *Sally always speaks straight from the shoulder. You never have to guess what she really means.* □ *Bill told the staff the financial facts—straight from the shoulder and brief.*

straight off right away, without thinking or considering. □ *I liked Mary's friend straight off.* □ *The boss knew straight off that Ben was the right man for the job.*

straight out frankly; directly. □ *Bob told Pam straight out that he didn't want to marry her.* □ *Jim was told straight out to start working harder.*

straighten someone or something out AND **straighten out someone or something 1.** [with *someone*] to reform someone. □ *The judge felt that a few years at hard labour would straighten out the thief.* □ *Most people think that jail never straightens anybody out.* **2.** [with *something*] to make a situation less confused. □ *John made a mess of the contract, so I helped him straighten it out.* □ *Please straighten out your accounts.*

straighten someone or something up AND **straighten up someone or something 1.** to put someone or something into an upright position. □ *The post is tilted. Please straighten it up.* □ *Bill, you're slouching again. Straighten yourself up.* **2.** to tidy up someone or something. □ *This room is a mess. Let's straighten it up.* □ *John straightened himself up a little before going on stage.*

strapped (for something) very much in need of money. (Slang.) □ *I'm strapped for cash. Can you loan me five pounds?* □ *Sorry, I'm a bit strapped, too.*

straw in the wind an indication or sign of what might happen in the future. □

The student's argument with the lecturer was a straw in the wind in terms of student-teacher relations. The students are planning a strike. □ *Two or three people getting the sack represents just a straw in the wind. I think the whole work-force will have to go.*

stretch a point to interpret a point flexibly and with great latitude. □ *Would it be stretching a point to suggest that everyone is invited to your picnic?* □ *Could you stretch a point and let the staff away early?*

stretch one's legs to walk around after sitting down or lying down for a time. (Informal.) □ *We wanted to stretch our legs during the theatre interval.* □ *After sitting in the car all day, the travellers decided to stretch their legs.*

strike a balance (between two things) to find a satisfactory compromise between two extremes. □ *The political party must strike a balance between the right wing and the left wing.* □ *Jane is overdressed for the party and Sally is underdressed. What a pity they didn't strike a balance.*

strike a bargain to reach an agreement on a price (for something). □ *They argued for a while and finally struck a bargain.* □ *They were unable to strike a bargain, so they left.*

strike a chord to cause someone to remember [someone or something]; to remind someone of [someone or something]; to be familiar. □ *The woman in the portrait struck a chord, and I realized that it was my grandmother.* □ *His name strikes a chord, but I don't know why.*

strike a happy medium to find a compromise position; to arrive at a position half-way between two unacceptable extremes. □ *Ann likes very spicy food, but Bob doesn't care for spicy food at all. We are trying to find a restaurant which strikes a happy medium.* □ *Tom is either very happy or very sad. He can't seem to strike a happy medium.*

strike a sour note to introduce something unpleasant. □ *Jane's sad announcement struck a sour note at the annual banquet.* □ *News of the crime struck a sour note in our holiday celebration.*

strike it lucky to have good fortune. (From finding gold while prospecting.) □ *Jack thought he'd be turned down for the job, but he struck it lucky.* □ *The hitch-hiker might strike it lucky and get a lift straight to London.*

strike it rich to acquire wealth suddenly. □ *If I could strike it rich, I wouldn't have to work any more.* □ *Sally ordered a dozen oysters and found a huge pearl in one of them. She struck it rich!*

strike out at someone or something (figuratively or literally) to hit at or attack someone or something. □ *She was so angry she struck out at the person she was arguing with.* □ *I was frantic. I wanted to strike out at everything and everybody.*

strike the right note to achieve the desired effect; to do something suitable or pleasing. (A musical reference.) □ *Meg struck the right note when she wore a dark suit to the interview.* □ *The politician's speech failed to strike the right note with the crowd.*

strike up a conversation to start a conversation (with someone). □ *I struck up an interesting conversation with someone on the bus yesterday.* □ *It's easy to strike up a conversation with someone when you're travelling.*

strike up a friendship to become friends (with someone). □ *I struck up a friendship with John while we were on a business trip together.* □ *If you're lonely, you should go out and try to strike up a friendship with someone you like.*

strike while the iron is hot to do something at the best possible time; to do something when the time is ripe. □ *He* was in a good mood, so I asked for a loan of £200. I thought I'd better strike while the iron was hot. □ *Please go to the bank and settle this matter now! They are willing to be reasonable. You've got to strike while the iron is hot.*

string along (with someone) to accompany someone; to run around with someone. (Informal.) □ *Sally seemed to know where she was going, so I decided to string along with her.* □ *She said it was okay if I strung along.*

string someone along to deceive someone in order to gain time. (Informal.) □ *Jane thinks that Bob is really in love with her, but he's just stringing her along until he meets the right girl.* □ *I think the firm is stringing Jack long. They are looking to see if there is a better candidate before they offer him the job.*

string something out AND **string out something** to draw something out (in time); to make something last a long time. (Informal.) □ *The meeting was long enough. There was no need to string it out further with all those speeches.* □ *They tried to string out the meeting to make things seem more important.*

stroke of luck a bit of luck; a lucky happening. □ *I had a stroke of luck and found Tom at home when I called. He's not usually there.* □ *Unless I have a stroke of luck, I'm not going to finish this report by tomorrow.*

stuck for something lacking something; unable to obtain something. (Informal.) □ *We're a bit stuck for money, but we have just enough to finish the building.* □ *The town council are stuck for land to build houses on.*

stuck on someone or something (Slang.) **1.** [with *someone*] to be fond of or in love with someone; to have a crush on someone. □ *John was stuck on Sally, but she didn't know it.* □ *He always gets stuck on the wrong person.* **2.** [with *something*] to be locked into an idea, cause, or purpose. □ *Mary is really* stuck on the idea of going to France this spring. □ *You've proposed a good plan, Jane, but don't get stuck on it. We may have to make some changes.*

stuck with someone or something burdened with someone or something; left having to care for someone or something. (Informal.) □ *Please don't leave me stuck with your aunt. She talks too much.* □ *My room-mate left college and left me stuck with the telephone bill.*

stuff and nonsense nonsense. (Informal.) □ *Come on! Don't give me all that stuff and nonsense!* □ *I don't understand this book. It's all stuff and nonsense as far as I am concerned.*

stumble across someone or something AND **stumble into someone or something; stumble on someone or something** to find someone or something, usually by accident. □ *I stumbled across an interesting book yesterday when I was shopping.* □ *Guess who I stumbled into at the library yesterday?* □ *I stumbled on a real bargain at the bookshop last week.*

stumble into someone or something See the previous entry.

stumble on someone or something See *stumble across someone or something.*

stumbling-block something that prevents or obstructs progress. □ *We'd like to buy that house, but the high price is the stumbling-block.* □ *Jim's age is a stumbling-block to getting another job. He's over sixty.*

subject to something 1. to depend on something. □ *Building is subject to planning approval.* □ *Tickets are subject to availability.* 2. likely to have or get something, usually a disease or ailment; to have a tendency towards something. □ *Bill is subject to fainting spells.* □ *Bob says he's subject to colds and the flu.*

such-and-such someone or something whose name has been forgotten or should not be said. (Informal.) □ *Mary said that such-and-such was coming to her party, but I forgot their names.* □ *If you walk into a shop and ask for such-and-such and they don't have it, you go to a different shop.*

such as it is in the imperfect state that one sees it; in the less-than-perfect condition in which one sees it. □ *This is where I live. This is my glorious home—such as it is.* □ *I've worked for days on this report, and I've done the best that I can do. It's my supreme effort—such as it is.*

Such is life! that is the way things happen. □ *Oh, well. Everything can't be perfect. Such is life!* □ *So I failed my test. Such is life! I can take it again sometime.*

sugar the pill AND **sweeten the pill** to make something unpleasant more pleasant. (From the sugar coating on some pills to disguise the bitter taste of the medicine.) □ *Mary's parents wouldn't let her go out and tried to sugar the pill by inviting some of her friends around.* □ *Tom hated boarding-school and his parents tried to sweeten the pill by giving him a lot of pocket-money.*

suit one's actions to one's words to behave in accordance with what one has said; to do what one has promised or threatened to do. □ *Mr. Smith suited his actions to his words and punished the children.* □ *John threatened to resign, but he didn't think he'd have to suit his actions to his words.*

suit someone down to the ground See the following entry.

suit someone to a T AND **suit someone down to the ground** to be very appropriate for someone. □ *This kind of employment suits me to a T.* □ *This is Sally's kind of house. It suits her down to the ground.*

suit yourself to do what one wants to do without considering other people's wishes or opinions. □ *Okay, if you* *don't want to do it my way, suit yourself.* □ *Either go or stay. Suit yourself.*

sum something up AND **sum up something** to summarize something. □ *At the end of the lecture, Dr. Williams summed the important points up for us.* □ *He said when he finished, "Well, that about sums it up."*

survival of the fittest the idea that the most able or fit will survive (while the less able and less fit will perish). (This is used literally as a part of the theory of evolution.) □ *In college, it's the survival of the fittest. You have to keep working in order to survive and graduate.* □ *I don't look after my houseplants very well, but the ones I have are really flourishing. It's the survival of the fittest, I suppose.*

swallow one's pride to forget one's pride and accept something humiliating. □ *I had to swallow my pride and admit that I was wrong.* □ *When you're a pupil, you find yourself swallowing your pride quite often.*

swallow something hook, line, and sinker to believe something completely. (Informal. These terms refer to fishing and fooling a fish into being caught.) □ *I made up a story about why I was so late. They all believed it hook, line, and sinker.* □ *I feel like a fool. I fell for the trick, hook, line, and sinker.*

swan around to go around in an idle and irresponsible way. (Informal.) □ *Mrs. Smith's swanning around abroad while her husband's in hospital here.* □ *Mary's not looking for a job. She's just swanning around visiting all her friends.*

swan-song the last work or performance of a playwright, musician, actor, etc., before death or retirement. □ *His portrayal of Lear was the actor's swan-song.* □ *We didn't know that her performance last night was the singer's swan-song.*

sweat blood to be very anxious and tense. (Slang.) □ *What a terrible test! I was really sweating blood at the end.* □

Bob is such a bad driver. I sweat blood every time I ride with him.

sweat something out AND **sweat out something** to endure or wait for something which causes tension or boredom. (Slang.) □ *I had to wait for her in the reception area. It was a long wait, but I managed to sweat it out.* □ *I took the test and then spent a week sweating out the results.*

sweep one off one's feet AND **knock one off one's feet** to overwhelm someone. (Informal.) □ *Mary is madly in love with Bill. He swept her off her feet.* □ *The news was so exciting that it knocked me off my feet.*

sweep something under the carpet AND **brush something under the carpet** to try to hide something unpleasant, shameful, etc., from the attention of others. □ *The boss said he couldn't sweep the theft under the carpet, that he'd have to call in the police.* □ *The headmaster tried to brush the children's truancy under the carpet, but the inspector wanted to investigate it.*

sweet nothings affectionate but unimportant or meaningless words spoken to a loved one. □ *Jack was whispering sweet nothings in Joan's ear when they were dancing.* □ *The two lovers sat in the cinema exchanging sweet nothings.*

sweet on someone fond of someone. (Informal.) □ *Tom is sweet on Mary. He may ask her to marry him.* □ *Mary's sweet on him, too.*

sweet-talk someone to talk convincingly to someone with much flattery. (Informal.) □ *I didn't want to help her, but she sweet-talked me into it.* □ *He sweet-talked her for a while, and she finally agreed to go to the dance with him.*

sweeten the pill See *sugar the pill.*

swim against the tide to do the opposite of everyone else; to go against the trend. □ *Bob tends to do what everybody else does. He isn't likely to swim against the tide.* □ *Mary always swims against the tide. She's a very contrary person.*

swing into action   See *go into action.*

swing something   to make something happen. (Slang.) □ *I hope I can swing a deal that will make us all a lot of money.* □ *We all hope you can swing it.*

swing the lead   to avoid one's work or to neglect one's duty, especially by making excuses. (Slang. *Lead* rhymes with *said.*) □ *Fred's bound to get the sack. He's always pretending to be ill and swinging the lead.* □ *Mary's avoided overtime by saying her mother's ill, but she's swinging the lead.*

T

tag along to go along with or follow someone, often when uninvited or unwanted. (Informal.) □ *Jean always tags along when Tim and Sally go out on a date.* □ *I took my children to the zoo and the neighbour's children tagged along.*

tail wagging the dog a situation where a small or minor part is controlling the whole thing. □ *John was just employed yesterday, and today he's bossing everyone around. It's a case of the tail wagging the dog.* □ *Why is this minor matter being given so much importance? Now the tail is wagging the dog!*

take a back seat (to someone) to defer to someone; to give control to someone. □ *I decided to take a back seat to Mary and let her manage the project.* □ *I had done the best I could, but it was time to take a back seat and let someone else run things.*

take a bow 1. to bow and receive credit for a good performance. □ *At the end of the concerto, the pianist rose and took a bow.* □ *The audience applauded wildly and demanded that the conductor come out and take a bow again.* 2. to receive recognition and congratulations for something one has done. □ *Take a bow. You've worked really well.* □ *You can take a bow now. The project has been a success.*

take a break to have a short rest period in one's work. □ *It's ten o'clock—time to take a break.* □ *I don't usually take a break. I prefer to work right through.*

take a chance AND **take a risk** to try something where failure or bad fortune is likely. □ *Come on, take a chance. You may lose, but it's worth trying.* □ *I'm not reckless, but I don't mind taking a risk now and then.*

take a dim view of something to disapprove of something; to regard something sceptically or pessimistically. □ *My aunt takes a dim view of most things that young people do.* □ *The manager took a dim view of my efforts on the project. I suppose I didn't try hard enough.*

take a fancy to someone or something AND **take a liking to someone or something; take a shine to someone or something** to develop a fondness or a preference for someone or something. (Informal.) □ *John began to take a fancy to Sally late last August at the picnic.* □ *I've never taken a liking to cooked carrots.* □ *I think my teacher has taken a shine to me.*

take a gander (at someone or something) to examine someone or something; to *take a look at someone or something*. (Slang.) □ *Fred, will you take a gander at that fancy car!* □ *Drive it over here so I can take a gander.*

take a hand in something to help in the planning or doing of something. □ *I was glad to take a hand in planning the picnic.* □ *Jane refused to take a hand in any of the work.* ALSO: **have a hand in something** to play a part in (doing) something. □ *I had a hand in the picnic plans.*

take a hard line (with someone) to be firm with someone; to have a firm policy for dealing with someone. □ *The manager takes a hard line with people who appear late.* □ *This is a serious matter. The police are likely to take a hard line.*

take a hint to understand a hint and behave accordingly. □ *I said I didn't want to see you any more. Can't you take a hint? I don't like you.* □ *Sure I can take a hint, but I'd rather be told directly.*

take a leaf out of someone's book to behave or to do something in the way that someone else would; to use someone as an example. □ *Take a leaf out of your brother's book and work hard.* □ *Eventually June took a leaf out of her friend's book and started dressing smartly.*

take a licking See *get a licking.*

take a liking to someone or something See *take a fancy to someone or something.*

take a look (at someone or something) to examine (briefly) someone or something. (Also with *have*, as in the examples.) □ *I asked the doctor to take a look at my ankle which has been hurting.* □ *"So your ankle's hurting," said the doctor. "Let's take a look."* □ *Please have a look at my car. It's not running well.*

take a new turn [for something] to begin a new course or direction. □ *When I received the telegram with the exciting news, my life took a new turn.* □ *With the merger of the firms, my career took a new turn.*

take a nosedive See *go into a nosedive.*

take a raincheck (on something) to accept (or request) a re-issuance of an invitation at a later date. (Said to someone who has invited you to something which you cannot attend now, but would like to attend at a later time. Originally American. From a piece of paper handed out to allow one to see a sporting event cancelled because of rain, at a later time.) □ *We would love to come to your house, but we are busy next Saturday. Could we take a raincheck on your kind invitation?* □ *Oh, yes. Please take a raincheck and come when you can.*

take a rise out of someone AND **get a rise out of someone** to get a response from someone, usually anger. (Informal.) □ *I can always get a rise out of him by pretending not to understand what he's saying.* □ *John doesn't really think Mary's freckles are ugly. He's just taking a rise out of her.*

take a risk See *take a chance.*

take a shine to someone or something See *take a fancy to someone or something.*

take a shot at something to shoot at something, as with a gun. (See also *have a try at something.*) □ *I aimed carefully and took a shot at the target.* □ *Be careful when you're in the woods during the hunting season, or a hunter might take a shot at you.*

take a spill to have a fall; to tip over. (Informal. Also with *bad, nasty, quite,* etc. Also with *have.*) □ *Ann tripped on the kerb and took a nasty spill.* □ *John had quite a spill when he fell off his bicycle.*

take a stab at something to make a try at something, sometimes without much hope of success. (Informal. Also with *have.*) □ *I don't know if I can do it, but I'll take a stab at it.* □ *Come on, Mary. Take a stab at catching a fish. You might end up liking fishing.* □ *Would you like to have a stab at this problem?*

take a stand (against someone or something) to take a position in opposition to someone or something; to oppose or resist someone or something. □ *The treasurer was forced to take a stand against the board because of its wasteful spending.* □ *The treasurer took a stand, and others agreed.*

take a turn for the better to start to improve; to start to get well. □ *She was very sick for a month; then suddenly she took a turn for the better.* □ *Things are taking a turn for the better at my shop. I may make a profit this year.*

take a turn for the worse to start to get worse. (The opposite of the previous entry.) □ *It appeared that she was going to get well; then, unfortunately, she took a turn for the worse.* □ *My job was going quite well; then last week things took a turn for the worse.*

take action (against someone or something) to do something against someone or something; to use the law—as in a law suit—against someone or something. □ *If you don't stop bothering me, I'll take action against you.* □ *We'll all have to take action against this threat.* □ *All of us will take action.*

take advantage of someone or something **1.** to exploit someone or something for one's own benefit or gain. □ *The shop owner took advantage of me when I was in a hurry, and I'm angry.* □ *He took advantage of my ignorance about the money system and overcharged me.* **2.** to utilize someone or something to one's own benefit. □ *Jane can be of great help to me, and I intend to take advantage of her talents.* □ *Try to take advantage of every opportunity which comes your way.*

take after someone to resemble a close, older relation. (Informal.) □ *Don't you think that Sally takes after her mother?* □ *No, Sally takes after her Aunt Ann.*

take aim (at someone or something) to aim (something) at someone or something. □ *The hunter took aim at the deer and pulled the trigger.* □ *You must take aim carefully before you shoot.*

take an interest (in something) to develop an interest in something. □ *I wish John would take an interest in his school work.* □ *We hoped you'd take an interest and join our club.*

take care of someone or something **1.** to look after someone or something; to see that someone or something is not harmed. □ *Please take care of my budgie while I'm away.* □ *Her mother takes care of Jean's baby during the day.* **2.** [with *something*] to settle or pay

something, such as a bill. (Informal.) □ *I have to take care of this bill.* □ *I'm taking care of my mother's gas bill.*

take charge (of someone or something) to take (over) control of someone or something. □ *The president came in late and took charge of the meeting.* □ *When the new manager took charge, things really began to happen.*

take coals to Newcastle See *carry coals to Newcastle.*

take effect See *go into effect.*

take exception to something to object to or take offence at something (which someone has said). □ *I take exception to your remarks, and I would like to discuss them with you.* □ *I'm sorry you took exception to Bob's behaviour. He was feeling ill.*

take five to take a five-minute rest period. (Slang.) □ *Okay, everybody. Take five!* □ *Look, Bob. I'm tired. Can we take five?*

take forty winks to take a nap; to go to sleep. (Informal.) □ *I think I'll go to bed and take forty winks. See you later.* □ *Why don't you go take forty winks and call me in about an hour?*

take heart to be brave; to have courage. □ *Take heart, John. Things could be worse!* □ *I told her to take heart and try again next time.*

take heed to take notice; to pay attention; to be careful. □ *Take heed when you are crossing the road.* □ *You will have to take heed this year. You have major exams.*

take hold of someone or something AND **get hold of someone or something** **1.** to grasp someone or something. □ *Take hold of the bat and swing it against the ball when it's bowled.* □ *Billy's mother took hold of him and dragged him away.* **2.** [with *someone*] to get control of oneself. □ *Take hold of yourself! Calm down and relax.* □ *She took a few minutes to get hold of herself, and then she spoke.*

take ill to become ill. □ *I took ill with an upset stomach last week.* □ *I hope I don't take ill before final exams.* ALSO: **taken ill** to be taken by an illness. □ *Bob was taken ill on the plane.*

take issue (with someone) to argue with someone; to dispute a point with someone. □ *I hate to take issue with you on such a minor point, but I'm quite sure you're wrong.* □ *I don't mind if you take issue, but I'm sure I'm right.*

take it away to start up a performance. (Slang. Typically a public announcement of the beginning of a musical performance. Also used literally.) □ *And now, here is the band playing* Song of Songs. *Take it away!* □ *Sally will now sing us a song. Take it away, Sally!*

take it easy on someone or something (Informal.) **1.** to be gentle with someone or something. □ *Take it easy on Mary. She's been sick.* □ *Please take it easy on the furniture. It has to last us many years.* **2.** [with *something*] to use less of something (rather than more). □ *Take it easy on the soup. There's just enough for one serving for each person.* □ *Please take it easy on the pencils. There are hardly any left.*

take it or leave it to accept it (the way it is) or forget about it. (Informal.) □ *This is my last offer. Take it or leave it.* □ *It's not much, but it's the only food we have. You can take it or leave it.*

take kindly to something to be agreeable to something. □ *My father doesn't take kindly to anyone using his tools.* □ *I hope they'll take kindly to our request.*

take leave of one's senses to become irrational. □ *What are you doing? Have you taken leave of your senses?* □ *What a terrible situation! It's enough to make one take leave of one's senses.*

take leave of someone See *take (one's) leave (of someone).*

take liberties with someone or something AND **make free with someone or something** to use or abuse someone or something. □ *You are overly familiar with me, Mr. Jones. One might think*

you were taking liberties with me. □ *I don't like it when you make free with my lawn-mower. You should at least ask when you want to borrow it.*

take note (of something) to observe and remember something. □ *Please take note of the point I'm about to make.* □ *Take note. You must be back by midnight.* □ *You must take note of these rules.*

take notice (of someone or something) to pay attention to someone or something. □ *I didn't take any notice of the rules. Everyone ignores them.* □ *Take no notice of her. She's just trying to hurt you.*

take off 1. [for an aeroplane or a rocket] to ascend into the air. □ *When do we take off?* □ *The rocket took off on schedule.* **2.** suddenly to begin to improve or be successful. (Informal. From the ascent of rockets or aeroplanes.) □ *The car-hire firm has really taken off.* □ *That new board game has unexpectedly taken off.*

take off (after someone or something) to begin to chase someone or something. (Informal.) □ *The bank guard took off after the robber.* □ *Did you see that police car take off?*

take off one's hat to someone AND **take one's hat off to someone** to offer praise for someone's good accomplishments. □ *I have to take off my hat to the headmistress. She has done an excellent job.* □ *We must take our hats off to people who survive on very little money.*

take offence (at someone or something) to become resentful at someone or something. □ *Bill took offence at Mary for her remarks about him.* □ *Almost everyone took offence at Bill's new book. It was written about people in the village.* □ *I'm sorry you took offence. I meant no harm.*

take office to begin serving as an elected or appointed official. □ *When did the mayor take office?* □ *All the elected officials took office just after the election.*

take one at one's word to believe what someone says and act accordingly. □ *She told me to get out for good, and I took her at her word.* □ *You shouldn't take her at her word. She frequently says things she doesn't really mean.*

take one's cue from someone to use someone else's behaviour or reactions as a guide to one's own. (From the theatrical cue as a signal to speak, etc.) □ *If you don't know which cutlery to use at the dinner, just take your cue from John.* □ *The other children took their cue from Tommy and ignored the new boy.*

take one's hands off (someone or something) See *get one's hands off (someone or something)*.

take (one's) leave (of someone) to say goodbye to someone and leave. □ *I took leave of my hosts and drove off.* □ *One by one, the guests took their leave.*

take one's medicine to accept the punishment or the bad fortune which one deserves. □ *I know I did wrong, and I know I have to take my medicine.* □ *Billy knew he was going to be punished, and he didn't want to take his medicine.*

take one's own life to kill oneself; to commit suicide. □ *Bob tried to take his own life, but he was rescued in time.* □ *John took his own life by taking an overdose of sleeping pills.*

take one's time to use as much time (to do something) as one wants. □ *There is no hurry. Please take your time.* □ *Take your time. You don't want to arrive early.*

take pains to do something to make a great effort to do something. □ *Tom took pains to decorate the room exactly right.* □ *We took pains to get there on time.*

take part (in something) to participate in something. □ *They invited me to take part in their celebration.* □ *I was quite pleased to take part.*

take pity (on someone or something) to feel sorry for someone or something; to have sympathy for someone or something; to show mercy to someone or something. □ *We took pity on the hungry people and gave them some warm food.* □ *She took pity on the little dog and brought it in to get warm.* □ *Please take pity! Please help us!*

take place to happen. □ *When will this party take place?* □ *It's taking place right now.*

take root to begin to take hold or have effect. (Also used literally referring to plants.) □ *Things will begin to change when my new policies take root.* □ *My ideas began to take root and influence other people.*

take sides to choose one side of an argument. □ *They were arguing, but I didn't want to take sides, so I left.* □ *I don't mind taking sides on important issues.*

take someone down a peg (or two) to reprimand someone who is acting in too arrogant a way. (Informal.) □ *The teacher's scolding took Bob down a peg or two.* □ *He was so rude that someone was bound to take him down a peg.*

take someone for a fool See *take someone for an idiot*.

take someone for a ride to trick or deceive someone. (Slang.) □ *Old people are being taken for a ride by bogus workmen.* □ *Whoever sold Tom that car took him for a ride. It needs a new engine.*

take someone for an idiot AND **take someone for a fool** to assume that someone is stupid. □ *I wouldn't do anything like that! Do you take me for an idiot?* □ *I don't take you for a fool. I think you're very clever.*

take someone for someone or something to mistake someone for someone or something. □ *I took Bill for his brother, Bob. They look so much alike!* □ *I took Mr. Brown for the gardener, and he was a little bit insulted.*

take someone in AND **take in someone** to deceive or cheat someone. (Informal.) □ *The salesman took in the old lady* *and got her to give him her money.* □ *Don't be taken in by his charm. He's dishonest.*

take someone off to imitate someone, often unkindly; to mock someone. (Informal.) □ *Jack was taking off the teacher when she entered the room.* □ *It's cruel to take off old Fred because of his handicap.*

take someone or something apart AND **take apart someone or something 1.** [with *something*] to disassemble something; to remove or disconnect the parts of something, one by one. □ *Bill took his radio apart to try to fix it.* □ *He takes apart everything he can so he can learn how things work.* **2.** to criticize someone or something severely. (Informal.) □ *The critic took the play apart.* □ *The teacher took John apart when he failed the exam.*

take someone or something by storm to overwhelm someone or something; to attract a great deal of attention from someone or something. □ *Jane is madly in love with Tom. He took her by storm at the office party, and they've been together ever since.* □ *The singer took the world of opera by storm with her performance in* La Boheme.

take someone or something by surprise to startle or surprise someone or something; to come upon someone or something unexpectedly. □ *She came into the room and took them by surprise.* □ *I took the little bird by surprise, and it flew away.*

take someone or something for granted to accept someone or something—without gratitude—as a matter of course. □ *We tend to take a lot of things for granted.* □ *Mrs. Franklin complained that Mr. Franklin takes her for granted.*

take someone or something into account AND **take into account someone or something** to remember to consider someone or something. □ *I hope you'll take Bill and Bob into account when you plan the party.* □ *I'll try to*

take into account all the things that are important in a situation like this.

take someone or something on AND **take on someone or something 1.** to undertake to deal with someone or something. (Informal.) □ *Mrs. Smith is such a problem. I don't feel like taking her on just now.* □ *I'm too busy to take on any new problems.* **2.** [with *someone*] to begin to employ someone. □ *I have taken on three new members of staff.* □ *The factory is not taking on any new workers. Three were taken on last week.*

take someone or something over AND **take over someone or something** to take charge of someone or something; to assume control of someone or something. □ *The new manager will take the office over next week.* □ *Will you please take over your children? I can't seem to control them.*

take someone out AND **take out someone** to take someone out on a date. □ *I hear that Tom has been taking Ann out.* □ *No, Tom has been taking out Mary.*

take someone to task to scold or reprimand someone. □ *The teacher took John to task for his bad behaviour.* □ *I lost a big contract, and the managing director took me to task in front of everyone.*

take someone to the cleaners to cause someone to lose or spend a great deal of money; to ruin someone. (Slang.) □ *His ex-wife took him to the cleaners with her divorce settlement.* □ *John really took the company to the cleaners when he sued them for wrongful dismissal.*

take someone under one's wing to take over and care for a person. □ *John wasn't doing well at school until an older pupil took him under her wing.* □ *I took the new workers under my wing, and they learned the job in no time.*

take someone up on something AND **take up someone on something** to take advantage of someone's offer of something. (Informal.) □ *I'd like to take you up on your offer to help.* □ *We*

319

took up the Browns on their invitation to come to dinner.

take someone's breath away to overwhelm someone with beauty or splendour. □ *The magnificent painting took my breath away.* □ *Ann looked so beautiful that she took my breath away.*

take someone's fancy to appeal to someone. □ *I'll have some ice-cream, please. Chocolate takes my fancy right now.* □ *Why don't you go to the record shop and buy a record album that takes your fancy?*

take something to endure something; to survive something. (Also used literally.) □ *I don't think I can take any more scolding today. I've been in trouble since I got up this morning.* □ *Mary was very insulting to Tom, but he can take it.*

take something amiss AND **take something the wrong way** to understand something as critical or insulting. □ *Would you take it amiss if I told you I thought you look lovely?* □ *Why would anyone take such a nice compliment amiss?* □ *I was afraid he'd take it the wrong way when I asked him to keep his lecture short.* □ *Jean took it the wrong way when I asked her to be tactful.*

take something as read to assume something or regard something as being understood and accepted without reading it out, stating it, or checking it. □ *Can we take the minutes of the meeting as read, or should I read them?* □ *I think we can take their agreement as read, but I'll check with them if you like.*

take something at face value to accept something just as it is presented. □ *You'll have to take what John says at face value. Don't look for a hidden motive.* □ *Jack made us a promise, and we took his word at face value.*

take something back AND **take back something** to withdraw or cancel one's statement. □ *I heard what you said, and I'm very insulted. Please take your remark back.* □ *Take back your words, or I'll never speak to you again!*

take something in one's stride to accept something as natural or expected. □ *The argument surprised him, but he took it in his stride.* □ *It was a very rude remark, but Mary took it in her stride.*

take something lying down to endure something unpleasant without fighting back. □ *He insulted me publicly. You don't expect me to take that lying down, do you?* □ *I'm not the kind of person who'll take something like that lying down.*

take something on the chin to experience and endure a blow stoically. (Informal.) □ *The bad news was a real shock, but John took it on the chin.* □ *The worst luck comes my way, but I always end up taking it on the chin.*

take something out on someone or something to direct (or redirect) one's anger or fear onto someone or something. (Informal.) □ *I don't care if you're angry with your brother. Don't take it out on me!* □ *John took his anger out on the wall by kicking it.*

take something the wrong way See *take something amiss.*

take something to heart to take something very seriously. □ *John took the criticism to heart and made an honest effort to improve.* □ *I know Bob said a lot of cruel things to you, but he was angry. You shouldn't take those things to heart.*

take something up AND **take up something** to make the bottom of a skirt or trouser turn-ups higher from the floor. □ *I'll have to take this skirt up. It's too long for me.* □ *Please take up my trouser turn-ups. They are an inch too long.*

take something up with someone AND **take up something with someone** to raise and discuss a matter with someone. □ *This is a very complicated problem. I'll have to take it up with the office manager.* □ *She'll take up this problem with the owner in the morning.*

take something (up)on oneself to make something one's responsibility. □ *I* took it upon myself to order more pencils since we were running out of them. □ *I'm glad that you took it on yourself to do that.*

take something with a grain of salt See the following entry.

take something with a pinch of salt AND **take something with a grain of salt** to listen to a story or an explanation with considerable doubt. □ *You must take anything she says with a grain of salt. She doesn't always tell the truth.* □ *They took my explanation with a pinch of salt. I was sure they didn't believe me.*

take steps (to prevent something) to do what is necessary to prevent something. □ *I took steps to prevent John from learning what we were talking about.* □ *I have to keep John from knowing what I've been doing. I can prevent it if I take steps.*

take stock (of someone or something) 1. to make an appraisal of the resources of someone or something. □ *I spent some time yesterday taking stock of my good and bad qualities.* □ *Take stock of your career prospects before leaving your job.* **2.** to consider something carefully. □ *You must take stock of the situation before proceeding.* □ *The general took stock of the terrain before ordering the army to attack.*

take the biscuit to be most remarkable; to be the worst example of something. (Slang.) □ *Her rudeness really takes the biscuit.* □ *The family are all bad-mannered, but the youngest child's behaviour takes the biscuit.*

take the bit between one's teeth to put oneself in charge; to approach a task boldly and confidently. □ *Someone needed to direct the project, so I took the bit between my teeth.* □ *If you want to get something done, you've got to take the bit between your teeth and get to work.*

take the bull by the horns to meet a challenge directly. □ *If we are going to solve this problem, someone is going to have to take the bull by the horns.* □

This threat isn't going to go away by itself. We are going to take the bull by the horns and settle this matter once and for all.

take the day off to choose not to go to work for one day. (Compare to *get the day off.*) □ *The sun was shining, and it was warm, so I took the day off and went fishing.* □ *Jane wasn't feeling well, so she took the day off.*

take the edge (off something) to reduce the strength or power of something; to dull something. □ *Jean's illness took the edge off our enjoyment of the dance.* □ *Eating sweets takes the edge off your appetite.*

take the floor 1. to stand up and address the audience. (Also with *have.* See the note at *get a black eye.*) □ *When I take the floor, I'll make a short speech.* □ *The last time you had the floor, you talked for an hour.* **2.** to go to the dance-floor in order to dance. □ *They took the floor for the foxtrot.* □ *When the band played, everyone took the floor.*

take the law into one's own hands to attempt to administer the law; to act as a judge and jury for someone who has done something wrong. □ *Citizens don't have the right to take the law into their own hands.* □ *The shopkeeper took the law into his own hands when he tried to arrest the thief.*

take the liberty of doing something to assume the right to do something. □ *Since I knew you were arriving late, I took the liberty of booking a hotel room for you.* □ *May I take the liberty of addressing you by your first name?*

take the lid off something to remove the secrecy from something. (Slang. Also used literally.) □ *When the press took the lid off the MP's private life, he resigned.* □ *The parents eventually took the lid off the goings-on at school.*

take the load off one's feet to sit down. (Slang.) □ *Come in, John. Sit down and take the load off your feet.* □ *Take the load off your feet when you have the chance.*

take the rap (for someone or something) (Slang, especially criminal slang.) **1.** [with *someone*] to take the blame (for doing something) for someone else. □ *I don't want to take the rap for you.* □ *John robbed the bank, but Tom took the rap for him.* **2.** [with *something*] to take the blame for (doing) something even though someone else did it. □ *I won't take the rap for the crime. I wasn't even in town.* □ *Who'll take the rap for it? Who did it?*

take the rough with the smooth to accept the bad things along with the good things. □ *We all have disappointments. You have to learn to take the rough with the smooth.* □ *There are good days and bad days, but every day you take the rough with the smooth. That's life.*

take the stand to go to and sit in the witness chair in a courtroom. □ *I was in court all day waiting to take the stand.* □ *The solicitor asked the witness to take the stand.*

take the trouble (to do something) to make an effort to do something (which one might not otherwise do). □ *I wish I had taken the trouble to study this matter more carefully.* □ *I just didn't have enough time to take the trouble.*

take the wind out of someone's sails to put an end to someone's boasting or arrogance and make the person feel embarrassed; to take an advantage away from someone. (Informal.) □ *John was bragging about how much money he earned until he learned that most of us make more. That took the wind out of his sails.* □ *Learning that one has been totally wrong about something can really take the wind out of one's sails.*

take the words out of one's mouth [for someone else] to say what you were going to say. (Also with *right*, as in the example below.) □ *John said exactly what I was going to say. He took the words out of my mouth.* □ *I agree with you. You took the words right out of my mouth.*

take time off not to work for a period of time—a few minutes or a longer period. (Compare to *get time off*.) □ *I had to*

take time off to go to the dentist. □ *Mary took time off to have tea.*

take time out to spend time away from studying or working. (Informal.) □ *He's taking time out between school and university.* □ *Mary's taking time out from her job to work abroad for a year.*

take to one's heels to run away. □ *The little boy said hello and then took to his heels.* □ *The man took to his heels to try to get to the bus-stop before the bus left.*

take to someone or something to become fond of or attracted to someone or something. (Informal.) □ *Mary didn't take to her new job, and she left after two weeks.* □ *Mary seemed to take to John right away.*

take too much on AND **take on too much** to undertake to do too much work or too many tasks. □ *Don't take too much on, or you won't be able to do any of it well.* □ *Ann tends to take on too much and get exhausted.*

take turns ((at) doing something) to do something, one (person) at a time (rather than everyone all at once). □ *Please take turns at reading the book.* □ *Everyone is taking turns looking at the picture.* □ *It's more orderly when everyone takes turns.*

take up a collection to collect some money for a specific project. □ *We wanted to send Bill some flowers, so we took up a collection.* □ *The office staff took up a collection to pay for the office party.*

take up arms (against someone or something) to prepare to fight against someone or something. □ *Everyone in the town took up arms against the enemy.* □ *They were all so angry that the leader persuaded them to take up arms.*

take up room See *take up space.*

take up someone's time to occupy someone's time and attention. □ *His work takes up all his time.* □ *I'm sorry. I didn't mean to take up so much of your time.* □ *This problem is taking up too much of my time.*

take up space AND **take up room** to fill or occupy space. (Note the variations in the examples.) □ *The piano is taking up too much room in our living-room.* □ *John, you're not being any help at all. You're just taking up space.*

take up the cudgels on behalf of someone or something to support or defend someone or something. □ *We'll have to take up cudgels on behalf of Jim or he'll lose the debate.* □ *Meg has taken up cudgels on behalf of an environmental movement.*

take up time to require or fill time. (Also without *up*.) □ *This project is taking up too much time.* □ *This kind of thing always takes up time.*

take up with someone to become a friend or companion to someone. (Informal.) □ *Billy's mother was afraid that he was taking up with the wrong kind of people.* □ *John and Bob took up with each other and became close friends.*

taken aback surprised and confused. □ *When Mary told me the news, I was taken aback for a moment.* □ *When I told my parents I was married, they were completely taken aback.*

taken for dead appearing to be dead; assumed to be dead. □ *I was so ill with the flu that I was almost taken for dead.* □ *The accident victims were so seriously injured that they were taken for dead at first.*

taken ill See under *take ill*.

taken short See under *caught short*.

talk back (to someone) to respond (to a rebuke) rudely or impertinently. □ *John got into trouble for talking back to the teacher.* □ *An employee never gains anything by talking back.*

talk big to brag or boast; to talk in an intimidating manner. (Slang.) □ *John is always talking big, but he hasn't really accomplished a lot in life.* □ *She talks big, but she's harmless.*

talk down to someone to speak to someone in a patronizing manner, using very simple language as though the person being spoken to were unintelligent. □ *The manager insulted everyone in the office by talking down to them.* □ *Please don't talk down to me. I can understand everything you have to say.*

talk nineteen to the dozen to talk a lot, usually quickly. (Informal.) □ *The old friends talk nineteen to the dozen when they meet once a year.* □ *You won't get Jean to stop chattering. She always talks nineteen to the dozen.*

talk of the town the subject of gossip; someone or something that everyone is talking about. □ *Joan's argument with the town council is the talk of the town.* □ *Fred's father is the talk of the town since the police arrested him.*

talk shop to talk about business matters at a social event (where business talk is out of place). (Informal.) □ *All right, everyone, we're not here to talk shop. Let's have a good time.* □ *Mary and Jane stood by the punch-bowl talking shop.*

talk someone into doing something to overcome someone's objections to doing something; to persuade someone to do something. □ *They talked me into going to the meeting, even though I didn't really have the time.* □ *No one can talk me into doing something illegal.*

talk someone out of doing something to persuade someone not to do something. □ *I tried to talk her out of going, but she insisted.* □ *Don't try to talk me out of leaving school. My mind is made up.*

talk someone out of something to persuade someone to give something up. □ *That is my decision, and you can't talk me out of it.* □ *I tried to talk her out of her piece of cake.*

talk someone's head off [for someone] to speak too much. (Slang.) □ *Why does John always talk his head off? Doesn't he know he bores people?* □ *She talks her head off and doesn't seem to know what she's saying.*

talk something out AND **talk out something** to talk about all aspects of a problem or disagreement. □ *Ann and*

Sally had a problem, so they agreed to talk it out. □ It's better to talk out a disagreement than to stay angry.

talk something over AND **talk over something** to discuss something. □ Come into my office so we can talk this over. □ We talked over the plans for nearly an hour.

talk through one's hat to talk nonsense. (Informal. See also the following entry.) □ John doesn't know anything about gardening. He's just talking through his hat. □ Jean said that the Smiths are emigrating, but she's talking through her hat.

talk through the back of one's head to talk nonsense; to *talk through one's hat*. □ She knows nothing about electronics. She is just talking through the back of her head. □ Tom is talking through the back of his head when he accuses the boss of victimizing him.

talk turkey to talk business; to talk frankly. (Slang.) □ Okay, Bob, we have business to discuss. Let's talk turkey. □ John wanted to talk turkey, but Jane just wanted to have a gossip.

talk until one is blue in the face to talk until one is exhausted. (Informal.) □ I talked until I was blue in the face, but I couldn't change her mind. □ She had to talk until she was blue in the face in order to convince him.

talking-shop a place or meeting where things are discussed, but at which no action is taken or decided on. (Informal.) □ Many people think the City Chambers is just a talking-shop. □ The firm's board meeting is always just a talking-shop. The chairman makes all the decisions himself.

tall story a story which is difficult or impossible to believe; a lie. □ Jim's alibi sounds like a tall story to me. □ Jack told a tall story about his grandmother dying to get a day off work. Both his grandmothers are already dead.

tan someone's hide to spank or beat someone. (Informal.) □ Billy's mother said she'd tan Billy's hide if he ever did

that again. □ "I'll tan your hide if you're late!" said Tom's father.

taper off (doing something) to stop doing something gradually. □ My doctor told me to taper off smoking cigarettes. □ Your course of pills must be tapered off.

tar and feather someone to chastise someone severely. (Also used literally at one time.) □ They threatened to tar and feather me if I ever came back into their town. □ I don't believe that they'd really tar and feather me, but they could be very unpleasant.

tarred with the same brush having the same faults or bad points as someone else. □ Jack and his brother are tarred with the same brush. They're both crooks. □ The Smith children are tarred with the same brush. They're all lazy.

teach one's grandmother to suck eggs to try to tell or show someone more knowledgeable or experienced than oneself how to do something. □ Don't suggest showing Mary how to knit. It will be teaching your grandmother to suck eggs. She's an expert. □ Don't teach your grandmother to suck eggs. Jack has been playing tennis for years.

teach someone a lesson to get even with someone for bad behaviour. □ John tripped me, so I punched him. That ought to teach him a lesson. □ That taught me a lesson. I won't do it again.

team up with someone to join with someone. □ I teamed up with Jane to write the report. □ I had never teamed up with anyone else before. I had always worked alone.

tear into someone or something (Slang.) **1.** [with *someone*] to criticize and scold someone. □ Tom tore into John and shouted at him for an hour. □ Don't tear into me like that. You have no right to speak to me that way. **2.** to attack or fight with someone or something. □ The boxer tore into his opponent. □ The lion tore into the herd of zebras.

tear off to leave or depart in a great hurry. (Informal.) □ *Well, excuse me. I have to tear off.* □ *Bob tore off down the street, chasing the fire engine.*

tear one's hair to be anxious, frustrated, or angry. (Not used literally.) □ *I was so nervous, I was about to tear my hair.* □ *I had better get home. My parents will be tearing their hair.*

tear something down AND **tear down something** to dismantle or destroy something. □ *They plan to tear the old building down and build a new one there.* □ *They'll tear down the building in about two weeks.*

teething troubles difficulties and problems experienced in the early stages of a project, activity, etc. □ *There have been a lot of teething troubles with the new computer system.* □ *We have got over the teething troubles connected with the new building complex.*

tell it to the marines I do not believe you (maybe the marines will). (Informal.) □ *That's silly. Tell it to the marines.* □ *I don't care how good you think your reason is. Tell it to the marines!*

tell its own story AND **tell its own tale** [for the state of something] to indicate clearly what has happened. □ *The upturned boat told its own tale. The oarsman had drowned.* □ *The girl's tear-stained face told its own story.*

tell on someone to report someone's bad behaviour; to tell tales on someone. □ *If you do that again, I'll tell on you!* □ *Please don't tell on me. I'm in enough trouble as it is.*

tell one to one's face to tell (something) to someone directly. □ *I'm sorry that Sally feels that way about me. I wish she had told me to my face.* □ *I won't tell Tom that you're angry with him. You should tell him to his face.*

tell people apart to distinguish one person or a group of people from another person or group of people. □ *Tom and John are brothers, and you can hardly tell them apart.* □ *Our team is wearing*

red, and the other team is wearing orange. I can't tell them apart.

tell someone a thing or two AND **tell someone where to get off** to scold someone; to express one's anger to someone; to *tell someone off.* (Informal.) □ *Wait till I see Sally. I'll tell her a thing or two!* □ *She told me where to get off and then started in scolding Tom.*

tell someone off AND **tell off someone** to scold someone; to attack someone verbally. □ *I was so angry with Bob that I told him off.* □ *By the end of the day, I had told off everyone else, too.*

tell someone on someone to report someone's bad behaviour to someone else. (Informal. See also *tell on someone.*) □ *Stop it, or I'll tell the teacher on you.* □ *Please don't tell the teacher on me! I'll have to stand in the corner.*

tell someone where to get off See *tell someone a thing or two.*

tell tales out of school to tell secrets or spread rumours. □ *I wish that John would keep quiet. He's telling tales out of school again.* □ *If you tell tales out of school a lot, people won't know when to believe you.*

tell the time to be able to read time from a clock or watch. □ *Billy is only 4. He can't tell the time yet.* □ *They are teaching the children to tell the time at school.*

tell things apart to distinguish one thing or a group of things from another thing or group of things. □ *This one is gold, and the others are brass. Can you tell them apart?* □ *Without their labels, I can't tell them apart.*

tell which is which See *know which is which.*

thank one's lucky stars to be thankful for one's luck. (Informal.) □ *You can thank your lucky stars that I was there to help you.* □ *I thank my lucky stars that I studied the right things for the test.*

thankful for small mercies grateful for any small benefits or advantages one has, especially in a generally difficult situation. □ *We have very little money, but we must be grateful for small mercies. At least we have enough food.* □ *Bob was badly injured in the accident, but at least he's still alive. Let's be grateful for small mercies.*

thanks to someone or something owing to someone or something; because of someone or something. (This does not refer to gratitude.) □ *Thanks to the storm, we have no electricity.* □ *Thanks to Mary, we have tickets to the game. She bought them early before they were sold out.*

That makes two of us. The same goes for me.; I, too. (Informal.) □ *So, you're going to the game? That makes two of us.* □ BILL: *I just passed my biology test.* BOB: *That makes two of us!*

That takes care of that. That is settled. □ *That takes care of that, and I'm glad it's over.* □ *I spent all morning dealing with this matter, and that takes care of that.*

That will do. That is enough.; Do no more. □ *That'll do, Billy. Stop your crying.* □ *"That will do," said Mr. Jones when he had heard enough of our arguing.*

That'll be the day. I don't believe that the day will ever come (when something will happen). (Informal.) □ *Do you really think that John will pass geometry? That'll be the day.* □ *John graduate? That'll be the day!*

That's about the size of it. It is final and correct. (Informal.) □ MARY: *Do you mean that you aren't going?* TOM: *That's about the size of it.* □ *At the end of his speech Bob said, "That's about the size of it."*

That's how it goes. That is the kind of thing that happens.; That is life. □ *Too bad about John and his problems. That's how it goes.* □ *I just lost a twenty-pound note, and I can't find it anywhere. That's how it goes.*

That's that. It is permanently settled and need not be dealt with again. □ *I*

said no, and that's that. □ *You can't come back. I told you to leave, and that's that.*

That's the last straw. AND **That's the straw that broke the camel's back.** That is the final thing. □ *Now it's raining! That's the last straw. The picnic is cancelled!* □ *When Sally became ill, that was the straw that broke the camel's back. The department closed down.*

That's the straw that broke the camel's back. See the previous entry.

That's the ticket. That is exactly what is needed. (Informal.) □ *That's the ticket, John. You're doing it just the way it should be done.* □ *That's the ticket! I knew you could do it.*

That's the way the cookie crumbles. Those things happen.; That's life. (Slang.) □ *Sorry to hear about your problems. That's the way the cookie crumbles.* □ *John crashed his car and then lost his job. That's the way the cookie crumbles.*

The boot is on the other foot. a proverb meaning that the situation has been reversed; the opposite of what was formerly the case has happened. □ *John used to be poor and Peter wealthy, but since John's promotion and Peter's bankruptcy, the boot is on the other foot.* □ *Mary used to be Jean's landlady, but now that she's bought the house from her, the boot is on the other foot.* □ *The teacher is taking a course in summer school and is finding out what it's like when the boot is on the other foot.* ALSO: **have the boot on the other foot.** □ *When the policeman was arrested, he learned what it was like to have the boot on the other foot.*

The cards are stacked against one. See under *have the cards stacked against one.*

The coast is clear. There is no visible danger. (Informal.) □ *I'm going to stay hidden here until the coast is clear.* □ *You can come out of your hiding-place now. The coast is clear.*

The early bird catches the worm. a proverb meaning that the early person will get the reward. (See also *early bird.*) □ *Don't be late again! Don't you know that the early bird catches the worm?* □ *I'll be there before the sun is up. After all, the early bird catches the worm.*

The fat is in the fire. a proverb meaning that serious trouble has broken out. □ *Now that Mary is leaving, the fat is in the fire. How can we get along without her?* □ *The fat's in the fire! There's £3,000 missing from the office safe.*

The heavens opened. It started to rain heavily. □ *The heavens opened, and we had to run for cover.* □ *We were waiting at the bus-stop when the heavens opened.*

The honeymoon is over. The early pleasant beginning has ended. □ *Okay, the honeymoon is over. It's time to settle down and do some hard work.* □ *I knew the honeymoon was over when they started shouting at me to work faster.*

The more the merrier. the more people there are, the happier they will be or the more enjoyable the occasion will be. □ *Of course you can have a lift with us! The more the merrier.* □ *The manager took on a new employee even though there's not enough work for all of us now. Oh well, the more the merrier.*

The odds are against one. Things are against one generally. One's chances are slim. □ *You can give it a try, but the odds are against you.* □ *I know the odds are against me, but I wish to run in the race anyway.*

The party's over. A happy or fortunate time has come to an end. (Informal.) □ *We go back to school tomorrow. The party's over.* □ *The staff did hardly any work under the old management, but they'll find the party's over now.*

The penny dropped. after a bit of time, something became clearly understood. (Informal. From a coin taking some time to operate a machine after being dropped in the slot.) □ *Fred didn't re-* alize what Joan was trying to say, but at last, the penny dropped. □ *Mary didn't know what was going on, but the penny soon dropped. They were planning a surprise party.*

The plot thickens. Things are becoming more complicated or interesting. □ *The police assumed that the woman was murdered by her ex-husband, but he has an alibi. The plot thickens.* □ *John is supposed to be going out with Mary, but I saw him last night with Sally. The plot thickens.*

The sky's the limit. There is no limit to the success that can be achieved or the money that can be gained or spent. (Informal.) □ *If you take a job with us, you'll find the promotion prospects very good. The sky's the limit, in fact.* □ *The insurance salesmen were told that the sky was the limit when it came to potential earnings.*

The spirit is willing (but the flesh is weak). a saying meaning that one may wish to do something but be physically unable to do it. (A biblical reference.) □ *I would like to join the climbing expedition, but I'm not fit enough. The spirit is willing but the flesh is weak.* □ *John would love to go to the party, but he is utterly exhausted. The spirit is willing, but the flesh is weak.* □ *It's not that I don't want to go. Certainly the spirit is willing.*

The world is someone's oyster. All the chances and opportunities in life are available to someone. (From Shakespeare's *The Merry Wives of Windsor.*) □ *When you are young the world is your oyster. You can go anywhere and do anything.* □ *Jane has just left university with a good degree and the world is her oyster.*

The worm (has) turned. Someone who is usually patient and humble has decided to stop being so. □ *Jane used to be treated badly by her husband and she just accepted it, but one day she hit him. The worm turned all right.* □ *Tom used to let the other boys bully him in the playground, but one day the worm* turned and he's now leader of their gang.

Them's fighting words. Those are words which will start a fight. (Slang. Note that *them is* is permissible in this expression.) □ *Better not talk like that around here. Them's fighting words.* □ *Them's fighting words, and you'd better be quiet unless you want trouble.*

then and there right then. □ *I asked him right then and there exactly what he meant.* □ *I decided to settle the matter then and there and not wait until Monday.*

There are plenty of other fish in the sea. There are other choices. (Used to refer to persons.) □ *When John broke up with Ann, I told her not to worry. There are plenty of other fish in the sea.* □ *It's too bad that your secretary left, but there are plenty of other fish in the sea.*

there is no doing something one is not permitted to do something. (Informal.) □ *There is no arguing with Bill.* □ *There is no cigarette smoking here.*

There is trouble brewing. See *Trouble is brewing.*

There will be the devil to pay. There will be lots of trouble. (Slang.) □ *If you damage my car, there will be the devil to pay.* □ *Bill broke a window, and now there will be the devil to pay.*

Thereby hangs a tale. There is an interesting story to be told about that. □ *Tommy has run away from home, and thereby hangs a tale.* □ *The Smiths have sold the manor and thereby hangs a tale.*

There's more than one way to kill a cat. AND **There's more than one way to skin a cat.** a proverb meaning that there is more than one way to do something. □ *If that way won't work, try another way. There's more than one way to kill a cat.* □ *Don't worry, I'll think of a way to get it done. There's more than one way to skin a cat.*

There's no accounting for taste. a proverb meaning that there is no explanation for people's preferences. □ *Look at that purple and orange car! There's no accounting for taste.* □ *Some people seemed to like the music, although I thought it was worse than noise. There's no accounting for taste.*

There's no smoke without fire. See *Where there's smoke there's fire.*

thick and fast in large numbers or amounts and at a rapid rate. □ *The enemy soldiers came thick and fast.* □ *New problems seem to come thick and fast.*

thick-skinned not easily upset or hurt; insensitive. (The opposite of *thin-skinned.*) □ *Tom won't worry about your insults. He's completely thick-skinned.* □ *Jane's so thick-skinned she didn't realize Fred was being rude to her.*

thin end of the wedge a minor or unimportant event or act that is the first stage in something more serious or unfortunate. □ *If you let Pam stay for a few days, it will be the thin end of the wedge. She'll stay for ages.* □ *The boss thinks that if he gives his secretary a rise, it will be the thin end of the wedge and all the staff will demand one.*

thin on the ground few in number; rare. □ *Jobs in that area are thin on the ground.* □ *Butterflies are thin on the ground here now.*

thin on top balding. (Informal.) □ *James is wearing a hat because he's getting thin on top.* □ *Father got a little thin on top as he got older.*

thin out to disperse; to become sparse. □ *As Tom grew older, his hair began to thin out.* □ *Soon after the accident, the crowd began to thin out.*

thin-skinned easily upset or hurt; sensitive. (The opposite of *thick-skinned.*) □ *You'll have to handle Mary's mother carefully. She's very thin-skinned.* □ *Jane weeps easily when people tease her. She's too thin-skinned.*

Things are looking up. Conditions are looking better. □ *Since I got a salary increase, things are looking up.* □

Things are looking up at school. I'm doing better in all my classes.

think a great deal of someone or something See the following entry.

think a lot of someone or something AND **think a great deal of someone or something; think highly of someone or something; think much of someone or something** to think well of someone or something. □ *The teacher thinks a lot of Mary and her talents.* □ *No one really thinks a great deal of the new policies.* □ *I think highly of John.* □ *The manager doesn't think much of John and says so to everyone.*

think back (on someone or something) to remember and think about someone or something. □ *When I think back on Sally and the good times we had together, I get very sad.* □ *I like to think back on my childhood and try to remember what it was like.* □ *Thinking back can be depressing.*

think better of something to reconsider something; to think again and decide not to do something. □ *Jack was going to escape, but he thought better of it.* □ *Jill had planned to resign, but thought better of it.*

think fit (to do something) AND **see fit (to do something)** to consider that a certain course of action is right or suitable. □ *He did not think fit to telephone before arriving.* □ *I'll go if I see fit.* □ *If I see fit to return, I'll bring Bill with me.*

think highly of someone or something See *think a lot of someone or something.*

think little of someone or something AND **think nothing of someone or something** to have a low opinion of someone or something. (See also *think nothing of doing something.*) □ *Most experts think little of Jane's theory.* □ *People may think nothing of it now, but in a few years everyone will praise it.* □ *No one thinks little of her now.*

think much of someone or something See *think a lot of someone or something.*

think nothing of doing something not to consider something difficult. □ *Mary thinks nothing of walking miles to work.* □ *Bob thinks nothing of working eighteen hours a day.*

think nothing of someone or something See *think little of someone or something.*

think on one's feet to think while one is talking. □ *If you want to be a successful teacher, you must be able to think on your feet.* □ *I have to write out everything I'm going to say, because I can't think on my feet too well.*

think out loud to say one's thoughts aloud. □ *Excuse me. I didn't really mean to say that. I was just thinking out loud.* □ *Mr. Johnson didn't prepare a speech. He just stood there and thought out loud. It was a terrible presentation.*

think something out AND **think out something** to think through something; to think something over. □ *This is an interesting problem. I'll have to take some time and think it out.* □ *We spent all morning thinking out our plan.*

think something over AND **think over something** to consider something; to think about something (before giving a decision). □ *Please think it over and give me your decision in the morning.* □ *I need more time to think over your offer.*

think something up AND **think up something** to contrive or invent something. □ *Don't worry. I'll find a way to do it. I can think something up in time to get it done.* □ *John thought up a way to solve our problem.*

think the world of someone or something to be very fond of someone or something. □ *Mary thinks the world of her little sister.* □ *The old lady thinks the world of her cats.*

think twice (before doing something) to consider carefully whether one should do something; to be cautious about doing something. □ *You should think twice before leaving your job.* □ *That's a serious decision, and you should certainly think twice.*

thrash something out AND **thrash out something** to discuss something thoroughly and solve any problems. □ *The committee took hours to thrash the whole matter out.* □ *Fred and Anne thrashed out the reasons for their constant disagreements.*

thrill someone to bits to please or excite someone very much. (Informal.) □ *John sent flowers to Ann and thrilled her to bits.* □ *Your wonderful comments thrilled me to bits.*

through and through thoroughly; completely. □ *I've studied this report through and through trying to find the facts you've mentioned.* □ *I was angry through and through, and I had to sit down and recover before I could talk to anyone.*

through hell and high water through all sorts of severe difficulties. (Informal.) □ *I came through hell and high water to get to this meeting. Why don't you start on time?* □ *You'll have to go through hell and high water to accomplish your goal, but it'll be worth it.*

through thick and thin through good times and bad times. (Informal.) □ *We've been together through thick and thin, and we won't desert each other now.* □ *Over the years, we went through thick and thin and enjoyed every minute of it.*

through with someone or something finished with someone or something. (Informal.) □ *I'm through with John. We had a big argument and said goodbye to each other.* □ *Where shall I put the paintbrush when I'm through with it?*

throw a fit to become very angry; to put on a display of anger. □ *Sally threw a fit when I showed up without the things she asked me to buy.* □ *My dad threw a fit when I got home three hours late.*

throw a party (for someone) to give or hold a party for someone. □ *Mary was leaving town, so we threw a party for her.* □ *Do you know a place where we could throw a party?*

throw a spanner in the works to cause problems for someone's plans. (Informal.) □ *I don't want to throw a spanner in the works, but have you checked your plans with a solicitor?* □ *When John refused to help us, he really threw a spanner in the works.*

throw caution to the winds to become very careless. □ *Jane, who is usually cautious, threw caution to the winds and went windsurfing.* □ *I don't mind taking a little chance now and then, but I'm not the type of person who throws caution to the winds.*

throw cold water on something See *pour cold water on something.*

throw down the gauntlet to challenge (someone) to an argument or (a figurative) combat. □ *When Bob challenged my conclusions, he threw down the gauntlet. I was ready for an argument.* □ *Frowning at Bob is the same as throwing down the gauntlet. He loves to get into a fight about something.*

throw good money after bad to waste additional money after wasting money once. □ *I bought a used car and then had to spend £300 on repairs. That was throwing good money after bad.* □ *The Browns are always throwing good money after bad. They bought a plot of land which turned out to be swamp, and then had to pay to have it filled in.*

throw in one's hand to give up or abandon a course of action. (From a player giving up in a card-game.) □ *I got tired of the tennis competition and threw in my hand.* □ *John spent only one year at university and then threw in his hand.*

throw in the sponge See the following entry.

throw in the towel AND **throw in the sponge** to give up (doing something). (Informal.) □ *When John could stand no more of Mary's bad temper, he threw in* the towel and left. □ *Don't give up now! It's too soon to throw in the sponge.*

throw one's hat into the ring AND **toss one's hat into the ring** to state that one is running for an elective office; to announce that one is a candidate in a contest. □ *Jane wanted to run for treasurer, so she tossed her hat into the ring.* □ *The mayor refused to toss his hat into the ring. Instead he announced his retirement.*

throw one's weight around to attempt to order people around; to give orders. (Informal.) □ *The district manager came to our office and tried to throw his weight around, but no one paid any attention to him.* □ *Don't try to throw your weight around in this office. We know who our employer is.*

throw oneself at someone to give oneself willingly to someone else for romance. (Informal.) □ *It looks like Mary really likes John. She practically threw herself at him when he came into the room.* □ *Everyone could see by the way Tom threw himself at Jane that he was going to ask her for a date.*

throw oneself at someone's feet to act towards someone in a very humble and respectful manner; to ask for mercy from someone else. (Used both figuratively and literally). □ *Do I have to throw myself at your feet in order to convince you that I'm sorry?* □ *Bob threw himself at his wife's feet and asked her to take him back.*

throw oneself at the mercy of someone to plead for mercy from someone. □ *When Jean's father threw her out, she threw herself at the mercy of her uncle.* □ *If you've lost your passport, you'll just have to throw yourself at the mercy of the British Council.*

throw someone to confuse someone. (Informal.) □ *You threw me for a minute when you asked for my identification. I thought you recognized me.* □ *The question the teacher asked was so hard that it threw me, and I became very nervous.*

throw someone off the track 1. to cause one to lose one's place in what one is doing. □ *The interruption threw me off the track for a moment, but I soon got started again with my presentation.* □ *Don't let little things throw you off the track. Concentrate on what you're doing.* 2. to cause someone to lose the trail (when following someone or something). □ *The fox threw us off the track by running across the stream.* □ *The robber threw the police off the track by leaving town.*

throw someone out (of something) to force a person to leave a place. (Also used literally.) □ *John behaved so badly that they threw him out of the party.* □ *I was very loud, but they didn't throw me out.*

throw someone over to end a romance with someone. (Informal.) □ *Jane threw Bill over. I think she met someone she likes better.* □ *Bill was about ready to throw her over, so it's just as well.*

throw someone to the wolves (figuratively) to sacrifice someone. □ *The press was demanding an explanation, so the mayor blamed the mess on John and threw him to the wolves.* □ *I wouldn't let them throw me to the wolves! I did nothing wrong, and I won't take the blame for their errors.*

throw someone's name around to mention the name of a famous or influential person in order to impress people. (Informal.) □ *You won't get anywhere around here by throwing the MP's name around.* □ *When you get to the meeting, just throw the boss's name around a bit, and people will pay attention to you.*

throw something in AND **throw in something** to include something in a deal or bargain. □ *To encourage me to buy a new car, the car dealer threw in a free radio.* □ *If you purchase three pounds of chocolates, I'll throw in one pound of salted nuts.*

throw something off AND **throw off something** to resist or recover from a disease. □ *It was a bad cold, but I managed to* throw it off in a few days. □ I can't seem to throw off my cold. I've had it for weeks.

throw something together AND **throw together something** to assemble or arrange something in haste. (Informal.) □ John went into the kitchen to throw something together for dinner. □ Don't throw something together! Take some care over it. □ You assembled this device very badly. It seems that you just threw it together.

throw something up at someone to mention a shortcoming to someone repeatedly. (Informal.) □ I know I'm thoughtless. Why do you keep throwing it up at me? □ Bill was always throwing Jane's faults up at her.

throw the book at someone to charge or convict someone with as many crimes as is possible; to reprimand or punish someone severely. □ I made the police officer angry, so he took me to the station and threw the book at me. □ The judge threatened to throw the book at me if I didn't stop insulting the police officer.

throw up to vomit. (Slang.) □ The meat was bad, and I threw up. □ The children always throw up when they travel in cars.

throw up one's hands in horror to be shocked; to raise one's hands as when shocked. □ When Bill heard the bad news, he threw up his hands in horror. □ I threw up my hands in horror when I saw the mess the burglars had made.

thumb a lift AND **hitch a lift** to get a lift from a passing motorist; to make a sign with one's thumb that indicates to passing drivers that one is asking for a lift. □ My car broke down on the motorway, and I had to thumb a lift to get back to town. □ Sometimes it's dangerous to hitch a lift with a stranger.

thumb one's nose at someone or something to make a rude gesture of disgust with one's thumb and nose at someone or something. (Both literal and figurative uses.) □ The tramp thumbed his nose at the lady and walked away. □ You can't just thumb your nose at peo-

ple who give you trouble. You've got to learn to get along with them.

thumb through something AND **leaf through something** to look through a book, magazine, or newspaper without reading it carefully. □ I've only thumbed through this book, but it looks very interesting. □ I leafed through a magazine while waiting to see the doctor.

tick over to move along at a quiet, even pace, without either stopping or going quickly. (Informal. From an engine ticking over.) □ The firm didn't make large profits, but it's ticking over. □ We must try to keep our finances ticking over until the recession ends.

tick someone off to scold or rebuke someone. (Informal.) □ I was ticked off by my mother for arriving late. □ You really ticked me off! ALSO: **give someone a ticking-off** □ The teacher gave the children a ticking-off for untidy work.

tickle someone pink AND **tickle someone to death** to please or entertain someone very much. (Informal. Never used literally.) □ Bill was tickled pink to meet his favourite film star. □ I know that these flowers will tickle her to death.

tickle someone to death See tickle someone pink.

tickle someone's fancy to interest someone; to attract someone. (Informal.) □ I have an interesting proposal here which I think will tickle your fancy. □ The idea of dancing doesn't exactly tickle my fancy.

tide someone over [for a portion of something] to last until someone can get some more. (Informal.) □ I don't get paid until next Wednesday. Could you lend me thirty pounds to tide me over? □ Could I borrow some tea to tide me over until I can get to the shops tomorrow?

tie someone down to restrict or hamper someone. □ I'd like to go fishing every week-end, but my family ties me down. □ I don't want to tie you down, but you do have responsibilities here at home.

tie someone in knots to make someone confused or upset. (Informal.) □ *The speaker tied herself in knots trying to explain her difficult subject in simple language.* □ *I was trying to be tactful, but I just tied myself in knots.*

tie someone or something up AND **tie up someone or something** (Informal.) **1.** [with *someone*] to keep someone busy or occupied. □ *Sorry, this matter will tie me up for about an hour.* □ *The same matter will tie up almost everyone in the office.* **2.** [with *something*] to conclude and finalize something. □ *Let's try to tie up this deal by Thursday.* □ *We'll manage to tie our business up by Wednesday at the latest.*

tie someone's hands to prevent someone from doing something. □ *I'd like to help you, but the headmaster has tied my hands.* □ *Please don't tie my hands with unnecessary restrictions. I'd like the freedom to do whatever is necessary.*

tie the knot to get married. (Informal.) □ *Well, I hear that you and John are going to tie the knot.* □ *My parents tied the knot almost forty years ago.*

tied to one's mother's apron-strings dominated by one's mother; dependent on one's mother. □ *Tom is still tied to his mother's apron-strings.* □ *Isn't he a little old to be tied to his mother's apron-strings?*

tighten one's belt to manage to spend less money. (Informal.) □ *Things are beginning to cost more and more. It looks as though we'll all have to tighten our belts.* □ *Times are hard, and prices are high. I can tighten my belt for only so long.*

till the cows come home for a very long time. (Cows are returned to the barn at the end of the day. Informal.) □ *We could discuss this till the cows come home and still reach no decisions.* □ *He could drink beer till the cows come home.*

tilt at windmills to fight battles with imaginary enemies; to struggle against imaginary opposition. (As with the fictional character Don Quixote, who attacked windmills.) □ *There are enough real problems in life without tilting at windmills.* □ *George is tilting at windmills. Actually all his colleagues agree with him.*

time after time AND **time and (time) again** repeatedly. □ *You've made the same error time after time! Please try to be more careful!* □ *I've told you time and again not to do that.* □ *You keep saying the same thing over and over, time and time again. Stop it!*

time and (time) again See the previous entry.

time flies time passes very quickly. (From the Latin *tempus fugit*.) □ *I didn't really think it was so late when the party ended. Doesn't time fly?* □ *Time simply flew when the old friends exchanged news.*

Time hangs heavy on someone's hands. Time seems to go slowly when one has nothing to do. (Note the variations in the examples.) □ *I don't like it when time hangs so heavily on my hands.* □ *John looks so bored. Time hangs heavy on his hands.*

Time is money. [My] time is valuable, so don't waste it. □ *I can't afford to spend a lot of time standing here talking. Time is money, you know!* □ *People who keep saying time is money may be working too hard.*

Time is up. The allotted time has run out. □ *You must stop now. Your time is up.* □ *Time's up! Turn in your test papers whether you're finished or not.*

time out of mind for a very long time; longer than anyone can remember. □ *There has been a church in the village time out of mind.* □ *The Smith family have lived in that house time out of mind.*

time was when there was a time when; at a time in the past. □ *Time was when old people were taken care of at home.* □ *Time was when people didn't travel around so much.*

Time will tell. a proverb meaning that something will become known in the course of time. □ *I don't know if things will improve. Time will tell.* □ *Who knows what the future will bring? Only time will tell.*

tip someone off AND **tip off someone** to give someone a hint; to warn someone. (Informal.) □ *I tipped John off that there would be a test in his algebra class.* □ *Bob tipped the rest of the class off about the test.*

tip someone the wink to give someone privileged or useful information in a secret or private manner. (Informal.) □ *John tipped Mary the wink that there was a vacancy in his department.* □ *Jack got his new house at a good price. A friend tipped him the wink that it was going on the market.*

tip the scales at something to weigh some amount. □ *Tom tips the scales at nearly 200 pounds.* □ *I'll be glad when I tip the scales at a few pounds less.*

to a great extent mainly; largely. □ *To a great extent, Mary is the cause of her own problems.* □ *To a great extent, the trouble has cleared up.*

to and fro towards and away from (something). (See also *back and forth*.) □ *The puppy was very active—running to and fro—wagging its tail.* □ *The lion in the cage moved to and fro, watching the people in front of the cage.*

to boot in addition; besides. □ *For breakfast I had my usual two eggs and a slice of ham to boot.* □ *When I left for school, my parents gave me a plane ticket and fifty pounds to boot.*

to date up to the present time. □ *How much have you accomplished to date?* □ *I've done everything I'm supposed to have done to date.*

to kick off with to start with. (Informal.) □ *To kick off with, I want a salary increase.* □ *The workers wanted better conditions to kick off with.*

to no avail AND **of no avail** with no effect; unsuccessful. □ *All of my efforts were to no avail.* □ *Everything I did to help was of no avail. Nothing worked.*

to one's heart's content as much as one wants. □ *John wanted a week's holiday so he could go to the lake and fish to his heart's content.* □ *I just sat there eating chocolate to my heart's content.*

to put it mildly to understate something; to say something politely. □ *She was angry with almost everyone—to put it mildly.* □ *To say she was angry is putting it mildly.* □ *To put it mildly, I disagree with you.*

to say nothing of someone or something not even to mention the importance of someone or something. □ *John and Mary had to be cared for, to say nothing of Bill, who would require even more attention.* □ *I'm having enough difficulty painting the house, to say nothing of the garage which is very much in need of paint.*

to say the least at the very least; without dwelling on the subject; *to put it mildly.* □ *We were not at all pleased with her work—to say the least.* □ *When they had an accident, they were upset to say the least.*

to some extent to some degree; in some amount; partly. □ *I've solved this problem to some extent.* □ *I can help you understand this to some extent.*

to someone's liking in a way which pleases someone. □ *I hope I've done the work to your liking.* □ *Sally didn't find the meal to her liking and didn't eat any of it.*

to someone's way of thinking in someone's opinion. □ *This isn't satisfactory to my way of thinking.* □ *To my way of thinking, this is the perfect kind of holiday.*

to the best of one's ability as well as one is able. □ *I did the work to the best of my ability.* □ *You should always work to the best of your ability.*

to the best of one's knowledge as far as one knows; from one's knowledge. □ *This is the true story to the best of my* knowledge. □ *To the best of my knowledge, John is the only person who can answer that question.*

to the bitter end to the very end. (Originally nautical. This originally had nothing to do with bitterness.) □ *I kept trying to the bitter end.* □ *It took me a long time to get through college, but I worked hard at it all the way to the bitter end.*

to the contrary as the opposite of what has been stated; contrary to what has been stated. (Compare to *on the contrary.*) □ *Of course she's right. I didn't say anything to the contrary.* □ *There could be an election. The prime minister has made no statement to the contrary.*

to the core all the way through; basically and essentially. (Usually with some negative sense, such as *evil, rotten,* etc.) □ *Bill said that John is evil to the core.* □ *This organization is rotten to the core.*

to the ends of the earth to the remotest and most inaccessible points on the earth. □ *I'll pursue him to the ends of the earth.* □ *We've explored almost the whole world. We've travelled to the ends of the earth trying to learn about our world.*

to the last to the end; to the conclusion. □ *All of us kept trying to the last.* □ *It was a very boring play, but I sat through it to the last.*

to the letter exactly as instructed; exactly as written. □ *I didn't make an error. I followed your instructions to the letter.* □ *We didn't prepare the recipe to the letter, but the cake still turned out very well.*

to the nth degree to the maximum amount; to the greatest extent possible. (Informal.) □ *Jane is a perfectionist and tries to be careful to the nth degree.* □ *This scientific instrument is accurate to the nth degree.*

to the tune of some amount of money a certain amount of money. (Informal.) □ *My bank account is overdrawn to the tune of £340.* □ *My wallet was stolen,* and I'm short of money to the tune of seventy pounds.

To the victors belong the spoils. a proverb meaning that the winners achieve power over people and property. □ *The new managing director took office and immediately sacked many workers and employed new ones. Everyone said, "To the victors belong the spoils."* □ *The office of treasurer includes many perks. To the victors belong the spoils.*

to whom it may concern to the person to whom this applies. (A formal form of address used when you do not know the name of the person who handles the kind of business you are writing about.) □ *The letter started out, "To whom it may concern."* □ *When you don't know whom to write to, just say, "To whom it may concern."*

toe the line to do what one is expected or required to do; to follow the rules. (Informal.) □ *You'll get ahead, Sally. Don't worry. Just toe the line, and everything will be okay.* □ *John finally got the sack. He just couldn't learn to toe the line.*

tone something down AND **tone down something** to make something less extreme. □ *That yellow is too bright. Please try to tone it down.* □ *Can you tone down your remarks? They seem quite strong for this situation.*

tongue-in-cheek insincere; joking. □ *Ann made a tongue-in-cheek remark to John, and he got angry because he thought she was serious.* □ *The play seemed very serious at first, but then everyone saw that it was tongue-in-cheek, and they began laughing.*

too big for one's boots AND **too big for one's britches** too haughty for one's status or age. (Informal.) □ *Bill's getting a little too big for his boots. He thinks he's better than anyone else.* □ *You're too big for your britches, young man! You had better be more respectful.*

too big for one's britches See the previous entry.

too close for comfort [for a misfortune or a threat] to be dangerously close. (See also *close to home*.) □ *That car nearly hit me! That was too close for comfort.* □ *When I was in hospital, I nearly died from pneumonia. Believe me, that was too close for comfort.*

too good to be true almost unbelievable; so good as to be unbelievable. □ *The news was too good to be true.* □ *When I finally got a big rise, it was too good to be true.*

Too many cooks spoil the broth. a proverb meaning that too many people trying to manage something simply spoil it. □ *Let's decide who is in charge around here. Too many cooks spoil the broth.* □ *Everyone is giving orders, but no one is following them! Too many cooks spoil the broth.*

too much of a good thing more of a thing than is good or useful. □ *I usually take short holidays. I can't stand too much of a good thing.* □ *Too much of a good thing can make you sick, especially if the good thing is chocolate.*

top someone or something to do or be better than someone or something. (Informal.) □ *Ann has done very well, but I don't think she can top Jane.* □ *Do you think your car tops mine when it comes to petrol use?*

toss one's hat into the ring See *throw one's hat into the ring.*

toss something off AND **shake off something; shake something off; toss off something** to ignore or resist the bad effects of something. □ *John insulted Bob, but Bob just tossed it off.* □ *If I couldn't shake off insults, I'd be miserable.*

total something up See *add something up.*

touch a sore point See the following entry.

touch a sore spot AND **touch a sore point** to refer to a sensitive matter which will upset someone. (Also used literally.) □ *I seem to have touched a sore spot. I'm sorry. I didn't mean to upset you.* □ *When you talk to him, avoid talking about money. It's best not to touch a sore point if possible.*

touch-and-go very uncertain or critical. □ *Things were touch-and-go at the office until a new manager was employed.* □ *Jane had a serious operation, and everything was touch-and-go for two days after her operation.*

touch on something to mention something; to talk about something briefly. □ *In tomorrow's lecture I'd like to touch on the matter of morality.* □ *The teacher only touched on the subject. There wasn't time to do more than that.*

touch someone for something to ask someone for a loan of something, usually a sum of money. (Informal.) □ *Fred's always trying to touch people for money.* □ *Jack touched John for £10.*

touch someone or something off AND **touch off someone or something** 1. [with *someone*] to make someone very angry. □ *Your rude comments touched Mary off. She's very angry with you.* □ *I didn't mean to touch off anyone. I was only being honest.* 2. [with *something*] to ignite something; to start something. □ *The argument touched off a serious fight.* □ *A few sparks touched all the fireworks off at once.*

touch something up AND **touch up something** to repair the paintwork on something; to freshen one's make-up. □ *We don't need to paint the whole room. We can just touch the walls up.* □ *You should touch up scratches on your car as soon as they occur.* □ *The model touched up her make-up before the photographs were taken.*

touch wood See *knock on wood.*

touched by someone or something emotionally affected or moved by someone or something. □ *Sally was very nice to me. I was very touched by her.* □ *I was really touched by your kind letter.*

touched (in the head) crazy. (Informal.) □ *Sometimes Bob acts as though he's touched in the head.* □ *In fact, I thought he was touched.*

tough act to follow a difficult presentation or performance to follow with one's own performance. □ *Bill's speech was excellent. It was a tough act to follow, but my speech was good also.* □ *In spite of the fact that I had a tough act to follow, I did my best.*

tough furrow to plough See *tough row to hoe.*

Tough luck! That is too bad! (Slang. Usually an insincere expression.) □ *So you were late and missed the bus. Tough luck!* □ *Tough luck, chum! Try again next time.*

tough nut to crack See *hard nut to crack.*

tough row to hoe AND **tough furrow to plough** a difficult task to undertake. □ *It was a tough row to hoe, but I finally got a college degree.* □ *Getting the contract signed is going to be a tough furrow to plough, but I'm sure I can do it.*

tower of strength a person who can always be depended on to provide support and encouragement, especially in times of trouble. □ *Mary was a tower of strength when Jean was in hospital. She looked after her whole family.* □ *Jack was a tower of strength during the time that his father was unemployed.*

toy with someone or something 1. [with *someone*] to tease someone; to deal lightly with someone's emotions. □ *Ann broke up with Tom because he was just toying with her. He was not serious at all.* □ *Don't toy with me! I won't have it!* 2. [with *something*] to play or fiddle with something. □ *Don't toy with your food. Eat it or leave it.* □ *John sat there toying with a pencil all through the meeting.*

track someone or something down AND **track down someone or something** to search for or pursue someone or something. □ *See if you can track Tom down for me. I need to talk to him.* □ *Please track down a red pencil for me.* □ *I can't seem to track down the file you want. Give me another few minutes.*

trade on something to use a fact or a situation to one's advantage. □ *Tom was able to trade on the fact that he had once been in the army.* □ *John traded on his poor eyesight to get a seat closer to the stage.*

trade something in (on something) AND **trade in something (on something)** to trade a used thing as part payment for a new thing. □ *I traded my old car in on a new one.* □ *Did you trade in the red one or the green one?*

tread on someone's toes See *step on someone's toes.*

trial and error trying repeatedly for success. □ *I finally found the right key after lots of trial and error.* □ *Sometimes trial and error is the only way to get something done.*

trip someone up AND **trip up someone** to cause someone to make a mistake or fail. □ *Bill tripped Tom up during the spelling contest, and Tom lost.* □ *I didn't mean to trip up anyone. I'm sorry I caused trouble.*

trot something out AND **trot out something** to mention something regularly or habitually, without giving it much thought. (Informal.) □ *Jack always trots out the same excuses for being late.* □ *When James disagreed with Mary, she simply trotted out her same old political arguments.*

Trouble is brewing. AND **There is trouble brewing.** Trouble is developing. □ *Trouble's brewing at the office. I have to get there early tomorrow.* □ *There is trouble brewing in the government. The prime minister may resign.*

trouble one's head about someone or something to worry about someone or something; to *trouble oneself about someone or something* which is none of one's business. (Also with *pretty,* as in the examples. Usually in the negative, meaning to mind one's own business.) □ *Now, now, don't trouble your pretty head about all these things.* □ *You needn't trouble your head about Sally.*

trouble oneself about someone or something to worry oneself about someone or something. (Usually in the negative.) □ *Please don't trouble yourself about me. I'm doing fine.* □ *I can't take time to trouble myself about this matter. Do it yourself.*

true to form exactly as expected; following the usual pattern. (Often with *running,* as in the examples.) □ *As usual, John is late. At least he's true to form.* □ *And true to form, Mary left before the meeting was adjourned.* □ *This winter season is running true to form—miserable!*

true to one's word keeping one's promise. □ *True to his word, Tom appeared at exactly eight o'clock.* □ *We'll soon know if Jane is true to her word. We'll see if she does what she promised.*

trumped-up false; fraudulently devised. □ *They tried to have Tom arrested on a trumped-up charge.* □ *Bob gave some trumped-up excuse for not being at the meeting.*

try it on to behave in a bold, disobedient, or unlawful manner in order to discover whether such behaviour will be allowed. (Informal.) □ *Tony knew he wouldn't get away with working only four days a week. He was just trying it on by asking the boss.* □ *The children really try it on when their mother's out.*

try one's hand (at something) to take a try at something. □ *Someday I'd like to try my hand at flying a plane.* □ *Give me a chance. Let me try my hand!*

try one's luck (at something) to attempt to do something (where success requires luck). □ *My grandfather came to California to try his luck at finding gold.* □ *I went into a gambling casino to try my luck.*

try one's wings to try to do something one has recently become qualified to do. (Like a young bird uses its wings to try to fly.) □ *John just got his driver's licence and wants to borrow the car to try his wings.* □ *I learned to skin-dive, and I want to go to the seaside to try my wings.*

try out (for something) to test one's fitness for a role in a play, a position on a sports team, etc. □ *I sing pretty well, so I thought I'd try out for the chorus.* □ *Hardly anyone else wanted to try out.*

try someone or something out AND **try out someone or something** to test someone or something for suitability (for some particular purpose). □ *John thought he could handle the job, so I thought I'd try him out.* □ *I'd like to try out that tool to see if it suits my purposes.*

try someone's patience to do something annoying which may cause someone to lose patience; to cause someone to be annoyed. □ *Stop whistling. You're trying my patience. Very soon I'm going to lose my temper.* □ *Some pupils think it's fun to try the teacher's patience.*

try something on AND **try on something** to put on a piece of clothing (or something else which fits on the body) to see if it fits. □ *Here, try this shirt on. I think it's your size.* □ *I tried on seven pairs of shoes before I found some that I liked.*

try something out (on someone) AND **try out something (on someone)** 1. to test something on someone (to see how it works or if it is liked). □ *I found a recipe for oyster stew and tried it out on my flat-mate.* □ *I'm glad you didn't try out that stuff on me!* 2. to tell about a plan or an idea and ask someone for an opinion about it. □ *I have a tremendous idea! Let me try it out on you.* □ *I want to try out my plan on you. Please give me your honest opinion.*

tuck into something to eat something with hunger and enjoyment. (Informal.) □ *The children really tucked into the ice-cream.* □ *Jean would like to have tucked into the cream cakes, but she's on a strict diet.*

tumble to something suddenly to understand or realize something. (Informal.) □ *I suddenly tumbled to the reason* *for his behaviour.* □ *When will Meg tumble to the fact that her husband is dishonest?*

tune something up AND **tune up something** to adjust an engine so that it runs the way it was meant to. (In the examples, *car* means "car engine.") □ *I need to find someone to tune my car up.* □ *I have a friend who tunes up cars.*

turn a blind eye to someone or something to ignore something and pretend you do not see it. □ *The usher turned a blind eye to the little boy who sneaked into the theatre.* □ *How can you turn a blind eye to all those starving children?*

turn a deaf ear (to something) to ignore what someone says; to ignore a cry for help. □ *How can you just turn a deaf ear to their cries for food and shelter?* □ *The government has turned a deaf ear.*

turn about one person after the other, each one taking a turn. □ *We baby-sit the children turn about.* □ *The parents drive the children to school turn about.*

turn against someone or something to become opposed to someone or something (after once supporting someone or something). □ *Bob turned against Mary after years of being her friend.* □ *I used to like small cars, but lately I've turned against them.*

turn in to go to bed. (Informal.) □ *It's late. I think I'll turn in.* □ *We usually turn in at about midnight.*

turn in one's grave See *turn (over) in one's grave.*

turn into something to become something. □ *The caterpillar turned into a butterfly.* □ *When the big lights came on, night turned into day.*

turn of the century the end of one century and the beginning of another. □ *It's just a few years until the turn of the century.* □ *People like to celebrate the turn of the century.*

turn on someone 1. to attack someone. □ *I thought the strange dog was friendly, but suddenly it turned on me*

and bit me. □ *Bob knows a lot about lions, and he says that no matter how well they are trained, there is always the danger that they'll turn on you.* 2. See *turn someone or something on.*

turn on the heat (on someone) AND **turn the heat on (someone)** to use force to persuade someone to do something; to increase the pressure on someone to do something. (Slang.) □ *The company are turning on the heat to increase production by threatening redundancies.* □ *The teacher really turned the heat on the pupils by saying that everyone would be punished if the real culprit was not found.*

turn on the waterworks to begin to cry. (Slang.) □ *Every time Billy got homesick, he turned on the waterworks.* □ *Sally hurt her knee and turned on the waterworks for about twenty minutes.*

turn one's back (on someone or something) to abandon or ignore someone or something. □ *Don't turn your back on your old friends.* □ *Bob has a tendency to turn his back on serious problems.* □ *This matter needs your attention. Please don't just turn your back.*

turn one's coat to change one's ideas or principles; to change sides and join the opposition. □ *Tom used to be a socialist, but he has turned his coat. Now he is a banker.* □ *We assumed that James would vote for us in the debate, but he turned his coat.*

turn one's nose up at someone or something AND **turn up one's nose at someone or something** to reject someone or something; to treat someone or something with contempt. □ *John turned his nose up at Ann, and that hurt her feelings.* □ *I never turn up my nose at dessert, no matter what it is.*

turn out (all right) AND **pan out; work out (all right)** to end satisfactorily. (Compare to *work out for the best.*) □ *I hope everything turns out all right.* □ *Oh, yes. It'll all pan out.* □ *Things usually work out, no matter how bad they seem.*

turn out to be someone or something to end up being someone or something; to be shown to be someone or something. □ *The most helpful person turned out to be Tom.* □ *The real cause of the frightening noise turned out to be the wind.*

turn over 1. AND **kick over** [for an engine] to start or to rotate. □ *My car engine was so cold that it wouldn't even turn over.* □ *The engine kicked over a few times and then stopped for good.* **2.** [for goods] to be stocked and sold (at a certain rate). □ *Don't order any more of those items. They turn over too slowly.* □ *Most of our items turn over very well, and this means that our business is good.*

turn over a new leaf to start again with the intention of doing better; to begin again, ignoring past errors. □ *Tom promised to turn over a new leaf and do better from now on.* □ *After a minor accident, Sally decided to turn over a new leaf and drive more carefully.*

turn (over) in one's grave [for a dead person] to be shocked or horrified. □ *If Beethoven heard Mary play one of his sonatas, he'd turn over in his grave.* □ *If Aunt Jane knew what you were doing with her favourite chair, she would turn in her grave.*

turn someone or something down AND **turn down someone or something 1.** [with *someone*] to refuse or deny someone. □ *I applied for employment with the town council, but they turned me down.* □ *They turned down Mary, who also applied.* **2.** [with *something*] to deny someone's request. □ *I offered her some help, but she turned it down.* □ *She had turned down John's offer of help, too.* **3.** [with *something*] to fold part of something downward. □ *The hotel maid turned down the bed while I was at dinner.* □ *In the mail-order catalogue, I always turn down a page which interests me.* **4.** [with *something*] to lower the volume or amount of something, such as heat, sound, water, air pressure, etc. □ *It's hot in here. Please*

turn down the heat. □ *Turn the stereo down. It's too loud.*

turn someone or something in AND **turn in someone or something 1.** [with *someone*] to give someone over to the authorities; to report someone's bad behaviour. (Informal.) □ *I knew who stole the money, so I turned him in.* □ *I know that Mr. Johnson cheated on his taxes, so I turned him in.* **2.** [with *something*] to give something back; to take something to the proper place. □ *I found a pair of gloves in the hallway, and I turned them in.* □ *I earned over five pounds when I turned in a lot of soft-drink bottles.*

turn someone or something into something to make someone or something become something. □ *My teachers tried to turn me into a scholar, but they failed.* □ *I can turn these vegetables into a delicious soup.*

turn someone or something off AND **turn off someone or something 1.** [with *someone*] to discourage or disgust someone. (Slang.) □ *His manner really turns me off.* □ *That man has a way of turning off everyone he comes in contact with.* **2.** [with *someone*] to destroy someone's sexual excitement. □ *Mary's stern manner really turned John off.* □ *That disgusting film did not excite me. It turned me off.* **3.** [with *something*] to switch off lights, a radio, a television, a stereo, etc. □ *Please turn that radio off and pay attention.* □ *John Johnson is talking on the television again. Please turn him off. I'm tired of hearing him.*

turn someone or something on AND **turn on someone or something 1.** [with *someone*] to excite someone. (Informal.) □ *The lecture was very good. It turned on the whole class.* □ *A new hobby might turn you on and help you enjoy life.* **2.** [with *someone*] to excite someone sexually. (Informal.) □ *Sally said she preferred not to watch films that attempted to turn people on.* □ *Are you trying to turn me on?* **2.** [with *something*] to switch on lights, a radio, television, stereo, etc. □ *Turn on the radio* *so we can listen to the news.* □ *Let's turn the telly on and watch a film.*

turn someone or something out AND **turn out someone or something** 1. [with *someone*] to send someone out of somewhere. □ *I didn't pay my rent, so the manager turned me out.* □ *I'm glad it's not winter. I'd hate to be turned out in the snow.* 2. [with *something*] to manufacture something; to produce something. □ *This machine can turn out thousands of items a day.* □ *John wasn't turning enough work out, so the manager had a talk with him.*

turn someone or something over (to someone) to hand over someone or something to someone. □ *The teacher turned over the pupils to the headmaster.* □ *Please turn over the extra money to me.*

turn someone or something up AND **turn up someone or something** 1. to search for and find someone or something. □ *Let me try to see if I can turn someone up who knows how to do the job.* □ *I turned up a number of interesting items when I went through Aunt Jane's attic.* 2. [with *something*] to increase the volume or amount of something, such as a light, heat, a radio, etc. □ *Don't turn your stereo up. It's too loud already.* □ *I'm going to turn up the heat. It's too cold in here.* ALSO: **turn up** to appear. □ *We'll send out invitations and see who turns up.*

turn someone's head to make someone conceited. □ *John's compliments really turned Sally's head.* □ *Victory in the competition is bound to turn Tom's head. He'll think he's too good for us.*

turn someone's stomach to make someone (figuratively or literally) ill. □ *This milk is sour. The smell of it turns my stomach.* □ *The play was so bad that it turned my stomach.*

turn something around to reverse the direction of something. □ *They turned the car around and headed in the other direction.* □ *The new manager took over and turned the business around. Suddenly we were making a profit.*

turn something to good account to use something in such a way that it is to one's advantage; to make good use of a situation, experience, etc. □ *Pam turned her illness to good account and did a lot of reading.* □ *Many people turn their retirement to good account and take up interesting hobbies.*

turn something to one's advantage to make an advantage for oneself out of something (which might otherwise be a disadvantage). □ *Sally found a way to turn the problem to her advantage.* □ *The ice-cream shop manager was able to turn the hot weather to her advantage.*

turn the other cheek to ignore abuse or an insult. □ *When Bob got angry with Mary and shouted at her, she just turned the other cheek.* □ *Usually I turn the other cheek when someone is rude to me.*

turn the tables (on someone) to cause a reversal in someone's plans; to reverse a situation and put someone in a different position, especially in a less advantageous position. □ *I went to Jane's house to help get ready for a surprise party for Bob. It turned out that the surprise party was for me! Jane really turned the tables on me!* □ *Turning the tables like that requires a lot of planning and a lot of secrecy.*

turn the tide to cause a reversal in the direction of events; to cause a reversal in public opinion. □ *It looked as though the team was going to lose, but near the end of the game, our star player turned the tide.* □ *At first, people were opposed to our plan. After a lot of discussion, we were able to turn the tide and get them to agree with us.*

turn to to begin to get busy. □ *Come on, folks! Turn to! Let's get to work.* □ *If you people will turn to, we can finish this work in no time at all.*

turn to someone or something (for something) 1. to seek something from someone or something. □ *I turned to Ann for help.* □ *Bill turned to aspirin for relief from his headache.* 2. [with *something*] to turn (pages) to find a particular thing. □ *I opened the book and turned to chapter seven.* □ *Please turn to the index. You can use it to find what you want.*

turn turtle to turn upside down. □ *The boat turned turtle, and everyone got soaked.* □ *The car ran off the road and turned turtle in the ditch.*

turn up See under *turn someone or something up.*

turn up one's toes to die. (Slang.) □ *When I turn up my toes, I want a big funeral with lots of flowers.* □ *Our cat turned up his toes during the night. He was nearly ten years old.*

turn up trumps to do the right or required thing, often unexpectedly or at the last minute. (Informal.) □ *I thought our team would let us down, but they turned up trumps in the second half of the match.* □ *We always thought the boss was mean, but he turned up trumps and made a large contribution to Mary's leaving present.*

twiddle one's thumbs to fill up time by playing with one's fingers. □ *What am I supposed to do while waiting for you? Sit here and twiddle my thumbs?* □ *Don't sit around twiddling your thumbs. Get busy!*

twist someone around one's little finger to manipulate and control someone. □ *Bob really fell for Jane. She can twist him around her little finger.* □ *Billy's mother has twisted him around her little finger. He's very dependent on her.*

twist someone's arm to force or persuade someone. □ *At first she refused, but after I twisted her arm a little, she agreed to help.* □ *I didn't want to stand for club president, but everyone twisted my arm.*

two a penny very common; easily obtained and therefore cheap. □ *People with qualifications like yours are two a penny. You should take another training course.* □ *Flats to rent here are no longer two a penny.*

two can play at that game See under *game at which two can play.*

two of a kind people or things of the same type or that are similar in character, attitude, etc. □ *Jack and Tom are two of a kind. They're both ambitious.* □ *The companies are two of a kind. They both pay their employees badly.*

two-time someone to cheat on or betray one's spouse or lover by dating or seeing someone else. (Slang.) □ *When Mrs. Franklin learned that Mr. Franklin was two-timing her, she left him.* □ *Ann told Bob that if he ever two-timed her, she would cause him a lot of trouble.*

two's company(, three's a crowd) a saying meaning that often two people would want to be alone and a third person would be in the way. □ *Two's company. I'm sure Tom and Jill won't want his sister to go to the cinema with them.* □ *John has been invited to join Jane and Peter on their picnic, but he says "Two's company, three's a crowd."*

U

under a cloud to be suspected of (doing) something. □ *Someone stole some money at work, and now everyone is under a cloud.* □ *Even the manager is under a cloud.*

under construction being built or repaired. □ *We cannot travel on this road because it's under construction.* □ *Our new home has been under construction all summer. We hope to move in next month.*

under fire being attacked; being criticized or blamed. □ *The government were under fire from the opposition party for their economic policy.* □ *Jack's new novel came under fire from the critics.*

under one's own steam by one's own power or effort. (Informal.) □ *I missed my lift to school, so I had to get there under my own steam.* □ *John will need some help with this project. He can't do it under his own steam.*

under someone's (very) nose AND **right under someone's nose 1.** right in front of someone. □ *I thought I'd lost my purse, but it was sitting on the table under my very nose.* □ *How did Mary fail to see the book? It was right under her nose.* **2.** in someone's presence. □ *The thief stole Jim's wallet right under his nose. He took it from the jacket he was wearing.* □ *The jewels were stolen from under the very noses of the security guards.*

under the circumstances in a particular situation; because of the circumstances. □ *I'm sorry to hear that you're ill. Under the circumstances, you may take the day off.* □ *We won't expect you to come to work for a few days, under the circumstances.*

under the counter [bought or sold] in secret or illegally. (Also used literally.) □ *The shopkeeper was selling illegal drugs under the counter.* □ *The newsagent was also selling dirty books under the counter.*

under the table drunk. (Informal.) □ *If you drink all that beer, you'll be under the table.* □ *By the end of the party, everyone was under the table.*

under the weather ill. □ *I'm a bit under the weather today, so I can't go to the office.* □ *My head is aching, and I feel a little under the weather.*

until all hours until very late. □ *Mary is out until all hours night after night.* □ *If I'm up until all hours two nights in a row, I'm just exhausted.*

up a blind alley at a dead end; on a route that leads nowhere. (Informal.) □ *I have been trying to find out something about my ancestors, but I'm up a blind alley. I can't find anything.* □ *The police are up a blind alley in their investigation of the crime.*

up a creek See *up the creek (without a paddle).*

up a gum-tree in a difficult situation and unable to get out. (Slang.) □ *I've lost my wallet. I'm really up a gum-tree.* □ *Bob's up a gum-tree. He has an appointment with his boss and he has forgotten the address.*

up against something having trouble with something. (The *something* is often *it*, meaning facing trouble in general.) ☐ *Jane is up against a serious problem.* ☐ *Yes, she really looks like she's up against it.*

up and about healthy and moving about—not sick in bed. ☐ *Mary is getting better. She should be up and about in a few days.* ☐ *She can't wait until she's up and about. She's tired of being in bed.*

up and at them to get up and go at people or things; to become active and get busy. (Informal. Usually *them* is *'em*.) ☐ *Come on, Bob—up and at 'em!* ☐ *There is a lot of work to be done around here. Up and at 'em, everybody!*

up-and-coming progressing well; likely to succeed. ☐ *We want to employ people who are up-and-coming.* ☐ *Bob is also an up-and-coming young man who is going to become well known.*

up and doing active and lively. ☐ *The children are always up and doing early in the morning.* ☐ *If Jean wants to be at work early, it's time she was up and doing.*

up for grabs available to anyone. (Slang.) ☐ *Mary resigned yesterday, and her job is up for grabs.* ☐ *Who's in charge around here? This whole organization is up for grabs.*

up-front (Slang.) **1.** sincere and open. ☐ *Ann is a very up-front kind of person. Everyone feels comfortable around her.* ☐ *It's hard to tell what Tom is really thinking. He's not very up-front.* **2.** in advance. ☐ *I ordered a new car, and they wanted 20 percent up-front.* ☐ *I couldn't afford to pay that much up-front. I'd have to make a smaller deposit.*

up in arms rising up in anger. ☐ *The citizens were up in arms, pounding on the gates of the palace, demanding justice.* ☐ *My father was really up in arms when he got his rates bill this year.*

up in the air undecided; uncertain. ☐ *I don't know what Sally plans to do. Things were sort of up in the air the last time we talked.* ☐ *Let's leave this question up in the air until next week.*

up in years AND **advanced in years; on in years** old; elderly. ☐ *My uncle is up in years and can't hear too well.* ☐ *Many people lose their hearing somewhat when they get on in years.*

up North to or at the northern part of the country or the world. (See also *down South*.) ☐ *I don't like living up North. I want to move down South where it's warm.* ☐ *They went up North from London a few years ago.*

up the creek (without a paddle) in a bad situation. (Slang.) ☐ *What a mess I'm in. I'm really up the creek without a paddle.* ☐ *I tried to prevent it, but I seem to be up the creek, too.*

up to date **1.** up to the current standards of fashion. ☐ *I'm having my living-room redecorated to bring it up to date.* ☐ *I don't care if my rooms are up to date. I just want them to be comfortable.* **2.** completed or dealt with up to the present time. ☐ *I like to keep my correspondence up to date.* ☐ *Your reports are not up to date.*

up to no good doing something bad or criminal. (Informal.) ☐ *I could tell from the look on Tom's face that he was up to no good.* ☐ *There are three boys in the front garden. I don't know what they are doing, but I think they are up to no good.*

up to one to be one's own choice. ☐ *She said I didn't have to go if I didn't want to. It's entirely up to me.* ☐ *It's up to Mary whether she takes the job or tries to find another one.*

up to one's ears (in something) See the following entry.

up to one's neck (in something) AND **up to one's ears (in something)** very much involved in something. (Informal. *Up to one's neck (in something)* usually refers to something bad.) ☐ *I can't come to the meeting. I'm up to my ears in these reports.* ☐ *Bob is up to his neck in the drug-smuggling business.*

up to par as good as the standard or average; up to standard. □ *I'm just not feeling up to par today. I must be coming down with something.* □ *The manager said that the report was not up to par and gave it back to Mary to do over again.*

up-to-the-minute the very latest or most recent. □ *I want to hear some up-to-the-minute news on the hostage situation.* □ *I just got an up-to-the-minute report on Tom's health.*

upper crust the higher levels of society; the upper class. (Informal. From the top, as opposed to the bottom, crust of a pie.) □ *Jane speaks like that because she pretends to be from the upper crust, but her father was a miner.* □ *James is from the upper crust, but he is penniless.* ALSO: **upper-crust** of the upper class; belonging to or typical of the upper class. (Informal.) □ *Pam has a grating upper-crust voice.* □ *People dislike Bob because of his snobbish, upper-crust attitude.*

ups and downs good fortune and bad fortune. □ *I've had my ups and downs, but in general life has been good to me.* □ *All people have their ups and downs.*

upset someone's plans to ruin someone's plans. □ *I hope it doesn't upset your plans if I'm late for the meeting.* □ *No, it won't upset my plans at all.*

upset the applecart to spoil or ruin something. □ *Tom really upset the applecart by telling Mary the truth about Jane.* □ *We were going abroad, but the* children upset the applecart by getting the mumps.

upshot of something the result or outcome of something. □ *The upshot of my criticism was a change in policy.* □ *The upshot of the argument was an agreement to employ a new secretary.*

upside down turned over with the top on the bottom. □ *The turtle was upside down and couldn't go anywhere.* □ *The book was upside down, and I couldn't see what the title was.*

use every trick in the book to use every method possible. (Informal.) □ *I used every trick in the book, but I still couldn't manage to get a ticket to the game Saturday.* □ *Bob tried to use every trick in the book to get Mary to go out with him, but he still failed.*

use one's head AND **use one's noodle** to use one's own intelligence. (The word *noodle* is a slang term for "head".) □ *You can find a way to get there if you'll just use your head.* □ *Jane uses her noodle and gets things done correctly and on time.*

use one's noodle See the previous entry.

use strong language to swear, threaten, or use abusive language. □ *I wish you wouldn't use strong language in front of the children.* □ *If you feel you have to use strong language with the manager, perhaps you had better let me do the talking.*

used to someone or something accustomed to someone or something. □ *I'm not used to Jane yet. She's a bit hard to get along with.* □ *How long does it take to get used to this weather?*

V

vanish into thin air   to disappear without leaving a trace. □ *My money gets spent so fast. It seems to vanish into thin air.* □ *When I came back, my car was gone. I had locked it, and it couldn't have vanished in thin air!*

Variety is the spice of life.   a proverb meaning that differences and changes make life interesting. □ *Mary reads all kinds of books. She says variety is the spice of life.* □ *The Franklins travel all over the world so they can learn how different people live. After all, variety is the spice of life.*

vent one's spleen on someone or something   to get rid of one's feelings of anger caused by someone or something by attacking someone or something else. □ *Jack vented his spleen at not getting the job by shouting at his wife.* □ *Peter kicked his car to vent his spleen for losing the race.*

verge on something   to be almost something. □ *Your blouse is a lovely colour. It seems to be blue verging on purple.* □ *Sally has a terrible case of the flu, and they are afraid it's verging on pneumonia.*

very thing   the exact thing that is required. □ *The vacuum cleaner is the very thing for cleaning the stairs.* □ *I have the very thing to remove that stain.*

vexed question   a difficult problem about which there is a lot of discussion without a solution being found. □ *The two brothers quarrelled over the vexed question of which of them should take charge of their father's firm.* □ *We've seen a house that we like, but there's the vexed question of where we'll get the money from.*

vicious circle   a situation in which the solution of one problem leads to a second problem, and the solution of the second problem brings back the first problem, etc. □ *One problem after another—it's a vicious circle.* □ *We are in a vicious circle trying to get ahead financially.*

villain of the piece   someone or something that is responsible for something bad or wrong. □ *I wondered who told the newspapers about the local scandal. I discovered that Joan was the villain of the piece.* □ *We couldn't think who had stolen the meat. The dog next door turned out to be the villain of the piece.*

vote of confidence   a poll taken to discover whether or not a person, party, etc., still has the majority's support. □ *The government easily won the vote of confidence called for by the opposition.* □ *The president of the club resigned when one of the members called for a vote of confidence in his leadership.*

vote of thanks   a speech expressing appreciation and thanks to a speaker, lecturer, organizer, etc., and inviting the audience to applaud. □ *John gave a vote of thanks to Professor Jones for his talk.* □ *Mary was given a vote of thanks for organizing the dance.*

vote someone in AND vote in someone   to elect someone. □ *The town voted in the same mayor year after year.* □ *I didn't really want to hold public office, but everyone voted me in, so I had to serve.*

vote someone out AND **vote out someone** to send someone out of elective office (by voting someone else into office). □ *Mr. Williams was a poor president, so they voted him out in the following club election.* □ *The constituency voted out the sitting MP.*

W

wade in(to something) to start in (doing) something immediately. (Informal.) □ *I need some preparation. I can't just wade into the job and start doing things correctly.* □ *We don't expect you to wade in. We'll tell you what to do.*

wait-and-see attitude a sceptical attitude; an uncertain attitude where someone will just wait and see what happens. □ *John thought that Mary couldn't do it, but he took a wait-and-see attitude.* □ *His wait-and-see attitude didn't impress me at all. I like to take action.*

wait on someone hand and foot to serve someone very well, often too well, attending to all personal needs. □ *I don't mind bringing you your tea, but I don't intend to wait on you hand and foot.* □ *I don't want anyone to wait on me hand and foot. I can look after myself.*

wait one's turn to keep from doing something until everyone ahead of you has done it. □ *You can't cross the intersection yet. You must wait your turn.* □ *I can't wait my turn. I'm in a tremendous hurry.*

wait up (for someone or something) to stay up late waiting for someone to arrive or something to happen. □ *I'll be home late. Don't wait up for me.* □ *We waited up for the coming of the New Year, and then we went to bed.*

waiting in the wings ready or prepared to do something, especially to take over someone else's job or position. (From waiting at the side of the stage to go on.) □ *Mr. Smith retires as manager next year, and Mr. Jones is just waiting in the wings.* □ *Jane was waiting in the wings, hoping that a member of the hockey team would drop out and she would get a place on the team.*

walk a tightrope to be in a situation where one must be very cautious. □ *I've been walking a tightrope all day trying to please both bosses. I need to relax.* □ *Our business is about to fail. We've been walking a tightrope for three months, trying to control our cash flow.*

walk all over someone to treat someone badly; to show no regard for other people's rights or feeling. (Informal.) □ *People are inclined to walk all over meek people.* □ *The manager had walked all over Ann for months. Finally she left.*

walk away with something to win something easily. (Informal.) □ *John won the tennis match with no difficulty. He walked away with it.* □ *Our team walked away with first place.*

walk it to win or succeed easily. (Slang.) □ *Don't worry about James losing the match. He'll walk it.* □ *Jean was worried about failing the exam but she walked it.*

walk off with something to take or steal something. (Informal.) □ *I think somebody just walked off with my purse!* □ *Somebody walked off with my daughter's bicycle.*

walk on air to be very happy; to be euphoric. □ *Ann was walking on air when she got the job.* □ *On the last day of school, all the children are walking on air.*

walk on eggs to be very cautious. (Informal. Never used literally.) □ *The manager is very hard to deal with. You really have to walk on eggs.* □ *I've been walking on eggs ever since I started working here. There's a very large staff turnover.*

walk out to leave a performance before it is over, usually because one does not like it. □ *We didn't like the play at all, so we walked out.* □ *John was giving a very dull speech, and a few people even walked out.*

walk out (on someone) to abandon someone; to leave one's spouse. □ *Mr. Franklin walked out on Mrs. Franklin last week.* □ *Mary didn't tell her husband she was leaving. She just walked out.*

walk the floor to pace nervously while waiting. □ *While Bill waited for news of the operation, he walked the floor for hours on end.* □ *Walking the floor won't help. You might as well sit down and relax.*

walls have ears we may be overheard. □ *Let's not discuss this matter here. Walls have ears, you know.* □ *Shhh. Walls have ears. Someone may be listening.*

want for nothing to lack nothing; to have everything one needs or wishes. □ *The Smiths don't have much money, but their children seem to want for nothing.* □ *Jean's husband spoils her. She wants for nothing.*

want out (of something) to want to remove oneself from a place or a situation. □ *The children want out of the house so they can play. Please let them go out.* □ *I took this position because I liked the work. Now I want out.*

warm the cockles of someone's heart to make someone feel pleased and happy. □ *It warms the cockles of my heart to hear you say that.* □ *Hearing that old song again warmed the cockles of her heart.*

warm up to become lively. □ *The party was boring at first, but it soon warmed up.* □ *The tennis game was slow to start with, but soon warmed up.*

warts and all including all the faults and disadvantages. □ *Jim has many faults, but Jean loves him, warts and all.* □ *The place where we went on holiday had some very run-down parts, but we liked it, warts and all.*

wash one's dirty linen in public See *air one's dirty linen in public.*

wash one's hands of someone or something to have nothing more to do with someone or something; to end one's association with someone or something. □ *I washed my hands of Tom. I wanted no more to do with him.* □ *That car was a real headache. I washed my hands of it long ago.*

wash someone or something up AND **wash up someone or something 1.** [for waves, wind, etc.] to carry someone or something to the shore. □ *A man drowned, and the waves washed him up.* □ *The storm washed up a lot of seaweed.* **2.** [with *someone*] to put an end to someone's career. (Informal.) □ *That poor performance washed up Tom's career.* □ *The last play washed up the team.* ALSO: **washed up** finished. (Informal.) □ *"You're finished, Tom," said the manager, "sacked—washed up!"* □ *My career is washed up. I shall have to stay at home and look after the children.*

wash something down AND **wash down something 1.** to rinse or wash something. □ *The car was dusty, so I washed it down.* □ *I used the hose to wash the driveway down.* **2.** to drink a liquid to aid in the swallowing of something. □ *I took a drink of milk to wash down my food.* □ *John washed the pizza down with a beer.*

washed out exhausted; lacking energy. (Informal.) □ *Pam was completely washed out after the birth of the baby.* □ *I feel washed out. I need a holiday.*

washed up See under *wash someone or something up.*

waste away to decline gradually; to become weak and feeble. □ *Our cat was very old, and she just wasted away over the last few years.* □ *The old lady wasted away when she got cancer.*

Waste not, want not. a saying meaning that if one never wastes anything, one will never be short of anything. □ *Bob always saves the used string from parcels. Waste not, want not, he says.* □ *Mary always reuses envelopes. We think she's mean, but she says that it's a case of waste not, want not.*

waste one's breath to waste one's time talking; to talk in vain. (Informal.) □ *Don't waste your breath talking to her. She won't listen.* □ *You can't persuade me. You're just wasting your breath.*

watch one's step to act with care and caution so as not to make a mistake or offend someone. □ *John had better watch his step with the new boss. He won't put up with his lateness.* □ *Mary was told by the lecturer to watch her step and stop missing classes or she would be asked to leave college.*

watch out for someone or something AND **look out for someone or something** 1. to be on guard for someone or something; to be on the watch for someone or something. □ *Watch out for someone wearing a white carnation.* □ *Look out for John and his friends. They'll be coming this way very soon.* 2. AND **look out; watch out** to try to avoid a confrontation with someone or something. □ *Watch out for that car! It nearly hit you!* □ *Look out for John. He's looking for you, and he's really angry.* □ *Thanks loads. I'd better look out.*

watch someone like a hawk to watch someone very carefully. □ *The teacher watched the pupils like a hawk to make sure they did not cheat on the exam.* □ *We have to watch our dog like a hawk in case he runs away.*

water something down AND **water down something** to dilute something; to thin something out and make it less strong. (Used figuratively and literally.) □ *The*

punch was good until someone watered it down. □ *Professor Jones sometimes waters down his lectures so people can understand them better.*

water under the bridge [something] past and forgotten. □ *Please don't worry about it any more. It's all water under the bridge.* □ *I can't change the past. It's water under the bridge.*

ways and means methods, often secret or underhanded, of doing something or of obtaining something. □ *You may find it difficult to get a visa, but there are ways and means of obtaining one.* □ *The secret police had ways and means of getting information out of people.*

We live and learn. We increase our knowledge by experience. (Informal. Usually said when one is surprised to learn something.) □ *I didn't know that snakes could swim. Well, we live and learn!* □ *John didn't know he should water his house-plants a little extra in the dry winter months. When they all died, he said, "We live and learn."*

wear and tear (on something) the process of wearing down or breaking down something; damage or the loss of quality or value caused by everyday use. □ *The car's in poor condition from the wear and tear of ten years.* □ *We need a new sofa. This one's had too much wear and tear.*

wear more than one hat to have more than one set of responsibilities; to hold more than one office. □ *The mayor is also the police chief. She wears more than one hat.* □ *I have too much to do to wear more than one hat.*

wear off to become less; to stop gradually. □ *The effects of the pain-killer wore off, and my tooth began to hurt.* □ *I was annoyed at first, but my anger wore off.*

wear one's heart on one's sleeve AND **have one's heart on one's sleeve** habitually to display one's feelings openly, rather than keep them private. □ *Jack wears his heart on his sleeve when he looks at*

Jane. □ *Because Mary has her heart on her sleeve, it's easy to hurt her feelings.*

wear out one's welcome to stay too long (at an event to which one has been invited); to visit somewhere too often. □ *Tom visited the Smiths so often that he wore out his welcome.* □ *At about midnight, I decided that I had worn out my welcome, so I went home.*

wear someone down AND **wear down someone** to overcome someone's objections; to persist until someone has been persuaded. □ *John didn't want to go, but we finally wore him down.* □ *We were unable to wear down John, and when we left, he was still insisting on running away from home.*

wear someone or something out AND **wear out someone or something 1.** [with *someone*] to exhaust someone; to make someone tired. □ *The coach made the team work until he wore them out.* □ *If he wears out everybody on the team, nobody will be left to play in the game.* **2.** [with *something*] to make something useless or unserviceable through wear or over-use. □ *Tom wore his car's tyres out by driving on bumpy roads.* □ *I wore out my favourite record by playing it too much.*

weasel out (of something) to get out or slide out of something. (Informal.) □ *I don't want to go to the meeting. I think I'll try to weasel out of it.* □ *You had better be there! Don't try to weasel out!*

weave in and out (of something) to move, drive, or walk in and out of something, such as traffic or a queue. □ *The car was dangerously weaving in and out of traffic.* □ *The deer ran rapidly through the forest, weaving in and out of the trees.*

weed someone or something out AND **weed out someone or something** to remove someone or something unwanted or undesirable from a group or collection. □ *The auditions were held to weed out the actors with least ability.* □ *I'm going through my books to weed out those that I don't read any more.*

week in, week out every week, week after week. (Informal.) □ *We have the same old food, week in, week out.* □ *I'm tired of this job. I've done the same thing—week in, week out—for three years.*

weep buckets to weep a great many tears. (Informal.) □ *The girls wept buckets at the sad film.* □ *Mary wept buckets when her dog died.*

weigh on someone's mind [for a worrying matter] to be constantly in a person's thoughts; [for something] to be bothering someone's thinking. □ *This problem has been weighing on my mind for many days now.* □ *I hate to have things weighing on my mind. I can't sleep when I'm worried.*

weigh one's words to consider one's own words carefully when speaking. □ *I always weigh my words when I speak in public.* □ *John was weighing his words carefully because he didn't want to be misunderstood.*

weigh someone down AND **weigh down someone** [for a thought] to worry or depress someone. (Also used literally.) □ *All these problems really weigh me down.* □ *Financial problems have been weighing down our entire family.*

weigh someone or something up to make an assessment of someone or something; to consider and calculate something. □ *Fred tried to weigh up his chances of winning.* □ *The selection committee spent some time weighing up the various applicants for the job.*

welcome someone with open arms See *receive someone with open arms.*

welcome to do something to be free to do something. □ *You're welcome to leave whenever you wish.* □ *He's welcome to join the club whenever he feels he's ready.*

Well and good. That is fine. □ *If you want to go, well and good. We'll soon replace you.* □ *You're going home? Well and good. I'll see you tomorrow.*

well-heeled AND **well off** wealthy; with sufficient money. □ *My uncle can afford a new car. He's well-heeled.* □ *Everyone in his family is well off.*

well off See the previous entry.

well-to-do wealthy and of good social position. (Often with *quite,* as in the examples.) □ *The Jones family is quite well-to-do.* □ *There is a gentleman waiting for you at the door. He appears quite well-to-do.*

well up in something having a great deal of knowledge about something. □ *Jane's husband is well up in computers.* □ *Joan's well up in car maintenance. She took lessons at night-school.*

wet behind the ears young and inexperienced. □ *John's too young to take on responsibility like this! He's still wet behind the ears!* □ *He may be wet behind the ears, but he's well trained and totally competent.*

wet blanket a dull or depressing person who spoils other people's enjoyment. (Informal.) □ *Jack's fun at parties, but his brother's a wet blanket.* □ *Anne was bringing a real wet blanket to the party.*

wet someone's whistle to take a drink of something. (Informal.) □ *Wow, am I thirsty! I need something to wet my whistle.* □ *Give her something to wet her whistle.*

What about (doing) something? Would you like to do something? □ *What about going on a picnic?* □ *What about a picnic?*

What about (having) something? Would you like to have something? □ *What about having another drink?* □ *What about another drink?*

What are you driving at? What are you implying?; What do you mean? (Informal.) □ *What are you driving at? What are you trying to say?* □ *Why are you asking me all these questions? What are you driving at?*

What difference does it make? Does it really matter?; Does it cause any trouble? □ *What if I choose to leave home? What difference does it make?* □ *So Jane dropped out of the club. What difference does it make?*

What is sauce for the goose is sauce for the gander. a proverb meaning that what is appropriate for one is appropriate for the other. □ *If John gets a new coat, I should get one, too. After all, what is sauce for the goose is sauce for the gander.* □ *If I get punished for breaking the window, so should Mary. What is sauce for the goose is sauce for the gander.*

what makes someone tick what motivates someone; what makes someone behave in a certain way. (Informal.) □ *William is strange. I don't know what makes him tick.* □ *When you get to know people, you find out what makes them tick.*

What of it? Why does it matter?; So what? (Informal.) □ *So I'm a few minutes late. What of it?* □ BILL: *Your hands are dirty.* BOB: *What of it?*

What price something? What is the value of something?; What good is something?; What part does something play? (Informal.) □ *Jane's best friend told us all about Jane's personal problems. What price friendship?* □ *Jack simply declared himself president of the political society. What price democracy?* □ *The government are behind in the opinion polls. What price an early election?*

what with because. □ *What with the children being at home and my parents coming to stay, I have too much to do.* □ *The Smiths find it difficult to manage financially, what with Mr. Smith losing his job and Mrs. Smith being too ill to work.*

What's cooking? AND **What's up?** What is happening? (Slang.) □ *What's going on around here? What's cooking?* □ *Are there any plans for this evening? What's up?*

What's done is done. It is final and in the past. □ *It's too late to change it now.*

What's done is done. □ *What's done is done. The past cannot be altered.*

What's eating you? What is bothering you? (Slang.) □ *What's wrong, Bob? What's eating you?* □ *You seem upset, Mary. What's eating you?*

What's going on? What is happening? □ *Things seem very busy here. What's going on?* □ *What's going on? Is someone causing trouble?*

What's got into someone? What has caused someone to behave in some way? □ *Why are you doing that? What's got into you?* □ *What's got into Bob? He's acting so strangely.*

What's the (big) idea? Why did you do that? (Informal. Usually said in anger.) □ *Please don't do that! What's the idea?* □ *Why did you shove me? What's the big idea?*

What's the good of something? What is the point of something?; Why bother with something? □ *What's the good of my going at all if I'll be late?* □ *There is no need to get there early. What's the good of that?*

What's up? See *What's cooking?*

wheeling and dealing taking part in clever but sometimes dishonest or immoral business deals. □ *John loves wheeling and dealing in the money markets.* □ *Jack's got tired of all the wheeling and dealing of big business and retired to run a pub in the country.*

wheels within wheels circumstances, often secret or personal, which all have an effect on each other and lead to a complicated, confusing situation. □ *This is not a staightforward matter of choosing the best person for the job. There are wheels within wheels and one of the applicants is the boss's son-in-law.* □ *I don't know why Jane was accepted by the college and Mary wasn't. There must have been wheels within wheels, because Mary has better qualifications.*

when all is said and done when everything is finished and settled; when everything is considered. □ *When all is said and done, this isn't such a bad part of the country to live in after all.* □ *When all is said and done, I believe I had a very enjoyable time on my holiday.*

When in Rome do as the Romans do. a proverb meaning that one should behave in the same way that the local people behave. □ *I don't usually eat lamb, but I did when I went to Australia. When in Rome do as the Romans do.* □ *I always carry an umbrella when I visit London. When in Rome do as the Romans do.*

when it comes right down to it all things considered; when one really thinks about something. □ *When it comes right down to it, I'd like to find a new job.* □ *When it comes right down to it, he can't really afford a new car.*

when it comes to something as for something; speaking about something. □ *When it comes to fishing, John is an expert.* □ *When it comes to trouble, Mary really knows how to cause it.*

when least expected when one does not expect (something). □ *An old car is likely to give you trouble when least expected.* □ *My pencil usually breaks when least expected.*

when one is good and ready when one is completely ready. □ *I'll be there when I'm good and ready.* □ *Ann will finish the job when she's good and ready and not a minute sooner.*

When the cat's away the mice will play. Some people will get into mischief when they are not being watched. □ *The pupils behaved very badly for the substitute teacher. When the cat's away the mice will play.* □ *John had a wild party at his house when his parents were out of town. When the cat's away the mice will play.*

when the time is ripe at exactly the right time. □ *I'll tell her the good news when the time is ripe.* □ *When the time is ripe, I'll bring up the subject again.*

Where there's a will there's a way. a proverb meaning that one can do something if one really wants to. □ *Don't give up, Ann. You can do it. Where there's a will there's a way.* □ *They told John he'd never walk again after his accident. He worked at it, and he was able to walk again! Where there's a will there's a way.*

Where there's smoke there's fire. AND **There's no smoke without fire.** a proverb meaning that some evidence of a problem probably indicates that there really is a problem. □ *There's a rumour around that Bob's leaving, and where there's smoke, there's fire.* □ *People are saying that Jean's having an affair, and there's no smoke without fire.*

whet someone's appetite to cause someone to be interested in something and to be eager to have, know, learn, etc., more about it. □ *Seeing that film really whetted my sister's appetite for horror films. She now sees as many as possible.* □ *My appetite for theatre was whetted when I was very young.*

while away the time AND **while the time away** to spend or waste time. □ *I like to read to while away the time.* □ *Jane whiles the time away by day-dreaming.*

whip something into shape See *lick something into shape.*

whip something up AND **whip up something** to prepare, create, or put something together quickly. (Informal.) □ *I haven't written my report yet, but I'll whip one up before the deadline.* □ *Come in and sit down. I'll go and whip up something to eat.*

whistle for something to expect or look for something with no hope of getting it. (Informal.) □ *I'm afraid you'll have to whistle for it if you want to borrow money. I don't have any.* □ *Jane's father told her to whistle for it when she asked him to buy her a car.*

white elephant something which is useless and which is either a nuisance or expensive to keep up. (From the gift of a white elephant by the Kings of Siam to courtiers who displeased them, knowing the cost of the upkeep would ruin them.)

□ *Bob's father-in-law has given him an old Rolls-Royce, but it's a real white elephant. He has no place to park it and can't afford the petrol for it.* □ *Those antique vases Aunt Mary gave me are white elephants. They're ugly and take ages to clean.*

whole (bang) shoot the whole lot. (Informal.) □ *They didn't even sort through the books. They just threw out the whole shoot.* □ *All these tables are damaged. Take the whole bang shoot away and replace them.*

whole shooting-match the entire affair or organization. (Informal.) □ *John's not a good manager. Instead of delegating jobs to others, he runs the whole shooting-match himself.* □ *There's not a hard worker in that whole shooting-match.*

whoop it up to enjoy oneself in a lively and noisy manner. (Informal.) □ *John's friends really whooped it up at his stag night.* □ *Jean wants to have a party and whoop it up to celebrate her promotion.*

whys and wherefores of something the reason or causes relating to something. □ *I refuse to discuss the whys and wherefores of my decision. It's final.* □ *Bob doesn't know the whys and wherefores of his contract. He just knows that it means he will get a lot of money when he finishes the work.*

wide awake completely awake; completely alert. □ *After the telephone rang, I was wide awake for an hour.* □ *Pilots have to be wide awake all the time at their job.*

wide of the mark 1. far from the target. □ *Tom's shot was wide of the mark.* □ *The ball was quite fast, but wide of the mark.* 2. inadequate; far from what is required or expected. □ *Jane's efforts were sincere, but wide of the mark.* □ *He failed the course because everything he did was wide of the mark.*

wild about someone or something enthusiastic about someone or something. (Informal.) □ *Bill is wild about* chocolate ice-cream. □ *Sally is wild about Tom and his new car.*

wild-goose chase a worthless hunt or chase; a futile pursuit. □ *I wasted all afternoon on a wild-goose chase.* □ *John was angry because he was sent out on a wild-goose chase.*

Wild horses couldn't drag someone. nothing could force someone (to go somewhere). (Informal.) □ *I refuse to go to that meeting! Wild horses couldn't drag me there.* □ *Wild horses couldn't drag her to that match.*

will not hear of something to refuse to tolerate or permit something. □ *You mustn't drive home alone. I won't hear of it.* □ *My parents won't hear of my staying out that late.*

win by a nose AND **win by a whisker** to win by the slightest amount of difference. (Informal. As in a horse-race where one horse wins with only its nose ahead of the horse which comes in second.) □ *I ran the fastest race I could, but I only won by a nose.* □ *Sally won the race, but she only won by a whisker.*

win by a whisker See the previous entry.

win someone over to succeed in gaining the support and sympathy of someone. □ *Jane's parents disapproved of her engagement at first, but she won them over.* □ *I'm trying to win the boss over and get him to give us the day off.*

win something hands down to do something easily and without opposition. □ *The mayor won the election hands down.* □ *She won the race hands down.*

win the day AND **carry the day** to be successful; to win a competition, argument, etc. (Originally meaning to win a battle.) □ *Our team didn't play well at first, but we won the day in the end.* □ *Hard work won the day and James passed his exams.*

win through to succeed. □ *After many setbacks, we won through in the end.* □ *The rescuers had difficulty reaching the injured climber, but they won through.*

wind down to decrease or diminish. □ *Things are very busy now, but they'll wind down in about an hour.* □ *I hope business winds down soon. I'm exhausted.*

wind something up AND **wind up something 1.** to conclude something. □ *I have a few items of business to wind up; then I'll be with you.* □ *Today we'll wind up that deal with the bank.* **2.** to bring a business to an end. □ *They've wound up the printing company. It was losing money.* □ *The sons wound up the business when the old man died.*

wind up (by) doing something See *end up (by) doing something.*

wind up somewhere See *end up somewhere.*

window-shopping the habit or practice of looking at goods in shop-windows without actually buying anything. □ *The girls do a lot of window-shopping in their lunch-hour, looking for things to buy when they get paid.* □ *Joan said she was just window-shopping, but she bought a new coat.*

wipe someone or something out AND **wipe out someone or something** to exterminate someone or something. (Slang.) □ *The hunters came and wiped out all the deer.* □ *The crooks wiped out the two witnesses.*

wipe the floor with someone to beat or defeat someone completely; to do much better than someone else. (Informal.) □ *Bob played tennis against Mary, and she wiped the floor with him.* □ *Our quiz team wiped the floor with their team.*

wipe the slate clean to erase or forget someone's (bad) record. □ *I'd like to wipe the slate clean at my job and start all over again.* □ *Bob did badly in high school, but he wiped the slate clean and did a good job in college.*

wise after the event knowledgeable of how a situation should have been dealt with only after it has passed. □ *I know now I should have agreed to help him, but that's being wise after the event. At the time I thought he was just being lazy.*

□ *Jack now realizes that he shouldn't have married Mary when they had nothing in common, but he didn't see it at the time. He's just being wise after the event.*

wise up (to someone or something) to begin to understand the truth about someone or something. (Slang.) □ *It was almost a week before I began to wise up to John. He's a total phony.* □ *You had better stay hidden for a while. The police are beginning to wise up.*

wish someone joy of something to express the hope that someone will enjoy having or doing something, usually while being glad that one does not have to have it or do it. □ *I wish you joy of that old car. I had one just like it and spent a fortune on repairs for it.* □ *Mary wished us joy of going to Nepal on holiday, but she preferred somewhere more comfortable.*

wish something off on someone AND **wish off something on someone** to pass something off onto someone else. (Informal.) □ *I don't want to have to deal with your problems. Don't wish them off on me.* □ *The shopkeeper wished off the defective watch on the very next customer who came in.*

wishful thinking believing that something is true or that something will happen just because one wishes that it were true or would happen. □ *Hoping for a car as a birthday present is just wishful thinking. Your parents can't afford it.* □ *Mary thinks that she is going to get a big rise, but that's wishful thinking. Her boss is so mean.*

with a heavy heart sadly. □ *With a heavy heart, she said goodbye.* □ *We left school on the last day with a heavy heart.*

with a vengeance with vigour; energetically, as if one were angry. □ *Bob is building that fence with a vengeance.* □ *Mary is really weeding her garden with a vengeance.*

with a view to doing something AND **with an eye to doing something** with the intention of doing something. □ *I came* to this school with a view to getting a degree. □ *The mayor took office with an eye to improving the town.*

with a will with determination and enthusiasm. □ *The children worked with a will to finish the project on time.* □ *The workers set about manufacturing the new products with a will.*

with all one's heart and soul very sincerely. □ *Oh Bill, I love you with all my heart and soul, and I always will!* □ *She thanked us with all her heart and soul for the gift.*

with an eye to doing something See *with a view to doing something.*

with both hands tied behind one's back See *with one hand tied behind one's back.*

with every other breath [saying something] repeatedly or continually. □ *Bob was out in the garden raking leaves and cursing with every other breath.* □ *The child was so grateful that she was thanking me with every other breath.*

with flying colours easily and excellently. □ *John passed his geometry test with flying colours.* □ *Sally qualified for the race with flying colours.*

with it 1. up to date; fashionable. (Slang.) □ *Bob thinks he's with it, but he's wearing sixties clothes.* □ *Mary's mother embarrasses her by trying to be with it. She wears clothes that are too young for her.* **2.** able to think clearly; able to understand things. (Informal.) □ *Jean's mother is not really with it any more. She's going senile.* □ *Peter's not with it yet. He's only just come round from the anaesthetic.* **3.** in addition. □ *Mr. Jones is very wealthy—and mean with it.* □ *Joan is pretty—and clever with it.*

with no strings attached AND **without any strings attached** unconditionally; with no obligations attached. □ *Mary said she would go out with Bob only if there were no strings attached.* □ *I want to accept this free holiday only if there are no strings attached.*

with one hand tied behind one's back AND **with both hands tied behind one's back** under whatever handicap; easily. □ *I could put an end to this argument with one hand tied behind my back.* □ *John could do this job with both hands tied behind his back.*

with respect to someone or something See *in reference to someone or something.*

with someone or something in tow See under *have someone or something in tow.*

with the best will in the world however much one wishes to do something or however hard one tries to do something. □ *With the best will in the world, Jack won't be able to help Mary get the job.* □ *With the best will in the world, they won't finish the job in time.*

wither on the vine [for something] to decline or fade away at an early stage of development. (Also used literally in reference to grapes or other fruit.) □ *You have a great plan, Tom. Let's keep it alive. Don't let it wither on the vine.* □ *The whole project withered on the vine when the contract was cancelled.*

within an inch of doing something very close to doing something. □ *I came within an inch of losing my job.* □ *Bob came within an inch of hitting Mike across the face.*

within an inch of one's life very close to death. □ *When Mary was seriously ill in the hospital, she came within an inch of her life.* □ *The thug beat up the old man to within an inch of his life.*

within hailing distance close enough to hear someone call out. □ *When the boat came within hailing distance, I asked if I could borrow some petrol.* □ *We weren't within calling distance, so I couldn't hear what you said to me.*

within limits up to a certain point; with certain restrictions. □ *You're free to do what you want—within limits, of course.* □ *We were allowed to do what we wanted—within limits.*

within reason up to a certain point. □ *You can do anything you want within reason.* □ *I'll pay any sum you ask— within reason.*

within someone's reach AND **within someone's grasp** almost in the possession of someone. □ *My goals are almost within my reach, so I know I'll succeed.* □ *We almost had the contract within our grasp, but the deal fell through at the last minute.*

without any strings attached See *with no strings attached.*

without batting an eye without showing surprise or emotion; without blinking an eye. □ *I knew I had insulted her, and she turned to me and asked me to leave without batting an eye.* □ *The child can tell lies without batting an eye.*

without fail for certain; definitely. □ *I'll do what you ask without fail.* □ *The plane leaves on time every day without fail.*

without further ado without further talk. (An overworked phrase usually heard in public announcements.) □ *And without further ado, I would like to introduce Mr. Bill Franklin!* □ *The time has come to leave, so without further ado, good evening and goodbye.*

without question absolutely; certainly. □ *She will be there without question.* □ *Without question, the suspect is guilty.*

without rhyme or reason without purpose, order, or reason. (See variations in the examples.) □ *The teacher said my report was disorganized. My paragraphs seemed to be without rhyme or reason.* □ *Everything you do seems to be without rhyme or reason.* □ *This procedure seems to have no rhyme or reason.*

without so much as doing something without even doing something. □ *Jane borrowed Bob's car without so much as asking his permission.* □ *Mary's husband walked out without so much as saying goodbye.*

woe betide someone someone will regret something very much. □ *Woe betide John if he's late. Mary will be angry.* □ *Woe betide the students if they don't work harder. They will be asked to leave college.*

Woe is me. I am unfortunate.; I am unhappy. (Usually humorous.) □ *Woe is me! I have to work when the rest of the family are on holiday.* □ *Woe is me. I have the flu and my friends have gone to a party.*

wolf in sheep's clothing someone dangerous or ruthless who appears kind and gentle. □ *Beware of the police chief. He seems polite, but he's a wolf in sheep's clothing.* □ *Bob's a real wolf in sheep's clothing. He is charming to Mary only because he wants to borrow money from her.*

woman to woman See *man to man.*

won't hold water to be inadequate, insubstantial, or ill-conceived. (Informal.) □ *Sorry, your ideas won't hold water. Nice try, though.* □ *The solicitor's case wouldn't hold water, so the defendant was released.*

wool-gathering day-dreaming. (From the practice of wandering along collecting tufts of sheep's wool from hedges.) □ *John never listens to the teacher. He's always wool-gathering.* □ *I wish my new secretary would get on with the work and stop wool-gathering.*

word for word in the exact words; verbatim. □ *I memorized the speech, word for word.* □ *I can't recall word for word what she told us.*

words to that effect [other] words which have about the same meaning. □ *She told me I ought to read more carefully— or words to that effect.* □ *I was instructed to go to the devil, or words to that effect.*

work like a horse to work very hard. □ *I've been working like a horse all day, and I'm tired.* □ *I'm too old to work like a horse. I'd prefer to relax more.*

work on someone to try to convince someone about something. (Informal.) □ *We worked on Tom for nearly an hour, but we couldn't get him to change his mind.* □ *I'll work on him for a while, and I'll change his mind.*

work one's fingers to the bone to work very hard. □ *I worked my fingers to the bone so you children could have everything you needed. Now look at the way you treat me!* □ *I spent the day working my fingers to the bone, and now I want to relax.*

work one's way into something to squeeze into something (literally or figuratively). □ *The skunk worked its way into the hollow log.* □ *Ann worked her way into the club, and now she's a member in good standing.*

work one's way up to advance in one's job or position, from the beginning level to a higher level. □ *I haven't always been managing director of this bank. I started as a clerk and worked my way up.* □ *She's started as a secretary, but she hopes to work her way up.*

work out to exercise. □ *I have to work out every day in order to keep healthy.* □ *Working out a lot gives me a big appetite.*

work out (all right) See *turn out (all right).*

work out for the best to end up in the best possible way. □ *Don't worry. Things will work out for the best.* □ *It seems bad now, but it'll work out for the best.*

work someone over AND **work over someone** to threaten, intimidate, or beat someone. (Slang, especially criminal slang.) □ *I thought they were really going to work me over, but they only asked a few questions.* □ *The police worked over Bill until he told where the money was hidden.*

work something into something to rub or knead something into something else. □ *You should work more butter into the dough before baking the bread.* □ *Work this lotion into your skin to make your sunburn stop hurting.*

work something off to get rid of something by taking physical exercise. □ *Bob put on weight on holiday and is trying to work it off by swimming regularly.* □ *Jane tried to work off her depression by having a game of tennis.*

work something out AND **work out something** to settle a problem. □ *It was a serious problem, but we managed to work it out.* □ *I'm glad we can work out our problems without fighting.*

worm one's way out of something to squeeze or wiggle out of a problem or a responsibility. (Informal.) □ *This is your job, and you can't worm your way out of it!* □ *I'm not trying to worm my way out of anything!*

worm something out of someone to get some kind of information out of someone. (Informal.) □ *He didn't want to tell me the truth, but I finally wormed it out of him.* □ *She succeeded in worming the secret out of me. I didn't mean to tell it.*

worn to a shadow exhausted and thin, often from overwork. □ *Working all day and looking after the children in the evening has left Pam worn to a shadow.* □ *Ruth's worn to a shadow worrying about her son who's very ill.*

Worse luck! Unfortunately!; The worst thing has happened! □ *I have an exam tomorrow, worse luck!* □ *We ran out of money on holiday, worse luck!*

worth its weight in gold very valuable. □ *This book is worth its weight in gold.* □ *Oh, Bill. You're wonderful. You're worth your weight in gold.*

worth one's salt worth one's salary; of any worth at all. □ *Tom doesn't work very hard, and he's just barely worth his salt, but he's very easy to get along with.* □ *Anyone worth his salt would refuse to work here.*

worth someone's while worth one's time and trouble. □ *The job pays so badly it's not worth your while even going for an interview.* □ *It's not worth Mary's while going all that way just for a one-hour meeting.*

worthy of the name that deserves or is good enough to be so called. □ *There was not an actor worthy of the name in that play.* □ *Any art critic worthy of the name would know that painting is a fake.*

would as soon do something See *had as soon do something.*

wouldn't dream of doing something would not even consider doing something. □ *I wouldn't dream of taking your money!* □ *I'm sure that John wouldn't dream of complaining to the manager.*

wrap something up AND **wrap up something** to terminate something; to bring something to an end. (Informal. See also *get something sewn up.*) □ *It's time to wrap this project up and move on to something else.* □ *Let's wrap up this discussion. It's time to go home.*

wrapped up in someone or something totally concerned and involved with someone or something. □ *Sally is wrapped up in her work.* □ *Ann is all wrapped up in her children and their activities.*

wreak havoc with something to cause a lot of trouble with something; to ruin or damage something. □ *Your attitude will wreak havoc with my project.* □ *The weather wreaked havoc with our picnic plans.*

write in for something to request something by mail, often in response to a radio or television advertisement. (Similar to *send away for something.*) □ *I wrote in for a record album which I saw advertised on television.* □ *I wrote in for a request on the radio.*

write off for something See *send off for something.*

write someone or something off AND **write off someone or something 1.** [with *something*] to absorb a debt or a loss in accounting. □ *The bill couldn't be collected, so we had to write it off.* □ *The bill was too large, and we couldn't write off the amount. We decided to sue.* **2.** to drop someone or something from consideration. □ *The manager wrote Tom off for a promotion.* □ *I wrote off that piece of land as worthless. It can't be used for anything.*

write something down AND **write down something** to write something; to make a note of something. (Also without *down*.) □ *If I write it down, I won't forget it.* □ *I wrote down everything she said.*

write something out AND **write out something** to spell or write a number or an abbreviation. □ *Don't just write 7, write it out.* □ *Please write out all abbreviations, such as* Doctor *for Dr.*

wrongfoot someone to take someone by surprise, placing the person in a difficult situation. □ *The chairman of the committee wrongfooted his opponents by calling a meeting when most of them were on holiday and had no time to prepare for it.* □ *The teacher wrongfooted the class by giving them a test the day before they were expecting it.*

X

X marks the spot this is the exact spot. (Can be used literally when someone draws an *X* to mark an exact spot.) □ *This is where the stone struck my car—X marks the spot.* □ *Now, please move that table over here. Yes, right here—X marks the spot.*

Y

year in, year out year after year, all year long. □ *I seem to have hay fever year in, year out. I never get over it.* □ *John wears the same old suit, year in, year out.*

You bet! AND You bet your boots!; You can bet on it! surely; absolutely. (Informal.) □ BILL: *Coming to the meeting next Saturday?* BOB: *You bet!* □ *You bet your boots I'll be there!*

You bet your boots! See the previous entry.

You can bet on it! See *You bet!*

You can say that again! AND You said it! That is certainly true!; You are absolutely correct! (Informal. The word *that* is emphasized.) □ MARY: *It sure is hot today.* JANE: *You can say that again!* □ BILL: *This cake is yummy!* BOB: *You said it!*

You can't take it with you. You should enjoy your money now, because it is no good when you're dead. □ *My uncle is a wealthy miser. I keep telling him, "You can't take it with you."* □ *If you have money, you should make out a will. You can't take it with you, you know!*

You can't teach an old dog new tricks. a proverb meaning that old people cannot learn anything new. □ *"Of course I can learn," bellowed Uncle John. "Who says you can't teach an old dog new tricks?"* □ *I'm sorry. I can't seem to learn to do this job properly. Oh, well. You can't teach an old dog new tricks.*

you know as you are aware, or should be aware. □ *This is a very valuable book, you know.* □ *Goldfish can be overfed, you know.*

You said it! See *You can say that again!*

Your guess is as good as mine. Your opinion is likely to be as correct as mine. (Informal.) □ *I don't know where the scissors are. Your guess is as good as mine.* □ *Your guess is as good as mine as to when the train will arrive.*

yours truly 1. a closing phrase at the end of a letter, just before the signature. □ *Yours truly, Tom Jones.* 2. oneself; I; me. (Informal.) □ *There's nobody here right now but yours truly.* □ *Everyone else got up and left the table, leaving yours truly to pay the bill.*

Z

zero hour the time at which something is due to begin; a crucial moment. □ *We'll know whether the new computer system works effectively at zero hour when we switch over to it.* □ *The runners are getting nervous as zero hour approaches. The starter's gun will soon go off.*

zero in on something AND **zoom in on something** to aim or focus directly on something. (Informal.) □ *"Now," said Mr. Smith, "I would like to zero in on another important point."* □ *Mary is very good about zeroing in on the most important and helpful ideas.* □ *Mr. Smith zoomed in on the heart of the problem.*

zonk out to pass out; to fall asleep. (Slang.) □ *I was so tired after playing rugby that I almost zonked out on the floor.* □ *I had a cup of coffee before the test to keep from zonking out in the middle of it.*

zoom in (on someone or something) 1. to fly or move rapidly at someone or something. (Slang.) □ *The hawk zoomed in on the sparrow.* □ *The angry bees zoomed in on Jane and stung her.* □ *When the door opened, the cat zoomed in.* **2.** [for a photographer] to use a zoom lens to get a closer view of someone or something. □ *Bill zoomed in on Sally's face just as she grinned.* □ *On the next shot I'll zoom in for a close-up.* **3.** [with *something*] See *zero in on something*.

PHRASE-FINDER INDEX

Use this index to find the form of a phrase that you want to look up in the dictionary. First, pick out any major word in the phrase you are seeking. Second, look that word up in this index to find the form of the phrase used in the dictionary. Third, look up the phrase in the dictionary. See Hints below.

Some of the words occurring in the dictionary entries do not occur as entries in this index. Some words are omitted because they occur so frequently that their lists cover many pages. In these instances, you should look up the phrase under some other word. Most of the grammar or function words are not indexed. In addition, the most numerous verbs, *be, get, go, have, make,* and *take* are not indexed.

USES

This index provides a convenient way to find the complete form of an entry from only a single major word in the entry phrase.

HINTS

1. When you are trying to find an expression in this index, look up the noun first, if there is one.

2. When you are looking for a noun, try first to find the singular form or the simplest form of the noun.

3. When you are looking for a verb, try first to find the present tense form or the simplest form of the verb.

4. In most expressions where a noun or pronoun is a variable part of an expression, it will be represented by the words "someone" or "something" in the form of the expression used in the Dictionary. If you do not find the noun you want in the index, it may, in fact, be a variable word.

5. This is an index of forms, not meanings. The expressions in an index entry do not usually have any meanings in common. Consult the dictionary for information about meaning.

ABACK
taken aback

ABANDON
abandon oneself to someone or something

ABC
ABC of something □ know one's ABC

ABET
aid and abet someone

ABIDE
abide by something

ABILITY
to the best of one's ability

ABLE
able to breathe again □ able to do something blindfold □ able to do something standing on one's head □ able to take a joke □ able to take something □ not able to call one's time one's own □ not able to go on □ not able to help something □ not able to make anything out of someone or something □ not able to see the wood for the trees □ not able to wait

ABREAST
be abreast (of something) □ keep abreast (of something)

ABSENCE
conspicuous by one's absence □ in the absence of someone or something

ABSENT
absent without leave

ACCIDENT
chapter of accidents □ have an accident

ACCORD
of one's own accord

ACCORDANCE
in accordance with something

ACCORDING
according to all accounts □ according to one's (own) lights □ cut one's coat according to one's cloth

ACCOUNT
according to all accounts □ blow-by-blow account □ by all accounts □ call someone to account □ give a good account of oneself □ give an account of someone or something □ hold someone accountable (for something) □ not on any account □ on account □ on account of someone or something □ on no account □ on someone's account □ square accounts (with someone) □ take someone or something into account □ There's no accounting for taste. □ turn something to good account

ACCOUNTABLE
hold someone accountable (for something)

ACE
come within an ace of doing something

ACHILLES
Achilles' heel

ACID
acid test

ACQUAINT
acquainted with someone or something

ACQUIRE
acquire a taste for something

ACROSS
across the board □ come across someone or something □ cut across something □ get someone or something across □ get something across (to someone) □ put one across someone □ put someone or something across □ run across someone or something □ shot across the bows □ stumble across someone or something

ACT
act of faith □ act of God □ act of war □ act one's age □ act something out □ act the goat □ act up □ catch someone in the act (of doing something) □ caught in the act □ clean up one's act □ get one's act together □ in the act (of doing something) □ keep up an act □ put on an act □ read someone the Riot Act □ tough act to follow

ACTION
Actions speak louder than words. □ go into action □ piece of the action □ suit one's actions to one's words □ swing into action □ take action (against someone or something)

ACTIVE

on active duty

ADAM

not know someone from Adam

ADD

add fuel to the fire □ add insult to injury □ add something up □ add up (to something)

ADDITION

in addition (to someone or something)

ADO

much ado about nothing □ without further ado

ADVANCE

advanced in years □ in advance (of someone or something) □ pay in advance

ADVANTAGE

get the advantage of someone □ have the advantage of someone (over someone) □ show something to advantage □ take advantage of someone or something □ turn something to one's advantage

ADVOCATE

play (the) devil's advocate

AFFAIR

fine state of affairs □ settle someone's affairs

AFRAID

afraid of one's own shadow

AFTER

after a fashion □ after all □ after all is said and done □ after hours □ after the fact □ after the style of someone or something □ chase after someone or something □ chase around (after someone or something) □ day after day □ get after someone □ go after someone or something □ inquire after someone □ keep after someone □ look after someone or something □ morning after (the night before) □ much sought after □ name someone after someone else □ run after someone □ take after someone □ take off (after someone or something) □ throw good money after bad □ time after time □ wise after the event

AGAIN

able to breathe again □ at it again □ be oneself again □ Breathe again! □ Come again? □ do something over (again) □ every now and again □ never darken my door again □ now and again □ off again, on again □ on again, off again □ over and over (again) □ something else (again) □ time and (time) again □ You can say that again!

AGAINST

against someone's will □ bang one's head against a brick wall □ bear a grudge (against someone) □ beat one's head against the wall □ dead set against someone or something □ go against the grain □ guard against someone or something □ have a case (against someone) □ have a grudge against someone □ have one's heart set against something □ have something against someone or something □ have the cards stacked against one □ hold a grudge (against someone) □ hold something against someone □ hope against hope □ nurse a grudge (against someone) □ one's heart is set against something □ pit someone or something against someone or something □ play both ends (against the middle) □ play someone off against someone else □ race against time □ raise a hand (against someone or something) □ run against the clock □ run up against a brick wall □ run up against a stone wall □ set one's heart against something □ side against someone □ smear campaign (against someone) □ speak out (against something) □ speak up (against something) □ stack the cards (against someone or something) □ stand out against someone or something □ stand up against someone or something □ swim against the tide □ take a stand (against someone or something) □ take action (against someone or something) □ take up arms (against someone or something) □ The cards are stacked against one. □ The odds are against one. □ turn against someone or something □ up against something

AGE

act one's age □ be of age □ come of

age □ donkey's ages □ in this day and age □ ripe old age

AGREEMENT
reach an agreement (with someone)

AHEAD
ahead of one's time □ ahead of time □ be ahead (of someone or something) □ full steam ahead □ get ahead (of someone or something) □ get the go-ahead □ give someone the go-ahead □ go ahead (with something) □ keep ahead (of someone or something) □ one jump ahead (of someone or something) □ one move ahead (of someone or something) □ pull ahead (of someone or something) □ stay ahead of someone or something

AID
aid and abet someone

AIM
aim to do something □ take aim (at someone or something)

AIR
air one's dirty linen in public □ air one's grievances □ airs and graces □ breath of fresh air □ build castles in the air □ clear the air □ full of hot air □ give oneself airs □ have one's nose in the air □ in the air □ keep one's nose in the air □ keep someone or something hanging in mid-air □ leave someone or something hanging in mid-air □ off the air □ on the air □ one's nose is in the air □ out of thin air □ pull something out of thin air □ put on airs □ up in the air □ vanish into thin air □ walk on air

AISLE
have them rolling in the aisles

ALERT
on the alert (for someone or something)

ALIKE
share and share alike

ALIVE
alive and kicking □ alive with someone or something □ skin someone alive

ALLEY
up a blind alley

ALLOW
allow for someone or something

ALLOWANCE
make allowances (for someone or something)

ALONE
go it alone □ leave someone or something alone □ leave well alone □ let alone someone or something □ let someone or something alone □ let well alone

ALONG
come along (with someone) □ get along □ get along (without (someone or something)) □ go along for the ride □ go along (with someone or something) □ inch along (something) □ jolly someone along □ play along with someone or something □ rub along with someone □ string along (with someone) □ string someone along □ tag along

ALONGSIDE
alongside (of) someone or something

ALTOGETHER
in the altogether

AMISS
take something amiss

AMONG
put the cat among the pigeons □ set the cat among the pigeons

AMOUNT
amount to something □ to the tune of some amount of money

ANGEL
fools rush in (where angels fear to tread)

ANOTHER
dance to another tune □ have another think coming □ horse of another colour □ keep something for another occasion □ leave something for another occasion □ One good turn deserves another. □ One man's meat is another man's poison. □ one way or another

ANSWER
answer someone's purpose □ answer to someone □ not take no for an answer

ANT
have ants in one's pants

ANY
any number of someone or something □
any port in a storm □ at any cost □ at
any rate □ go to any lengths □ in any
case □ in any event □ not on any account □ without any strings attached

ANYONE
(as) far as anyone knows □ not give a
hang about anyone or anything □ not
give a hoot about anyone or anything □
so far as anyone knows

ANYTHING
can't do anything with someone or something □ not able to make anything out
of someone or something □ not for anything in the world □ not give a hang
about anyone or anything □ not give a
hoot about anyone or anything

APART
be poles apart □ come apart at the
seams □ fall apart □ fall apart at the
seams □ joking apart □ take someone or something apart □ tell people
apart □ tell things apart

APE
go ape (over someone or something)

APPEARANCE
by all appearances □ make an appearance □ put in an appearance

APPETITE
whet someone's appetite

APPLE
apple of someone's eye □ in apple-pie
order

APPLECART
upset the applecart

APPOINTMENT
make an appointment (with someone)

APPROVAL
on approval

APRON
tied to one's mother's apron-strings

AREA
grey area

ARGUMENT
get into an argument (with someone) □
have an argument (with someone)

ARM
arm in arm □ armed to the teeth □
babe in arms □ chance one's arm □
cost an arm and a leg □ give one's
right arm (for someone or something)
□ keep someone or something at arm's
length □ pay an arm and a leg (for
something) □ put the arm on someone
□ receive someone with open arms □
shot in the arm □ take up arms
(against someone or something) □
twist someone's arm □ up in arms □
welcome someone with open arms □
armed to the teeth

ARMOUR
chink in one's armour

ARRANGEMENT
make an arrangement (with someone)
□ make arrangements (to do something) □ make the arrangements (for
someone or something)

ARREARS
in arrears

ASIDE
aside from someone or something □
lay something aside □ put something
aside □ set something aside

ASK
ask for something □ ask for the moon
□ ask for trouble □ ask someone out
□ for the asking

ASLEEP
asleep at the wheel □ fall asleep

ASS
make an ass of someone

ASSURE
rest assured

ASTRAY
go astray

ATTACH
with no strings attached □ without
any strings attached

ATTENDANCE
dance attendance on someone

ATTENTION
call someone's attention to something ☐
pay attention (to someone or something)

ATTITUDE
devil-may-care attitude ☐ wait-and-see
attitude

AUCTION
Dutch auction

AVAIL
of no avail ☐ to no avail

AVAILABLE
make someone or something available to
someone

AVERAGE
on average

AVOID
avoid someone or something like the
plague

AWAKE
wide awake

AWAY
break something away ☐ carried away
☐ come away empty-handed ☐ die
away ☐ do away with someone ☐
draw the fire away from someone or
something ☐ eat away at someone ☐
explain something away ☐ far and
away ☐ Fire away! ☐ get away (from
it all) ☐ get away (from someone or
something) ☐ get away with something ☐ get carried away ☐ give
away something ☐ give someone or
something away ☐ give the bride away
☐ give the game away ☐ go away
empty-handed ☐ hammer away (at
someone or something) ☐ keep away
(from someone or something) ☐ pass
away ☐ peg away (at something) ☐
plug away (at something) ☐ put someone or something away ☐ right away
☐ run away (with someone or something) ☐ salt something away ☐ send
away for something ☐ shy away (from
someone or something) ☐ slip away
☐ squirrel something away ☐ stay
away (from someone or something) ☐
stone's throw away ☐ stow away ☐
straight away ☐ take it away ☐ take
someone's breath away ☐ walk away
with something ☐ waste away ☐

When the cat's away the mice will play.
☐ while away the time

AWE
in awe (of someone or something) ☐
stand in awe of someone or something

AXE
get the axe ☐ give someone the axe ☐
have an axe to grind (with someone)

BABE
babe in arms ☐ babe in the woods

BABY
(as) soft as a baby's bottom ☐ leave
someone holding the baby

BACK
back and forth ☐ back down (from
something) ☐ back in circulation ☐
back of the beyond ☐ back out (of
something) ☐ back someone or something up ☐ back to the drawing-board
☐ back to the salt mines ☐ behind
someone's back ☐ break the back of
something ☐ call (someone) back ☐
cut back ☐ cut back (on something) ☐
date back (to sometime) ☐ double back
(on one's tracks) ☐ drop back ☐ fall
back (from something) ☐ fall back on
someone or something ☐ get a pat on
the back ☐ get back (at someone) ☐
get back on one's feet ☐ get back to
someone ☐ Get off someone's back! ☐
get someone's back up ☐ get something
back ☐ give someone a pat on the back
☐ give someone the shirt off one's back
☐ go back on one's word ☐ hang back
☐ hark(en) back to something ☐ have
eyes in the back of one's head ☐ have
one's back to the wall ☐ hold someone
or something back ☐ hurry back ☐ in
the back ☐ keep someone or something
back ☐ knock something back ☐
know someone or something like the back
of one's hand ☐ laid back ☐ like water
off a duck's back ☐ look back on someone or something ☐ make a come-back
☐ on someone's back ☐ pat someone
on the back ☐ pin someone's ears back
☐ put one's back into something ☐ put
something on the back burner ☐ scratch
someone's back ☐ set one back on one's
heels ☐ set someone or something back
☐ sit back and let something happen ☐

stab someone in the back □ take a back seat (to someone) □ take something back □ talk back (to someone) □ talk through the back of one's head □ That's the straw that broke the camel's back. □ think back (on someone or something) □ turn one's back (on someone or something) □ with both hands tied behind one's back □ with one hand tied behind one's back

BACKWARDS
bend over backwards to do something □ fall over backwards to do something □ lean over backwards to do something

BACKYARD
in one's (own) backyard

BACON
bring home the bacon

BAD
as bad as all that □ bad-mouth someone or something □ be off to a bad start □ come to a bad end □ get off to a bad start □ go bad □ go from bad to worse □ good riddance (to bad rubbish) □ in a bad mood □ in a bad way □ in bad faith □ in bad taste □ leave a bad taste in someone's mouth □ not half bad □ throw good money after bad

BAG
bag and baggage □ bag of tricks □ in the bag □ let the cat out of the bag □ mixed bag

BAGGAGE
bag and baggage

BAIL
bail out (of something) □ bail someone or something out □ jump bail □ out on bail □ skip bail

BALANCE
balance the books □ hang in the balance □ in the balance □ strike a balance (between two things)

BALE
bale out (of something) □ bale something out

BALL
ball and chain □ ball of fire □ get the ball rolling □ have a ball □ keep one's

eye on the ball □ keep the ball rolling □ new ball game □ on the ball □ play ball (with someone) □ set the ball rolling □ start the ball rolling

BALLOON
go down like a lead balloon □ send up a trial balloon

BANANA
go bananas

BAND
beat the band

BANDWAGON
climb on the bandwagon □ jump on the bandwagon

BANDY
bandy something about

BANG
bang one's head against a brick wall □ whole (bang) shoot

BANK
bank on something □ break the bank

BAPTISM
baptism of fire

BAR
all over bar the shouting □ no holds barred

BARGAIN
bargain for something □ drive a hard bargain □ in the bargain □ keep one's end of the bargain □ keep one's side of the bargain □ strike a bargain

BARGE
barge in (on someone or something)

BARK
bark up the wrong tree □ One's bark is worse than one's bite.

BARREL
get someone over a barrel □ have someone over a barrel □ lock, stock, and barrel □ more fun than a barrel of monkeys □ packed (in) like herring in a barrel □ scrape the bottom of the barrel

BASIS
on a first-name basis (with someone)

371

BASKET
put all one's eggs in one basket

BAT
(as) blind as a bat □ have bats in one's belfry □ like a bat out of hell □ without batting an eye

BAWL
bawl someone out

BAY
hold someone or something at bay □ keep someone or something at bay

BEAM
on the beam

BEAN
full of beans □ spill the beans

BEAR
bear a grudge (against someone) □ bear fruit □ bear one's cross □ bear someone or something in mind □ bear something out □ bear the brunt (of something) □ bear up □ bear with someone or something □ grin and bear it

BEARD
beard the lion in his den

BEAT
beat a (hasty) retreat □ beat a path to someone's door □ beat about the bush □ beat one's brains out (to do something) □ beat one's head against the wall □ beat someone to it □ beat someone to the draw □ beat someone up □ beat someone's brains out □ beat the band □ beat the living daylights out of someone □ beat the stuffing out of someone □ off the beaten track □ one's heart misses a beat □ one's heart skips a beat □ pound a beat

BEAUTY
Beauty is only skin deep.

BEAVER
eager beaver

BECK
at someone's beck and call

BECOMING
be becoming to someone

BED
bed of roses □ Early to bed, early to rise, makes a man healthy, wealthy, and wise. □ get out of the wrong side of the bed □ go to bed (with someone) □ make someone's bed □ make the bed □ put someone or something to bed □ sick in bed

BEE
(as) busy as a bee □ birds and the bees □ have a bee in one's bonnet □ make a bee-line for someone or something

BEEF
beef something up

BEFORE
before you can say Jack Robinson □ before you know it □ carry all before one □ Cast (one's) pearls before swine. □ count one's chickens before they are hatched □ cross a bridge before one comes to it □ cry before one is hurt □ morning after (the night before) □ Pride goes before a fall. □ put the cart before the horse □ think twice (before doing something)

BEG
beg off □ beg the question □ go begging

BEGGAR
beggar description □ Beggars can't be choosers.

BEGIN
begin to see daylight □ begin to see the light □ Charity begins at home.

BEHALF
on behalf of someone □ on someone's behalf □ take up the cudgels on behalf of someone or something

BEHAVIOUR
get time off for good behaviour □ on one's best behaviour

BEHIND
behind someone's back □ behind the scenes □ burn one's bridges (behind one) □ come up from behind □ driving force (behind someone or something) □ fall behind (with something) □ get behind (with something) □ lag behind (someone or something) □

372

leave someone or something behind ☐ power behind the throne ☐ wet behind the ears ☐ with both hands tied behind one's back ☐ with one hand tied behind one's back

BEHOVE
it behoves one to do something

BELFRY
have bats in one's belfry

BELIEVE
believe it or not ☐ lead someone to believe something ☐ seeing is believing

BELL
(as) sound as a bell ☐ ring a bell ☐ saved by the bell

BELONG
To the victors belong the spoils.

BELOW
hit (someone) below the belt

BELT
belt something out ☐ get something under one's belt ☐ hit (someone) below the belt ☐ tighten one's belt

BENCH
on the bench

BEND
bend over backwards to do something ☐ bend someone's ear ☐ go (a)round the bend

BENEATH
feel it beneath one (to do something)

BENEFIT
get the benefit of the doubt ☐ give someone the benefit of the doubt ☐ of benefit (to someone)

BENT
be bent on doing something

BERTH
give someone or something a wide berth

BESIDE
be beside oneself ☐ beside the point

BEST
at best ☐ at one's best ☐ at (the) best ☐ best bib and tucker ☐ come off second-best ☐ do one's best ☐ get the best of someone ☐ give something

one's best shot ☐ had best do something ☐ in one's (own) (best) interests ☐ in one's Sunday best ☐ in the best of health ☐ make the best of something ☐ on one's best behaviour ☐ past someone's or something's best ☐ put one's best foot forward ☐ to the best of one's ability ☐ to the best of one's knowledge ☐ with the best will in the world ☐ work out for the best

BET
bet one's bottom dollar ☐ bet one's life ☐ hedge one's bets ☐ You bet! ☐ You bet your boots! ☐ You can bet on it!

BETIDE
woe betide someone

BETTER
all better now ☐ be better off doing something ☐ be better off somewhere ☐ better late than never ☐ for better or for worse ☐ get better ☐ get the better of someone ☐ go one better ☐ had better do something ☐ Half a loaf is better than none. ☐ have seen better days ☐ know better ☐ one's better half ☐ so much the better ☐ take a turn for the better ☐ think better of something

BETTY
all my eye (and Betty Martin)

BETWEEN
between the devil and the deep blue sea ☐ betwixt and between ☐ come between someone and someone else ☐ draw a line between something and something else ☐ fall between two stools ☐ few and far between ☐ have one's tail between one's legs ☐ hit someone between the eyes ☐ no love lost (between someone and someone else) ☐ one's tail is between one's legs ☐ read between the lines ☐ strike a balance (between two things) ☐ take the bit between one's teeth

BETWIXT
betwixt and between

BEYOND
(above and) beyond the call of duty ☐ back of the beyond ☐ beyond measure

□ beyond one's ken □ beyond one's means □ beyond reasonable doubt □ beyond the call of duty □ beyond the pale □ beyond the shadow of a doubt □ beyond words □ can't see beyond the end of one's nose □ live beyond one's means

BIB
best bib and tucker

BIDE
bide one's time

BIG
be given a big send-off □ big fish in a small pond □ get a big hand for something □ get a big send-off □ give someone a big hand for something □ give someone a big send-off □ have a big mouth □ have eyes bigger than one's stomach □ make a big deal about something □ one's eyes are bigger than one's stomach □ talk big □ too big for one's boots □ too big for one's britches □ What's the (big) idea?

BILL
fill the bill □ foot the bill □ get a clean bill of health □ give someone a clean bill of health

BINGE
go on a binge

BIRD
A bird in the hand is worth two in the bush. □ A little bird told me. □ (as) free as a bird □ birds and the bees □ bird's-eye view □ Birds of a feather flock together. □ early bird □ eat like a bird □ Fine feathers make fine birds. □ for the birds □ kill two birds with one stone □ The early bird catches the worm.

BIRTH
give birth to someone or something

BIRTHDAY
in one's birthday suit

BISCUIT
take the biscuit

BIT
champ at the bit □ do one's bit □ hair of the dog that bit one □ Not a bit (of it). □ quite a bit □ take the bit

between one's teeth □ thrill someone to bits

BITE
bite off more than one can chew □ bite one's nails □ bite someone's head off □ bite the bullet □ bite the dust □ bite the hand that feeds one □ hair of the dog that bit one □ One's bark is worse than one's bite. □ put the bite on someone

BITTER
bitter pill to swallow □ to the bitter end

BLACK
(as) black as one is painted □ (as) black as pitch □ black and blue □ black out □ black sheep (of the family) □ get a black eye □ give someone a black eye □ in black and white □ in the black □ pot calling the kettle black

BLAME
lay the blame on someone or something □ place the blame on someone or something □ put the blame on someone or something

BLANCHE
carte blanche

BLANK
blank cheque □ draw a blank

BLANKET
wet blanket

BLAST
(at) full blast

BLAZE
blaze a trail

BLEEP
bleep something out

BLESSING
blessing in disguise

BLIND
(a case of) the blind leading the blind □ (as) blind as a bat □ blind leading the blind □ turn a blind eye to someone or something □ up a blind alley

BLINDFOLD
able to do something blindfold

BLINK

on the blink

BLOCK

chip off the old block □ knock someone's block off □ stumbling-block

BLOOD

blue blood □ draw blood □ flesh and blood □ fresh blood □ in cold blood □ in one's blood □ in the blood □ make someone's blood boil □ make someone's blood run cold □ new blood □ some new blood □ sweat blood

BLOW

blow-by-blow account □ blow-by-blow description □ blow hot and cold □ blow off steam □ blow one's own trumpet □ blow one's top □ blow over □ blow someone's brains out □ blow someone's cover □ blow someone's mind □ blow something out of all proportion □ blow the gaff □ blow the lid off (something) □ blow the whistle (on someone or something) □ blow up □ blow up in someone's face □ come to blows (over something) □ have a blow-out □ land a blow (somewhere)

BLUE

between the devil and the deep blue sea □ black and blue □ blue blood □ cry blue murder □ get the blues □ have the blues □ like a bolt out of the blue □ once in a blue moon □ out of the blue □ scream blue murder □ talk until one is blue in the face

BLUFF

call someone's bluff

BOARD

above-board □ across the board □ back to the drawing-board □ go by the board □ on board □ open and above-board

BOAT

burn one's boats □ in the same boat □ miss the boat □ rock the boat

BODY

go in a body □ in a body □ keep body and soul together □ over my dead body

BOG

get bogged down

BOGGLE

boggle someone's mind

BOIL

A watched pot never boils. □ boil down to something □ have a low boiling-point □ make someone's blood boil

BOLD

(as) bold as brass

BOLT

get down to the nuts and bolts □ like a bolt out of the blue □ nuts and bolts (of something)

BOMBSHELL

drop a bombshell

BONE

all skin and bones □ bone of contention □ bone up (on something) □ chilled to the bone □ cut something to the bone □ feel something in one's bones □ have a bone to pick (with someone) □ make no bones about something □ near the bone □ nothing but skin and bones □ work one's fingers to the bone

BONNET

have a bee in one's bonnet

BOOK

balance the books □ by the book □ cook the books □ have one's nose in a book □ in one's book □ know someone or something like a book □ make book on something □ one for the record (books) □ open book □ read someone like a book □ take a leaf out of someone's book □ throw the book at someone □ use every trick in the book

BOOT

(as) tough as old boots □ boot someone or something out □ die with one's boots on □ get the boot □ give someone the boot □ have one's heart in one's boots □ have the boot on the other foot □ The boot is on the other foot. □ to boot □ too big for one's boots □ You bet your boots!

375

BOOTSTRAP
pull oneself up by one's bootstraps

BORE
bore someone stiff □ bore someone to death

BOREDOM
die of boredom

BORN
born with a silver spoon in one's mouth □ in all one's born days □ not born yesterday

BORROW
live on borrowed time

BOSS
boss someone around

BOTCH
botch something up

BOTH
burn the candle at both ends □ cut both ways □ have a foot in both camps □ have it both ways □ land on both feet □ make (both) ends meet □ play both ends (against the middle) □ with both hands tied behind one's back

BOTHER
bother with someone or something □ hot and bothered

BOTTLE
bottle something up □ crack a bottle

BOTTOM
(as) soft as a baby's bottom □ at the bottom of the ladder □ bet one's bottom dollar □ bottom line □ bottom out □ from the bottom of one's heart □ from top to bottom □ get to the bottom of something □ hit bottom □ learn something from the bottom up □ scrape the bottom of the barrel

BOUND
bound for somewhere □ bound hand and foot □ by leaps and bounds □ duty-bound (to do something) □ out of bounds

BOW
bow and scrape □ bow out □ shot across the bows □ take a bow

BOWL
bowl someone over

BOX
Box and Cox □ open Pandora's box

BOY
All work and no play makes Jack a dull boy. □ separate the men from the boys

BRAIN
beat one's brains out (to do something) □ beat someone's brains out □ blow someone's brains out □ have something on the brain □ rack one's brains

BRANCH
branch out (into something) □ hold out the olive branch □ root and branch

BRASS
(as) bold as brass □ get down to brass tacks

BRAVE
put a brave face on it □ put up a (brave) front

BREACH
step in(to the breach)

BREAD
bread and butter □ know which side one's bread is buttered on

BREADTH
by a hair's breadth

BREAK
at the break of dawn □ Break a leg! □ break camp □ break down □ break even □ break in (on someone or something) □ break in(to something) □ break into tears □ break it off □ break loose (from someone or something) □ break new ground □ break off with someone □ break one's duck □ break one's neck (to do something) □ break one's word □ break out in a cold sweat □ break out in something □ break out (of something) □ break someone or something in □ break someone's fall □ break someone's heart □ break something away □ break something loose □ break something off □ break the back of something □ break the bank □ break the ice □ break the news (to someone) □

break up (with someone) □ broken reed □ die of a broken heart □ get a lucky break □ Give someone a break! □ go broke □ make a break for something or somewhere □ make or break someone □ take a break □ That's the straw that broke the camel's back.

BREAST
make a clean breast of something

BREATH
all in one breath □ breath of fresh air □ catch one's breath □ Don't hold your breath. □ get time to catch one's breath □ have time to catch one's breath □ hold one's breath □ in the same breath □ out of breath □ save one's breath □ say something under one's breath □ take someone's breath away □ waste one's breath □ with every other breath

BREATHE
able to breathe again □ Breathe again! □ breathe down someone's neck □ breathe one's last □ hardly have time to breathe □ not breathe a word (about someone or something)

BREED
Familiarity breeds contempt.

BREW
There is trouble brewing. □ Trouble is brewing.

BRICK
bang one's head against a brick wall □ drop a brick □ hit (someone or something) like a ton of bricks □ run up against a brick wall

BRIDE
give the bride away

BRIDGE
burn one's bridges (behind one) □ cross a bridge before one comes to it □ cross a bridge when one comes to it □ water under the bridge

BRIEF
hold no brief for someone or something □ in brief

BRIGHT
(as) bright as a button □ bright and early □ get a bright idea □ have a bright idea

BRING
bring down the curtain (on something) □ bring home the bacon □ bring someone or something up □ bring someone round □ bring someone to □ bring someone up to date (on someone or something) □ bring something about □ bring something crashing down (around one('s ears)) □ bring something home to someone □ bring something into question □ bring something off □ bring something to a close □ bring something to a halt □ bring something to a head □ bring something to an end □ bring something to light □ bring the house down □ bring up the rear

BRISTOL
shipshape (and Bristol fashion)

BRITCHES
too big for one's britches

BROAD
in broad daylight

BROKE
broken reed □ die of a broken heart □ go broke □ That's the straw that broke the camel's back.

BROTH
Too many cooks spoil the broth.

BROW
by the sweat of one's brow □ knit one's brow

BRUNT
bear the brunt (of something)

BRUSH
brush something under the carpet □ brush up on something □ get the brush-off □ have a brush with something □ tarred with the same brush

BRUSHOFF
give someone the brushoff

BUCK
buck up □ make a fast buck □ pass the buck

BUCKET
drop in the bucket □ kick the bucket □ weep buckets

BUCKLE
buckle down to something □ buckle to

BUD
nip something in the bud

BUFF
in the buff

BUG
(as) snug as a bug (in a rug) □ bug someone

BUILD
build castles in Spain □ build castles in the air □ build someone or something up □ build up for something □ build up to something

BUILT
Rome wasn't built in a day.

BULL
bull in a china shop □ cock-and-bull story □ hit the bull's-eye □ take the bull by the horns

BULLET
bite the bullet

BUMP
bump into someone □ bump someone off

BUNDLE
bundle someone up

BUNK
do a bunk

BURN
burn one's boats □ burn one's bridges (behind one) □ burn (oneself) out □ burn the candle at both ends □ burn the midnight oil □ fiddle while Rome burns □ get one's fingers burned □ have money to burn □ keep the home fires burning □ Money burns a hole in someone's pocket.

BURNER
put something on the back burner

BURST
be bursting at the seams □ be bursting with joy □ be bursting with pride □ burst at the seams □ burst in (on someone or something) □ burst into flames □ burst into tears □ burst out crying □ burst out laughing □ burst with joy □ burst with pride

BURY
bury one's head in the sand □ bury the hatchet □ dead and buried

BUSH
A bird in the hand is worth two in the bush. □ beat about the bush □ be bushed □ bush telegraph

BUSHEL
hide one's light under a bushel

BUSINESS
be about one's business □ business end of something □ funny business □ get down to business □ get one's nose out of someone's business □ go about one's business □ have no business doing something □ keep one's nose out of someone's business □ mind one's own business □ monkey business □ one means business □ send one about one's business □ set someone up (in business)

BUSMAN
busman's holiday

BUSY
(as) busy as a bee

BUT
everything but the kitchen sink □ It never rains but it pours. □ last but not least □ no buts about it □ nothing but □ nothing but skin and bones □ The spirit is willing (but the flesh is weak).

BUTT
butt in (on something)

BUTTER
bread and butter □ butter someone up □ Fine words butter no parsnips. □ know which side one's bread is buttered on □ look as if butter wouldn't melt in one's mouth

BUTTERFLIES
get butterflies in one's stomach □ give one butterflies in one's stomach □ have butterflies in one's stomach

BUTTON

(as) bright as a button □ button one's lip □ not worth a button □ on the button □ press the panic button □ push the panic button

BUY

buy a pig in a poke □ buy someone off □ buy someone or something out □ buy something □ buy something for a song □ buy something on credit □ buy something up □ not buy something

BUZZ

give someone a buzz

BYGONES

Let bygones be bygones.

CAHOOTS

in cahoots (with someone)

CAIN

raise Cain (with someone or something)

CAKE

(as) nutty as a fruit-cake □ eat one's cake and have it too □ have one's cake and eat it too □ piece of cake □ sell like hot cakes □ slice of the cake

CALF

kill the fatted calf

CALL

(above and) beyond the call of duty □ at someone's beck and call □ beyond the call of duty □ call a halt (to something) □ call a meeting □ call a spade a spade □ call it a day □ call it quits □ call of nature □ call (someone) back □ call someone in □ call someone names □ call someone or something off □ call someone or something up □ call someone to account □ call someone's attention to something □ call someone's bluff □ call something into question □ call the dogs off □ call the meeting to order □ call the shots □ call the tune □ have a close call □ He who pays the piper calls the tune. □ not able to call one's time one's own □ on call □ pot calling the kettle black

CALM

(as) calm as a millpond

CAMEL

That's the straw that broke the camel's back.

CAMP

break camp □ have a foot in both camps

CAMPAIGN

smear campaign (against someone)

CAN

before you can say Jack Robinson □ Beggars can't be choosers. □ bite off more than one can chew □ can't do anything with someone or something □ can't hold a candle to someone □ can't make head or tail of someone or something □ can't see beyond the end of one's nose □ can't see one's hand in front of one's face □ can't stand (the sight of) someone or something □ can't stomach someone or something □ catch-as-catch-can □ game at which two can play □ no can do □ open a can of worms □ two can play at that game □ You can bet on it! □ You can say that again! □ You can't take it with you. □ You can't teach an old dog new tricks.

CANARY

look like the cat that swallowed the canary

CANCEL

cancel something out

CANDLE

burn the candle at both ends □ can't hold a candle to someone

CANOE

paddle one's own canoe

CAP

cap in hand □ feather in one's cap □ If the cap fits, wear it. □ put on one's thinking-cap

CARD

have the cards stacked against one □ hold all the cards □ lay one's cards on the table □ on the cards □ play one's cards close to one's chest □ play one's cards right □ play one's trump card □ put one's cards on the table □ stack the cards (against someone or something) □ The cards are stacked against one.

CARE
care about someone or something □ care for someone or something □ care nothing about someone or something □ care nothing for someone or something □ care of someone □ couldn't care less □ devil-may-care attitude □ devil-may-care manner □ for all I care □ in the care of someone □ not care two hoots about someone or something □ not have a care in the world □ take care of someone or something □ That takes care of that.

CAREFUL
be careful not to do something □ be careful (with something)

CARPET
brush something under the carpet □ get the red carpet treatment □ give someone the red carpet treatment □ roll out the red carpet for someone □ sweep something under the carpet

CARRY
carried away □ carry a torch (for someone) □ carry all before one □ carry coals to Newcastle □ carry on □ carry on about someone or something □ carry on (with someone) □ carry one's cross □ carry one's (own) weight □ carry over □ carry something off □ carry something over □ carry the day □ carry the weight of the world on one's shoulders □ carry weight (with someone) □ cash and carry □ get carried away

CART
put the cart before the horse

CARTE
carte blanche

CASE
(a case of) the blind leading the blind □ case in point □ have a case (against someone) □ in any case □ in case of something □ in the case of someone or something □ just in case □ open-and-shut case

CASH
cash and carry □ cash in on something

□ cash in one's chips □ cash something in □ hard cash

CAST
cast about for someone or something □ cast around for someone or something □ cast doubt (on someone or something) □ cast in the same mould □ cast one's lot in with someone □ Cast (one's) pearls before swine. □ cast the first stone

CASTLE
build castles in Spain □ build castles in the air

CAT
be a copy-cat □ Cat got your tongue? □ Curiosity killed the cat. □ let the cat out of the bag □ look like the cat that swallowed the canary □ not enough room to swing a cat □ play cat and mouse (with someone) □ put the cat among the pigeons □ rain cats and dogs □ set the cat among the pigeons □ There's more than one way to kill a cat. □ When the cat's away the mice will play.

CATCH
catch-as-catch-can □ catch cold □ catch fire □ catch forty winks □ catch hold of someone or something □ catch it □ catch on (to someone or something) □ catch one off one's guard □ catch one with one's pants down □ catch one with one's trousers down □ catch one's breath □ catch one's death (of cold) □ catch sight of someone or something □ catch someone in the act (of doing something) □ catch someone napping □ catch someone off guard □ catch someone on the hop □ catch someone red-handed □ catch someone's eye □ catch the sun □ catch up (with someone or something) □ caught in the act □ caught in the cross-fire □ caught in the middle □ caught red-handed □ caught short □ get time to catch one's breath □ have time to catch one's breath □ The early bird catches the worm.

CAUGHT
caught in the act □ caught in the cross-

fire □ caught in the middle □ caught red-handed □ caught short

CAUSE
cause a commotion □ cause a stir □ cause eyebrows to raise □ cause raised eyebrows □ cause tongues to wag

CAUTION
throw caution to the winds

CAVE
cave in (to something)

CEILING
hit the ceiling

CENT
not worth a cent

CENTRE
dead centre □ left, right, and centre □ off-centre

CENTURY
turn of the century

CEREMONY
stand on ceremony

CHAFF
separate the grain from the chaff

CHAIN
ball and chain

CHALK
(as) different as chalk from cheese □ chalk something up □ chalk something up to someone or something □ chalk something up to something

CHAMP
champ at the bit

CHANCE
by chance □ chance one's arm □ chance something □ chance (up)on someone or something □ fancy someone's chances □ fat chance □ fighting chance □ ghost of a chance □ have a snowball's chance in hell □ jump at the chance (to do something) □ let the chance slip by □ on the off chance □ once-in-a-lifetime chance □ sporting chance □ stand a chance □ take a chance

CHANGE
change colour □ change hands □ change horses in mid-stream □ change

someone's mind □ change someone's tune □ change the subject □ chop and change □ ring the changes

CHANNEL
go through the proper channels

CHAPTER
chapter and verse □ chapter of accidents

CHARACTER
in character □ out of character

CHARGE
charge off □ charge something to someone or something □ have charge (of someone or something) □ in charge (of someone or something) □ in the charge of someone □ take charge (of someone or something)

CHARITY
(as) cold as charity □ Charity begins at home.

CHASE
chase after someone or something □ chase around (after someone or something) □ give chase (to someone or something) □ go chase oneself □ lead someone on a merry chase □ wild-goose chase

CHEAP
dirt cheap

CHECK
check in(to something) □ check on someone or something □ check out (of something) □ check someone in □ check someone or something off □ check someone or something out □ check up on someone or something □ check with someone □ get a check-up □ give someone a check-up □ hold someone or something in check □ keep someone or something in check

CHEEK
cheek by jowl □ tongue-in-cheek □ turn the other cheek

CHEER
cheer someone on □ cheer someone up □ cheer up

CHEESE
(as) different as chalk from cheese □ cheese-paring □ cheesed off

CHEQUE
blank cheque ☐ honour someone's cheque ☐ make a cheque out (to someone)

CHEST
get something off one's chest ☐ play one's cards close to one's chest

CHEW
bite off more than one can chew ☐ chew the cud ☐ chew the fat ☐ chew the rag

CHICKEN
chicken out (of something) ☐ count one's chickens before they are hatched ☐ for chicken-feed ☐ no spring chicken ☐ run around like a chicken with its head cut off

CHILD
child's play ☐ expecting (a child)

CHILDHOOD
in one's second childhood

CHILL
chilled to the bone ☐ chilled to the marrow

CHIME
chime in

CHINA
bull in a china shop

CHIN
keep one's chin up ☐ take something on the chin

CHINK
chink in one's armour

CHIP
cash in one's chips ☐ chip in (something) ☐ chip off the old block ☐ have a chip on one's shoulder

CHOICE
by choice ☐ Hobson's choice

CHOKE
choke someone off

CHOOSE
Beggars can't be choosers. ☐ choose sides ☐ pick and choose

CHOP
chop and change ☐ chop someone or something up

CHORD
strike a chord

CHURCH
(as) poor as a church mouse

CIRCLE
come full circle ☐ go (a)round in circles ☐ go round in circles ☐ run around in circles ☐ run circles around someone ☐ vicious circle

CIRCULATION
back in circulation ☐ out of circulation

CIRCUMSTANCE
extenuating circumstances ☐ under the circumstances

CIRCUS
like a three-ring circus

CIVIL
keep a civil tongue (in one's head)

CLAIM
stake a claim (on something)

CLAM
clam up

CLAMP
clamp down (on someone or something) ☐ put the clamps on (someone)

CLANGER
drop a clanger

CLAP
clap eyes on someone or something

CLAY
have feet of clay

CLEAN
(as) clean as a whistle ☐ clean out of something ☐ clean someone out ☐ clean something up ☐ clean up ☐ clean up one's act ☐ come clean (with someone) ☐ get a clean bill of health ☐ give someone a clean bill of health ☐ have a clean conscience (about someone or something) ☐ have clean hands ☐ keep one's nose clean ☐ make a clean breast of something ☐ make a clean sweep ☐ start (off) with a clean slate ☐ wipe the slate clean

CLEANERS
take someone to the cleaners

CLEAR
(as) clear as crystal □ (as) clear as mud □ clear out □ clear someone's name □ clear something up □ clear the air □ clear the table □ clear up □ have a clear conscience (about someone or something) □ in the clear □ make someone's position clear □ see one's way clear (to do something) □ steer clear (of someone or something) □ The coast is clear.

CLIMB
climb down □ climb on the bandwagon □ climb the wall

CLIP
clip someone's wings

CLOAK
cloak-and-dagger

CLOCK
(a)round the clock □ run against the clock

CLOCKWORK
(as) regular as clockwork □ go like clockwork

CLOSE
at close range □ bring something to a close □ close at hand □ close in (on someone or something) □ close one's eyes to something □ close ranks □ close something down □ close the door on something □ close to home □ close to someone □ close up shop □ come too close to home □ get close (to someone or something) □ have a close call □ have a close shave □ play one's cards close to one's chest □ too close for comfort

CLOSET
come out (of the closet) □ skeleton in the closet

CLOTH
cut one's coat according to one's cloth □ cut one's coat to suit one's cloth

CLOTHING
wolf in sheep's clothing

CLOUD
Cloud-cuckoo-land □ Every cloud has a silver lining. □ have one's head in the clouds □ on cloud nine □ under a cloud

CLOVER
in clover

CLUB
Join the club!

CLUTCH
clutch at straws

COACH
drive a coach and horses through something

COAL
carry coals to Newcastle □ haul someone over the coals □ take coals to Newcastle

COAST
The coast is clear.

COAT
cut one's coat according to one's cloth □ cut one's coat to suit one's cloth □ hang on someone's coat-tails □ turn one's coat

COCK
cock a snook at someone □ cock-and-bull story □ cock of the walk □ go off at half cock

COCKLES
warm the cockles of someone's heart

COFFIN
nail in someone's or something's coffin

COLD
(as) cold as charity □ be a cold fish □ blow hot and cold □ break out in a cold sweat □ catch cold □ catch one's death (of cold) □ cold comfort □ cold turkey □ get cold feet □ get the cold shoulder □ give someone the cold shoulder □ go cold turkey □ have cold feet □ in cold blood □ keep someone out in the cold □ knock someone cold □ leave someone out in the cold □ make someone's blood run cold □ out cold □ pour cold water on something □ throw cold water on something

COLLAR
hot under the collar

COLLECTION
take up a collection

COLOUR
change colour □ horse of a different colour □ horse of another colour □ nail one's colours to the mast □ off colour □ sail under false colours □ see the colour of someone's money □ show oneself in one's true colours □ with flying colours

COMB
go over something with a fine-tooth comb □ search something with a fine-tooth comb

COME
come a cropper □ come about □ come across someone or something □ Come again? □ come along (with someone) □ Come and get it! □ come apart at the seams □ come at someone or something □ come away empty-handed □ come between someone and someone else □ come by something □ come clean (with someone) □ come down hard on someone or something □ come down in the world □ come down to earth □ come down to something □ come down with something □ come from far and wide □ come full circle □ come hell or high water □ come home to roost □ come in for something □ come in handy □ come into one's or its own □ come into something □ come of age □ come off □ Come off it! □ come off second-best □ come on □ come out □ come out in the wash □ come out of nowhere □ come out of one's shell □ come out (of the closet) □ come out with something □ come round □ come someone's way □ come to □ come to a bad end □ come to a head □ come to a pretty pass □ come to a standstill □ come to an end □ come to an understanding (with someone) □ come to an untimely end □ come to blows (over something) □ come to grief □ come to grips with something □ come to life □ come to light □ come to mind □ come to

naught □ come to nothing □ come to one's senses □ come to pass □ come to rest □ come to terms with something □ come to the fore □ come to the point □ come to think of it □ come too close to home □ come true □ come up □ come up from behind □ come up in the world □ come up with someone or something □ come (up)on someone or something □ come what may □ come within an ace of doing something □ come within an inch of doing something □ cross a bridge before one comes to it □ cross a bridge when one comes to it □ dream come true □ easy come, easy go □ easy to come by □ First come, first served. □ get one's come-uppance □ get what is coming to one □ give one what's coming to one □ have another think coming □ have come a long way □ have something coming (to one) □ if the worst comes to the worst □ johnny-come-lately □ make a comeback □ not know if one is coming or going □ not know whether one is coming or going □ till the cows come home □ up-and-coming □ when it comes right down to it □ when it comes to something

COMFORT
cold comfort □ too close for comfort

COMFORTER
Job's comforter

COMMAND
have a good command of something

COMMISSION
out of commission

COMMIT
commit something to memory

COMMON
have something in common (with someone or something)

COMMOTION
cause a commotion

COMPANY
keep company with someone □ keep someone company □ part company (with someone) □ two's company(, three's a crowd)

COMPLAIN
nothing to complain about

COMPLIMENT
fish for compliments ☐ pay someone a compliment ☐ pay someone a left-handed compliment ☐ return the compliment

COMPOSURE
regain one's composure

CONCERN
as far as someone is concerned ☐ so far as someone is concerned ☐ to whom it may concern

CONCERT
in concert (with someone)

CONCLUSION
jump to conclusions ☐ leap to conclusions

CONDITION
in an interesting condition ☐ in condition ☐ in good condition ☐ in mint condition ☐ in the pink (of condition) ☐ out of condition

CONFIDE
confide in someone

CONFIDENCE
vote of confidence

CONFORMITY
in conformity with something

CONK
conk out

CONSCIENCE
have a clean conscience (about someone or something) ☐ have a clear conscience (about someone or something)

CONSEQUENCE
in consequence (of something)

CONSIDERATION
in consideration of something ☐ out of consideration (for someone or something)

CONSPICUOUS
conspicuous by one's absence ☐ make oneself conspicuous

CONSTRUCTION
under construction

CONTEMPT
Familiarity breeds contempt.

CONTEND
contend with someone or something

CONTENT
to one's heart's content

CONTENTION
bone of contention

CONTRADICTION
contradiction in terms

CONTRARY
on the contrary ☐ to the contrary

CONTROL
control the purse-strings ☐ out of control

CONVENIENCE
at someone's earliest convenience

CONVERSATION
strike up a conversation

CONVERT
preach to the converted

CONVICTION
have the courage of one's convictions

COOK
cook someone's goose ☐ cook something up ☐ cook the books ☐ Too many cooks spoil the broth. ☐ What's cooking?

COOKIE
That's the way the cookie crumbles.

COOL
(as) cool as a cucumber ☐ cool down ☐ Cool it! ☐ cool off ☐ cool one's heels ☐ cool someone or something down ☐ cool someone or something off ☐ keep cool ☐ lose one's cool ☐ play it cool

COOP
fly the coop

COP
cop it ☐ cop out

COPY
be a copy-cat

CORE
to the core

CORNER

cut corners □ have turned the corner □ hole-and-corner □ hole-in-the-corner □ out of the corner of one's eye

CORRECT

stand corrected

COST

at all costs □ at any cost □ cost a pretty penny □ cost an arm and a leg □ cost the earth

COUGH

cough something up

COULD

could do with someone or something □ couldn't care less □ so still you could hear a pin drop □ Wild horses couldn't drag someone.

COUNSEL

keep one's own counsel

COUNT

count heads □ count off □ count on someone or something □ count one's chickens before they are hatched □ count someone (in for something) □ count someone or something off □ count someone out (for something) □ count something up □ every minute counts □ every moment counts □ stand up and be counted

COUNTER

run counter to something □ under the counter

COURAGE

Dutch courage □ have the courage of one's convictions □ pluck up (one's) courage □ screw up one's courage

COURSE

as a matter of course □ in due course □ in the course of time □ par for the course

COURT

laugh something out of court

COURTESY

out of courtesy (to someone)

COVENTRY

send someone to Coventry

COVER

blow someone's cover □ cover a lot of ground □ cover for someone □ cover someone's tracks (up) □ cover something up

COW

sacred cow □ till the cows come home

COX

Box and Cox

CRACK

at the crack of dawn □ crack a bottle □ crack a joke □ crack down (on someone or something) □ crack something wide open □ crack up □ fair crack of the whip □ get cracking □ hard nut to crack □ have a crack at something □ make cracks (about someone or something) □ not all it is cracked up to be □ not what it is cracked up to be □ paper over the cracks (in something) □ tough nut to crack

CRADLE

cradle-snatch

CRAMP

cramp someone's style

CRASH

bring something crashing down (around one('s ears))

CRAW

something sticks in one's craw

CRAZY

crazy about someone or something □ drive someone crazy □ like crazy

CREATE

create a scene □ create a stink (about something) □ create an uproar

CREATION

in creation

CREDENCE

give credence to something

CREDIT

buy something on credit □ do credit to someone □ do someone credit □ extend credit (to someone) □ get credit (for something) □ give credit where credit is due □ give someone credit (for something)

CREEK
up a creek □ up the creek (without a paddle)

CREEP
creep up on someone or something □ get the creeps □ give someone the creeps

CRIME
Crime doesn't pay.

CROCODILE
shed crocodile tears

CROOK
by hook or by crook

CROP
crop up

CROPPER
come a cropper

CROSS
at cross purposes □ bear one's cross □ carry one's cross □ caught in the cross-fire □ cross a bridge before one comes to it □ cross a bridge when one comes to it □ cross-examine someone □ cross one's fingers □ cross one's heart (and hope to die) □ cross someone or something off □ cross someone or something out □ cross someone's mind □ cross swords (with someone) □ cross the Rubicon □ double-cross someone □ keep one's fingers crossed (for someone or something)

CROW
as the crow flies □ make someone eat crow

CROWD
two's company(, three's a crowd)

CRUMBLE
That's the way the cookie crumbles.

CRUSH
crushed by something □ get a crush on someone □ have a crush on someone

CRUST
upper crust

CRUX
crux of the matter

CRY
burst out crying □ cry before one is

hurt □ cry blue murder □ cry for the moon □ cry one's eyes out □ cry over spilled milk □ cry wolf □ far cry from something □ hue and cry

CRYSTAL
(as) clear as crystal

CUCKOO
Cloud-cuckoo-land

CUCUMBER
(as) cool as a cucumber

CUD
chew the cud

CUDGEL
take up the cudgels on behalf of someone or something

CUE
cue someone in □ take one's cue from someone

CUFF
off the cuff □ speak off the cuff

CULTURE
culture vulture

CUNNING
(as) cunning as a fox

CUP
in one's cups □ not someone's cup of tea

CUPBOARD
cupboard love

CURIOSITY
Curiosity killed the cat.

CURL
curl someone's hair □ curl up (and die) □ make someone's hair curl

CURRY
curry favour (with someone)

CURTAIN
be curtains for someone or something □ bring down the curtain (on something) □ ring down the curtain (on something)

CUT
cut a fine figure □ cut above someone or something □ cut across something □ cut and dried □ cut and thrust □ cut back □ cut back (on something)

□ cut both ways □ cut corners □ cut down (on something) □ cut in (on someone or something) □ cut in(to something) □ Cut it out! □ cut it (too) fine □ cut loose (from someone or something) □ cut no ice □ cut off □ cut off one's nose to spite one's face □ cut one's coat according to one's cloth □ cut one's coat to suit one's cloth □ cut one's eye-teeth on something □ cut one's teeth on something □ cut out for something □ cut out to be something □ cut someone dead □ cut someone down to size □ cut someone in □ cut someone or something off □ cut someone or something (off) short □ cut someone or something out □ cut someone or something to pieces □ cut someone to the quick □ cut someone's losses □ cut someone's throat □ cut something to the bone □ cut teeth □ cut the ground out from under someone □ cut up rough □ cut up someone or something □ have one's work cut out (for one) □ one's work is cut out (for one) □ run around like a chicken with its head cut off

CYLINDER
firing on all cylinders

DAB
smack dab in the middle

DADDY
daddy of them all

DAGGER
cloak-and-dagger □ look daggers at someone

DAILY
daily dozen □ daily grind

DAISY
pushing up the daisies

DAMMIT
(as) near as dammit

DAMN
damn someone or something with faint praise

DAMP
damp squib

DANCE
dance attendance on someone □ dance

to another tune □ lead someone a merry dance

DANDER
get someone's dander up

DANGEROUS
A little knowledge is a dangerous thing. □ A little learning is a dangerous thing.

DARBY
Darby and Joan

DARK
dark horse □ in the dark (about someone or something) □ never darken my door again □ not to darken someone's door □ shot in the dark

DASH
dash something off

DATE
at an early date □ bring someone up to date (on someone or something) □ date back (to sometime) □ out of date □ past someone's or something's sell-by date □ to date □ up to date

DAVY
Davy Jones's Locker □ go to Davy Jones's locker

DAWN
at the break of dawn □ at the crack of dawn □ dawn on someone

DAY
all day long □ all hours (of the day and night) □ all in a day's work □ all the livelong day □ (as) different as night and day □ (as) happy as the day is long □ at the end of the day □ by the day □ call it a day □ carry the day □ day after day □ day and night □ day in and day out □ day-to-day □ Every dog has its day. □ for days on end □ forever and a day □ from day to day □ from this day forward □ from this day on □ get the day off □ have had its day □ have seen better days □ have the day off □ in all one's born days □ in this day and age □ late in the day □ make a day of doing something □ night and day □ nine days' wonder □ not give someone the time of day □ one of these days □ one's days are numbered □ order of

the day □ pass the time of day (with someone) □ Rome wasn't built in a day. □ save something for a rainy day □ save the day □ see the light of day □ take the day off □ That'll be the day. □ win the day

DAYLIGHT
beat the living daylights out of someone □ begin to see daylight □ daylight robbery □ in broad daylight □ scare the (living) daylights out of someone

DEAD
(as) dead as a dodo □ (as) dead as a doornail □ be a dead duck □ cut someone dead □ dead and buried □ dead centre □ dead loss □ dead on one's or its feet □ dead set against someone or something □ dead to the world □ drop dead □ fill dead men's shoes □ flog a dead horse □ in a dead heat □ knock someone dead □ leave someone for dead □ over my dead body □ step into dead men's shoes □ stop one dead in one's tracks □ stop something dead in its tracks □ taken for dead

DEAF
turn a deaf ear (to something)

DEAL
get a raw deal □ give someone a raw deal □ It's a deal. □ make a big deal about something □ square deal □ think a great deal of someone or something □ wheeling and dealing

DEATH
at death's door □ be death to something □ bore someone to death □ catch one's death (of cold) □ death to something □ die a natural death □ fight to the death □ frighten someone to death □ kiss of death □ matter of life and death □ scare someone to death □ scared to death □ sign one's own death-warrant □ tickle someone to death

DEBT
pay one's debt to society

DECISION
eleventh-hour decision

DECK
on deck

DEEP
Beauty is only skin deep. □ between the devil and the deep blue sea □ go off the deep end □ in deep □ in deep water □ jump off the deep end □ Still waters run deep.

DEFIANCE
in defiance of someone or something

DEGREE
get the third degree □ give someone the third degree □ to the nth degree

DELIVERED
signed, sealed, and delivered

DEN
beard the lion in his den

DENT
make a dent in something

DEPOSIT
on deposit

DESCRIPTION
beggar description □ blow-by-blow description

DESERT
desert a sinking ship

DESERVE
One good turn deserves another.

DESIGN
have designs on someone or something

DESIRE
leave a lot to be desired

DESPAIR
sink into despair

DESSERT
get one's just desserts

DEVIL
between the devil and the deep blue sea □ devil-may-care attitude □ devil-may-care manner □ devil of a job □ devil's own job □ full of the devil □ give the devil his due □ go to the devil □ have the devil to pay □ play (the) devil's advocate □ speak of the devil □ There will be the devil to pay.

389

DICE
No dice.

DICK
(every) Tom, Dick, and Harry

DIE
cross one's heart (and hope to die) □ curl up (and die) □ die a natural death □ die away □ die down □ die laughing □ die of a broken heart □ die of boredom □ die off □ die out □ die with one's boots on □ dying to do something

DIET
on a diet

DIFFERENCE
make no difference (to someone) □ sink our differences □ split the difference □ What difference does it make?

DIFFERENT
(as) different as chalk from cheese □ (as) different as night and day □ horse of a different colour □ sing a different tune

DIG
dig in □ dig in one's heels □ dig one's own grave □ dig some dirt up on someone □ dig someone or something □ dig someone or something up □ dig something out □ give someone a dig

DILEMMA
on the horns of a dilemma

DIM
take a dim view of something

DINE
dine out □ dine out on something

DINT
by dint of something

DIP
dip into something □ lucky dip

DIRT
dig some dirt up on someone □ dirt cheap

DIRTY
air one's dirty linen in public □ dirty look □ dirty old man □ dirty one's hands □ dirty word □ dirty work □ wash one's dirty linen in public

DISEASE
down with a disease

DISGUISE
blessing in disguise

DISH
(as) dull as dish-water □ dish something out □ do the dishes

DISPOSAL
put someone or something at someone's disposal

DISTANCE
go the distance □ keep one's distance (from someone or something) □ keep someone or something at a distance □ stay the distance □ within hailing distance

DITCH
last-ditch effort

DIVIDE
divide something fifty-fifty

DOCTOR
just what the doctor ordered

DODO
(as) dead as a dodo

DOG
(as) sick as a dog □ call the dogs off □ dog-eat-dog □ dog in the manger □ Every dog has its day. □ go to the dogs □ hair of the dog that bit one □ lead a dog's life □ Let sleeping dogs lie. □ live a dog's life □ rain cats and dogs □ see a man about a dog □ shaggy-dog story □ tail wagging the dog □ You can't teach an old dog new tricks.

DOGHOUSE
in the doghouse

DOLDRUM
in the doldrums

DOLLAR
bet one's bottom dollar □ feel like a million dollars □ look like a million dollars

DOLLED
get (all) dolled up

DONKEY

donkey-work □ donkey's ages □ donkey's years

DOOR

at death's door □ beat a path to someone's door □ close the door on something □ get one's foot in the door □ have one's foot in the door □ keep the wolf from the door □ live next door (to someone) □ never darken my door again □ not to darken someone's door □ open the door to something □ see someone to the door □ show someone the door □ show someone to the door □ shut the door on something

DOORNAIL

(as) dead as a doornail

DOORSTEP

at someone's doorstep □ on someone's doorstep

DOSE

dose of one's own medicine

DOT

from the year dot □ on the dot □ sign on the dotted line □ since the year dot

DOUBLE

do a double take □ double back (on one's tracks) □ double-cross someone □ double Dutch □ double up (with someone) □ on the double □ see double

DOUBT

beyond reasonable doubt □ beyond the shadow of a doubt □ cast doubt (on someone or something) □ doubting Thomas □ get the benefit of the doubt □ give someone the benefit of the doubt □ no doubt

DOWNHILL

go downhill

DOZE

doze off

DOZEN

by the dozen □ daily dozen □ six of one and half a dozen of the other □ talk nineteen to the dozen

DRAB

dribs and drabs

DRAG

be a drag □ drag on □ drag one's feet □ drag out □ drag something out □ Wild horses couldn't drag someone.

DRAIN

down the drain □ pour money down the drain

DRAUGHT

feel the draught

DRAW

back to the drawing-board □ beat someone to the draw □ draw a blank □ draw a line between something and something else □ draw a red herring □ draw blood □ draw someone or something up □ draw something up □ draw the fire away from someone or something □ draw the line (at something) □ quick on the draw

DREAM

dream come true □ dream something up □ pipe-dream □ wouldn't dream of doing something

DRESS

all dressed up □ dress someone or something up □ dress up □ dressed to kill □ dressed (up) to the nines □ dressing down

DRIB

dribs and drabs

DRIED

cut and dried

DRIFT

drift off (to sleep)

DRINK

drink something up □ drink to excess □ drink up

DRIVE

(as) pure as the driven snow □ (as) white as the driven snow □ drive a coach and horses through something □ drive a hard bargain □ drive someone crazy □ drive someone mad □ drive someone to the wall □ drive someone up the wall □ drive something home □ driving force (behind someone or something) □ What are you driving at?

DROP

at the drop of a hat □ drop a bomb-shell □ drop a brick □ drop a clanger □ drop back □ drop dead □ drop in (on someone) □ drop in one's tracks □ drop in the bucket □ drop in the ocean □ drop off (to sleep) □ drop out (of something) □ drop someone □ drop someone a line □ drop someone or something off □ drop someone's name □ drop the name of someone □ name-dropping □ so still you could hear a pin drop □ The penny dropped.

DROWN

drown one's sorrows □ drown some-one or something out

DRUG

drug on the market

DRUM

drum someone out of something □ drum something into someone □ drum something up

DRY

cut and dried □ dry run □ dry some-one out □ dry up □ home and dry □ leave someone high and dry

DUCK

as a duck takes to water □ be a dead duck □ break one's duck □ lame duck □ like a sitting duck □ like sit-ting ducks □ like water off a duck's back □ lovely weather for ducks

DUE

give credit where credit is due □ give the devil his due □ in due course □ in due time □ pay one's dues

DULL

All work and no play makes Jack a dull boy. □ (as) dull as dish-water

DUMP

down in the dumps

DUST

bite the dust □ dust someone or some-thing down

DUTCH

double Dutch □ Dutch auction □ Dutch courage □ Dutch treat □ Dutch uncle □ go Dutch

DUTY

(above and) beyond the call of duty □ beyond the call of duty □ do one's duty □ duty-bound (to do something) □ in the line of duty □ off duty □ on active duty □ on duty □ shirk one's duty

DWELL

dwell (up)on something

DYE

dyed-in-the-wool

EACH

made for each other

EAGER

eager beaver

EAGLE

eagle eye

EAR

be all ears □ be all eyes (and ears) □ bend someone's ear □ bring something crashing down (around one('s ears)) □ flea in one's ear □ get someone's ear □ go in one ear and out the other □ have one's ear to the ground □ have someone's ear □ in one ear and out the other □ keep one's ear to the ground □ lend an ear (to someone) □ Make a silk purse out of a sow's ear. □ pin someone's ears back □ play by ear □ play something by ear □ prick up one's ears □ turn a deaf ear (to something) □ up to one's ears (in something) □ walls have ears □ wet behind the ears

EARLY

at an early date □ at someone's earliest convenience □ bright and early □ early bird □ Early to bed, early to rise(, makes a man healthy, wealthy, and wise). □ The early bird catches the worm.

EARN

A penny saved is a penny earned. □ earn one's keep

EARNEST

in earnest

EARTH

come down to earth □ cost the earth □ down to earth □ like nothing on earth □ move heaven and earth to do something □ on earth □ pay the earth □ run someone or something to earth □ salt of the earth □ to the ends of the earth

EASE

at ease □ ease someone out □ ill at ease

EASY

(as) easy as falling off a log □ (as) easy as pie □ easier said than done □ easy come, easy go □ Easy does it. □ easy to come by □ free and easy □ go easy (on someone or something) □ on Easy Street □ take it easy on someone or something

EAT

dog-eat-dog □ eat away at someone □ eat humble pie □ eat like a bird □ eat like a horse □ eat one's cake and have it too □ eat one's hat □ eat one's heart out □ eat one's words □ eat out □ eat out of someone's hands □ eat someone out of house and home □ have one's cake and eat it too □ make someone eat crow □ What's eating you?

EDGE

edge someone or something out □ get the edge on someone □ have the edge on someone □ on edge □ set someone's teeth on edge □ take the edge (off something)

EDGEWAYS

get a word in (edgeways)

EEL

(as) slippery as an eel

EFFECT

go into effect □ something to that effect □ take effect □ words to that effect

EFFORT

all out effort □ last-ditch effort □ make an all out effort

EGG

egg someone on □ have egg on one's face □ kill the goose that laid the golden egg □ lay an egg □ put all one's eggs in one basket □ teach one's grandmother to suck eggs □ walk on eggs

EITHER

either feast or famine

ELBOW

elbow-grease

ELEMENT

in one's element □ out of one's element

ELEPHANT

white elephant

ELEVENTH

at the eleventh hour □ eleventh-hour decision

ELSE

come between someone and someone else □ draw a line between something and something else □ in someone else's place □ in someone else's shoes □ mistake someone for someone else □ mistake something for something else □ mix someone up with someone else □ mix something up with something else □ name someone after someone else □ no love lost (between someone and someone else) □ play someone off against someone else □ put oneself in someone else's place □ something else □ something else (again)

EMPTY

come away empty-handed □ Empty vessels make the most noise. □ go away empty-handed

END

All's well that ends well. □ at a loose end □ at one's wits' end □ at the end of one's tether □ at the end of the day □ be an end in itself □ bring something to an end □ burn the candle at both ends □ business end of something □ can't see beyond the end of one's nose □ come to a bad end □ come to an end □ come to an untimely end □ end of the line □ end of the road □ end up (by) doing something □ end up somewhere □ end up with the short end of the stick □ for days on end □ for hours on end □ get the short end of the stick □ go off the deep end □ jump off the deep end □ keep one's end of the bargain □ make (both) ends meet □ make someone's hair stand on end □ meet one's end □ no end of something □ not see further than the end of one's nose □ play both ends (against the middle) □ put an end to something □ see the light at the end of the tunnel □ thin end of the wedge □ to the bitter end □ to the ends of the earth

ENGLISH
in plain English

ENLARGE
enlarge on something

ENOUGH
enough is as good as a feast □ Enough is enough. □ enough to go (a)round □ get up enough nerve (to do something) □ good enough for someone or something □ have had enough □ Hot enough for you? □ not enough room to swing a cat □ old enough to be someone's father □ old enough to be someone's mother

ENTER
enter one's mind □ enter the lists

ENVY
green with envy

EQUAL
equal to someone or something

ERRAND
go on an errand □ on a fool's errand □ run an errand □ send someone (out) on an errand

ERROR
trial and error

ESCAPE
escape someone's notice

ETERNAL
eternal triangle

EVE
on the eve of something

EVEN
be even-steven □ break even □ get even (with someone) □ keep on an

even keel □ keep something on an even keel

EVENT
in any event □ in the event of something □ in the unlikely event of something □ wise after the event

EVER
forever and ever

EVERY
at every turn □ Every cloud has a silver lining. □ Every dog has its day. □ every inch a something □ every last one □ every living soul □ every man jack (of someone) □ every minute counts □ every moment counts □ every mother's son (of someone) □ every now and again □ every now and then □ every once in a while □ every time one turns around □ (every) Tom, Dick, and Harry □ hang on someone's every word □ use every trick in the book □ with every other breath

EVERYTHING
everything but the kitchen sink □ everything from A to Z

EVIDENCE
much in evidence

EVIL
Money is the root of all evil.

EXAMINE
cross-examine someone

EXAMPLE
hold someone or something up as an example □ make an example of someone

EXCEPTION
exception that proves the rule □ make an exception (for someone) □ take exception to something

EXCESS
drink to excess

EXCHANGE
in exchange (for someone or something)

EXPAND
expand on something

EXPECT
expecting (a child) □ when least expected

EXPECTATION

measure up (to someone's expectations)

EXPENSE

at the expense of someone or something ☐ expense is no object ☐ go to the expense of doing something ☐ out-of-pocket expenses

EXPLAIN

explain oneself ☐ explain something away

EXTEND

extend credit (to someone) ☐ extend one's sympathy (to someone)

EXTENT

to a great extent ☐ to some extent

EXTENUATING

extenuating circumstances

EYE

all my eye (and Betty Martin) ☐ An eye for an eye (and a tooth for a tooth). ☐ apple of someone's eye ☐ be all eyes (and ears) ☐ bird's-eye view ☐ catch someone's eye ☐ clap eyes on someone or something ☐ close one's eyes to something ☐ cry one's eyes out ☐ cut one's eye-teeth on something ☐ eagle eye ☐ feast one's eyes (on someone or something) ☐ get a black eye ☐ get someone's eye ☐ get stars in one's eyes ☐ give someone a black eye ☐ give someone the eye ☐ give the glad eye to someone ☐ have an eye for someone or something ☐ have an eye on someone or something ☐ have eyes bigger than one's stomach ☐ have eyes in the back of one's head ☐ have one's eye on someone or something ☐ have stars in one's eyes ☐ hit someone between the eyes ☐ hit the bull's-eye ☐ in one's mind's eye ☐ in the public eye ☐ in the twinkling of an eye ☐ keep an eye on someone or something ☐ keep an eye out (for someone or something) ☐ keep one's eye on someone or something ☐ keep one's eye on the ball ☐ keep one's eyes open (for someone or something) ☐ keep one's eyes peeled (for someone or something) ☐ keep one's weather eye open ☐ lay eyes on someone or something ☐ look someone in the eye ☐ make eyes (at some-

one) ☐ more (to something) than meets the eye ☐ naked eye ☐ one in the eye for someone ☐ one's eyes are bigger than one's stomach ☐ only have eyes for someone ☐ open someone's eyes (to something) ☐ out of the corner of one's eye ☐ pull the wool over someone's eyes ☐ see eye to eye (about something) ☐ see something with half an eye ☐ set eyes on someone or something ☐ sight for sore eyes ☐ smack in the eye ☐ turn a blind eye to someone or something ☐ with an eye to doing something ☐ without batting an eye

EYEBALL

eyeball to eyeball

EYEBROW

cause eyebrows to raise ☐ cause raised eyebrows ☐ raise a few eyebrows

FACE

(as) plain as the nose on one's face ☐ blow up in someone's face ☐ can't see one's hand in front of one's face ☐ cut off one's nose to spite one's face ☐ do an about-face ☐ face someone down ☐ face the music ☐ face to face ☐ face up to someone or something ☐ face value ☐ fall flat (on one's face) ☐ feed one's face ☐ fly in the face of someone or something ☐ get a red face ☐ give someone a red face ☐ have a red face ☐ have egg on one's face ☐ hide one's face in shame ☐ keep a straight face ☐ look someone in the face ☐ lose face ☐ make a face ☐ make a face (at someone) ☐ not show one's face ☐ on the face of it ☐ pull a face ☐ put a brave face on it ☐ red in the face ☐ save (one's) face ☐ say something (right) to someone's face ☐ slap in the face ☐ stare someone in the face ☐ take something at face value ☐ talk until one is blue in the face ☐ tell one to one's face

FACT

after the fact ☐ as a matter of fact ☐ facts of life ☐ matter-of-fact

FAIL

without fail

FAINT
damn someone or something with faint praise

FAIR
fair crack of the whip □ fair do's □ fair game □ fair-to-middling □ fair-weather friend □ play fair

FAITH
act of faith □ in bad faith □ in good faith □ pin one's faith on someone or something □ show good faith

FALL
(as) easy as falling off a log □ break someone's fall □ fall about □ fall apart □ fall apart at the seams □ fall asleep □ fall back (from something) □ fall back on someone or something □ fall behind (with something) □ fall between two stools □ fall by the way-side □ fall down on the job □ fall flat (on one's face) □ fall for someone or something □ fall foul of someone or something □ fall from grace □ fall in □ fall in love (with someone) □ fall in with someone or something □ fall into line □ fall in(to) place □ fall into the trap of doing something □ fall off □ fall out □ fall out (with someone) (over something) □ fall over backwards to do something □ fall over oneself □ fall short (of something) □ fall through □ fall to □ fall to pieces □ fall to someone □ fall (up)on someone or something □ have a falling-out (with someone) (over something) □ Pride goes before a fall. □ riding for a fall

FALSE
lull someone into a false sense of security □ sail under false colours

FAMILIAR
have a familiar ring

FAMILIARITY
Familiarity breeds contempt.

FAMILY
black sheep (of the family) □ in the family □ in the family way □ like one of the family □ run in the family

FAMINE
either feast or famine

FAN
be a fan of someone □ fan the flames (of something)

FANCY
fancy someone's chances □ flight of fancy □ footloose and fancy-free □ take a fancy to someone or something □ take someone's fancy □ tickle someone's fancy

FAR
(as) far as anyone knows □ as far as it goes □ as far as possible □ as far as someone is concerned □ come from far and wide □ far and away □ far be it from me to do something □ far cry from something □ far from it □ far into the night □ far out □ few and far between □ go so far as to say something □ go too far □ so far as anyone knows □ so far as possible □ so far as someone is concerned □ So far, so good.

FARM
farm someone or something out

FASHION
after a fashion □ out of fashion □ parrot-fashion □ shipshape (and Bristol fashion)

FAST
get nowhere fast □ hard-and-fast rule □ make a fast buck □ make fast work of someone or something □ play fast and loose (with someone or something) □ pull a fast one □ thick and fast

FAT
chew the fat □ fat chance □ kill the fatted calf □ live off the fat of the land □ The fat is in the fire.

FATE
leave one to one's fate

FATHER
old enough to be someone's father

FAULT
find fault (with someone or something) □ generous to a fault

FAVOUR
curry favour (with someone) □ in favour of someone □ in favour (of someone or something) □ in some-

one's favour □ out of favour (with someone) □ return the favour

FEAR
fools rush in (where angels fear to tread) □ in fear and trembling □ never fear

FEAST
either feast or famine □ enough is as good as a feast □ feast one's eyes (on someone or something)

FEATHER
(as) light as a feather □ Birds of a feather flock together. □ feather in one's cap □ feather one's (own) nest □ Fine feathers make fine birds. □ in fine feather □ knock someone down with a feather □ make the feathers fly □ ruffle someone's feathers □ show the white feather □ tar and feather someone

FEED
bite the hand that feeds one □ fed up to somewhere with someone or something □ fed up (with someone or something) □ feed one's face □ for chicken-feed □ spoon-feed

FEEL
feel fit □ feel free to do something □ feel it beneath one (to do something) □ feel like a million dollars □ feel like a new person □ feel like something □ feel out of place □ feel put upon □ feel something in one's bones □ feel the draught □ feel the pinch □ feel up to something □ get the feel of something □ have the feel of something

FEELERS
put out (some) feelers

FEELING
have mixed feelings (about someone or something) □ hurt someone's feelings □ no hard feelings

FEET
dead on one's or its feet □ drag one's feet □ find one's feet □ get back on one's feet □ get cold feet □ get to one's feet □ have cold feet □ have feet of clay □ have one's feet on the ground □ keep one's feet on the ground □ knock one off one's feet □ land on both feet □ land on one's feet

□ let the grass grow under one's feet □ on one's feet □ pull the rug out from under someone('s feet) □ regain one's feet □ sit at someone's feet □ stand on one's own two feet □ sweep one off one's feet □ take the load off one's feet □ think on one's feet □ throw oneself at someone's feet

FELL
at one fell swoop □ in one fell swoop

FELLOW
hail-fellow-well-met

FENCE
fence someone in □ fenced in □ mend (one's) fences □ rush one's fences □ sit on the fence

FEND
fend for oneself

FERRET
ferret something out of someone or something

FEVER
run a fever

FEW
few and far between □ precious few □ raise a few eyebrows

FIDDLE
(as) fit as a fiddle □ fiddle around (with something) □ fiddle while Rome burns □ play second fiddle (to someone)

FIELD
(fresh fields and) pastures new □ play the field

FIFTY
divide something fifty-fifty □ split something fifty-fifty

FIGHT
fight shy of something □ fight someone or something hammer and tongs □ fight someone or something tooth and nail □ fight to the death □ fighting chance □ go down fighting □ Them's fighting words.

FIGURE
cut a fine figure □ figure in something □ in round figures □ It figures.

FILE

have something on file □ (in) single file □ rank and file □ single file

FILL

fill dead men's shoes □ fill in (for someone) □ fill out □ fill someone in (on someone or something) □ fill someone or something in □ fill someone's shoes □ fill something out □ fill the bill □ get one's fill of someone or something □ have one's fill of someone or something

FINAL

final fling □ get the final word

FIND

find fault (with someone or something) □ find it in one's heart to do something □ find one's feet □ find one's own level □ find one's tongue □ find oneself □ find someone out □ find something out the hard way □ find time for someone or something

FINDER

Finders keepers(, losers weepers).

FINE

cut a fine figure □ cut it (too) fine □ Fine feathers make fine birds. □ fine kettle of fish □ fine state of affairs □ Fine words butter no parsnips. □ go over something with a fine-tooth comb □ in fine feather □ search something with a fine-tooth comb

FINGER

cross one's fingers □ get one's fingers burned □ have green fingers □ have one's finger in the pie □ have sticky fingers □ keep one's fingers crossed (for someone or something) □ lay a finger on someone or something □ lay the finger on someone □ not lift a finger (to help someone) □ point the finger at someone □ put one's finger on something □ put the finger on someone □ slip through someone's fingers □ twist someone around one's little finger □ work one's fingers to the bone

FINGERTIP

have something at one's fingertips

FIRE

add fuel to the fire □ ball of fire □ baptism of fire □ catch fire □ caught in the cross-fire □ draw the fire away from someone or something □ Fire away! □ firing on all cylinders □ hang fire □ have too many irons in the fire □ hold one's fire □ keep the home fires burning □ like a house on fire □ open fire (on someone) □ out of the frying-pan into the fire □ play with fire □ set fire to someone or something □ set someone or something on fire □ set the world on fire □ The fat is in the fire. □ There's no smoke without fire. □ under fire □ Where there's smoke there's fire.

FIRST

at first glance □ cast the first stone □ first and foremost □ First come, first served. □ first off □ first thing (in the morning) □ first things first □ in the first instance □ in the first place □ love at first sight □ not know the first thing about someone or something □ of the first water □ on a first-name basis (with someone) □ on first-name terms (with someone)

FISH

be a cold fish □ big fish in a small pond □ fine kettle of fish □ fish for compliments □ fish for something □ fish in troubled waters □ have other fish to fry □ like a fish out of water □ neither fish nor fowl □ There are plenty of other fish in the sea.

FIST

hand over fist

FIT

(as) fit as a fiddle □ by fits and starts □ feel fit □ fit for a king □ fit in (with someone or something) □ fit like a glove □ fit someone in(to something) □ fit someone or something out (with something) □ fit to be tied □ have a fit □ If the cap fits, wear it. □ see fit (to do something) □ survival of the fittest □ think fit (to do something) □ throw a fit

FIVE

nine-to-five job □ take five

FIX
fix someone up (with something) ☐ fix something up (for someone) ☐ in a fix

FLAG
show the flag

FLAME
burst into flames ☐ fan the flames (of something) ☐ go up in flames

FLARE
flare up

FLASH
(as) quick as a flash ☐ flash in the pan ☐ in a flash

FLAT
(as) flat as a pancake ☐ fall flat (on one's face) ☐ flat out ☐ leave someone flat

FLEA
flea in one's ear

FLESH
flesh and blood ☐ flesh something out ☐ in the flesh ☐ The spirit is willing (but the flesh is weak).

FLIGHT
flight of fancy

FLING
final fling ☐ fling oneself at someone

FLIP
flip one's lid

FLOCK
Birds of a feather flock together.

FLOG
flog a dead horse

FLOOR
get in on the ground floor ☐ take the floor ☐ walk the floor ☐ wipe the floor with someone

FLUFF
fluff one's lines

FLY
as the crow flies ☐ be flying high ☐ fly a kite ☐ fly-by-night ☐ fly high ☐ fly in the face of someone or something ☐ fly in the ointment ☐ fly off the handle ☐ fly the coop ☐ flying visit ☐ get off to a flying start ☐

high-flyer ☐ make the feathers fly ☐ make the fur fly ☐ pigs might fly ☐ time flies ☐ with flying colours

FOAM
foam at the mouth

FOB
fob something off (on someone)

FOLLOW
follow in someone's footsteps ☐ follow one's heart ☐ follow one's nose ☐ follow something through ☐ follow something up ☐ follow suit ☐ follow-through ☐ tough act to follow

FOOD
food for thought

FOOL
A fool and his money are soon parted. ☐ fool around (with someone or something) ☐ fool's paradise ☐ fools rush in (where angels fear to tread) ☐ make a fool out of someone ☐ More fool you! ☐ nobody's fool ☐ on a fool's errand ☐ play the fool ☐ take someone for a fool

FOOLISH
penny wise and pound foolish

FOOT
be off on the wrong foot ☐ bound hand and foot ☐ dead on one's or its feet ☐ drag one's feet ☐ find one's feet ☐ foot the bill ☐ get back on one's feet ☐ get cold feet ☐ get off on the wrong foot ☐ get one's foot in the door ☐ get to one's feet ☐ have a foot in both camps ☐ have cold feet ☐ have feet of clay ☐ have one's feet on the ground ☐ have one's foot in the door ☐ have the boot on the other foot ☐ keep one's feet on the ground ☐ knock one off one's feet ☐ land on both feet ☐ land on one's feet ☐ let the grass grow under one's feet ☐ not set foot somewhere ☐ on foot ☐ on one's feet ☐ pull the rug out from under someone('s feet) ☐ put one's best foot forward ☐ put one's foot down (about something) ☐ put one's foot in it ☐ regain one's feet ☐ set foot somewhere ☐ sit at someone's feet ☐ stand on one's own two feet ☐ sweep

one off one's feet □ take the load off one's feet □ The boot is on the other foot. □ think on one's feet □ throw oneself at someone's feet □ wait on someone hand and foot

FOOTLOOSE
footloose and fancy-free

FOOTSIE
play footsie (with someone)

FOOTSTEPS
follow in someone's footsteps

FORBIDDEN
forbidden fruit

FORCE
driving force (behind someone or something) □ force someone's hand □ in force □ join forces (with someone) □ out in force

FORE
come to the fore

FOREMOST
first and foremost

FOREVER
forever and a day □ forever and ever

FORGET
forget oneself □ forgive and forget

FORGIVE
forgive and forget

FORK
fork money out (for something) □ speak with a forked tongue

FORM
form an opinion □ true to form

FORT
hold the fort

FORTH
back and forth □ hold forth □ launch forth (into something) □ launch forth (on something) □ set forth (on something)

FORTY
catch forty winks □ forty winks □ have forty winks □ take forty winks

FORWARD
from this day forward □ look forward

to something □ put one's best foot forward □ put something forward

FOUL
fall foul of someone or something □ foul one's own nest □ foul play □ foul someone or something up □ foul up

FOUR
on all fours

FOWL
neither fish nor fowl

FOX
(as) cunning as a fox

FREE
(as) free as a bird □ be given a free hand (with something) □ feel free to do something □ footloose and fancy-free □ free and easy □ free-for-all □ get off scot-free □ give a free rein to someone □ give someone a free hand (with something) □ go scot-free □ make free (with someone or something) □ of one's own free will □ set someone or something free

FREEDOM
give one one's freedom

FRESH
breath of fresh air □ fresh blood □ (fresh fields and) pastures new □ get fresh (with someone)

FRIEND
A friend in need is a friend indeed. □ fair-weather friend □ make friends (with someone)

FRIENDSHIP
strike up a friendship

FRIGHTEN
frighten one out of one's wits □ frighten someone to death □ frighten the wits out of someone

FRO
to and fro

FROG
frog in one's throat

FROM
(as) different as chalk from cheese □ aside from someone or something □

back down (from something) □ break loose (from someone or something) □ come from far and wide □ come up from behind □ cut loose (from someone or something) □ cut the ground out from under someone □ draw the fire away from someone or something □ everything from A to Z □ fall back (from something) □ fall from grace □ far be it from me to do something □ far cry from something □ far from it □ from day to day □ from pillar to post □ from rags to riches □ from stem to stern □ from the bottom of one's heart □ from the ground up □ from the heart □ from the word go □ from the year dot □ from this day forward □ from this day on □ from time to time □ from top to bottom □ get away (from it all) □ get away (from someone or something) □ get out from under someone or something □ go from bad to worse □ hail from somewhere □ hear from someone □ keep away (from someone or something) □ keep one's distance (from someone or something) □ keep someone from doing something □ keep the wolf from the door □ know something from memory □ learn something from the bottom up □ live from hand to mouth □ make something from scratch □ manna from heaven □ not know someone from Adam □ out from under (something) □ pull the rug out from under someone('s feet) □ separate the grain from the chaff □ separate the men from the boys □ separate the sheep from the goats □ shoot from the hip □ shy away (from someone or something) □ start from scratch □ stay away (from someone or something) □ step down (from something) □ straight from the horse's mouth □ straight from the shoulder □ take one's cue from someone

FRONT
can't see one's hand in front of one's face □ in front (of someone or something) □ put up a (brave) front □ up-front

FRUIT
(as) nutty as a fruit-cake □ bear fruit □ forbidden fruit

FRY
have other fish to fry □ out of the frying-pan into the fire □ small fry

FUEL
add fuel to the fire

FULL
(at) full blast □ at full speed □ at full stretch □ at full tilt □ come full circle □ full of beans □ full of hot air □ full of oneself □ full of the devil □ full steam ahead □ get into full swing □ have one's hands full (with someone or something) □ in full swing

FUN
fun and games □ make fun of someone or something □ more fun than a barrel of monkeys □ poke fun (at someone or something)

FUNNY
funny business □ funny ha-ha □ funny peculiar

FUR
make the fur fly

FURROW
tough furrow to plough

FURTHER
not see further than the end of one's nose □ without further ado

FUSS
fuss over someone or something □ kick up a fuss □ make a fuss (over someone or something)

FUTURE
in the near future

GAB
have the gift of gab

GAFF
blow the gaff

GAIN
gain ground □ gain on someone or something □ ill-gotten gains □ Nothing ventured, nothing gained.

GALLERY
play to the gallery

GAME
fair game □ fun and games □ game

401

at which two can play □ give the game away □ mug's game □ name of the game □ new ball game □ play the game □ two can play at that game

GANDER
take a gander (at someone or something) □ What is sauce for the goose is sauce for the gander.

GANG
gang up (on someone) □ press-gang someone into doing something

GARDEN
lead someone up the garden path

GATHER
A rolling stone gathers no moss. □ wool-gathering

GAUNTLET
throw down the gauntlet

GEAR
in high gear

GENERAL
as a (general) rule

GENEROUS
generous to a fault

GHOST
ghost of a chance □ give up the ghost

GIFT
Don't look a gift horse in the mouth. □ have the gift of gab

GILD
gild the lily

GILL
green around the gills □ pale around the gills

GIRD
gird (up) one's loins

GIVE
be given a big send-off □ be given a free hand (with something) □ be given a hard time □ be given to understand □ give a free rein to someone □ give a good account of oneself □ give an account of someone or something □ give as good as one gets □ give away something □ give birth to someone or something □ give chase (to someone or something) □ give credence to some-

thing □ give credit where credit is due □ give ground □ give in (to someone or something) □ give it to someone straight □ give of oneself □ give off something □ give one a run for one's money □ Give one an inch, and one will take a mile. □ give one butterflies in one's stomach □ give one one's freedom □ give one one's marching orders □ give one what's coming to one □ give one's right arm (for someone or something) □ give oneself airs □ give oneself up (to someone or something) □ give out □ give rise to something □ give someone a big hand for something □ give someone a big send-off □ give someone a black eye □ Give someone a break! □ give someone a buzz □ give someone a check-up □ give someone a clean bill of health □ give someone a dig □ give someone a free hand (with something) □ give someone a hand (with something) □ give someone a hard time □ give someone a head start (on someone or something) □ give someone a kick □ give someone a licking □ give someone a pain □ give someone a pat on the back □ give someone a piece of one's mind □ give someone a raw deal □ give someone a red face □ give someone a reputation (as a something) □ give someone a reputation for doing something □ give someone a ring □ give someone a rough idea (about something) □ give someone a slap on the wrist □ give someone a start □ give someone a swelled head □ give someone a ticking-off □ give someone a tongue-lashing □ give someone credit (for something) □ give someone grey hair(s) □ give someone hell □ give someone or something a wide berth □ give someone or something away □ give someone or something the once-over □ give someone or something up □ give someone pause □ give someone the axe □ give someone the benefit of the doubt □ give someone the boot □ give someone the brushoff □ give someone the cold shoulder □ give someone the creeps □ give someone the eye □ give someone the go-ahead □ give someone the go-by □ give someone the green light □ give someone the hard sell □ give someone the low-down on someone or something □ give someone the (old) heave ho □ give someone the once-over □ give someone the red carpet treatment □ give someone the runaround □ give someone the sack □ give someone the shirt off one's back □ give someone the slip □ give someone the third degree □ give someone the willies □ give someone the works □ give someone tit for tat □ give someone to understand something □ give someone what for □ give something a lick and a promise □ give something a miss □ give something one's best shot □ give something out □ give the bride away □ give the devil his due □ give the game away □ give the glad eye to someone □ give up □ give up the ghost □ give vent to something □ give voice to something □ give way (to someone or something) □ given to understand □ If you give one an inch, one will take a mile. □ not give a hang about anyone or anything □ not give a hoot about anyone or anything □ not give someone the time of day □ not give two hoots about someone or something

GLAD
give the glad eye to someone

GLANCE
at first glance

GLITTER
All that glitters is not gold.

GLORY
in one's glory

GLOSS
gloss over something

GLOVE
fit like a glove □ hand in glove (with someone) □ handle someone with kid gloves □ iron hand in the velvet glove

GLUTTON
glutton for punishment

GOAT
act the goat □ get someone's goat □ separate the sheep from the goats

GOD
act of God

GOLD
All that glitters is not gold. □ (as)

good as gold □ have a heart of gold □ worth its weight in gold

GOLDEN
kill the goose that laid the golden egg

GONER
be a goner

GOOD
all in good time □ all to the good □ as good as done □ (as) good as gold □ as good as one's word □ do someone a good turn □ do someone good □ do someone's heart good □ enough is as good as a feast □ for good □ for good measure □ get a good run for one's money □ get on the good side of someone □ get time off for good behaviour □ give a good account of oneself □ give as good as one gets □ good and something □ good enough for someone or something □ good-for-nothing □ good riddance (to bad rubbish) □ have a good command of something □ have a good head on one's shoulders □ have a good thing going □ in good condition □ in good faith □ in good shape □ in good time □ keep good time □ keep on the good side of someone □ make good □ make good as something □ make good money □ make good time □ make someone look good □ never had it so good □ No news is good news. □ on good terms (with someone) □ One good turn deserves another. □ put in a good word for someone □ put something to (good) use □ show good faith □ So far, so good. □ stand someone in good stead □ throw good money after bad □ too good to be true □ too much of a good thing □ turn something to good account □ up to no good □ Well and good. □ What's the good of something? □ when one is good and ready □ Your guess is as good as mine.

GOODBYE
kiss something goodbye

GOODNESS
honest to goodness

GOOSE
cook someone's goose □ get goose-

pimples □ kill the goose that laid the golden egg □ What is sauce for the goose is sauce for the gander. □ wild-goose chase

GOOSEBERRY
play gooseberry

GOT
Cat got your tongue? □ What's got into someone?

GOTTEN
ill-gotten gains

GRAB
up for grabs

GRACE
airs and graces □ fall from grace

GRADE
make the grade

GRAIN
go against the grain □ separate the grain from the chaff □ take something with a grain of salt

GRANDMOTHER
teach one's grandmother to suck eggs

GRANTED
take someone or something for granted

GRASP
grasp the nettle □ have a grasp of something

GRASS
let the grass grow under one's feet □ snake in the grass

GRASSHOPPER
knee-high to a grasshopper

GRAVE
(as) quiet as the grave □ dig one's own grave □ turn in one's grave □ turn (over) in one's grave

GREASE
(as) quick as (greased) lightning □ elbow-grease □ grease someone's palm

GREAT
go great guns □ in great haste □ make a great show of something □ no great shakes □ set great store by someone or something □ think a great deal

of someone or something □ to a great extent

GREEK
Greek to me

GREEN
get the green light □ give someone the green light □ green around the gills □ green with envy □ have green fingers

GREY
get grey hair(s) □ give someone grey hair(s) □ grey area □ grey matter

GRIEF
come to grief

GRIEVANCE
air one's grievances

GRIN
grin and bear it

GRIND
daily grind □ grind to a halt □ have an axe to grind (with someone)

GRINDSTONE
keep one's nose to the grindstone

GRIP
come to grips with something □ lose one's grip

GRIST
grist to the mill

GRIT
grit one's teeth

GRITTY
get down to the nitty-gritty

GROUND
break new ground □ cover a lot of ground □ cut the ground out from under someone □ from the ground up □ gain ground □ get in on the ground floor □ get something off the ground □ give ground □ ground someone □ have one's ear to the ground □ have one's feet on the ground □ keep one's ear to the ground □ keep one's feet on the ground □ lose ground □ one's old stamping-ground □ shift one's ground □ stand one's ground □ suit someone down to the ground □ thin on the ground

GROW

grow on someone ☐ grow out of something ☐ grow up ☐ have growing pains ☐ let the grass grow under one's feet

GRUDGE

bear a grudge (against someone) ☐ have a grudge against someone ☐ hold a grudge (against someone) ☐ nurse a grudge (against someone)

GUARD

catch one off one's guard ☐ catch someone off guard ☐ guard against someone or something ☐ on one's guard

GUESS

guess at something ☐ Your guess is as good as mine.

GUINEA

serve as a guinea pig

GUM

gum something up ☐ gum up the works ☐ up a gum-tree

GUN

go great guns ☐ gun for someone ☐ jump the gun ☐ shot-gun wedding ☐ spike someone's guns ☐ stick to one's guns

GUT

hate someone's guts

GUTTER

in the gutter

HA

funny ha-ha

HABIT

kick a habit ☐ kick the habit

HACKLE

get someone's hackles up

HAIL

hail-fellow-well-met ☐ hail from somewhere ☐ within hailing distance

HAIR

by a hair's breadth ☐ curl someone's hair ☐ get grey hair(s) ☐ get in someone's hair ☐ give someone grey hair(s) ☐ hair of the dog that bit one ☐ hang by a hair ☐ let one's hair down ☐ make someone's hair curl ☐ make someone's hair stand on end ☐ neither hide nor hair ☐ split hairs ☐ tear one's hair

HALE

hale and hearty

HALF

at half-mast ☐ be half-hearted about someone or something ☐ go off at half cock ☐ Half a loaf is better than none. ☐ have half a mind to do something ☐ meet someone half-way ☐ not half bad ☐ one's better half ☐ see something with half an eye ☐ six of one and half a dozen of the other

HALFPENNIES

put in one's two halfpennies (worth)

HALT

bring something to a halt ☐ call a halt (to something) ☐ grind to a halt

HAM

ham something up

HAMMER

fight someone or something hammer and tongs ☐ go at it hammer and tongs ☐ hammer away (at someone or something) ☐ hammer something home ☐ hammer something out

HAND

A bird in the hand is worth two in the bush. ☐ at hand ☐ at second hand ☐ be given a free hand (with something) ☐ bite the hand that feeds one ☐ bound hand and foot ☐ can't see one's hand in front of one's face ☐ cap in hand ☐ catch someone red-handed ☐ caught red-handed ☐ change hands ☐ close at hand ☐ come away empty-handed ☐ dirty one's hands ☐ do something by hand ☐ eat out of someone's hands ☐ force someone's hand ☐ get a big hand for something ☐ get a hand with something ☐ get one's hands off (someone or something) ☐ get one's hands on someone or something ☐ get the upper hand (over someone) ☐ give someone a big hand for something ☐ give someone a free hand (with something) ☐ give someone a hand (with something) □ go away empty-handed □ go hand in hand □ hand in glove (with someone) □ hand in hand □ hand it to someone □ hand-me-down □ hand over fist □ hand over hand □ hand something down to someone □ hand something in □ hand something on (to someone) □ hand something out (to someone) □ hand something over □ Hands off! □ Hands up! □ have a hand for someone or something □ have a hand in something □ have clean hands □ have one's hand in the till □ have one's hands full (with someone or something) □ have one's hands tied □ have someone or something in one's hands □ have something at hand □ have something in hand □ have something on one's hands □ have the upper hand on someone □ iron hand in the velvet glove □ keep one's hand in (something) □ keep one's hands off (someone or something) □ know someone or something like the back of one's hand □ know someone or something like the palm of one's hand □ lay one's hands on someone or something □ lend a hand □ lend (someone) a hand □ live from hand to mouth □ Many hands make light work. □ near at hand □ old hand at doing something □ on the one hand □ on the other hand □ one's hands are tied □ out of hand □ pay someone a left-handed compliment □ play into someone's hands □ put one's hand to the plough □ put one's hand(s) on something □ putty in someone's hands □ raise a hand (against someone or something) □ shake (hands) on something □ shake hands (with someone) □ show of hands □ show one's hand □ sit on one's hands □ soil one's hands □ take a hand in something □ take one's hands off (someone or something) □ take the law into one's own hands □ throw in one's hand □ tie someone's hands □ Time hangs heavy on someone's hands. □ try one's hand (at something) □ wait on someone hand and foot □ wash one's hands of someone or something □ win something hands down □ with both hands tied behind one's back □ with one hand tied behind one's back

HANDBASKET
go to hell in a handbasket

HANDLE
fly off the handle □ handle someone with kid gloves

HANDSOME
Handsome is as handsome does.

HANDY
come in handy

HANG
get the hang of something □ hang around (with someone) □ hang back □ hang by a hair □ hang fire □ hang in the balance □ hang in there □ hang loose □ hang on □ hang on someone's coat-tails □ hang on someone's every word □ hang on to someone or something □ Hang on to your hat! □ hang one's hat up somewhere □ hang out (somewhere) □ hang out with someone □ hang together □ hang up □ have something hanging over one's head □ keep someone or something hanging in mid-air □ leave someone or something hanging in mid-air □ let it all hang out □ not give a hang about anyone or anything □ Thereby hangs a tale. □ Time hangs heavy on someone's hands.

HA'PORTH
spoil the ship for a ha'porth of tar

HAPPEN
happen on someone or something □ no matter what (happens) □ sit back and let something happen

HAPPY
(as) happy as a lark □ (as) happy as a sandboy □ (as) happy as Larry □ (as) happy as the day is long □ strike a happy medium

HARD
(as) hard as nails □ be given a hard time □ come down hard on someone or something □ do something the hard way □ drive a hard bargain □ find something out the hard way □ get the hard sell □ give someone a hard time

□ give someone the hard sell □ hard-and-fast rule □ hard cash □ hard nut to crack □ hard on someone's heels □ hard on the heels of something □ hard pressed (to do something) □ hard put (to do something) □ hard up for something □ learn something the hard way □ no hard feelings □ play hard to get □ take a hard line (with someone)

HARDLY
hardly have time to breathe

HARE
(as) mad as a March hare

HARKEN
hark(en) back to something

HARP
harp on about something

HARRY
(every) Tom, Dick, and Harry

HASTE
Haste makes waste. □ in great haste

HASTY
beat a (hasty) retreat

HAT
at the drop of a hat □ be old hat □ eat one's hat □ Hang on to your hat! □ hang one's hat up somewhere □ Hold on to your hat! □ keep something under one's hat □ pass the hat round □ pull something out of a hat □ take off one's hat to someone □ talk through one's hat □ throw one's hat into the ring □ toss one's hat into the ring □ wear more than one hat

HATCH
count one's chickens before they are hatched □ Down the hatch!

HATCHET
bury the hatchet

HATE
hate someone's guts

HATTER
(as) mad as a hatter

HAUL
haul someone in □ haul someone over the coals

HAVOC
play havoc (with someone or something) □ wreak havoc with something

HAW
hem and haw □ hum and haw

HAWK
watch someone like a hawk

HAY
hit the hay □ Make hay while the sun shines.

HAYSTACK
like looking for a needle in a haystack

HAYWIRE
go haywire

HEAD
able to do something standing on one's head □ above someone's head □ bang one's head against a brick wall □ beat one's head against the wall □ bite someone's head off □ bring something to a head □ bury one's head in the sand □ can't make head or tail of someone or something □ come to a head □ count heads □ get a head start (on someone or something) □ get a swelled head □ get one's head above water □ get something into someone's thick head □ give someone a head start (on someone or something) □ give someone a swelled head □ go over someone's head □ go to someone's head □ have a good head on one's shoulders □ have a head start on someone or something □ have a price on one's head □ have a swelled head □ have eyes in the back of one's head □ have one's head in the clouds □ have something hanging over one's head □ head and shoulders above someone or something □ head for someone or something □ head over heels in love (with someone) □ head someone or something off □ head something up □ heads will roll □ hide one's head in the sand □ hit the nail on the head □ hold one's head up □ in over one's head □ keep a civil tongue (in one's head) □ keep one's head above water □ knock people's heads together □ lose one's head (over someone or something) □ make someone's head spin

□ make someone's head swim □ off the top of one's head □ on one's (own) head be it □ out of one's head □ put ideas into someone's head □ rear its ugly head □ run around like a chicken with its head cut off □ talk someone's head off □ talk through the back of one's head □ touched (in the head) □ trouble one's head about someone or something □ turn someone's head □ use one's head

HEALTH

Early to bed, early to rise(, makes a man healthy, wealthy, and wise). □ get a clean bill of health □ give someone a clean bill of health □ in the best of health

HEAR

hear from someone □ hear of someone or something □ so still you could hear a pin drop □ will not hear of something

HEART

be half-hearted about someone or something □ break someone's heart □ cross one's heart (and hope to die) □ die of a broken heart □ do someone's heart good □ eat one's heart out □ find it in one's heart to do something □ follow one's heart □ from the bottom of one's heart □ from the heart □ get to the heart of the matter □ have a heart □ have a heart of gold □ have a heart of stone □ have a heart-to-heart (talk) □ have one's heart in one's boots □ have one's heart in the right place □ have one's heart on one's sleeve □ have one's heart set against something □ have one's heart set on something □ know something by heart □ learn something by heart □ lose heart □ One's heart goes out to someone. □ one's heart is in one's mouth □ one's heart is in the right place □ one's heart is set against something □ one's heart is set on something □ one's heart misses a beat □ one's heart skips a beat □ one's heart stands still □ open one's heart (to someone) □ pour one's heart out (to someone) □ set one's heart against something □ set one's heart on something □ take

heart □ take something to heart □ to one's heart's content □ warm the cockles of someone's heart □ wear one's heart on one's sleeve □ with a heavy heart □ with all one's heart and soul

HEARTY

hale and hearty

HEAT

in a dead heat □ in heat □ put the heat on (someone) □ turn on the heat (on someone)

HEAVE

get the (old) heave ho □ give someone the (old) heave ho

HEAVEN

in seventh heaven □ manna from heaven □ move heaven and earth to do something □ The heavens opened.

HEAVY

heavy going □ Time hangs heavy on someone's hands. □ with a heavy heart

HEDGE

hedge one's bets

HEED

take heed

HEEL

Achilles' heel □ cool one's heels □ dig in one's heels □ down at heel □ hard on someone's heels □ hard on the heels of something □ head over heels in love (with someone) □ kick one's heels □ kick up one's heels □ set one back on one's heels □ take to one's heels □ well-heeled

HELL

(as) hot as hell □ (as) mad as hell □ come hell or high water □ for the hell of it □ get hell □ give someone hell □ go to hell □ go to hell in a handbasket □ have a snowball's chance in hell □ have hell to pay □ hell for leather □ like a bat out of hell □ raise hell (with someone or something) □ through hell and high water

HELP

help oneself □ help someone or something out (with someone or something) □ not able to help something □ not lift a finger (to help someone) □ pitch in (and help)

HEM
hem and haw □ hem someone or something in □ hemmed in

HEN
(as) rare as hen's teeth

HERE
have had it (up to here) □ here and now □ here and there □ here's to someone or something □ neither here nor there □ same here

HERRING
draw a red herring □ packed (in) like herring in a barrel □ red herring

HIDE
have someone's hide □ hide one's face in shame □ hide one's head in the sand □ hide one's light under a bushel □ neither hide nor hair □ tan someone's hide

HIGH
(as) high as a kite □ be flying high □ come hell or high water □ fly high □ go sky-high □ have (high) hopes of something □ high and mighty □ high-flyer □ high on something □ high spot □ high-tail it out of somewhere □ hit the high spots □ hunt high and low for someone or something □ in high gear □ it's high time □ knee-high to a grasshopper □ leave someone high and dry □ look for someone or something high and low □ look high and low (for someone or something) □ run high □ search high and low for someone or something □ speak highly of someone or something □ think highly of someone or something □ through hell and high water

HILL
(as) old as the hills □ over the hill

HINGE
hinge on something

HINT
take a hint

HIP
shoot from the hip

HISTORY
go down in history

HIT
hit a snag □ hit and miss □ hit bottom □ hit it off (with someone) □ hit on something □ hit or miss □ hit (someone) below the belt □ hit someone between the eyes □ hit (someone or something) like a ton of bricks □ hit the bull's-eye □ hit the ceiling □ hit the hay □ hit the high spots □ hit the jackpot □ hit the nail on the head □ hit the roof □ hit the spot □ hit (up)on something □ make a hit (with someone or something)

HITCH
hitch a lift

HO
get the (old) heave ho □ give someone the (old) heave ho

HOBSON'S
Hobson's choice

HOE
tough row to hoe

HOG
go the whole hog □ road-hog

HOIST
hoist with one's own petard

HOLD
can't hold a candle to someone □ catch hold of someone or something □ Don't hold your breath. □ get hold of someone or something □ have hold of someone or something □ hold a grudge (against someone) □ hold a meeting □ hold all the cards □ hold forth □ Hold it! □ hold no brief for someone or something □ hold off (doing something) □ hold on □ hold (on) tight □ hold on to someone or something □ Hold on to your hat! □ hold one's breath □ hold one's fire □ hold one's head up □ hold one's own □ hold one's peace □ hold one's temper □ hold one's tongue □ hold out □ hold out (for someone or something) □ hold out the olive branch □ hold someone accountable (for something) □ hold someone down □ hold someone or something at bay □ hold some-

one or something back □ hold someone or something in check □ hold someone or something off □ hold someone or something up □ hold someone or something up as an example □ hold something against someone □ hold still □ hold still (for someone or something) □ hold the fort □ hold true □ hold up □ hold water □ hold with something □ Hold your horses! □ lay hold of someone or something □ leave someone holding the baby □ no holds barred □ not hold water □ on hold □ put someone or something on hold □ take hold of someone or something □ won't hold water

HOLE

hole-and-corner □ hole in one □ hole-in-the-corner □ hole up (somewhere) □ in a hole □ Money burns a hole in someone's pocket. □ pick holes in something □ square peg in a round hole

HOLIDAY

busman's holiday □ on holiday

HOLY

holier-than-thou

HOME

at home with someone or something □ bring home the bacon □ bring something home to someone □ Charity begins at home. □ close to home □ come home to roost □ come too close to home □ drive something home □ eat someone out of house and home □ hammer something home □ home and dry □ home in (on someone or something) □ keep the home fires burning □ make oneself at home □ nothing to write home about □ romp home □ see someone home □ till the cows come home

HONEST

honest to goodness

HONEYMOON

The honeymoon is over.

HONOUR

do the honours □ honour someone's

cheque □ in honour of someone or something □ on one's honour

HOOF

do something on the hoof

HOOK

by hook or by crook □ get off the hook □ get someone off the hook □ hook something up □ hooked on something □ let someone off (the hook) □ swallow something hook, line, and sinker

HOOKEY

play hookey

HOOP

jump through a hoop

HOOT

not care two hoots about someone or something □ not give a hoot about anyone or anything □ not give two hoots about someone or something

HOP

catch someone on the hop □ Hop it!

HOPE

cross one's heart (and hope to die) □ have (high) hopes of something □ hope against hope

HORIZON

on the horizon

HORN

horn in (on something) □ lock horns (with someone) □ on the horns of a dilemma □ take the bull by the horns

HORNET

stir up a hornets' nest

HORSE

change horses in mid-stream □ dark horse □ Don't look a gift horse in the mouth. □ drive a coach and horses through something □ eat like a horse □ flog a dead horse □ Hold your horses! □ horse around □ horse of a different colour □ horse of another colour □ horse-play □ horse sense □ put the cart before the horse □ straight from the horse's mouth □ Wild horses couldn't drag someone. □ work like a horse

HOT
(as) hot as hell ☐ blow hot and cold
☐ full of hot air ☐ hot and bothered
☐ Hot enough for you? ☐ hot on
something ☐ hot under the collar ☐
in hot water ☐ in the hot seat ☐
make it hot for someone ☐ on the hot
seat ☐ sell like hot cakes ☐ strike
while the iron is hot

HOTFOOT
hotfoot it out of somewhere

HOUR
after hours ☐ all hours (of the day and
night) ☐ at the eleventh hour ☐ by
the hour ☐ eleventh-hour decision ☐
for hours on end ☐ keep late hours ☐
on the hour ☐ small hours ☐ until
all hours ☐ zero hour

HOUSE
(as) safe as houses ☐ bring the house
down ☐ eat someone out of house and
home ☐ house-proud ☐ keep house
☐ like a house on fire ☐ on the house
☐ put one's house in order

HOVER
hover over someone or something

HOW
know-how ☐ That's how it goes.

HUE
hue and cry

HUFF
in a huff

HUM
hum and haw

HUMAN
milk of human kindness

HUMBLE
eat humble pie

HUMP
over the hump

HUNDRED
one in a hundred

HUNG
hung up (on someone or something)

HUNGRY
(as) hungry as a hunter

HUNT
hunt high and low for someone or
something

HUNTER
(as) hungry as a hunter

HURRY
hurry back

HURT
cry before one is hurt ☐ hurt someone's feelings

HUSH
hush-money ☐ hush someone or
something up

HYDE
Jekyll and Hyde

ICE
break the ice ☐ cut no ice ☐ put
something on ice ☐ (skating) on thin
ice

IDEA
get a bright idea ☐ get a rough idea
(about something) ☐ give someone a
rough idea (about something) ☐ have
a bright idea ☐ have a rough idea
about something ☐ put ideas into
someone's head ☐ What's the (big)
idea?

IDIOT
take someone for an idiot

IDLY
sit (idly) by

IF
If the cap fits, wear it. ☐ if the worst
comes to the worst ☐ If you give one
an inch, one will take a mile. ☐ look as
if butter wouldn't melt in one's mouth
☐ make as if to do something ☐ no
ifs about it ☐ not know if one is coming or going

ILL
ill at ease ☐ ill-gotten gains ☐ take ill
☐ taken ill

IMAGE
be the spit and image of someone ☐ be
the spitting image of someone ☐ spitting image

IMPOSE
impose on someone ☐ impose something on someone

IMPRESSION
make an impression (on someone)

IMPROVE
improve (up)on something

INCH
come within an inch of doing something ☐ every inch a something ☐ Give one an inch, and one will take a mile. ☐ If you give one an inch, one will take a mile. ☐ inch along (something) ☐ inch by inch ☐ within an inch of doing something ☐ within an inch of one's life

INCUMBENT
incumbent upon someone to do something

INDEED
A friend in need is a friend indeed.

INFORMATION
mine of information

INJURY
add insult to injury

INNOCENT
(as) innocent as a lamb

INQUIRE
inquire after someone

INS
ins and outs of something

INSIDE
know something inside out

INSTANCE
in the first instance

INSTRUMENTAL
instrumental in doing something

INSULT
add insult to injury

INTEREST
have a vested interest in something ☐ in an interesting condition ☐ in one's (own) (best) interests ☐ in the interest(s) of someone or something ☐ take an interest (in something)

INVOLVE
be involved with someone or something

☐ get involved (with someone or something)

IRON
have too many irons in the fire ☐ iron hand in the velvet glove ☐ iron something out ☐ rule someone or something with a rod of iron ☐ strike while the iron is hot

ISSUE
make an issue of something ☐ take issue (with someone)

ITCHY
have an itchy palm

IVORY
live in an ivory tower

JACK
All work and no play makes Jack a dull boy. ☐ before you can say Jack Robinson ☐ every man jack (of someone) ☐ jack of all trades ☐ jack something in ☐ jack something up

JACKPOT
hit the jackpot

JAM
get out of a jam ☐ get someone out of a jam ☐ in a jam ☐ jam tomorrow ☐ money for jam

JAZZ
jazz something up

JEKYLL
Jekyll and Hyde

JIFFY
in a jiffy

JOAN
Darby and Joan

JOB
devil of a job ☐ devil's own job ☐ fall down on the job ☐ job lot ☐ Job's comforter ☐ just the job ☐ lie down on the job ☐ nine-to-five job ☐ on the job ☐ put-up job

JOCKEY
jockey for position

JOHNNY
johnny-come-lately

JOIN
join forces (with someone) □ Join the club!

JOINT
put someone's nose out of joint

JOKE
able to take a joke □ crack a joke □ joking apart □ no joke □ standing joke

JOLLY
jolly someone along

JONES
Davy Jones's Locker □ go to Davy Jones's locker □ keep up (with the Joneses)

JOWL
cheek by jowl

JOY
be bursting with joy □ burst with joy □ wish someone joy of something

JUDGE
(as) sober as a judge □ judge one on one's own merit(s) □ judge something on its own merit(s) □ judging by something

JUICE
stew in one's own juice

JUMP
jump at something □ jump at the chance (to do something) □ jump at the opportunity (to do something) □ jump bail □ jump down someone's throat □ jump off the deep end □ jump on the bandwagon □ jump out of one's skin □ jump the gun □ jump through a hoop □ jump to conclusions □ jump to it □ jumping-off point □ one jump ahead (of someone or something)

JUST
get one's just desserts □ in (just) a second □ just as soon do something □ just in case □ just one of those things □ just so □ just the job □ just the same □ just what the doctor ordered

JUSTICE
do justice to something □ miscarriage of justice □ poetic justice

KEEL
keel over □ keep on an even keel □ keep something on an even keel

KEEP
earn one's keep □ for keeps □ in keeping (with something) □ keep a civil tongue (in one's head) □ keep a stiff upper lip □ keep a straight face □ keep abreast (of something) □ keep after someone □ keep ahead (of someone or something) □ keep an eye on someone or something □ keep an eye out (for someone or something) □ keep at someone □ keep at someone or something □ keep away (from someone or something) □ keep body and soul together □ keep company with someone □ keep cool □ keep good time □ keep house □ keep in touch (with someone) □ keep in with someone □ keep late hours □ keep off (something) □ keep on an even keel □ keep on (doing something) □ keep on someone □ keep on the good side of someone □ keep on (with something) □ keep one's chin up □ keep one's distance (from someone or something) □ keep one's ear to the ground □ keep one's end of the bargain □ keep one's eye on someone or something □ keep one's eye on the ball □ keep one's eyes open (for someone or something) □ keep one's eyes peeled (for someone or something) □ keep one's feet on the ground □ keep one's fingers crossed (for someone or something) □ keep one's hand in (something) □ keep one's hands off (someone or something) □ keep one's head above water □ keep one's mouth shut (about someone or something) □ keep one's nose clean □ keep one's nose in the air □ keep one's nose out of someone's business □ keep one's nose to the grindstone □ keep one's own counsel □ keep one's side of the bargain □ keep one's temper □ keep one's weather eye open □ keep one's wits about one □ keep one's word □ keep oneself to oneself □ keep out (of something or somewhere) □ keep pace (with someone or something) □ keep quiet (about someone or something) □

keep someone company □ keep someone from doing something □ keep someone in line □ keep someone in stitches □ keep someone on tenterhooks □ keep someone or something at a distance □ keep someone or something at arm's length □ keep someone or something at bay □ keep someone or something back □ keep someone or something down □ keep someone or something hanging in mid-air □ keep someone or something in check □ keep someone or something in mind □ keep someone or something off □ keep someone or something out of the way □ keep someone or something quiet □ keep someone or something up □ keep someone out in the cold □ keep someone posted □ keep something for another occasion □ keep something on an even keel □ keep something to oneself □ keep something under one's hat □ keep something under wraps □ keep still □ keep still about someone or something □ keep tab(s) (on someone or something) □ keep the ball rolling □ keep the home fires burning □ keep the lid on something □ keep the wolf from the door □ keep time □ keep to oneself □ keep track (of someone or something) □ keep up an act □ keep up (with someone or something) □ keep up (with the Joneses) □ keep up (with the times) □ keep watch (on someone or something) □ keep watch (over someone or something) □ Keep your shirt on! □ out of keeping with something

KEEPER
Finders keepers(, losers weepers).

KEG
sitting on a powder keg

KEN
beyond one's ken

KETTLE
fine kettle of fish □ pot calling the kettle black

KEY
keyed up

KIBOSH
put the kibosh on something

KICK
alive and kicking □ for kicks □ get a kick out of someone or something □ give someone a kick □ kick a habit □ kick off □ kick one's heels □ kick oneself (for doing something) □ kick over □ kick someone or something around □ kick someone or something out □ kick something in □ kick the bucket □ kick the habit □ kick up a fuss □ kick up a row □ kick up one's heels □ to kick off with

KID
handle someone with kid gloves □ kid's stuff □ no kidding

KILL
Curiosity killed the cat. □ dressed to kill □ in at the kill □ kill someone or something off □ kill the fatted calf □ kill the goose that laid the golden egg □ kill time □ kill two birds with one stone □ make a killing □ There's more than one way to kill a cat.

KILLER
lady-killer

KILTER
out of kilter

KIND
in kind □ kind of (something) □ nothing of the kind □ take kindly to something □ two of a kind

KINDNESS
milk of human kindness

KING
fit for a king

KISS
kiss and make up □ kiss of death □ kiss something goodbye

KITCHEN
everything but the kitchen sink

KITE
(as) high as a kite □ fly a kite

KITTEN
(as) weak as a kitten

KNEE
knee-high to a grasshopper

KNIFE
go under the knife

KNIT
knit one's brow

KNOCK
knock about (somewhere) □ knock it off □ knock off work □ knock on wood □ knock one off one's feet □ knock people's heads together □ knock someone cold □ knock someone dead □ knock someone down with a feather □ knock someone or something about □ knock someone or something around □ knock someone or something down □ knock someone or something off □ knock someone or something out □ knock someone's block off □ knock something back

KNOT
at a rate of knots □ tie someone in knots □ tie the knot

KNOW
(as) far as anyone knows □ before you know it □ in the know □ know a thing or two (about someone or something) □ know all the tricks of the trade □ know better □ know-how □ know one's ABC □ know one's onions □ know one's place □ know one's stuff □ know one's way about □ know one's way around □ know someone by sight □ know someone or something like a book □ know someone or something like the back of one's hand □ know someone or something like the palm of one's hand □ know something by heart □ know something from memory □ know something inside out □ know something only too well □ know the ropes □ know the score □ know what's what □ know where someone stands (on someone or something) □ know which is which □ know which side one's bread is buttered on □ not know if one is coming or going □ not know someone from Adam □ not know the first thing about someone or something □ not know where to turn □ not know

whether one is coming or going □ not know which way to turn □ so far as anyone knows □ you know

KNOWLEDGE
A little knowledge is a dangerous thing. □ to the best of one's knowledge

KNUCKLE
get one's knuckles rapped □ have one's knuckles rapped □ knuckle down (to something) □ knuckle under (to someone or something) □ near the knuckle □ rap someone's knuckles

LABOUR
labour of love

LACE
lace into someone or something

LADDER
at the bottom of the ladder

LADIES
ladies' man

LADY
lady-killer

LAG
lag behind (someone or something)

LAID
kill the goose that laid the golden egg □ laid back □ laid up

LAMB
(as) innocent as a lamb □ in two shakes of a lamb's tail □ like a lamb to the slaughter

LAME
lame duck

LAMP
smell of the lamp

LAND
Cloud-cuckoo-land □ land a blow (somewhere) □ land of Nod □ land on both feet □ land on one's feet □ land someone with someone or something □ land up somehow or somewhere □ live off the fat of the land

LANDSLIDE
landslide victory

LANGUAGE
speak the same language ☐ use strong language

LAP
in the lap of luxury ☐ lap something up

LARGE
(as) large as life ☐ (as) large as life (and twice as ugly) ☐ at large ☐ by and large ☐ loom large

LARK
(as) happy as a lark

LARRY
(as) happy as Larry

LASH
get a tongue-lashing ☐ give someone a tongue-lashing ☐ lash out (at someone or something)

LAST
as a last resort ☐ at (long) last ☐ at the last minute ☐ be the last person ☐ breathe one's last ☐ every last one ☐ get the last laugh ☐ get the last word ☐ have the last laugh ☐ have the last word ☐ He who laughs last laughs longest. ☐ last but not least ☐ last-ditch effort ☐ last something out ☐ on someone's or something's last legs ☐ see the last of someone or something ☐ That's the last straw. ☐ to the last

LATE
at the latest ☐ better late than never ☐ johnny-come-lately ☐ keep late hours ☐ late in life ☐ late in the day ☐ of late ☐ sooner or later

LATHER
in a lather

LAUGH
burst out laughing ☐ die laughing ☐ get the last laugh ☐ have the last laugh ☐ He who laughs last laughs longest. ☐ laugh out of the other side of one's mouth ☐ laugh something off ☐ laugh something out of court ☐ laugh up one's sleeve ☐ no laughing matter

LAUNCH
launch forth (into something) ☐ launch forth (on something) ☐ launch into something

LAUREL
look to one's laurels ☐ rest on one's laurels

LAW
law unto oneself ☐ lay down the law ☐ Possession is nine points of the law. ☐ take the law into one's own hands

LAY
kill the goose that laid the golden egg ☐ laid back ☐ laid up ☐ lay a finger on someone or something ☐ lay about one ☐ lay an egg ☐ lay down one's life (for someone or something) ☐ lay down the law ☐ lay eyes on someone or something ☐ lay hold of someone or something ☐ lay into someone or something ☐ lay it on thick ☐ lay off (someone or something) ☐ lay one's cards on the table ☐ lay one's hands on someone or something ☐ lay someone off ☐ lay someone or something out ☐ lay someone up ☐ lay something aside ☐ lay something by ☐ lay something down ☐ lay something in ☐ lay something on the line ☐ lay something to rest ☐ lay something to waste ☐ lay something up ☐ lay the blame on someone or something ☐ lay the finger on someone

LEAD
(a case of) the blind leading the blind ☐ All roads lead to Rome. ☐ blind leading the blind ☐ go down like a lead balloon ☐ lead a dog's life ☐ lead off ☐ lead someone a merry dance ☐ lead someone by the nose ☐ lead someone on ☐ lead someone on a merry chase ☐ lead someone to believe something ☐ lead someone to do something ☐ lead someone up the garden path ☐ lead the life of Riley ☐ lead the way ☐ lead up to something ☐ swing the lead

LEAF
leaf through something ☐ take a leaf out of someone's book ☐ turn over a new leaf

LEAGUE
in league (with someone) ☐ not in the same league as someone or something

LEAK
leak something (out)

LEAN
lean on someone ☐ lean over backwards to do something

LEAP
by leaps and bounds ☐ leap at the opportunity (to do something) ☐ leap to conclusions

LEARN
A little learning is a dangerous thing. ☐ learn something by heart ☐ learn something by rote ☐ learn something from the bottom up ☐ learn something the hard way ☐ learn the ropes ☐ We live and learn.

LEASE
new lease on life

LEAST
last but not least ☐ least of all ☐ Least said soonest mended. ☐ line of least resistance ☐ not in the least ☐ to say the least ☐ when least expected

LEATHER
hell for leather

LEAVE
absent without leave ☐ leave a bad taste in someone's mouth ☐ leave a lot to be desired ☐ leave a sinking ship ☐ leave no stone unturned ☐ leave off (doing something) ☐ leave one to one's fate ☐ leave oneself wide open for something ☐ leave someone flat ☐ leave someone for dead ☐ leave someone high and dry ☐ leave someone holding the baby ☐ leave someone in peace ☐ leave someone in the lurch ☐ leave someone or something alone ☐ leave someone or something behind ☐ leave someone or something hanging in mid-air ☐ leave someone or something out ☐ leave someone out in the cold ☐ leave something for another occasion ☐ leave something on ☐ leave well alone ☐ leave word (with someone) ☐ take it or leave it ☐ take leave of one's senses ☐ take leave of someone ☐ take (one's) leave (of someone)

LEFT
have something left ☐ left, right, and centre ☐ pay someone a left-handed compliment ☐ right and left

LEG
Break a leg! ☐ cost an arm and a leg ☐ have one's tail between one's legs ☐ not have a leg to stand on ☐ on someone's or something's last legs ☐ one's tail is between one's legs ☐ pay an arm and a leg (for something) ☐ pull someone's leg ☐ stretch one's legs

LEISURE
at (one's) leisure

LEND
lend a hand ☐ lend an ear (to someone) ☐ lend oneself or itself to something ☐ lend (someone) a hand

LENGTH
at length ☐ at some length ☐ go to any lengths ☐ keep someone or something at arm's length

LESS
couldn't care less ☐ in less than no time ☐ less than pleased ☐ more or less

LESSON
teach someone a lesson

LET
let alone someone or something ☐ Let bygones be bygones. ☐ let go (of someone or something) ☐ let her rip ☐ let it all hang out ☐ let it rip ☐ let off steam ☐ let on ☐ let one's hair down ☐ let oneself go ☐ Let sleeping dogs lie. ☐ let someone down ☐ let someone have it ☐ let someone in for something ☐ let someone in on something ☐ let someone off (the hook) ☐ let someone or something alone ☐ let someone or something be ☐ let someone or something go ☐ let someone or something in ☐ let someone or something loose ☐ let someone or something off ☐ let someone or something out ☐ let something get out ☐ let something ride ☐ let something slide ☐ let something slip by ☐ let something slip (out) ☐ let the cat out of the bag ☐ let the chance slip by ☐ let the grass grow under one's feet ☐ let up (on someone or something) ☐ let well alone ☐ live and let live ☐ sit back and let something happen

LETTER
to the letter

LEVEL
find one's own level □ level off □ level something off □ level with someone □ on the level

LIBERTY
at liberty □ take liberties with someone or something □ take the liberty of doing something

LICK
get a licking □ give someone a licking □ give something a lick and a promise □ lick one's lips □ lick something into shape □ take a licking

LID
blow the lid off (something) □ flip one's lid □ keep the lid on something □ take the lid off something

LIE
Let sleeping dogs lie. □ lie down on the job □ lie in state □ lie in wait for someone or something □ lie low □ lie through one's teeth □ take something lying down

LIEU
in lieu of something

LIFE
all walks of life □ (as) large as life □ (as) large as life (and twice as ugly) □ bet one's life □ come to life □ facts of life □ for the life of one □ get the shock of one's life □ have the time of one's life □ in the prime of life □ late in life □ lay down one's life (for someone or something) □ lead a dog's life □ lead the life of Riley □ life (and soul) of the party □ live a dog's life □ make life miserable for someone □ matter of life and death □ milestone in someone's life □ never in one's life □ new lease on life □ not on your life □ one's way of life □ run for one's life □ seamy side of life □ Such is life! □ take one's own life □ Variety is the spice of life. □ within an inch of one's life

LIFETIME
once-in-a-lifetime chance

LIFT
hitch a lift □ not lift a finger (to help someone) □ thumb a lift

LIGHT
according to one's (own) lights □ (as) light as a feather □ begin to see the light □ bring something to light □ come to light □ get the green light □ give someone the green light □ hide one's light under a bushel □ in the light of something □ light into someone or something □ light out (for somewhere) □ light out (of somewhere) □ make light of something □ Many hands make light work. □ out like a light □ see the light □ see the light at the end of the tunnel □ see the light of day □ shed (some) light on something

LIGHTLY
get off lightly

LIGHTNING
(as) quick as (greased) lightning □ Lightning never strikes twice (in the same place).

LIKE
and the like □ avoid someone or something like the plague □ eat like a bird □ eat like a horse □ feel like a million dollars □ feel like a new person □ feel like something □ fit like a glove □ go down like a lead balloon □ go like clockwork □ hit (someone or something) like a ton of bricks □ know someone or something like a book □ know someone or something like the back of one's hand □ know someone or something like the palm of one's hand □ like a bat out of hell □ like a bolt out of the blue □ like a fish out of water □ like a house on fire □ like a lamb to the slaughter □ like a sitting duck □ like a three-ring circus □ like crazy □ like it or lump it □ like looking for a needle in a haystack □ like mad □ like nothing on earth □ like one of the family □ like sitting ducks □ like water off a duck's back □ likes of someone □ look like a million dollars □ look like someone or something □ look like the cat that swallowed the canary □ out like a light □ packed

(in) like herring in a barrel □ packed
(in) like sardines □ read someone like
a book □ run around like a chicken
with its head cut off □ sell like hot
cakes □ sleep like a log □ sleep like a
top □ spread like wildfire □ stick
out like a sore thumb □ take a liking to
someone or something □ to someone's
liking □ watch someone like a hawk
□ work like a horse

LIKELY
(as) likely as not

LILY
gild the lily

LIMB
out on a limb

LIMBO
in limbo

LIMELIGHT
in the limelight

LIMIT
go to the limit □ off limits □ The
sky's the limit. □ within limits

LINE
bottom line □ draw a line between
something and something else □ draw
the line (at something) □ drop someone
a line □ end of the line □ fall into line
□ fluff one's lines □ in line with something □ in the line of duty □ keep
someone in line □ lay something on the
line □ line of least resistance □ line
one's own pockets □ line someone or
something up with something □ line
someone up for something □ line up
(with something) □ make a bee-line for
someone or something □ muff one's
lines □ out of line □ out of line (with
something) □ party line □ read between the lines □ shoot a line □ sign
on the dotted line □ step out of line □
swallow something hook, line, and sinker
□ take a hard line (with someone) □
toe the line

LINEN
air one's dirty linen in public □ wash
one's dirty linen in public

LINING
Every cloud has a silver lining.

LION
beard the lion in his den □ lion's share
(of something)

LIP
button one's lip □ keep a stiff upper
lip □ lick one's lips □ pay lip-service
(to something)

LIST
enter the lists □ on the waiting-list

LISTEN
listen in (on someone or something) □
listen to reason

LITTLE
A little bird told me. □ A little knowledge is a dangerous thing. □ He who
laughs last laughs longest. □ A little
learning is a dangerous thing. □ little
by little □ make little of someone or
something □ precious little □ think
little of someone or something □ twist
someone around one's little finger

LIVE
beat the living daylights out of someone
□ every living soul □ have to live
with something □ live a dog's life □
live and let live □ live beyond one's
means □ live by one's wits □ live for
the moment □ live from hand to
mouth □ live in □ live in an ivory
tower □ live it up □ live next door
(to someone) □ live off someone or
something □ live off the fat of the
land □ live on borrowed time □ live
on something □ live out of a suitcase
□ live something down □ live
through something □ live up to something □ live within one's means □
make a living □ not a living soul □
scare the (living) daylights out of someone □ We live and learn.

LIVELONG
all the livelong day

LOAD
get a load of someone or something □
load off one's mind □ take the load off
one's feet

LOAF
Half a loaf is better than none.

LOCK

lock horns (with someone) □ lock someone or something in something □ lock someone or something up □ lock, stock, and barrel

LOCKER

Davy Jones's locker □ go to Davy Jones's locker

LOG

(as) easy as falling off a log □ sleep like a log

LOGGERHEADS

at loggerheads (with someone)

LOIN

gird (up) one's loins

LONG

all day long □ all night long □ (as) happy as the day is long □ at (long) last □ go a long way in doing something □ go a long way towards doing something □ have come a long way □ He who laughs last laughs longest. □ in the long run □ Long time no see. □ make a long story short □ not by a long shot □ not long for this world □ so long

LOOK

dirty look □ Don't look a gift horse in the mouth. □ like looking for a needle in a haystack □ look after someone or something □ look as if butter wouldn't melt in one's mouth □ look back on someone or something □ look daggers at someone □ look down on someone or something □ look down one's nose at someone or something □ look for someone or something □ look for someone or something high and low □ look for trouble □ look forward to something □ look high and low (for someone or something) □ look in (on someone or something) □ look into something □ look like a million dollars □ look like someone or something □ look like the cat that swallowed the canary □ look on (at something) □ look on someone as something □ look out for someone or something □ look someone in the eye □ look someone in the face □ look someone or something over □ look someone or something up

look the other way □ look to one's laurels □ look to someone or something (for something) □ look up and down something □ look up to someone □ make someone look good □ make someone look ridiculous □ on the look-out (for someone or something) □ take a look (at someone or something) □ Things are looking up.

LOOM

loom large

LOOSE

at a loose end □ break loose (from someone or something) □ break something loose □ cut loose (from someone or something) □ hang loose □ have a screw loose □ let someone or something loose □ on the loose □ play fast and loose (with someone or something)

LORD

lord it over someone

LOSE

lose face □ lose ground □ lose heart □ lose one's cool □ lose one's grip □ lose one's head (over someone or something) □ lose one's marbles □ lose one's mind □ lose one's reason □ lose one's shirt □ lose one's temper □ lose one's touch (with someone or something) □ lose one's train of thought □ lose oneself in something □ lose out (on something) □ lose out to someone or something □ lose sight of someone or something □ lose sleep over someone or something □ lose touch (with someone or something) □ lose track (of someone or something)

LOSER

Finders keepers(, losers weepers).

LOSS

at a loss for words □ cut someone's losses □ dead loss

LOST

get lost □ lost in thought □ lost on someone □ lost to something □ make up for lost time □ no love lost (between someone and someone else)

LOT

cast one's lot in with someone □ cover a lot of ground □ have a lot going for one □ have a lot of promise □ have a lot on one's mind □ job lot □ leave a lot to be desired □ quite a lot □ think a lot of someone or something

LOUD
Actions speak louder than words. □ say something out loud □ think out loud

LOUSE
louse something up

LOUSY
lousy with something

LOVE
cupboard love □ fall in love (with someone) □ head over heels in love (with someone) □ in love (with someone or something) □ labour of love □ love at first sight □ make love (to someone) □ no love lost (between someone and someone else) □ not for love nor money

LOVELY
lovely weather for ducks

LOW
get the low-down (on someone or something) □ give someone the low-down on someone or something □ have a low boiling-point □ hunt high and low for someone or something □ lie low □ look for someone or something high and low □ look high and low (for someone or something) □ lower one's sights □ lower one's voice □ search high and low for someone or something

LUCK
(as) luck would have it □ down on one's luck □ in luck □ luck out □ one's luck runs out □ out of luck □ press one's luck □ push one's luck □ stroke of luck □ Tough luck! □ try one's luck (at something) □ Worse luck!

LUCKY
get a lucky break □ lucky dip □ strike it lucky □ thank one's lucky stars

LULL
lull someone into a false sense of security

LUMP
get a lump in one's throat □ have a lump in one's throat □ like it or lump it

LUNCH
out to lunch

LURCH
leave someone in the lurch

LUTE
rift in the lute

LUXURY
in the lap of luxury

MAD
(as) mad as a hatter □ (as) mad as a March hare □ (as) mad as hell □ drive someone mad □ in a mad rush □ like mad

MADE
have something made □ made for doing something □ made for each other □ made to measure □ made to order

MADNESS
method in one's madness

MAIDEN
maiden speech □ maiden voyage

MAN
dirty old man □ Early to bed, early to rise(, makes a man healthy, wealthy, and wise). □ every man jack (of someone) □ ladies' man □ man about town □ man in the street □ man to man □ marked man □ odd man out □ One man's meat is another man's poison. □ see a man about a dog

MANGER
dog in the manger

MANNA
manna from heaven

MANNER
all manner of someone or something □ devil-may-care manner

MANY
have too many irons in the fire □ in so many words □ Many hands make light work. □ many is the time □ Too many cooks spoil the broth.

MARBLE
lose one's marbles ☐ not have all one's marbles

MARCH
(as) mad as a March hare ☐ get one's marching orders ☐ get one's marching papers ☐ give one one's marching orders ☐ steal a march on someone

MARE
by shank's mare

MARINE
tell it to the marines

MARK
mark my word(s) ☐ mark someone or something down ☐ mark something up ☐ marked man ☐ wide of the mark ☐ X marks the spot

MARKET
drug on the market ☐ in the market (for something) ☐ on the market ☐ play the market

MARROW
chilled to the marrow

MARTIN
all my eye (and Betty Martin)

MAST
at half-mast ☐ nail one's colours to the mast

MASTER
be a past master at something

MATCH
meet one's match ☐ slanging match ☐ whole shooting-match

MATTER
as a matter of course ☐ as a matter of fact ☐ crux of the matter ☐ for that matter ☐ get to the heart of the matter ☐ grey matter ☐ matter-of-fact ☐ matter of life and death ☐ matter of opinion ☐ no laughing matter ☐ no matter what (happens)

MAY
come what may ☐ devil-may-care attitude ☐ devil-may-care manner ☐ to whom it may concern

MEAL
make a meal of something ☐ square meal

MEALY
mealy-mouthed

MEAN
beyond one's means ☐ by all means ☐ by no means ☐ live beyond one's means ☐ live within one's means ☐ mean nothing (to someone) ☐ mean something (to someone) ☐ mean to (do something) ☐ one means business ☐ ways and means

MEASURE
beyond measure ☐ for good measure ☐ made to measure ☐ measure up (to someone or something) ☐ measure up (to someone's expectations)

MEAT
One man's meat is another man's poison.

MECCA
Mecca for someone

MEDICINE
dose of one's own medicine ☐ take one's medicine

MEDIUM
strike a happy medium

MEET
call a meeting ☐ call the meeting to order ☐ hold a meeting ☐ make (both) ends meet ☐ meet one's end ☐ meet one's match ☐ meet one's Waterloo ☐ meet someone half-way ☐ meet the requirements (for something) ☐ more (to something) than meets the eye

MELT
look as if butter wouldn't melt in one's mouth ☐ melt in one's mouth

MEMORY
commit something to memory ☐ know something from memory

MEN
fill dead men's shoes ☐ separate the men from the boys ☐ step into dead men's shoes

MEND
Least said soonest mended. ☐ mend

(one's) fences □ mend one's ways □ on the mend

MENTION
mention something in passing

MERCY
at someone's mercy □ at the mercy of someone □ thankful for small mercies □ throw oneself at the mercy of someone

MERIT
judge one on one's own merit(s) □ judge something on its own merit(s)

MERRY
lead someone a merry dance □ lead someone on a merry chase □ make merry □ The more the merrier.

MESS
get into a mess □ get out of a mess □ make a mess (of something) □ mess about (with someone or something) □ mess around (with someone or something) □ mess something up

MESSAGE
get the message

MET
hail-fellow-well-met

METHOD
method in one's madness

MICE
When the cat's away the mice will play.

MID
change horses in mid-stream □ keep someone or something hanging in mid-air □ leave someone or something hanging in mid-air

MIDAS
have the Midas touch

MIDDLE
caught in the middle □ in the middle of nowhere □ middle-of-the-road □ pig(gy)-in-the-middle □ play both ends (against the middle) □ smack dab in the middle

MIDDLING
fair-to-middling

MIDNIGHT
burn the midnight oil

MIGHT
pigs might fly

MIGHTY
high and mighty

MILDLY
to put it mildly

MILE
by a mile □ Give one an inch, and one will take a mile. □ If you give one an inch, one will take a mile. □ miss (something) by a mile □ stand out a mile □ stick out a mile

MILESTONE
milestone in someone's life

MILK
cry over spilled milk □ milk of human kindness

MILL
grist to the mill □ have been through the mill □ run of the mill

MILLION
feel like a million dollars □ look like a million dollars □ one in a million

MILLPOND
(as) calm as a millpond

MILLSTONE
millstone about one's neck

MINCE
mince (one's) words

MINCEMEAT
make mincemeat of someone

MIND
bear someone or something in mind □ blow someone's mind □ boggle someone's mind □ change someone's mind □ come to mind □ cross someone's mind □ enter one's mind □ get someone or something out of one's mind □ give someone a piece of one's mind □ have a lot on one's mind □ have half a mind to do something □ have someone or something on one's mind □ have something in mind □ in one's mind's eye □ in one's right mind □ keep someone or something in mind □ load off one's mind □ lose one's mind □ make someone's mind up □ mind one's own business □ mind one's P's and Q's □ mind

423

you □ never mind □ on one's mind □ one-track mind □ out of one's mind □ Out of sight, out of mind. □ pass through someone's mind □ presence of mind □ put someone in mind of someone or something □ put someone or something out of one's mind □ read someone's mind □ slip one's mind □ speak one's mind □ time out of mind □ weigh on someone's mind

MINE
back to the salt mines □ mine of information □ Your guess is as good as mine.

MINT
in mint condition

MINUTE
at the last minute □ every minute counts □ up-to-the-minute

MISCARRIAGE
miscarriage of justice

MISCHIEF
make mischief

MISERABLE
make life miserable for someone □ make oneself miserable

MISS
give something a miss □ have a near miss □ hit and miss □ hit or miss □ miss out (on something) □ miss (something) by a mile □ miss the boat □ miss the point □ one's heart misses a beat

MISTAKE
make no mistake about it □ mistake someone for someone else □ mistake something for something else

MIX
get mixed up □ have mixed feelings (about someone or something) □ mix it □ mix someone or something up □ mix someone up with someone else □ mix something up with something else □ mixed bag

MOLEHILL
make a mountain out of a molehill

MOMENT
every moment counts □ live for the moment □ moment of truth □ on the spur of the moment

MONEY
A fool and his money are soon parted. □ fork money out (for something) □ get a good run for one's money □ get one's money's worth □ give one a run for one's money □ have money to burn □ hush-money □ in the money □ make good money □ Money burns a hole in someone's pocket. □ money for jam □ money for old rope □ money is no object □ Money is the root of all evil. □ money talks □ not for love nor money □ pour money down the drain □ Put your money where your mouth is! □ see the colour of someone's money □ throw good money after bad □ Time is money. □ to the tune of some amount of money

MONKEY
make a monkey out of someone □ monkey around with someone or something □ monkey business □ more fun than a barrel of monkeys

MONTH
by the month □ in a month of Sundays

MOOD
in a bad mood □ in no mood to do something □ in the mood (for something)

MOON
ask for the moon □ cry for the moon □ once in a blue moon □ promise the moon (to someone)

MOPE
mope around

MORE
bite off more than one can chew □ More fool you! □ more fun than a barrel of monkeys □ more often than not □ more or less □ more (to something) than meets the eye □ more's the pity □ The more the merrier. □ There's more than one way to kill a cat. □ wear more than one hat

MORNING
first thing (in the morning) □ morning after (the night before)

MOSS
A rolling stone gathers no moss.

MOST
at most □ at (the) most □ Empty vessels make the most noise. □ make the most of something □ most of all

MOTHER
every mother's son (of someone) □ old enough to be someone's mother □ tied to one's mother's apron-strings

MOTION
go through the motions

MOULD
cast in the same mould

MOUNTAIN
make a mountain out of a molehill

MOUSE
(as) poor as a church mouse □ (as) quiet as a mouse □ play cat and mouse (with someone)

MOUTH
bad-mouth someone or something □ born with a silver spoon in one's mouth □ by word of mouth □ Don't look a gift horse in the mouth. □ down in the mouth □ foam at the mouth □ have a big mouth □ keep one's mouth shut (about someone or something) □ laugh out of the other side of one's mouth □ leave a bad taste in someone's mouth □ live from hand to mouth □ look as if butter wouldn't melt in one's mouth □ make someone's mouth water □ mealy-mouthed □ melt in one's mouth □ not open one's mouth □ one's heart is in one's mouth □ put words into someone's mouth □ Put your money where your mouth is! □ shoot one's mouth off □ straight from the horse's mouth □ take the words out of one's mouth

MOUTHFUL
say a mouthful

MOVE
get a move on □ get moving □ move heaven and earth to do something □ move in(to something) □ move on □ move out □ move up (in the world) □ not move a muscle □ on the move □ one move ahead (of someone or something) □ prime mover

MUCH
much ado about nothing □ much in evidence □ much of a muchness □ much sought after □ so much for someone or something □ so much the better □ take too much on □ think much of someone or something □ too much of a good thing □ without so much as doing something

MUCHNESS
much of a muchness

MUCK
make a muck of something □ muck in (with someone)

MUD
(as) clear as mud □ one's name is mud □ stick-in-the-mud

MUFF
muff one's lines

MUG
mug's game

MULE
(as) stubborn as a mule

MULL
mull something over

MUM
mum's the word

MURDER
cry blue murder □ scream blue murder

MUSCLE
muscle in (on something) □ not move a muscle

MUSIC
face the music

MUST
be a must □ needs must

MUSTER
pass muster

NAIL
(as) hard as nails □ bite one's nails □ fight someone or something tooth and nail □ go at it tooth and nail □ hit the nail on the head □ nail in someone's or something's coffin □ nail

NAKED

one's colours to the mast □ nail someone or something down

NAKED
naked eye

NAME
call someone names □ clear someone's name □ drop someone's name □ drop the name of someone □ in name only □ in someone's name □ make a name for oneself □ name-dropping □ name of the game □ name someone after someone else □ on a first-name basis (with someone) □ on first-name terms (with someone) □ one's name is mud □ throw someone's name around □ worthy of the name

NAP
catch someone napping

NATURAL
die a natural death

NATURE
call of nature □ second nature to someone

NAUGHT
come to naught

NEAR
(as) near as dammit □ have a near miss □ in the near future □ near at hand □ near the bone □ near the knuckle □ nowhere near

NECESSITY
out of necessity

NECK
break one's neck (to do something) □ breathe down someone's neck □ get it in the neck □ in some neck of the woods □ millstone about one's neck □ neck and neck □ pain in the neck □ risk one's neck (to do something) □ stick one's neck out □ up to one's neck (in something)

NEED
A friend in need is a friend indeed. □ needs must

NEEDLE
like looking for a needle in a haystack □ on pins and needles □ pins and needles

NEITHER
neither fish nor fowl □ neither here nor there □ neither hide nor hair

NELLY
Not on your Nelly!

NERVE
get on someone's nerves □ get up enough nerve (to do something) □ of all the nerve

NEST
feather one's (own) nest □ foul one's own nest □ stir up a hornets' nest

NETTLE
grasp the nettle

NEVER
A watched pot never boils. □ better late than never □ It never rains but it pours. □ Lightning never strikes twice (in the same place). □ never darken my door again □ never fear □ never had it so good □ never in one's life □ never mind □ now or never

NEW
break new ground □ break the news (to someone) □ feel like a new person □ (fresh fields and) pastures new □ new ball game □ new blood □ new lease on life □ new one on someone □ No news is good news. □ pastures new □ ring in the New Year □ some new blood □ take a new turn □ turn over a new leaf □ You can't teach an old dog new tricks.

NEWCASTLE
carry coals to Newcastle □ take coals to Newcastle

NEXT
live next door (to someone) □ next to nothing

NICK
in the nick of time

NIGHT
all hours (of the day and night) □ all night long □ (as) different as night and day □ day and night □ far into the night □ fly-by-night □ make a night of doing something □ morning after (the night before) □ night and day □ night on the town □ night-owl □

one-night stand ☐ , ships that pass in the night

NINE
A stitch in time (saves nine). ☐ dressed (up) to the nines ☐ nine days' wonder ☐ nine-to-five job ☐ on cloud nine ☐ Possession is nine points of the law.

NINETEEN
talk nineteen to the dozen

NIP
nip something in the bud

NITTY
get down to the nitty-gritty

NO
A rolling stone gathers no moss. ☐ All work and no play makes Jack a dull boy. ☐ by no means ☐ cut no ice ☐ expense is no object ☐ Fine words butter no parsnips. ☐ have no business doing something ☐ have no staying-power ☐ have no time for someone or something ☐ have no use for someone or something ☐ hold no brief for someone or something ☐ in less than no time ☐ in no mood to do something ☐ in no time (at all) ☐ in no uncertain terms ☐ it's no use (doing something) ☐ leave no stone unturned ☐ Long time no see. ☐ make no bones about something ☐ make no difference (to someone) ☐ make no mistake about it ☐ money is no object ☐ no buts about it ☐ no can do ☐ No dice. ☐ no doubt ☐ no end of something ☐ no great shakes ☐ no hard feelings ☐ no holds barred ☐ no ifs about it ☐ no joke ☐ no kidding ☐ no laughing matter ☐ no love lost (between someone and someone else) ☐ no matter what (happens) ☐ No news is good news. ☐ no problem ☐ no skin off someone's nose ☐ no sooner said than done ☐ no spring chicken ☐ no sweat ☐ no trespassing ☐ no two ways about it ☐ no way ☐ no wonder ☐ not take no for an answer ☐ of no avail ☐ on no account ☐ see no objection (to something) ☐ there is no doing something ☐ There's no accounting for taste. ☐ There's no smoke without fire. ☐ to no avail ☐ up to no good ☐ with no strings attached

NOBODY
nobody's fool

NOD
land of Nod ☐ nod off

NOISE
Empty vessels make the most noise.

NONE
Half a loaf is better than none. ☐ have none of something ☐ none other than ☐ none the wiser ☐ none the worse for wear ☐ none to speak of ☐ none too something ☐ second to none

NONSENSE
stuff and nonsense

NOODLE
use one's noodle

NOR
neither fish nor fowl ☐ neither here nor there ☐ neither hide nor hair ☐ not for love nor money

NORTH
up North

NOSE
(as) plain as the nose on one's face ☐ can't see beyond the end of one's nose ☐ cut off one's nose to spite one's face ☐ follow one's nose ☐ get one's nose out of someone's business ☐ have one's nose in a book ☐ have one's nose in the air ☐ keep one's nose clean ☐ keep one's nose in the air ☐ keep one's nose out of someone's business ☐ keep one's nose to the grindstone ☐ lead someone by the nose ☐ look down one's nose at someone or something ☐ no skin off someone's nose ☐ nose about ☐ nose around ☐ nose in(to something) ☐ nose something in(to something) ☐ not see further than the end of one's nose ☐ on the nose ☐ one's nose is in the air ☐ pay through the nose for something ☐ poke one's nose in(to something) ☐ put someone's nose out of joint ☐ right under someone's nose ☐ rub someone's nose in it ☐ stick one's nose in(to something) ☐ thumb one's nose at someone or something ☐ turn one's nose up at someone or something ☐ under someone's (very) nose ☐ win by a nose

NOSEDIVE
go into a nosedive □ take a nosedive

NOT
All that glitters is not gold. □ (as) likely as not □ be careful not to do something □ believe it or not □ last but not least □ more often than not □ Not a bit (of it). □ not a living soul □ not able □ not able to call one's time one's own □ not able to go on □ not able to help something □ not able to make anything out of someone or something □ not able to see the wood for the trees □ not able to wait □ not all it is cracked up to be □ not all there □ not at all □ not born yesterday □ not breathe a word (about someone or something) □ not buy something □ not by a long shot □ not care two hoots about someone or something □ not enough room to swing a cat □ not for anything in the world □ not for love nor money □ not for the world □ not give a hang about anyone or anything □ not give a hoot about anyone or anything □ not give someone the time of day □ not give two hoots about someone or something □ not half bad □ not have a care in the world □ not have a leg to stand on □ not have all one's marbles □ not hold water □ not in the least □ not in the same league as someone or something □ not know if one is coming or going □ not know someone from Adam □ not know the first thing about someone or something □ not know where to turn □ not know whether one is coming or going □ not know which way to turn □ not lift a finger (to help someone) □ not long for this world □ not move a muscle □ not on any account □ not on your life □ Not on your Nelly! □ not open one's mouth □ not see further than the end of one's nose □ not set foot somewhere □ not show one's face □ not sleep a wink □ not someone's cup of tea □ not take no for an answer □ not to darken someone's door □ not up to scratch □ not utter a word □ not what it is cracked up to be □ not worth a button □ not worth a cent □ not worth a

penny □ Waste not, want not. □ will not hear of something

NOTE
make a note of something □ strike a sour note □ strike the right note □ take note (of something)

NOTHING
care nothing about someone or something □ care nothing for someone or something □ come to nothing □ good-for-nothing □ have nothing on someone or something □ have nothing to do with someone or something □ like nothing on earth □ make nothing of it □ make something out of nothing □ mean nothing (to someone) □ much ado about nothing □ next to nothing □ nothing but □ nothing but skin and bones □ nothing doing □ nothing of the kind □ nothing short of something □ nothing to complain about □ nothing to it □ nothing to sneeze at □ nothing to speak of □ nothing to write home about □ Nothing ventured, nothing gained. □ stop at nothing □ sweet nothings □ think nothing of doing something □ think nothing of someone or something □ to say nothing of someone or something □ want for nothing

NOTICE
escape someone's notice □ serve notice □ sit up and take notice □ take notice (of someone or something)

NOW
all better now □ every now and again □ every now and then □ here and now □ now and again □ now and then □ now or never

NOWHERE
come out of nowhere □ get nowhere fast □ in the middle of nowhere □ nowhere near

NTH
to the nth degree

NUISANCE
make a nuisance of oneself

NULL
null and void

NUMBER
any number of someone or something □ get someone's number □ have someone's number □ in round numbers □ one's days are numbered □ one's number is up □ quite a number

NURSE
nurse a grudge (against someone)

NUT
do one's nut □ get down to the nuts and bolts □ hard nut to crack □ nuts □ nuts and bolts (of something) □ off one's nut □ tough nut to crack

NUTSHELL
in a nutshell

NUTTY
(as) nutty as a fruit-cake

OAR
put one's oar in □ rest on one's oars □ stick one's oar in

OAT
off one's oats □ sow one's wild oats

OBJECT
expense is no object □ money is no object

OBJECTION
raise an objection (to someone or something) □ see no objection (to something)

OBLIGATE
obligated to someone

OCCASION
keep something for another occasion □ leave something for another occasion □ on occasions □ rise to the occasion

OCCUR
occur to someone

OCEAN
drop in the ocean

ODD
at odds (with someone) □ odd man out □ over the odds □ The odds are against one.

ODOUR
odour of sanctity

OFFENCE
take offence (at someone or something)

OFFICE
take office

OFFING
in the offing

OFTEN
more often than not

OIL
burn the midnight oil □ oil someone's palm □ oil the wheels □ pour oil on troubled waters

OINTMENT
fly in the ointment

OLD
(as) old as the hills □ (as) tough as old boots □ be old hat □ chip off the old block □ dirty old man □ get the (old) heave ho □ give someone the (old) heave ho □ money for old rope □ of the old school □ old enough to be someone's father □ old enough to be someone's mother □ old hand at doing something □ one's old stamping-ground □ ripe old age □ same old story □ You can't teach an old dog new tricks.

OLIVE
hold out the olive branch

ONCE
every once in a while □ get the once-over □ give someone or something the once-over □ give someone the once-over □ once and for all □ once in a blue moon □ once-in-a-lifetime chance □ once in a while □ once upon a time

ONION
know one's onions

ONLY
Beauty is only skin deep. □ in name only □ know something only too well □ one and only □ only have eyes for someone

OPEN
crack something wide open □ get something out in the open □ keep one's eyes open (for someone or something) □ keep one's weather eye open □ leave oneself wide open for something □ not open one's mouth □

open a can of worms ☐ open and above-board ☐ open-and-shut case ☐ open book ☐ open fire (on someone) ☐ open one's heart (to someone) ☐ open Pandora's box ☐ open season for something ☐ open secret ☐ open someone's eyes (to something) ☐ open something up ☐ open the door to something ☐ open up ☐ open up (on someone or something) ☐ open up (to someone) ☐ open up (with someone) ☐ open with something ☐ receive someone with open arms ☐ The heavens opened. ☐ welcome someone with open arms

OPENERS
for openers

OPINION
form an opinion ☐ in one's opinion ☐ matter of opinion

OPPORTUNITY
jump at the opportunity (to do something) ☐ leap at the opportunity (to do something) ☐ seize the opportunity

OPPOSITE
opposite sex

OPPOSITION
in opposition (to someone or something)

ORBIT
go into orbit ☐ in orbit

ORDER
call the meeting to order ☐ get one's marching orders ☐ get something in order ☐ give one one's marching orders ☐ in apple-pie order ☐ in order to do something ☐ just what the doctor ordered ☐ made to order ☐ make something to order ☐ on order ☐ order of the day ☐ order someone about ☐ order someone around ☐ out of order ☐ put one's house in order ☐ put something in order

ORDINARY
out of the ordinary

OTHER
go in one ear and out the other ☐ have other fish to fry ☐ have the boot on the other foot ☐ in one ear and out the other ☐ in other words ☐ laugh out

of the other side of one's mouth ☐ look the other way ☐ made for each other ☐ none other than ☐ on the other hand ☐ other way round ☐ six of one and half a dozen of the other ☐ something or other ☐ The boot is on the other foot. ☐ There are plenty of other fish in the sea. ☐ turn the other cheek ☐ with every other breath

OUTGROW
outgrow something

OUTS
ins and outs of something

OUTSET
at the outset

OUTSIDE
at the outside

OVERBOARD
go overboard

OWL
(as) wise as an owl ☐ night-owl

OWN
according to one's (own) lights ☐ afraid of one's own shadow ☐ blow one's own trumpet ☐ carry one's (own) weight ☐ come into one's or its own ☐ devil's own job ☐ dig one's own grave ☐ do one's (own) thing ☐ dose of one's own medicine ☐ feather one's (own) nest ☐ find one's own level ☐ for one's (own) part ☐ for one's (own) sake ☐ foul one's own nest ☐ hoist with one's own petard ☐ hold one's own ☐ in a world of one's own ☐ in one's (own) backyard ☐ in one's (own) (best) interests ☐ in one's own time ☐ in one's own way ☐ judge one on one's own merit(s) ☐ judge something on its own merit(s) ☐ keep one's own counsel ☐ line one's own pockets ☐ mind one's own business ☐ not able to call one's time one's own ☐ of one's own accord ☐ of one's own free will ☐ on one's own ☐ on one's (own) head be it ☐ own up (to something) ☐ paddle one's own canoe ☐ pay one's own way ☐ Pick on someone your own size! ☐ sign one's own death-warrant ☐ stand on one's own two feet ☐ stew in one's own juice ☐ take one's own life ☐

430

take the law into one's own hands □ tell its own story □ under one's own steam

OX

(as) strong as an ox

OYSTER

The world is someone's oyster.

PACE

at a snail's pace □ keep pace (with someone or something) □ put one through one's paces □ put something through its paces □ show one's paces

PACK

pack a punch □ pack a wallop □ pack it in □ pack someone off (to somewhere) □ pack someone or something in □ pack them in □ pack up □ packed (in) like herring in a barrel □ packed (in) like sardines □ packed out □ send someone packing

PACKET

make a packet

PADDLE

paddle one's own canoe □ up the creek (without a paddle)

PAIN

give someone a pain □ have growing pains □ pain in the neck □ take pains to do something

PAINT

(as) black as one is painted □ paint the town red

PAIR

pair off (with someone) □ pair up (with someone)

PAL

pal around (with someone)

PALE

beyond the pale □ pale around the gills

PALM

grease someone's palm □ have an itchy palm □ know someone or something like the palm of one's hand □ oil someone's palm □ palm someone or something off (on someone)

PAN

flash in the pan □ out of the frying-pan into the fire □ pan out

PANCAKE

(as) flat as a pancake

PANDORA

open Pandora's box

PANIC

press the panic button □ push the panic button

PANTS

by the seat of one's pants □ catch one with one's pants down □ have ants in one's pants

PAPER

get one's marching papers □ get one's walking papers □ paper over the cracks (in something) □ put something on paper

PAR

on a par with someone or something □ par for the course □ up to par

PARADISE

fool's paradise

PARCEL

parcel someone or something out □ part and parcel (of something)

PARING

cheese-paring

PAROLE

out on parole

PARROT

(as) sick as a parrot □ parrot-fashion

PARSNIP

Fine words butter no parsnips.

PART

A fool and his money are soon parted. □ for one's (own) part □ in part □ part and parcel (of something) □ part company (with someone) □ part with someone or something □ parting of the ways □ take part (in something)

PARTAKE

partake of something

PARTY

life (and soul) of the party □ party line

□ The party's over. □ throw a party (for someone)

PASS

come to a pretty pass □ come to pass □ in passing □ make a pass at someone □ mention something in passing □ pass as someone or something □ pass away □ pass muster □ pass on □ pass out □ pass over someone or something □ pass someone or something by □ pass someone or something over □ pass someone or something up □ pass something off (as something) □ pass something off (on someone) (as something) □ pass something on □ pass something out □ pass the buck □ pass the hat round □ pass the time □ pass the time of day (with someone) □ pass through someone's mind □ ships that pass in the night

PASSANT

en passant

PAST

be a past master at something □ past it □ past someone's or something's best □ past someone's or something's sell-by date

PASTURE

(fresh fields and) pastures new □ pastures new □ put someone or something out to pasture

PAT

get a pat on the back □ give someone a pat on the back □ pat someone on the back

PATCH

patch someone or something up

PATH

beat a path to someone's door □ lead someone up the garden path □ on the war-path

PATIENCE

try someone's patience

PAUL

rob Peter to pay Paul

PAUSE

give someone pause

PAVE

pave the way (for someone or something)

PAY

Crime doesn't pay. □ have hell to pay □ have the devil to pay □ He who pays the piper calls the tune. □ pay a visit (to someone) □ pay an arm and a leg (for something) □ pay as you go □ pay attention (to someone or something) □ pay for something □ pay in advance □ pay lip-service (to something) □ pay one's debt to society □ pay one's dues □ pay one's own way □ pay someone a compliment □ pay someone a left-handed compliment □ pay someone a visit □ pay someone or something off □ pay someone's way □ pay the earth □ pay the piper □ pay through the nose for something □ Pay up! □ put paid to something □ rob Peter to pay Paul □ There will be the devil to pay.

PEACE

hold one's peace □ leave someone in peace □ make peace (with someone)

PEACOCK

(as) proud as a peacock

PEANUT

for peanuts

PEARL

Cast (one's) pearls before swine.

PECULIAR

funny peculiar

PEDESTAL

put someone on a pedestal

PEEL

keep one's eyes peeled (for someone or something)

PEG

peg away (at something) □ square peg in a round hole □ take someone down a peg (or two)

PENCHANT

have a penchant for doing something

PENNY

A penny for your thoughts. □ A penny saved is a penny earned. □ cost a pretty penny □ not worth a penny □

penny wise and pound foolish ☐ spend a penny ☐ The penny dropped. ☐ two a penny

PEOPLE
knock people's heads together ☐ split people up ☐ tell people apart

PERFECT
Practice makes perfect.

PERISH
Perish the thought.

PERK
perk someone or something up

PERSON
be the last person ☐ do something in person ☐ feel like a new person

PET
be the teacher's pet

PETARD
hoist with one's own petard

PETER
peter out ☐ rob Peter to pay Paul

PHASE
phase someone or something out

PHYSICAL
get physical (with someone)

PICK
have a bone to pick (with someone) ☐ have a pick-me-up ☐ pick a quarrel (with someone) ☐ pick and choose ☐ pick at something ☐ pick holes in something ☐ pick on someone ☐ Pick on someone your own size! ☐ pick one's way through something ☐ pick someone or something off ☐ pick someone or something out ☐ pick someone or something up ☐ pick something over ☐ pick up

PICKLE
in a (pretty) pickle

PICTURE
(as) pretty as a picture ☐ get the picture ☐ put someone in the picture

PIE
(as) easy as pie ☐ eat humble pie ☐ have one's finger in the pie ☐ in apple-pie order ☐ pie in the sky

PIECE
all in one piece ☐ cut someone or something to pieces ☐ fall to pieces ☐ give someone a piece of one's mind ☐ go to pieces ☐ piece of cake ☐ piece of the action ☐ piece something together ☐ villain of the piece

PIG
buy a pig in a poke ☐ pigs might fly ☐ serve as a guinea pig

PIGEON
put the cat among the pigeons ☐ set the cat among the pigeons

PIGGY
pig(gy)-in-the-middle

PIKESTAFF
(as) plain as a pikestaff

PILE
make a pile ☐ pile in(to something) ☐ pile on something ☐ pile out (of something) ☐ pile something on (someone or something) ☐ pile up

PILL
bitter pill to swallow ☐ sugar the pill ☐ sweeten the pill

PILLAR
from pillar to post

PIMPLE
get goose-pimples

PIN
on pins and needles ☐ pin one's faith on someone or something ☐ pin someone or something down (on something) ☐ pin someone's ears back ☐ pin something on someone ☐ pins and needles ☐ so still you could hear a pin drop

PINCH
at a pinch ☐ feel the pinch ☐ pinch and scrape ☐ take something with a pinch of salt

PINK
in the pink (of condition) ☐ tickle someone pink

PIPE
pipe down ☐ pipe-dream ☐ pipe up (with something) ☐ Put that in your pipe and smoke it!

PIPER

He who pays the piper calls the tune. □ pay the piper

PIPPED

pipped at the post

PIT

pit someone or something against someone or something

PITCH

(as) black as pitch □ make a pitch for someone or something □ pitch in (and help)

PITY

more's the pity □ take pity (on someone or something)

PLACE

all over the place □ fall in(to) place □ feel out of place □ go places □ have one's heart in the right place □ in place □ in place of someone or something □ in someone else's place □ in the first place □ in the second place □ know one's place □ Lightning never strikes twice (in the same place). □ one's heart is in the right place □ out of place □ place the blame on someone or something □ pride of place □ put one in one's place □ put oneself in someone else's place □ take place

PLAGUE

avoid someone or something like the plague

PLAIN

(as) plain as a pikestaff □ (as) plain as the nose on one's face □ in plain English □ plain sailing □ put something plainly

PLAN

plan on something □ upset someone's plans

PLANK

(as) thick as two short planks

PLAY

All work and no play makes Jack a dull boy. □ child's play □ foul play □ game at which two can play □ horseplay □ make a play for someone □ play about (with someone or something) □ play along with someone or some-thing □ play around (with someone or something) □ play ball (with someone) □ play both ends (against the middle) □ play by ear □ play cat and mouse (with someone) □ play fair □ play fast and loose (with someone or some-thing) □ play footsie (with someone) □ play gooseberry □ play hard to get □ play havoc (with someone or some-thing) □ play hookey □ play into someone's hands □ play it cool □ play it safe □ play on something □ play one's cards close to one's chest □ play one's cards right □ play one's trump card □ play politics □ play possum □ play second fiddle (to some-one) □ play someone off against someone else □ play someone or something down □ play someone or something up □ play someone up □ play something by ear □ play (the) devil's advocate □ play the field □ play the fool □ play the game □ play the market □ play to the gallery □ play tricks (on someone) □ play up □ play up to someone □ play with fire □ played out □ two can play at that game □ When the cat's away the mice will play.

PLEASE

(as) pleased as Punch □ less than pleased □ please oneself

PLENTY

There are plenty of other fish in the sea.

PLOT

The plot thickens.

PLOUGH

plough into someone or something □ put one's hand to the plough □ tough furrow to plough

PLUCK

pluck up (one's) courage

PLUG

plug away (at something) □ plug something in □ plug something up □ pull the plug (on someone or something)

POCKET

have someone in one's pocket □ line one's own pockets □ Money burns a hole in someone's pocket. ☐ out-of-pocket expenses

POETIC
poetic justice

POINT
at the point of doing something ☐ at this point (in time) ☐ beside the point ☐ case in point ☐ come to the point ☐ get to the point ☐ have a low boiling-point ☐ jumping-off point ☐ make a point ☐ make a point of (doing) something ☐ miss the point ☐ on the point of doing something ☐ point someone or something out ☐ point the finger at someone ☐ point up something ☐ Possession is nine points of the law. ☐ stretch a point ☐ touch a sore point

POISON
One man's meat is another man's poison.

POKE
buy a pig in a poke ☐ poke about ☐ poke around ☐ poke fun (at someone or something) ☐ poke one's nose in(to something)

POLE
be poles apart

POLISH
polish something off

POLITICS
play politics

POND
big fish in a small pond

PONY
by shank's pony

POOR
(as) poor as a church mouse ☐ in poor taste

POP
pop off ☐ pop the question ☐ pop up

PORT
any port in a storm

POSITION
jockey for position ☐ make someone's position clear

POSSESS
possessed by something ☐ possessed of something

POSSESSION
Possession is nine points of the law.

POSSIBLE
as far as possible ☐ so far as possible

POSSUM
play possum

POST
by return post ☐ from pillar to post ☐ keep someone posted ☐ pipped at the post

POT
A watched pot never boils. ☐ go to pot ☐ pot calling the kettle black

POUND
penny wise and pound foolish ☐ pound a beat ☐ pound for pound ☐ pound something out ☐ pound the streets

POUR
It never rains but it pours. ☐ pour cold water on something ☐ pour it on thick ☐ pour money down the drain ☐ pour oil on troubled waters ☐ pour one's heart out (to someone)

POWDER
sitting on a powder keg

POWER
have no staying-power ☐ power behind the throne ☐ powers that be

PRACTICE
in practice ☐ make a practice of something ☐ out of practice ☐ Practice makes perfect. ☐ put something into practice ☐ sharp practice

PRACTISE
practise what you preach

PRAISE
damn someone or something with faint praise ☐ praise someone or something to the skies ☐ sing someone's praises

PREACH
practise what you preach ☐ preach to the converted

PRECEDENT
set a precedent

PRECIOUS
precious few ☐ precious little

PREMIUM
at a premium

PRESENCE
presence of mind

PRESENT
at present ☐ at the present time

PRESS
hard pressed (to do something) ☐ press-gang someone into doing something ☐ press one's luck ☐ press the panic button

PRETTY
(as) pretty as a picture ☐ come to a pretty pass ☐ cost a pretty penny ☐ in a (pretty) pickle ☐ sitting pretty

PREVAIL
prevail (up)on someone ☐ take steps (to prevent something)

PREY
prey (up)on someone or something

PRICE
have a price on one's head ☐ What price something?

PRICK
prick up one's ears

PRIDE
be bursting with pride ☐ burst with pride ☐ Pride goes before a fall. ☐ pride of place ☐ pride oneself on something ☐ swallow one's pride

PRIME
in one's or its prime ☐ in the prime of life ☐ prime mover

PRINT
in print ☐ out of print ☐ put something into print ☐ small print

PROBABILITY
in all probability

PROBLEM
no problem

PROGRESS
in progress

PROMISE
give something a lick and a promise ☐ have a lot of promise ☐ promise the moon (to someone) ☐ show promise

PROPER
go through the proper channels

PROPORTION
blow something out of all proportion ☐ out of all proportion

PROUD
(as) proud as a peacock ☐ do someone proud ☐ house-proud

PROVE
exception that proves the rule

PSYCH
psych someone out ☐ psych someone up ☐ psyched up

PUBLIC
air one's dirty linen in public ☐ in the public eye ☐ wash one's dirty linen in public

PULL
have pull with someone ☐ pull a face ☐ pull a fast one ☐ pull a stunt ☐ pull ahead (of someone or something) ☐ pull in (somewhere) ☐ pull one's punches ☐ pull one's socks up ☐ pull one's weight ☐ pull oneself together ☐ pull oneself up by one's bootstraps ☐ pull out all the stops ☐ pull out (of something) ☐ pull over ☐ pull rank (on someone) ☐ pull someone or something down ☐ pull someone through (something) ☐ pull someone's leg ☐ pull someone's or something's teeth ☐ pull something off ☐ pull something on someone ☐ pull something out of a hat ☐ pull something out of thin air ☐ pull strings ☐ pull the plug (on someone or something) ☐ pull the rug out from under someone('s feet) ☐ pull the wool over someone's eyes ☐ pull through ☐ pull up (somewhere)

PUNCH
(as) pleased as Punch ☐ pack a punch ☐ pull one's punches

PUNISHMENT
glutton for punishment

PUP

sell someone a pup

PURE

(as) pure as the driven snow

PURPOSE

answer someone's purpose ☐ at cross purposes ☐ serve someone's purpose

PURSE

control the purse-strings ☐ Make a silk purse out of a sow's ear.

PURSUIT

in pursuit of something

PUSH

push off ☐ push one's luck ☐ push someone to the wall ☐ push the panic button ☐ pushing up the daisies

PUT

feel put upon ☐ hard put (to do something) ☐ put a brave face on it ☐ put a stop to something ☐ put all one's eggs in one basket ☐ put an end to something ☐ put ideas into someone's head ☐ put in a good word for someone ☐ put in an appearance ☐ put in one's two halfpennies (worth) ☐ put it on ☐ put off by someone or something ☐ put on airs ☐ put on an act ☐ put on one's thinking-cap ☐ put on weight ☐ put one across someone ☐ put one in one's place ☐ put one over (on someone) ☐ put one through one's paces ☐ put one's back into something ☐ put one's best foot forward ☐ put one's cards on the table ☐ put one's finger on something ☐ put one's foot down (about something) ☐ put one's foot in it ☐ put one's hand to the plough ☐ put one's hand(s) on something ☐ put one's house in order ☐ put one's oar in ☐ put one's shoulder to the wheel ☐ put oneself in someone else's place ☐ put out ☐ put out (some) feelers ☐ put paid to something ☐ put someone down as something ☐ put someone down (for something) ☐ put someone in mind of someone or something ☐ put someone in the picture ☐ put someone on a pedestal ☐ put someone on the spot ☐ put someone or something across ☐ put someone or something at someone's disposal

☐ put someone or something away ☐ put someone or something down ☐ put someone or something off ☐ put someone or something on hold ☐ put someone or something out ☐ put someone or something out of one's mind ☐ put someone or something out to pasture ☐ put someone or something to bed ☐ put someone or something to sleep ☐ put someone or something up ☐ put someone through the wringer ☐ put someone to shame ☐ put someone to the test ☐ put someone up to something ☐ put someone wise to someone or something ☐ put someone's nose out of joint ☐ put something aside ☐ put something by ☐ put something down to something ☐ put something forward ☐ put something in ☐ put something in order ☐ put something in the way (of someone or something) ☐ put something into practice ☐ put something into print ☐ put something into words ☐ put something on ice ☐ put something on paper ☐ put something on the back burner ☐ put something over ☐ put something plainly ☐ put something right ☐ put something straight ☐ put something through its paces ☐ put something to (good) use ☐ put something to rest ☐ put something together ☐ Put that in your pipe and smoke it! ☐ put the arm on someone ☐ put the bite on someone ☐ put the blame on someone or something ☐ put the cart before the horse ☐ put the cat among the pigeons ☐ put the clamps on (someone) ☐ put the finger on someone ☐ put the heat on (someone) ☐ put the kibosh on something ☐ put the screws on someone ☐ put the skids on something ☐ put the squeeze on someone ☐ put two and two together ☐ put up a (brave) front ☐ put-up job ☐ put up with someone or something ☐ put upon someone ☐ put words into someone's mouth ☐ Put your money where your mouth is! ☐ stay put ☐ to put it mildly

PUTTY

putty in someone's hands

QUAKE

quake in one's shoes

QUANDARY
in a quandary

QUANTITY
be an unknown quantity

QUARREL
pick a quarrel (with someone)

QUEER
in Queer Street

QUEST
in quest of someone or something

QUESTION
beg the question □ bring something into question □ call something into question □ out of the question □ pop the question □ vexed question □ without question

QUEUE
queue up

QUICK
(as) quick as a flash □ (as) quick as (greased) lightning □ cut someone to the quick □ quick on the draw □ quick on the uptake

QUID
quids in with someone

QUIET
(as) quiet as a mouse □ (as) quiet as the grave □ keep quiet (about someone or something) □ keep someone or something quiet

QUIT
call it quits

QUITE
quite a bit □ quite a lot □ quite a number □ quite something

RACE
race against time □ rat race □ Slow and steady wins the race.

RACK
go to rack and ruin □ rack one's brains

RAG
chew the rag □ from rags to riches □ in rags □ run someone ragged

RAGE
all the rage

RAGGED
run someone ragged

RAIN
(as) right as rain □ It never rains but it pours. □ rain cats and dogs □ rain or shine □ rained off

RAINCHECK
take a raincheck (on something)

RAINY
save something for a rainy day

RAISE
cause eyebrows to raise □ cause raised eyebrows □ raise a few eyebrows □ raise a hand (against someone or something) □ raise a stink about something □ raise an objection (to someone or something) □ raise Cain (with someone or something) □ raise hell (with someone or something) □ raise one's sights □ raise one's voice (to someone) □ raise the wind for something

RAKE
(as) thin as a rake □ rake something up

RALLY
rally round someone or something

RAM
ram someone or something down someone's throat

RAMBLE
ramble on (about something)

RANDOM
at random

RANGE
at close range

RANK
close ranks □ pull rank (on someone) □ rank and file

RANT
rant and rave

RAP
get one's knuckles rapped □ have one's knuckles rapped □ rap someone's knuckles □ take the rap (for someone or something)

RARE
(as) rare as hen's teeth

RARING
rarin' to go

RAT
rat on someone □ rat race □ smell a rat

RATE
at a rate of knots □ at any rate □ at that rate □ at this rate □ rate someone □ second-rate

RATHER
had rather do something

RATTLE
rattle something off

RAVE
rant and rave □ rave about someone or something

RAW
get a raw deal □ give someone a raw deal □ in the raw

RAZOR
(as) sharp as a razor

REACH
out of reach □ reach an agreement (with someone) □ reach for the sky □ within someone's reach

READ
read between the lines □ read someone like a book □ read someone the Riot Act □ read someone's mind □ read something into something □ read something through □ read up (on someone or something) □ take something as read

READY
get ready (to do something) □ when one is good and ready

REAR
bring up the rear □ rear its ugly head

REASON
beyond reasonable doubt □ have reason (to do something) □ listen to reason □ lose one's reason □ stand to reason □ within reason □ without rhyme or reason

REASONABLE
beyond reasonable doubt

RECEIVE
receive someone with open arms

RECKON
reckon with someone

RECORD
for the record □ off the record □ on record □ one for the record (books) □ set the record straight

RED
catch someone red-handed □ caught red-handed □ draw a red herring □ get a red face □ get the red carpet treatment □ give someone a red face □ give someone the red carpet treatment □ have a red face □ in the red □ paint the town red □ red herring □ red in the face □ red tape □ roll out the red carpet for someone □ see red

REDBRICK
redbrick university

REED
broken reed

REEL
reel something off

REFERENCE
in reference to someone or something

REGAIN
regain one's composure □ regain one's feet

REGARD
in regard to someone or something

REGULAR
(as) regular as clockwork

REIN
give a free rein to someone

RELATION
in relation to someone or something

RELATIVE
relative to someone or something

RELIGION
get religion

REPUTATION
get a reputation (as a something) □ get a reputation (for doing something) □ give someone a reputation (as a some-

thing) □ give someone a reputation for doing something □ have a reputation as a something □ have a reputation for doing something

REQUEST
at someone's request

REQUIREMENT
meet the requirements (for something)

RESIGN
resign oneself to something

RESISTANCE
line of least resistance

RESORT
as a last resort

RESPECT
with respect to someone or something

REST
come to rest □ lay something to rest □ put something to rest □ rest assured □ rest on one's laurels □ rest on one's oars

RESULT
result in something

RETREAT
beat a (hasty) retreat

RETURN
by return post □ in return (for someone or something) □ return the compliment □ return the favour □ return ticket

REV
rev something up

RHYME
without rhyme or reason

RICH
from rags to riches □ strike it rich

RID
get rid of someone or something

RIDDANCE
good riddance (to bad rubbish)

RIDE
go along for the ride □ let something ride □ ride roughshod over someone or something □ ride something out □ riding for a fall □ take someone for a ride

RIDICULOUS
make someone look ridiculous

RIFT
rift in the lute

RIGHT
all right □ all right with someone □ (as) right as rain □ give one's right arm (for someone or something) □ have a right to do something □ have one's heart in the right place □ have the right of way □ in one's right mind □ in the right □ left, right, and centre □ one's heart is in the right place □ play one's cards right □ put something right □ right and left □ right away □ Right on! □ right on time □ right side up □ right under someone's nose □ right up someone's street □ say something (right) to someone's face □ serve someone right □ set something right □ step (right) up □ strike the right note □ turn out (all right) □ when it comes right down to it □ work out (all right)

RILEY
lead the life of Riley

RING
give someone a ring □ have a familiar ring □ like a three-ring circus □ ring a bell □ ring down the curtain (on something) □ ring in the New Year □ ring off □ ring someone or something up □ ring the changes □ ring true □ run rings around someone □ throw one's hat into the ring □ toss one's hat into the ring

RIOT
read someone the Riot Act □ run riot

RIP
let her rip □ let it rip □ rip into someone or something □ rip someone or something off

RIPE
ripe old age □ when the time is ripe

RISE
Early to bed, early to rise(, makes a man healthy, wealthy, and wise). □ get a rise out of someone □ give rise to something □ rise and shine □ rise to

the occasion □ take a rise out of someone

RISK
risk one's neck (to do something) □
run a risk (of something) □ take a risk

RIVER
sell someone down the river

ROAD
All roads lead to Rome. □ end of the
road □ get the show on the road □
middle-of-the-road □ road-hog

ROB
rob Peter to pay Paul

ROBBERY
daylight robbery

ROBINSON
before you can say Jack Robinson

ROCK
(as) steady as a rock □ rock the boat

ROCKER
off one's rocker

ROD
rule someone or something with a rod of
iron

ROLL
A rolling stone gathers no moss. □ get
the ball rolling □ have them rolling in
the aisles □ heads will roll □ keep
the ball rolling □ roll in □ roll on
something □ roll one's sleeves up □
roll out the red carpet for someone □
rolling in something □ set the ball rolling □ start the ball rolling

ROMAN
When in Rome do as the Romans do.

ROME
All roads lead to Rome. □ fiddle while
Rome burns □ Rome wasn't built in a
day. □ When in Rome do as the Romans do.

ROMP
romp home

ROOF
go through the roof □ hit the roof

ROOM
not enough room to swing a cat □ take
up room

ROOST
come home to roost □ rule the roost

ROOT
Money is the root of all evil. □ root
and branch □ root for someone or
something □ root something out □
rooted to the spot □ take root

ROPE
know the ropes □ learn the ropes □
money for old rope □ rope someone
into doing something □ show someone the ropes

ROSE
bed of roses

ROTE
learn something by rote

ROUGH
cut up rough □ get a rough idea (about
something) □ give someone a rough
idea (about something) □ have a
rough idea about something □ have a
rough time (of it) □ rough it □
rough someone up □ take the rough
with the smooth

ROUGHSHOD
ride roughshod over someone or
something

ROUND
all year round □ bring someone round
□ come round □ go round in circles
□ in round figures □ in round numbers □ other way round □ pass the
hat round □ rally round someone or
something □ round on someone □
round something off □ round something up □ square peg in a round hole

ROUNDABOUT
say something in a roundabout way

ROW
kick up a row □ tough row to hoe

RUB
rub along with someone □ rub off (on
someone) □ rub salt in the wound □
rub shoulders (with someone) □ rub
someone or something down □ rub

someone out □ rub someone up the wrong way □ rub someone's nose in it □ rub something in

RUBBISH
good riddance (to bad rubbish)

RUBICON
cross the Rubicon

RUFFLE
ruffle someone's feathers

RUG
(as) snug as a bug (in a rug) □ pull the rug out from under someone('s feet)

RUIN
go to rack and ruin □ go to wrack and ruin

RULE
as a (general) rule □ as a rule □ exception that proves the rule □ hard-and-fast rule □ rule of thumb □ rule someone or something out □ rule someone or something with a rod of iron □ rule the roost

RUN
do something on the run □ dry run □ get a good run for one's money □ give one a run for one's money □ in the long run □ in the running □ in the short run □ make a run for it □ make someone's blood run cold □ off to a running start □ one's luck runs out □ out of the running □ run a fever □ run a risk (of something) □ run a temperature □ run a tight ship □ run across someone or something □ run after someone □ run against the clock □ run an errand □ run around in circles □ run around like a chicken with its head cut off □ run around with someone □ run away (with someone or something) □ run circles around someone □ run counter to something □ run down □ run-down □ run for it □ run for one's life □ run high □ run in the family □ run into someone □ run of the mill □ run off with someone or something □ run out of something □ run out of time □ run over someone or something □ run rings around someone □ run riot □ run short (of something)

□ run someone in □ run someone or something down □ run someone or something to earth □ run someone ragged □ run something up □ run through something □ run to seed □ run to something □ run up against a brick wall □ run up against a stone wall □ run wild □ Still waters run deep.

RUNAROUND
get the runaround □ give someone the runaround

RUSH
fools rush in (where angels fear to tread) □ in a mad rush □ rush one's fences

RUSTLE
rustle something up

SACK
get the sack □ give someone the sack

SACRED
sacred cow

SADDLE
saddle someone with something

SAFE
(as) safe as houses □ play it safe □ safe and sound

SAID
after all is said and done □ easier said than done □ Least said soonest mended. □ no sooner said than done □ when all is said and done □ You said it!

SAIL
plain sailing □ sail through something □ sail under false colours □ set sail (for somewhere) □ take the wind out of someone's sails

SAKE
for one's (own) sake □ for the sake of someone or something

SALE
for sale □ on sale

SALT
back to the salt mines □ rub salt in the wound □ salt of the earth □ salt something away □ take something with a grain of salt □ take something with a pinch of salt □ worth one's salt

SAME

all the same ☐ all the same (to some-one) ☐ at the same time ☐ by the same token ☐ cast in the same mould ☐ in the same boat ☐ in the same breath ☐ just the same ☐ Lightning never strikes twice (in the same place). ☐ not in the same league as someone or something ☐ same here ☐ same old story ☐ same to you ☐ speak the same language ☐ tarred with the same brush

SANCTITY

odour of sanctity

SAND

bury one's head in the sand ☐ hide one's head in the sand

SANDBOY

(as) happy as a sandboy

SARDINE

packed (in) like sardines

SAUCE

What is sauce for the goose is sauce for the gander.

SAVE

A penny saved is a penny earned. ☐ A stitch in time (saves nine). ☐ save one's breath ☐ save (one's) face ☐ save someone's skin ☐ save something for a rainy day ☐ save something up ☐ save the day ☐ save up (for something) ☐ saved by the bell ☐ scrimp and save

SAY

after all is said and done ☐ before you can say Jack Robinson ☐ easier said than done ☐ get one's say ☐ go so far as to say something ☐ goes without saying ☐ have a say (in something) ☐ have one's say ☐ Least said soonest mended. ☐ no sooner said than done ☐ on someone's say-so ☐ say a mouthful ☐ say something in a round-about way ☐ say something out loud ☐ say something (right) to someone's face ☐ say something under one's breath ☐ say the word ☐ to say noth-ing of someone or something ☐ to say the least ☐ when all is said and done ☐ You can say that again! ☐ You said it!

SCALE

scale something down ☐ tip the scales at something

SCARCE

make oneself scarce

SCARE

scare one out of one's wits ☐ scare someone stiff ☐ scare someone to death ☐ scare the (living) daylights out of someone ☐ scare the wits out of someone ☐ scared stiff ☐ scared to death

SCENE

behind the scenes ☐ create a scene ☐ make a scene

SCHEDULE

on schedule

SCHOOL

of the old school ☐ tell tales out of school

SCORE

have a score to settle with someone ☐ know the score ☐ settle a score (with someone)

SCOT

get off scot-free ☐ go scot-free

SCRAPE

bow and scrape ☐ pinch and scrape ☐ scrape something together ☐ scrape the bottom of the barrel

SCRATCH

make something from scratch ☐ not up to scratch ☐ scratch around (for something) ☐ scratch someone's back ☐ scratch the surface ☐ start from scratch

SCREAM

scream blue murder

SCREW

have a screw loose ☐ put the screws on someone ☐ screw someone or some-thing up ☐ screw up one's courage

SCRIMP

scrimp and save

SEA

at sea (about something) ☐ between

the devil and the deep blue sea □
There are plenty of other fish in the sea.

SEAL
signed, sealed, and delivered

SEAM
be bursting at the seams □ burst at the seams □ come apart at the seams □ fall apart at the seams

SEAMY
seamy side of life

SEARCH
in search of someone or something □ search high and low for someone or something □ Search me. □ search someone or something out □ search something with a fine-tooth comb

SEASON
in season □ open season for something □ out of season □ silly season

SEAT
by the seat of one's pants □ in the hot seat □ on the hot seat □ take a back seat (to someone)

SECOND
at second hand □ come off second-best □ get one's second wind □ get second thoughts about someone or something □ have second thoughts about someone or something □ in a split second □ in (just) a second □ in one's second childhood □ in the second place □ on second thoughts □ play second fiddle (to someone) □ second nature to someone □ second-rate □ second sight □ second to none

SECRET
open secret

SECURITY
lull someone into a false sense of security

SEE
begin to see daylight □ begin to see the light □ can't see beyond the end of one's nose □ can't see one's hand in front of one's face □ have seen better days □ Long time no see. □ not able to see the wood for the trees □ not see further than the end of one's nose □ see a man about a dog □ see about something □ see double □ see eye to eye (about something) □ see fit (to do something) □ see into something □ see no objection (to something) □ see one's way clear (to do something) □ see over something □ see red □ see someone home □ see someone off □ see someone out □ see someone to the door □ see something through □ see something with half an eye □ see stars □ see the colour of someone's money □ see the last of someone or something □ see the light □ see the light at the end of the tunnel □ see the light of day □ see the sights □ see the writing on the wall □ see things □ see through someone or something □ see to someone or something □ seeing is believing □ seeing that □ wait-and-see attitude

SEED
go to seed □ run to seed

SEEK
much sought after

SEIZE
seize on something □ seize the opportunity □ seize up

SELL
get the hard sell □ give someone the hard sell □ past someone's or something's sell-by date □ sell like hot cakes □ sell someone a pup □ sell someone down the river □ sell someone or something short □ sell someone something □ sell something off

SEND
be given a big send-off □ get a big send-off □ give someone a big send-off □ send away for something □ send off for something □ send one about one's business □ send out for someone or something □ send someone or something up □ send someone (out) on an errand □ send someone packing □ send someone to Coventry □ send something C.O.D. □ send something off □ send up a trial balloon □ send word (to someone)

SENSE
come to one's senses □ horse sense □ in a sense □ lull someone into a false sense of security □ make sense out of

someone or something □ sixth sense □ take leave of one's senses

SEPARATE
separate the grain from the chaff □ separate the men from the boys □ separate the sheep from the goats

SERVE
First come, first served. □ serve as a guinea pig □ serve notice □ serve someone right □ serve someone's purpose □ serve something up

SERVICE
be at someone's service □ be of service (to someone) □ out of service □ pay lip-service (to something)

SET
all set (to do something) □ dead set against someone or something □ get set □ have one's heart set against something □ have one's heart set on something □ not set foot somewhere □ one's heart is set against something □ one's heart is set on something □ set a precedent □ set about doing something □ set about someone or something □ set eyes on someone or something □ set fire to someone or something □ set foot somewhere □ set forth (on something) □ set great store by someone or something □ set in □ set off (for somewhere) □ set one back on one's heels □ set one's heart against something □ set one's heart on something □ set one's sights on something □ set out (for somewhere) □ set sail (for somewhere) □ set someone or something back □ set someone or something free □ set someone or something off □ set someone or something on fire □ set someone or something up □ set someone straight □ set someone up as something □ set someone up (in business) □ set someone's teeth on edge □ set something aside □ set something down to something □ set something out □ set something right □ set something straight □ set the ball rolling □ set the cat among the pigeons □ set the record straight □ set the stage for something □ set the table □ set the world on fire □ set up shop

somewhere □ set upon someone or something

SETTLE
have a score to settle with someone □ settle a score (with someone) □ settle down □ settle for something □ settle on something □ settle someone's affairs □ settle up with someone

SEVEN
at sixes and sevens

SEVENTH
in seventh heaven

SEW
get something sewn up □ have something sewn up □ sew something up

SEX
opposite sex

SHACK
shack up (with someone)

SHADE
shades of someone or something

SHADOW
afraid of one's own shadow □ beyond the shadow of a doubt □ worn to a shadow

SHAGGY
shaggy-dog story

SHAKE
in two shakes of a lamb's tail □ no great shakes □ shake (hands) on something □ shake hands (with someone) □ shake in one's shoes □ shake someone or something off □ shake someone up □ shake something off

SHAME
For shame! □ hide one's face in shame □ put someone to shame □ Shame on someone.

SHANK
by shank's mare □ by shank's pony

SHAPE
in good shape □ in shape □ lick something into shape □ out of shape □ shape up □ whip something into shape

SHARE
lion's share (of something) ☐ share and share alike

SHARP
(as) sharp as a razor ☐ at sometime sharp ☐ sharp practice

SHAVE
have a close shave

SHED
shed crocodile tears ☐ shed (some) light on something

SHEEP
black sheep (of the family) ☐ separate the sheep from the goats ☐ wolf in sheep's clothing

SHEET
(as) white as a sheet

SHELL
come out of one's shell ☐ shell something out

SHIFT
shift for oneself ☐ shift one's ground

SHINE
Make hay while the sun shines. ☐ rain or shine ☐ rise and shine ☐ take a shine to someone or something

SHIP
desert a sinking ship ☐ leave a sinking ship ☐ run a tight ship ☐ ships that pass in the night ☐ spoil the ship for a ha'porth of tar

SHIPSHAPE
shipshape (and Bristol fashion)

SHIRK
shirk one's duty

SHIRT
give someone the shirt off one's back ☐ Keep your shirt on! ☐ lose one's shirt

SHOCK
get the shock of one's life

SHOE
fill dead men's shoes ☐ fill someone's shoes ☐ get by (on a shoe-string) ☐ in someone else's shoes ☐ quake in one's shoes ☐ shake in one's shoes ☐ step into dead men's shoes

SHOOT
shoot a line ☐ shoot from the hip ☐ shoot one's mouth off ☐ whole (bang) shoot ☐ whole shooting-match

SHOP
bull in a china shop ☐ close up shop ☐ set up shop somewhere ☐ shop around (for something) ☐ talk shop ☐ talking-shop ☐ window-shopping

SHORE
shore someone or something up

SHORT
(as) thick as two short planks ☐ caught short ☐ cut someone or something (off) short ☐ end up with the short end of the stick ☐ fall short (of something) ☐ for short ☐ get the short end of the stick ☐ in short ☐ in short supply ☐ in the short run ☐ make a long story short ☐ make short work of someone or something ☐ nothing short of something ☐ run short (of something) ☐ sell someone or something short ☐ short and sweet ☐ short of something ☐ stop short of doing something ☐ taken short

SHOT
call the shots ☐ give something one's best shot ☐ have a shot at something ☐ not by a long shot ☐ shot across the bows ☐ shot-gun wedding ☐ shot in the arm ☐ shot in the dark ☐ shot through with something ☐ take a shot at something

SHOULDER
carry the weight of the world on one's shoulders ☐ get the cold shoulder ☐ give someone the cold shoulder ☐ have a chip on one's shoulder ☐ have a good head on one's shoulders ☐ head and shoulders above someone or something ☐ on someone's shoulders ☐ put one's shoulder to the wheel ☐ rub shoulders (with someone) ☐ shoulder to shoulder ☐ straight from the shoulder

SHOUT
all over bar the shouting ☐ shout someone or something down

SHOVE

shove off □ shove someone or something down someone's throat

SHOW

get the show on the road □ goes to show (someone) □ make a great show of something □ not show one's face □ show good faith □ show of hands □ show off □ show one's hand □ show one's paces □ show one's teeth □ show oneself in one's true colours □ show promise □ show signs of something □ show someone around □ show someone into somewhere □ show someone or something off □ show someone out □ show someone the door □ show someone the ropes □ show someone to the door □ show someone up □ show someone up as something □ show something to advantage □ show the flag □ show the white feather □ show up □ steal the show

SHRUG

shrug something off (as something)

SHUT

keep one's mouth shut (about someone or something) □ open-and-shut case □ shut someone or something out □ shut someone up □ shut something down □ shut the door on something □ Shut up!

SHY

fight shy of something □ shy away (from someone or something)

SICK

(as) sick as a dog □ (as) sick as a parrot □ get sick □ sick and tired of someone or something □ sick in bed

SIDE

be a thorn in someone's side □ choose sides □ get on the good side of someone □ get out of the wrong side of the bed □ keep on the good side of someone □ keep one's side of the bargain □ know which side one's bread is buttered on □ laugh out of the other side of one's mouth □ right side up □ seamy side of life □ side against someone □ side with someone □ take sides

SIGHT

can't stand (the sight of) someone or something □ catch sight of someone or something □ know someone by sight □ lose sight of someone or something □ love at first sight □ lower one's sights □ out of sight □ Out of sight, out of mind. □ raise one's sights □ second sight □ see the sights □ set one's sights on something □ sight for sore eyes

SIGN

show signs of something □ sign in □ sign off □ sign on □ sign on the dotted line □ sign one's own death-warrant □ sign someone in □ sign someone on □ sign something over (to someone) □ sign up (for something) □ signed, sealed, and delivered

SILK

Make a silk purse out of a sow's ear.

SILLY

silly season

SILVER

born with a silver spoon in one's mouth □ Every cloud has a silver lining.

SIMMER

simmer down

SIN

(as) ugly as sin

SINCE

since the year dot

SING

sing a different tune □ sing someone's praises

SINGLE

(in) single file □ single file □ single someone or something out

SINK

desert a sinking ship □ everything but the kitchen sink □ leave a sinking ship □ sink in □ sink into despair □ sink one's teeth into something □ sink or swim □ sink our differences

SINKER

swallow something hook, line, and sinker

SIT

like a sitting duck □ like sitting ducks □ sit at someone's feet □ sit back and let something happen □ sit (idly) by □ sit in for someone □ sit in (on something) □ sit on one's hands □ sit on something □ sit on the fence □ sit something out □ sit through something □ sit tight □ sit up and take notice □ sit up with someone □ sit with someone □ sitting on a powder keg □ (sitting) on top of the world □ sitting pretty □ sitting target

SIX

at sixes and sevens □ six of one and half a dozen of the other □ sixth sense

SIZE

cut someone down to size □ Pick on someone your own size! □ size someone or something up □ That's about the size of it.

SKATE

skate over something □ (skating) on thin ice

SKELETON

skeleton in the closet

SKID

put the skids on something

SKIN

all skin and bones □ Beauty is only skin deep. □ by the skin of one's teeth □ get under someone's skin □ jump out of one's skin □ no skin off someone's nose □ nothing but skin and bones □ save someone's skin □ skin someone alive □ soaked to the skin □ thick-skinned □ thin-skinned

SKIP

one's heart skips a beat □ skip bail □ Skip it!

SKULL

get something into someone's thick skull

SKY

go sky-high □ pie in the sky □ praise someone or something to the skies □ reach for the sky □ The sky's the limit.

SLACK

slack off

SLANG

slanging match

SLAP

get a slap on the wrist □ give someone a slap on the wrist □ slap in the face □ slap someone down □ slap someone's wrist

SLATE

slate something □ start (off) with a clean slate □ wipe the slate clean

SLAUGHTER

like a lamb to the slaughter

SLEEP

drift off (to sleep) □ drop off (to sleep) □ Let sleeping dogs lie. □ lose sleep over someone or something □ not sleep a wink □ put someone or something to sleep □ sleep in □ sleep like a log □ sleep like a top □ sleep on something □ sleep something off □ sleep with someone

SLEEVE

have one's heart on one's sleeve □ have something up one's sleeve □ laugh up one's sleeve □ roll one's sleeves up □ wear one's heart on one's sleeve

SLICE

slice of the cake

SLIDE

let something slide

SLIP

get the slip □ give someone the slip □ let something slip by □ let something slip (out) □ let the chance slip by □ slip away □ slip of the tongue □ slip off □ slip one's mind □ slip out □ slip through someone's fingers □ slip up

SLIPPERY

(as) slippery as an eel

SLOPE

slope off

SLOUGH

slough something off

SLOW

Slow and steady wins the race. □ slow on the uptake

SLY
on the sly

SMACK
smack dab in the middle □ smack in the eye

SMALL
big fish in a small pond □ small fry □ small hours □ small print □ small talk □ small time □ thankful for small mercies

SMEAR
smear campaign (against someone)

SMELL
smell a rat □ smell of the lamp

SMILE
smile on someone or something

SMOKE
go up in smoke □ have a smoke □ Put that in your pipe and smoke it! □ smoke someone or something out □ There's no smoke without fire. □ Where there's smoke there's fire.

SMOOTH
smooth something out □ smooth something over □ take the rough with the smooth

SNAG
hit a snag

SNAIL
at a snail's pace

SNAKE
snake in the grass

SNAP
snap out of something □ snap something up

SNAPPY
Make it snappy!

SNATCH
cradle-snatch

SNEAK
sneak up on someone or something

SNEEZE
nothing to sneeze at

SNOOK
cock a snook at someone

SNOW
(as) pure as the driven snow □ (as) white as the driven snow □ snowed in □ snowed under

SNOWBALL'S
have a snowball's chance in hell

SNUG
(as) snug as a bug (in a rug)

SO
be so □ do so □ go so far as to say something □ in so many words □ just so □ never had it so good □ on someone's say-so □ so-and-so □ so be it □ so far as anyone knows □ so far as possible □ so far as someone is concerned □ So far, so good. □ so long □ so much for someone or something □ so much the better □ so-so □ so still you could hear a pin drop □ so to speak □ without so much as doing something

SOAK
soak something up □ soaked to the skin

SOBER
(as) sober as a judge

SOCIETY
pay one's debt to society

SOCKS
pull one's socks up

SOFT
(as) soft as a baby's bottom □ have a soft spot for someone or something

SOIL
soil one's hands

SOME
and then some □ at some length □ dig some dirt up on someone □ in some neck of the woods □ put out (some) feelers □ shed (some) light on something □ some new blood □ to some extent □ to the tune of some amount of money

SOMEHOW
do somehow by someone □ land up somehow or somewhere

SON
every mother's son (of someone)

SONG

buy something for a song □ swan-song

SOON

A fool and his money are soon parted. □ had as soon do something □ had sooner do something □ just as soon do something □ Least said soonest mended. □ no sooner said than done □ sooner or later □ would as soon do something

SORE

sight for sore eyes □ stick out like a sore thumb □ touch a sore point □ touch a sore spot

SORROW

drown one's sorrows

SORT

out of sorts □ something of the sort □ sort of (something) □ sort something out

SOUGHT

much sought after

SOUL

every living soul □ keep body and soul together □ life (and soul) of the party □ not a living soul □ with all one's heart and soul

SOUND

(as) sound as a bell □ safe and sound □ sound off □ sound someone out

SOUP

in the soup □ soup something up

SOUR

strike a sour note

SOUTH

down South

SOW

Make a silk purse out of a sow's ear. □ sow one's wild oats

SPACE

spaced out □ take up space

SPADE

call a spade a spade

SPAIN

build castles in Spain

SPAN

spick and span

SPANNER

throw a spanner in the works

SPARE

have something to spare □ in one's spare time

SPEAK

Actions speak louder than words. □ none to speak of □ nothing to speak of □ on speaking terms (with someone) □ so to speak □ speak for itself □ speak highly of someone or something □ speak of the devil □ speak off the cuff □ speak one's mind □ speak out (against something) □ speak out of turn □ speak the same language □ speak up □ speak up (against something) □ speak with a forked tongue □ spoken for

SPEECH

maiden speech

SPEED

at full speed □ speed someone or something up

SPELL

spell something out □ spell trouble

SPEND

spend a penny

SPICE

Variety is the spice of life.

SPICK

spick and span

SPIKE

spike someone's guns

SPILL

cry over spilled milk □ spill the beans □ take a spill

SPIN

go into a tail-spin □ make someone's head spin □ spin something out

SPIRIT

The spirit is willing (but the flesh is weak).

SPIT

be the spit and image of someone □ be

the spitting image of someone □ spitting image

SPITE
cut off one's nose to spite one's face □ in spite of someone or something

SPLASH
splash out on something

SPLEEN
vent one's spleen on someone or something

SPLIT
in a split second □ split hairs □ split people up □ split something fifty-fifty □ split the difference □ split up

SPOIL
spoil the ship for a ha'porth of tar □ To the victors belong the spoils. □ Too many cooks spoil the broth.

SPONGE
throw in the sponge

SPOON
born with a silver spoon in one's mouth □ spoon-feed

SPORT
sporting chance

SPOT
have a soft spot for someone or something □ high spot □ hit the high spots □ hit the spot □ in a spot □ in a (tight) spot □ on the spot □ put someone on the spot □ rooted to the spot □ spot on □ touch a sore spot □ X marks the spot

SPOUT
spout off (about someone or something)

SPREAD
spread it on thick □ spread like wildfire □ spread oneself too thin

SPRING
no spring chicken □ spring something on someone

SPUR
on the spur of the moment

SQUARE
square accounts (with someone) □ square deal □ square meal □ square peg in a round hole □ square up (for

something) □ square up to someone or something □ square up with someone

SQUEEZE
put the squeeze on someone

SQUIB
damp squib

SQUIRREL
squirrel something away

STAB
have a stab at something □ stab someone in the back □ take a stab at something

STACK
have the cards stacked against one □ stack the cards (against someone or something) □ The cards are stacked against one.

STAGE
at this stage □ in a stage whisper □ set the stage for something

STAKE
at stake □ stake a claim (on something)

STAMP
one's old stamping-ground □ stamp something out

STAND
able to do something standing on one's head □ can't stand (the sight of) someone or something □ know where someone stands (on someone or something) □ make someone's hair stand on end □ not have a leg to stand on □ one-night stand □ one's heart stands still □ stand a chance □ stand by □ stand by someone □ stand corrected □ stand down □ stand for something □ stand-in □ stand in awe of someone or something □ stand in (for someone) □ stand in someone's way □ stand on ceremony □ stand on one's own two feet □ stand one's ground □ stand out □ stand out a mile □ stand out against someone or something □ stand over someone □ stand someone in good stead □ stand someone something □ stand someone up □ stand still (for someone or something) □ stand to reason □ stand up against someone or something □ stand

up and be counted □ stand up for someone or something □ stand up to someone or something □ standing joke □ take a stand (against someone or something) □ take the stand

STANDSTILL
come to a standstill

STAR
get stars in one's eyes □ have stars in one's eyes □ see stars □ thank one's lucky stars

STARE
stare someone in the face

START
be off to a bad start □ by fits and starts □ get a head start (on someone or something) □ get a start □ get off to a bad start □ get off to a flying start □ get one's start □ give someone a head start (on someone or something) □ give someone a start □ have a head start on someone or something □ off to a running start □ start from scratch □ start (off) with a clean slate □ start out (as something) □ start something □ start something up □ start the ball rolling

STARTERS
for starters

STATE
fine state of affairs □ lie in state

STATION
above one's station

STAY
have no staying-power □ stay ahead of someone or something □ stay away (from someone or something) □ stay out (of something or somewhere) □ stay put □ stay the distance

STEAD
stand someone in good stead

STEADY
(as) steady as a rock □ go steady (with someone) □ Slow and steady wins the race.

STEAL
steal a march on someone □ steal someone's thunder □ steal the show

STEAM
blow off steam □ full steam ahead □ let off steam □ steamed up □ under one's own steam

STEER
steer clear (of someone or something)

STEM
from stem to stern

STEP
in step (with someone or something) □ out of step (with someone or something) □ step by step □ step down (from something) □ step into dead men's shoes □ step in(to the breach) □ step on it □ step on someone's toes □ step out of line □ step (right) up □ step something up □ take steps (to prevent something) □ watch one's step

STERN
from stem to stern

STEVEN
be even-steven

STEW
in a stew (about someone or something) □ stew in one's own juice

STICK
end up with the short end of the stick □ get the short end of the stick □ one's words stick in one's throat □ something sticks in one's craw □ stick around □ stick by someone or something □ Stick 'em up! □ stick-in-the-mud □ stick it out □ stick one's neck out □ stick one's nose in(to something) □ stick one's oar in □ stick out a mile □ stick out for something □ stick out like a sore thumb □ stick someone or something up □ stick to one's guns □ stick together □ stick up for someone or something □ stick with someone or something

STICKY
have sticky fingers

STIFF
bore someone stiff □ keep a stiff upper lip □ scare someone stiff □ scared stiff

STILL
hold still □ hold still (for someone or

something) ☐ keep still ☐ keep still about someone or something ☐ one's heart stands still ☐ so still you could hear a pin drop ☐ stand still (for someone or something) ☐ Still waters run deep.

STINK
create a stink (about something) ☐ make a stink (about something) ☐ raise a stink about something

STIR
cause a stir ☐ stir one's stumps ☐ stir up a hornets' nest

STITCH
A stitch in time (saves nine). ☐ keep someone in stitches

STOCK
have something in stock ☐ in stock ☐ lock, stock, and barrel ☐ out of stock ☐ stock up (on something) ☐ take stock (of someone or something)

STOMACH
can't stomach someone or something ☐ get butterflies in one's stomach ☐ give one butterflies in one's stomach ☐ have butterflies in one's stomach ☐ have eyes bigger than one's stomach ☐ one's eyes are bigger than one's stomach ☐ turn someone's stomach

STONE
A rolling stone gathers no moss. ☐ cast the first stone ☐ have a heart of stone ☐ kill two birds with one stone ☐ leave no stone unturned ☐ run up against a stone wall ☐ stone's throw away

STOOL
fall between two stools

STOOP
stoop to (doing) something

STOP
pull out all the stops ☐ put a stop to something ☐ stop at nothing ☐ stop off (somewhere) ☐ stop one dead in one's tracks ☐ stop over (somewhere) ☐ stop short of doing something ☐ stop something dead in its tracks

STOPOVER
stopover

STORE
have something in store (for someone) ☐ set great store by someone or something

STORM
any port in a storm ☐ storm in a teacup ☐ take someone or something by storm

STORY
cock-and-bull story ☐ make a long story short ☐ same old story ☐ shaggy-dog story ☐ tall story ☐ tell its own story

STOW
stow away

STRAIGHT
get something straight ☐ give it to someone straight ☐ go straight ☐ keep a straight face ☐ put something straight ☐ set someone straight ☐ set something straight ☐ set the record straight ☐ straight away ☐ straight from the horse's mouth ☐ straight from the shoulder ☐ straight off ☐ straight out ☐ straighten someone or something out ☐ straighten someone or something up

STRAP
strapped (for something)

STRAW
clutch at straws ☐ straw in the wind ☐ That's the last straw. ☐ That's the straw that broke the camel's back.

STREAM
change horses in mid-stream

STREET
in Queer Street ☐ man in the street ☐ on Easy Street ☐ pound the streets ☐ right up someone's street

STRENGTH
on the strength of something ☐ tower of strength

STRETCH
at a stretch ☐ at full stretch ☐ stretch a point ☐ stretch one's legs

STRIDE
take something in one's stride

STRIKE
go (out) on strike ☐ Lightning never

strikes twice (in the same place). □
strike a balance (between two things) □
strike a bargain □ strike a chord □
strike a happy medium □ strike a sour
note □ strike it lucky □ strike it rich
□ strike out at someone or something
□ strike the right note □ strike up a
conversation □ strike up a friendship
□ strike while the iron is hot

STRING
control the purse-strings □ get by (on
a shoe-string) □ have someone on a
string □ pull strings □ string along
(with someone) □ string someone
along □ string something out □ tied
to one's mother's apron-strings □ with
no strings attached □ without any
strings attached

STROKE
have a stroke □ stroke of luck

STRONG
(as) strong as an ox □ use strong
language

STUBBORN
(as) stubborn as a mule

STUCK
stuck for something □ stuck on someone or something □ stuck with someone or something

STUFF
beat the stuffing out of someone □
kid's stuff □ know one's stuff □
stuff and nonsense

STUMBLE
stumble across someone or something
□ stumble into someone or something
□ stumble on someone or something
□ stumbling-block

STUMP
stir one's stumps

STUNT
pull a stunt

STYLE
after the style of someone or something
□ cramp someone's style □ in style

SUBJECT
change the subject □ subject to
something

SUCH
such-and-such □ such as it is □ Such
is life! □ teach one's grandmother to
suck eggs

SUDDEN
all of a sudden

SUGAR
sugar the pill

SUIT
cut one's coat to suit one's cloth □ follow suit □ in one's birthday suit □
suit one's actions to one's words □ suit
someone down to the ground □ suit
someone to a T □ suit yourself

SUITCASE
live out of a suitcase

SUM
sum something up

SUN
catch the sun □ Make hay while the
sun shines.

SUNDAY
in a month of Sundays □ in one's Sunday best

SUNDRY
all and sundry

SUPPLY
in short supply

SURE
for sure

SURFACE
scratch the surface

SURPRISE
take someone or something by surprise

SURVIVAL
survival of the fittest

SUSPICION
above suspicion

SWALLOW
bitter pill to swallow □ look like the
cat that swallowed the canary □ swallow one's pride □ swallow something
hook, line, and sinker

SWAN
swan around □ swan-song

SWEAT

break out in a cold sweat □ by the sweat of one's brow □ no sweat □ sweat blood □ sweat something out

SWEEP

make a clean sweep □ sweep one off one's feet □ sweep something under the carpet

SWEET

have a sweet tooth □ short and sweet □ sweet nothings □ sweet on someone □ sweet-talk someone □ sweeten the pill

SWELL

get a swelled head □ give someone a swelled head □ have a swelled head

SWIM

in the swim (of things) □ make someone's head swim □ out of the swim of things □ sink or swim □ swim against the tide

SWINE

Cast (one's) pearls before swine.

SWING

get into full swing □ get into the swing of things □ in full swing □ not enough room to swing a cat □ swing into action □ swing something □ swing the lead

SWOOP

at one fell swoop □ in one fell swoop

SWORD

cross swords (with someone)

SYMPATHY

extend one's sympathy (to someone)

SYSTEM

all systems go □ get something out of one's system

TAB

keep tab(s) (on someone or something)

TABLE

clear the table □ lay one's cards on the table □ put one's cards on the table □ set the table □ turn the tables (on someone) □ under the table

TACK

get down to brass tacks

TAG

tag along

TAIL

can't make head or tail of someone or something □ go into a tail-spin □ hang on someone's coat-tails □ have one's tail between one's legs □ high-tail it out of somewhere □ in two shakes of a lamb's tail □ one's tail is between one's legs □ tail wagging the dog

TALE

tell tales out of school □ Thereby hangs a tale.

TALK

all talk □ have a heart-to-heart (talk) □ money talks □ small talk □ sweet-talk someone □ talk back (to someone) □ talk big □ talk down to someone □ talk nineteen to the dozen □ talk of the town □ talk shop □ talk someone into doing something □ talk someone out of doing something □ talk someone out of something □ talk someone's head off □ talk something out □ talk something over □ talk through one's hat □ talk through the back of one's head □ talk turkey □ talk until one is blue in the face □ talking-shop

TALL

tall story

TAN

tan someone's hide

TANGENT

go off at a tangent

TAPE

red tape

TAPER

taper off (doing something)

TAR

spoil the ship for a ha'porth of tar □ tar and feather someone □ tarred with the same brush

TARGET

on target □ sitting target

TASK

take someone to task

TASTE
acquire a taste for something ☐ in bad taste ☐ in poor taste ☐ leave a bad taste in someone's mouth ☐ There's no accounting for taste.

TAT
give someone tit for tat

TEA
not someone's cup of tea

TEACH
teach one's grandmother to suck eggs ☐ teach someone a lesson ☐ You can't teach an old dog new tricks.

TEACHER
be the teacher's pet

TEACUP
storm in a teacup

TEAM
team up with someone

TEAR
break into tears ☐ burst into tears ☐ shed crocodile tears ☐ tear into someone or something ☐ tear off ☐ tear one's hair ☐ tear something down ☐ wear and tear (on something)

TEETH
armed to the teeth ☐ (as) rare as hen's teeth ☐ by the skin of one's teeth ☐ cut one's eye-teeth on something ☐ cut one's teeth on something ☐ cut teeth ☐ get one's teeth into something ☐ grit one's teeth ☐ lie through one's teeth ☐ pull someone's or something's teeth ☐ set someone's teeth on edge ☐ show one's teeth ☐ sink one's teeth into something

TEETHING
teething troubles

TELEGRAPH
bush telegraph

TELEPHONE
on the telephone

TELL
A little bird told me. ☐ all told ☐ tell it to the marines ☐ tell its own story ☐ tell on someone ☐ tell one to one's face ☐ tell people apart ☐ tell someone a thing or two ☐ tell someone off ☐ tell someone on someone ☐ tell someone where to get off ☐ tell tales out of school ☐ tell the time ☐ tell things apart ☐ tell which is which ☐ Time will tell.

TEMPER
hold one's temper ☐ keep one's temper ☐ lose one's temper

TEMPERATURE
run a temperature

TENTERHOOKS
keep someone on tenterhooks

TERM
come to terms with something ☐ contradiction in terms ☐ in no uncertain terms ☐ in terms of something ☐ on first-name terms (with someone) ☐ on good terms (with someone) ☐ on speaking terms (with someone)

TEST
acid test ☐ put someone to the test

TETHER
at the end of one's tether

THAN
Actions speak louder than words. ☐ better late than never ☐ bite off more than one can chew ☐ easier said than done ☐ Half a loaf is better than none. ☐ have eyes bigger than one's stomach ☐ holier-than-thou ☐ in less than no time ☐ less than pleased ☐ more fun than a barrel of monkeys ☐ more often than not ☐ more (to something) than meets the eye ☐ no sooner said than done ☐ none other than ☐ not see further than the end of one's nose ☐ One's bark is worse than one's bite. ☐ one's eyes are bigger than one's stomach ☐ There's more than one way to kill a cat. ☐ wear more than one hat

THANK
thank one's lucky stars ☐ thanks to someone or something ☐ vote of thanks

THANKFUL
thankful for small mercies

THEN
and then some ☐ every now and then ☐ now and then ☐ then and there

THERE

hang in there □ here and there □
neither here nor there □ not all there
□ then and there □ There are plenty
of other fish in the sea. □ there is no
doing something □ There is trouble
brewing. □ There will be the devil to
pay. □ There's more than one way to
kill a cat. □ There's no accounting for
taste. □ There's no smoke without fire.
□ Where there's a will there's a way. □
Where there's smoke there's fire.

THEREBY

Thereby hangs a tale.

THICK

(as) thick as thieves □ (as) thick as two
short planks □ get something into
someone's thick head □ get something
into someone's thick skull □ lay it on
thick □ pour it on thick □ spread it
on thick □ thick and fast □ thick-
skinned □ through thick and thin

THICKEN

The plot thickens.

THIEF

(as) thick as thieves

THIN

(as) thin as a rake □ have a thin time
(of it) □ out of thin air □ pull something out of thin air □ (skating) on
thin ice □ spread oneself too thin □
thin end of the wedge □ thin on the
ground □ thin on top □ thin out □
thin-skinned □ through thick and thin
□ vanish into thin air

THING

A little knowledge is a dangerous thing.
□ A little learning is a dangerous thing.
□ do one's (own) thing □ first thing
(in the morning) □ first things first □
get into the swing of things □ have a
good thing going □ have a thing about
someone or something □ have a thing
going (with someone) □ in the swim
(of things) □ in thing (to do) □ just
one of those things □ know a thing or
two (about someone or something) □
not know the first thing about someone
or something □ Of all things! □ out
of the swim of things □ see things □
strike a balance (between two things) □

tell someone a thing or two □ tell
things apart □ Things are looking up.
□ too much of a good thing □ very
thing

THINK

come to think of it □ have another think
coming □ put on one's thinking-cap □
think a great deal of someone or something □ think a lot of someone or something □ think back (on someone or
something) □ think better of something
□ think fit (to do something) □ think
highly of someone or something □ think
little of someone or something □ think
much of someone or something □ think
nothing of doing something □ think
nothing of someone or something □
think on one's feet □ think out loud □
think something out □ think something
over □ think something up □ think
the world of someone or something □
think twice (before doing something) □
to someone's way of thinking □ wishful
thinking

THIRD

get the third degree □ give someone
the third degree

THOMAS

doubting Thomas

THORN

be a thorn in someone's side

THOSE

just one of those things

THOU

holier-than-thou

THOUGHT

A penny for your thoughts. □ food for
thought □ get second thoughts about
someone or something □ have second
thoughts about someone or something
□ lose one's train of thought □ lost in
thought □ on second thoughts □
Perish the thought.

THOUSAND

one in a thousand

THRASH

thrash something out

THREE
like a three-ring circus ☐ two's company(, three's a crowd)

THRILL
thrill someone to bits

THROAT
cut someone's throat ☐ frog in one's throat ☐ get a lump in one's throat ☐ have a lump in one's throat ☐ jump down someone's throat ☐ one's words stick in one's throat ☐ ram someone or something down someone's throat ☐ shove someone or something down someone's throat

THRONE
power behind the throne

THROUGH
be through with something ☐ drive a coach and horses through something ☐ fall through ☐ follow something through ☐ follow-through ☐ get through something ☐ get through (to someone) ☐ go through ☐ go through something ☐ go through the motions ☐ go through the proper channels ☐ go through the roof ☐ go through with something ☐ have been through the mill ☐ jump through a hoop ☐ leaf through something ☐ lie through one's teeth ☐ live through something ☐ make one's way (through something) ☐ pass through someone's mind ☐ pay through the nose for something ☐ pick one's way through something ☐ pull someone through (something) ☐ pull through ☐ put one through one's paces ☐ put someone through the wringer ☐ put something through its paces ☐ read something through ☐ run through something ☐ sail through something ☐ see something through ☐ see through someone or something ☐ shot through with something ☐ sit through something ☐ slip through someone's fingers ☐ talk through one's hat ☐ talk through the back of one's head ☐ through and through ☐ through hell and high water ☐ through thick and thin ☐ through with someone or something ☐ thumb through something ☐ win through

THROW
stone's throw away ☐ throw a fit ☐ throw a party (for someone) ☐ throw a spanner in the works ☐ throw caution to the winds ☐ throw cold water on something ☐ throw down the gauntlet ☐ throw good money after bad ☐ throw in one's hand ☐ throw in the sponge ☐ throw in the towel ☐ throw one's hat into the ring ☐ throw one's weight around ☐ throw oneself at someone ☐ throw oneself at someone's feet ☐ throw oneself at the mercy of someone ☐ throw someone ☐ throw someone off the track ☐ throw someone out (of something) ☐ throw someone over ☐ throw someone to the wolves ☐ throw someone's name around ☐ throw something in ☐ throw something off ☐ throw something together ☐ throw something up at someone ☐ throw the book at someone ☐ throw up

THRUST
cut and thrust

THUMB
all thumbs ☐ get someone under one's thumb ☐ have someone under one's thumb ☐ rule of thumb ☐ stick out like a sore thumb ☐ thumb a lift ☐ thumb one's nose at someone or something ☐ thumb through something ☐ twiddle one's thumbs

THUNDER
steal someone's thunder

TICK
(as) tight as a tick ☐ give someone a ticking-off ☐ make someone or something tick ☐ tick over ☐ tick someone off ☐ what makes someone tick

TICKET
return ticket ☐ That's the ticket.

TICKLE
tickle someone pink ☐ tickle someone to death ☐ tickle someone's fancy

TIDE
swim against the tide ☐ tide someone over ☐ turn the tide

TIE
fit to be tied ☐ have one's hands tied ☐ one's hands are tied ☐ tie someone

down □ tie someone in knots □ tie someone or something up □ tie someone's hands □ tie the knot □ tied to one's mother's apron-strings □ with both hands tied behind one's back □ with one hand tied behind one's back

TIGHT
(as) tight as a tick □ hold (on) tight □ in a (tight) spot □ run a tight ship □ sit tight □ tighten one's belt

TIGHTROPE
walk a tightrope

TILL
have one's hand in the till □ till the cows come home

TILT
at full tilt □ tilt at windmills

TIME
A stitch in time (saves nine). □ ahead of one's time □ ahead of time □ all in good time □ all the time □ at the present time □ at the same time □ at this point (in time) □ at times □ be given a hard time □ bide one's time □ every time one turns around □ find time for someone or something □ for the time being □ from time to time □ get time off □ get time off for good behaviour □ get time to catch one's breath □ give someone a hard time □ hardly have time to breathe □ have a rough time (of it) □ have a thin time (of it) □ have a whale of a time □ have no time for someone or something □ have the time of one's life □ have time off □ have time to catch one's breath □ in due time □ in good time □ in less than no time □ in no time (at all) □ in one's own time □ in one's spare time □ in the course of time □ in the nick of time □ in time □ in time (with someone or something) □ It's about time! □ it's high time □ keep good time □ keep time □ keep up (with the times) □ kill time □ live on borrowed time □ Long time no see. □ make good time □ make up for lost time □ many is the time □ not able to call one's time one's own □ not give someone the time of day □ on time □ once upon a time □ one at a

time □ out of time □ pass the time □ pass the time of day (with someone) □ race against time □ right on time □ run out of time □ small time □ take one's time □ take time off □ take time out □ take up someone's time □ take up time □ tell the time □ time after time □ time and (time) again □ time flies □ Time hangs heavy on someone's hands. □ Time is money. □ Time is up. □ time out of mind □ time was when □ Time will tell. □ two-time someone □ when the time is ripe □ while away the time

TIP
on the tip of one's tongue □ tip someone off □ tip someone the wink □ tip the scales at something

TIPTOE
on tiptoe

TIRED
sick and tired of someone or something

TIT
give someone tit for tat

TOAST
(as) warm as toast

TOE
on one's toes □ step on someone's toes □ toe the line □ tread on someone's toes □ turn up one's toes

TOGETHER
Birds of a feather flock together. □ get it (all) together □ get one's act together □ get together (with someone) □ go together □ hang together □ keep body and soul together □ knock people's heads together □ piece something together □ pull oneself together □ put something together □ put two and two together □ scrape something together □ stick together □ throw something together

TOILET
go to the toilet

TOKEN
as a token of something □ by the same token

TOLD
A little bird told me. □ all told

459

TOM

(every) Tom, Dick, and Harry

TOMORROW

jam tomorrow

TON

hit (someone or something) like a ton of bricks

TONE

tone something down

TONG

fight someone or something hammer and tongs □ go at it hammer and tongs

TONGUE

Cat got your tongue? □ cause tongues to wag □ find one's tongue □ get a tongue-lashing □ give someone a tongue-lashing □ hold one's tongue □ keep a civil tongue (in one's head) □ on the tip of one's tongue □ slip of the tongue □ speak with a forked tongue □ tongue-in-cheek

TOO

be too □ come too close to home □ cut it (too) fine □ do too □ eat one's cake and have it too □ go too far □ have one's cake and eat it too □ have too □ have too many irons in the fire □ know something only too well □ none too something □ spread oneself too thin □ take too much on □ too big for one's boots □ too big for one's britches □ too close for comfort □ too good to be true □ Too many cooks spoil the broth. □ too much of a good thing

TOOTH

An eye for an eye (and a tooth for a tooth). □ armed to the teeth □ (as) rare as hen's teeth □ by the skin of one's teeth □ cut one's eye-teeth on something □ cut one's teeth on something □ cut teeth □ fight someone or something tooth and nail □ get one's teeth into something □ go at it tooth and nail □ go over something with a fine-tooth comb □ grit one's teeth □ have a sweet tooth □ lie through one's teeth □ pull someone's or something's teeth □ search some-thing with a fine-tooth comb □ set someone's teeth on edge □ show one's teeth □ sink one's teeth into something □ take the bit between one's teeth

TOP

at the top of one's voice □ blow one's top □ from top to bottom □ go over the top □ off the top of one's head □ on top □ on top of something □ on top of the world □ over the top □ (sitting) on top of the world □ sleep like a top □ thin on top □ top someone or something

TORCH

carry a torch (for someone)

TOSS

toss one's hat into the ring □ toss something off

TOTAL

total something up

TOUCH

get in touch (with someone) □ have the Midas touch □ keep in touch (with someone) □ lose one's touch (with someone or something) □ lose touch (with someone or something) □ out of touch (with someone or something) □ touch a sore point □ touch a sore spot □ touch-and-go □ touch on something □ touch someone for something □ touch someone or something off □ touch something up □ touch wood □ touched by someone or something □ touched (in the head)

TOUGH

(as) tough as old boots □ get tough (with someone) □ tough act to follow □ tough furrow to plough □ Tough luck! □ tough nut to crack □ tough row to hoe

TOW

have someone or something in tow □ with someone or something in tow

TOWARDS

go a long way towards doing something

TOWEL

throw in the towel

TOWER
live in an ivory tower ☐ tower of strength

TOWN
go to town ☐ man about town ☐ night on the town ☐ out of town ☐ out on the town ☐ paint the town red ☐ talk of the town

TOY
toy with someone or something

TRACK
cover someone's tracks (up) ☐ double back (on one's tracks) ☐ drop in one's tracks ☐ keep track (of someone or something) ☐ lose track (of someone or something) ☐ make tracks (somewhere) ☐ off the beaten track ☐ on the track of someone or something ☐ on the wrong track ☐ one-track mind ☐ stop one dead in one's tracks ☐ stop something dead in its tracks ☐ throw someone off the track ☐ track someone or something down

TRADE
jack of all trades ☐ know all the tricks of the trade ☐ trade on something ☐ trade something in (on something)

TRAIL
blaze a trail ☐ on the trail of someone or something

TRAIN
lose one's train of thought

TRAP
fall into the trap of doing something

TREAD
fools rush in (where angels fear to tread) ☐ tread on someone's toes

TREAT
Dutch treat

TREATMENT
get the red carpet treatment ☐ give someone the red carpet treatment

TREE
bark up the wrong tree ☐ not able to see the wood for the trees ☐ up a gum-tree

TREMBLE
in fear and trembling

TRESPASS
no trespassing

TRIAL
on trial ☐ send up a trial balloon ☐ trial and error

TRIANGLE
eternal triangle

TRICK
bag of tricks ☐ do the trick ☐ know all the tricks of the trade ☐ play tricks (on someone) ☐ use every trick in the book ☐ You can't teach an old dog new tricks.

TRIP
trip someone up

TROLLEY
off one's trolley

TROT
trot something out

TROUBLE
ask for trouble ☐ fish in troubled waters ☐ go to the trouble (of doing something) ☐ go to the trouble (to do something) ☐ look for trouble ☐ pour oil on troubled waters ☐ spell trouble ☐ take the trouble (to do something) ☐ teething troubles ☐ There is trouble brewing. ☐ Trouble is brewing. ☐ trouble one's head about someone or something ☐ trouble oneself about someone or something

TROUSERS
catch one with one's trousers down

TRUE
come true ☐ dream come true ☐ hold true ☐ ring true ☐ show oneself in one's true colours ☐ too good to be true ☐ true to form ☐ true to one's word

TRULY
yours truly

TRUMP
play one's trump card ☐ trumped-up ☐ turn up trumps

TRUMPET
blow one's own trumpet

TRUTH
moment of truth

TRY
have a try at something □ try it on □ try one's hand (at something) □ try one's luck (at something) □ try one's wings □ try out (for something) □ try someone or something out □ try someone's patience □ try something on □ try something out (on someone)

TUBE
down the tube

TUCK
tuck into something

TUCKER
best bib and tucker

TUMBLE
tumble to something

TUNE
call the tune □ change someone's tune □ dance to another tune □ He who pays the piper calls the tune. □ in tune (with someone or something) □ out of tune (with someone or something) □ sing a different tune □ to the tune of some amount of money □ tune something up

TUNNEL
see the light at the end of the tunnel

TURKEY
cold turkey □ go cold turkey □ talk turkey

TURN
at every turn □ do someone a good turn □ done to a turn □ every time one turns around □ have turned the corner □ in turn □ not know where to turn □ not know which way to turn □ One good turn deserves another. □ out of turn □ speak out of turn □ take a new turn □ take a turn for the better □ take a turn for the worse □ take turns ((at) doing something) □ The worm (has) turned. □ turn a blind eye to someone or something □ turn a deaf ear (to something) □ turn about □ turn against someone or something □ turn in □ turn in one's grave □ turn into something □ turn of the century □ turn on

someone □ turn on the heat (on someone) □ turn on the waterworks □ turn one's back (on someone or something) □ turn one's coat □ turn one's nose up at someone or something □ turn out (all right) □ turn out to be someone or something □ turn over □ turn over a new leaf □ turn (over) in one's grave □ turn someone or something down □ turn someone or something in □ turn someone or something into something □ turn someone or something off □ turn someone or something on □ turn someone or something out □ turn someone or something over (to someone) □ turn someone or something up □ turn someone's head □ turn someone's stomach □ turn something around □ turn something to good account □ turn something to one's advantage □ turn the other cheek □ turn the tables (on someone) □ turn the tide □ turn to □ turn to someone or something (for something) □ turn turtle □ turn up □ turn up one's toes □ turn up trumps □ wait one's turn

TURTLE
turn turtle

TWICE
(as) large as life (and twice as ugly) □ Lightning never strikes twice (in the same place). □ think twice (before doing something)

TWIDDLE
twiddle one's thumbs

TWINKLE
in the twinkling of an eye

TWIST
twist someone around one's little finger □ twist someone's arm

TWO
A bird in the hand is worth two in the bush. □ (as) thick as two short planks □ fall between two stools □ game at which two can play □ in two shakes of a lamb's tail □ kill two birds with one stone □ know a thing or two (about someone or something) □ no two ways about it □ not care two hoots about someone or something □ not give two hoots about someone or something □

put in one's two halfpennies (worth) □ put two and two together □ stand on one's own two feet □ strike a balance (between two things) □ take someone down a peg (or two) □ tell someone a thing or two □ That makes two of us. □ two a penny □ two can play at that game □ two of a kind □ two-time someone □ two's company(, three's a crowd)

UGLY
(as) large as life (and twice as ugly) □ (as) ugly as sin □ rear its ugly head

UNCERTAIN
in no uncertain terms

UNCLE
Dutch uncle

UNDERSTAND
be given to understand □ come to an understanding (with someone) □ give someone to understand something □ given to understand

UNIVERSITY
redbrick university

UNKNOWN
be an unknown quantity

UNLIKELY
in the unlikely event of something

UNTIL
talk until one is blue in the face □ until all hours

UNTIMELY
come to an untimely end

UNTO
law unto oneself

UNTURNED
leave no stone unturned

UPON
chance (up)on someone or something □ come (up)on someone or something □ dwell (up)on something □ fall (up)on someone or something □ feel put upon □ hit (up)on something □ improve (up)on something □ incumbent upon someone to do something □ once upon a time □ prevail (up)on someone □ prey (up)on someone or something □ put upon someone □

set upon someone or something □ take something (up)on oneself

UPPANCE
get one's come-uppance

UPPER
get the upper hand (over someone) □ have the upper hand on someone □ keep a stiff upper lip □ upper crust

UPROAR
create an uproar □ make an uproar

UPS
ups and downs

UPSET
upset someone's plans □ upset the applecart

UPSHOT
upshot of something

UPSIDE
upside down

UPTAKE
quick on the uptake □ slow on the uptake

USE
get used to someone or something □ have no use for someone or something □ it's no use (doing something) □ make use of someone or something □ put something to (good) use □ use every trick in the book □ use one's head □ use one's noodle □ use strong language □ used to someone or something

UTTER
not utter a word

VAIN
in vain

VALUE
face value □ take something at face value

VANISH
vanish into thin air

VARIETY
Variety is the spice of life.

VELVET
iron hand in the velvet glove

VENGEANCE
with a vengeance

VENT
give vent to something □ vent one's spleen on someone or something

VENTURE
Nothing ventured, nothing gained.

VERGE
on the verge of (doing) something □ verge on something

VERSE
chapter and verse

VERY
under someone's (very) nose □ very thing

VESSEL
Empty vessels make the most noise.

VESTED
have a vested interest in something

VEX
vexed question

VICIOUS
vicious circle

VICTOR
To the victors belong the spoils.

VICTORY
landslide victory

VIEW
bird's-eye view □ in view of something □ on view □ take a dim view of something □ with a view to doing something

VILLAIN
villain of the piece

VINE
wither on the vine

VIRTUE
by virtue of something

VISIT
flying visit □ pay a visit (to someone) □ pay someone a visit

VOICE
at the top of one's voice □ give voice to something □ have a voice (in some-thing) □ lower one's voice □ raise one's voice (to someone)

VOID
null and void

VOTE
vote of confidence □ vote of thanks □ vote someone in □ vote someone out

VOYAGE
maiden voyage

VULTURE
culture vulture

WADE
wade in(to something)

WAG
cause tongues to wag □ tail wagging the dog

WAGON
on the wagon

WAIT
lie in wait for someone or something □ not able to wait □ on the waiting-list □ wait-and-see attitude □ wait on someone hand and foot □ wait one's turn □ wait up (for someone or some-thing) □ waiting in the wings

WAKE
in the wake of something

WALK
all walks of life □ cock of the walk □ get one's walking papers □ walk a tightrope □ walk all over someone □ walk away with something □ walk it □ walk off with something □ walk on air □ walk on eggs □ walk out □ walk out (on someone) □ walk the floor

WALL
bang one's head against a brick wall □ beat one's head against the wall □ climb the wall □ drive someone to the wall □ drive someone up the wall □ go to the wall □ have one's back to the wall □ off the wall □ push someone to the wall □ run up against a brick wall □ run up against a stone wall □ see the writing on the wall □ walls have ears

WALLOP
pack a wallop

WANT
want for nothing □ want out (of something) □ Waste not, want not.

WAR
act of war □ all out war □ on the war-path

WARM
(as) warm as toast □ warm the cockles of someone's heart □ warm up

WARRANT
sign one's own death-warrant

WART
warts and all

WAS
time was when

WASH
come out in the wash □ wash one's dirty linen in public □ wash one's hands of someone or something □ wash someone or something up □ wash something down □ washed out □ washed up

WASTE
go to waste □ Haste makes waste. □ lay something to waste □ waste away □ Waste not, want not. □ waste one's breath

WATCH
A watched pot never boils. □ keep watch (on someone or something) □ keep watch (over someone or something) □ on the watch for someone or something □ watch one's step □ watch out for someone or something □ watch someone like a hawk

WATER
as a duck takes to water □ (as) dull as dish-water □ come hell or high water □ fish in troubled waters □ get one's head above water □ hold water □ in deep water □ in hot water □ keep one's head above water □ like a fish out of water □ like water off a duck's back □ make someone's mouth water □ not hold water □ of the first water □ pour cold water on something □ pour oil on troubled waters □ Still waters run deep. □ through hell and high water □ throw cold water on something □ water something down □ water under the bridge □ won't hold water

WATERLOO
meet one's Waterloo

WATERWORKS
turn on the waterworks

WAVE
make waves

WAY
by the way □ by way of something □ come someone's way □ cut both ways □ do something the hard way □ find something out the hard way □ get in someone's way □ get one's way (with someone or something) □ get out of someone's way □ get someone or something out of the way □ get something under-way □ get under-way □ give way (to someone or something) □ go a long way in doing something □ go a long way towards doing something □ go all the way (to somewhere) □ go all the way (with someone) □ go out of one's way (to do something) □ have a way with someone or something □ have come a long way □ have it both ways □ have one's way (with someone or something) □ have the right of way □ in a bad way □ in one's own way □ in someone's or something's way □ in the family way □ in the way □ in the way of someone or something □ keep someone or something out of the way □ know one's way about □ know one's way around □ lead the way □ learn something the hard way □ look the other way □ make one's way (through something) □ make way □ make way (for someone or something) □ meet someone half-way □ mend one's ways □ no two ways about it □ no way □ not know which way to turn □ on one's way (somewhere) □ on one's way (to doing something) □ on the way (somewhere) □ on the way (to doing something) □ one way or another □ one's way of life □ other way round □ out of the way □ parting of the ways □ pave the way (for someone or something) □ pay one's own way □

pay someone's way □ pick one's way through something □ put something in the way (of someone or something) □ rub someone up the wrong way □ say something in a roundabout way □ see one's way clear (to do something) □ stand in someone's way □ take something the wrong way □ That's the way the cookie crumbles. □ There's more than one way to kill a cat. □ to someone's way of thinking □ ways and means □ Where there's a will there's a way. □ work one's way into something □ work one's way up □ worm one's way out of something

WAYSIDE
fall by the wayside

WEAK
(as) weak as a kitten □ The spirit is willing (but the flesh is weak).

WEAKNESS
have a weakness for someone or something

WEALTHY
Early to bed, early to rise(, makes a man healthy, wealthy, and wise).

WEAR
If the cap fits, wear it. □ none the worse for wear □ wear and tear (on something) □ wear more than one hat □ wear off □ wear one's heart on one's sleeve □ wear out one's welcome □ wear someone down □ wear someone or something out □ worn to a shadow

WEASEL
weasel out (of something)

WEATHER
fair-weather friend □ keep one's weather eye open □ lovely weather for ducks □ under the weather

WEAVE
weave in and out (of something)

WEDDING
shot-gun wedding

WEDGE
thin end of the wedge

WEED
weed someone or something out

WEEK
by the week □ week in, week out

WEEP
weep buckets

WEEPER
Finders keepers(, losers weepers).

WEIGH
weigh on someone's mind □ weigh one's words □ weigh someone down □ weigh someone or something up

WEIGHT
carry one's (own) weight □ carry the weight of the world on one's shoulders □ carry weight (with someone) □ pull one's weight □ put on weight □ throw one's weight around □ worth its weight in gold

WELCOME
wear out one's welcome □ welcome someone with open arms □ welcome to do something

WELL
All's well that ends well. □ get well □ hail-fellow-well-met □ know something only too well □ leave well alone □ let well alone □ Well and good. □ well-heeled □ well off □ well-to-do □ well up in something

WET
get wet □ wet behind the ears □ wet blanket □ wet someone's whistle

WHALE
have a whale of a time

WHAT
and what have you □ come what may □ for what it's worth □ get what for □ get what is coming to one □ give one what's coming to one □ give someone what for □ have what it takes □ just what the doctor ordered □ know what's what □ no matter what (happens) □ not what it is cracked up to be □ practise what you preach □ What about (doing) something? □ What about (having) something? □ What are you driving at? □ What difference does it make? □ What is sauce

for the goose is sauce for the gander. □ what makes someone tick □ What of it? □ What price something? □ what with □ What's cooking? □ What's done is done. □ What's eating you? □ What's going on? □ What's got into someone? □ What's the (big) idea? □ What's the good of something? □ What's up?

WHEEL
asleep at the wheel □ oil the wheels □ put one's shoulder to the wheel □ wheeling and dealing □ wheels within wheels

WHEN
cross a bridge when one comes to it □ time was when □ when all is said and done □ When in Rome do as the Romans do. □ when it comes right down to it □ when it comes to something □ when least expected □ when one is good and ready □ When the cat's away the mice will play. □ when the time is ripe

WHERE
fools rush in (where angels fear to tread) □ give credit where credit is due □ know where someone stands (on someone or something) □ not know where to turn □ Put your money where your mouth is! □ tell someone where to get off □ Where there's a will there's a way. □ Where there's smoke there's fire.

WHEREFORES
whys and wherefores of something

WHEREWITHAL
have the wherewithal (to do something)

WHET
whet someone's appetite

WHETHER
not know whether one is coming or going

WHICH
game at which two can play □ know which is which □ know which side one's bread is buttered on □ not know which way to turn □ tell which is which

WHILE
every once in a while □ fiddle while Rome burns □ Make hay while the sun shines. □ make it worth someone's while □ once in a while □ strike while the iron is hot □ while away the time □ worth someone's while

WHIP
fair crack of the whip □ whip something into shape □ whip something up

WHISKER
by a whisker □ win by a whisker

WHISPER
in a stage whisper

WHISTLE
(as) clean as a whistle □ blow the whistle (on someone or something) □ wet someone's whistle □ whistle for something

WHITE
(as) white as a sheet □ (as) white as the driven snow □ in black and white □ show the white feather □ white elephant

WHO
He who laughs last laughs longest. □ He who pays the piper calls the tune.

WHOLE
go the whole hog □ on the whole □ whole (bang) shoot □ whole shooting-match

WHOM
to whom it may concern

WHOOP
whoop it up

WHYS
whys and wherefores of something

WIDE
come from far and wide □ crack something wide open □ give someone or something a wide berth □ leave oneself wide open for something □ wide awake □ wide of the mark

WILD
run wild □ sow one's wild oats □ wild about someone or something □ wild-goose chase □ Wild horses couldn't drag someone.

WILDFIRE
spread like wildfire

WILL
against someone's will □ at will □
Give one an inch, and one will take a
mile. □ heads will roll □ If you give
one an inch, one will take a mile. □ of
one's own free will □ That will do. □
There will be the devil to pay. □ Time
will tell. □ When the cat's away the
mice will play. □ Where there's a will
there's a way. □ will not hear of something □ with a will □ with the best
will in the world □ won't hold water

WILLIES
get the willies □ give someone the willies

WILLING
The spirit is willing (but the flesh is
weak).

WIN
Slow and steady wins the race. □ win
by a nose □ win by a whisker □ win
someone over □ win something hands
down □ win the day □ win through

WIND
get one's second wind □ get wind of
something □ in the wind □ raise the
wind for something □ straw in the
wind □ take the wind out of someone's
sails □ throw caution to the winds □
wind down □ wind something up □
wind up (by) doing something □ wind
up somewhere

WINDMILL
tilt at windmills

WINDOW
window-shopping

WING
clip someone's wings □ on the wing
□ take someone under one's wing □
try one's wings □ waiting in the wings

WINK
catch forty winks □ forty winks □
have forty winks □ not sleep a wink
□ take forty winks □ tip someone the
wink

WIPE
wipe someone or something out □

wipe the floor with someone □ wipe
the slate clean

WISE
(as) wise as an owl □ Early to bed,
early to rise(, makes a man healthy,
wealthy, and wise). □ get wise to
someone or something □ none the
wiser □ penny wise and pound foolish
□ put someone wise to someone or
something □ wise after the event □
wise up (to someone or something)

WISH
wish someone joy of something □
wish something off on someone

WISHFUL
wishful thinking

WIT
at one's wits' end □ frighten one out
of one's wits □ frighten the wits out of
someone □ have one's wits about one
□ keep one's wits about one □ live by
one's wits □ scare one out of one's wits
□ scare the wits out of someone

WITHER
wither on the vine

WITHIN
come within an ace of doing something
□ come within an inch of doing something □ live within one's means □
wheels within wheels □ within an inch
of doing something □ within an inch
of one's life □ within hailing distance
□ within limits □ within reason □
within someone's reach

WITHOUT
absent without leave □ do without
(someone or something) □ get along
(without (someone or something)) □
go without (something) □ goes without saying □ There's no smoke without
fire. □ up the creek (without a paddle)
□ without any strings attached □
without batting an eye □ without fail
□ without further ado □ without
question □ without rhyme or reason
□ without so much as doing something

WOE
woe betide someone □ Woe is me.

WOLF
cry wolf □ keep the wolf from the door □ throw someone to the wolves □ wolf in sheep's clothing

WOMAN
woman to woman

WONDER
nine days' wonder □ no wonder

WON'T
won't hold water

WOOD
babe in the woods □ in some neck of the woods □ knock on wood □ not able to see the wood for the trees □ out of the woods □ touch wood

WOOL
dyed-in-the-wool □ pull the wool over someone's eyes □ wool-gathering

WORD
Actions speak louder than words. □ as good as one's word □ at a loss for words □ beyond words □ break one's word □ by word of mouth □ dirty word □ eat one's words □ Fine words butter no parsnips. □ from the word go □ get a word in (edgeways) □ get the final word □ get the last word □ go back on one's word □ hang on someone's every word □ have a word with someone □ have the last word □ in a word □ in other words □ in so many words □ keep one's word □ leave word (with someone) □ mark my word(s) □ mince (one's) words □ mum's the word □ not breathe a word (about someone or something) □ not utter a word □ one's words stick in one's throat □ put in a good word for someone □ put something into words □ put words into someone's mouth □ say the word □ send word (to someone) □ suit one's actions to one's words □ take one at one's word □ take the words out of one's mouth □ Them's fighting words. □ true to one's word □ weigh one's words □ word for word □ words to that effect

WORK
all in a day's work □ All work and no play makes Jack a dull boy. □ all worked up (over something) □ dirty work □ donkey-work □ get the works □ get worked up (over something) □ give someone the works □ gum up the works □ have one's work cut out (for one) □ knock off work □ make fast work of someone or something □ make short work of someone or something □ Many hands make light work. □ one's work is cut out (for one) □ out of work □ throw a spanner in the works □ work like a horse □ work on someone □ work one's fingers to the bone □ work one's way into something □ work one's way up □ work out □ work out (all right) □ work out for the best □ work someone over □ work something into something □ work something off □ work something out

WORLD
carry the weight of the world on one's shoulders □ come down in the world □ come up in the world □ dead to the world □ for all the world □ in a world of one's own □ in the world □ move up (in the world) □ not for anything in the world □ not for the world □ not have a care in the world □ not long for this world □ on top of the world □ out of this world □ set the world on fire □ (sitting) on top of the world □ The world is someone's oyster. □ think the world of someone or something □ with the best will in the world

WORM
open a can of worms □ The early bird catches the worm. □ The worm (has) turned. □ worm one's way out of something □ worm something out of someone

WORN
worn to a shadow

WORSE
for better or for worse □ go from bad to worse □ none the worse for wear □ One's bark is worse than one's bite. □ take a turn for the worse □ Worse luck!

WORST

at (the) worst □ get the worst of something □ if the worst comes to the worst

WORTH

A bird in the hand is worth two in the bush. □ for all it's worth □ for what it's worth □ get one's money's worth □ make it worth someone's while □ not worth a button □ not worth a cent □ not worth a penny □ put in one's two halfpennies (worth) □ worth its weight in gold □ worth one's salt □ worth someone's while

WORTHY

worthy of the name

WOULD

(as) luck would have it □ look as if butter wouldn't melt in one's mouth □ would as soon do something □ wouldn't dream of doing something

WOUND

rub salt in the wound

WRACK

go to wrack and ruin

WRAP

get something wrapped up □ have something wrapped up □ keep something under wraps □ wrap something up □ wrapped up in someone or something

WREAK

wreak havoc with something

WRINGER

put someone through the wringer

WRIST

get a slap on the wrist □ give someone a slap on the wrist □ slap someone's wrist

WRITE

nothing to write home about □ see the writing on the wall □ write in for something □ write off for something □ write someone or something off □ write something down □ write something out

WRONG

bark up the wrong tree □ be off on the wrong foot □ get off on the wrong foot □ get out of the wrong side of the bed □ go wrong □ in the wrong □ on the wrong track □ rub someone up the wrong way □ take something the wrong way

WRONGFOOT

wrongfoot someone

YEAR

advanced in years □ all year round □ by the year □ donkey's years □ from the year dot □ get on (in years) □ on in years □ ring in the New Year □ since the year dot □ up in years □ year in, year out

YESTERDAY

not born yesterday

ZERO

zero hour □ zero in on something

ZONK

zonk out

ZOOM

zoom in (on someone or something)